# MACROECONOMICS

# MACROEC

# ONOMICS

**Richard B. McKenzie**

*Clemson University*

*Visiting Professor of American Business,*
*Washington University in St. Louis*

**Houghton Mifflin Company Boston**

Dallas Geneva, Illinois Lawrenceville, New Jersey Palo Alto

Cover painting: Frank Stella, "River of Ponds I."
(11-color lithograph, 38 × 38 inches, 1970, edition: 78)
Copyright 1970, Gemini G. E. L., Los Angeles.



Printed in the U.S.A.

Library of Congress Catalog Card Number: 85-71107

ISBN: 0-395-35527-3

ABCDEFGHIJ-RM-898765

**Dedicated to**

*Professor Hugh H. Macaulay*

## Chapter Epigraphs

*Chapter* 1. Frank H. Knight, "Economics, Political Science, and Education," in *Freedom and Reform: Essays in Economics and Social Philosophy* (Indianapolis, Ind.: Liberty Press, 1982), p. 386.

*Chapter* 2. Lionel Robbins, *The Nature and Significance of Economic Science,* 2nd ed. (New York: Macmillan, 1973), p. 16.

*Chapter* 3. Friedrich A. Hayek, *Law, Legislation, and Liberty* (Chicago: University of Chicago Press, 1979) III, p. 74.

*Chapter* 4. John Locke, *The Second Treatise of Government,* ed. Thomas P. Peardon (New York: The Liberal Arts Press, 1954), pp. 32–33.

*Chapter* 5. Lewis Carroll, *Through the Looking Glass and What Alice Found There* (A number of modern sources are available.)

*Chapter* 6. Henry C. Wallich, "Honest Money," *Macroeconomics 1979: Readings on Contemporary Issues* (Ithaca, N.Y.: Cornell University Press, 1979), p. 43.

*Chapter* 7. David T. Bazelon, *The Paper Economy* (New York: Vintage Books, 1965), p. 73.

*Chapter* 8. Milton Friedman, *Dollars and Deficits: Inflation, Monetary Policy, and the Balance of Payments* (Englewood Cliffs, N.J.: Prentice-Hall, 1968), p. 165.

*Chapter* 9. Roger Leroy Miller, Raburn M. Williams, *The Economics of National Issues* (San Francisco: Canfield Press, 1972), p. 114.

*Chapter* 10. E. Ray Canterbery, *Economics on a New Frontier* (Belmont, Calif.: Wadsworth Publishing, 1968), p. i.

*Chapter* 11. Alvin H. Hansen, "The General Theory," in M. G. Mueller, ed., *Readings in Macroeconomics,* 2nd ed. (New York: Holt, Rinehart and Winston, 1971), p. 23.

*Chapter* 12. Walter W. Heller, "Ford's Budget and the Economy," *Wall Street Journal* (February 5, 1976), p. 18.

*Chapter* 13. Arthur Okun, *The Political Economy of Prosperity* (New York: W. W. Norton, 1970), p. 100.

*Chapter* 14. Darryl R. Francis, "The Role of Monetary Policy in Dealing with Inflation and High Interest Rates," *Federal Reserve Bank of St. Louis Review* (August 1974), p. 2.

*Chapter* 15. George Guilder, *Wealth and Poverty* (New York: Basic Books, 1981), p. 28.

*Chapter* 16. Abraham Lincoln, speech in Clinton, Illinois, September 8, 1858.

*Chapter* 17. David Ricardo, *Notes on Malthus' Principles of Political Economy,* quoted in Jacob Viner, *Studies in the Theory of International Trade* (New York: Augustus M. Kelly, 1965), p. 441.

*Chapter* 18. Robert Z. Aliber, *The International Money Game* (New York: Basic Books, 1973), p. 12.

*Chapter* 19. Barry Commoner, *The Poverty of Power: Energy and the Economic Crisis* (New York: Alfred A. Knopf, 1976), p. 257.

*Chapter 20.* Karl Marx, *The Communist Manifesto* (Chicago: Henry Regnery, 1954), p. 23.

*Chapter 21.* Saul K. Padover, ed., *Thomas Jefferson on Democracy* (New York: Appleton-Century, 1939), p. 19.

## *Acknowledgments*

James Bovard. "Can Sunkist Wrap Up the Lemon Industry?" from *The Wall Street Journal,* January 24, 1985 reprinted by permission of *The Wall Street Journal.* © Dow Jones & Company, 1985. All rights reserved.

Cato Institute. Table from *Policy Analysis* reprinted by permission of the Institute.

Robert J. Barro. "A Deficit Nearly on Target," from *The Wall Street Journal,* January 30, 1985 reprinted by permission of *The Wall Street Journal.* © Dow Jones & Company, 1985. All rights reserved.

Paul Davidson. "The Statistical Assault Against the Elderly," from *The New York Times,* February 14, 1985. © 1985 by The New York Times Company. Reprinted by permission.

Robert D. Hershey, Jr. "Economic Scene: Modern Myths about the Elderly," from *The New York Times,* February 6, 1985. © 1985 by The New York Times Company. Reprinted by permission.

Mary M. Kent & Carl Haub. Table from "1984 Population Data Sheet" reprinted by permission of the Population Reference Bureau.

Henry F. Myers. "High Unemployment Is Likely to Linger On" from *The Wall Street Journal,* February 25, 1985 reprinted by permission of *The Wall Street Journal.* © Dow Jones & Company, 1985. All rights reserved.

Organization for Economic Cooperation and Development. Table 15.1. from *OECD Revenue Statistics.* Reprinted by permission.

Alan Reynolds. "Less Will Get You More" from *The Wall Street Journal,* January 23, 1985 reprinted by permission of *The Wall Street Journal.* © Dow Jones & Company, 1985. All rights reserved.

Stephanie Saul. "Employment at Will" copyright 1985, Newsday, Inc. Reprinted by permission.

Harry Schwartz. "How Much Is a Life Worth?" from *The Wall Street Journal,* September 15, 1980 reprinted by permission of *The Wall Street Journal.* © Dow Jones & Company, 1980. All rights reserved.

Richard Vedder and Lowell Gallaway. "Soaking the Rich Through Tax Cuts" from *The Wall Street Journal,* March 21, 1985 reprinted by permission of *The Wall Street Journal.* © Dow Jones & Company, 1985. All rights reserved.

Table 35.1. from *The Wall Street Journal,* March 1, 1985, reprinted by permission of *The Wall Street Journal.* © Dow Jones & Company, 1985. All rights reserved.

World Bank. Six tables from *World Development Report 1984* reprinted by permission of the Oxford University Press and the World Bank.

# Preface

Every day, the media carry stories about the national, international, and local economies—how they work, or fail to work, to produce the goods and services people want. Whether the headlines are "unemployment," "inflation," "protectionism," "budget deficit," "tax reform," or "farm debt crisis," they indicate the prominent role economics has come to play in people's daily lives.

One central purpose in writing this text is to explore, with the aid of economic theory, the basic issues that underlie these headlines. Using theory as the "engine of analysis" to provide the necessary structure and methodology, this text applies it to the economic problems and policies of today. The intent is that students completing this text will have a better understanding of why inflation and unemployment occur, how the market power of a monopoly affects the way a market works, the power and the limits of governments to remedy economic problems, and other issues.

Consensus among economists has been hard to achieve in the 1980s. Old solutions have failed to work, new solutions have been proposed, and we are typically confronted by several quite different answers to any given question. But another central purpose of this text is to show students that a surprisingly small number of concepts, principles, and models are common to *any* proposed solution, and that the different views of different economists are more a matter of interpretation than of methodology.

## The Text

With these central purposes in mind, *Economics* has been designed to be comprehensive and adaptable to most curricula, to be rich in applications, and to make economics easier to learn.

### A text that is comprehensive, and adaptable to most curricula

Part I forms an introduction to macroeconomics (Parts II–V) or microeconomics (Parts VI–IX), so *Economics* is equally suited to a macro/micro sequence or a micro/macro sequence in the two-term principles course.

### *Macro*

Parts II–IV form the core of the macro section, and treat money and monetary policy *before* covering national income and fiscal policy. Part IV ends with a thorough development of aggregate supply and demand, which was introduced first in Chapter 6. In Part V "Alternative Views of the Macroeconomy," monetarism, supply-side economics, and rational expectations theory are covered in three self-contained chapters. They are unified by reference to the aggregate supply/demand model, but each is complete in itself, allowing instructors to choose whether or not to assign any or all of these chapters.

### *Micro*

Parts VI through VIII form the core of the micro section. Appendices treating indifference curves, isoquants, isocosts, and several other optional topics allow instructors to choose whether or not to cover them in their principles course. In Part IX, optional chapters covering market failures, government controls, agriculture, and public choice provide further flexibility in choosing specific areas of microeconomics applications.

## A text that is rich in issues and applications

"Perspectives on Economics"—most written specifically for this text—draw on the experience and insight of a wide range of economists to illuminate current issues, applications, and historical background. Flat tax proposals, sexual discrimination, the federal deficit, and many other topics are covered. Informative, authoritative, and thought-provoking, these short essays show the many perspectives of economic analysis, and acquaint students with the kinds of questions economists ask, and some of the answers they propose.

## A text that makes economics easier to learn

Right from Chapter 1, in which the concepts of scarcity and choice are clarified through an eyewitness account of life in a prisoner-of-war camp, abstract terms are presented in the context of realistic, integrated examples.

All key terms are highlighted, defined immediately in the margins, and defined again in an alphabetical end-of-text glossary. In addition, the index indicates the page on which each term is initially defined in context.

Each chapter begins by asking the *central question* the chapter will provide answers to. *Key terms* are also previewed before the student encounters them in the text. All figures appear near the pertinent discussion of them in the text, and have full descriptive captions as well. Each chapter ends with a *summary, major conclusions,* and *discussion questions.*

## Acknowledgments

Several of my colleagues helped bring economic issues to life by contributing articles for the boxed inserts in the text. For their assistance, I would like to thank (in order of first appearance): Delores T. Martin, Clark Nardinelli, Dennis Placone, Dwight R. Lee, N. Keith Womer, Thomas M. Humbert, William F. Shughart II, Clinton H. Whitehurst Jr., Bruce Yandle, Adele Ernst Wick, Catherine England, John Warner, Terry L. Anderson, Robert Valero, B. H. Robinson, Clifford M. Hardin, Cotton M. Lindsay, Edward L. Hudgins, Katsuro Sakoh, Laurence S. Moss, Russell Shannon, and Martin Schnitzer.

Finally, a word about Professor Hugh Macaulay, who will complete his thirty-seventh year of college and university teaching in 1986. He is the type of professor every student should have for their introductory economics course. Although he can barely be seen behind most normal size podiums, there are few professors who can stand higher in the minds of their students. His students may not always agree with him, but they are not able to ignore him or dismiss him. In and out of class, Professor Macaulay exudes excitement: for a new-found twist on an old argument, for an economist joke that he can turn on himself. By sheer example—by constantly putting his students first and giving of himself in helping his colleagues with their work at the expense of his own—Professor Macaulay has been a moral force among those who have known him. He is, simply stated, a person to be emulated. For this reason, I am proud to be able to dedicate this book to him.

**Professor John E. Anderson**
*Eastern Michigan University*

**Professor Richard G. Anderson**
*Ohio State University*

**Professor Ronald G. Brandolini**
*Valencia Community College*

**Professor Wallace Broome**
*Community College of Rhode Island*

**Professor Marshall Colberg**
*Florida State University*

**Professor Douglas W. Copeland**
*Kansas State University*

**Professor Eleanor D. Craig**
*University of Delaware*

**Professor Lawrence Daellenbach**
*University of Wisconsin, La Crosse*

**Professor Mary Jane Gorman**
*Furman University*

**Professor A. R. Gutowsky**
*California State University, Sacramento*

# Acknowledgments

Many reviewers read the manuscript of *Economics* at various stages of its development and offered valuable suggestions for its enrichment.
I appreciate the help of these reviewers.

**Professor Richard B. Hansen**
*University of Northern Iowa*

**Professor Roy B. Helfgott**
*New Jersey Institute of Technology*

**Professor Willard W. Howard**
*Maricopa County Community College, Phoenix College*

**Professor Maryann O. Keating**
*University of Notre Dame*

**Professor Anatoli Kuprianov**
*Virginia Polytechnic Institute and State University*

**Professor Patrick Lenihan**
*Eastern Illinois University*

**Professor James R. Marchand**
*University of Mississippi*

**Professor Kent W. Olson**
*Oklahoma State University*

**Professor Robert Payne**
*Portland Community College*

**Professor James T. Peach**
*New Mexico State University*

**Professor Stanley C. Sofas**
*Santa Barbara City College*

**Professor Richard A. Yach**
*Des Moines Area Community College*

**Economics,**
The hardcover text.

**Macroeconomics** and **Microeconomics,** paperbacks.
Both volumes include chapters on introduction to economics, public choice economics, international trade and finance, comparative economic systems, and economic development.

**Study Guide,** by Douglas W. Copeland, Kansas State University.
For each chapter, provides:
Chapter Summary
Chapter Objectives
Review Terms and Concepts
Completion Exercises
Problems and Applications
True/False Questions
Multiple Choice Questions
Discussion Questions

# The Complete Teaching/Learning System

**Instructor's Manual**, prepared by the author.
For each chapter, provides:
Chapter Objectives
Key Terms
Chapter Conclusions and Teaching Tips
Suggested Answers to all discussion questions in the text

**Transparency Masters** for every figure in the book and instructions for using the computerized Test Bank are also provided in the Instructor's Manual.

**Test Bank,** by Douglas W. Copeland, Kansas State University
Contains over 2,000 items in two separate files, A and B, providing two alternative sets of test items for each chapter.

**Computerized Test Bank**
Available for mainframes, minicomputers, and IBM PC, Apple II, and TRS-80 microcomputers.

**Two-Color Overhead Transparencies**
One hundred key figures from the text, reproduced on mylar for clear, legible projection.

**Quadrant I**
A computerized color graphics package that can generate virtually any graph commonly used in economics. Suitable for both classroom demonstration and for making custom overhead transparencies.

# Contents in Brief

| *Chapter Number In:* | *Economics* | *Macroeconomics* | *Microeconomics* |
|---|---|---|---|
| **Alternative Views of the Macroeconomy** | | | |
| The Monetarist View of Unemployment and Inflation | 14 | 14 | |
| Supply-Side Economics | 15 | 15 | |
| Rational Expectations | 16 | 16 | |
| **Principles of Consumer Behavior and the Theory of Demand** | | | |
| Principles of Individual Behavior | 17 | | 5 |
| Consumer Choice and Demand | 18 | | 6 |
| **Costs and the Firm in the Market Economy** | | | |
| Business Organizations | 19 | | 7 |
| Cost and Producer Choice | 20 | | 8 |
| Cost in the Short Run and the Long Run | 21 | | 9 |
| Perfect Competition | 22 | | 10 |
| Pure Monopoly | 23 | | 11 |
| Imperfect Competition | 24 | | 12 |
| Business Regulation | 25 | | 13 |
| **Resource Markets** | | | |
| The Competitive Labor Market | 26 | | 14 |

| *Chapter Number In:* | *Economics* | *Macroeconomics* | *Microeconomics* |
|---|---|---|---|
| Monopsonies and Unions | 27 | | 15 |
| Rent, Interest, and Profit | 28 | | 16 |
| Poverty and Poverty Relief | 29 | | 17 |
| **Applications of Microeconomic Theory** | | | |
| Market Failures: External Costs and Benefits | 30 | | 18 |
| Government Controls: Price Controls and Consumer Protection | 31 | | 19 |
| Agriculture and Government Agricultural Policy | 32 | | 20 |
| Public Choice: The Economics of Government | 33 | 21 | 21 |
| **The International Economy** | | | |
| International Trade | 34 | 17 | 22 |
| International Finance | 35 | 18 | 23 |
| Comparative Economic Systems | 36 | 19 | 24 |
| Economic Growth and Development | 37 | 20 | 25 |

# Contents

# MACROECONOMICS

# Part I

# Introduction

## Central Question

*What is economics?*

## Key Terms

**Market**

**Entrepreneur**

**Resources**

**Land**

**Labor**

**Capital**

**Technology**

**Scarcity**

**Economics**

**Theory**

**Positive economics**

**Normative economics**

**Microeconomics**

**Macroeconomics**

# Chapter 1

# The Economic Way of Thinking

*In economics in particular, education seems to be largely a matter of unlearning and "disteaching" rather than constructive action. A once famous American humorist observed that "it's not ignorance does so much damage; it's knowin' so derned much that ain't so." . . . It seems that the hardest things to learn and to teach are things that everyone already knows.*

*Frank H. Knight*

**Market:** the process by which buyers and sellers determine what they are willing to buy and sell, on what terms. That is, the process by which buyers and sellers decide the prices and quantities of goods to be bought and sold.

Economic systems spring from necessity. R. A. Radford, an American soldier who was captured and imprisoned during the Second World War, left a vivid account of the primitive market for goods and services that grew up in his prisoner-of-war camp.[1] A **market** is the process by which buyers and sellers determine what they are willing to buy and sell, on what terms. That is, it is the process by which buyers and sellers decide the prices and quantities of goods that are to be bought and sold. Because the inmates had few opportunities to produce the things they wanted, they turned to a system of exchanges based on the cigarettes, toiletries, chocolate, and other rations distributed to them periodically by the Red Cross.

The Red Cross distributed the supplies equally among the prisoners, but "very soon after capture . . . [the prisoners] realized that it was both undesirable and unnecessary, in view of the limited size and the equality of supplies, to give away or to accept gifts of cigarettes or food. Goodwill developed into trading as a more equitable means of maximizing individual satisfaction."[2] As the weeks went by, trade expanded and the prices of goods stabilized. A soldier who hoped to receive a high price for his soap found he had to compete with others who also wanted to trade soap. Soon shops emerged, and middlemen began to take advantage of discrepancies in the prices offered in different bungalows.

A priest, for example, found that he could exchange a pack of cigarettes for a pound of cheese in one bungalow, trade the cheese for a pack and a half of cigarettes in a second bungalow, and return home with more cigarettes than he had begun with. Although he was acting in his own self-interest, he had provided the people in the second bungalow with something they wanted—more cheese than they would otherwise have had. In fact, prices for cheese and cigarettes differed partly because prisoners had different desires, and partly because they could not all interact freely. In exploiting the discrepancy in prices, the priest moved the camp's store of cheese from the first bungalow, where it was worth less, to the second bungalow, where it was worth more. Everyone involved in the trade benefited from the priest's enterprise.

**Entrepreneur:** an enterprising person who discovers profitable opportunities and organizes, directs, and manages productive ventures.

A few entrepreneurs in the camp hoarded cigarettes and used them to buy up the troops' rations shortly after issue—and then sold the rations just before the next issue, at higher prices. An **entrepreneur** is an enterprising person who discovers profitable opportunities and organizes, directs, and manages productive ventures. Though these entrepreneurs were pursuing their own private interest, like the priest, they were providing a service to the other prisoners. They bought the rations when people wanted to get rid of them and sold them when people were running short. The difference between the low price at which they bought and the high price at which they sold gave them the incentive they needed to make the trades, hold on to the rations, and assume the risk that the price of rations might not rise.

1. R. A. Radford, "The Economic Organization of a P.O.W. Camp," *Economica,* (November, 1945), pp. 180–201.
2. Ibid., p. 190.

Soon the troops began to use cigarettes as money, quoting prices in packs or fractions of packs. (Only the less desirable brands of cigarette were used this way; the better brands were smoked.) Because cigarettes were generally acceptable, the soldier who wanted soap no longer had to search out those who might want his jam; he could buy the soap with cigarettes. Even nonsmokers began to accept cigarettes in trade.

This makeshift monetary system adjusted itself to allow for changes in the money supply. On the day the Red Cross distributed new supplies of cigarettes, prices rose, reflecting the influx of new money. After nights spent listening to nearby bombing, when the nervous prisoners had smoked up their holdings of cigarettes, prices fell. Radford saw a form of social order emerging in these spontaneous, voluntary, and completely undirected efforts. Even in this unlikely environment, the human tendency toward mutually advantageous interaction had asserted itself.

Today markets for numerous new and used products spring up spontaneously in much the same way. At the end of each semester college students can be found trading books among themselves, or standing in line at the bookstore to resell books they bought at the beginning of the semester. Garage sales are now common in practically all communities. Indeed, like the priest in the POW camp, many people go to garage sales to buy what they believe they can resell—at a higher price, of course.

More than two hundred years ago, Adam Smith outlined a society that resembled these POW camp markets in his classic *Wealth of Nations*. Smith, considered the first economist, asked why markets arise and how they contribute to the social welfare. In answering that question, he defined the economic problem.

## The Economic Problem

Our world is not nearly as restrictive as Radford's prison, but it is no Garden of Eden either. Most of us are constantly occupied in securing the food, clothing, and shelter we need to exist, to say nothing of those things we would only like to have—a tape deck, a night on the town. Indeed if we think seriously about the world around us, we can make two general observations.

**Resources:** things used in the production of goods and services.

First, the world is more or less fixed in size and limited in its resources. **Resources** are things used in the production of goods and services. There are only so many acres of land, gallons of water, trees, rivers, wind currents, oil and mineral deposits, trained workers, and machines that can be used in any one period to produce the things we need and want. We can plant more trees, find more oil, and increase our stock of human talent. But still there are limits on what we can accomplish with the resources at our disposal.

**Land:** the surface area of the world and everything in nature—minerals, chemicals, plants—that is useful in the production process.

Economists group resources into four broad categories: land, labor, capital (also called investment goods), and technology. **Land** includes the surface area of the world and everything in nature—minerals, chemicals, plants—that is useful in the production process. **Labor** includes any way in which human energy, physical or mental, can be usefully expended.

**Labor:** any way in which human energy, physical or mental, can be usefully expended.

## Economists in History: Adam Smith (1723–1790)

"It is not from the benevolence of the butcher, the brewer, or the baker, that we expect our dinner, but from their regard to their own interest. We address ourselves, not to their humanity but to their self-love, and never talk to them of our own necessities but of their advantages."

When this passage from Adam Smith's *An Inquiry into the Nature and Causes of the Wealth of Nations* (1776) is taken out of context, as it so often is, it may convey a narrow and cynical view of human behavior. Understood in context, however, Smith's statement is merely a logical one. In a complex society, one simply cannot rely on the kindness of others for all one's wants and needs. People are charitable—at least most people are—but they have their limits. As Smith wrote, the individual "at all times stands in need of the cooperation and assistance of great multitudes [of people], while his whole life is scarcely sufficient to gain the friendship of a few persons . . . He will more likely prevail if he can interest their self-love in his favor, and show them that it is for their own advantage to do what he requires of them."

Smith saw the market as a means of enlisting cooperation among strangers. "Give me what I want and I will give you what you want" is the proposition that lies at the base of every market transaction. The butcher, the brewer, and the baker may not know their customers, but by pursuing their own interest, they provide the meat, beer, and bread that others need in order to put dinner on the table.

Prevailing opinion in Smith's time held that in a market exchange, one party profits at the expense of the other. Smith, however, reasoned that if both parties enter into an exchange *voluntarily*, and each gives up something of value for something else of value, both parties benefit. They may not be as well off as they would like to be, but their welfare has been improved by the transaction. Through trade, they have each obtained something they want but cannot produce themselves.

Smith's ideas also conflicted with the mercantilist philosophy of trade, which held that the unregulated pursuit of private interest would inevitably lead to disorder. In Europe in the seventeenth and eighteenth centuries, wages, prices, interest rates, employment, foreign trade, and the quality of goods and services were all strictly controlled by government. The object of this control was to ensure the ruling class's vision of social justice through the administration of what was produced and how it was produced and distributed. Yet to Smith, self-interest was obviously a constructive, coordinating force. In the drive to fulfill their own needs, self-interested people had to appeal to the interests of others. Self-interest is an incentive, a reason to cooperate and coordinate one's activities with others'.

**Capital** (investment goods): any output of a production process that is designed to be used later in other production processes. Includes plant and equipment.

**Capital** (investment goods) includes any output of a production process that is designed to be used later in other production processes. Plant and equipment—things produced to produce other things—are examples of these manufactured means of production. **Technology** is the knowledge of how resources can be combined in productive ways.

To this list some economists would add a fifth category, entrepreneurial talent. The entrepreneur is critical to the success of any economy, especially if it relies heavily on markets. Because entrepreneurs discover more effective and profitable ways of organizing resources to produce the goods and services people want, they are often considered a resource in themselves.

Critics of the market system saw profit as an unfair drain on workers' earnings, but Smith viewed it as an incentive, the reward that encourages the producer to meet the interests of others. He felt that competition among producers would keep profits and prices low, so consumers would not be overcharged. In Smith's words, self-interest acts like an "invisible hand," guiding individuals to work for the common interest in the pursuit of their own gain.

Smith saw government as necessary, but only to provide for national defense, for the administration of law and justice, and for certain essential public works that cannot be provided efficiently by the market, such as roads and education. He objected to further government involvement in the market for three reasons. First, government means collective decision making, which runs counter to the individual self-interest that is the foundation of the market system. To Smith, individual choices were important. Leaving decisions to the individual seemed the best way to ensure that good choices would be made.

Second, Smith argued that government restrictions on the market can prevent mutually beneficial trades and reduce the welfare of potential traders. Government-imposed tariffs on imports are a good example of this negative effect. Tariffs increase the price of imports, encouraging consumers to buy more domestic substitutes than they would otherwise, at a higher price. As a result, consumers get less for their dollar.

Third, Smith felt that businessmen would exploit any government power over the economy to further their own interests. He once wrote, "The proposal of any new law or regulations of commerce which comes from this order [of entrepreneurs], ought always to be listened to with great precaution, and ought never to be adopted till after having been long and carefully examined . . . with the most suspicious attention. It comes from an order of men . . . who have generally an interest to deceive and even to oppress the public. . . ." Businessmen, said Smith, seldom come together except to conspire against the public—that is, to restrict trade in their favor. He felt that the competition inherent in the market system would help to minimize such collusion.

Although he may never have used the word, Smith was well aware of the imperfections of the market system. He recognized the risk of monopoly, which he saw as an evil fostered primarily by government. And he acknowledged that the market often adjusts slowly to change and may fail to produce adequate quantities of certain goods without government intervention. *The Wealth of Nations* did not attempt to prove that the free market system is perfect. Rather, it was a classic statement of the relative merits of the market system, compared with the alternatives.

**Technology:** the knowledge of how resources can be combined in productive ways.

Our second general observation is that in contrast to the world's physical limitations, human wants abound. You yourself would probably like to have books, notebooks, pens, and a calculator; perhaps even a computer with 512K worth of memory and two double-sided disk drives. A stereo system, a car, more clothes, a plane ticket home, a seat at a big concert or ballgame—you could probably go on for a long time, especially when you realize how many basics, like three good meals a day, you normally take for granted.

In fact, most people want far more than they can ever have. One of the unavoidable conditions of life is the fundamental fact of scarcity.

**Scarcity:** the fact that we cannot all have everything we want all the time.

**Scarcity** is the fact that we cannot all have everything we want all the time. Put simply, there isn't enough of everything to go around. Consequently society must face several unavoidable questions:

1. What will be produced? More guns or more butter? More schools or more prisons? More cars or more art, more textbooks or more "Saturday night specials"?
2. How will those things be produced, considering the resources at our disposal? Shall we use a great deal of labor and little mechanical power, or vice versa?
3. Who will receive the goods and services produced? Shall we distribute them equally? If not, then on what other basis shall we distribute them?
4. Perhaps most important, how shall we answer all these questions? Shall we allow for individual freedom of choice, or shall we make all these decisions collectively?

These questions have no easy answers. Most of us spend our lives attempting to come to grips with them on an individual level. What should I do with my time today—study or walk through the woods? How should I study—in the library or at home with the stereo on? Who is going to benefit from my efforts—me or my mother, who wants me to succeed? Am I going to live by principle or by habit? Take each day as it comes or plan ahead? In a broader sense, these questions are fundamental not just to the individual but to all the social sciences, economics in particular. Scarcity is the root of economics. **Economics** is the study of how people cope with scarcity—with the pressing problem of how to allocate their limited resources among their competing wants so as to satisfy as many of those wants as possible.

**Economics:** the study of how people cope with scarcity—with the pressing problem of how to allocate their limited resources among their competing wants so as to satisfy as many of those wants as possible.

Markets like the one in the POW camp emerge in direct response to scarcity. Because people want more than is immediately available, they produce some goods and services for trade. By exchanging things they like less for things they like more, they reallocate their resources, enhancing their welfare as individuals.

## The Scope of Economics

Beginning students often associate economics with a rather narrow portion of the human experience: the pursuit of wealth; money and taxes; commercial and industrial life. And critics often suggest that economists are oblivious to the aesthetic and ethical dimensions of human experience. Such criticism is not altogether unjustified. But increasingly, economists are expanding their horizons and applying the laws of economics to the full spectrum of human activities.

The struggle to improve one's lot is not limited to the attainment of material goals. Though most economic principles have to do with the pursuit of material gain, they can be relevant to aesthetic and humanistic goals as well. The appreciation of a poem or play can be the subject of economic inquiry. Poems and plays, and the time in which to appreciate them, are also scarce.

Jacob Viner, an economist active in the first half of this century, once defined economics as what economists do. Today economists study an increasingly diverse array of topics. As always, they are involved in describing market processes, methods of trade, and commercial and industrial patterns. But they also pay considerable attention to poverty and wealth; to racial, sexual, and religious discrimination; to politics and bureaucracy; to crime and crime law; and to revolution. There is even an economics of group interaction, in which economic principles are applied to marital and family problems. Thus though economists are still working on the conventional problems of inflation, unemployment, and international monetary problems, they are also studying the delivery of health care to the very young and the elderly, or of housing to the disadvantaged. In one way or another, today's economists are tackling a wide variety of subjects, from committee structure to the criminal justice system, ethics, voting rules, and the legislative process.

What is the unifying factor in these diverse inquiries? What ties them all together and distinguishes the economist's work from that of other social scientists? Economists take a distinctive approach to the study of human behavior. They employ a mode of analysis based on certain presuppositions about human behavior. For example, much economic analysis starts with the general proposition that people prefer more to less of those things they want; that they seek to maximize their welfare by making reasonably consistent choices in the things they buy and sell. These propositions enable economists to derive the "law of demand" (people will buy more of any good at a lower price than at a higher price, and vice versa), and many other principles of human behavior.

One purpose of this book is to describe this special approach in considerable detail—to develop in precise terms the commonly accepted principles of economic analysis, and to demonstrate how they can be used to understand a variety of problems, including pollution, unemployment, crime, and ticket scalping. In every case, economic analysis is useful only if it is based on a sound theory that can be evaluated in terms of real-world experience.

## Developing and Using Economic Theories

The real world of economics is staggeringly complex. Each day millions of people engage in innumerable transactions, only some of them involving money, and many of them undertaken for contradictory reasons. To make sense of all these activities, economists turn to theory.

**Theory:** a set of abstractions about the real world. An economic theory is a simplified explanation of how the economy, or part of the economy, functions or would function under specific conditions.

A theory is a model of how the world is put together, an attempt to uncover some order in the seemingly random events of daily life. Economic theory is abstract, but not in the sense that its models lack concreteness. On the contrary, good models are laid out with great precision. But economic theories are simplified models *abstracted from* the complexity of the real world. The economist deliberately concentrates on just a few outstanding features of a problem in an effort to discover the laws that govern their relationship. A **theory** is a set of abstractions about the real world. An economic theory is a simplified explanation of how the economy, or part of the economy, functions or would function under specific conditions.

Quite often the economist must also make unproved assumptions, called simplifying assumptions, about the parts of the economy under study. For example, in examining the effects of price and availability on the amount of food sold, the economist might assume that people eat only oranges and bananas in the model society in question. Such a simplifying assumption is permissible in constructing a model for two reasons. First, it makes the discussion more manageable. Second, it does not alter the problem under study or destroy its relevance to the real world.

As following chapters will reveal, economic theorizing is largely deductive—that is, the analysis proceeds from very general propositions (such as "more is preferred to less") to much more precise statements or predictions (for example, "the quantity purchased will rise when the price falls").[3] Economic theories sometimes vary in their premises and conclusions, but all develop through the following three steps.

First, a few very general premises or propositions are stated. "More is preferred to less" or "People will seek to maximize their welfare" are examples of such propositions. The premises tend to be so general that they are beyond dispute, at least for the economists developing the theory.

Second, logical deductions, which are tentative predictions about behavior, are drawn from the premises. From the premise "People will seek to maximize their welfare" we can deduce how people will tend to allocate their incomes, at certain prices. We can then conclude that they will purchase more of a good when its price falls. Mathematics and graphic analysis are often very useful in deducing the consequences of premises.

Third, the predictions are tested against observable experience. Theory may tell us that people buy more at lower prices than at higher prices, but the critical question is whether that prediction is borne out in the real world. Do people actually buy more apples when the price falls? Empirical tests require data to be carefully selected and statistically analyzed.

Empirical tests can never prove a theory's validity. The behavior that is observed—more apples purchased, for instance—may be caused by factors not considered in the theory. That is, the quantity of apples purchased may increase for some reason other than a drop in price. Empirical tests can only fail to disprove a theory. If a theory is repeatedly evaluated in different circumstances and is not disproven, however, its usefulness and general applicability increase. Economists have considerable confidence in the proposition that price and quantity purchased are inversely related because it has been repeatedly tested and found to be accurate.

Though a theory is not a complete and realistic description of the real world, a good theory should incorporate enough data to simulate real life. That is, it should provide some explanation for past experiences and

---

3. In contrast, inductive theorizing proceeds from very precise statements about observable relationships (such as "people are laid off when plants close") to much more general propositions (for example, "plant closings increase unemployment").

permit reasonably accurate predictions of the future. When you evaluate a new theory, ask yourself: Does this theory explain what has been observed? Does it provide a better basis for prediction than other theories?

## Positive and Normative Economics

Economic thinking is often divided into two categories, positive and normative. **Positive economics** is that branch of economic inquiry that is concerned with the world as it is rather than as it should be. It deals only with the consequences of changes in economic conditions or policies. A positive economist suspends questions of values when dealing with issues like crime or minimum wage laws. The object is to predict the effect of changes in the criminal code or the minimum wage rate—not to evaluate the fairness of such changes. **Normative economics** is that branch of economic inquiry that deals with value judgments—with what prices, production levels, incomes, and government policies *ought* to be. A normative economist does not shrink from the question of what the minimum wage rate ought to be. To arrive at an answer, the economist weighs the results of various minimum wage rates on the groups affected by them—the unemployed, employers, taxpayers, and so on. Then, on the basis of value judgments of the relative need or merit of each group, the normative economist recommends a specific minimum wage rate. Of course, values differ from one person to the next. In the analytical jump from recognizing the alternatives to prescribing a solution, scientific thinking gives way to ethical judgment.

**Positive economics:** that branch of economic inquiry that is concerned with the world as it is rather than as it should be. Deals only with the consequences of changes in economic conditions or policies.

**Normative economics:** that branch of economic inquiry that deals with value judgments—with what prices, production levels, incomes, and government policies ought to be.

## Microeconomics and Macroeconomics

The discipline of economics is divided into two main parts: microeconomics and macroeconomics. As the term *micro* (as in microscope) suggests, **microeconomics** is the study of the individual markets—for corn, records, books, and so forth—that operate within the broad national economy. When economists measure, explain, and predict the demand for specific products like bicycles and hand calculators, they are dealing with microeconomics. Much of the work of economists is concerned with microeconomic analysis—that is, with the interpretation of events in the marketplace and of personal choices among products.

**Microeconomics:** the study of the individual markets—for corn, records, books, and so forth—that operate within the broad national economy.

Questions of interest to microeconomists include:

What determines the price of particular goods and services?

What determines the output of individual firms and industries?

What determines the wages workers receive? The interest rates lenders receive? The profits businesses receive?

How do government policies—like minimum wage laws, price controls, tariffs, and excise taxes—affect the price and output levels of individual markets?

**Macroeconomics:** the study of the national economy as a whole, or of its major components. Deals with the "big picture," not the details, of the nation's economic activity.

Economists are also interested in measuring, explaining, and predicting the performance of the economic system itself. To do so they study broad subdivisions of the economy, such as the total output of all firms that produce goods and services. **Macroeconomics** is the study of the national economy as a whole, or of its major components. It deals with the "big picture," not the details, of the nation's economic activity.

Instead of concentrating on how many bicycles or hand calculators are sold, macroeconomists watch how many goods and services consumers purchase in total, or how much money all producers spend on new plant and equipment. Instead of tracking the price of a particular good in a particular market, macroeconomics monitors the general price level or average of all prices. And instead of focusing on the wage rate and the number of people employed as plumbers or engineers, macroeconomists study incomes of all employees and the total number of people employed throughout the economy. In short, macroeconomics involves the study of national production, unemployment, and inflation. For that reason it is often referred to as aggregate economics.

Typical macroeconomic questions include:

What determines the general price level? The rate of inflation?

What determines national income and production levels?

What determines national employment and unemployment levels?

What effects do government monetary and budgetary policies have on the general price, income, production, employment, and unemployment levels?

What, if anything, can government do to combat inflation, unemployment, and recession?

These questions are of more than academic interest. The theories that have been developed to answer them can be applied to problems and issues of the real world. Throughout this book, as well as in specific chapters on topics like inflation, regulation and deregulation, and price controls and consumer protection, we will examine the practical applications of economic theory. In some basic way, scarcity—and the economic question of how to deal with it—touches all of us.

## Summary and Extensions

Economics is a discipline best described as the study of human interaction in the context of scarcity. It is the study of how, individually and collectively, people use their scarce resources to satisfy as many of their wants as possible. The economic method is founded in a set of presuppositions about human behavior, on the basis of which economists construct theoretical models. A major purpose of this book is to describe the analytical tools economists use, and in that way to show how they study human behavior.

## Major Conclusions

1. Economics can be defined as the study of human behavior in the context of scarcity. It is the study of how individuals, confronted by scarcity, allocate their resources among competing wants.
2. Economic thinking is founded on the assumption that people's needs and wants are limitless, but resources, goods, and services are scarce. Thus people must choose among the many things they want—they cannot have everything. Individually or collectively, they must decide what to produce, how to produce it, and for whom to produce it.
3. Resources are things useful in producing the goods and services people want. Economists divide resources into four categories: land, labor, capital, and technology.
4. Economists construct theories, or simplified models of the real world, in order to highlight the relationships among a few outstanding features of the economy.
5. Positive economics deals with the economy as it is, specifically with the consequences of a change in economic conditions or policy. Normative economics deals with value judgments, or with what economic policy and conditions ought to be.
6. Microeconomics is the study of individual markets, specifically their price levels, resource inputs, and product outputs. Macroeconomics is the study of economic activity across many markets, specifically the national price, output, employment, and unemployment levels.

## Questions to Ponder

1. In the prison camp described on pages 6–7, rations were distributed equally. Why did trade within and among bungalows result?
2. Recall the priest who traded cigarettes for cheese, and cheese for cigarettes, so that he ended up with more cigarettes than he had initially. Did someone else in the camp lose by the priest's activities? How was the priest able to end up better off than when he began? What did his activities do to the price of cheese in the different bungalows?
3. Theories may be defective, but economists continue to use them. Why?
4. An introductory economics book could include theories more complex than those in this book. What might be the tradeoffs in dealing with more complex theories?
5. How can values influence scientific inquiry? How can value-free (positive) economic analysis affect the assessment of policy?

## Central Question

*Given the scarcity of resources and the limitlessness of human wants, how does society decide what to produce?*

## Key Terms

Cost
Production possibilities curve
Consumption goods
Private goods
Public goods
Specialization of labor
Economies of scale
Diseconomies of scale
Money
Comparative advantage
Circular flow of income

# Chapter 2

# Scarcity and Production Possibilities

*Economics is the science which studies human behavior as a relationship between ends and scarce means which have alternative uses.*
Lionel Robbins

The last chapter introduced the basic economic problem: the conflict between unlimited human wants and limited resources. Using graphic analysis, this chapter examines the decisions that must be made individually and collectively as a result of the conflict. Two concepts, the production possibilities curve and the circular flow of income, are particularly important to the discussion.

The appendix at the end of this chapter outlines the basic features and uses of graphs. If you are unsure how to use or read graphs, turn to page 36 before reading further.

## The Implications of Scarcity

Scarcity is a fact of life. Individually and collectively we cannot have all that we want; we are forced to live within our means. So the essential economic problem is this: Our ability to imagine the goods and services we would like to have far exceeds our ability to produce them—that is, to transform the resources at our disposal into the goods and services we want.

From the basic observation of scarcity, three conclusions flow. First, there is always more than one use for a resource. Time not spent studying can be used to farm, to run computers, or to raise a family. There is always something constructive for people (or machinery, or land) to do. Economically speaking, a person is unemployed because some barrier—distance or lack of skill—separates him or her from productive work, not because none exists. Technological change may eliminate the need for labor in a given industry, but it also frees labor to do other things, satisfy other wants.

Second, we must choose among alternative uses for resources. Choice is an inescapable, sometimes agonizing, part of the economic process. Whenever we do anything, we forgo the opportunity to do other things. If we go to a movie, we choose not to study. If we produce textiles, we forgo the chance to make machines or a variety of other products and services. And if we expand public education, we must do without extra police protection—or raise taxes and do without private goods. "You can't have your cake and eat it too" is a well-worn adage, but an economically apt one.

Third, every choice has a cost. Though often stated in dollars and cents, an item's cost is more accurately defined as the value of what could have been purchased instead. Dollars and cents are only a means of measuring this opportunity cost. **Cost** (or, more precisely, opportunity cost) is the value of the most highly preferred alternative not taken.

**Cost** (opportunity cost): the value of the most highly preferred alternative not taken.

As long as resources are scarce and we can choose among them, everything we do will have a cost. There is a cost to studying, to producing textiles, and to providing public education. Although we talk about cost in terms of dollars and cents, cost itself will never be seen—can never be seen—for it is the option not taken, the value of what we could have done, but didn't.

## The Production Possibilities Curve

The limitations and choices inherent in the economy can be represented graphically. Assume that a nation can produce only two goods, guns (measured in numbers of guns) and butter (measured in pounds). Although this economy can produce only so much, choices among alternatives do exist. Resources can be shifted from one line of production to another, changing the combination of guns and butter produced. At one extreme, the nation can devote all its resources to making guns, producing no butter at all. Alternatively, it can make only butter. Or resources can be divided between the two production processes, yielding some combination of guns and butter. If all possible production combinations are plotted on a graph (with guns on the horizontal axis and butter on the vertical), the result is a production possibilities curve. A **production possibilities curve** (sometimes called a production possibilities frontier or a product transformation curve) is a graphical representation of the various combinations of goods that can be produced when all resources are fully and efficiently employed. It shows all the production combinations possible when all resources available are used in the most productive way possible, given the best known technology (see Figure 2.1).

**Production possibilities curve** (production possibilities frontier): a graphical representation of the various combinations of goods that can be produced when all resources are fully and efficiently employed.

### Linear Production Possibilities Curves

The production possibilities curve can take several shapes, two of which are shown in Figure 2.1. All are downward sloping from left to right. (Such curves are said to have a *negative slope*—see the Appendix, page 36, for an explanation of the term *slope*.) Why? Suppose we are using all our resources to produce guns; that is, we are at point *a* in Figure 2.1, panel (a). Then the only way we can produce butter is to move some resources away from the production of guns. Such a shift necessarily means a cut in the number of guns produced. We move from point *a* to point *b*—upward and to the left.

The movement from *a* to *b* on the curve in Figure 2.1(a) can be seen as the cost of producing the butter. That is, the cost of the 80 pounds of butter gained is the *value* of the 50 guns given up. It is important to remember that cost is the value, not the number, of what is given up. In Figure 2.1(a), the slope of the curve, $-80/50$, or $-8/5$, is constant (because the curve is straight). Therefore the *number* of guns forgone for each additional unit of butter remains constant. The value of additional units of butter, in economic terms, does not necessarily remain constant, however.

In fact, as we move up along the curve, acquiring more butter and giving up more guns, the relative value of guns and butter is almost certain to change. As more guns are given up, they will be taken away from uses that are increasingly valuable. Hence the cost of additional units of butter will tend to rise as more are produced. At the same time, the relative value of the additional units of butter will tend to fall, since they will be

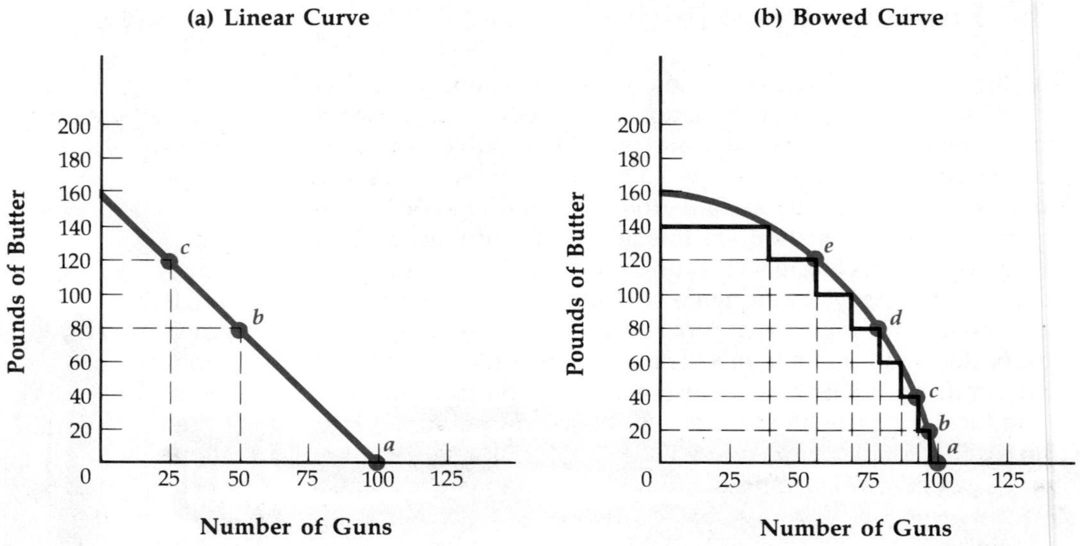


**Figure 2.1.** Production Possibilities Curves.
All production possibilities curves slope downward from the left to the right. When resources are fully and efficiently employed, more of one good, like guns, can be produced only by giving up some of another good, like butter.

A production possibilities curve that takes the form of a straight line—as in panel (a)—indicates that the number of goods that must be given up for a specific amount of a second good remains constant as production increases. A production possibilities curve that is bowed out—as in panel (b)—indicates that as production increases, more and more goods must be given up to gain the same amount of the second good.

used for less and less valuable purposes. Just how far up the curve we will go depends entirely on the relative values of the two commodities. If we stop at *c*, that is the point where additional units of butter are not worth their cost to us.

## Bowed Production Possibilities Curves

The curve in Figure 2.1(b) is bowed out from (or, to use mathematical jargon, "concave to") the origin. What does such a shape imply? As the curve approaches the intersection on the vertical axis, it becomes flatter, or lower in slope. The number of guns that must be forgone for each additional unit of butter goes up progressively. When we moved from *a* to *b*, expanding our production of butter by 20 pounds, we gave up only 5 guns. If we move further up the curve from *b* to *c*, however, we must forgo significantly more guns than before—7 instead of 5—to get 20 more pounds of butter. Similarly, as we move up the curve from *c* to *d* and from *d* to *e*, we give up proportionally more guns for each 20 pounds of butter.

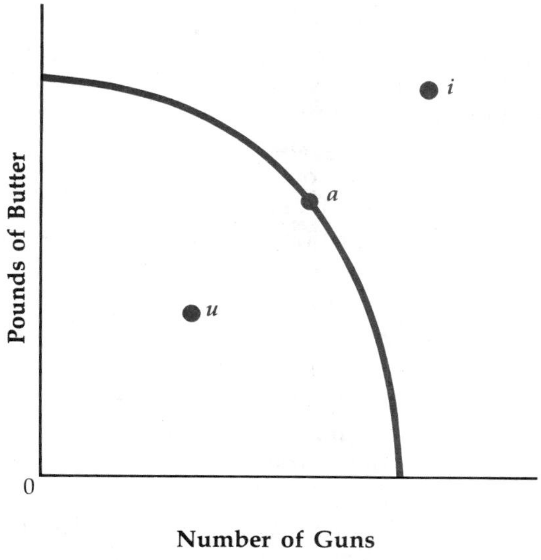


**Figure 2.2.** Maximizing Production.
Any point on a production possibilities curve (such as *a*) represents full and efficient use of resources. Points inside the production possibilities curve (such as *u*) represent incomplete or inefficient use of at least one resource. Points outside the curve (*i*, for instance) are beyond an economy's resources.

These increases in the number of units forgone stem from the tendency to use resources as efficiently as possible. As we divide up our resources between butter and guns, we put those resources that are better suited to butter production into the butter industry, and those better suited to guns into the gun industry. If we then want to increase butter production, we must move some resources from guns to butter. But we have already put the most suitable resources into butter; now we must add resources that are less suitable. Thus for each additional pound of butter, we must give up progressively more of our gun resources.

In Figure 2.1(b), the *cost* of producing each additional unit of butter increases for two reasons. First, as in Figure 2.1(a), the value of the guns forgone rises. Second, each time butter production is expanded, the resources transferred from guns will be less efficient for butter production; thus more and more guns must be given up.

## Points Inside and Outside the Curve

The production possibilities curve assumes that resources are fully and efficiently employed. (That is, they are used where they will do the most good, in terms of what people want most.) If those two conditions are not met, then the economy will not be operating on the production possibilities curve, but at some point within it, like point *u* in Figure 2.2. At point *u*, fewer goods than possible are being produced. From such a point, we should be able to move to a point on the curve, like *a*, expanding the production of both guns and butter at the same time. In that respect, a movement from *u* to *a* is costless—nothing is forgone to increase production. Making sure that our economy is not functioning somewhere in the interior of the production possibilities curve, where resources are underutilized, is one of the major tasks for economic policymakers.

Points outside, or to the right of, the production possibilities curve are by definition impossible to achieve. To suggest, for instance, that we should choose to produce at a point like *i* is equivalent to saying that we should produce more than we are capable of producing (*i* stands for "impossible"). In the heat of debate, our political leaders sometimes seem to suggest just such impossible goals. Our production limitations (and the problems of choice) cannot be escaped. We cannot move to a point like *i* by printing more money. The additional dollars add nothing to our stock of real resources.

Partly because economists are constantly insisting that we recognize the obvious, economics is often referred to as the "dismal science." In fact we are generally either on or close to our production possibilities frontier. Getting more of one thing thus means giving up something else. We do have options, but they are options constrained by reality. To borrow the words of Ben Franklin, choices are as certain as death and taxes.

## The Choice Between Investment and Consumption

Choices span the spectrum of goods and services. We must choose not only between the goods and services we can have today, but between current goods and services and those we can have in the future. When we choose an apple from our barrel, we also choose to have one less apple for the future. In the same way, our choices between capital or investment goods and consumption goods influence both our present and future incomes, and our consumption patterns over time. Recall from Chapter 1 that an investment or capital good is any output of a production process that is designed to be used in other production processes—for example, plant and equipment. Investment goods are manufactured means of production. A **consumption good** is any good that is produced to be used and enjoyed more or less immediately by its purchaser, like ice cream.

**Consumption goods:** goods that are produced to be used and enjoyed more or less immediately by their purchasers.

Figure 2.3 shows the economic consequences of various levels of investment. Assume that a nation's production possibilities curve is $C_2I_3$. Assume also that the nation chooses to produce at point *a*, representing $C_1$ consumption goods and $I_1$ investment goods. Several consequences follow from such a decision.

First, like consumption goods, investment goods come at a cost. That cost is the value of the consumption goods forgone, in this case, $C_2 - C_1$.

Second, investment goods are means of production; they add to a nation's stock of plant and equipment. As long as the level of investment—in this case, $I_1$—does more than replace old, worn-out plant and equipment, it increases future production capabilities. That is, because of the new

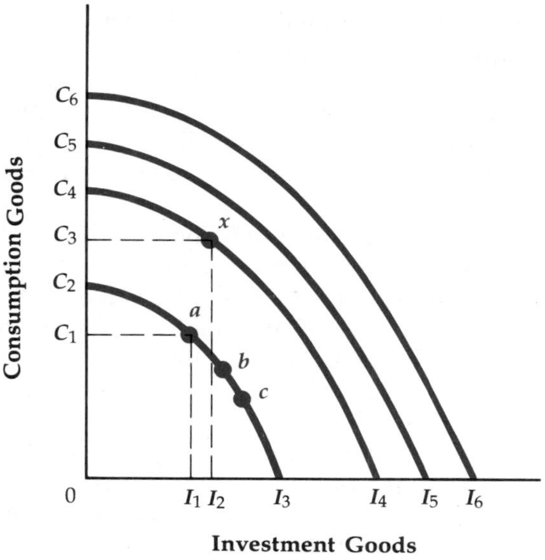


**Figure 2.3.** Investment Versus Consumption.
A nation's future production capability depends on the choices it makes between consumption and investment goods. The more investment goods it produces, the further to the right its production possibilities curve will shift. If a nation produces at point *a* on curve $C_2I_2$, its production possibilities curve will shift to $C_4I_4$. If it chooses point *b*, its curve will shift to $C_5I_5$; from point *c*, it will shift to $C_6I_6$.

plant and equipment, the nation's production possibilities curve will gradually shift to the right, perhaps to $C_4I_4$. This rightward shift of the production possibilities curve indicates economic growth.

Third, when the production possibilities curve shifts to the right, a nation's ability to afford consumption goods increases. When a nation that was producing initially at point *a* moves to point *x*, consumption increases from $C_1$ to $C_3$. Thus by forgoing a small amount of consumption goods ($C_2 - C_1$) in the beginning, a nation gains a larger amount of consumption goods ($C_3 - C_2$) in the future. This increased future consumption does not require a decrease in future investment. Investment increases too, from $I_1$ to $I_2$.

Fourth, this greater investment capability increases the potential for future growth. Every time investment increases, the production possibilities curve shifts further to the right—to $C_5I_5$, $C_6I_6$, and so on.

Fifth, the more a nation invests initially, the greater the shift in its future production possibilities. If a nation chooses to invest more than $I_1$—for example, choosing point *b* instead of point *a* on curve $C_2I_3$—its production possibilities curve will shift further to the right, perhaps to $C_5I_5$, than it would with $I_1$ investment. Choosing point *c* can cause the curve to shift still further, perhaps to $C_6I_6$. The more a nation invests initially, however, the more it must forgo in the way of consumption goods.

Thus a nation's long-term economic growth depends heavily on its ability to forgo current consumption in order to invest. Suppose three nations—A, B, and C—start out on the same production possibilities curve, $C_2I_3$. Simply by choosing different points on that curve—*a, b,* or *c*—they can end up with vastly different future production possibilities curves and future consumption patterns. What happens tomorrow depends critically on the choices made today.

Ideally, at what point should a nation produce initially: *a, b,* or *c*? At first it may seem that the answer is obviously *c* (and if not *c*, then *b*). But does the value of the future consumption gained exceed the value of the current consumption forgone? Not necessarily. If a nation chooses to produce at point *a* when it could have produced at point *c*, we must presume that its citizens do not value the benefits of future consumption as much as current consumption.

The position of the production possibilities curve also depends on the types of investment projects that are undertaken. A nation that merely duplicates existing plant and equipment, rather than improving them, will not do as well in the future as a nation that invests heavily in research and innovative technology. Of course innovation can be risky; not all new ideas are better ideas. Again the benefits of increased investment must be weighed against the cost to those who will pay for it.

In the United States, investment goods accounted for 14–16 percent of the total market value of all goods and services produced over the past two decades. That was higher than the percentage for economically stagnant Great Britain, but significantly lower than the percentage for dynamic Japan. During the early 1980s, the United States invested slightly less of its output (13 percent) in investment goods. The reasons cited most frequently for the drop in investment were the uncertainties produced by inflation; the reduced willingness of Americans to save (there can be no investment without saving); higher taxes; greater government regulation of industry; high interest rates; and reduced industry profits. In the mid-1980s, the decline in investment as a percentage of national output was reversed.

## The Choice Between Private and Public Goods

Just as a society must decide between consumption and investment, it must choose between individual and collective consumption or investment. Politicians may be fond of so-called free lunch programs, and local officials may vie with each other for "federal handouts" with which to finance municipal projects. But these publicly funded goods are "free" only in a very limited sense. When a particular city receives federal funds, local taxpayers' federal income tax bills may not change very much. Nevertheless federal programs always involve a cost. One task of the economist is to spot that cost and bring it to the attention of decision makers.

**Private goods:** goods that are bought or produced and used by people as individuals or as members of small voluntary groups.

Figure 2.4 shows the production possibilities curve for private goods and public goods. **Private goods** are goods that are bought or produced and used by people as individuals or as members of small voluntary

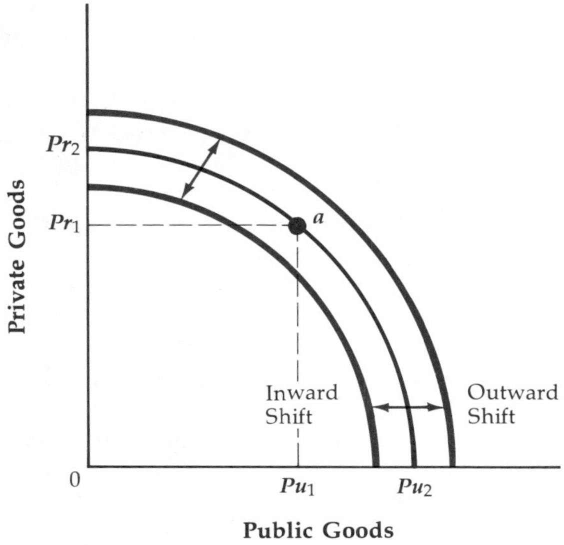


**Figure 2.4.** Public Versus Private Goods.
A nation's future production possibilities curve depends on the choices it makes between public and private goods. Production of some public goods—for example, pollution control devices or police protection—can shift the production possibilities curve outward. But production of other public goods—welfare assistance that discourages people from working or acquiring education, for example—can shift the production possibilities curve inward.

groups, like baseballs and food. **Public goods** are goods that are bought or produced and used by large groups of people or governments, like police protection or national defense. Public goods can benefit many people at once. As with other production possibilities curves, a society can operate at any point along the curve. Operating at point *a* will produce a combination of $Pr_1$ private goods and $Pu_1$ public goods. In this case, the cost of the public goods is the difference between $Pr_2$ and $Pr_1$ on the vertical axis. That is, to obtain $Pu_1$ public goods, we must give up $Pr_2 - Pr_1$ private goods. As individuals, we forgo so many cars, stereos, or computers to get missiles and water treatment plants instead.

**Public goods:** goods that are bought or produced and used by large groups of people or by governments.

Our choices between public and private goods can also (but do not necessarily) affect our nation's future production possibilities curve. The purchase of public goods can shift the curve in either direction. The curve may shift to the right, for instance, if government-provided goods allow the private sector to operate more efficiently, by reducing the costs businesses have to bear. Up to a point, police protection enables producers to devote more of their resources to production and investment and fewer to protecting their property from thieves and vandals. If government-provided goods increase the nation's stock of plant and equipment (for example, dams, hospitals, and sewer systems) or enhance people's ability to produce (through student loans, for example), the curve may shift to the right. Government-enforced environmental controls may also have a positive effect, if they make producers and consumers more aware of the environmental costs of products, and thus less wasteful of resources.

Government-provided goods may shift the nation's production possibilities curve to the left, however, if they discourage people from working or reduce the resources available for production. If welfare allows people to remain out of work longer than they need to, for instance, it reduces the nation's production possibilities. Government-provided goods may also have a negative effect if, like taxes on the interest earned on savings accounts, they reduce people's incentive to save, increasing consumption at the expense of investment. Finally, government production of goods may be wasteful. If resources are idle or underutilized because of political maneuvering, fewer goods, public and private, will be produced than is possible.

The exact extent to which government affects the movement of the production possibilities curve has been the subject of considerable study by economists, but no consensus has been reached. This question can have no simple answer.

## Shifting the Production Possibilities Curve

Given limited resources and unlimited wants, people have become quite creative in devising ways to get the most out of scarce resources and expand their production possibilities. Among the wide variety of techniques they have developed, several deserve to be mentioned.

### Substitution of Resources

People have discovered new resources and substituted them where possible for scarce ones. Chemists developed fertilizers to increase the yield of farmland, freeing scarce land for other uses. Prospectors developed hydrocarbon fuels as a substitute for scarce human and animal energy. More recently scientists invented solar energy collectors to replace dwindling hydrocarbon fuels. The progressive substitution of nonhuman for human energy sources has increased society's production possibilities.

### Cost Sharing

To share the cost of capital equipment ("spread the overhead") and the risk that must be assumed by investors, people have developed a variety of social structures, from families and cooperatives to corporations and insurance companies.

**Specialization of labor:** the process of dividing and assigning different production tasks to individuals with differing skills and talents.

### Specialization of Labor

To increase the productivity of labor, people have learned to divide up the tasks of production, a process called specialization of labor. **Specialization of labor** is the process of dividing and assigning different production tasks to individuals with differing skills and talents. Specialization usually (but not always) increases production because when people concentrate on a limited number of tasks, they tend to become more proficient at them. They spend more time in actual production and less in shifting from one task to another. Specialization also reduces the duplication of tools that is necessary when people attempt to be self-sufficient.

## Economies of Scale

Partly because it promotes specialization, production on a large, even massive, scale can reduce the cost per unit of production. **Economies of scale** are decreases in per unit cost due to an increase in the rate of production when the use of all resources is expanded. Economies of scale occur when an increase in resource inputs brings a proportionally greater increase in output during a given period of time. Large-scale production also allows the use of larger, faster, more efficient equipment. For example, if large computers can be fully used twenty-four hours a day, their speed—hundreds of thousands of calculations per second—makes up for their expense. When they are fully used, their cost per unit of calculation is less than the cost per unit of a desk-top calculator.

**Economies of scale:** decreases in per-unit cost due to an increase in the rate of production when the use of all resources is expanded.

There are limits, of course, to a firm's ability to reduce costs by expanding its scale of operation. Beyond some point, expansion brings an increase in the cost of producing each unit, called a diseconomy of scale. **Diseconomies of scale** are increases in per unit cost due to an increase in the rate of production when the use of all resources is expanded. Diseconomies of scale occur when an increase in resource inputs is not matched by a proportionate increase in output. Diseconomies of scale are generally attributed to the communication problems that plague large, bureaucratic organizations. When those at the top of the organizational hierarchy lose touch with those at the bottom, the firm functions less efficiently.

**Diseconomies of scale:** increases in per-unit cost due to an increase in the rate of production when the use of all resources is expanded.

## Trade

As the priest in the POW camp found (see pages 6–7), the inconveniences associated with scarcity can be reduced by trade. Commerce allows people to exchange goods and services they value less for those they value more. It also increases people's opportunity to specialize, expand the scale of their operations, and take advantage of resulting economies of scale. But perhaps most important, trade allows people to capitalize on any advantage they may have in production cost.

## Money as a Resource

In a very simple economy, barter (the exchange of goods for goods) is an acceptable means of trade. But it requires a double coincidence of wants. A person who has a good to sell, say pigs, must find someone who not only wants that particular good, but wants to give up something the pig

## *Economists in History: David Ricardo (1772–1823)*

***Delores T. Martin***

At the beginning of the nineteenth century, English economic thought remained much as it had been in the preceding century. Since the publication of Adam Smith's classic treatise *An Inquiry into the Nature and Causes of the Wealth of Nations* (1776), many able economists had developed economic principles and applied them to the social problems of the day. But not until David Ricardo wrote his *Principles of Political Economy and Taxation* (1817) was Smith's classical theory seriously refined and advanced. In that work, Ricardo's great powers of abstraction and synthesis established a standard that permanently altered the method of economic analysis.

Ricardo had little formal education, but considerable native ability. At the age of twenty he became a stock broker; by his mid-twenties he had amassed a large fortune. Ricardo first encountered Smith's *Wealth of Nations* in 1799, while on vacation. Within ten years he was analyzing economic problems in pamphlets and the press. He quickly became one of the most influential economists of his time.

Ricardo was the first of the classical economists to formulate a theory of economic development. He recognized that invention and the formation of capital spurred industrial production. The pursuit of profit thus created seed money for development. Ricardo opposed the taxation of profits, arguing that it drained an economy's capacity for growth.

It was Ricardo's attack on protectionist trade policies that made his reputation. At that time Britain was attempting to export more than it

owner desires—chickens, perhaps. The time the pig farmer spends searching for a compatible trader is time that cannot be spent farming and producing.

Money was developed to make trading more efficient and to reduce the time spent looking for traders. Instead of searching for someone who wants pork and has chickens to sell, a pig farmer can sell his pigs for cash and use the cash to buy chickens. With the time he saves, he can produce more food. Money can serve as a medium of exchange because it is an accepted store of purchasing power. That is, people who want to postpone consumption can leave their money in a safe place, knowing that when they do want to spend it, it will still be valuable. **Money** is any generally accepted medium of exchange or trade that also serves as a store of purchasing power.

**Money:** any generally accepted medium of exchange or trade that also serves as a store of purchasing power.

Without money, people would have to save for future purchases by holding on to a variety of goods that could be used in trade. Their resources would be tied up in storage and would be unavailable for the production of other goods and services. Money, however, can be used productively while it is being stored for future use. A banker can lend it to someone who needs to buy a new machine, for instance. Thus money frees resources to be used in productive activity. It expands society's production possibilities frontier.

imported in order to accumulate hard currency. An elaborate system of tariffs and quotas supported this strategy. The so-called Corn Laws, for example, severely limited the importation of grain except in times of unusually high prices. But Ricardo demonstrated the mutual benefits of international exchange. His law of comparative advantage became the core of the classical free trade doctrine. "Under a system of perfectly free commerce," he wrote,

> each country naturally devotes its capital and labour to such employments as are most beneficial to each. This pursuit of individual advantage is admirably connected with the universal good of the whole. By stimulating industry, by rewarding ingenuity, and by using efficaciously the peculiar powers bestowed by nature, it distributes labour most effectively and most economically: while, by increasing the general mass of productions, it diffuses general benefit, and binds together in one common tie of interest and intercourse, the universal society of nations throughout the civilized world. It is this principle which determines that wine shall be made in France and Portugal, that corn shall be grown in America and Poland, and that hardware and other goods shall be manufactured in England.[1]

Ricardo's influence on economic theory was enormous. As John Maynard Keynes put it in a biographical sketch, "Ricardo conquered England the way that the Holy Inquisition conquered Spain."[2]

1. David Ricardo, "On Foreign Trade," in *The Principles of Political Economy and Taxation* (Homewood, Ill.: Richard D. Irwin, 1963), pp. 70–71.
2. John Maynard Keynes, *Essays in Biography* (London: Macmillan, 1933), p. 143.

## Taking Advantage of Comparative Advantage

One of the benefits of trade is that it allows people to capitalize on any advantages they may have in cost of production. Consider a world in which there are only two people, Fred and Harry. Let's imagine that they live on an island and that they can produce only two goods, coconuts and papayas. The table below shows how much each man can produce. In one hour Fred can produce four coconuts or eight papayas; Harry can produce six coconuts or twenty-four papayas. Harry is more productive than Fred in either case. Yet both can gain by specializing and trading with each other.

| | Number of Coconuts Produced per Hour | Number of Papayas Produced per Hour |
|---|---|---|
| Fred | 4 | 8 |
| Harry | 6 | 24 |

To see why, we must look at the relative cost of producing coconuts and papayas. If Fred produces four coconuts, he loses the opportunity to produce eight papayas. In other words, the cost of the four coconuts is eight papayas—or to put it another way, the cost of one coconut is two papayas. Fred would be better off if he could trade one coconut for more than two papayas, because two papayas is what he has to give up to produce the coconut.

From Harry's point of view, the cost of one coconut is four papayas. (To produce six coconuts, Harry has to give up twenty-four papayas.) If Harry could get a coconut for less than four papayas, he would be better off. He could produce four papayas, trade some for a coconut, and have some left over to eat.

The cost of producing coconuts may be summarized as follows:

Fred: 1 coconut = 2 papayas

Harry: 1 coconut = 4 papayas

Fred can produce one coconut at less cost (in terms of the papayas that must be given up) than Harry can. Similarly, one papaya is less costly to produce (in terms of the coconuts that must be given up) for Harry than for Fred. In terms of the relative cost of production, Fred has a comparative advantage in the production of coconuts, and Harry has a comparative advantage in papaya production. A **comparative advantage** is a relatively lower cost of production, or the capacity to produce a product at a lower cost than a competitor, in terms of the goods that must be given up.

**Comparative advantage:** a relatively lower cost of production, or the capacity to produce a product at a lower cost than a competitor, in terms of the goods that must be given up.

If Fred and Harry specialize in the fruits for which they have a comparative advantage and then trade with each other, each will benefit. Remember that Fred would be better off if he could trade one coconut for more than two papayas. Thus if he and Harry agree to an exchange at the rate of one coconut for three papayas, he will obviously benefit. He will produce one coconut, giving up two papayas in the process, but will get three papayas in return from Harry. Harry will also benefit. He can produce four papayas, giving up one coconut in the process, and trade three of those papayas to Fred for one coconut. Harry will end up with the same number of coconuts he would have had if he had produced coconuts instead of papayas, but he will have one papaya as well.

If both Fred and Harry are better off, their total production must have increased. Through specialization and trade Fred and Harry have cut their cost of production and moved closer to their joint production possibilities frontier. They have used scarce resources more efficiently than they would have otherwise.

## The Circular Flow of Income

**Circular flow of income:** the integrated flow of resources, goods, and services between or among broad sectors of the economy, like producers, consumers, and government.

Trade not only enhances people's welfare, but increases their dependence on one another. This interdependence can be illustrated by what is called a circular flow diagram (see Figure 2.5). The **circular flow of income** is the integrated flow of resources, goods, and services between or among broad sectors of the economy, like producers, consumers, and government. In simplified form, this diagram shows the flow of resources, goods, and services between two sectors of the private economy, producers (bottom)

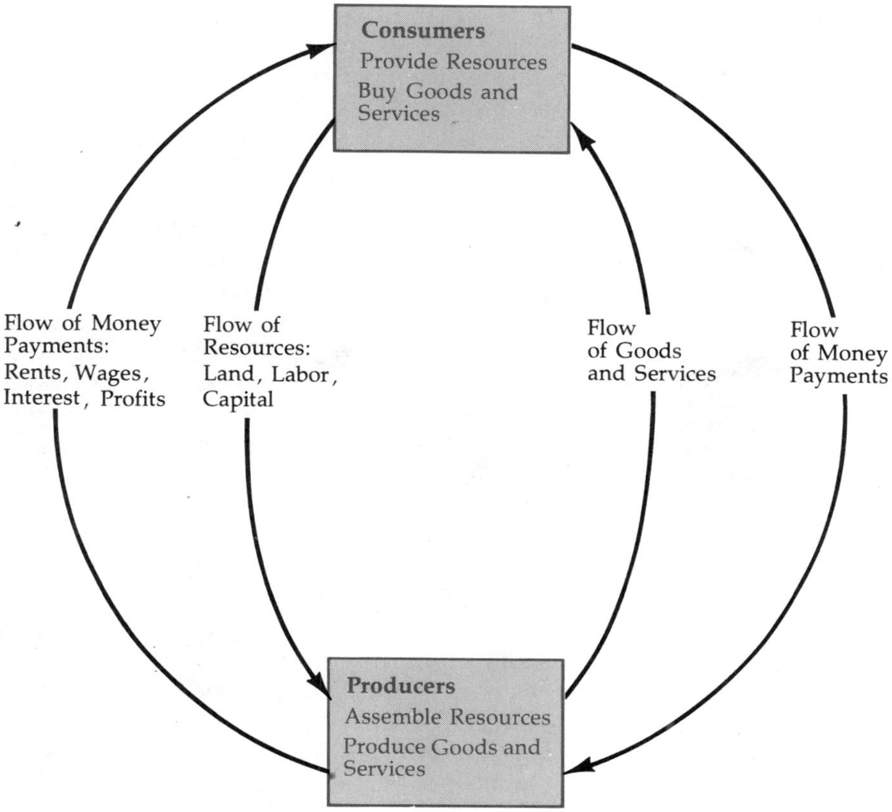


**Figure 2.5.** The Circular Flow of Income.
Consumers and producers generate opposing flows of resources and money payments for those resources, in the form of wages, rents, interest, and profits (left-hand side). In the same way, they generate opposing flows of goods and services and money payments for those goods and services (right-hand side).

and consumers (top). The consumers have two basic functions: to provide the resources (land, labor, and capital) needed by the producers and to consume the goods and services produced. The producers also have two basic functions: to assemble the necessary resources provided by consumers and to produce the goods and services consumers want. The integrated nature of the economy is symbolized by the arrows that represent the flows of resources, final products, and money payments to and from consumers and producers.

For a barter economy, the diagram would be even simpler. There would be only two arrows, one representing the flow of resources from the consumer to the producer, the other representing the flow of goods and services from the producer back to the consumer. In this primitive economy, the goods on the right-hand side of the diagram would trade for the resources on the left-hand side. The price of labor, for example, would be stated in so many gadgets produced, and the price of gadgets would be stated in so many hours of labor. Such a system would be extremely inefficient, for people would waste a great deal of time searching for beneficial trades.

Though money eases the difficulties of trading, it tends to obscure the interdependence of producers and consumers. When money is used for trade, producers secure their income from particular consumers, not caring whether those consumers work for them or provide them with resources. Laborers secure a money payment for their services from producers, which they use to buy goods from a variety of producers, not necessarily those they work for. Prices are stated in terms of dollars (or pounds sterling, or lira), and people may get the mistaken impression that their incomes are unrelated to production, except in a remote and tenuous way. After all, they don't get paid with the goods they produce.

Yet the two sectors are closely interrelated. The health of the business sector (producers) clearly depends on the expenditures made by the consuming sector. Without that flow of money payments from consumers, producers would be unable to pay for the resources they buy from consumers. Likewise, conditions in the consuming sector depend on the success of firms in the business sector. If the business sector cannot sell its goods and services, producers will not be able to pay workers' salaries. Thus an integrated, money-based trade can multiply the effects of disruptions in trade. If the circular flow of money is interrupted, production may slow, consumption may fall off, and laborers may be thrown out of work. Such interruptions in the circular flow, called recessions, are a subject of considerable concern to macroeconomists.

Figure 2.5 does not reflect the full complexity of the exchange relationships that exist among people. In the real world, the business sector has internal flows of its own. Producers funnel resources to other producers in the form of raw materials and investment goods like machinery. They make payments to each other in the form of money. A more realistic, though still incomplete description of the circular flow is contained in Figure 2.6. Producers have been divided into three representative groups: farmers, millers, and bakers. All three buy certain resources, like labor, from consumers. But in addition, the millers buy their basic resource, wheat, from the farmers, and the bakers buy their basic resource, flour, from the millers.

Actual trading arrangements are extraordinarily complex. Farmers, for example, must buy machinery to produce wheat. Farm equipment producers must buy metal, plastics, and hundreds of other resources to produce the machinery they sell to the farmers. Metal producers must buy equipment to process and finish their product. Both metal producers and equipment manufacturers must have food to live on. Furthermore, all these trades must be handled by a communications and transportation network that can deliver all the resources and products needed to the

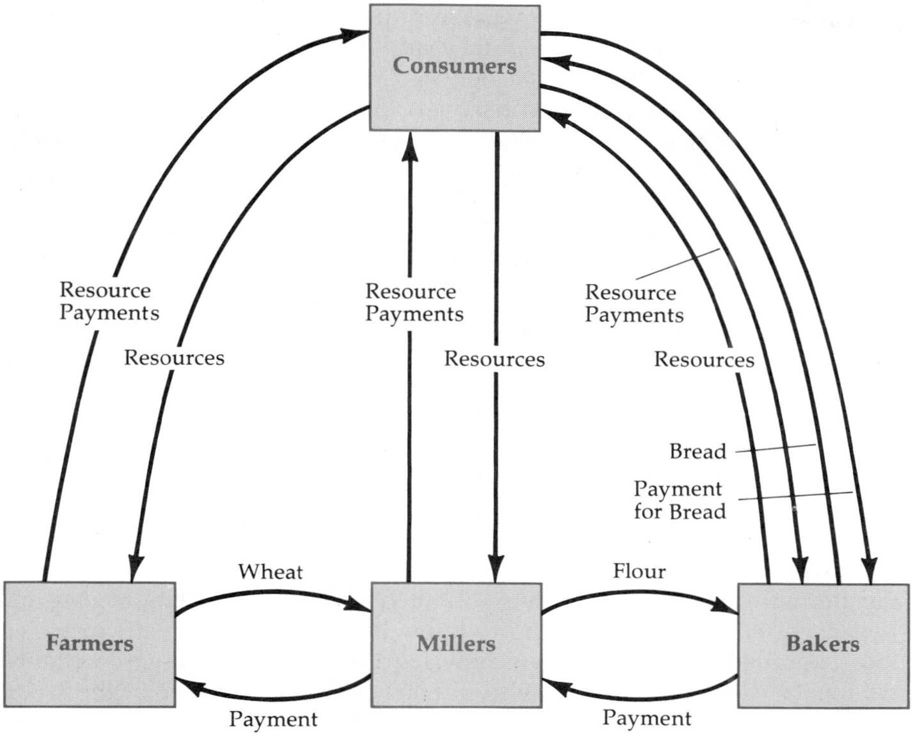


**Figure 2.6.** The Circular Flow of Income: A More Complicated Model. Resources (goods and services) and money payments for them flow not just between consumers and producers, but among producers as well. All producers buy resources from households with money payments. Farmers, for instance, receive resources from consumer households, for which they make money payments. But they also sell their wheat to millers, who make flour and sell it to bakers—who then make bread and sell it to consumers.

appropriate destinations at the appropriate time. And traders must be able to adjust their relationships to changes in consumer demand.

Government further complicates the circular flow by drawing off money in the form of taxes and then injecting it back into the circular flow in the form of government purchases, for everything from planes to welfare checks. There is also private saving, which channels purchasing power through banks to consumers of cars, houses, and furniture and through stock and bond markets to investors in inventory, plant, and equipment. It is a wonder that the system works at all. The economy is an extraordinarily complex web of fragile but productive interrelationships, all formed for one overriding purpose: to make the most of society's production possibilities, given the inescapable fact of scarcity.

## Summary and Extensions

Like scarcity, choice is pervasive. We must choose between a variety of goods and services, between public and private goods, between consumption and investment, and between old and new technology. The choices we make have huge consequences for both the present and the future. Our ability to grow and become more productive tomorrow depends on our willingness to save today. Greater future output does not necessarily imply greater welfare over time, however. Tomorrow's growth may not be worth today's sacrifice, in terms of consumption forgone.

Production possibilities curves can be useful in illustrating these and other choices we must make. But they can easily be misunderstood. The production possibilities curve may suggest that society's choices are more or less apparent: we simply have to plot the curve, observe the options, and choose. For several reasons, our economic difficulties cannot be solved so easily.

First, we lack a great deal of information about what our society can produce at the limit. If we produced only two goods, finding the production possibilities frontier might be relatively simple. But we produce millions of products, requiring many kinds of resources. The tradeoffs among those resources and the goods made from them are extraordinarily complex. Furthermore, we do not know very much about the quantity of existing resources. For instance, we do not know how much labor really exists in total, because we do not know how hard and long people are actually willing to work. The people who interact with one another in the labor market are the ones who know the answer to that question. Social scientists and policymakers may know something about the operation of the economy, but there is a great deal they do not and cannot know.

In short, though production possibilities curves help us to envision the types of choices we must make, the actual options open to us do not result from the curves, but from the economic process. They are the product of the millions of interrelated choices made daily by individuals, groups, and government. Our resources and our choices as to how those resources will be employed determine our production possibilities and our position on the production possibilities curve. In the next chapter we will see how people make choices through the market process and how, through the pricing system, they determine their society's production possibilities.

## Major Conclusions

1. A decision to consume goods and services implies a decision to forgo investment goods. Since investment goods are used to produce other goods and services, the level of investment we choose will affect the position of our production possibilities curve in the future. In this way, current and future choices are inextricably related.
2. A decision to produce public goods is a decision to forgo private goods. The production of public goods can shift the future production possibilities curve to the left or right, depending on how those public goods affect people's tendency to produce, work, save, and invest.

3. People have devised a number of ways to improve the productivity of resources in the face of scarcity. They have developed substitute resources, organized to share costs, specialized their labor, and expanded in order to realize economies of scale. They have developed trading relationships based on comparative advantages in cost of production and used money to put idle resources to work. Trade increases production by encouraging the most efficient use of resources.
4. Circular flow diagrams show the economic interdependence of consumers and producers. Producers depend on consumer expenditures, and consumers depend on payment from producers for their land, labor, and capital.

## Questions to Ponder

1. What determines the shape and position of a nation's production possibilities curve?
2. Suppose a nation is producing at some point inside the production possibilities curve. If the government implements a policy that moves the nation onto the production frontier, is there a cost to the additional goods produced?
3. Suppose a nation's yearly purchase of investment goods is less than its yearly loss of investment goods through wear and tear. What will happen to the nation's production possibilities curve?
4. Evaluate the following statement: "Greater investment today will enable this nation to produce more in the future. It will reduce the cost of future investment and enable us to grow even faster in the future. Our government should therefore devise a policy that will stimulate business investment."
5. Does a nation's production possibilities curve depend on its distribution of wealth and income? On the existence and distribution of property rights? On the level of taxation and type of tax levied?
6. Suppose that Joan's and Terry's hourly production rates for squashes and turnips are as follows:

| **Case I** | Squashes | Turnips |
|---|---|---|
| Joan | 10 | 50 |
| Terry | 40 | 800 |

| **Case II** | Squashes | Turnips |
|---|---|---|
| Joan | 20 | 30 |
| Terry | 100 | 50 |

For each case, determine who should specialize in producing squashes and then suggest an exchange rate for squashes and turnips that will benefit both Joan and Terry.

# Appendix: Graphic Analysis

Economists often use graphs to illustrate the relationships between and among economic variables. Graphs are pictorial representations of the presumed relationships between or among variables. Graphs can display a great deal of information in a small area; they show at a glance how two or more variables are related.

## The Features of Graphs

The major features of a graph are shown in Figure 2.A1. In the lower left-hand corner is the *origin,* the point at which the value of both variables represented in the graph is zero. Extending out from the origin are the horizontal, or *X,* axis (also called the abscissa) and the vertical, or *Y,* axis (also called the ordinate). The relationship among variables is shown graphically by a series of points in the interior of the graph (between the vertical and horizontal axes). The points combine various values scaled along the two axes.

For example, suppose we scale the number of bushels of apples consumers will buy at different prices along the horizontal axis, and the various prices per bushel along the vertical axis. If consumers buy 50 bushels of apples a day when the price of apples is $5 a bushel, that price-quantity combination can be represented by point *a* on the graph. Other price-quantity combinations like *b* and *c* can be plotted and connected to form a line, or curve, like the one in color in the figure.

## The Slope of Curves

The curves plotted on a graph can have almost any shape. One important characteristic of their shape is the slope. The *slope* is the ratio of the vertical movement up a curve (sometimes called the "rise") to the corresponding horizontal movement along the curve (also called the "run"). Mathematically, the slope can be expressed as follows:

$$\text{slope} = \frac{\text{rise}}{\text{run}} = \frac{\text{change in } y}{\text{change in } x}$$

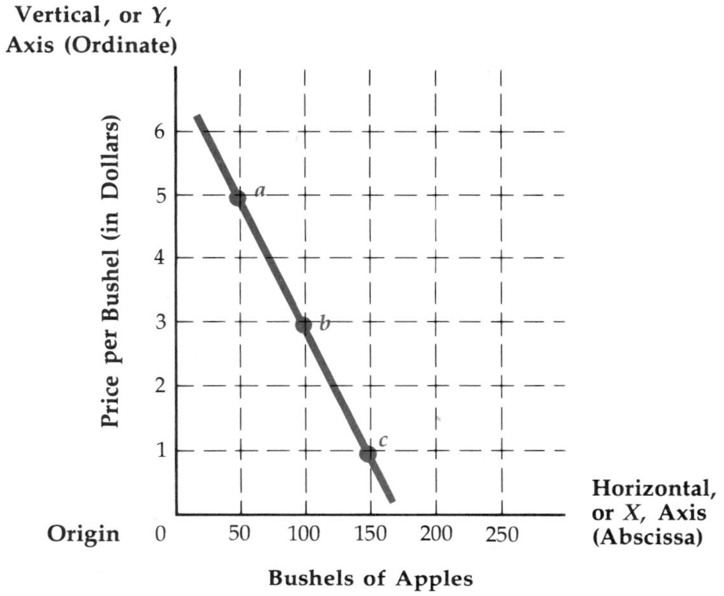


**Figure 2.A1.** Features of a Graph.
The vertical axis of a graph is sometimes called the *Y* axis, or the ordinate. The horizontal axis is called the *X* axis, or the abscissa. The point of intersection of the two axes is called the origin. A series of points inside the graph portray assumed or deduced relationships between the variables on the *X* and *Y* axes, like the price and quantity of apples sold. The line that connects those points is called a curve. The curve shown here has a negative slope (moves downward from left to right).

That is, the slope is equal to the ratio of the change in the value on the vertical axis to the change in the value on the horizontal axis.

The slope can be either positive or negative, depending on which way the curve slants. It is said to be positive when the curve moves up toward the right and negative when it moves down toward the right. Figure 2.A1 shows a curve with a negative slope. As the price per bushel goes down (vertical axis), the number of bushels sold goes up (horizontal axis). This kind of relationship, called an inverse relationship, produces a negative slope. If the price of a bushel of apples falls from \$5 to \$3 while the quantity consumers purchase rises from 50 to 100 bushels, the slope of the curve will be $\frac{-2}{50}$, or $-0.04$:

$$\text{slope} = \frac{\text{change in } y}{\text{change in } x} = \frac{P_1 - P_2}{Q_1 - Q_2} = \frac{(\$3 - \$5)}{(100 - 50)} = \frac{-2}{50} = -0.04$$

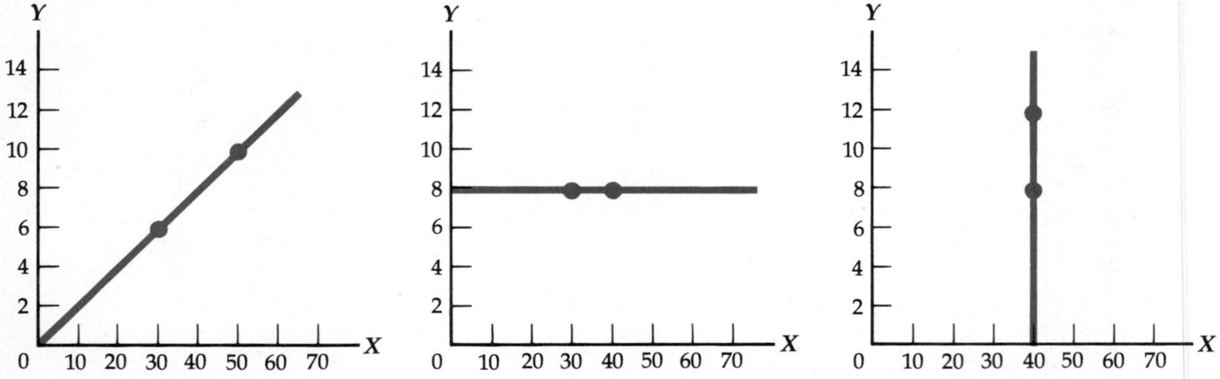

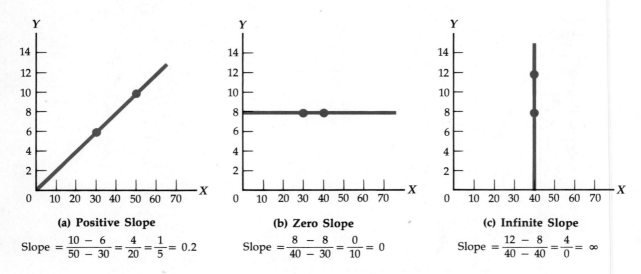

**(a) Positive Slope**

$$\text{Slope} = \frac{10 - 6}{50 - 30} = \frac{4}{20} = \frac{1}{5} = 0.2$$

**(b) Zero Slope**

$$\text{Slope} = \frac{8 - 8}{40 - 30} = \frac{0}{10} = 0$$

**(c) Infinite Slope**

$$\text{Slope} = \frac{12 - 8}{40 - 40} = \frac{4}{0} = \infty$$

Figure 2.A2. Curves with Various Slopes.
Curves that move upward from the left to the right—panel (a)—are said to have a positive slope. Curves that are horizontal to the *X* axis—panel (b)—have a zero slope; curves that are vertical to the *X* axis—panel (c)—have an infinite slope.

When the change in both $x$ and $y$ is positive, the ratio, or slope, is positive, and the relationship between $x$ and $y$ is said to be direct. The curve slants up toward the right, as in Figure 2.A2(a).

A curve that runs parallel to the horizontal axis has a slope of zero—it has no vertical rise or fall (see Figure 2.A2(b)). When its zero numerator (the rise) is divided by a positive denominator, the result is zero. A curve that runs perpendicular to the horizontal axis has a slope of infinity—even with no horizontal movement, it continues upward indefinitely (see Figure 2.A2(c)). When its positive numerator is divided by a zero denominator, the result is infinity.

## Curves with Changing Slopes

Straight curves (sometimes called linear curves) like the ones in Figures 2.A1 and 2.A2 have the same slope at all points. The rise is always the same for any given run, no matter where on the curve it is measured. Thus the ratio of the rise to the run is said to be constant. But not all curves are straight lines. The slope of the curve in Figure 2.A3, for example, is steeper near the origin than at the other end. Because the slope of a curve like this is constantly changing, it must be measured at specific points on the curve.

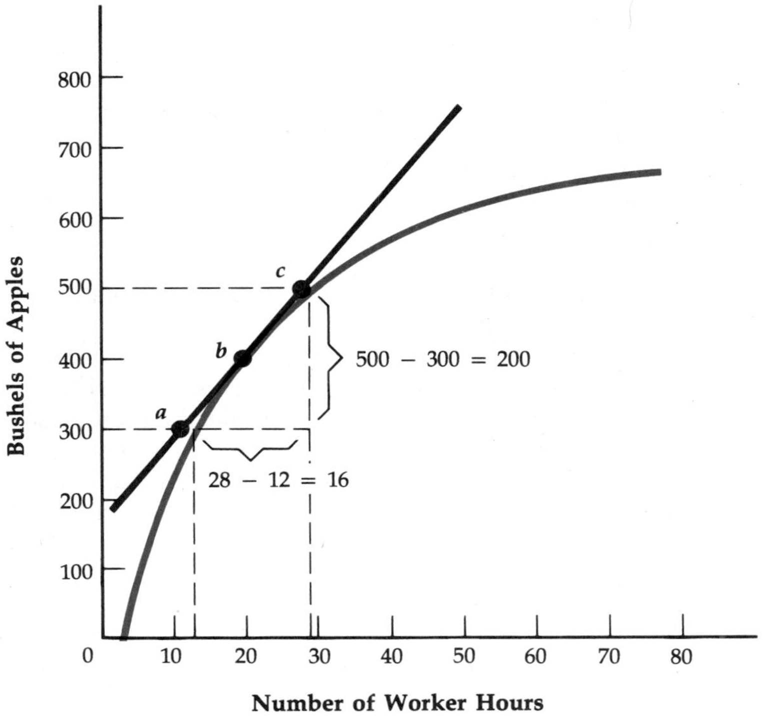


Figure 2.A3. Curves with a Changing Slope.
Because this curve bends downward as it moves from the left up to the right, it is said to have a decreasing positive slope. (Slope at $b = \frac{200}{16} = \frac{25}{2} = 12.5$)

To obtain the slope at any given point on such a curve, draw a straight line tangent to the curve, as in Figure 2.A3. Measure the rise and the run between any two points on that tangent straight line, and divide the rise by the run. In Figure 2.A3, the rise of the line tangent to point *b*, measured between points *a* and *c*, is 200; the run is 16 (28 − 12). Hence the slope is:

$$\frac{200}{16}, \text{ or } \frac{25}{2}.$$

The changing slope of a curve has practical implications. In Figure 2.A3, the rising curve shows the contribution made by additional worker hours to the total output of apples. As the curve rises past point *b*, its slope becomes progressively flatter. In other words, beyond a certain point, as the number of hours worked grows, each new hour adds less to total output.

## The Uses and Misuses of Graphs

A comparison of Table 2.A1 and Figure 2.A4 demonstrates the efficiency of graphs in displaying economic variables. The table and the graph both show a measure of the nation's overall price level, the consumer price index, over time. By scrutinizing the figures in the table, you can determine that the price level rose and fell several times during the nineteenth century, before skyrocketing in the second half of this century. Figure 2.A4 shows the same trend at a glance, however. The dramatic upward surge in prices from 1940 on, visible immediately, shows that inflation is, to a significant extent, a modern phenomenon.

Graphs, like statistics, can be misused. The mere plotting of two variables on a graph does not establish a cause-and-effect relationship between them. For instance, the number of major-league home runs hit each season can be plotted against the annual snowfalls in Rochester, New York—but the resulting curve will make no sense, regardless of its shape and slope. A graph proves nothing about the way in which two variables are influenced by one another. Relationships are established by theory.

**Table 2.A1.** U.S. Price Level, 1800–1984

| Year | CPI[a] | Year | CPI | Year | CPI |
|---|---|---|---|---|---|
| 1800 | 51 | 1865 | 46 | 1930 | 50 |
| 1805 | 45 | 1870 | 38 | 1935 | 41 |
| 1810 | 47 | 1875 | 33 | 1940 | 42 |
| 1815 | 55 | 1880 | 29 | 1945 | 54 |
| 1820 | 42 | 1885 | 27 | 1950 | 72 |
| 1825 | 34 | 1890 | 27 | 1955 | 80 |
| 1830 | 32 | 1895 | 25 | 1960 | 89 |
| 1835 | 31 | 1900 | 25 | 1965 | 95 |
| 1840 | 30 | 1905 | 27 | 1970 | 116 |
| 1845 | 28 | 1910 | 28 | 1975 | 161 |
| 1850 | 25 | 1915 | 30 | 1980 | 247 |
| 1855 | 28 | 1920 | 60 | 1984 | 311 |
| 1860 | 27 | 1925 | 53 | | |

[a] CPI stands for consumer price index; 1967 = 100.

**Sources:** U.S. Bureau of the Census, *Historical Statistics of the United States: Colonial Times to 1970* (Washington, D.C.: U.S. Government Printing Office, 1975), pp. 210, 211; *Economic Report of the President* (Washington, D.C.: U.S. Government Printing Office, 1985), p. 291.

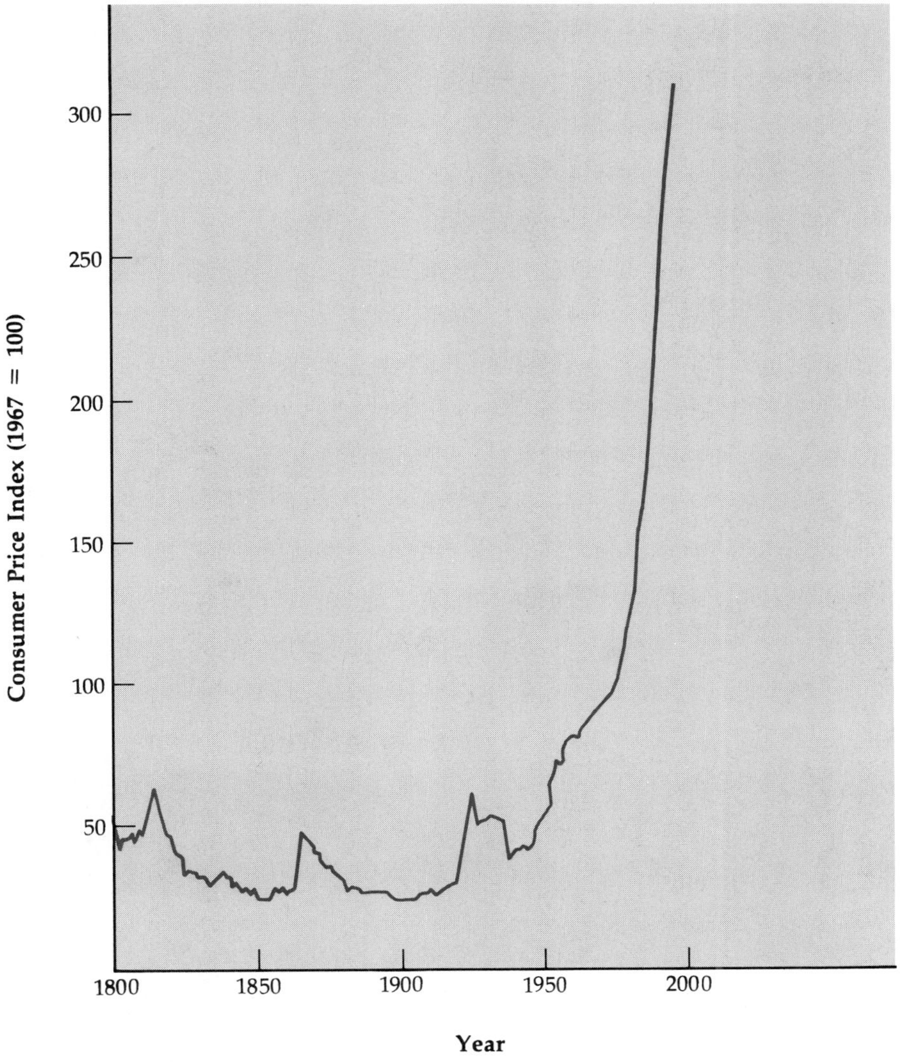


**Figure 2.A4.** U.S. Price Level, 1880–1984.
The general movement of prices over a long period of time can be shown graphically by plotting the consumer price index (vertical axis) for each year (horizontal axis). At a glance one can see that the price level moved up and down at relatively low levels between 1800 and 1940. Over recent decades, however, it has risen sharply.
**Sources:** U.S. Bureau of the Census, *Historical Statistics of the United States* (Washington, D.C.: U.S. Government Printing Office, 1975), pp. 210–211; *Economic Report of the President* (Washington, D.C.: U.S. Government Printing Office, 1985), p. 291.

## Central Question

*How does the competitive market work?*

## Key Terms

Competition
Perfect competition
Demand
Increase in demand
Decrease in demand
Supply
Increase in supply
Decrease in supply
Market surplus
Equilibrium price
Equilibrium quantity
Market shortage
Efficiency
Price ceiling
Price floor
Short-run equilibrium
Long-run equilibrium

# Chapter 3

# The Elements of Supply and Demand

*Competition, if not prevented, tends to bring about a state of affairs in which:* first, *everything will be produced which somebody knows how to produce and which he can sell profitably at a price at which buyers will prefer it to the available alternatives;* second, *everything that is being produced is produced by persons who can do so at least as cheaply as anybody else who in fact is not producing it; and* third, *that everything will be sold at prices lower than, or at least as low as, those at which it could be sold by anybody who in fact does not do so.*

*Friedrich Hayek*

In the heart of New York City, Fred Lieberman's small grocery is dwarfed by the tall buildings that surround it. Yet it is remarkable for what it accomplishes. Lieberman's carries thousands of items, most of which are not produced locally, and some of which come thousands of miles from other parts of this country or abroad. A man of modest means, with little knowledge of production processes, Fred Lieberman has nevertheless been able to stock his store with many if not most of the foods and toiletries his customers need and want. Occasionally Lieberman's runs out of certain items, but most of the time the stock is ample. Its supply is so dependable that customers tend to take it for granted, forgetting that Lieberman's is one small strand in an extremely complex economic network.

How does Fred Lieberman get the goods he sells, and how does he know which ones to sell and at what price? The simplest answer is that the goods he offers and the prices at which they sell are determined through the market process, the interaction of many buyers and sellers trading what they have (their labor or other resources) for what they want. Lieberman stocks his store by appealing to the private interests of suppliers—by paying them competitive prices. His customers pay him extra for the convenience of purchasing goods in their neighborhood grocery—in the process appealing to his private interests. To determine what he should buy, Fred Lieberman considers his suppliers' prices. To determine what and how much they should buy, his customers consider the prices he charges. The Nobel Prize–winning economist Friedrich Hayek has suggested that the market process is manageable for people like Fred Lieberman precisely because prices condense into usable form a great deal of information, signaling quickly what people want, what goods cost, and what resources are readily available. Prices guide and coordinate the sellers' production decisions and consumers' purchases.

But how are prices determined? In competitive markets, as this chapter describes, prices are established by the forces of supply and demand.

## The Competitive Market Process

So far, our discussion of markets and their consequences has been rather casual. In this section we will define precisely such terms as *market* and *competition*. In later sections we will examine the way markets work and learn why, in a limited sense, markets can be considered efficient systems for determining what and how much to produce.

### The Market Setting

Most people tend to think of a market as a geographical location—a shopping center, an auction barn, a business district. From an economic perspective, however, it is more useful to think of a market as a process. You may recall from Chapter 1 that a market is defined as the process by which buyers and sellers determine what they are willing to buy and sell, on what terms. That is, it is the process by which buyers and sellers decide the prices and quantities of goods to be bought and sold.

In this process, individual market participants search for information relevant to their own interests. Buyers ask about the models, sizes, colors, and quantities available and the prices they must pay for them. Sellers inquire about the types of goods and services buyers want and the prices they are willing to pay.

This market process is self-correcting. Buyers and sellers routinely revise their plans on the basis of experience. As Israel Kirzner has written:

> The overambitious plans of one period will be replaced by more realistic ones; market opportunities overlooked in one period will be exploited in the next. In other words, even without changes in the basic data of the market (i.e., in consumer tastes, technological possibilities, and resource availabilities), the decisions made in one period of time generate systematic alterations in corresponding decisions for the succeeding period.[1]

The market is made up of people, consumers and entrepreneurs, attempting to buy and sell on the best terms possible. Through the groping process of give and take, they move from relative ignorance about others' wants and needs to a reasonably accurate understanding of how much can be bought and sold and at what price. The market functions as an ongoing information and exchange system.

## Competition Among Buyers and Among Sellers

Part and parcel of the market process is the concept of competition. **Competition** is the process by which market participants, in pursuing their own interests, attempt to outdo, outprice, outproduce, and outmaneuver each other. By extension, competition is also the process by which market participants attempt to avoid being outdone, outpriced, outproduced, or outmaneuvered by others.

**Competition:** the process by which market participants, in pursuing their own interests, attempt to outdo, outprice, outproduce, and outmaneuver each other.

Competition does not occur between buyer and seller, but among buyers or among sellers. Buyers compete with other buyers for the limited number of goods on the market. To compete, they must discover what other buyers are bidding and offer the seller better terms—a higher price or the same price for a lower-quality product. Sellers compete with other sellers for the consumer's dollar. They must learn what their rivals are doing and attempt to do it better or differently—to lower the price or enhance the product's appeal.

This kind of competition stimulates the exchange of information, forcing competitors to reveal their plans to prospective buyers or sellers. The exchange of information can be seen clearly at auctions. Before the bidding begins, buyers look over the merchandise and the other buyers, attempting to determine how high others might be willing to bid for a particular piece. During the auction, this specific information is revealed as buyers call out their bids and others try to top them. Information exchange is less apparent

1. Israel Kirzner, *Competition and Entrepreneurship* (Chicago: University of Chicago Press, 1973), p. 10.

in department stores, where competition is often restricted. Even there, however, comparison shopping will often reveal some sellers who are offering lower prices in an attempt to attract consumers.

In competing with each other, sellers reveal information that is ultimately of use to buyers, and vice versa. From the consumer's point of view,

> The function of competition is here precisely to teach us *who* will serve us well: which grocer or travel agent, which department store or hotel, which doctor or solicitor, we can expect to provide the most satisfactory solution for whatever particular personal problem we may have to face.[2]

From the seller's point of view—say the auctioneer's—competition among buyers brings the highest prices possible.

Competition among sellers takes many forms, including the price, quality, weight, volume, color, texture, power, durability, and smell of products, as well as the credit terms offered to buyers. Sellers also compete for consumers' attention by appealing to their hunger and sex drives or their fear of death, pain, and loud noises. All these forms of competition can be divided into two basic categories, price and nonprice competition. Price competition is of particular interest to economists, who see it as an important source of information for market participants, a coordinating force that brings the quantity produced into line with the quantity consumers are willing and able to buy. In the following sections, we will construct a model of the competitive market and use it to explore the process of price competition. Nonprice competition will be covered in a later section.

## Supply and Demand: A Market Model

**Perfect competition:** a market composed of numerous sellers and buyers of an identical product, such that no one individual or buyer has the ability to affect the market price by changing the production level. Entry into and exit from a perfectly competitive market is unrestricted.

A fully competitive market is made up of many buyers and sellers searching for opportunities or ready to enter the market when opportunities arise. To be described as competitive, therefore, a market must include a significant number of actual or potential competitors. A fully competitive market offers freedom of entry: there are no legal or economic barriers to producing and selling goods in the market.

Our market model assumes perfect competition, an ideal situation that is seldom, if ever, achieved in real life but that will simplify our calculations. **Perfect competition** is a market composed of numerous sellers and buyers of an identical product, such that no one individual seller or buyer has the ability to affect the market price by changing the production level. Entry into and exit from a perfectly competitive market is unrestricted. Producers can start up or shut down production at will. Anyone can enter the market, duplicate the good, and compete for consumers' dollars. Since each competitor produces only a small share of the total output, the individual competitor cannot significantly influence the degree of competition or the market price by entering or leaving the market.

---

2. Friedrich H. Hayek, "The Meaning of Competition," *Individualism and Economic Order* (Chicago: University of Chicago Press, 1948), p. 97.

This kind of market is well suited to graphic analysis. Our discussion will concentrate on how buyers and sellers interact to determine the price of tomatoes, a product Mr. Lieberman almost always carries. It will employ two curves. The first represents buyers' behavior, which is called their demand for the product.

## The Elements of Demand

To the general public, demand is simply what people want. But to economists, demand has a much more technical meaning. **Demand** is the assumed inverse relationship between the price of a good or service and the quantity consumers are willing and able to buy during a given period, all other things held constant.

**Demand:** the assumed inverse relationship between the price of a good or service and the quantity consumers are willing and able to buy during a given period, all other things held constant.

### *Demand as a Relationship*

The relationship between price and quantity is normally assumed to be inverse. That is, when the price of a good rises, the quantity sold, *ceteris paribus* (Latin for "everything else held constant"), will go down. Conversely, when the price of a good falls, the quantity sold goes up. Demand is not a quantity, but a relationship. A given quantity sold at a particular price is properly called *quantity demanded.*

Both tables and graphs can be used to describe the assumed inverse relationship between price and quantity.

### *Demand as a Table or a Graph*

Demand may be thought of as a schedule of the various quantities of a particular good consumers will buy at various prices. As the price goes down, the quantity purchased goes up, and vice versa. Table 3.1 contains a hypothetical schedule of the demand for tomatoes in the New York area during a typical week. The middle column shows prices that might be charged. The right-hand column shows the number of bushels consumers will buy at those prices. Note that as the price rises from zero to $11 a bushel, the number of bushels purchased drops from 110,000 to zero.

Demand may also be thought of as a curve. If price is scaled on a graph's vertical axis and quantity on the horizontal axis, the demand curve has a negative slope (downward and to the right), reflecting the assumed inverse relationship between price and quantity. The general shape of the demand curve is shown in Figure 3.1, which is based on the data from Table 3.1. Points *a* through *l* on the graph correspond to the price-quantity combinations *A* through *L* in the table. Note that as the price falls from $P_2$ ($8) to $P_1$ ($5), consumers move down their demand curve from a quantity of $Q_1$ (30) to the larger quantity $Q_2$ (60).[3]

3. Mathematically, the demand relationship may be stated as $Q_d = a - bP$, where $Q_d$ is the quantity demanded at each and every price; *a* is the quantity consumers will buy when the price is zero; *b* is the slope of the demand curve; and *P* is the price of the good. Thus the demand for tomatoes described in Table 3.1 and Figure 3.1 may be written as $Q_d = 110{,}000 - 10{,}000\,P$.

**Table 3.1.** Demand for Tomatoes

| Price–Quantity Combinations | Price per Bushel | Number of Bushels |
|---|---|---|
| A | $ 0 | 110,000 |
| B | 1 | 100,000 |
| C | 2 | 90,000 |
| D | 3 | 80,000 |
| E | 4 | 70,000 |
| F | 5 | 60,000 |
| G | 6 | 50,000 |
| H | 7 | 40,000 |
| I | 8 | 30,000 |
| J | 9 | 20,000 |
| K | 10 | 10,000 |
| L | 11 | 0 |

### *The Slope and Determinants of Demand*

Price and quantity are assumed to be inversely related for two reasons.

First, as the price of a good decreases (and the prices of all other goods stay the same—remember *ceteris paribus*), the purchasing power of consumer incomes rises. More consumers are able to buy the good, and many will buy more of most goods. (This response is called the income effect.)

In addition, as the price of a good decreases (and the prices of all other goods remain the same), the good becomes relatively cheaper, and consumers will substitute that good for others. (This response is called the substitution effect.)

In sum, when the price of tomatoes (or razorblades, or any other good) falls, more tomatoes will be purchased, because more people will be buying them for more purposes.

Although price is an important part of the definition of demand, it is not the only determinant of how much of a good people will want. It may not even be the most important. The major nonprice factors that affect demand are called determinants of demand. They are:

consumer tastes or preferences

the prices of other goods

consumer incomes

number of consumers

expectations concerning future prices and incomes

A host of other factors, like weather, may also influence the demand for particular goods—ice cream, for instance.

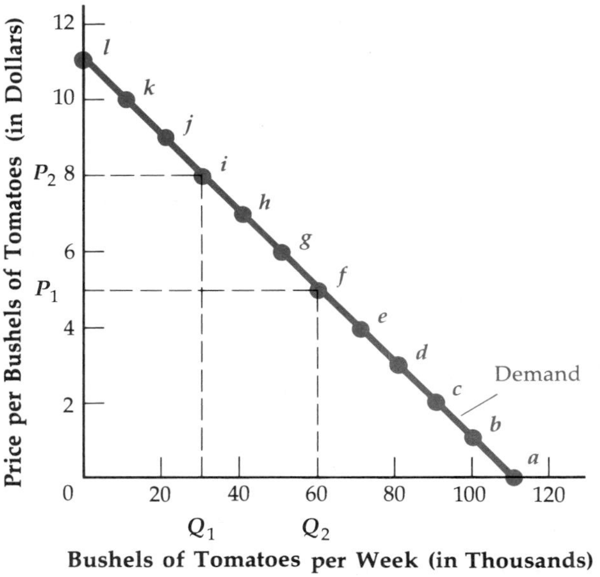


**Figure 3.1.** Demand for Tomatoes.
Demand, the assumed inverse relationship between price and quantity purchased, can be represented by a curve that slopes down toward the right. Here, as the price falls from $11 to zero, the number of bushels of tomatoes purchased per week rises from zero to 110,000.

A change in any of these determinants of demand will cause either an increase or a decrease in demand. An **increase in demand** is an increase in the quantity demanded at each and every price. It is represented graphically by a rightward, or outward, shift in the demand curve. A **decrease in demand** is a decrease in the quantity demanded at each and every price. It is represented graphically by a leftward, or inward, shift of the demand curve. Figure 3.2 illustrates the shifts in the demand curve that result from a change in one of the determinants of demand. The outward shift from $D_1$ to $D_2$ indicates an increase in demand: consumers now want more of a good at each and every price. For example, they want $Q_3$ instead of $Q_2$ tomatoes at price $P_2$. Consumers are also willing to pay a higher price now for any quantity. For example, they will pay $P_3$ instead of $P_2$ for $Q_2$ tomatoes. The inward shift from $D_1$ to $D_3$ indicates a decrease in demand: consumers want less of a good at each and every price—$Q_1$ instead of $Q_2$ tomatoes at price $P_2$. And they are willing to pay less than before for any quantity—$P_1$ instead of $P_2$ for $Q_2$ tomatoes.

**Increase in demand:** an increase in the quantity demanded at each and every price, represented graphically by a rightward, or outward, shift in the demand curve.

**Decrease in demand:** a decrease in the quantity demanded at each and every price, represented graphically by a leftward, or inward, shift of the demand curve.

A change in a determinant of demand may be translated into an increase or decrease in demand in numerous ways. An increase in demand can be caused by:

An increase in consumers' desire for the good. If people truly want the good more, they will buy more of the good at any given price, or pay a higher price for any given quantity.

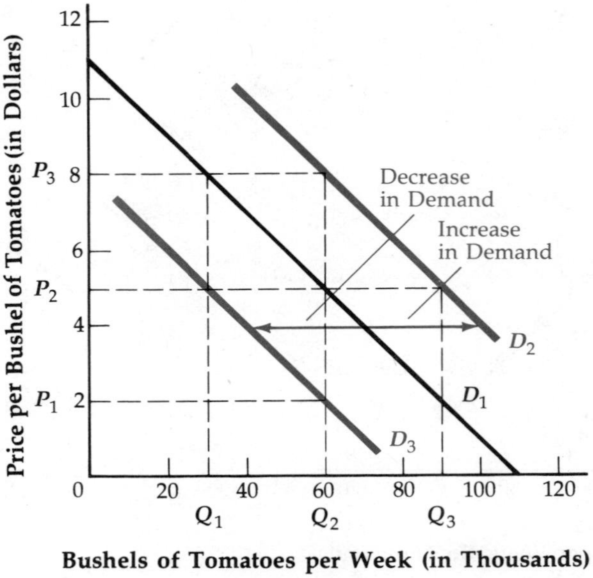


**Figure 3.2.** Shifts in the Demand Curve.
An increase in demand is represented by a rightward, or outward, shift in the demand curve, from $D_1$ to $D_2$. A decrease in demand is represented by a leftward, or inward, shift in the demand curve, from $D_1$ to $D_3$.

An increase in the number of buyers. If more people will buy the good at any given price, they will also pay a higher price for any given quantity.

An increase in the price of substitute goods (which can be used in place of the good in question). If the price of oranges increases, the demand for grapefruit will increase.

A decrease in the price of complement goods (which are used in conjunction with the good in question). If the price of records or tapes falls, the demand for stereo systems will rise.

Generally speaking (but not always), an increase in consumer incomes. An increase in people's incomes may increase the demand for luxury goods, such as new cars. But it may also decrease demand for low-quality goods (like hamburger) because people can now afford better-quality products (like steak).

An expected increase in the future price of the good in question. If people expect the price of cars to rise faster than the prices of other goods, then (depending on exactly when they expect the increase) they may buy more cars now, thus avoiding the expected additional cost in the future.

An expected decrease in the future price of a substitute good. If people expect the price of oranges to fall in the future, then (depending on exactly when they expect the price decrease) they may reduce their current demand for grapefruit, so they can buy more oranges in the future.

An expected increase in future incomes of buyers. College seniors' demand for cars tends to increase as graduation approaches and they anticipate a rise in income.

The determinants of a decrease in demand are just the opposite:

A decrease in consumers' desire or taste for the good.

A decrease in the number of buyers.

A decrease in the price of substitute goods.

An increase in the price of complement goods.

Generally speaking (but not always), a decrease in consumer incomes.

An expected decrease in the future price of the good in question.

An expected decrease in the future price of a substitute good.

An expected decrease in future incomes of buyers.

## The Elements of Supply

On the other side of the market are producers of goods. The average person thinks of supply as the quantity of a good producers are willing to sell. But to economists, supply means something quite different. **Supply** is the assumed relationship between the quantity of a good producers are willing to offer during a given period and the price, all else being equal. Generally, because managerial costs tend to rise with expanded production, this relationship is presumed to be positive. Like demand, supply is not a given quantity—that is called quantity supplied. Rather it is a relationship between price and quantity. As the price of a good rises, producers are generally willing to offer a larger quantity. The reverse is equally true: as price decreases, so does quantity supplied. Like demand, supply can also be described in a table or a graph.

**Supply:** the assumed relationship between the quantity of a good producers are willing and able to offer during a given period and the price, everything else held constant.

### *Supply as a Table or a Graph*

Supply may be described as a schedule of the quantities producers will offer at various prices during a given period of time. Table 3.2 shows such a supply schedule. As the price of tomatoes goes up from zero to $11 a bushel, the quantity offered rises from zero to 110,000, reflecting the assumed positive relationship between price and quantity.

Supply may also be thought of as a curve. If the quantity producers will offer is scaled on the horizontal axis of a graph and the price of the good is scaled on the vertical axis, the supply curve will slope upward to the right, reflecting the assumed positive relationship between price and

**Table 3.2.** Supply of Tomatoes

| Price–Quantity Combination | Price per Bushel | Number of Bushels |
|---|---|---|
| A | 0 | 0 |
| B | 1 | 10 |
| C | 2 | 20 |
| D | 3 | 30 |
| E | 4 | 40 |
| F | 5 | 50 |
| G | 6 | 60 |
| H | 7 | 70 |
| I | 8 | 80 |
| J | 9 | 90 |
| K | 10 | 100 |
| L | 11 | 110 |

quantity. In Figure 3.3, which was plotted from the data in Table 3.2, points *a* through *l* represent the price-quantity combinations *A* through *L*. Note how a change in the price causes a movement along the supply curve.[4]

*The Slope and Determinants of Supply*

The quantity producers will offer on the market depends on their production costs. Obviously the total cost of production will rise when more is produced, since more resources will be required to expand output. But the additional or marginal cost of each additional bushel produced also tends to rise as total output expands. In other words, it costs more to produce the second bushel of tomatoes than the first, and more to produce the third than the second. Firms will not expand their output unless they can cover their higher unit costs with a higher price. This is the reason the supply curve is thought to slope upward.

Anything that affects production costs will influence supply and the position of the supply curve. Such factors, which are called determinants of supply, include:

A change in productivity due to a change in technology.

A change in the profitability of producing other goods.

A change in the scarcity of various production resources.

4. Mathematically, the supply relationship may be stated as $Q_s = a + bP$, where $Q_s$ is the quantity supplied; $a$ is the quantity producers will supply when the price is zero; $b$ is the slope; and $P$ is the price. Thus the supply of tomatoes represented in Table 3.3 and Figure 3.3 may be written $Q_s = 0 + 10{,}000\ P$.

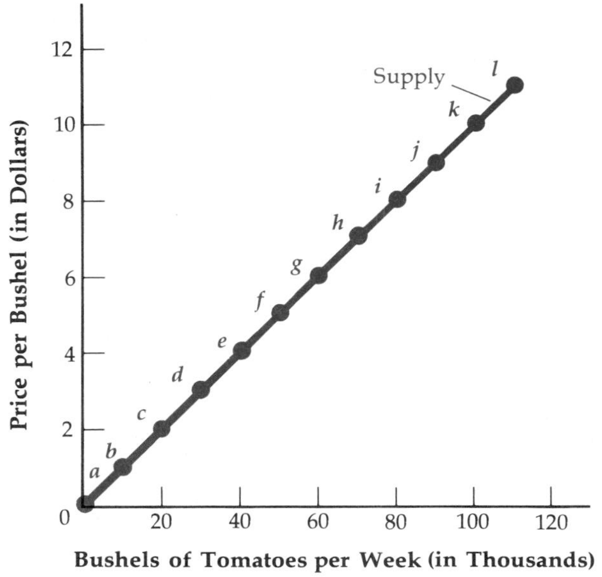


**Figure 3.3.** Supply of Tomatoes.
Supply, the assumed relationship between price and quantity produced, can be represented by a curve that slopes up toward the right. Here, as the price rises from zero to $11, the number of bushels of tomatoes offered for sale during the course of a week rises from zero to 110,000.

Many other factors, such as weather, can also affect production costs. A change in any of these determinants of supply can either increase or decrease supply. An **increase in supply** is an increase in the quantity producers are willing and able to offer at each and every price. It is represented graphically by a rightward, or outward, shift in the supply curve. A **decrease in supply** is a decrease in the quantity producers are willing and able to offer at each and every price. It is represented graphically by a leftward, or inward, shift of the supply curve.

In Figure 3.4, an increase in supply is represented by the shift from $S_1$ to $S_2$. Producers are willing to produce a larger quantity at each price—$Q_3$ instead of $Q_2$ at price $P_2$, for example. They will also accept a lower price for each quantity—$P_1$ instead of $P_2$ for quantity $Q_2$. Conversely, the decrease in supply represented by the shift from $S_1$ to $S_3$ means that producers will offer less at each price—$Q_1$ instead of $Q_2$ at price $P_2$. They must also have a higher price for each quantity—$P_3$ instead of $P_2$ for quantity $Q_2$.

A few examples will illustrate the impact of changes in the determinants of supply. If firms learn how to produce more goods with the same or fewer resources, the cost of producing any given quantity will fall. Because of the technological improvement, firms will be able to offer a larger quantity at any given price, or the same quantity at a lower price. The supply will increase, shifting the supply curve outward to the right.

**Increase in supply:** an increase in the quantity producers are willing and able to offer at each and every price, represented graphically by a rightward, or outward, shift in the supply curve.

**Decrease in supply:** a decrease in the quantity producers are willing and able to offer at each and every price, represented graphically by a leftward, or inward, shift of the supply curve.

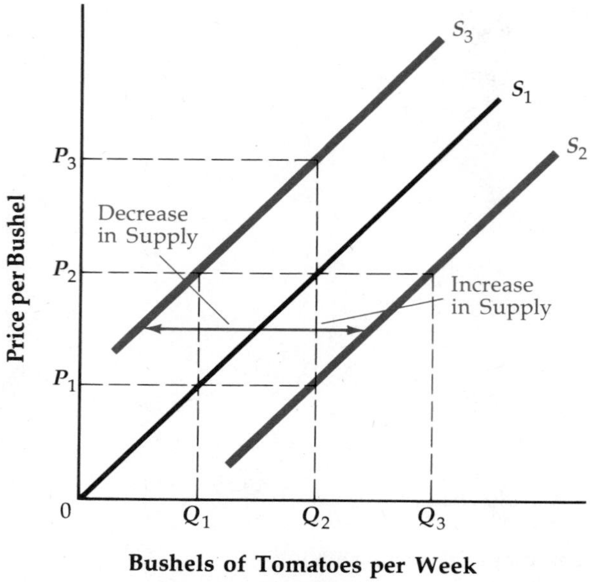


**Figure 3.4.** Shifts in the Supply Curve.
A rightward, or outward, shift in the supply curve, from $S_1$ to $S_2$, represents an increase in supply. A leftward, or inward, shift in the supply curve, from $S_1$ to $S_3$, represents a decrease in supply.

Similarly, if the profitability of producing oranges increases relative to grapefruit, grapefruit producers will shift their resources to oranges. The supply of oranges will increase, shifting the supply curve to the right. Finally, if lumber (or labor or equipment) becomes scarcer, its price will rise, increasing the cost of new housing and reducing the supply. The supply curve will shift inward to the left.

## Market Equilibrium

Supply and demand represent the two sides of the market, sellers and buyers. By plotting the supply and demand curves together, as in Figure 3.5, we can predict how buyers and sellers will interact with one another. At any price other than the one at the intersection of the two curves, the desires of buyers and sellers will be inconsistent, and a market surplus or shortage of tomatoes will result.

**Market surplus:** the amount by which the quantity supplied exceeds the quantity demanded at a given price. Graphically, the excess supply that occurs at any price above the intersection of the supply and demand curves.

### *Market Surpluses*

Suppose that the price of a bushel of tomatoes is \$9, or $P_2$ in Figure 3.5. At this price the quantity demanded by consumers is 20,000 bushels, much less than the quantity offered by producers, 90,000. There is a market surplus, or excess supply, of 70,000 bushels. A **market surplus** is the

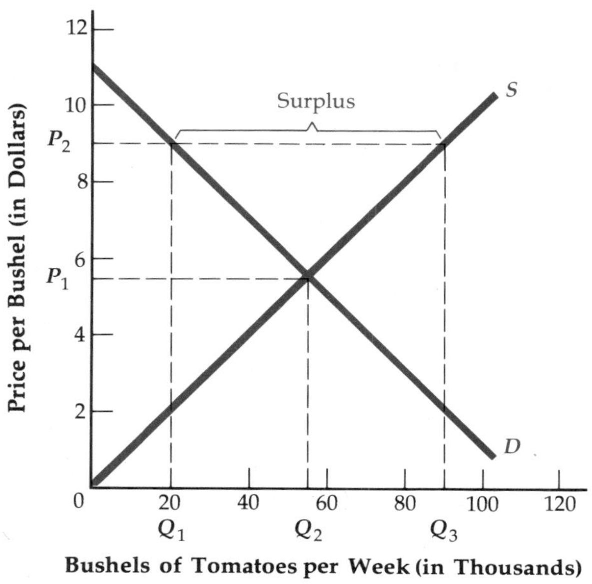


**Figure 3.5.** Market Surplus.
If a price is higher than the intersection of the supply and demand curves, a market surplus—a greater quantity supplied, $Q_3$, than demanded, $Q_1$—results. Competitive pressure will push the price down to the equilibrium price $P_1$, the price at which the quantity supplied equals the quantity demanded ($Q_2$).

amount by which the quantity supplied exceeds the quantity demanded at any given price. Graphically, it is the excess supply that occurs at any price above the intersection of the supply and demand curves.

What will happen in this situation? Producers who cannot sell their tomatoes will have to compete by offering to sell at a lower price, forcing other producers to follow suit. As the competitive process forces the price down, the quantity consumers are willing to buy will expand, while the quantity producers are willing to sell will decrease. The result will be a contraction of the surplus, until it is finally eliminated at a price of $5.50 or $P_1$ (at the intersection of the two curves). At that price, producers will be selling all they want to; they will see no reason to lower prices further. Similarly, consumers will see no reason to pay more; they will be buying all they want. This point, where the wants of buyers and sellers intersect, is called the equilibrium price. The **equilibrium price** is the price toward which a competitive market will move, and at which it will remain once there, everything else held constant. It is the price at which the market "clears"—that is, at which the quantity demanded by consumers is matched exactly by the quantity offered by producers. At the equilibrium price, the quantities desired by buyers and sellers are also equal. This is the equilibrium quantity. The **equilibrium quantity** is the output (or sales) level toward which the market will move, and at which it will remain once there, everything else held constant.

**Equilibrium price:** the price toward which a competitive market will move, and at which it will remain once there, everything else held constant. The price at which the market "clears"—that is, at which the quantity demanded by consumers is matched exactly by the quantity offered by producers.

**Equilibrium quantity:** the output (or sales) level toward which the market will move, and at which it will remain once there, everything else held constant. Reached when the quantity demanded equals the quantity supplied (at the equilibrium price).

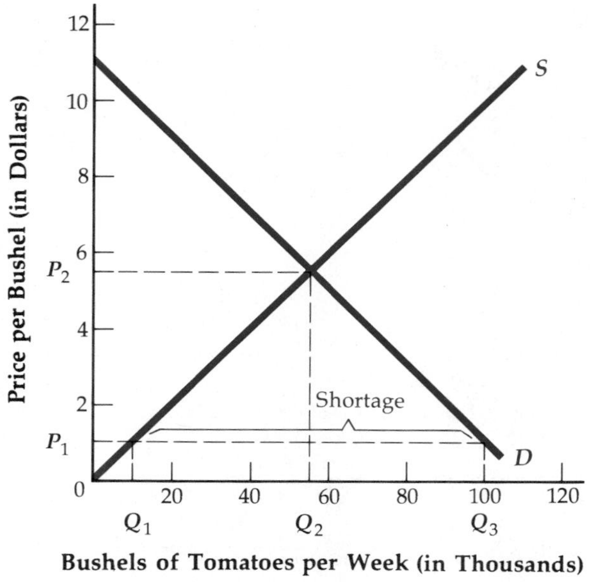


**Figure 3.6.** Market Shortage.
A price that is below the intersection of the supply and demand curves will create a shortage—a greater quantity demanded, $Q_3$, than supplied, $Q_1$. Competitive pressure will push the price up to the equilibrium price $P_2$, the price at which the quantity supplied equals the quantity demanded.

In sum, a surplus emerges when the price asked is above the equilibrium price. It will be eliminated, through competition among sellers, when the price drops to the equilibrium price.

### *Market Shortages*

**Market shortage:** the amount by which the quantity demanded exceeds the quantity supplied at a given price. Graphically, the shortfall in supply that occurs at any price below the intersection of the supply and demand curves.

Suppose the price asked is below the equilibrium price, as in Figure 3.6. At the relatively low price of \$1, or $P_1$, buyers want to purchase 100,000 bushels—substantially more than the 10,000 bushels producers are willing to offer. The result is a market shortage. A **market shortage** is the amount by which the quantity demanded exceeds the quantity supplied at any given price. Graphically, it is the shortfall that occurs at any price below the intersection of the supply and demand curves.

As with a market surplus, competition will correct the discrepancy between buyers' and sellers' plans. Buyers who want tomatoes but are unable to get them at a price of \$1 will bid higher prices, as at an auction. As the price rises, a larger quantity will be supplied, because suppliers will be better able to cover their increasing production costs. At the same time the quantity demanded will contract as buyers seek substitutes that are now relatively less expensive compared with tomatoes. At the equilibrium price of \$5.50, or $P_2$, the market shortage will be eliminated. Buyers will have no reason to bid prices up further, for they will be getting all the tomatoes they want at that price. Sellers will have no reason to expand production further; they will be selling all they want to at that price. The equilibrium price will remain the same until some force shifts the position of either the supply or the demand curve. If such a shift occurs, the price will move toward a new equilibrium at the new intersection of the supply and demand curves.

### *The Effect of Changes in Demand and Supply*

Figure 3.7 shows the effects of shifts in demand and supply on the equilibrium price and quantity. In panel (a), an increase in demand from $D_1$ to $D_2$ raises the equilibrium price from $P_1$ to $P_2$ and quantity from $Q_1$ to $Q_2$. In panel (b), a decrease in demand from $D_1$ to $D_2$ has the opposite effect, lowering price from $P_2$ to $P_1$ and quantity from $Q_2$ to $Q_1$.

An increase in supply from $S_1$ to $S_2$—panel (c)—has a different effect. The equilibrium quantity rises from $Q_1$ to $Q_2$, but the equilibrium price falls from $P_2$ to $P_1$. A decrease in supply from $S_1$ to $S_2$—panel (d)—causes the opposite effect: the equilibrium quantity falls from $Q_2$ to $Q_1$, and the equilibrium price rises from $P_1$ to $P_2$.

## The Efficiency of the Competitive Market Model

Early in this chapter we asked how Fred Lieberman knows what prices to charge for the goods he sells. The answer is now apparent: he adjusts his prices until his customers buy the quantities that he wants to sell. If he cannot sell all the fruits and vegetables he has, he lowers his price to attract customers and cuts back on his orders for those goods. If he runs short, he knows he can raise his prices and increase his orders. His customers then adjust their purchases accordingly. Similar actions by other producers and customers all over the city move the market for produce toward equilibrium. And the information provided by the orders, reorders, and cancellations from stores like Lieberman's eventually reach the suppliers of goods and then the suppliers of resources. Similarly wholesale prices give Fred Lieberman information on suppliers' costs of production and the relative scarcity and productivity of resources.

The use of the competitive market system to determine what and how much to produce has two advantages. First, it is tolerably accurate. Much of the time the amount produced in a competitive market system tends to equal the amount consumers want—no more, no less. Second, the market system maximizes output.

In Figure 3.8(a), note that all price-quantity combinations acceptable to consumers lie either on or below the market demand curve, in the shaded area. (If consumers are willing to pay $P_2$ for $Q_1$ then they should also be willing to pay less for that quantity—for example, $P_1$.) Furthermore, all price-quantity combinations acceptable to producers lie either on or above the supply curve, in the shaded area shown in Figure 3.7(b). (If producers are willing to accept $P_1$ for quantity $Q_1$, then they should also be willing to accept a higher price—for example, $P_2$). When supply and demand

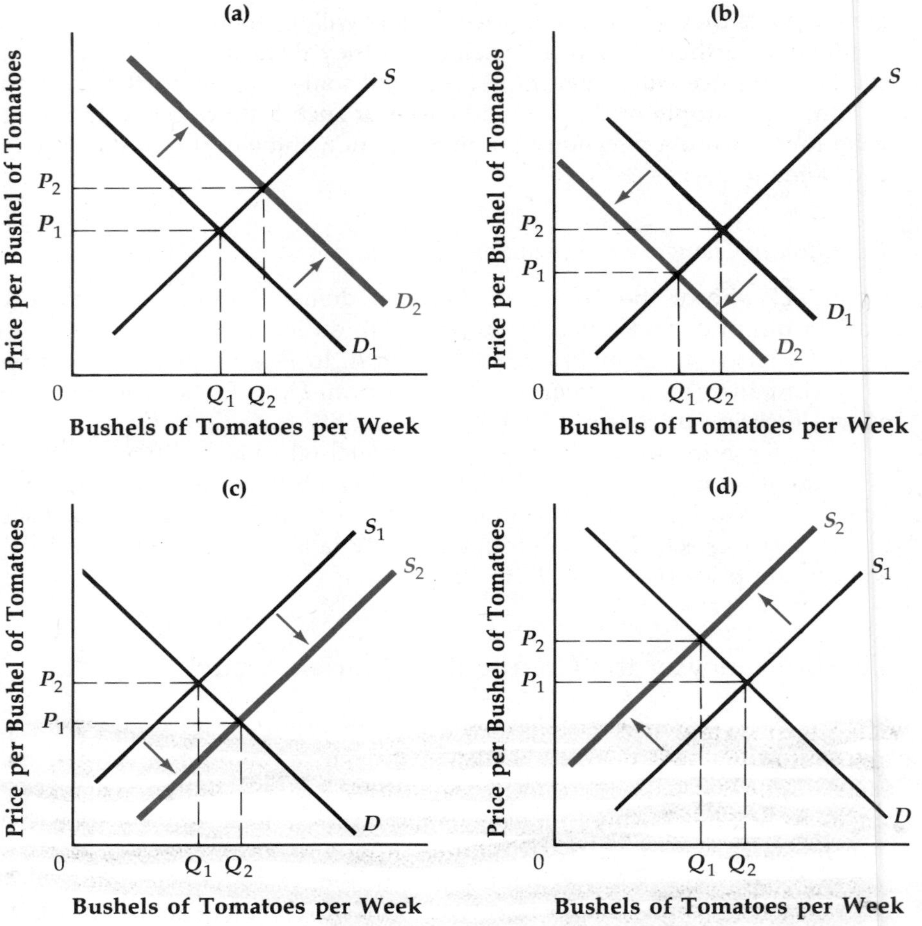


**Figure 3.7.** The Effects of Changes in Supply and Demand.
An increase in demand—panel (a)—raises both the equilibrium price and the equilibrium quantity. A decrease in demand—panel (b)—has the opposite effect: a decrease in the equilibrium price and quantity. An increase in supply—panel (c)—causes the equilibrium quantity to rise but the equilibrium price to fall. A decrease in supply—panel (d)—has the opposite effect: a rise in the equilibrium price and a fall in the equilibrium quantity.

**Efficiency:** the maximization of output through careful allocation of resources, given the constraints of supply (producers' costs) and demand (consumers' preferences).

curves are combined in Figure 3.8(c), we see that all price-quantity combinations acceptable to both consumers and producers lie in the darkest shaded triangular area. From all those acceptable output levels, the competitive market produces $Q_1$, the maximum output level that can be produced given what producers and consumers are willing and able to do. In this respect, the competitive market can be said to be efficient, or to allocate resources efficiently. **Efficiency** is the maximization of output through careful allocation of resources, given the constraints of supply

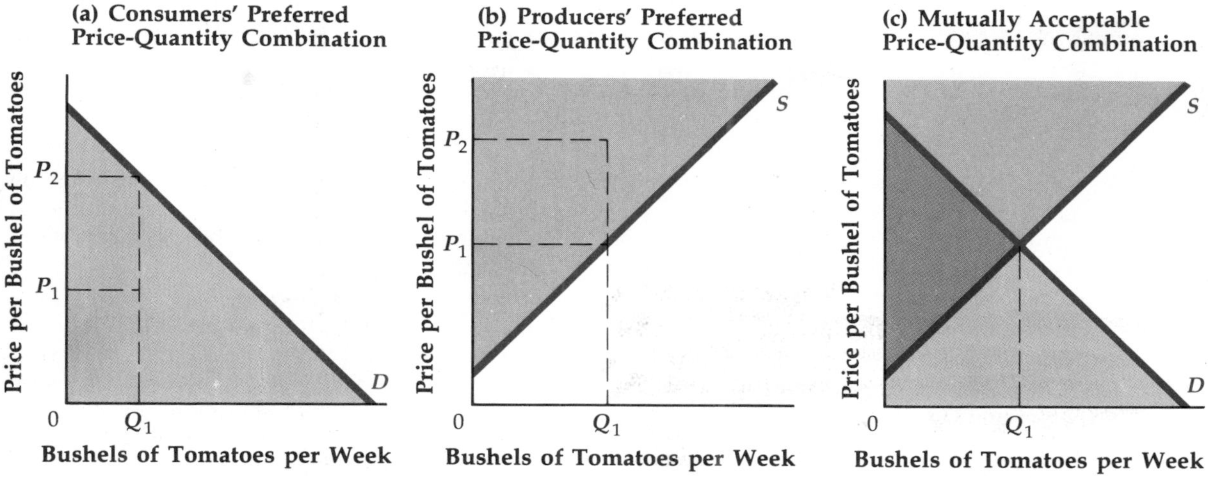


**Figure 3.8.** The Efficiency of the Competitive Market.
Only those price-quantity combinations on or below the demand curve—panel (a)—are acceptable to buyers. But only those price-quantity combinations on or above the supply curve—panel (b)—are acceptable to producers. Those price-quantity combinations that are acceptable to both buyers and producers are shown in the darkest shaded area of panel (c). The competitive market is efficient in the sense that it results in output $Q_1$, the maximum output level acceptable to both buyers and producers.

(producers' costs) and demand (consumers' preferences). The achievement of efficiency means that consumers' or producers' welfare will be reduced by an expansion or contraction of output.

The market system exploits all possible trades between buyers and sellers. Up to the equilibrium quantity, buyers will pay more than suppliers require (those points on the demand curve lie above the supply curve). Beyond $Q_1$, buyers will not pay as much as suppliers need to produce more (those points on the supply curve lie above the demand curve). Again the market can be called efficient.

## Nonprice Competition

Markets in which suppliers compete solely in terms of price are relatively rare. Table salt is a relatively uniform commodity sold in a market in which price is an important competitive tool. But even producers of salt compete in terms of real or imagined quality differences and the reputation and recognition of brand names. In most industries, competition is through a wide range of product features, such as quality or the appearance of it, design, and durability. In general, competitors can be expected to choose the mix of features that gives them the greatest profit.

## Perspectives in Economics: Price Floors and Price Ceilings

Political leaders have occasionally objected to the prices charged in open, competitive markets and have mandated the prices at which goods must be sold. That is, the government has enforced price ceilings and price floors. A **price ceiling** is a government-determined price above which a specified good cannot be sold. A **price floor** is a government-determined price below which a specified good cannot be sold. Supply and demand graphs can illustrate the consequences of price ceilings and floors. For example, some cities impose ceilings on the rents (or prices) for apartments. Such a ceiling must be below the equilibrium price—somewhere below $P_1$ in Figure 3.9(a). (If the ceiling were above equilibrium, it would be above the market price and would serve no purpose.) As the graph shows, such a price control creates a market shortage. The number of people wanting apartments, $Q_2$, is greater than the number of apartments available, $Q_1$. Because of the shortage, landlords will be less concerned about maintaining their units, for they will be able to rent them in any case.

If the government imposes a price *floor*—on a commodity like milk, for example—the price must be above the equilibrium price, $P_1$ in Figure 3.9(b). (A price floor below $P_1$ would be irrelevant, because the market would clear at a higher level on its own.) The result of such a price edict is a market surplus. Producers want to sell more milk, $Q_2$, than consumers are willing to buy, $Q_1$. Some producers—those caught holding the surplus ($Q_2 - Q_1$)—will be unable to sell all they want to sell. Eventually someone must bear the cost of destroying or storing the surplus—and in fact the government holds vast quantities of grain, cotton, and dairy products because of its past efforts to support an equilibrium price for those products.

In fact, price competition is not always the best method of competition, not only because price reductions mean lower average revenues, but because the reductions can be costly to communicate to consumers. Advertising is expensive, and consumers may not notice price reductions as readily as they do improvements in quality. Quality changes, furthermore, are not so easily duplicated as price changes. Consumers' preferences for quality over price should be reflected in the profitability of making such improvements. If consumers prefer a top-of-the-line calculator to a cheaper basic model, then producing the more sophisticated model could, depending on the cost of the extra features, be more profitable than producing the basic model and communicating its lower price to consumers.

If all consumers had exactly the same preferences—size, color, and so on—producers would presumably make uniform products and compete through price alone. But for most products, people's preferences differ. To keep the analysis manageable, we will explore nonprice competition in terms of just one feature, product size. Suppose that in the market for television sets, consumer preferences are distributed along the continuum shown in Figure 3.10. The curve is bell shaped, indicating that most

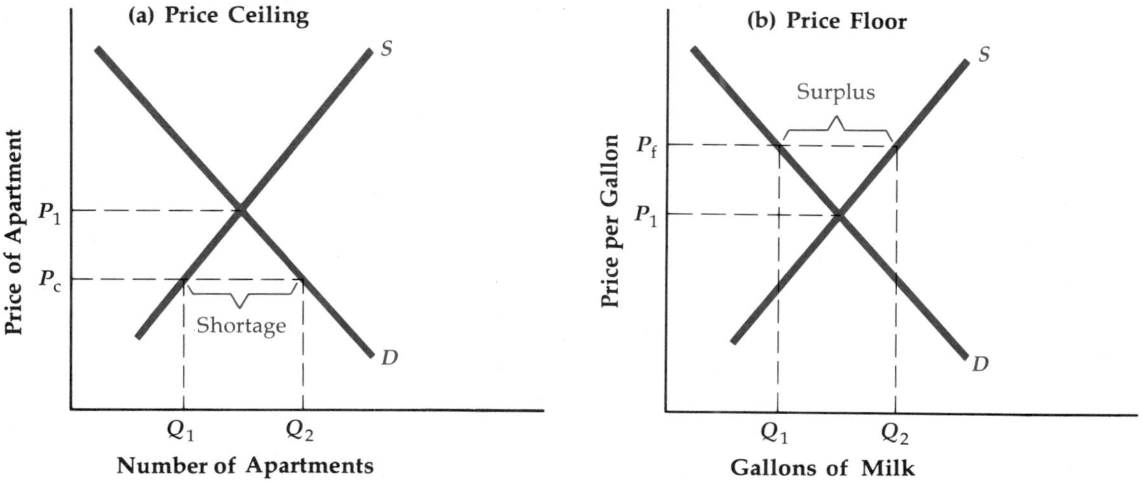


**Figure 3.9.** Price Ceilings and Floors.
A price ceiling $P_c$—panel (a)—will create a market shortage equal to $Q_2 - Q_1$. A price floor $P_f$—panel (b)—will create a market surplus equal to $Q_2 - Q_1$.

consumers are clustered in the middle of the distribution and want a middle-sized television. Fewer consumers want a giant screen or a mini-television.

Everything else being equal, the first producer to enter the market, Terrific TV, will probably offer a product that falls somewhere in the middle of the distribution—for example, at *T* in Figure 3.10. In this way, Terrific TV offers a product that reflects the preferences of the largest number of people. Furthermore, as long as there are no competitors, the firm can expect to pick up customers to the left and right of center. (Terrific TV's product may not come very close to satisfying the wants of consumers who prefer a very large or very small television, but it is the only one available.) The more Terrific TV can meet the preferences of the greatest number of consumers, everything else being equal, the higher the price it can charge and the greater the profit it can make. (Because consumers value the product more highly, they will pay a higher price for it.)

The first few competitors that enter the market may also locate close to the center—in fact, several may virtually duplicate Terrific TV's product. These firms may conclude that they will enjoy a larger market by sharing

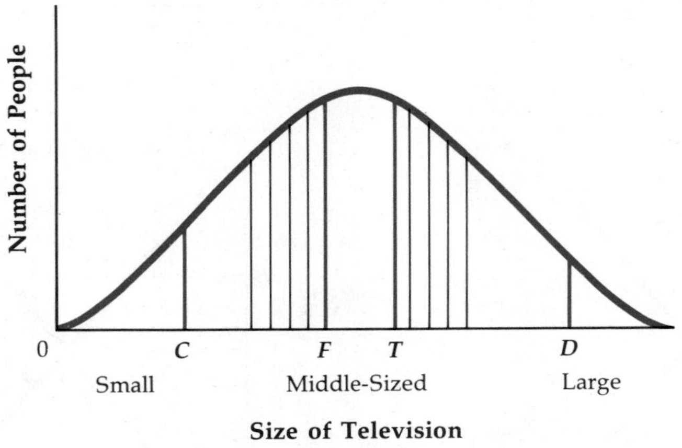


**Figure 3.10.** Consumer Preference in Television Size.
Consumers differ in their wants, but most desire a medium-sized television. Only a few want very small or large televisions.

the center with several competitors than by moving out into the wings of the distribution. And they are probably right. Though they may be able to charge more for a giant screen or a mini-television that closely reflects some consumers' preferences, there are fewer potential customers for those products.

To illustrate, assume that competitor Fabulous Focus locates at *F*, close to *T*. It can then appeal to consumers on the left side of the curve, because its product will reflect those consumers' preferences more closely than does Terrific TV's. Terrific TV can still appeal to consumers on the right half of the curve. If Fabulous Focus had located at *C*, however, it would have direct appeal only to consumers to the left of *C*, as well as to a few between *C* and *T*. Terrific TV would have appealed to more of the consumers on the left, between *C* and *T*, than in the first case. In short, Fabulous Focus has a larger potential market at *F* than at *C*.

However, as more competitors move into the market, the center will become so crowded that new competitors will find it advantageous to move away from the center, to *C* or *D*. At those points the market will not be as large as it is in the center, but competition will be less intense. If producers do not have to compete directly with as many competitors, they can charge higher prices. How far out into the wings they move will depend on the tradeoffs they must make between the number of customers they can appeal to and the price they can charge.

Like price reductions, the movement of competitors into the wings of the distribution benefits consumers whose tastes differ from those of the people in the middle. These atypical consumers now have a product that comes closer to or even directly reflects their preferences.

Our discussion has assumed free entry into the market. If entry is restricted by monopoly of a strategic resource or by government regulation, the variety of products offered will not be as great as in an open, competitive market. If there are only two or three competitors in a market, everything else being equal, we would expect them to cluster in the middle of a bell-shaped distribution. That tendency has been seen in the past in the broadcasting industry, when the number of television stations permitted in a given geographical area was strictly regulated by the Federal Communications Commission. Not surprisingly, stations carried programs that appealed predominantly to a mass audience—that is, to the middle of the distribution of television watchers. The Public Broadcasting System, PBS, was organized by the government partly to provide programs with less than mass appeal to satisfy viewers on the outer sections of the curve. When cable television companies were permitted to break into local television markets, television programs became more varied.

Even with free market entry, product variety depends on the cost of production and the prices people will pay for variations. Magazine and newsstand operators would behave very much like past television managers if they could carry only two or three magazines. They would choose *Newsweek* or some other magazine that appeals to the largest number of people. Most motel operators, for instance, have room for only a very small newsstand, and so they tend to carry the mass-circulation weeklies and monthlies.

For their own reasons, consumers may also prefer such a compromise. Though they may desire a product that perfectly reflects their tastes, they may buy a product that is not perfectly suitable if they can get it at a lower price. Producers can offer such a product at a lower price because of the economies of scale gained from selling to a large market. For example, most students take predesigned classes in large lecture halls instead of private tutorials. They do so largely because the mass lecture, although perhaps less effective, is substantially cheaper. In a market that is open to entry, producers will take advantage of such opportunities.

If producers in one part of a distribution attempt to charge a higher price than necessary, other producers can move into that segment of the market and push the price down; or consumers can switch to other products. In this way, an optimal variety of products will eventually emerge in a free, reasonably competitive market. Thus the argument for a free market is an argument for the optimal product mix. Without freedom of entry, we cannot tell whether it is possible to improve on the existing combination of products. A free, competitive market gives rival firms a chance to better that combination.

The case for the free market becomes even stronger when we recognize that market conditions—and therefore the optimal product mix—are constantly changing.

## Competition in the Short Run and the Long Run

One of the best examples of the workings of both price and nonprice competition is the market for hand calculators. Since the first model was introduced in the United States in 1969, the growth in sales, advancement in technology and design, and decline in prices in this market have been spectacular. The early calculators were simple—some did not even have a division key—and bulky by today's standards. By 1976 they had shrunk from the size of a large paperback book to a tiny two by three-and-a-half inches for one model, and sales exceeded 16 million.

While quality improved, prices fell. The first calculator, which Hewlett-Packard sold for $395, had an eight-digit display and performed only four basic functions, addition, subtraction, division, and multiplication. By December 1971, Bowmar was offering an eight-digit, four-function model for $240. The next year, in an attempt to maintain its high prices, Hewlett-Packard introduced a sophisticated model that could perform many more functions, still for $395. But by the end of the year, Bowmar, Sears, and other firms had broken the $100 barrier, and firms were offering built-in memories, AC adapters, and 1,500-hour batteries to shore up prices. At the year's end, Casio announced a basic model for $59.95.

In 1973 prices continued to fall. By the end of the year, National Semiconductor was offering a six-digit, four-function model for $29.95, and Hewlett-Packard had lowered the price of its special model by $100 and added extra features. In 1974, six-digit, four-function models sold for as little as $16.95. Eight-digit models that would have sold for over $300 three or four years earlier carried price tags of $19.95. By 1976, consumers could buy a six-digit model for just $6.95. All this happened during a period when prices in general rose at a rate unprecedented in the United States during peacetime. Thus the relative prices of calculators fell by even more than their dramatic price reductions suggest.

Yet the drop in the price of calculators was to be expected. Although the high prices of the first calculators partly reflected high production costs, they also brought high profits and tempted many other firms into the industry. These new firms duplicated and then improved the existing technology and increased their productivity in order to beat the competition or avoid being beaten themselves. Firms unwilling to move with the competition quickly lost their share of the market.

**Short-run equilibrium:** the price–quantity combination that will exist so long as producers do not have time to change their production facilities (or some other resource that is fixed in the short run).

The increase in competition in the calculator market can be represented visually with supply and demand curves. Such an analysis permits us to observe long-run changes in market equilibrium. Given the limited technology and the small number of firms producing calculators in 1969, as well as restricted demand for this new product, let us assume that the supply and demand curves were initially $S_1$ and $D_1$ in Figure 3.11. The initial equilibrium price would then be $P_2$, the quantity sold, $Q_1$. This is the short-run equilibrium. **Short-run equilibrium** is the price–quantity combination that will exist so long as producers do not have time to change their production facilities (or some other resource that is fixed in the short run).

Short-run equilibrium did not last long. In the years following 1969, firms expanded production, building new plants and converting facilities that had been producing other small electronic devices. Economies of scale resulted, and technological breakthroughs lowered the cost of production still further. Several $150 circuits were reduced to very small $2 chips. The increased supply shifted the supply curve to the right, from $S_1$ to $S_2$ (see

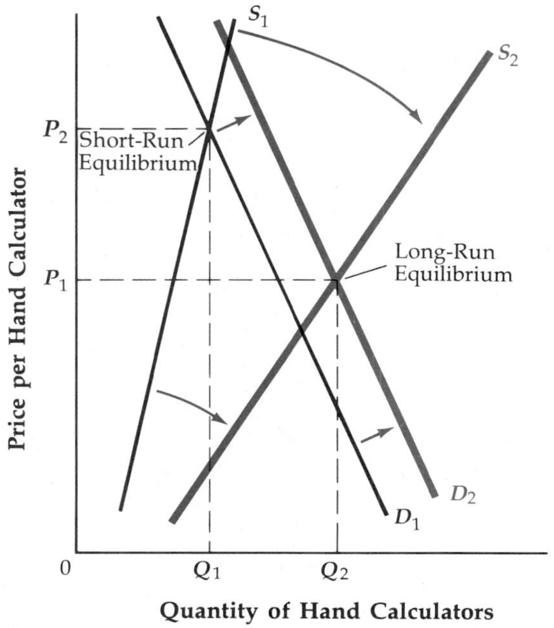


**Figure 3.11.** Long-Run Market for Calculators.
With supply and demand for calculators at $D_1$ and $S_1$, the short-run equilibrium price and quantity will be $P_2$ and $Q_1$. But as existing firms expand production and new firms enter the industry, the supply curve shifts to $S_2$. Simultaneously, an increase in consumer awareness of the product shifts the demand curve to $D_2$. The resulting long-run equilibrium price and quantity are $P_1$ and $Q_2$.

Figure 3.11). Meanwhile, because of advertising and word of mouth, people became familiar with the product and market demand increased, shifting the demand curve from $D_1$ to $D_2$. Because supply increased more than demand, the price fell from $P_2$ to $P_1$, and quantity rose from $Q_1$ to $Q_2$. The new equilibrium price and quantity, $P_1$ and $Q_2$, marked the new long-run market equilibrium. **Long-run equilibrium** is the price–quantity combination that will exist after firms have had time to change their production facilities (or some other resource that is fixed in the short run).

**Long-run equilibrium:** the price–quantity combination that will exist after firms have had time to change their production facilities (or some other resource that is fixed in the short run).

The market does not always move smoothly from the short run to the long run. Because firms do not know exactly what other firms are doing, or exactly what consumer demand will be, they may produce a product that cannot be sold at a price that will cover production costs. In fact, in the mid-1970s prices fell enough that several companies were losing money. Long-run improvements sometimes come at the expense of short-run losses.

In this example, a long-run market adjustment caused a drop in price (because supply increased more than demand). The opposite can occur: demand can increase more than supply, causing a rise in the price and

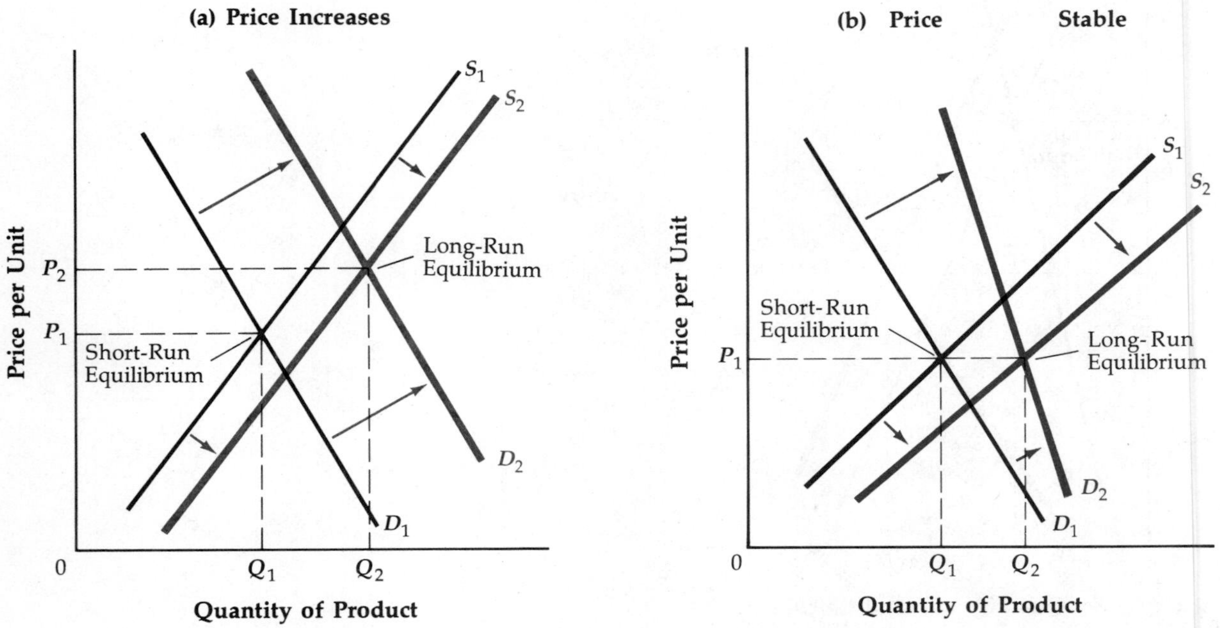


**Figure 3.12.** Prices in the Long Run.
If demand increases more than supply, the price will rise along with the quantity sold—panel (a). If supply keeps up with demand, however, the price will remain the same even though the quantity sold increases—panel (b).

the quantity produced. In Figure 3.12(a), when the supply curve shifts to $S_2$ and the demand curve shifts to $D_2$, price increases from $P_1$ to $P_2$ and quantity produced rises from $Q_1$ to $Q_2$. Supply and demand may also adjust so that price remains constant while quantity increases. (Figure 3.12(b).)

## Shortcomings of Competitive Markets

Though the competitive market may promote long-run improvements in product prices, quality, and output levels, it has deficiencies, and we must note several before closing. (Market deficiencies will be discussed further in later chapters.)

First, the competitive market process can be quite efficient because production is maximized. Consumer demand, however, depends on the way income is distributed. If market forces or government programs distort income distribution, the demand for goods and resources will also be distorted. If, for example, income is concentrated in the hands of a few, the demand for luxury items will be high, but the demand for household appliances and new housing will be low. In such a situation, the results of competition may be efficient in a strict economic sense, but whether these results are socially desirable is a matter of values—of normative, rather than positive, economics.

Second, the outcome of competition will not be efficient to the extent that production costs are imposed on people who do not consume a product. People whose house paint peels because of industrial pollution bear a portion of the offending firm's production cost, whether or not they buy its product. At the same time, the price consumers pay for the product is lower than it would be if all costs, including pollution costs, were incurred by the producer. Because of the low price, consumers will buy more than the efficient quantity. In a sense, this is an example of overproduction. Because all the costs of production have not been included in the producer's cost calculations, the price is artificially low.

Third, in a free market, competition can promote socially undesirable products or services. A competitive market in an addictive drug like alcohol or heroin can lead to lower prices and greater quantities consumed—and thus increase in social problems associated with addiction. Competition can be desirable only when it promotes the production of things people consider beneficial. But what is beneficial is a matter of values.

Fourth, opponents of the market system contend that competition sometimes leads to "product proliferation"—too many versions of essentially the same product, such as aspirin—and to waste in production and advertisement. Because so many types of the same product are available, production of each takes place on a very small scale, and no plant is fully utilized. This may be true. But the validity of this objection hinges on whether the range of choice in products compensates for the inefficiencies in production. The question is whether firms should be forced to standardize their products and to compete solely in terms of price. What about people who want something different from the standard product?

Fifth, unscrupulous competitors can take advantage of customers' ignorance. A competitor may employ unethical techniques, such as circulating false information about rivals or using bait-and-switch promotional tactics (advertising very low-priced, low-quality products to attract customers, in hope of switching them to higher-priced products when they get into the store). Competition can control some of these abuses. For instance, competitors will generally let consumers know when their rivals are misrepresenting their products. Still, fraudulent sellers can move from one market to another, keeping one step ahead of their reputations.

## Summary and Extensions

The market is a system that provides producers with incentives to deliver goods and services to others. To respond to those incentives, producers must meet the needs of society. They must compete with other producers to deliver their goods and services in the most cost-effective manner.

A market implies that sellers and buyers can freely respond to incentives, that they have options and can choose among them. It does not mean, however, that behavior is totally unconstrained, that producers can choose from unlimited options. What a competitor can do may be severely limited by what rival firms are willing to do.

The market system is not perfect. Producers may have difficulty acquiring enough information to make reliable production decisions. People take time to respond to incentives, and producers can make high profits while others are gathering their resources to respond to an opportunity. In the electronics industry, three or four years were required to reduce the price of a basic calculator from $300 to $40. Some consumers still may not be getting exactly the kind of calculator they want.

An uncontrolled market system also carries with it the very real prospect that one firm will acquire monopoly power, restricting the ability of others to respond to incentives, produce more, and push prices and profits down.

## Major Conclusions

1. The competitive market can best be defined as a process through which buyers and sellers, pursuing their own interests, attempt to outwit, outdistance, or outmaneuver other buyers and sellers. In this process, market rivals are forced to reveal the limits of what they will accept in terms of price, quantity, quality, and so on.
2. Price competition among producers will push the price and quantity toward the intersection of the market supply and demand curves, called the equilibrium point.
3. Market shortages will occur if a market price is below the equilibrium price. Market surpluses will occur if a market price is above the equilibrium price.
4. When the market price and quantity move toward the equilibrium price and quantity, the market is said to be operating efficiently.
5. Nonprice competition leads to a greater variety of goods that meet the demands of different buyers.

## Questions to Ponder

1. Why does the demand curve have a negative slope and the supply curve a positive slope?
2. The mercantilists argued that a country's wealth consisted of its holdings of "gold bullion" (money). To keep gold in a country, they proposed tariffs and quotas to restrict imported goods and services. How do you react to that argument?
3. Suppose that supply and demand are represented by the following formulas:

$$Q_d = 110 - 10P$$

$$Q_s = 10 + 10P$$

   What is the equilibrium price and quantity?
4. In what sense can competition in the production of undesirable goods be bad?
5. List what you consider to be the deficiencies of the free market system. Do the deficiencies outweigh the benefits?
6. Why will the competitive market tend to move toward the price-quantity combination at the intersection of the supply and demand curves? What might keep the market from moving all the way to that equilibrium point?
7. Under what conditions could competition cause market prices to move away from equilibrium?
8. Suppose the demand for blue jeans suddenly increases. Discuss the possible short-run and long-run movements of the market.
9. If the government imposes a price ceiling on gasoline, what would be the result?
10. If the government imposes a price floor on whole milk and buys the resulting surplus, can it later sell what it has bought and recoup its expenditure? What else can the government do with the milk surplus?

## Central Question

*From an economic perspective, what are the functions of government?*

## Key Terms

**Private sector**
**Public sector**
**Budget deficit**
**Budget surplus**
**Property rights**
**Personal income taxes**
**Corporate income taxes**
**Excise taxes**
**General sales tax**
**Property tax**
**Progressive tax system**
**Regressive tax system**
**Proportional tax system**
**Marginal tax rate**
**Average tax rate**
**Externalities**
**External benefits**
**External costs**
**Common access resources**
**Monopoly**
**Macroeconomic policy**
**Fiscal policy**
**Monetary policy**

# Chapter 4

# The Public Sector

*The end of law is not to abolish or restrain but to preserve and enlarge freedom; for in all the states of created beings capable of laws, where there is no law, there is no freedom. For liberty is to be free from restraint and violence of others, which cannot be where there is no law; but freedom is not, as we are told: a liberty for every man to do what he lists—for who could be free, when every man's humor might domineer over him?—but a liberty to dispose and order as he lists his . . . actions, possessions, and his whole property, within the allowance of those laws under which he is.*

John Locke

Our study of markets in the last chapter may have suggested that all economic decisions are made by individuals acting in their own self-interest, constrained by the forces of supply and demand. Nothing could be further from the truth. Many economic decisions are made by government, which allocates tax revenue for various public uses, such as national defense, retirement income, education, and garbage collection. Government decisions also influence the types of products we buy, the quality of the air we breathe and the water we drink, the safety of our workplaces, and the number of goods we can buy from foreign countries. In all these ways, government influences how scarce resources are allocated among competing public and private ends.

Because government is so powerful, it must be considered in any economics course. We need to ask why, from an economic perspective, government exists in the first place and how its policies affect private economic activity. After distinguishing the public and private sectors, we will briefly survey the extent of government taxation and expenditure. We will conclude by examining the economic justification for government's various roles.

## An Overview of the Public Sector

In most Western nations, economic life from year to year depends critically on trillions of decisions by millions of individuals acting on their own and as members of social and business organizations. This complex private sector, from which most of us draw a substantial portion of our livelihood, is largely an unintended consequence of purposeful individual action. The **private sector** encompasses all the economic transactions undertaken voluntarily by individuals, either alone or in association with others. Some economists have characterized activity in the private sector as "ordered anarchy," (for its myriad individual actions tend somehow toward economic stability). Others have called it "spontaneous order" (because it occurs without direction) or "self-generating order" (because it emerges on its own and is self-perpetuating). Without some help from government, however, the private economy may not be very orderly, spontaneous, or self-generating.

**Private sector:** all the economic transactions undertaken voluntarily by individuals, either alone or in association with others.

Many crucial decisions are not made by individuals acting independently, but by people acting collectively through government. Government decisions are binding on all citizens, and government activities are paid for by forced taxation. The lack of individual control in the public sector is necessary partly because not everyone agrees with government decisions, and partly because the benefits of many government activities, such as highways and national defense, cannot be distributed selectively. Without taxation, those who benefit from government activities would be unlikely to pay for the services voluntarily, and the services might never be provided. (More will be said about this later.) The **public sector** includes the activities of federal, state, and local government. Government decisions are normally made collectively, either by voters in a referendum or by Congress, and are financed primarily by forced taxation.

**Public sector:** the activities of federal, state, and local government.

At all levels of government—federal, state, and local—government in the United States is big business. All told, it accounts for approximately one-third of the nation's total output. In its 1986 budget (see Table 4.1), which was proposed in early 1985, the federal government planned to spend approximately $974 billion in fiscal year 1986; $286 billion (or 29 percent) of this total was to be spent on national defense and $399 (or 41

**Table 4.1.** Federal Government Outlays and Receipts, 1986[a] (in millions of dollars)

| | |
|---|---|
| **Budget Receipts** | 793,729 |
| Individual income taxes | 358,889 |
| Corporation income taxes | 74,088 |
| Social insurance taxes and contributions | 289,436 |
| Excise taxes | 34,998 |
| Estate and gift taxes | 5,345 |
| Customs duties | 12,342 |
| Miscellaneous receipts: | |
| Deposits of earnings by Federal Reserve System | 16,932 |
| All other | 1,698 |
| **Budget Outlays** | 973,725 |
| National defense | 285,669 |
| International affairs | 18,349 |
| General science, space, and technology | 9,285 |
| Energy | 4,671 |
| Natural resources and environment | 11,884 |
| Agriculture | 12,629 |
| Commerce and housing credit | 2,206 |
| Transportation | 25,860 |
| Community and regional development | 7,323 |
| Education, training, employment, and social services | 29,288 |
| Health | 34,920 |
| Social security and medicare | 269,404 |
| Social security | 202,245 |
| Medicare | 67,158 |
| Income security | 115,769 |
| Veterans benefits and services | 26,769 |
| Administration of justice | 6,587 |
| General government | 4,845 |
| General purpose fiscal assistance | 2,797 |
| Net interest | 142,550 |
| Allowances | 399 |
| Undistributed offsetting receipts | −37,478 |

[a] Estimates available in 1985.

**Source:** Executive Office of the President, Office of Management and Budget, *Budget of the United States Government, Fiscal Year 1986* (Washington, D.C.: U.S. Government Printing Office, 1985), pp. 9–12, 9–13.

**Table 4.2.** Federal Government Receipts, Selected Years, 1900–1985

| Year | Billion Dollars | Year | Billion Dollars |
|---|---|---|---|
| 1900 | 0.6 | 1950 | 39.5 |
| 1905 | 0.5 | 1955 | 65.5 |
| 1910 | 0.7 | 1960 | 92.5 |
| 1915 | 0.7 | 1965 | 116.8 |
| 1920 | 6.6 | 1970 | 193.7 |
| 1925 | 3.6 | 1975 | 279.1 |
| 1930 | 4.1 | 1980 | 517.1 |
| 1935 | 3.7 | 1985 | 736.9 |
| 1940 | 6.4 | 1986 | 793.7 |
| 1945 | 45.2 | | |

**Sources:** U.S. Bureau of the Census, *Historical Statistics of the United States* (Washington, D.C.: U.S. Government Printing Office, 1975), pp. 1104–1105; *Economic Report of the President* (Washington, D.C.: U.S. Government Printing Office, 1985), pp. 316–317; Executive Office of the President, Office of Management and Budget, *Budget of the United States Government, Fiscal Year 1986* (Washington, D.C.: U.S. Government Printing Office, 1985), p. 9–10.

percent) was to be paid directly to individuals under a variety of programs. Social security and income security outlays, which include retirement benefits, payments to disabled workers, and medical care for a wide range of people, were budgeted at $485 billion (or 50 percent of total federal outlays). The federal government also planned to spend $29 billion on education and $13 billion on agriculture. Billions more were budgeted for energy, international affairs, transportation, and housing.

Of the $794 billion that were expected to be collected in revenues in 1986, most ($359 billion, or 45 percent) were expected to come from individual income taxes. Another $74 billion (or 9 percent) were to come from corporate income taxes, and Social Security taxes were expected to add $289 billion, or 36 percent. Significant revenues were expected to come from excise taxes on products like gasoline, tobacco, and alcohol, and on inheritance.

**Budget deficit:** the amount by which outlays exceed receipts during any given accounting period.

**Budget surplus:** the amount by which receipts exceed outlays during a given accounting period.

As Table 4.2 shows, federal receipts have grown substantially, rising from less than $600 million in 1900 to $794 billion in 1986. Most of this growth has occurred since the 1930s. Though inflation has played a large part—dollars are worth much less now than they were in the 1930s—much of the growth is due to an expansion in the federal government's activities. Growth in federal outlays has been even more dramatic than growth in receipts. As a consequence, the federal budget deficit has mushroomed. A **budget deficit** is the amount by which outlays exceed receipts during any given accounting period. It is the opposite of a **budget surplus,** the amount by which receipts exceed outlays during a given accounting period.

Figure 4.1 shows federal outlays and receipts since 1970. Between 1970 and 1984, outlays grew from 20 to over 23 percent of total domestic production. The growing reliance on deficit spending is indicated by the

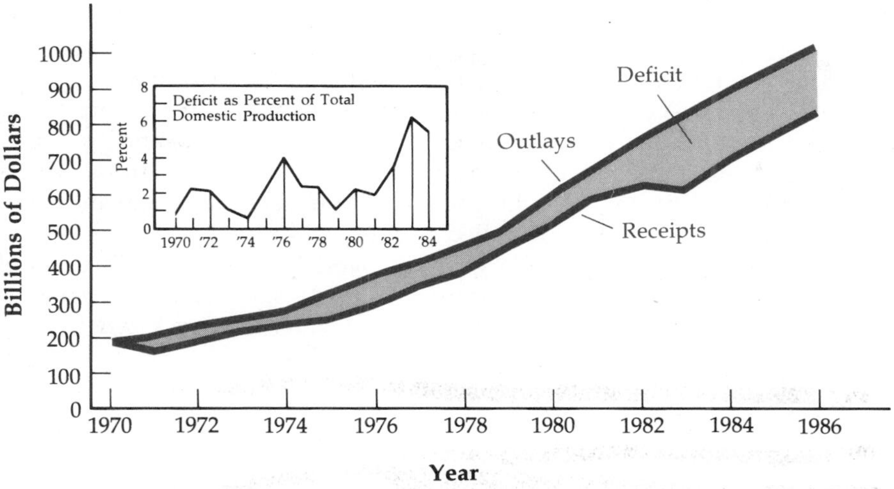


**Figure 4.1.** Federal Budget Receipts and Outlays, 1970–1986.
Federal outlays have risen substantially over the past fifteen years. Because they have risen faster than receipts, the budget deficit (shaded area) has also grown.
Note: Estimated figures for 1985 and 1986.
**Sources:** U.S. Bureau of the Census, *Statistical Abstract of the United States* (Washington, D.C.: U.S. Government Printing Office, 1985), p. 300; Executive Office of the President, Office of Management and Budget, *Budget of the United States Government, Fiscal Year 1986* (Washington, D.C.: U.S. Government Printing Office, 1985), p. 9–10.

shaded area. The federal deficit expanded from one to two percent of total domestic production in the early 1970s to five to six percent of total domestic production in the early 1980s (see the insert in Figure 4.1).

In 1981 the fifty state governments spent a total of $170 billion, most of which went for roads, education, police protection, and local government. They obtained their revenue largely from state income and sales taxes. To their revenue from local property taxes and fees for services provided, the eighty-five thousand local governments (counties, cities, and towns) added $107 billion received from the state and the federal governments, to spend a total of $254 billion. Most local expenditures went for services such as police and fire protection, roads, sewers, and water systems. A relatively small percentage went to welfare programs.

Besides making its own expenditures, government regulates private production. According to one estimate, federal regulation of business activities, including pollution, occupational safety, and product design, costs the private sector over $100 billion annually in added production expenses. State and local regulations increased the bill.

Governments also influence the use of resources through tax exemptions. For example, individuals can deduct the interest paid on borrowed money from their federally taxable incomes. Thus their taxes go down when they take out loans and mortgages. The economic effect of such a deduction is to reduce the after-tax price of many vacations, cars, and houses, and to increase sales of those goods. Businesses can also reduce their federal tax bills, by up to 10 percent of the cost of new plant and equipment. The so-called Investment Tax Credit (which the Reagan administration proposed in 1984 to abolish) encourages the formation of capital and the updating or expansion of industrial equipment. Like government tax and spending decisions, these tax deductions and credits divert resources from private to public uses. Private expenditures made in order to take advantage of tax deductions and credits are called "tax expenditures."

Government decisions loom large in the overall economy, adding to and subtracting from individuals' incentives to work, save, and invest for the future. As government budgets increase, citizens must ask whether all governmental activities are necessary and justifiable.

Several functions traditionally belong to government:

to define and protect property rights;

to protect the public from crime and bring criminals to justice;

to provide for the national defense;

to educate the general public; and

to establish a stable monetary system.

In modern times, however, government responsibilities have expanded to include other functions:

to stabilize the economy—that is, moderate the swings in general economic activity and unemployment;

to control the use of the environment, regulate industry, and protect consumers from perceived abuses of the competitive market process; and

to provide income security and health insurance.

We will examine most of these governmental functions, starting with the traditional function of protecting property.

## Minimal Government: Protection of Property

Although the last chapter's discussion of the market system rarely mentioned government, it was actually based on the existence of some collective authority. In the market system, what is really sold is not tomatoes or hand calculators, but the property rights to tomatoes and hand calculators—and property rights are generally established and protected by government. **Property rights** define the permissible uses of resources, goods, and services, both privately and collectively.

**Property rights:** legally defined and permissible uses, both private and collective, of resources, goods, and services.

Property rights are a social phenomenon—a response to the problem of living peaceably in a world where few have everything they want. In places where people are separated from one another by natural barriers, or where resources are abundant, property rights have no meaning. To

Robinson Crusoe, shipwrecked on a lonely island, property rights were inconsequential. His behavior was restricted only by the resources he found on the island, the tools he took from his wrecked ship, and his own ingenuity. Though he encountered problems in allocating his time efficiently—between food gathering, shelter building, and so on—the notion of property never restrained his behavior. He simply took from the ship, with impunity, whatever seemed most useful.[1]

With the arrival of Friday, it became necessary to establish some restrictions on behavior. The problem was particularly acute because Friday was a cannibal. Clearly each man had to establish property rights to his body. Then the two had to work out a system of ownership for the various possessions on the island.

The property rights traded in the market system are based ultimately on the need for social order. These rights bring obligations as well as privileges. A person who buys a house is actually buying the right to live in the house under certain conditions—for example, so long as he or she does not disturb others, or does not allow the property to deteriorate so much as to threaten the neighbors' safety. These rights and obligations of property owners draw their legitimacy, to a significant degree, from government enforcement of the law.

Just how much markets depend on government for the protection of private property rights is hard to determine. Markets existed in the Old West, which lacked formally instituted government. Even today, we cannot depend on government to arbitrate all questions of property rights. In college dormitories, disputes over property rights are usually settled before they reach the student council, to say nothing of the dean's office or the police station. In society at large, most conflicts over property are resolved personally, and many never arise because people conform to socially accepted standards of behavior.

Nevertheless government definition of property rights represents an important difference between the public and private sectors. When government defines or redefines property rights, it changes the economic circumstances—including the wealth—of individuals in the private sector. For instance, when the federal government imposes price ceilings, as it did in 1971, it restrains the freedom of buyers and sellers in the market system. One purpose of economics is to analyze the effects of a government-ordered realignment of property rights on the efficiency of production.

We are inclined to think of property rights as being natural, a part of our birthright. The Declaration of Independence speaks of "certain unalienable rights," and it is hard to imagine a world without rights to property. But, in addition, government enforcement of property rights has an economic basis.

---

1. The absence of other human beings affected Crusoe's idea of what was useful. Discovering a coffer of gold and silver coins on the ship, he exclaimed, "Thou art not worth to me, no, not the taking off of the ground; one of those knives is worth all this heap." On second thought, however—perhaps after considering the possibility of rescue—Crusoe took the coins.

## Perspectives in Economics: Sources of Income in the Public Sector

Government at all levels—local, state, and federal—is a major user of the nation's resources, and a major buyer of its goods and services. It secures the funds for massive expenditures by borrowing money and by levying taxes on income, sales, and property.

At the national and state levels, most tax revenues come from personal and corporate income taxes. **Personal income taxes** are government revenues collected from individual earnings, after allowance for certain exemptions and deductions. Under federal tax law in 1985, individuals pay taxes on their gross earnings minus exemptions for dependents (taxpayer, spouse, and children) and deductions for certain expenses (interest payments on home mortgages and loans, charitable contributions, and business expenses, among others). **Corporate income taxes** are government revenues collected on a corporation's computed profits, as reported on its profit and loss statements. A corporation's taxable profits are computed by subtracting its business expenses from its sales revenues.

Because of exemptions and deductions many people, including high income earners, pay no federal income taxes. In 1983, 299 millionaires paid no federal taxes. Many other high income earners paid only a small percentage of their income in taxes. Most high income earners who paid little or no tax did so by purchasing municipal bonds, the interest on which is not taxed; or by investing in real estate and taking deductions for depreciation. Other ways of reducing taxes might include charitable contributions, deductions for legitimate business expenses (for example, office supplies and business travel), and personal expenses disguised as business expenses (lunches, home office expenses, and vacations).

Taxes on sales of various commodities also provide income for government. **Excise taxes** are taxes levied on specific products or services, for specific purposes. For instance, an excise tax on gasoline might be used to fund road construction and repair. Sometimes an excise tax is levied to discourage consumption of a product: many liquor taxes serve this purpose. Excise taxes are levied at all levels of government, primarily federal and state. They are normally a percentage of the purchase price. The **general sales tax,** a tax on most, but not necessarily all, consumer purchases, is another type of levy on sales. The tax is usually imposed by states, but in some areas local governments may share its revenues or raise the tax slightly. The amount of the sales tax varies from place to place, ranging from 2 to 8.5 cents on the dollar (1984) in states that have sales tax.

The third source of tax revenues, property, is a major source of revenue for local government, as well as a minor source of revenue for most states and the federal government. The **property tax** is a tax on specified assets, usually real estate, cars and boats, household goods, bank account balances, and stocks and bonds.

The economic effect of all these taxes varies according to the way they are administered. In general, tax systems may be described as progressive, regressive, or proportional. A **progressive tax system** is any means of collecting government

Recall the imaginary island world of only two people, Fred and Harry. Let's assume that initially, like Crusoe and Friday, they have neither rules nor natural barriers to divide their spheres of interest. Furthermore, each man wants more than he can produce by himself. Each has two fundamental options for increasing his welfare. He can use his labor and other resources to produce goods and services, or he can steal. Fred and Harry can be expected to allocate their time in the most productive way. With no social revenues in which the percentage of income that is paid in taxes rises with income. For example, a tax system in which the tax rate rises from 10 to 50 percent as income rises from $15,000 to $100,000 a year is progressive. Personal income taxes are generally progressive, as are corporate income taxes at the federal level. Property taxes are also progressive, since people with higher incomes tend to save and invest a higher percentage of their income in taxable property.

A **regressive tax system** is any means of collecting government revenues in which the percentage of income that is paid in taxes declines as income rises. Under a regressive tax system, as income rises from $15,000 to $100,000, the tax rate would fall—from 20 to 10 percent, for instance. The general sales tax is considered regressive, because lower income groups tend to spend a higher percentage of their incomes on consumer purchases than higher income groups. If a man earning $10,000 a year spends 98 percent of his income, a 5 percent general sales tax on those purchases constitutes 4.9 percent of his earned income. If a woman earning $100,000 a year spends 75 percent of her income, the same 5 percent sales tax works out to only 3.75 percent of her earned income.

A **proportional tax system** is any means of collecting government revenues in which all income earners pay the same tax rate. Under a proportional tax system, the tax rate might be 10 or 20 percent across the board. At the state level, corporate income taxes are often proportional. In South Carolina in 1985, the corporate income tax was a straight 7 percent.

The economic effect of a tax depends largely on the marginal (as opposed to average) tax rate. A **marginal tax rate** is the percentage of any additional income that is subject to taxation. An **average tax rate** is the percentage of total income that is paid in taxes. It is obtained by dividing total taxes paid by total taxable income. The federal income tax system is founded on progressive marginal tax rates. As income rises, additional earned income is taxed at higher and higher rates, up to a limit of 50 percent as of 1985. Thus the more income a person earns, the more tax he or she is forced to pay.

In all their forms, taxes tend to discourage the economic activity they are levied on. Income taxes, especially if they are progressive, can discourage people from earning a taxable income, or from seeking a higher income through education or job training. Generally speaking, the higher the income tax rate, the less the incentive to earn an income, and the more the incentive to avoid taxes. High corporate taxes can discourage investment in corporations, and retard the growth of industry. As already mentioned, excise taxes can—and are often intended to—reduce consumption of certain goods and services. General sales taxes can encourage consumer spending on the relatively few products and services—for example, food or clothing—that are not subject to the sales tax. And property taxes can discourage people from accumulating property and can encourage them to consume instead. In all of these ways, government tax policies can have a significant impact on general economic activity.

or ethical barriers restricting their behavior, each man will steal from the other as long as theft is more rewarding than the production of goods and services. Each will then have to divert some of his resources into protecting what he has produced (or stolen). Presumably this approach will eventually become counterproductive. And each will be investing so much in attacks and counterattacks that neither one of them will find further investment in the activity profitable.

In a limited economic sense, the resources Fred and Harry spend on stealing and preventing theft are wasted, for they are taken away from the production of new goods and services. If those resources were applied to production, total output would rise, and both Fred and Harry would be better off. The wastefulness of plunder is the economic principle that underlies the establishment of property rights. Through social contracts people restrict their behavior so as to avoid the heavier restraints associated with anarchy. The fear of being attacked on the streets at night can be far more confining than laws that restrict people from attacking one another. As John Locke wrote, "The end of law is not to abolish or restrain but to preserve and enlarge freedom."

Even when they recognize the benefits of a social contract, Fred and Harry may be tempted to chisel on the agreement. Fred may find that although he benefits from agreeing to property rights, he benefits even more if he then violates those rights (that is, as long as Harry does not retaliate). By stealing or otherwise ignoring Harry's rights, Fred can redistribute some of Harry's wealth to himself. Of course, if Harry retaliates, the two producers could end up back in a state of anarchy.

Thus the social contract can disintegrate because of individuals' offensive actions as they seek to improve their own positions. But defensive actions can also lead to a return to anarchy. Each citizen must consider what the other might do. Neither would want to be caught upholding an agreement while the other violates it. If Fred thinks Harry might violate his rights, he may violate Harry's rights first, or vice versa. Many wars and battles, both on the street and internationally, have been fought because one party was afraid the other would attack first.

To prevent violations both offensive and defensive, societies have developed police, court, and penal systems to protect the rights specified in the social contract. The costs of such systems may be high, but they are less than the costs of anarchy, in which resources would be diverted to predatory and defensive uses. The costs of making and enforcing the contract will determine just how extensive the contract is.

The social contract that defines property rights establishes only the limits of permissible behavior. Fred and Harry may not be satisfied with the property rights they have, even if they respect them. Both men will try to improve their individual well-being, most likely through socially approved trading arrangements. Suppose the only goods on their island are coconuts and papayas. The social contract specifies the division of fruits between Fred and Harry—whatever each can produce. Suppose also that the additional satisfaction each receives from the last coconut and papaya in his possession is as follows:

| | Coconut | Papaya |
|---|---|---|
| Fred | 10 utils | 15 utils |
| Harry | 90 utils | 30 utils |

Fred receives more satisfaction from his last papaya (15 utils) than from his last coconut (10 utils). He would be better off if he could trade a coconut (sacrificing 10 utils) for a papaya (gaining 15).[2] Harry, on the other hand, would receive more satisfaction from his last coconut; he would gladly trade a papaya for one more coconut. Thus Fred and Harry can be expected to exchange coconut and papaya rights until they can no longer gain from trade. We can also expect them to specialize in producing the fruit in which they have a comparative advantage (see Chapter 2 for a review of comparative advantage).

## Government Production of Public Goods

The protection of property rights that undergirds Fred and Harry's system of specialization and trade requires certain services, such as police and court systems. These services, called public goods, are generally produced by government. They include goods and services that benefit all members of the community. By their nature, no one can be excluded from the benefits of public goods.

Unlike public goods, private goods benefit only those individuals who possess them. The benefits of a Snickers bar, for example, are received exclusively by the person who eats it. If someone else wants a Snickers bar, a new one will have to be produced and purchased; it cannot be consumed simultaneously by two people. Because only one person can eat a particular candy bar, the producer can withhold it until payment is made, just as Fred and Harry can withhold fruit from the market until a favorable rate of exchange has been established. That is why private firms are willing and able to sell private goods.

By their very nature, public goods are not suited to private production. National defense is one of the best examples. No citizen can be denied the benefits of national defense; all are protected by it, more or less simultaneously. Thus the benefits of defense cannot be withheld from consumers until payment is made, as is usual in a free market system. Most people would not pay for goods that they could get free. Instead, they would take the free benefits and assume their payment would be so small that it would not be missed. In other words, they would free-ride on the payments of others. Few private firms would be willing to produce under such conditions, for they could not sell enough even to recover their costs. Consequently government must undertake the production and payment for this public good.

National defense is a relatively pure public good, in the sense that almost everyone in the community can benefit from it. Many government services are only partially shared, however, and not necessarily by those who provide the good. Care of the environment, education, and poverty relief would fall into this category. The argument for government provision here is that market exchanges in certain goods and services affect people

2. A util is the economist's name for a unit of satisfaction. We have no idea what a unit of satisfaction is, but it provides a measure that we need to make our point.

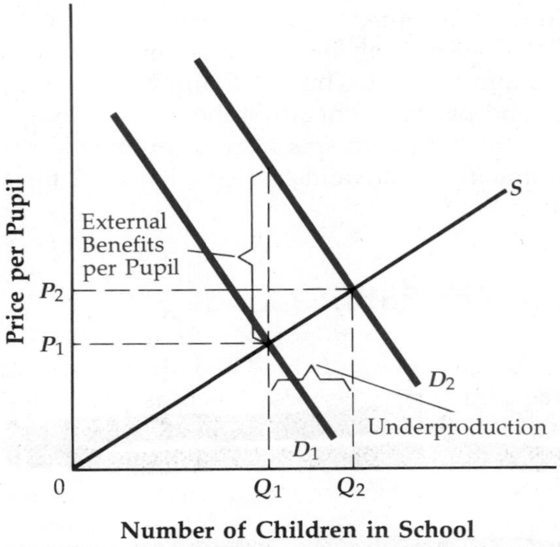


**Figure 4.2.** The External Benefits of Education.
Given market supply and demand curves $D_1$ and $S$, only $Q_1$ people will be educated. If the external benefits of education were recognized by the market, demand would be $D_2$, and the number of people educated would be $Q_2$. Without government intervention in this market, education will be underproduced. The misallocation of resources can be corrected by a per pupil subsidy equal to the vertical distance between $D_1$ and $D_2$.

**Externalities:** the positive (beneficial) or negative (harmful) effects that market exchanges have on people who do not participate directly in those exchanges. Third-party, or "spillover," effects.

other than the buyers and sellers. To use an economic term, the benefits (or costs) of such transactions are "externalized." Externalized costs are often referred to as externalities. **Externalities** are the positive (beneficial) or negative (harmful) effects that market exchanges have on people who do not participate directly in those exchanges. Externalities are third-party, or "spillover," effects.

## External Benefits

**External benefits:** benefits of production and consumption that are received by people not directly involved in the production, consumption, or exchange of a good. Positive effects on some third party.

Beneficial externalities are called external benefits. **External benefits** are benefits of production and consumption that are received by people not directly involved in the production, consumption, or exchange of a good. They are positive effects on some third party. Education is a good example of a service that provides external benefits. It helps both students and others in the community. Education equips people for more productive jobs and prepares them for their civic responsibilities.

The effects of external benefits can be illustrated graphically. Suppose the demand curve $D_1$ in Figure 4.2 reflects parents' private benefit from and demand for their children's education. The supply curve $S$ reflects the supply of places in school. Without government intervention in the education market, the number of children attending school would be $Q_1$. However, if the external benefits of an education were added to parents' demand, demand would be $D_2$ instead of $D_1$. The vertical distance between $D_1$ and $D_2$ indicates the external benefits that are not being captured by the market system. Education is being underproduced by $Q_2 - Q_1$ places.

The government could remedy the underproduction by using some of its tax receipts to provide subsidies to parents with children in school. This move would push the demand for education to $D_2$, thus increasing the number of children in school to $Q_2$. Such a scheme would spread the cost of the external benefits among the people in the community who receive them.

Notice that the government need not become directly involved in the production of education (that is, in running the schools) in order to correct the misallocation of resources. Education can be encouraged through subsidies to private schools or the pupils who attend them. Garbage collection, which captures external health benefits, is often procured through contracts with private firms. Fire, police, and even penal correction services can be secured through government contract rather than government production.

## External Costs

Harmful externalities are called external costs. **External costs** are costs of production and consumption that are imposed on people not directly involved in the production, consumption, or exchange of a good. These are negative effects on some third party. Smoke pollution is an example of an external cost. It results from a process that benefits the producers of the pollution and consumers, but harms others in the area.

**External costs:** costs of production and consumption that are imposed on people not directly involved in the production, consumption, or exchange of a good. Negative effects on some third party.

The external cost of pollution can be shown graphically. Suppose that in Figure 4.3, the demand curve $D$ represents car owners' demand for gasoline, which depends on their demand for driving, and that $S_1$ represents the costs refineries incur in producing the gasoline. In the competitive market, the equilibrium price will be $P_1$ and the equilibrium quantity will be $Q_2$. But when car owners drive, they pollute the atmosphere, causing other people discomfort or even ill health. This cost of gasoline use is just as real as refiners' costs of hiring labor and buying crude oil, but *it is not paid by refiners or drivers* and so is not included in supply curve $S_1$. If it were, the supply curve would shift to $S_2$, and the equilibrium gasoline price and quantity would be $P_2$ and $Q_1$. In other words, consumers of gasoline would have to pay a higher price and would cut back on their use of the product.

Thus if producers and consumers are not required to pay for pollution costs, they will overuse gasoline by $Q_2 - Q_1$ gallons. In this sense, resources have been misallocated. Social welfare would be increased if less gasoline were used. The overuse might be corrected with a tax on gasoline production, equal to the vertical distance between $S_1$ and $S_2$. If producers have to pay such a tax, the supply curve will shift to $S_2$, the price will be bid up, and consumers will cut back on their consumption of gasoline.

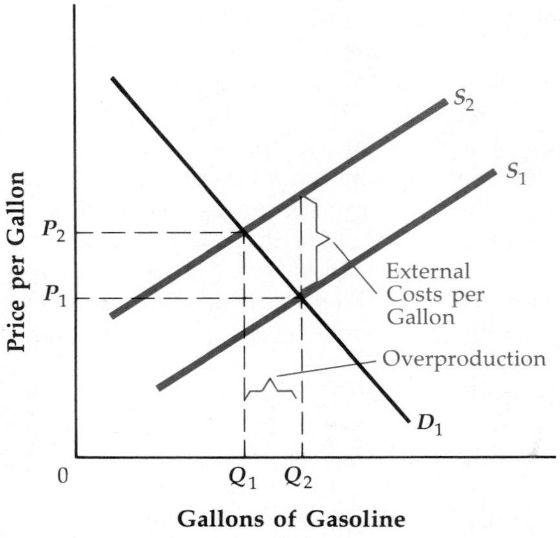


**Figure 4.3.** The External Costs of Pollution.
Given market supply and demand curves $S_1$ and $D$, the number of gallons of gasoline sold will be $Q_2$. If producers had to pay the external costs of pollution associated with gasoline use, however, the supply curve would be $S_2$ and the number of gallons sold would be $Q_1$. Without government intervention, gasoline will be overproduced. To correct the misallocation of resources, government can impose a tax on each gallon of gasoline sold, which will shift the supply curve to $S_2$ and reduce the quantity of gasoline sold to $Q_1$.

## Government Protection of Common Access Resources

**Common access resources:** resources owned in common instead of privately by individuals. Thus individuals may not be excluded from their use.

It may seem that in the ideal economy everyone would have the right to use all resources, goods, and services, and no one—not even the state—would have the right to exclude anyone from their use. In fact, the rights to many scarce resources are held "in common," or communally, with only minimal restrictions, if any, on their use. When access to resources is open to almost everyone, they are called common access resources. **Common access resources** are resources that are owned in common instead of privately by individuals. Thus individuals may not be excluded from their use. Rights to the use of a college or university's facilities are frequently held in common. So long as a student conforms to certain rules and regulations, he or she cannot be excluded from the use of the library, the parking lots, and other common facilities. The rights to city parks are also held communally. For several millennia before whites immigrated to this continent, Indian tribes held communal rights to hunting grounds. During the early part of the nineteenth century, whites living on the prairie held communal grazing rights. Anyone could let cattle loose on the plains. (The United States government claimed the right to exclude people from the plains, but did not exercise it.)

Communal property rights can be employed efficiently if (1) there is more than enough of the resource to go around—in other words, there is no cost to its use; or (2) the people who use the resource account fully for the effects of their use on others. Unless one of these two conditions is met, the resource will tend to be overused.

While a common access resource is being used, it is in effect the temporary private property of the user. Yet the users pay nothing for the privilege. Freeway drivers get a toll-free trip on a well-engineered road. If they are rational, they will use the road until the trip is not worth the cost to them in time and gas. One cost they may overlook, however, especially as it applies to themselves personally, is the alternative use to which their space might have been put by other drivers. (Environmentalists argue that many roads should never have been built. The alternative use in that case would have been scenery.) Increased highway congestion and the discomfort of other drivers are other hidden costs. These external costs, sometimes called social costs, of driving are just as important as other costs. But because drivers do not incur such costs themselves, they are effectively subsidized by others. Thus drivers will tend to overuse the road.

To lessen highway congestion the government could impose a tax on gasoline or a toll on road use. Drivers might then have to pay the true cost of their use of the road and would be encouraged to cut back on their driving. Or the government could turn the road into private property, giving the new owners the right to charge for its use. Such a solution would have essentially the same effect, reducing the use of the road. The main difference is that the revenues collected would go directly to individuals instead of to the government—a result that is either good or bad depending on one's personal values.

If the road is privately owned and no alternate mode of transportation is available, the owners may overcharge. In doing so they would be exploiting a monopoly on transportation. A **monopoly** is a sole seller of a good or service. Because a monopoly has no competitors, it can cut back on production (thus limiting the quantity supplied), charge higher prices, and reap greater profits than other firms. But for that matter, the state may also overcharge, acting like a monopolist. Though state agencies may not make a profit in the normal sense of the term, their revenues can be used to improve the salaries and working conditions of state employees. The question is whether the drawbacks of state or private use outweigh the drawbacks of communal use.

**Monopoly:** a sole seller of a good or service. Because a monopoly has no competitors, it can cut back on production (thus limiting the quantity supplied), charge higher prices, and reap greater profits than other firms.

Some additional examples will help clarify the problems associated with communal ownership of common access resources.

## Air and Water

Though federal and state governments hold the rights to the nation's water and airways, until recently they have not asserted much control over the use of these communal resources. Pollution has been the unhappy result. In dumping waste into the air and rivers, polluters are using a common access resource as if it were their own. Owners of private property generally exact payments for its use. But when polluters draw a common access resource away from an alternative use, like unspoiled scenery, no one reimburses society for the loss. No one compensates the people who live next to a plant with billowing smokestacks for their eye irritation or the additional paint jobs their homes require.

Pollution is often seen as a product of antisocial behavior, as indeed it often may be. Many who pollute simply do not care about what they do to others. However, much pollution results from a failure to recognize that individual behavior has an affect on the environment. The person who drops a cigarette butt to the ground may believe that littering on that scale cannot materially affect anyone's sensibilities. If everyone follows the same line of reasoning, however, the cigarette butts will accumulate into an eyesore. Even then an individual may reason that his own behavior has little effect one way or the other. This type of reasoning, of course, is a powerful argument against communal rights.

## Endangered Species

The hunting grounds of the Labrador Peninsula were originally held in common by Indian tribes. All Indians could hunt as they wished without fear of exclusion. Because of the difficulty of hunting and the limited demand for meat, skins, and bones, the area was not overhunted, and wildlife flourished. With the emergence of the European fur trade, however, the value of skins skyrocketed, encouraging the Indians to hunt beyond the area's natural capacity.

Once again communal rights were to blame. Hunters did not have to consider how their actions affected other hunters' ability to trap and hunt. Yet when one hunter killed a beaver, the task of hunting was made more difficult for others. Unlimited hunting imposed a social cost much like the cost imposed by unlimited driving. Moreover, hunters had little incentive to avoid excessive trapping. If one hunter did not kill a beaver, surely another would.

The Labrador Indians solved the problem of overkill by assigning private property rights to portions of their hunting grounds. Because he could exclude others, each hunter then had an incentive to control his take from the land.

Not all endangered species can be saved so easily. Whales have been hunted for centuries, but the threat of extinction is relatively recent. Until about two hundred years ago people did not have the technology to kill whales faster than the whales could reproduce. Theoretically, the problem could be solved in the same way as the beaver problem, through the establishment of private property rights. Some whales, however, migrate through six thousand miles of ocean annually. Establishing and enforcing private property rights over such a wide expanse, to say nothing of working out the international legal complications, would doubtless prove costly.

Whales will probably remain communal property, and the species' survival will continue to be threatened.

Communal property rights can also influence the methods of hunters. In the 1970s the Canadian government in effect declared the first fifty thousand baby seals killed annually to be a common access resource. Rights to the seals were allocated communally on a first-come, first-served basis, a rationing system that encouraged hunters to act quickly and ruthlessly.

The Canadian government permitted no more than 50,000 animals to be taken, so hunters worked with speed to make their kills before the legal maximum was reached. They swarmed over the ice floes and crushed the babies' skulls with heavy clubs. Government offices received many protests that the seals were unhumanly clubbed (by humans) and often skinned alive.[3]

## Public Property

In a condominium development in Blacksburg, Virginia, most of the grounds are held communally by the owners' association. By contract, all owners must become dues-paying members of the association and contribute their share toward the cost of upkeep. Thus no one can free-ride on the groundskeeping efforts of others, and the grounds are reasonably well kept, even though communally owned.

Not all the land in the development is held communally, however. Each unit comes with its own small back yard, which is the unit owner's responsibility. To encourage the upkeep of these yards, the condominium association bought lawn mowers, garden tools, and grass seed and stored them in a communal shed. This communal property was abused. Within a few months the garden tools had mysteriously disappeared. After a year the lawn mowers fell apart from rough use and lack of maintenance. The grass seed too seemed to disappear rapidly, though enough had been purchased to cover the entire community several times.

The argument for the purchase of communally held tools and seed had been economies of scale. It seemed more efficient to have one lawn mower for all than one for each small back yard. The system never achieved the planned economies, however, because residents had no incentive to use communal property with care. Like the whale and seal hunters, the members of the association fell victim to the negative effects inherent in communal property rights.

Communal property rights do not always bring this type of problem. The family is an institution in which much property is owned communally and with tolerably efficient results. In many cases, however, government intervention of some kind is necessary to prevent overuse and abuse of common access resources.

---

3. Armen A. Alchian and Harold Demsetz, "The Property Rights Paradigm," *Journal of Economic History*, 33 (March 1973), 20.

## Economists in History: Thomas Malthus (1766–1834)

The Reverend Thomas Robert Malthus was born in England in 1766, ten years before the publication of Adam Smith's *Wealth of Nations*. Though Malthus was educated for the ministry, he devoted his life to teaching history and political economy (the original name for economics).

Malthus's most famous work, his *An Essay on the Principle of Population,* was published anonymously in 1798. The book depicts a bleak future for the human race. Malthus contended that the production of food tends to grow arithmetically (by the addition of a constant number), whereas population tends to grow geometrically (by the multiplication of a constant number). Sooner or later, he warned, people's capacity to reproduce themselves would outstrip their ability to feed and house themselves. The result would be war, famine, and pestilence.

Malthus also argued that the rapid growth of the population would ultimately lower workers' wages to subsistence level (no more than necessary to sustain life). New and better ways of producing

## Government Provision of Income Security and Health Insurance

Government programs to guarantee incomes and provide health insurance are often justified on ethical grounds. If enough people feel that citizens are entitled to a minimum standard of living, income security can be viewed as a good for which there is a demand, like any other good. Government simply produces this good for the same reason a farmer produces apples.

In addition to helping recipients, some argue, income security increases the general social welfare. As income rises, the value of each additional dollar of income diminishes, for people generally satisfy their most pressing needs and wants first. Additional income is used to satisfy less pressing needs and wants. Hence if some income is taken from the well-off and given to the poor, the transferred money will be put to better use. Opponents of income redistribution would counter that the value of income is just as great for the well-off as for the poor. Therefore income redistribution would not improve societal welfare.

Suppose we accept that income security is a worthwhile service. Why should it be provided by government? The answer generally given is that externalities make private provision unworkable. If contributions to welfare programs were private and voluntary, many people might refrain from contributing, reasoning that they would not gain as much benefit from the program as others. Others might reason that they as individuals could abstain without jeopardizing the benefits to others. If enough people goods would be found, increasing profits and hence wages. But the higher wages would lead to more births and longer lives, and the growing supply of workers would eventually drive wages back down to subsistence level.

With Malthus's theory in mind, Thomas Carlyle described the new discipline of economics as the "dismal science," a name that persists to this day. Even so, Malthus's thinking influenced the two most powerful political ideologies of the twentieth century. His theory of population became a cornerstone of Karl Marx's theory of the exploitation of labor and the inevitable demise of capitalism, first outlined in the *Communist Manifesto* (1848). And Malthus's suggestion that recessions (periods of high unemployment and low production) sprang from inadequate demand for goods and services predated John Maynard Keynes's thinking on the use of government expenditure and tax policy to lower unemployment. Keynes's theory has greatly influenced the macroeconomic policies of capitalist governments for the past half-century.

withheld support, contributions might not cover the benefits paid out under the program. From this perspective, income security programs can be seen as an effort to overcome the external benefit problem—that is, underproduction in the private sector.

## Government Stabilization of the Economy

Throughout history, the general level of economic activity has fluctuated in business cycles. Sometimes overall economic activity rises, increasing the nation's output and employment. At other times it declines, decreasing production and throwing people out of work. Until recently the U.S. government has generally not attempted to interfere with these economic swings. But since the 1940s, the federal government has increasingly tried to use macroeconomic policy to control the overall level of economic activity, including prices, output, and employment and unemployment. **Macroeconomic policy** is the manipulation of taxes, federal expenditures, and the money supply to promote a high and stable level of employment and production, price level stability, and economic growth.

**Macroeconomic policy:** the manipulation of taxes, federal expenditures, and the money supply to promote a high and stable level of employment and production, price level stability, and economic growth.

This change in attitude was spurred by the writings of John Maynard Keynes, a British economist whose theory of business cycles was published during the Great Depression. Keynes believed that swings in economic activity were caused by changes in the demand for goods and services by consumers, government, and business. Government could moderate those swings, he taught, by monitoring and if necessary stimulating or restraining demand for goods and services.

**Fiscal policy:** the manipulation of federal expenditures and taxes to promote a high and stable level of employment and production, price level stability, and economic growth.

**Monetary policy:** the manipulation of the rate of growth of the nation's money supply to promote price level stability and a high and stable level of employment and production.

Just what the government should do to moderate swings in the economy remains a highly controversial question. Keynesians argue for the manipulation of fiscal policy, meaning taxes and expenditures. **Fiscal policy** (also called budgetary policy) is the manipulation of federal expenditures and taxes to promote a high and stable level of employment and production, price level stability, and economic growth. Monetarists, in contrast, maintain that business swings are caused largely by changes in the rate of growth of the nation's money stock. These economists recommend that the government moderate the swings through monetary policy. **Monetary policy** is the manipulation of the rate of growth of the nation's money supply to promote price stability and a high and stable level of employment and production. Much of our study of economics will involve the implications of these and other theories for government policy. Here we need only stress that stabilization of the nation's economic activity has come to be a major function of government.

## The Shortcomings of Government Action

In this and the last chapter, we discussed some of the shortcomings of the market system: an inability to provide public goods; the existence of external costs and benefits; and distortion in the allocation of resources by monopolies. The free market system does not always use the economy's scarce resources efficiently. But it does not follow that government should always attempt to correct market failures. Government too has its shortcomings.

All government action requires the use of scarce resources—and they will not necessarily be used more efficiently than in the private sector. A private monopoly may distort the allocation of resources, but the distortion may be slight compared with the cost of an antitrust suit against the monopoly. Cigarette smokers may throw their butts on the ground, but the cost of their pollution may be less than that of an antilitter campaign.

Government is itself a kind of monopoly. Because it faces no competition in many of its activities, it can become quite inefficient, distorting the allocation of resources, reducing the quality of the goods and services produced, or increasing their price. The U.S. Postal Service can afford to charge monopoly prices for first-class mail service precisely because the law prohibits private firms from entering that market.

## Summary and Extensions

Markets depend on property rights, which form the basis of trade. The private sector of our economy depends on the government to define and enforce property rights. In establishing the political and economic framework for trade, government performs an essential economic function.

Government has many other functions, some more essential than others. Government sometimes acts as a producer in order to correct for inefficiencies created by external costs and benefits, or to produce public goods that cannot be provided privately. It may also use its power to tax to provide goods and services not traditionally among its responsibilities, such as public welfare services. Though economists are certainly not opposed to the relief of economic distress, many of them are becoming more and more concerned with the inefficiencies of government attempts to promote the national well-being.

## Major Conclusions

1. The economic functions of government include: defining and protecting property rights; providing public goods like national defense; reducing the inefficiencies associated with external costs and benefits; protecting common access resources; providing for the public's health and security; and stabilizing overall economic activity.
2. Government establishment and enforcement of property rights increases production by freeing producers from the need to engage in wasteful conflicts over property.
3. Where property rights are defined and protected, markets will emerge, and mutually beneficial trades will be made.
4. Failure to define property rights frequently results in overuse and abuse of resources. Common access resources are inefficiently used partly because no one has to pay for their use.
5. Economists disagree as to whether and how government should act to stabilize the economy. Some recommend the use of fiscal policy, others the use of monetary policy.
6. Like the free market system it sometimes attempts to correct, government is far from perfect in an economic sense. Its actions can be costly or even monopolistic.

## Questions to Ponder

1. What are property rights? Why do they exist?
2. In economic terms, describe the causes of the pollution of some portion of your environment.
3. How is the cost of enforcement related to the existence of property rights? What might be the effect of an increase in the cost of enforcement? A decrease?
4. "Government can correct for inefficiencies due to external benefits by subsidizing producers and/or consumers." Do you agree? Illustrate your answer with supply and demand curves.
5. "Government can correct for the external costs of pollution by imposing taxes on the pollutants firms emit or on the products they produce." Do you agree? Explain your answer with supply and demand curves.
6. Economists frequently refer to national defense as a public good. What does that term mean? If national defense benefits everyone, why do so many people demonstrate against it?
7. Name ten government-administered programs and give an economic justification for each. Which if any of those programs could be "privatized"—that is, turned over to private firms or produced by private firms with government subsidies?

# Part II

# The Macroeconomy

## Central Question

*What are the major ways of measuring overall economic activity in the United States?*

## Key Terms

Gross national product (GNP)

Final goods and services

Intermediate goods and services

Real (constant dollar) gross national product

Net national product (NNP)

National income

Personal income

Disposable income

Unemployment rate

Labor force

Labor force participation rate

Inflation

Consumer price index

# Chapter 5

# Measurements of the Macroeconomy

*"But 'glory' doesn't mean 'a nice knock-down argument,'" Alice objected.*

*"When I use a word," Humpty Dumpty said in a rather scornful tone, "it means just what I choose it to mean—neither more nor less."*

*"The question is," said Alice, "whether you can make words mean so many different things."*

*"The question is," said Humpty Dumpty, "which is to be the master—that's all."*

Lewis Carroll

Our era is replete with macroeconomic problems. In newspaper headlines and news broadcasts, these problems are referred to as "recession," "unemployment," "inflation," "idle industrial capacity," "retarded economic growth," and "stagflation." In plainer language, they are lost production, lost income, rising prices, quiet factories, a stalled standard of living, and economic stagnation coupled with rising prices.

What can and should be done to correct these problems? That is the central question of the macroeconomic policy debates that greet us almost daily in the news media, and the central question of macroeconomics itself. Twenty years ago, economists generally agreed on the policies the government should follow to reach acceptable levels of national production, employment, and inflation. But years of high inflation and unemployment, both here and abroad, have shown how difficult it is for government, constrained by political reality, to achieve its stated policy objectives. In fact, many economists now suspect that government policy has increased unemployment and inflation—that the nation would have been better off without the government's attempts to alter overall economic performance. Others argue that to reduce unemployment and inflation, government must exercise even more powerful and direct control over the economy.

The following chapters attempt to develop an understanding of this issue. But first, to appreciate the magnitude and complexity of our macroeconomic problems, we must consider the problem of how to measure macroeconomic activity. This chapter covers macroeconomic measurement, and Chapter 6 outlines macroeconomic problems and policies. Then we must understand how the macroeconomy works, or how conditions in the various parts of the economy affect general economic activity—employment, production, incomes, and prices. Finally, we must appreciate the conflicts and tradeoffs that accompany policymakers' attempts to manipulate the macroeconomy. Macroeconomic theory and policy are treated in depth in Chapters 8 through 16.

Measurement is important in macroeconomics, for inaccurate or misleading measures can distort the statistics on which government policy decisions are based. Among the many ways of measuring macroeconomic activity, the most important are:

1. Gross national product, a measure of overall national production.
2. National personal and disposable income, measures of consumer buying power before and after taxes.
3. The unemployment rate, a measure of people's inability to find work.
4. The consumer price index, a measure of change in the general price level.

## Gross National Product (GNP)

Measuring gross national product, or total production of goods and services, allows economists and policymakers to evaluate a nation's economic progress over a period of years and to monitor the impact of government policy on production and incomes. It also enables economists to test their theories of how the macroeconomy works against real-world data. And it allows government officials to develop policies that will increase the nation's production.

Business people use general economic data as they plan for future production. They understand that the sales of their product depend in part on the level of production in the economy as a whole. Automobile producers, for example, realize that the income and productivity of workers in other industries will influence the number of cars sold. If production is down elsewhere, people will earn less money and have less to spend on automobiles. With data on recent and current economic activity, business people can estimate roughly how much they should produce to meet future market demand, or how much to spend on raw materials and labor.

Thus any measurement of the nation's economic activity does more than record what has happened in the past; it also influences future policy. Figures showing that prices have been rising too fast can create public dissatisfaction, which may well influence future government policy. If figures show that production has dropped sharply in some sectors of the economy, businesses in other sectors of the economy may cut back on their production, thereby contributing to the slump. In short, economic measures like the GNP have an effect on the economy themselves. The methods used in calculating such data are therefore crucial to macroeconomic policy debates.

## Definition of GNP

Though there are many ways of measuring the nation's general level of economic activity, the one used most often in developing government policy, and cited most often in the news media, is the gross national product (GNP). **Gross national product (GNP)** is the current market value in dollars of all final goods and services produced in the economy in a given period. Certain key words in this definition must be stressed. First, national production is measured in terms of current market value, which means current market prices. Market prices sometimes overstate, and sometimes understate, the intrinsic value of goods. To that extent, GNP may be distorted as a measure of general social welfare. GNP also includes the social "bads" that result from production, such as pollution and congestion, as well as goods designed to remedy them.

Second, only final goods and services are included in GNP. **Final goods and services** are those goods and services that are purchased for consumption rather than for further processing or resale. That is, GNP excludes the dollar value of intermediate goods used in the production process. **Intermediate goods and services** are goods and services that are purchased for further processing or resale. If intermediate goods were included in GNP, the total value of the nation's production would be vastly overstated. All intermediate goods would be counted at least twice—once when they are sold to be used in the production of final goods and again when the final products are sold.

**Gross national product (GNP):** the current market value in dollars of all final goods and services produced in the economy in a given period.

**Final goods and services:** those goods and services that are purchased for consumption rather than for further processing or resale.

**Intermediate goods and services:** goods and services that are purchased for further processing or resale.

Consider the intermediate good wheat, for instance. Wheat is used to make flour, an intermediate good used to make bread. The table below shows sales prices of given quantities of wheat, flour, and bread. If we add the value of all three transactions, our measure of total economic activity will be $600.

| | |
|---|---|
| Wheat sold to the miller | $100 |
| Flour sold to the baker | 200 |
| Bread sold to the consumer | 300 |
| | $600 |

But this procedure counts the value of the wheat three times: once by itself, once as part of the flour, and once as part of the bread. Because the value of the bread includes the value of the wheat and flour as well, total production can be measured by the market value of the final product alone—the bread.

Furthermore, if intermediate goods were included in GNP, that measure would change with changes in the structure of an industry. For example, if wheat production, flour milling, and baking were originally three separate businesses, but were later consolidated into one firm, our measure of total economic activity would fall from $600 to $300. Yet economic activity would not have changed. The farmer and miller would still be producing their products. But because they were now parts of a single firm, no market value would be attached to their activities.

## Computation of GNP

Gross national product is normally stated in annual terms, though data are also compiled quarterly. Table 5.1 shows the gross national product for 1984, along with the figures used to calculate it. As in the example of bread production, the value of the nation's final products is stated as their dollar value at the time of sale. Of the $3,661 billion total, over $2,342 billion was consumer purchases ("personal consumption expenditures").

**Table 5.1.** Gross National Product, 1984[a]

| | Billions of Dollars |
|---|---|
| Personal consumption expenditures | 2,342.3 |
| Gross private domestic investment | 637.3 |
| Government purchases of goods and services | 748.0 |
| Net exports (exports minus imports) | −66.3 |
| Total | 3,661.3 |

[a] Preliminary estimate.

**Source:** *Economic Report of the President* (Washington, D.C.: U.S. Government Printing Office, 1985), pp. 232–233.

Another $637 billion was purchased by businesses, in the form of plant and equipment and additions to inventory, and by households, in the form of new houses ("gross private domestic investment"). Federal, state, and local governments spent a little over $748 billion on goods and services ("government purchases of goods and services").

The negative figure in the last category of expenditures, "net exports," shows that exports from the United States totaled $66 billion less than imports into the nation. Since all exports are a part of U.S. production, you may wonder why only *net* exports are tabulated here. It is because other categories of expenditures include goods imported into the United States. For instance, when imported clothing is purchased by consumers, it is counted as a personal consumption expenditure. Yet imports are not part of U.S. production. They are the output of foreign countries, and should be subtracted from any measure of U.S. economic activity. By subtracting imports from exports, the net exports figure does just that.

Because the dollar amount buyers spend on goods and services must equal the dollar amount received by producers, total expenditures must equal the total value of goods produced. When added together, then, the four major categories of expenditures shown in Table 5.1 yield the gross national product.

Figure 5.1 shows GNP from 1929 to 1984. To a limited extent, this graph indicates the nation's economic progress over the long term. We can see, for example, that the Great Depression of the early 1930s was a substantial blow to the nation's economic activity. Furthermore we can see that production has grown irregularly, rising and then leveling out before rising again. By studying such data, economists can begin to draw some conclusions about the relationship between business and government policy and national production.

## Shortcomings of the GNP

Though the gross national product is probably the best available measure of overall production in the United States, it is by no means perfect. One of its deficiencies, the fact that it omits entirely certain sectors of the economy, is of increasing concern to economists.

### *Nonmarket Production*

With a few exceptions, the gross national product includes only final goods and services that are bought and sold in the market.[1] It excludes people's unpaid activities that benefit themselves, their families, and their friends. For instance, GNP includes the price paid for meat, potatoes, and lettuce,

1. The Department of Commerce assigns a value to the farm products that farmers grow and consume themselves. It also estimates the rental value of homes occupied by their owners. Both those figures are included in personal consumption expenditures.

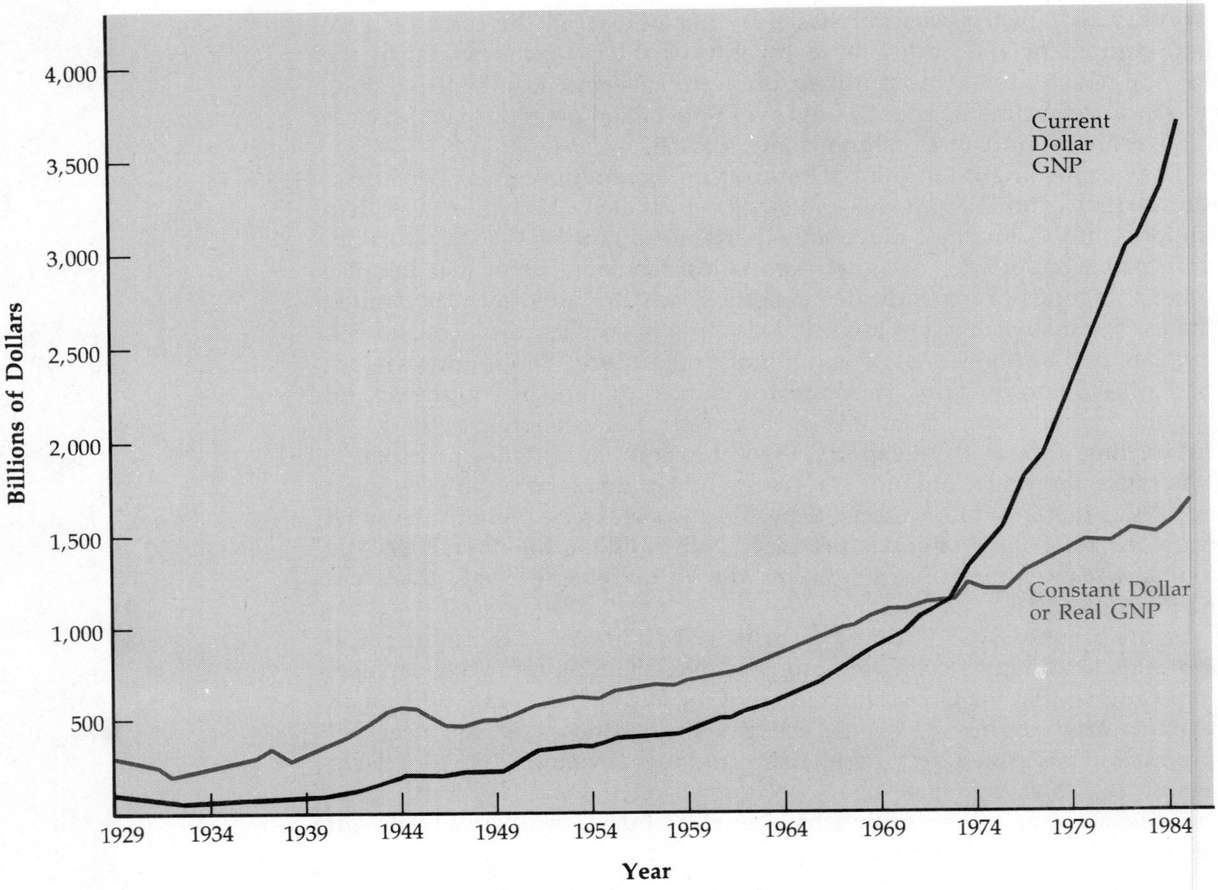


**Figure 5.1.** Gross National Product, 1929–1984.
The gross national product has increased significantly over the past five or six decades.
**Source:** *Economic Report of the President* (Washington, D.C.: U.S. Government Printing Office, 1985), pp. 232, 234.

but not the value of the work done to prepare a meal. (It does include the price of meals purchased at restaurants.) GNP includes the price paid for landscaping, but not the value of yard work done by homeowners.

Two reasons have been given for excluding nonmarket activities from GNP. First, it is extremely difficult to assign a value to the services people provide for themselves, because the quality of those services varies greatly from person to person. Second, economists have found it difficult to decide which nonmarket activities should be included. Perhaps dishwashing, clothes washing, and garbage removal should be included, but what about tooth brushing? That service, when performed by a dentist, has a market value—but few of us think we are adding to national production when we brush our teeth.

Because nonmarket activities are excluded, trends in GNP may not accurately reflect changes in social welfare. For example, during the Great Depression, GNP fell from $103.1 billion in 1929 to $55.6 billion in 1933. Although people were much worse off in 1933 than in 1929, total production, including both market and nonmarket activity, had not fallen as much as GNP indicates. People who lost their jobs invested more time in maintaining their households. More people kept bigger gardens and did more repair work around the house than they had before the economic downturn. Although such activities could not compensate fully for lost income, people were able to offset their losses in part. But this increase in home-related productive activity was not included in GNP.

### *The Underground Economy*

Many goods and services—hard drugs, moonshine liquor, and prostitution, for instance—are illegal in most areas of the United States. Nonetheless, they are part of the nation's total production—and because they are produced surreptitiously, they escape measurement. Other transactions are not counted because people are trying to evade taxation. To avoid taxes, many people trade rather than sell the goods they produce for the things they want. Others sell their goods and services for cash but do not report the income to the Internal Revenue Service. Waiters and waitresses, for example, often report only part of their tips; producers of firewood do not always declare the cash they receive; and many wealthy people store earnings from foreign assets in Swiss bank accounts closed to IRS inspection. Estimates of the size of the so-called underground economy vary. Some economists believe that the value of productive activity in this sector may be as high as a quarter of GNP.

### *Leisure Time*

GNP makes no allowances for changes in the amount of time workers spend at their jobs. During this century the length of the work week (the average number of hours worked by each laborer each week) has gradually decreased, from about sixty hours in 1900 to just under forty hours in 1984. The value of today's workers' greater leisure time is not reflected in GNP. If people were still working as many hours as they once did, the total value of the nation's production would be much higher.

### *Production of "Bads"*

In the course of producing goods and services, the economy also produces "bads"—things that detract from the quality of life. For example, steel mills often pollute the environment. Other industrial processes create solid wastes that are difficult to dispose of. The negative value of these by-products is not subtracted from the gross national product. Equipment purchased to clean up a pollution problem, however, is counted as part of GNP. Thus a snowfall in New York City or a flood in Lincoln, Nebraska, can lead to greater national production, but not greater national welfare.

**Table 5.2.** Gross National Product, 1929–1984

| Year | GNP in Current Dollars (billions) (1) | GNP in Constant 1972 Dollars (billions) (2) | U.S. Population (millions) (3) | Per Capita GNP in Constant 1972 Dollars [(2) ÷ (3)] (4) |
|---|---|---|---|---|
| 1929 | $ 103.4 | $ 315.7 | 121.8 | $2,591 |
| 1933 | 55.8 | 222.1 | 125.6 | 1,768 |
| 1940 | 100.0 | 344.1 | 132.1 | 2,604 |
| 1950 | 286.5 | 534.8 | 152.3 | 3,511 |
| 1960 | 506.5 | 737.2 | 180.7 | 4,079 |
| 1970 | 992.7 | 1,085.6 | 205.1 | 5,293 |
| 1980 | 2,631.7 | 1,475.0 | 227.7 | 6,477 |
| 1984 | 3,661.3 | 1,639.0 | 236.6 | 6,927 |

**Source:** *Economic Report of the President* (Washington, D.C.: U.S. Government Printing Office, 1985), pp. 232–235, 265.

### *Prices of Goods and Services*

Because GNP is computed in terms of current prices, comparisons over time are distorted by inflation. If prices rise, the GNP will reflect the inflation, exaggerating the increase in production of actual goods and services.

In Table 5.2, Column 1 shows the current-dollar value of the GNP for selected years from 1929 to 1984. At first glance, it appears that U.S. production was over 35 times greater in 1984 than in 1929. Output appears to have fallen by nearly 50 percent between 1929 and 1933, and to have risen by almost 270 percent between 1970 and 1984. Much of this apparent change in production is actually a change in prices, however. Prices fell significantly between 1929 and 1933, magnifying the underlying real drop in output. During the 1970s, prices rose at unprecedented peacetime rates, puffing the rather modest increases in total production out of proportion.

To eliminate distortions caused by price changes, the Department of Commerce adjusts GNP figures against various price indexes. These indexes measure changes in the price levels in particular sectors of the economy—such as lumber, agriculture, and energy—in relation to some base year, like 1972. For example, if the price of lumber rose 87 percent between 1972 and 1984, the price index for lumber would be 1.87 in 1984. To eliminate the influence of inflation, the Department of Commerce divides the 1984 production figure by 1.87. Similar adjustments are made for all sectors, and the resulting figures are then summed to obtain real, or constant dollar GNP. **Real (or constant dollar) gross national product** is the gross national product adjusted for price changes. Once such adjustments have been made for all years, changes in GNP over time will reflect changes in actual production, not changes in price.

**Real (constant dollar) gross national product:** the gross national product adjusted for price changes.

**Table 5.3.** Method of Computing Current Dollar Gross National Product and Real, or Constant Dollar, Gross National Product

| Year | GNP in Current Prices (1) | GNP in Constant 1972 Prices (2) |
|---|---|---|
| 1929 | $P_{29} \times Q_{29}$ | $P_{72} \times Q_{29}$ |
| 1933 | $P_{33} \times Q_{33}$ | $P_{72} \times Q_{33}$ |
| 1940 | $P_{40} \times Q_{40}$ | $P_{72} \times Q_{40}$ |
| 1950 | $P_{50} \times Q_{50}$ | $P_{72} \times Q_{50}$ |
| 1960 | $P_{60} \times Q_{60}$ | $P_{72} \times Q_{60}$ |
| 1970 | $P_{70} \times Q_{70}$ | $P_{72} \times Q_{70}$ |
| 1980 | $P_{80} \times Q_{80}$ | $P_{72} \times Q_{80}$ |
| 1984 | $P_{84} \times Q_{84}$ | $P_{72} \times Q_{84}$ |

Note: $P$ = price; $Q$ = quantity.

Table 5.3 shows the way real GNP is computed. The *P*s and *Q*s stand for prices and quantities, respectively; the subscripts indicate the year. Notice that the values in column 1 vary with changes in both price and quantity, whereas the values in column 2 vary only with changes in quantity. If such adjustments are made for all the figures in column 1 of Table 5.2, we arrive at column 2 of Table 5.2, GNP in constant 1972 dollars. Constant dollar, or real, GNP figures for 1929 to 1984 are also plotted in Figure 5.1.

The absolute values of the figures represented in Figure 5.1 and in column 2 of Table 5.2 are less meaningful than their relative value. These constant dollar figures show that production in the United States was indeed greater in 1984 than in 1929—slightly more than 5 times greater. They also show that between 1929 and 1933, total production of goods and services fell less than current dollar figures would suggest—by approximately 30 percent rather than 50 percent. And between 1970 and 1984 output grew much less than the price-inflated figures in column 1 suggest. This can be illustrated by comparing the curves in Figure 5.1.

Note that in 1982 real GNP actually declined. Table 5.4 shows GNP for each quarter-year from 1981 to 1984. Real output fell by 3 percent between the third quarter (III) of 1981, when it was $1,525.8 billion, to the fourth quarter (IV) of 1982, when it was only $1,480.7 billion. Real GNP began to rise again in 1983; by the final quarter of 1984, it was nearly 12 percent above its 1982 low.

### *Population Growth*

Real gross national product may increase over time, but if population grows faster, people will not be better off. To determine whether production

**Table 5.4.** Gross National Product by Quarter, 1981–1984

| Year | Quarter | GNP in Current Dollars (billions) (1) | GNP in Constant 1972 Dollars (billions) (2) |
|---|---|---|---|
| 1981 | I | 2,866.6 | 1,510.1 |
| | II | 2,912.5 | 1,512.5 |
| | III | 3,004.9 | 1,525.8 |
| | IV | 3,032.2 | 1,506.9 |
| 1982 | I | 3,021.4 | 1,485.8 |
| | II | 3,070.2 | 1,489.3 |
| | III | 3,090.7 | 1,485.7 |
| | IV | 3,109.2 | 1,480.7 |
| 1983 | I | 3,171.5 | 1,490.1 |
| | II | 3,272.0 | 1,525.1 |
| | III | 3,362.2 | 1,553.4 |
| | IV | 3,432.0 | 1,570.5 |
| 1984 | I | 3,553.3 | 1,610.9 |
| | II | 3,644.7 | 1,638.8 |
| | III | 3,694.6 | 1,645.2 |
| | IV[a] | 3,752.5 | 1,661.6 |

[a] Preliminary estimate.
**Source:** *Economic Report of the President* (Washington, D.C.: U.S. Government Printing Office, 1985), p. 232.

per capita (per person) is increasing, we must divide real GNP by yearly population figures. This procedure yields per capita real GNP, shown in column 4 of Table 5.2. On a per capita basis, U.S. production increased less than threefold between 1929 and 1984—less than the figures in columns 1 and 2 would suggest. Per capita figures offer no insight into how the national output is distributed among the population, however.

### *Quality of Goods and Services*

GNP estimates the money value of goods and services. But prices do not necessarily reflect changes in the quality of goods, especially over a long period of time. As we have seen, the prices of calculators declined while their quality improved. Nor do prices reflect the division of output between consumer goods and government purchases. If a nation shifts production from consumer goods in peacetime to war equipment in wartime, the average citizen's standard of living may suffer, even though factories are operating night and day. Production increased dramatically during the Second World War, but many consumer goods, such as butter and hosiery, were so scarce they had to be rationed. And while some people may have

**Table 5.5.** Gross National Product, Net National Product, and Disposable Personal Income, 1929–1984 (in current dollars)

| Year | Gross National Product (billions) (1) | Net National Product (billions) (2) | Disposable Personal Income (billions) (3) | Per Capita Disposable Personal Income (4) |
|---|---|---|---|---|
| 1929 | 103.4 | 93.7 | 82.3 | 676 |
| 1933 | 55.8 | 48.3 | 45.5 | 363 |
| 1940 | 100.0 | 91.0 | 75.2 | 570 |
| 1950 | 286.5 | 262.3 | 205.5 | 1,362 |
| 1960 | 506.5 | 460.2 | 352.0 | 1,947 |
| 1970 | 992.7 | 904.7 | 695.3 | 3,390 |
| 1980 | 2,631.7 | 2,338.5 | 1,829.9 | 8,032 |
| 1981 | 3,073.0 | 2,713.8 | 2,176.5 | 8,874 |
| 1982 | 2,954.1 | 2,624.5 | 2,047.6 | 9,385 |
| 1983 | 3,304.8 | 2,927.7 | 2,340.1 | 9,977 |
| 1984[a] | 3,661.3 | 3,258.4 | 2,578.1 | 10,893 |

[a] Preliminary estimate.
**Source:** *Economic Report of the President* (Washington, D.C.: U.S. Government Printing Office, 1985), pp. 254–261.

benefited because the demand for war materials increased the demand for and the price of their services, others—those who paid higher taxes to finance the war—may have been worse off.

## Net National Product (NNP)

Gross national product includes the current value of all final goods and services, including plant and equipment (sometimes called capital goods) purchased by businesses to replace worn-out plant and equipment. Because replacement plant and equipment is included, GNP overstates the actual increase in total goods and services. To estimate the increase more accurately, the Department of Commerce subtracts the value of worn-out plant and equipment (called the capital consumption, or depreciation, allowance) from the gross national product. This adjusted measure is called net national product (NNP). **Net national product (NNP)** equals gross national product minus an allowance for replacement of worn-out plant and equipment (called the capital consumption allowance). Because replacement of old equipment has been subtracted, net national product is a better measure of the real growth of production than gross national product.

**Net national product (NNP):** gross national product minus an allowance for replacement of worn-out plant and equipment (called the capital consumption allowance).

Net national product usually amounts to between 91 and 92 percent of gross national product (see Table 5.5, column 2). The two measures are equally good indicators of change in production over time.

Net national product is a reasonably good indicator of national production over time, but it is not the best available measure of social welfare. It does not tell us how much of the rewards of production ends up in people's pockets. To see how much money people have to spend, and therefore how much of the gross national product they can buy, we must look at measures of national income.

## National Income

National income is another way of measuring productive activity in the macroeconomy. When people produce goods and services, they generate wages and salaries that reflect their contribution to production. The rewards of production must ultimately be distributed to these people—employees, managers, or owners of capital assets. Thus total income received must equal the total value of goods and services produced. For instance, if $100 worth of goods is produced, the people who produce them must earn a total of $100 in income. The figure for national income is not obtained by summing individual incomes, however, but by making technical adjustments to net national product. **National income** is the total payment made to owners of productive resources for the use of those resources during a given period. It is equal to the total cost of producing the goods and services included in the net national product.

**National income:** the total payment made to owners of productive resources for the use of those resources during a given period.

Table 5.6 shows the method for computing national income from NNP. The most significant adjustment is the subtraction of indirect business taxes, like federal excise taxes on liquor and local property taxes, which are not considered to be payments to resource owners.

National income does not tell us how much money consumers earn. That figure is called personal income. **Personal income** is that part of national income which is paid to individuals as opposed to businesses.

**Personal income:** the part of national income that is paid to individuals as opposed to businesses.

Corporate profits, interest payments that do not go directly to individuals, and Social Security taxes must be subtracted from national income to obtain the figure for personal income. Then government transfer payments, interest income, corporate dividend payments, and business transfer payments received by individuals must be added (see Table 5.6). The method of accounting is somewhat arbitrary; Social Security taxes are deducted but personal income taxes are not. (No good reason has been given for the discrepancy.)

Personal income still does not tell us how much money people have to spend. Because of taxation, people's take-home pay is usually much less than their total income. A better measure of their welfare may be what they take home after taxes for use in the purchase of goods and services. This measure is called disposable (personal) income. **Disposable income** is personal income minus personal income tax payments.

**Disposable income:** personal income minus personal income tax payments.

Disposable income in the United States is shown in columns 3 and 4 of Table 5.5. In 1984, Americans received a total disposable income of $2,578 billion, or approximately 70 percent of the gross national product for that year. Of that amount, consumers spent $2,421 billion and about $157

**Table 5.6.** Relationship of Net National Product, National Income, Personal Income, and Disposable Income, 1984[a] (in billions of dollars)

| | |
|---|---|
| *Gross national product* | 3,661.1 |
| Less: Capital consumption allowances | 402.9 |
| Equals: *Net national product* | 3,258.4 |
| Less: Indirect business taxes | 304.3 |
| Business transfers | 17.3 |
| Statistical discrepancy | −8.2 |
| Plus: Subsidies less current surplus of government enterprises | 14.4 |
| Equals: *National income* | 2,959.4 |
| Less: Corporate profits | 284.5 |
| Net interest | 285.0 |
| Contributions for social insurance | 305.9 |
| Wage accruals less disbursement | .0 |
| Plus: Government transfer payments to persons | 399.5 |
| Personal interest income | 434.8 |
| Personal dividend income | 77.7 |
| Business transfer payments | 17.3 |
| Equals: *Personal income* | 3,013.2 |
| Less: Personal tax and nontax payments | 435.1 |
| Equals: *Disposable personal income* | 2,578.1 |
| Composed of: Personal outlays | 2,421.2 |
| Personal saving | 156.9 |

[a] Preliminary estimate.
**Source:** *Economic Report of the President* (Washington, D.C.: U.S. Government Printing Office, 1985), pp. 254–260.

billion (6.1 percent) was saved. In 1929, by contrast, Americans received approximately 80 percent of GNP as disposable income. The 10 percentage-point drop in personal income between 1929 and 1984 is mostly because taxes were higher in 1984 than in 1929.

Disposable income figures must be adjusted for price changes and population growth before they can accurately reflect changes in consumer purchasing power. (See column 4 of Table 5.5 for per capita disposable income in current dollar terms.)

## The Unemployment Rate

Gross national product and national income are positive measures of the nation's economic activity. The unemployment rate, on the other hand, estimates economic activity that is not occurring. This negative measure indicates the portion of the nation's labor force that is out of work.

Unemployment data are compiled monthly by the Bureau of Labor Statistics. Table 5.7 shows the average monthly unemployment rate for selected years from 1950 to 1984. The 1950 unemployment rate of 5.3 percent was considered high at the time. Two decades later the rate had fallen slightly to 4.8. But in 1975, the rate hit an alarming 8.3 percent, and by the early 1980s it had almost doubled its 1970 level.

Like GNP, the unemployment rate is interpreted by the press, by the public, by government officials, and by business people as a sign of how successfully public policy goals are being met. Almost everyone thinks that an increase in the unemployment rate is a sign of worsening economic activity and increasing social hardship. Like a drop in GNP, a rise in unemployment could induce some businesses to curtail their production plans in anticipation of reduced consumer demand—perhaps causing even more workers to be laid off. Worsening unemployment can be a boon to opposition candidates in election years. In 1980 President Reagan scored political points with the unemployed, unions, and other worker groups by stressing the apparent failure of the Carter administration to control unemployment, then at 7 percent.

In evaluating the unemployment rate and the statements of politicians, it helps to remember Humpty Dumpty's remark in Lewis Carroll's *Through the Looking Glass.* "When I use a word, it means just what I choose it to mean—neither more nor less." When the Bureau of Labor Statistics uses the term "unemployment rate," the bureau chooses it to mean something very specific. The rate is computed using precise definitions of "employed" and "unemployed," which have a significant effect on its numerical value.

## Computing the Unemployment Rate

**Unemployment rate:** the ratio of the number of people estimated to be unemployed to the number of people estimated to be in the labor force, stated as a percentage.

**Labor force:** all persons sixteen years of age or older who are willing and able to work and who are counted as either unemployed or employed.

Stated rigorously, the **unemployment rate** is the ratio of the number of people estimated to be unemployed to the number of people estimated to be in the labor force, stated as a percentage, or

$$\text{unemployment rate} = \frac{\text{number unemployed}}{\text{labor force}}$$

Labor force also has a very specific meaning: the **labor force** consists of all persons sixteen years of age or older who are willing and able to work and who are counted as either unemployed or employed,[2] or

$$\text{labor force} = \text{number unemployed} + \text{number employed}$$

Specifically, the only people who can be counted as employed or unemployed are those who are at least sixteen years old and who are not institutionalized—that is, do not reside in a penal or mental institution or

2. The civilian labor force equals the labor force minus the members of the armed forces of the United States. The civilian unemployment rate is the number unemployed divided by the civilian labor force.

**Table 5.7.** Number of People Employed and Unemployed, and the Unemployment Rate, 1950–1984

| Year | Millions of People Employed (1) | Millions of People Unemployed (2) | Millions of People in the Labor Force [(1) + (2)] (3) | Unemployment Rate (percent) [(2) ÷ (1)] (4) | Labor Force Participation Rate[a] (percent) (5) |
|---|---|---|---|---|---|
| 1950 | 58.9 | 3.3 | 62.2 | 5.9 | 59.2 |
| 1960 | 65.8 | 3.9 | 69.7 | 5.6 | 59.4 |
| 1970 | 78.7 | 4.1 | 82.8 | 5.0 | 60.4 |
| 1980 | 99.3 | 7.6 | 106.9 | 7.1 | 63.8 |
| 1981 | 100.4 | 8.3 | 108.7 | 7.6 | 63.9 |
| 1982 | 99.5 | 10.7 | 110.4 | 9.7 | 64.0 |
| 1983 | 100.8 | 10.7 | 111.5 | 9.6 | 64.0 |
| 1984 | 106.7 | 8.5 | 115.2 | 7.4 | 64.7 |

[a] Labor force participation rate = labor force ÷ noninstitutionalized population.
**Source:** *Economic Report of the President* (Washington, D.C.: U.S. Government Printing Office, 1985), p. 266.

a home for the aged, infirm, or needy. The Bureau of Labor Statistics excludes persons under sixteen years of age because child labor laws, compulsory education, and general social customs prevent most of them from working.

Subject to the restrictions indicated above, employed persons include:

1. All persons who, during the week in which the survey was taken, did any work at all for pay, or who worked at least fifteen hours without pay in a family-operated business.
2. All persons who were not working during the survey week, but who were temporarily absent from their jobs or businesses because of illness, bad weather, vacation, strikes, or a number of personal reasons.
3. Members of the military.

Unemployed persons include:

1. All persons who did not work at all during the week of the survey, but who were looking for work and were available for work.
2. All persons who had made some effort to find work in the past four weeks (such as filling out an application) and were waiting for the results.
3. All persons who (a) were waiting to be called back to a job from which they had been laid off, (b) were waiting to report to a new job within the next thirty days, or (c) would have been looking for work if they had not been sick.

Classified as "not in the labor force" are all those who are not considered either employed or unemployed, and who are not in the military. This group includes people who

are under 16 years of age, or are full-time students

are homemakers

are unable to work

are retired

work fewer than fifteen hours a week without pay for their family business

work without pay for a charitable or religious organization

do seasonal work and are idle because it is off season

are scheduled to report to a new job in more than thirty days

Columns 1 and 2 of Table 5.7 show the numbers of people employed and unemployed, from which the yearly unemployment rates in column 4 were computed.

Unemployment statistics are gathered from a survey of a representative sample of people in approximately fifty-five thousand housing units located in nearly one thousand counties and cities throughout the nation. They include data on over one hundred thousand people sixteen years of age or older. Each household is interviewed for four consecutive months, dropped for the next eight months, and then interviewed again for four more months. In gathering the data, the Bureau of Labor Statistics relies on the voluntary cooperation of those who are questioned.

## Shortcomings of Employment and Unemployment Statistics

Like any data, employment and unemployment figures are no more reliable than the workers who administer the survey and those who are interviewed. If survey procedures are changed or if survey workers do not follow established procedures—that is, if they vary the wording or emphasis of the questions—the results of the survey will be distorted. If those who are interviewed conceal their true employment status, the results will be distorted further. Small changes in unemployment rates from month to month may reflect errors and procedural changes as much as true changes in the number of people employed and unemployed.

Unemployment statistics do not measure the hardship borne by the underemployed. Anyone who has worked for pay at all during the survey week is counted as employed—even those who have worked only five or ten hours. If production cuts in the automobile industry drastically reduce the number of days or hours its employees can work, unemployment figures for auto workers will not be affected.

Finally unemployment statistics are not adjusted for changes in the relative size of the labor force. One reason for the increase in the unemployment rate over the last three decades is that a growing percentage of the working-age population has been looking for jobs. For a more accurate picture of national employment, we must look at the labor force participation rate. The **labor force participation rate** is the number of people employed divided by the number of people in the labor force. Table 5.7 shows that the labor force participation rate increased almost 5 percentage points from 1950 to 1984, slightly more than the increase in the unemployment rate.

**Labor force participation rate:** the number of people employed divided by the number of people in the labor force.

### Reducing the Unemployment Rate

For several reasons, the unemployment rate as defined by the Bureau of Labor Statistics, can never be reduced to zero. In a dynamic economy people will always be changing jobs. Among them will be some who expect to report to a new job within thirty days, but are classified as unemployed by the government. Others may decline a job that is offered in hope of finding a better one. Some who are willingly unemployed may claim they are still job hunting so that their unemployment pay will continue. Those who are employed in the illegal underground economy may not admit they are working. And finally, some people simply do not have the skills to earn the minimum wage rate for even the most menial jobs. In short, because of government procedures, voluntary unemployment, and unreported employment, the unemployment rate may exaggerate the extent of economic hardship in the nation.

For these reasons, it is doubtful that the unemployment rate, as currently defined, can be reduced much below 5 percent (some would say 6 percent). Others contend that unless some changes are made—like the elimination of the minimum wage law and of union barriers to entry into various labor markets—the unemployment rate will not fall much below 7 percent for very long.

## The Consumer Price Index (CPI)

Another negative measure of the nation's economic well-being is the inflation rate. **Inflation** is a rise in the general level of prices over a period of time. If the prices of some goods rise but others fall, the general price level has not necessarily risen, although the relative prices of goods have changed. Inflation occurs when a rise in the prices of many goods and services is not offset by a decrease in the prices of other goods and services. In other words, during inflationary times, the price level, or weighted average of all prices, rises.

**Inflation:** a rise in the general level of prices over a period of time.

The measurement of price levels and ultimately inflation rates depends on what prices are averaged and how they are weighted. The consumer price index (CPI), computed by the Bureau of Labor Statistics, is the measure of price level most often cited. The **consumer price index (CPI)** is the ratio of the cost of specific consumer items in any one year to the cost of those items in the base year, 1967. Because the CPI includes things consumers buy regularly, it is frequently called the cost of living index. The index does not, however, represent everyone's cost of living. It is

**Consumer price index (CPI):** the ratio of the cost of specific consumer items in any one year to the cost of those items in the base year, 1967.

designed to represent the changes in the prices of specific goods that are bought in large quantities by people who work and shop in cities, like craftsmen, factory supervisors, carpenters, and salespeople.

The CPI provides a reasonably accurate estimate of the price level of thousands of items produced by twenty-four thousand businesses in eighty-five urban areas, however. The so-called market basket, or list of items covered by the survey, includes most goods and services urban consumers buy. Food, clothing, automobiles, homes, house furnishings, household supplies, fuel, drugs, and recreational goods; fees to doctors, lawyers, and beauty shops; rent, repair costs, transportation fares, public utility rates, and sales, property, and excise taxes are all included. Prices are weighted according to their importance in a typical family budget in the years 1971–1973.[3] Then the index figure is obtained by dividing the cost of the market basket for the year by its cost in 1967, the base year, and multiplying by 100. For example, the consumer price index for 1984 will be figured this way:

$$\text{consumer price index} = \frac{\text{cost of market basket in 1984}}{\text{cost of market basket in 1967}} \times 100$$

The index figure for 1967 is equal to 100 (that is, the cost of the market basket for 1967 divided by the cost of the same basket of goods, which equals 1, multiplied by 100). Because prices were lower in the years before 1967, the index figures for those years are less than 100. Since 1967 prices have been higher, and the index figures are greater than 100.

Table 5.8 gives the consumer price index for selected years from 1929 to 1984. Prices fell by around 24 percent between 1929 and 1933, the period of the Great Depression. They nearly tripled in the three decades between 1933 and 1967, and more than tripled again in the decade-and-a-half between 1967 and 1984. From a yearly rate of 1.6 percent in 1960, inflation jumped to 13.5 percent in 1980 before dropping to 4.0 percent in 1984.

## Summary and Extensions

The gross national product, the unemployment rate, and the consumer price index measure the performance of the U.S. economy in terms of national production, the percentage of the work force without jobs, and the level of prices. These figures will always be rough approximations of the variables they measure. The method used for determining gross national product dictates that much productive activity will go unmeasured, for we lack a reasonable means of estimating the monetary value of the goods and services we produce for ourselves and for the underground economy. And the method used for calculating the unemployment and employment rates counts as employed some people who are hard hit by economic decline, whereas others who are working (in the underground exonomy) are considered unemployed.

3. The Bureau of Labor Statistics found that the average family of four allocated its budget as follows: 24.8 percent for food, 22.5 percent for housing, 8.4 percent for transportation, and 44.5 percent for medical care, services, and clothing.

**Table 5.8.** Consumer Price Index, 1929–1984 (base year 1967)

| Year | Consumer Price Index (1) | Annual (year-to-year) Percentage Change in Consumer Price Index (2) |
|---|---|---|
| 1929 | 51.3 | 0.0 |
| 1933 | 38.8 | −5.1 |
| 1940 | 42.0 | 1.0 |
| 1950 | 72.1 | 1.0 |
| 1960 | 88.7 | 1.6 |
| 1967 | 100.0 | 2.9 |
| 1970 | 116.3 | 5.9 |
| 1980 | 246.8 | 13.5 |
| 1984 | 311.1 | 4.3 |

**Sources:** U.S. Bureau of the Census, *Historical Statistics of the United States* (Washington, D.C.: U.S. Government Printing Office, 1975), pp. 210–211; *Economic Report of the President* (Washington, D.C.: U.S. Government Printing Office, 1985), pp. 294, 296.

Slight inaccuracies like these are unavoidable. All-inclusive surveys of employment and price levels would be prohibitively costly. The Bureau of Labor Statistics cannot interview every potential worker in the United States every month. Nor can it hope to record the monthly prices of all the millions of goods and services produced by the economy. Thus the Bureau has adopted sampling procedures based on broad categories of employment status and a representative selection of consumer goods.

As rough as they are, macroeconomic statistics can influence the nation's economic performance. Changes in the gross national product and other indexes can cause businesses to alter their production plans and support or undermine the public's confidence in the economy. If the statistics look bad, politicians may feel compelled to do something to demonstrate their concern, even though their response may be inadequately planned, ill-timed, and perhaps unwarranted. Unless we understand the meaning of these statistics—their sample base, limitations, and deficiencies—they may become our masters, as Humpty Dumpty suggested. People unfamiliar with the definition of *unemployed* may ask why government does not try to reduce unemployment to zero, for instance. They may expect more of government than it can possibly deliver.

## Major Conclusions

1. Gross national product is a measure of total production of final goods and services in the United States during a specified period of time—usually one calendar year. GNP is deficient in several respects: it values goods in terms of their market prices; does not include all production in the economy; does not allow for changes in the amount of time people spend at work; is not adjusted for the production of economic

"bads"; and does not reflect the impact of changes in the price level and in population.
2. The computation of real GNP corrects for price changes. The calculation of per capita GNP corrects for population changes.
3. Net national product is obtained by subtracting a capital consumption allowance for replacement of old equipment from gross national product. NNP measures real growth in production rather than maintenance of existing productive capacity.
4. National production can be computed by adding up either the total market value of the goods and services sold, or the total expenditures made on those goods and services. Because the market value of goods is determined by the amount of money people spend on goods and services, the two measures must be equal.
5. National income is a measure of the income received by all resources. Personal income is a measure of the income people receive before personal taxes. Disposable income is a measure of the amount of income people have available to spend after taxes.
6. The unemployment rate is an indicator of lost production as well as a measure of the economic hardship suffered by workers. The calculated unemployment rate is based on very precise definitions of who is and is not employed and unemployed. Because of the definition of unemployed used by the Bureau of Labor Statistics, the unemployment rate cannot be expected to fall to zero.
7. Because the unemployment rate does not recognize partial employment or underemployment, it does not capture the full extent of social hardship and forgone production. The unemployment rate also fails to reflect changes in the size of the labor force.
8. The consumer price index is a means of measuring inflation. Because it is based on a survey of goods and services that are not bought in the same proportions by everyone, the CPI does not give a true indication of changes in the cost of living for all consumers.

## Questions to Ponder

1. Are absolute current-dollar GNP figures meaningful?
2. Using the definitions of employed, unemployed, and not in the labor force, classify each of the following:
   a. A person who works twenty hours a week without pay in a family-owned drugstore.
   b. A person who works ten hours a week for a charitable organization.
   c. A person who works six hours a week for pay.
   d. A person who is on strike.
   e. A steel worker who has been laid off because of a strike in the automobile industry.
   f. A person who expects to report back to work within ten days.
   g. A person who is not working but who expects to report to a new job within sixty days.
   h. A person whose hours have been cut from forty to twenty per week.
   i. A person who is not working but who expects to report to a new job within fifteen days.
   j. A full-time college student.
   k. A person out of work because of sickness.
   l. A person fifteen years old who works thirty hours a week for pay.
   m. A person seventeen years old who works fourteen hours a week on his family's farm.
3. Presuming the data in question 2 cover the whole labor force, determine the unemployment rate.
4. Should much importance be attached to small month-to-month changes in the unemployment rate and consumer price index? Why? How may government interpret such changes? How may an opposition party interpret them?
5. Do people have sufficient incentive to learn about the limitations and deficiencies of economic statistics? Given your answer, how may these statistics be used by politicians?

## Central Question

*What major macroeconomic problems does our nation face, and what macroeconomic policies have been designed to solve them?*

## Key Terms

Demand-pull inflation
Cost-push inflation
Structural inflation
Transitional (frictional) unemployment
Cyclical unemployment
Structural unemployment
Natural rate of unemployment
Phillips curve
Stagflation
Trend
Business cycle
Recession
Trough
Recovery
Peak
Leading indicator
Aggregate demand
Aggregate supply

## Chapter 6

# Macroeconomic Problems and Policies

*What can be done [about inflation]? Before we look for remedies, we must examine the causes. Inflation is like cancer: many substances are carcinogenic, and many activities generate inflation. The sources of inflation can be diagnosed at several levels. . . . Inflation usually is the final link in the chain of well-meant actions. Inflation is the long-run consequence of short-run expediencies. Life, to be sure, is a succession of short runs, but every moment is also the long run of some expedience of long ago. We are now experiencing the long-run consequences of the short-run policies of the past. These consequences are as unacceptable as rain on weekends, and just as easy to change.*

Henry Wallich

The last chapter described several ways economists measure macroeconomic activity—or the lack of it. In this chapter we will use those measures to explore the depth and breadth of the economic problems our nation faces, as well as various theories about the causes and cures of those problems.

A macroeconomic policy to improve the welfare of much or all of a nation's population must pursue goals that have achieved some general consent. Macroeconomic goals on which policymakers and the public generally agree include:

1. Full and stable employment
2. Price stability
3. High and rising incomes

Attaining these goals is no simple matter, however.

The opening chapters of this book noted that every economic endeavor has a cost. This is certainly the case with macroeconomic policy. The pursuit of stable prices may require that we forgo some jobs. Attempts to stabilize employment may reduce economic growth. The search for macroeconomic stability may also require that we sacrifice some individual freedoms, since no government policy ever enjoys the consent of all citizens. Therefore, in considering our macroeconomic problems and the policies available to us, we might ask:

How serious is the problem?

What can be done about it?

At what costs will the problem be resolved?

## Macroeconomic Problems

In recent decades, the United States and most other nations have failed to reach their macroeconomic goals. In varying degrees, they have faced inflation, unemployment, or both of those problems simultaneously—a macroeconomic condition that has been called stagflation. Economic growth has been sluggish in many parts of the world. We will examine the effects and suspected causes of each of these problems in turn.

### Inflation

The price level has been changing throughout U.S. history. Periods of increasing prices have alternated with periods of decreasing prices (see Figure 6.1). Most episodes of rapid inflation have occurred during wartime: the War of 1812, the Civil War, the two world wars, and the Korean and Vietnam wars (1950–1953 and 1961–1973).

Persistent growth in the peacetime inflation rate is a recent problem. Over the nineteenth century, prices drifted gradually downward. In 1800

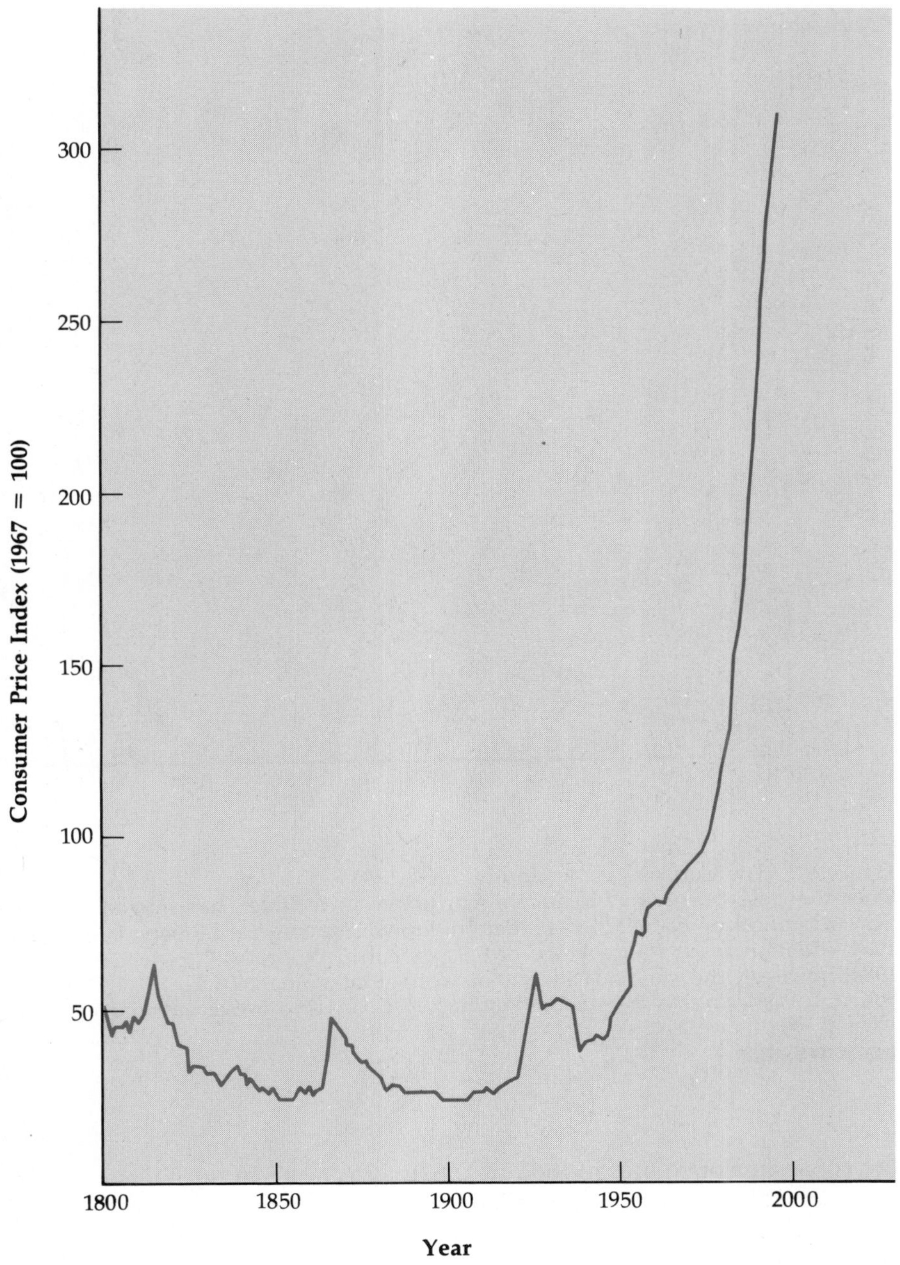


**Figure 6.1.** The Consumer Price Index, 1800–1984.
Over the past two centuries the price level has moved both up and down. Many of the fluctuations occurred during times of major change in the nation's monetary institutions.
**Sources:** U.S. Bureau of the Census, *Historical Statistics of the United States* (Washington, D.C.: U.S. Government Printing Office, 1975), pp. 210–211; *Economic Report of the President* (Washington, D.C.: U.S. Government Printing Office, 1985), p. 291.

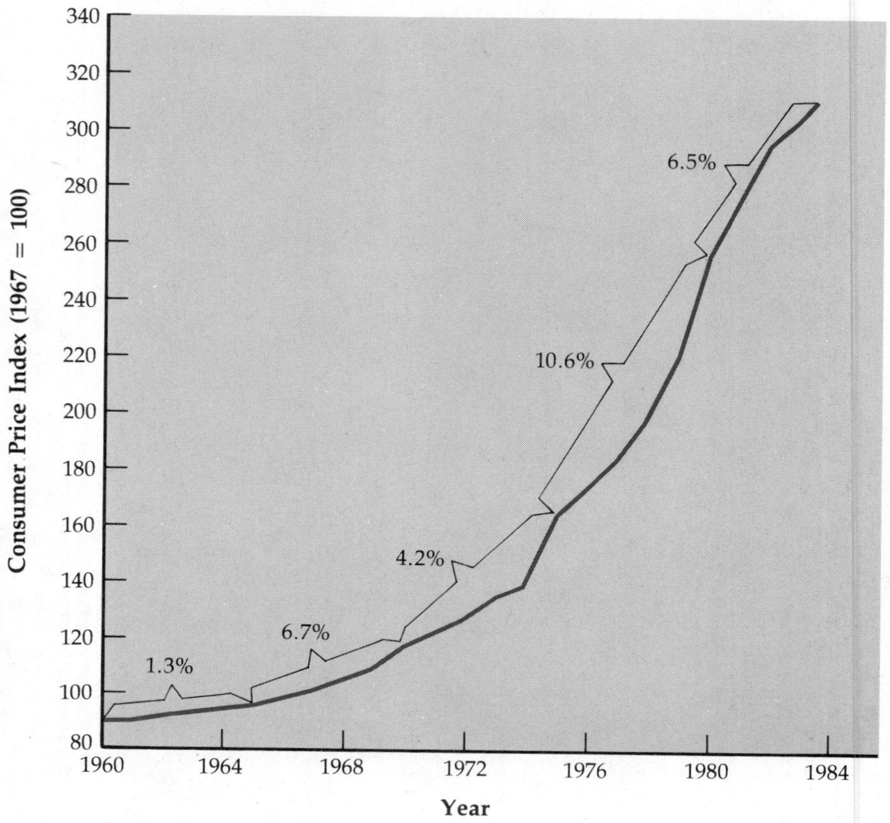


**Figure 6.2.** The Consumer Price Index, 1960–1984.
Over the past twenty-five years the consumer price index has moved sharply upward, reflecting rising rates of inflation. From an average of 1.3 percent in 1960–1964, inflation rose to an average of 8.9 percent in the last half of the 1970s. By 1984, however, the rate had fallen to an average of 6.5 percent.
**Source:** *Economic Report of the President* (Washington, D.C.: U.S. Government Printing Office, 1985), p. 291.

the consumer price index stood at less than 40; one hundred years later, after several periods of ups and downs, it was only 25.[1] Not until the 1920s did the index regain its 1800 level. But by 1950, the CPI stood at 72—44 percent higher than it had been just twenty years earlier. And in the next decade alone, the price level rose 23 percent.

The generally upward course of prices over the last twenty-five years is shown more clearly in Figure 6.2. During the first half of the 1960s, the inflation rate was a modest 1.3 percent. But in the second half of the

1. The index figures for the years before 1930, when data were not gathered regularly, are rough estimates only.

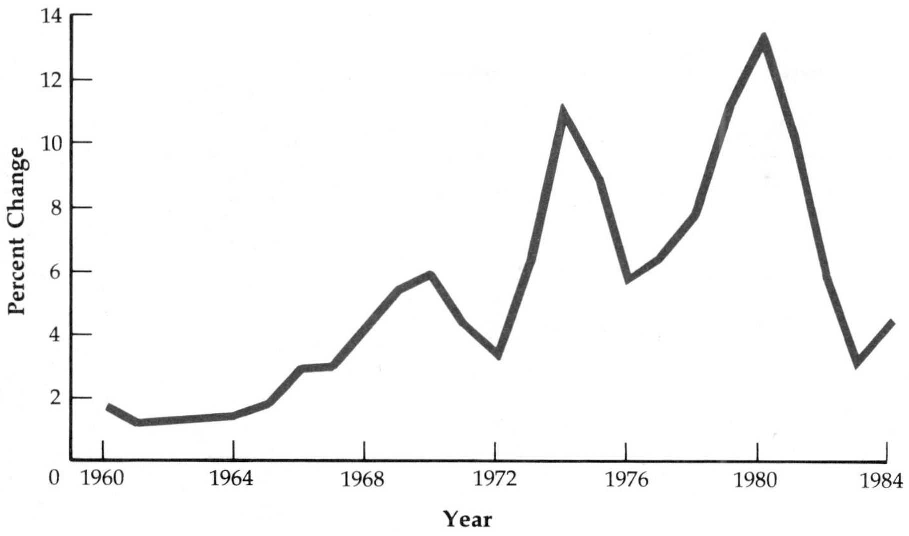


**Figure 6.3.** Percent Change in the Consumer Price Index, 1960–1984.
The inflation rate, as measured by the percentage change in the consumer price index, generally moved sharply upward during the 1960s and 1970s. However, the pace of price increases was very irregular, especially during the 1970s. On an annual basis, the inflation rate peaked at an average of 11 percent in 1974, only to fall to 5.8 percent in 1976. In 1980 it peaked again at an annual average of 13.5 percent. On a month-to-month basis, the inflation rate in 1980 was even more volatile: it fell from 18.2 percent in January to 1.2 percent in July, and then rose to 14 percent in November.
**Source:** *Economic Report of the President* (Washington, D.C.: U.S. Government Printing Office, 1985), p. 295.

decade, as the war in Vietnam escalated, prices began to move sharply upward. The average rate of inflation for the period 1965 to 1970 was 4.2 percent. For the early 1970s, despite government-imposed price controls, the rate was even higher, 6.7 percent. In 1974, it hit a shocking 11 percent, and for the rest of the decade inflation continued high, at an average of 10.6 percent. Not until the early 1980s—a decade after the end of the Vietnam War—did inflation return to the levels of the late 1960s.

The generally rising inflation rate was all the more difficult to deal with because it varied from year to year. It might reach 6 percent in one year and fall to 4 percent the next, and then rise to double-digit levels. At times during 1979 and 1980, the rate of inflation rose to 15 to 18 percent. Predicting future inflation rates became an exercise in crystal-ball gazing, and planning future purchases became a risky endeavor for both consumers and business people. The volatile annual U.S. inflation rates are shown in Figure 6.3.

U.S. inflation has been lower than that of many other nations (See Table 6.1). During the late 1950s and most of the 1960s, the United States had one of the world's lowest compound inflation rates, 2 percent. The

**Table 6.1.** Inflation Rates in Selected Countries, 1955–1982

| | Compound Annual Rate of Change in Consumer Prices | | | | |
|---|---|---|---|---|---|
| Country | 1955–1968 | 1969–1974 | 1975–1978 | 1980–1981 | 1981–1982 |
| Chile | 28 | 225 | 180 | 20 | 10 |
| Argentina | 27 | 32 | 244 | 105 | 165 |
| Brazil | 38 | 21 | 36 | 106 | 98 |
| Colombia | 10 | 15 | 23 | 28 | 25 |
| Ecuador | 2 | 11 | 13 | 16 | 16 |
| Peru | 9 | 9 | 38 | 75 | 65 |
| France | 5 | 7 | 10 | 13 | 12 |
| West Germany | 2 | 6 | 4 | 6 | 5 |
| Italy | 3 | 8 | 15 | 18 | 17 |
| Japan | 4 | 10 | 7 | 5 | 3 |
| Switzerland | 2 | 7 | 7 | 7 | 6 |
| United Kingdom | 3 | 9 | 15 | 12 | 9 |
| Canada | 2 | 5 | 8 | 12 | 11 |
| United States | 2 | 6 | 7 | 10 | 6 |

**Source:** U.S. Congress, Joint Economic Committee, *Industrial Policy Movement in the United States: Is It the Answer?* 98th Congress, 2nd Session (Washington, D.C.: U.S. Government Printing Office, June 8, 1984), p. 24.

compound rate was higher in 1970, 7 percent, but still one of the world's lowest. Even the double-digit rate of 1980–1981 was below the rates of most other nations.

The record of the past two-and-a-half decades nevertheless raises some questions:

What causes inflation?

Why has inflation risen so dramatically in the last several decades?

How does inflation affect our ability to produce and earn a living?

What are the costs and benefits of inflation?

What role does government policy play in creating inflation?

What can government do to stop or at least moderate inflation?

These questions have no easy answers. If they did, inflation would surely not be such a persistent problem. As the Wallich quotation at the opening of this chapter suggests, part of the difficulty is that inflation has many causes.

**Demand-pull inflation:** a general rise in prices that occurs when total planned expenditures increase faster than total production.

*Types of Inflation*

There are three types of inflation: demand-pull, cost-push, and structural. Each has a different cause. **Demand-pull inflation** occurs when total planned expenditures increase faster than total production. That is, people want to buy more than the economy is producing. In bidding for the limited number of goods and services available, they pull prices up. Demand-pull inflation may be stimulated by increases in the supply of money or in government expenditures—a subject to which we will return in later chapters.

**Cost-push inflation:** a general rise in prices that occurs when restrictions are placed on the supply of one or more resources, or when the price of one or more resources is increased.

**Cost-push inflation** occurs when restrictions are placed on the supply of one or more resources, or when the price of one or more resources is increased. For example, cost-push inflation may result from a cutoff in oil imports because of war or political disturbances. Competition for the restricted supply pushes oil prices up. Or it may arise from a curtailment of food supplies, like wheat or soy beans, because of poor weather. Cost-push inflation may also stem from wage increases that are not matched by productivity increases or from price fixing on the part of monopolies and oligopolies. In all these instances, output is restricted, either physically, or as in the last two cases, because a higher price reduces the demand for a resource. Competition among consumers for the limited output then forces the general price level up.

**Structural inflation:** a general rise in prices that occurs when producers cannot shift production in response to changes in the structure of the economy.

**Structural inflation** occurs when producers cannot readily shift production in response to changes in the structure of the economy. Changes in the demand for a product, in the technology of its production, and in the competition producers face can all cause structural inflation. Structural inflation may result when the overall composition of what consumers, businesses, and governments want to buy changes and producers cannot readily alter their employment of resources and their product mix. It may also be caused by the introduction of a major production innovation—for example, the advent of trains or the development of assembly-line robots. Changes in the structure of the economy create strategic shortages, or bottlenecks, in production supply lines. If a good like steel is caught in such a bottleneck, its price will rise, and that increase will then be transmitted to the prices of many other goods that use steel.

### *Reducing Inflation*

There are two major problems in dealing with inflation. The first is identifying which type of inflation is at work, because each type needs a different response. Demand-pull inflation may be tackled by reducing total spending—for example, by cutting government expenditures or increasing income taxes (since higher taxes will reduce consumer spending). Programs to increase the supply of certain key products, such as oil, may relieve cost-push inflation. Structural inflation may be attacked by eliminating the problems workers encounter in moving among different industries.

The second problem is to overcome political objections to implementing the appropriate policies. If inflation is caused by increases in the amount of money in circulation or by excessive government spending, then the obvious solution is to control the money supply and the government's tendency to overspend. But such steps may be politically unpopular. As long as citizens believe in the existence of the free lunch, governmental belt tightening—especially when it hits one's favorite government program—is bound to be controversial.

## Unemployment

During most of the years from 1959 to 1970, unemployment fluctuated between 3 and 7 percent. After 1970, however, the rate moved irregularly upward, peaking above 10 percent in 1982 (see Figure 6.4).

Unemployment means lost output as well as personal hardship for those who are out of work. Besides reducing output, unemployment triggers higher government expenditures on unemployment compensation and welfare programs. Eventually those expenditures are translated into higher taxes for the reduced working population—a problem in itself.

As in the case of inflation, the data on national production and unemployment raise many questions:

Why is the national production level not greater than it is? Why is it not smaller?

Why is the unemployment rate so high? Why has the rate not fallen below 4 percent more often? Why does the economy seem unable to operate with unemployment of less than 3 percent?

How has government policy affected the nation's unemployment and production levels?

Why has a growing percentage of the labor force sought employment outside the home? Why has the economy not provided all such people with jobs?

### *Types of Unemployment*

**Transitional (frictional) unemployment:** unemployment that occurs when people move from one job to another requiring similar skills.

**Cyclical unemployment:** unemployment that is caused by downswings of the business cycle—that is, by a broad-based reduction in the over-all level of spending in the economy.

**Structural unemployment:** unemployment that occurs with major changes in the skills needed by workers.

Unemployment has various causes, each requiring its own remedy. Unemployment may be transitional (frictional), cyclical, or structural. **Transitional (frictional) unemployment** occurs when people move from one job to another requiring similar skills. Transitional unemployment is caused by normal shifts in the supply of and demand for products. It is generally temporary, lasting a few days to a few weeks. **Cyclical unemployment** is caused by downswings of the business cycle—that is, by a broad-based reduction in the overall level of spending in the economy. It generally lasts for a period of weeks or months, until an increase in business activity raises national output and increases demand for labor. **Structural unemployment** is caused by major changes in the skills needed by workers, because of technological innovation or changes in the relative competitiveness of an industry. Structural unemployment can last for years, until workers are retrained for new jobs.

### *Reducing Unemployment*

The three types of unemployment require different solutions. Transitional unemployment may be shortened by providing information on jobs—for example, through Job Service offices. Manipulation of government spending and tax policies can moderate business cycles, thus reducing cyclical

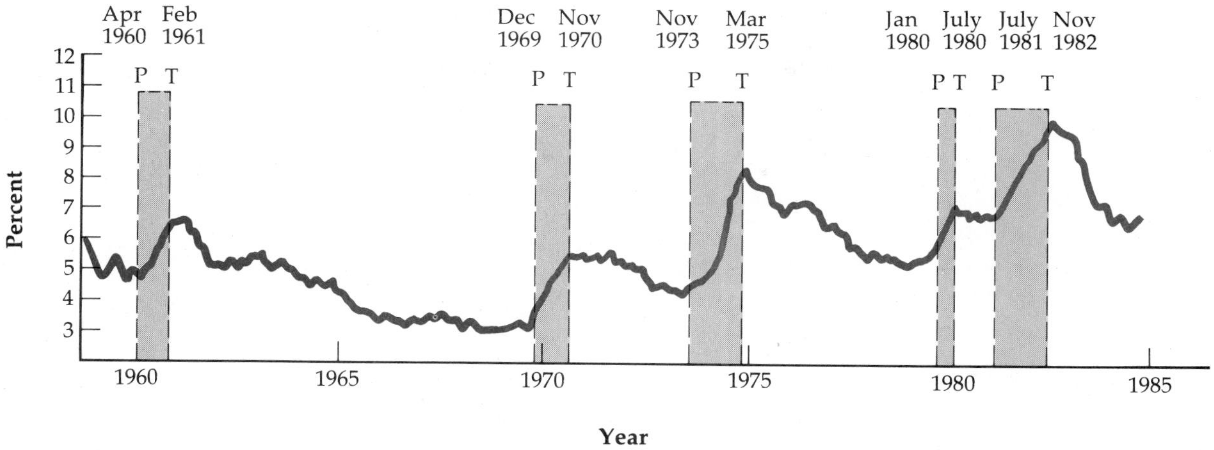


**Figure 6.4.** Unemployment in the United States.
Over the past twenty-five years, the unemployment rate has rarely dropped below 4 percent. Since the late 1960s, the rate has gradually increased, rising to unusually high levels during times of recession (the shaded areas). The *P*s correspond to peaks, the *T*s to troughs.
**Source:** U.S. Department of Commerce, Bureau of Economic Analysis, *Business Conditions Digest* (February 1985), p. 18.

unemployment. Relief of structural unemployment may require the introduction of special training programs or changes in the educational system.

Realistically, however, unemployment can never be completely eliminated. The natural rate of unemployment is always higher than zero. The **natural rate of unemployment** is that minimum percentage of the labor force that is unemployed because of structural problems in the economy and transitional movement among jobs. As we saw in the preceding chapter, the unemployment rate is really a snapshot of the economy at a given point in time. At any particular moment, some people will be caught changing jobs. Others will be counted as unemployed because of the way the Department of Commerce defines unemployed. In a dynamic economy, furthermore, some workers are bound to be out of work because of changes in the structure of the economy. That is, their skills are no longer easily employed where they live. Until they adjust their skills or location, they will be counted among the unemployed.

**Natural rate of unemployment:** the minimum percentage of the labor force that is unemployed because of structural problems in the economy and transitional movement among jobs.

Economists generally agree that the natural rate of unemployment is several percentage points above zero. But they do not agree on exactly what the figure might be, and whether or not it has been rising over time. (See the box on the rise in the natural unemployment rate, pages 136–137.) In the 1960s, many economists felt that the natural unemployment rate might be as low as 3 or 4 percent. Nowadays, many believe it is at least 6 percent, if not 7 percent or more.

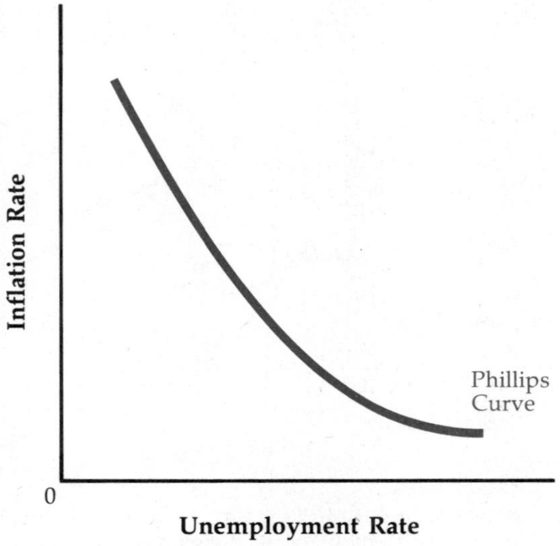


**Figure 6.5.** The Tradeoff Between Inflation and Unemployment.
The Phillips curve illustrates the presumed inverse relationship between unemployment and inflation. Theoretically, the inflation rate rises when the unemployment rate falls, and vice versa.

## Stagflation

As recently as twenty years ago, most economists and government policymakers believed that high unemployment would be accompanied by low rates of inflation, and vice versa. During periods of high unemployment, they reasoned, workers would be competing for a restricted number of jobs and thus would lose much of their ability to drive up wages. (Wage increases would be passed on to consumers as higher prices.) High unemployment would also depress people's incomes, and thus the demand for goods and services. Lower demand would mean less upward pressure on prices.

**Phillips curve:** a graphical representation of the presumed inverse relationship between unemployment and inflation.

This presumed relationship between unemployment and inflation is shown graphically by the Phillips curve, named for the British economist who first observed it (see Figure 6.5). The **Phillips curve** is a graphical representation of the presumed inverse relationship between unemployment and inflation. Since the 1960s, much of government policy has been based on the idea that a lower unemployment rate could be traded for a higher inflation rate, and vice versa. In other words, using government fiscal and monetary powers, policymakers could move the macroeconomy up or down the Phillips curve at will. The only question facing policymakers was which combination of unemployment and inflation they should seek.

Events of the 1970s and early 1980s disproved that line of thinking, however. As Figure 6.6 shows, inflation and unemployment were not inversely related in those years—at least not for more than a few months.

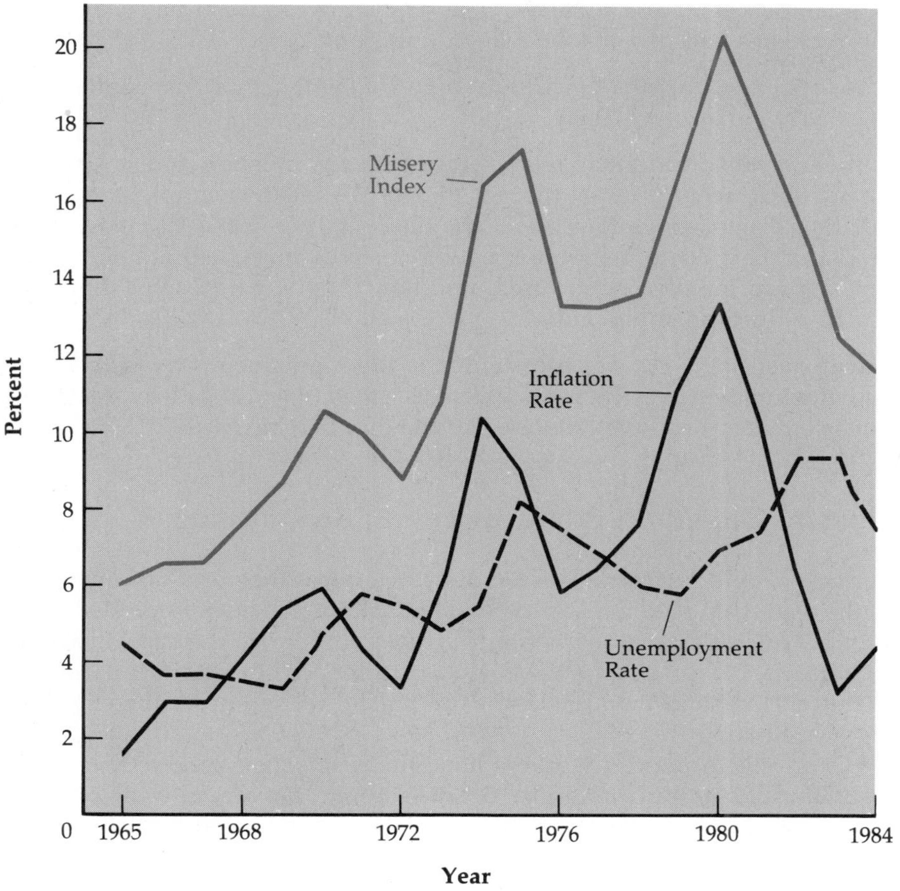


**Figure 6.6.** The Misery Index, 1965–1984.
Over the past twenty years both unemployment and inflation have tended to move upward. The misery index—the sum of the unemployment and inflation rates—has therefore moved upward as well. The experience of the last two decades suggests that unemployment and inflation may not be inversely related, as economists once thought.
**Source:** *Economic Report of the President* (Washington, D.C.: U.S. Government Printing Office, 1985), pp. 269, 291.

From 1965 to 1984, both unemployment and inflation followed a general upward trend. In fact, in the 1970s the overall relationship may well have been positive. That is, the higher the inflation rate, the higher the unemployment rate, and vice versa. The long-run positive tendency is particularly striking if the two rates are summed to obtain the so-called misery index (see Figure 6.6).

**Stagflation:** the combination of persistently high rates of unemployment and inflation.

This twin problem of high unemployment and high inflation is often called stagflation. **Stagflation** is the combination of persistently high rates of unemployment and inflation. This economic condition has challenged old remedies and posed a new set of questions:

How can high unemployment and high inflation coexist? Is stagflation a peculiarly modern problem?

Is there a cause-and-effect relationship between inflation and unemployment? If so, what is it? Is there a tradeoff between unemployment and inflation disguised somewhere in the data for 1970–1984? Can the unemployment part of stagflation be reduced by reducing the inflation rate? If so, how can inflation be lowered, and how long will it take for the lower rate to reduce unemployment?

Have government policies contributed to the simultaneous rise of inflation and unemployment? To what extent is stagflation caused by economic forces outside the United States, like the oil price increases of 1974?

## Lagging Growth in Productivity and Real Income

Because people's incomes are tied directly to what they produce, increases in the aggregate national income must be tied to increases in productivity. Without an increase in worker output, there can be no increase in worker income. People can be given more dollars to spend. But without an increase in output to spend them on, the extra dollars will go up in the smoke of higher prices.

Historically American workers have increased their productivity gradually through improved skills, the use of greater amounts of physical capital, and the discovery of new and less costly sources of energy. Between 1947 and 1970, for instance, output per man-hour in the private sector expanded at an average annual rate of 2.3 percent. After 1970, however, growth in worker productivity dipped below 2 percent per year and almost ground to a halt during the last three years of the 1970s. That slowdown in productivity growth diminished the growth of real purchasing power. Beginning in 1983, worker productivity turned upward again, along with the increase in general economic activity that began then.

Table 6.2 shows the rate of growth in real GNP in several industrialized nations from 1960 to 1983. In the 1960s, output grew more slowly in the United States than in most other nations. In the late 1970s, however, only Japan had a noticeably higher growth rate than the United States. The baby boom generation reached working age in the 1970s, and the labor force participation rate rose as more women took jobs outside the home. The result was a sharp increase in the size of the U.S. work force.

Still more questions suggest themselves:

What caused the slowdown in the growth of worker productivity during the 1970s?

Is worker productivity affected by the rate of inflation? By tax increases? By government policy? If so, how?

What can government do, if anything, to promote growth in productivity?

**Table 6.2.** Rate of Growth in Real Gross National Product, 1960–1983 (percent change)

| | Annual Average | | | | | | |
|---|---|---|---|---|---|---|---|
| Country | 1961–1965 | 1966–1970 | 1971–1975 | 1976–1980 | 1981 | 1982 | 1983 |
| United States | 4.7% | 3.2% | 2.6% | 3.7% | 2.6% | −1.9% | 3.4% |
| Canada | 5.7 | 4.8 | 5.0 | 3.1 | 3.8 | −5.0 | 3.8 |
| Japan | 10.0 | 11.2 | 4.6 | 5.0 | 3.2 | 2.5 | 2.0 |
| France | 5.8 | 5.4 | 4.0 | 3.3 | 0.2 | 1.5 | 0.5 |
| West Germany | 5.0 | 4.2 | 2.2 | 3.5 | 0.2 | −1.2 | 1.2 |
| Italy | 5.2 | 6.2 | 2.4 | 3.8 | −0.1 | −0.3 | −1.5 |
| United Kingdom | 3.1 | 2.5 | 2.1 | 1.6 | −2.0 | 0.5 | 2.5 |

**Source:** U.S. Congress, Joint Economic Committee, *Industrial Policy Movement in the United States: Is It the Answer?* 98th Congress, 2nd Session (Washington, D.C.: U.S. Government Printing Office, June 8, 1984), p. 26.

How will policies to promote growth in productivity affect the inflation and unemployment rates?

## Business Cycles

As Figures 6.3 and 6.4 show, recent economic activity has proceeded in fits and starts. In fact, the history of the U.S. economy has been one of ups and downs, booms and busts. Figure 6.7 shows the irregular path of the nation's annual rates of growth in real GNP from 1910 to 1984. The Great Depression of the 1930s, the rather large shaded area in the middle of the graph, stands out as this century's longest period of economic distress. In recent decades, business activity has been substantially higher than the overall trend. Much of that apparent surge in activity can be ascribed to inflation, however.

The long-run upward movement of economic activity seen in Figure 6.4 is called a trend. A **trend** is a long-run directional change, up or down, in some economic variable—for example, real GNP. Because they are long-run measures, trends may be obscured by the small irregularities, or ups and downs, in year-to-year business conditions. These smaller movements, which can last for several years, within the long-term trend are called business cycles. A **business cycle** is a recurring but irregular swing in general economic activity, a smaller pattern of ups and downs within a major long-term trend.

Business cycles have four phases: a recession, a trough, a recovery, and a peak (see Figure 6.8). The cycle begins with a downturn in activity, called a recession. A **recession** is a downward movement in general economic activity, especially in national production and employment. The Department of Commerce defines a recession as a downward movement in real GNP that lasts at least six months. An especially severe recession, with a substantial decline in real production and an unemployment rate of 15 percent or more, is called a depression.

**Trend:** a long-run directional change, up or down, in some economic variable—for example, real GNP.

**Business cycle:** a recurring swing in general economic activity, a smaller pattern of ups and downs within a major long-term trend.

**Recession:** a downward movement in general economic activity, especially in national production and employment.

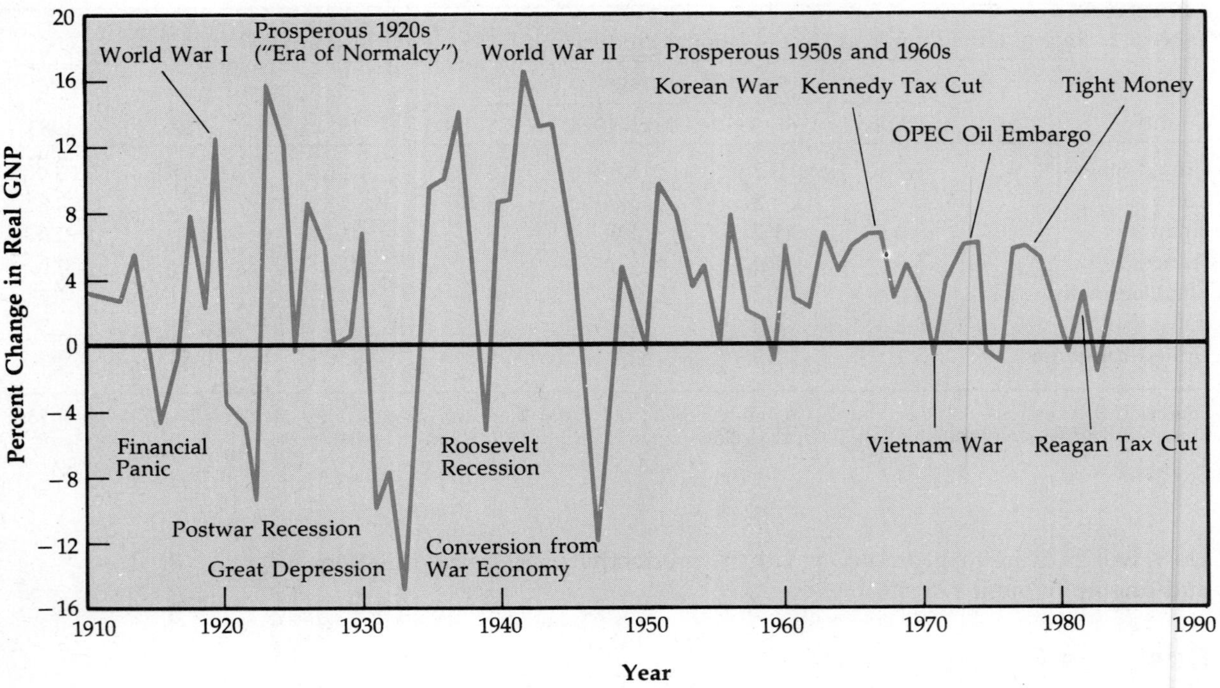


Figure 6.7. Business Cycles in the United States, 1910–1985.
Overall, economic activity in the United States has expanded over the last century. But the generally upward trend includes many boom-and-bust cycles, the most severe of which led to the Great Depression of the 1930s.
**Sources:** U.S. Bureau of the Census, *Historical Statistics of the United States* (Washington, D.C.: U.S. Government Printing Office, 1975), pp. 226–227; *Economic Report of the President* (Washington, D.C.: U.S. Government Printing Office, 1985), p. 234.

**Trough:** the bottom of the business cycle, the point at which general economic activity ceases to fall.

**Recovery:** an upward movement in general economic activity, especially in national production and employment.

**Peak:** the phase of the business cycle that occurs when general economic activity is no longer rising.

When real GNP stops falling and unemployment stops rising, the trough of the business cycle has been reached. The **trough** is the bottom of the business cycle, the point at which general economic activity ceases to fall. Once the economy hits bottom, it may shift upward almost immediately or languish there for several months. When real GNP begins to rise and unemployment to fall, the economy has entered the recovery phase. A **recovery** is an upward movement in general economic activity (real GNP and employment). A recovery may continue until full employment is approached or it may be aborted fairly quickly by another recession.

The business cycle ends when the recovery phase reaches its peak. A **peak** occurs when general economic activity is no longer rising. The peak is the top of the business cycle, the transition from the recovery phase of one cycle to the recession phase of another. Thus a peak cannot be identified until a new recession has been declared—at least six months after real GNP begins to fall.

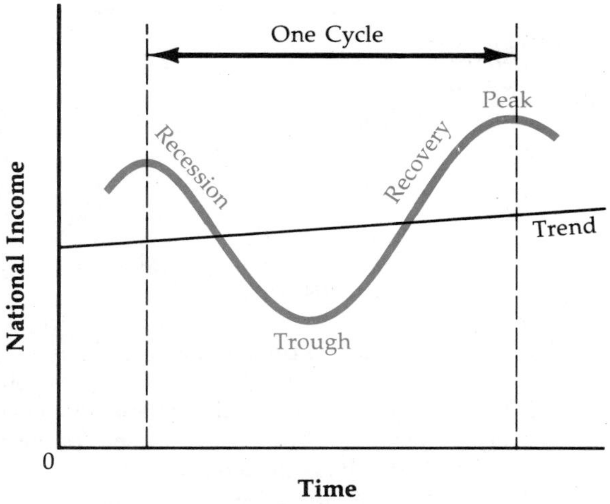


Figure 6.8. The Business Cycle.
A complete business cycle has four phases: recession, trough, recovery, and peak.

**Table 6.3.** Business Cycles in the United States, 1926–1982

| Peak | Trough | Length of Cycle from Peak to Peak (in months) |
|---|---|---|
| October 1926 | November 1927 | 41 |
| August 1929 | March 1933 | 34 |
| May 1937 | June 1938 | 93 |
| February 1945 | October 1945 | 93 |
| November 1948 | October 1949 | 45 |
| July 1953 | May 1954 | 56 |
| August 1957 | April 1958 | 49 |
| April 1960 | February 1961 | 32 |
| December 1969 | November 1970 | 116 |
| November 1973 | March 1975 | 47 |
| January 1980 | July 1980 | 62 |
| July 1981 | November 1982 | 18 |

**Source:** U.S. Department of Commerce, Bureau of Economic Analysis, *Business Conditions Digest* (February 1985 and earlier issues).

The length of a business cycle is measured from peak to peak. As Table 6.3 shows, recent U.S. business cycles have varied significantly in length, from one to several years. Look again at Figure 6.7. No two business cycles are exactly alike in depth or timing. These variations make predicting future business conditions an imperfect science at best.

## Perspectives in Economics: Economic Instability in the Twentieth Century

*Clark Nardinelli*

During the twentieth century the real gross national product of the United States has grown at a modest rate of about 3 percent a year. But although the overall trend has been positive, annual growth rates have fluctuated widely (see Figure 6.7). Especially in the first half of the century, the economy swung back and forth between rapid growth and negative growth.

These swings were not random, but related to historical events. The first major downswing of the century, the recession of 1913 to 1914, was due partly to a financial panic that caused a run on the banks. Both the panic and the recession were short-lived. They were followed by a period of inflationary growth, caused by mobilization for the First World War. When the war ended in 1918 the price level fell, and the nation had to convert its factories back to peacetime production. The result was a new downturn, the recession of 1919 to 1921. But the gains made after that recession more than offset its losses.

The 1920s were years of rapid economic growth. But the postwar boom halted abruptly with the onset of the Great Depression of 1929 to 1933, the greatest peacetime cataclysm in American history. In just four years the nominal gross national product fell from \$104.6 billion to \$56.1 billion. Even allowing for the simultaneous fall in prices, real GNP dropped at a precipitous rate.

Like earlier recessions, the Great Depression was followed by an economic expansion. This recovery, however, did not advance the economy past earlier highs. Its gains almost, but not quite, made up for depression losses. (The chart shows that the upswing following 1933 is of almost the same magnitude as the downswing preceding 1933.) In 1938, real GNP was almost the same as it had been in 1929.

The stagnation of the 1930s ended with mobilization for the Second World War (1939–1945), which brought another inflationary boom. Real GNP, the price level, and manufacturing output all rose rapidly after 1940. Once the United States became an active participant in the war (1941), unemployment virtually disappeared. As had happened after the First World War, the end of the hostilities was followed by deflation and problems of readjustment to peacetime production. The result was a short but severe recession from 1945 to 1947. Recovery was rapid, however, and growth

**Leading indicator:** an index of business activity that tends to move up or down several months before measures of general economic activity, like real GNP, do so.

Among the tools economists use in predicting business conditions are measures called leading indicators. A **leading indicator** is an index of business activity that tends to move up or down several months before measures of general economic activity, like real GNP, do so. The composite index of leading economic indicators for the 1964–1985 (first quarter) shown in Figure 6.9 combines information on stock prices, size of the money stock, unemployment, building permits, housing starts, commercial and industrial loans, and so forth, into a single measure of economic activity that tends to forecast changes in real GNP. By watching the index, as well as the individual indexes that go into the composite, economists and policymakers can get some clues as to what will happen in the future. If had resumed by the 1950s, aided somewhat by the expansion accompanying the Korean War (1950–1953). Growth remained positive throughout the decade, except for a brief recession in 1954 following the end of the Korean War.

The 1960s witnessed sustained economic growth, leading some economists to conclude that business cycles were a thing of the past. Indeed, the chart shows a moderation of the wide swings of the first half of the century. Though the Vietnam War brought the usual wartime inflation, it did not produce the rapid economic expansion associated with previous wartime eras.

The naive belief that the business cycle was obsolete collapsed in 1974–1975, when the Arab oil embargo plunged the United States and other industrial nations into the most severe recession since the 1940s. But though the ensuing recovery more than offset the losses of that recession, it was accompanied by the century's highest rate of peacetime inflation. In 1980 the consumer price index rose an alarming 13.5 percent. The recession that followed in 1981–1982 may have been caused in part by the adoption of anti-inflationary policies in the early 1980s.

Though events of the 1970s and 1980s have shown that the business cycle is not dead, the rate of change in real GNP has clearly been much steadier since 1950 than before. Why has the business cycle become less extreme? One possibility is that since 1950, the nation has experienced no events as catastrophic as the Great Depression or the Second World War. The U.S. economy may be more stable because the world as a whole is more stable. Another possibility is that the countercyclical policies the federal government has pursued in the last few decades have moderated the effects of business cycles. As government policymakers learn more about macroeconomics, their effectiveness may be increasing. Finally, the moderation of business cycles may stem from the increasing size of government itself. Government economic activity tends to be more stable than private economic activity, and the government's share of real GNP has been growing in the latter half of the century.

Whatever the reason, the U.S. economy has become more stable since 1950. Most economists believe that this greater stability will continue through the end of the century.

the composite index turns down for several months, economists can predict a recession with some confidence.

Our survey of business cycles raises still more questions about the macroeconomy.

What causes the ups and downs in general business activity? Why is the overall upward trend not a smooth one?

What can government do to make recessions less likely or less severe?

Do government policies contribute to the length and severity of business cycles?

## Macroeconomic Policies

Economists differ widely on what should be done to remedy the macroeconomic problems we have been discussing. In later chapters we will explain their views in considerable detail. Here we will simply outline them briefly.

### The Classical School

Before the 1930s, most economists believed that the forces of supply and demand would eventually remedy problems of unemployment and low levels of production. According to classical theory, a rise in unemployment would depress wage rates, for more workers would be competing for fewer jobs. When the price of labor fell, employers would hire more workers, lowering the unemployment rate and boosting production. Classical economists blame persistent unemployment and underproduction on unions and laws that prevent wage rates from falling in response to falling demand. Their prescription is straightforward: eliminate all legal impediments to flexibility in prices and wages.

Lagging growth in productivity can also be solved by the free market system, according to classical economists. If people want more goods and services enough to pay for them, then businesses will invest more, and the newer, more efficient equipment will permit a rise in productivity and future output. In the view of classical economists, lagging productivity indicates that consumers are not willing to pay for greater future output by forgoing current consumption. (For more on the classical school of economics, see Chapter 10.)

### The Keynesian School

Keynesian economists—followers of the British economist John Maynard Keynes—believe that the principal cause of low production and unemployment is inadequate total spending. Together, consumers, businesses, and government do not demand enough goods and services to employ the labor force fully. Keynesians would say that the fluctuations in macroeconomic activity reflect the fluctuations in demand, especially the demand for investment in capital goods. Their solution for unemployment is to increase total spending in any of several ways. One possibility is to reduce taxes, thereby increasing consumer and business purchasing power (and ultimately demand). Another is to increase government spending. A third is to lower interest rates by increasing the money stock, thereby encouraging businesses and consumers to obtain loans for new purchases. In fact, Keynesians believe any policy that stimulates the demand for investment will ultimately increase both production and the rate of growth in worker productivity.

Keynesians also tend to see inflation as primarily a demand problem. Consumers demand more in total than the economy can produce, putting

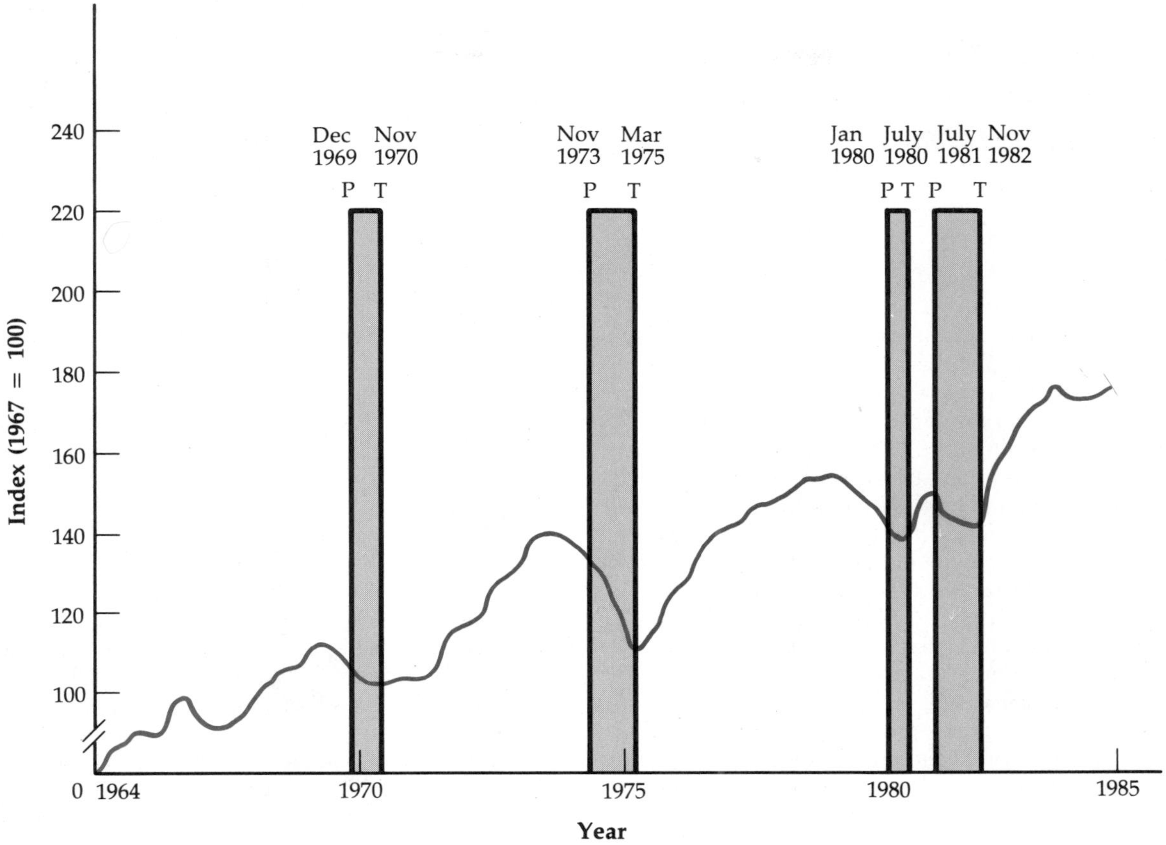


**Figure 6.9.** Composite Index of Leading Economic Indicators.
The composite index of leading economic indicators is compiled from indexes that economists find useful as predictors, including indexes of stock prices, size of the money stock, unemployment, building permits, housing starts, and commercial and industrial loans. The composite index tends to change direction several months before a change in general economic activity—for example, a change in real GNP. Thus it aids economists in forecasting future economic conditions.
Note: The shaded areas correspond to recessions, with *P* for the peaks and *T* for the troughs of the business cycles.
**Source:** U.S. Department of Commerce, Bureau of Economic Analysis, *Business Conditions Digest* (February 1985), p. 10.

upward pressure on prices. The solution: reduce total demand by reversing the policies prescribed to reduce unemployment. Raise taxes, dampening consumer and business spending; or reduce government spending; or raise interest rates, reducing business and consumer loans and purchases. Unfortunately, according to traditional Keynesian theory, policies designed to reduce inflation will tend to raise unemployment, and vice versa. (See Chapters 11–13 for more on the Keynesian model of the macroeconomy.)

# Perspectives in Economics: The Rising Natural Rate of Unemployment

*Henry F. Myers*

Does the rise in unemployment to 7.4% of the civilian labor force last month [January 1985] indicate that we have already seen the lows in joblessness for the current business expansion? Do we face a rerun of the 1970s and early 1980s, when the low achieved in each succeeding business cycle was consistently higher than in the previous one?

Most economists don't expect much improvement in unemployment figures anytime soon. The latest consensus forecast by the four dozen analysts surveyed monthly by Blue Chip Economic Indicators, a Sedona, Arizona, newsletter, envisioned unemployment averaging 7.1% this year [1985] and next year [1986].

However, Audrey Freedman, a senior research associate at the Conference Board, notes that her own prediction that unemployment "will sit around 7.2% this year" isn't a prediction that nothing will be going on. Far from it. Just to keep unemployment from rising, she says, "you will have to create 1.5 million jobs" to match the growth in the labor force. She expects those jobs to be created, but not many more—not enough to reduce unemployment further—because "the recovery is aging and flattening out."

So far in this cycle, the unemployment rate hit its low, 7.1%, last June [1984] and again last November [1984]. That may well be as far down as it gets; unemployment tends to be a leading indicator at cyclical peaks. Moreover, that low substantially exceeds the highest monthly rate, 6.1%, during the 1969–70 recession.

Here is how the unemployment rate lows have been trending during the four previous business expansions:

| Cycle Peak | Lowest Rate | Month |
|---|---|---|
| Dec. '69 | 3.4% | Jan.–May '69 |
| Nov. '73 | 4.6 | Oct. '73 |
| Jan. '80 | 5.6 | May '79 |
| July '81 | 7.2 | Apr. '81 |

Analyzing such trends, economists try to filter out cyclical joblessness from the unemployment lingering on even during booms—often called the natural rate of unemployment. That unemployment, which can't be reduced without unleashing steep inflation, is divided into frictional unemployment—the 3% or so of workers voluntarily between jobs—and structural unemployment—workers with inadequate skills.

During the 1970s, most economists believe, the natural rate of unemployment rose. Michael Wachter of the University of Pennsylvania cites three reasons:

—Unfavorable demographics. Baby boomers and women flooded into the labor force, and jobs couldn't be created fast enough. Moreover, youths and women tend to be less attached to the labor force, and as they float in and out of jobs, frictional unemployment rises.

—Rising government transfer payments. As unemployment compensation, welfare and Social Security benefits increased, the unemployed could be choosier about jobs.

—Inflationary shocks. Surges in oil and food prices hit when many labor and commodity markets were already tight, and the government felt forced to clamp down and fight inflation more quickly—at the cost of jobs—than it would in a slack economy.

Now, Professor Wachter estimates, the natural rate of unemployment probably has dropped to about 5¾% from perhaps 6¼% in the late 1970s. He notes that the surge of new job-seekers has slowed, and in the future "the demographics will continue to be favorable." So they will. According to the Bureau of Labor Statistics, the labor force aged 16 and over, which grew 1.3% a year in 1950–60, 1.7% in 1960–70 and 2.6% in 1970–80, is rising only 1.6% in 1980–90 and will increase just 1% annually in 1990–95.

Furthermore, President Reagan has halted the increase in inflation-adjusted transfer payments. And inflation is down, although Professor Wachter notes the danger posed by steep federal budget deficits.

Other factors may also be paring the natural rate of unemployment. Professor Wachter observes that the minimum wage, often said to inhibit hiring of low-skilled workers, has been eroded by inflation since its last increase, to $3.35 an hour, in January 1981. If the minimum had kept up with the 16.5% gain in nonsupervisory production workers' average pay since then, it "would now be $3.90," he adds.

Meanwhile, the youths and women who earlier swamped the labor market have acquired wider job skills and now presumably could, if laid off, find new jobs more quickly. And as actual unemployment drops, their increasing skills may reduce the natural rate.

Moreover, as Mrs. Freedman noted in a recent paper, "Union power to set industrywide wage rates has clearly decreased during the past four years." Unions thus have lost some of their ability to keep real wages from falling enough to enable employers to hire most of the jobless.

But tending to raise the natural rate of unemployment has been rapid technological change, which forces more job switching. In fact, a study by Michael Podgursky of the University of Massachusetts found that by the late 1970s, the primary source of structural unemployment had shifted from youths to prime-age males; unions couldn't halt surging imports, factory automation or the decline of smokestack industries. High-tech industry can't replace lost basic-industry jobs and, by lifting productivity, it enables output to rise faster than employment.

Economists figure that the economy must grow about 3% annually merely to provide jobs for new labor-force entrants, but the Blue Chip group, on the average, expects growth only slightly above that this year and below that next year. Without a new surge of growth, we may be stuck with 7%-plus unemployment for some time.

Henry F. Myers, "High Unemployment Is Likely to Linger On," *Wall Street Journal* (February 25, 1985), p. 1.

## The Monetarist School

The monetarists tend to see inflation and economic instability as largely a monetary problem. They believe that inflation results when too many dollars are pumped into the economy by government authorities (in the United States, principally the Federal Reserve System, which controls the money stock). The monetarists' solution is to reduce the growth in the amount of money in the economy.

The monetarists also believe many irregularities in economic activity stem from the irregular growth of the money stock. They argue that the Great Depression was worsened by the Federal Reserve's contraction of the money stock by as much as a third during the early 1930s. Prices and wages simply could not adjust downward as rapidly as the money stock contracted; the result was severe unemployment.

Although they emphasize variations in the growth of the money stock, the monetarists share many of the views of the classical school of economics. Much of modern unemployment, they believe, is due to legal restrictions like minimum wage laws, which keep wage rates from falling and labor markets from reaching equilibrium. Monetarists also believe some unemployment must be expected, given people's attempts to find the best jobs available and the existence of unemployment compensation and welfare benefits. In fact, if unemployment benefits and the growth of the money stock increase simultaneously, the monetarists would predict a rise in both inflation and unemployment. (Details of the monetarist theory are founded on the principles of money creation and control developed in Chapters 7, 8, and 9, and on theoretical points presented in Chapter 14.)

## The Supply-Side School

Rcently some analysts have begun to suspect that much of our unemployment and inflation is due to problems with supply (not demand, as the Keynesians would argue). These supply-side economists see high income tax rates as an important cause of low production and unemployment. Because government takes a relatively high percentage of what citizens earn, they reason, people have inadequate incentive to work, save, invest, and create jobs. Supply-side economists also see inflation as partly a supply problem. Price increases, they point out, can be moderated by an increase in production—in the supply of goods and services people want.

A supply-side solution to unemployment, inflation, and productivity problems is to reduce tax rates, increasing people's willingness to work, save, and invest. Reduced unemployment and greater national output should result; and if the number of dollars in circulation stays constant or rises less than output, the increase supply of goods and services should exert downward pressure on prices. Reducing the tax rate may also (but will not necessarily) increase government revenues, for the rise in disposable income may more than offset the lower tax rate. (See Chapter 15 for more information on supply-side economics).

## The Rational Expectations School

Although people's expectations play a role in the Keynesian, monetarist, and supply-side models, they are a central element in the rational expectations model of the macroeconomy. Rational expectations theorists assume that people will acquire some rationally determined amount of information on the impact of government policies and will act on that information. For example, if people observe that government deficits and interest rates are positively related, they will try to borrow money when the government deficit goes up, expecting a rise in interest rates.

Unfortunately the increased demand for borrowed funds will drive interest rates up almost immediately, not some time in the future. So while Keynesian theory predicts that an increase in the government deficit will raise national production (because demand rises with greater government spending), rational expectations theorists would expect a higher deficit to lead to higher interest rates and an offsetting reduction in investment spending. Similarly government efforts to change the money stock will be offset by people's defensive reaction, based on their expectations of what will happen to interest rates, prices, and production costs. Pushed to its logical limits, rational expectations theory suggests that government is virtually incapable of affecting national production and employment levels, even in the short run, by varying taxes, expenditures, or the money stock. (More will be said about rational expectations theory in Chapter 16.)

## Common Ground Among Theories

Our discussion of the various schools of macroeconomic thought has emphasized the differences among the Keynesian, monetarist, supply-side, and rational expectations theories. Those differences explain why economists often disagree about the policies government should adopt toward unemployment, inflation, and lagging growth. They disagree because they subscribe to different theories.

Discussing schools of thought separately has allowed us to highlight macroeconomic variables and their probable effects. Keynesian economics focuses on the impact of demand on production, income, and employment. Monetarism considers how growth in the money supply influences inflation. Supply-side economics stresses factors that affect aggregate supply, and rational expectations theory emphasizes the influence of people's expectations on interest rates, inflation, and unemployment.

Readers should not conclude, however, that Keynesians are unconcerned with prices and expectations; or that monetarists do not recognize government budgets' effect on prices; or that supply-side economists ignore the effect of demand on production; or that rational expectations theorists do not recognize influences other than people's expectations. Almost all macroeconomic theories allow for the interplay of a combination of economic forces. Those forces invariably include money, aggregate demand, aggregate suply, and expectations. Theories differ primarily in their relative emphasis on these forces.

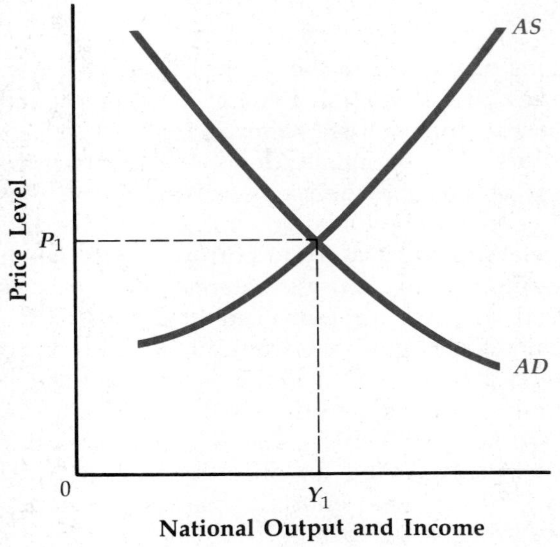


**Figure 6.10.** Aggregate Demand and Aggregate Supply.
Aggregate demand and supply relate the nation's price level to its output. Here the macroeconomy will be in equilibrium at a price level of $P_1$ and a national output level of $Y_1$. At any price level above $P_1$, the goods and services available will exceed the quantity demanded by households, firms, and government. Competitive pressure will force the price level back down to $P_1$. At any price level below $P_1$, the quantity of goods and services demanded will exceed the quantity supplied. Competitive pressure will force the price level back up to $P_1$.

## Aggregate Demand and Supply: A Macroeconomic Model

Chapter 3 showed how the laws of supply and demand determine the prices and quantities of particular goods in a market economy. Similar concepts can be applied to macroeconomics. In future chapters, we will see how aggregate (total) demand and aggregate (total) supply determine the general price level, national output, and national income. The aggregate demand and supply model will prove a useful tool for analyzing the various schools of macroeconomic thought.

### Aggregate Demand

Graphically, aggregate demand can be described as a downward sloping curve, like the curve labeled *AD* in Figure 6.10. It looks much like the demand curve for individual products. The market demand curve and the

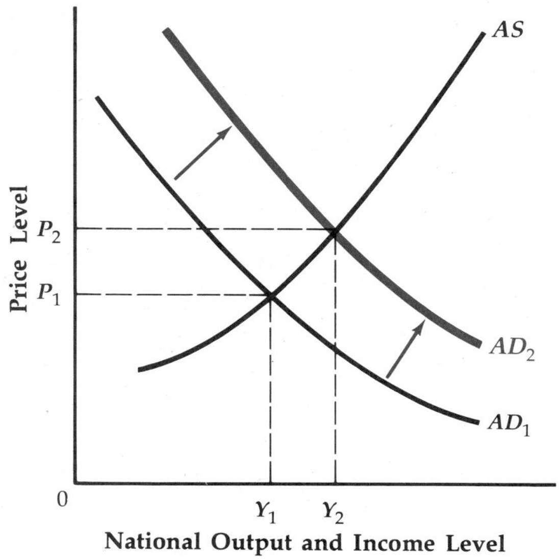


**Figure 6.11.** Effects of an Increase in Aggregate Demand.
If aggregate demand rises from $AD_1$ to $AD_2$, the equilibrium price level will rise from $P_1$ to $P_2$, and the national output level will rise from $Y_1$ to $Y_2$.

aggregate demand curve are two different concepts, however. The market demand curve relates the price of a given good to its consumption level; the aggregate demand curve relates the general price level to total desired spending on national output. **Aggregate demand** is the presumed negative relationship between the general price level and the total quantity of goods and services consumers, business, and government want to buy.

**Aggregate demand:** the presumed negative relationship between the general price level and the total quantity of goods and services consumers, business, and government want to buy.

The two curves slope downward for different reasons. The individual demand curve slopes downward because changes in price cause income and substitution effects. The aggregate demand curve slopes downward because changes in the general price level affect people's wealth (not because the market demands for individual products slope downward). When the price level falls, people can buy more with their cash, stocks and bonds, and other monetary assets; their aggregate real wealth rises, and they will buy more goods and services. Conversely, when the general price level goes up, aggregate purchases will decline along with aggregate real wealth.

## Aggregate Supply

**Aggregate supply:** the presumed positive relationship between the general price level and the total quantity of goods and services produced in the economy during a given period of time.

Aggregate supply relates national output to the general price level. **Aggregate supply** is the presumed positive relationship between the general price level and the total quantity of goods and services produced

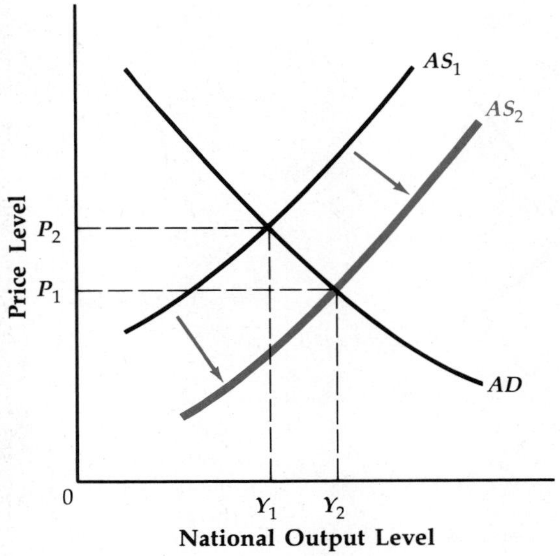


Figure 6.12. Effects of an Increase in Aggregate Supply.
If aggregate supply increases from $AS_1$ to $AS_2$, the price level will fall from $P_2$ to $P_1$, yet the national output level will rise from $Y_1$ to $Y_2$.

in the economy during a given period of time. The short-run aggregate supply curve slopes upward, like the curve labeled *AS* in Figure 6.10. In the short run, production may be expected to rise with an increase in the price level, because price increases may take time to be translated into cost increases. Until costs catch up, producers will expand production to reap extra profits. In the long run, cost increases usually do catch up with price increases, and supply contracts.

## Aggregate Demand and Supply

Analysis of aggregate demand and supply resembles analysis of market supply and demand in one important respect: equilibrium occurs at the intersection of the supply and demand curves. In Figure 6.10 the equilibrium national output level is $Y_1$, the equilibrium price level $P_1$. If the price level is higher than $P_1$, the aggregate quantity of goods and services demanded will not meet the quantity producers offer on the market. The price level will fall, increasing the quantity business, government, and consumers will buy and decreasing the quantity producers will offer. If the price level is lower than $P_1$, all sectors of the economy will demand more than producers offer. Total production will expand, and the total amount all sectors want to buy will contract.

The following chapters will discuss the details of how price and output levels adjust, and how changes in aggregate demand and supply affect production, employment, and the price level. Briefly, an increase in government demand for goods and services (unless offset by a reduction in consumer and business demand) can cause an expansion in national production and possibly an increase in the price level. The increase in government demand will shift the aggregate demand curve out, say from $AD_1$ to $AD_2$ in Figure 6.11. At the initial price level, total planned spending will be greater than total supply; the price level will rise, prompting producers to expand production. A decrease in taxes could cause the same result. If disposable income rises, increasing aggregate demand, price levels and national output will increase.

The price level may also fall, as a result of an increase in aggregate supply. If tax rates are reduced, increasing people's willingness to work and produce, the aggregate supply curve will shift outward to the right, say from $AS_1$ to $AS_2$ in Figure 6.12. A higher national output level, $Y_2$, but a lower price level, $P_1$, will result.

Just how and why aggregate demand and supply change is the subject of considerable dispute among economists. Many suspect that business cycles are caused by these shifts in aggregate demand and supply. When aggregate demand or supply shifts back and forth, everything else held constant, general economic activity will pick up or slow down. In fact macroeconomics is largely the study of how broad sectors of the economy affect one another through their effect on aggregate demand and supply. More will be said about aggregate demand and supply in Chapter 13.

## Summary and Extensions

Inflation, unemployment, and lagging growth in productivity affect almost all of us to some extent. We must all cope with uncertainty about future prices. And to the extent that unemployment means lost output—that is, unsatisfied wants—it also affects everyone. Reductions in productivity growth will make us all less well off in the future than we might have been.

What should we do about these problems? Economists disagree not only on which theory should guide policy, but on what goals government should pursue. Some believe government should do virtually nothing aside from creating a stable monetary system. They contend that, despite good intentions, government action has left us worse off on balance.

Most economists believe government bears some responsibility for promoting full employment, high productivity, and price stability. They do not always agree on how those goals should be achieved, however, for they base their policies on different theories. We would all be happier if the solutions to macroeconomic problems could be presented in a few pages. Unfortunately, the policy debate is not yet resolved, and probably will not be for some time.

## Major Conclusions

1. Persistent high peacetime inflation is a relatively recent phenomenon in the United States. Though the inflation rate has varied considerably from month to month and year to year, over the last two decades the overall trend has been upward.
2. Since the Second World War, the U.S. economy has operated below capacity much of the time. The gap between actual real GNP and potential real GNP reflects the unusually high rates of unemployment during this period.
3. In the last two decades, policymakers have confronted the problem of stagflation, or high inflation combined with high unemployment. Economists disagree on the causes of stagflation.
4. Economists differ on what should be done about inflation and unemployment. The classical, Keynesian, monetarist, supply-side, and rational expectations schools of thought stress different factors as the primary cause of economic difficulties.

## Questions To Ponder

1. Can you think of a macroeconomic problem not mentioned in this chapter?
2. Look up aggregate business expenditures in the most recent issue of *The Statistical Abstract of the United States*, published by the Department of Commerce. Then graph investment expenditures over the last twenty years. Do the same for the prime interest rate. Do the two measures seem to be related?
3. Find several articles on macroeconomic problems in recent issues of the *Wall Street Journal*. Classify the statements of the economists quoted in those articles by school of thought. Do the articles represent a variety of theories?
4. What actions has the government taken recently to deal with inflation, unemployment, and low productivity? How are those actions supposed to affect the economy?
5. Are there tradeoffs in dealing with inflation, unemployment, and low productivity? If so, explain how the problems may be interrelated.

# Part III

# Money and Monetary Policy

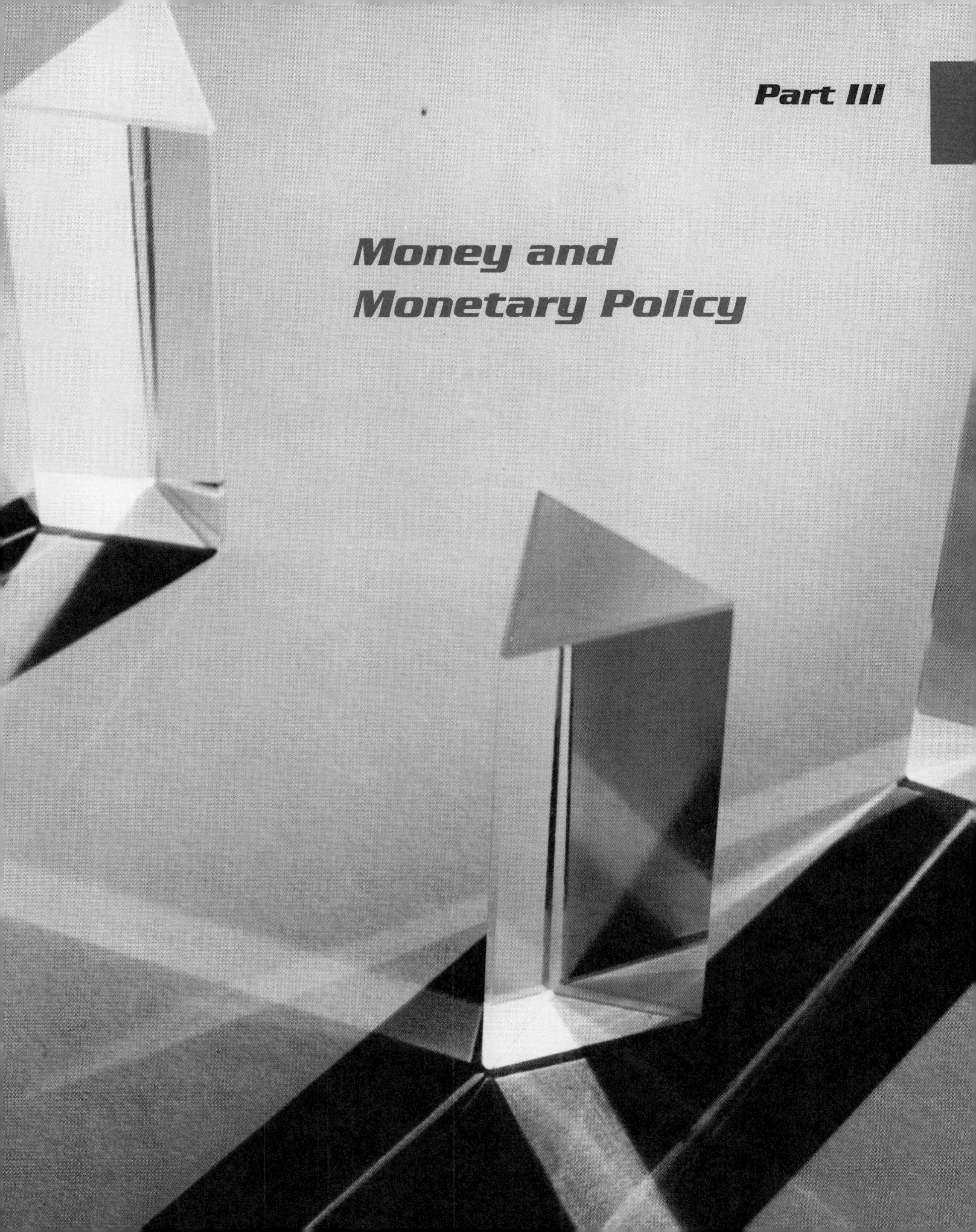

## Central Question

*What is money and how is it created?*

## Key Terms

Liquidity

Transactions demand for money

Precautionary demand for money

Speculative demand for money

Money stock

M1

M2

Full-bodied commodity money

Representative commodity money

Fiat money

Reserves

Reserve deposits

Reserve requirement

Excess reserves

Chapter 7

# The Meaning and Creation of Money

*Money is a contract—the freest, most gorgeous contract of them all. Money is somebody else's promise to pay, to give me what I want, when I want it. What a magnificent conception! . . . Whatever else history may ultimately record of the Western Bourgeoisie, this honor most certainly must be accorded them: They perfected modern money, which is a contract with parties unknown for the future delivery of pleasures undecided upon.*

David Bazelon

**Y**ou may not think the dollar is very valuable, but you are likely to be more concerned about losing one than about losing a plain piece of paper. Have you ever wondered why dollars have value—why, for example, you are willing to buy a wallet to protect them? Do you know how they are created? What form does the money in your bank account take, and what are you actually giving when you hand someone a check? How can banks make loans to some people at the same time others are withdrawing their deposits?

Though superficially there is nothing baffling about money, its effects on the macroeconomy are sufficiently mysterious to occupy the time of a great many economists. (More will be said on that subject in Chapters 8 and 9.)

## The Meaning of Money

Money is a social phenomenon that has taken different forms in different cultures. In the United States, we think of money in terms of dollars. In Great Britain, it is the pound sterling; in France, the franc. At other times and in other places, money has been anything from silver to cigarettes, beads, or seashells. Today in some parts of Tanzania, the monetary unit is the cow or bull, and cattle are used in exchange just as we use dollar bills.

Money can be traded to obtain the things we want or held until we decide we want to use it: that is its essence. Because it is used so widely, however, money also serves as a unit of account. It is, in other words, a kind of common denominator in which the relative values of most other goods and services can be expressed. In all its different forms, money is both a readily acceptable medium of exchange (means of making payment) and a financial asset—a form of savings that represents a store of readily usable purchasing power.

Money is so commonplace in our society that people take for granted the convenience it bestows. As we have stressed before, in a barter economy—one that uses no money—goods trade only for other goods, and people are paid for their labor with the goods they and others produce. In barter, the buyer must find a seller who not only offers the desired goods but also wants the goods the buyer has to trade. For instance, the person who has turkeys to sell and wants pigs must find someone who has pigs to sell and wants turkeys. The person who is paid in corn must trade it to people who are paid in the goods and services he or she wants. Needless to say, barter is a very complicated, time-consuming, and costly way to trade.

When money is used as a medium of exchange, it facilitates trade and contributes to national production. If money is readily accepted by others, people with money need only find the things they want to buy. Those who receive money for what they sell can in turn use money to buy the things they want. The cost (time and effort) of searching for mutually beneficial trades is reduced, and the time saved can be used to produce goods and services.

In this indirect way, money contributes to national production. If money is withdrawn from an economy for some reason, we would expect people to spend much more time consummating trades and much less time producing goods. That is what happened in Germany in the years after both world wars. National output fell dramatically, in part because of the destruction of plant and equipment, but also because the German currency lost its acceptability in trade. When output rose again, it was partially because the government instituted a new, more acceptable currency.

As a store of purchasing power, money gives its owner another kind of convenience, called liquidity. **Liquidity** is the ease with which any asset can be converted into another form, especially into money. The owner of money can quickly and inexpensively convert it into other assets, like furniture, a loaf of bread, or even stock in a corporation. At little or no cost, money can be traded for practically anything else. Other financial assets, such as corporate bonds, cannot be as easily converted. To exchange a bond for a car, the owner must typically sell the bond for money and then use the money to buy the car. The extra transaction takes time, and the seller may have to pay a fee to the agent or brokerage house that sells the bond. A house is even less liquid than a corporate bond; it may take weeks or months to sell.

**Liquidity:** the ease with which any asset can be converted into another form, especially into money.

For money to be a good means of storing purchasing power, its value—that is, how much it will buy—must be reasonably stable. If prices rise rapidly, the purchasing power of stored money will deteriorate rapidly. Instead of holding on to their money, people will use it to buy goods and services, like gold, jewels, and stocks, before its purchasing power deteriorates even further. Conversely if prices fall rapidly, people will want to hold on to more money than usual. They will delay their purchases, hoping to buy things at lower prices.

## The Value of Money

Why does money have value, in the sense that people will accept it in exchange for goods and services? Obviously, dollar bills themselves have no intrinsic value. Dollars in bank accounts cannot have intrinsic value—they are just figures on paper. And though the paper used for dollar bills is tough and relatively expensive, the purchasing power of the dollar is far greater than the value of the paper used.

Furthermore, the dollar's value is not based on some kind of "gold backing"—there is no such thing. Contrary to popular belief, the government no longer holds gold in Fort Knox to back the dollar. Until 1971, the government was required to hold $0.25 in gold for every dollar outstanding. Even then, however, the gold did not determine the value of the money, since $0.25 in gold cannot give a dollar bill a dollar's worth of value.

From an individual standpoint, trading goods for dollars and vice versa is quite sensible. The dollars received can always be traded to someone else. Dollars are valuable simply because people have confidence that others will accept them. The same was true of gold and silver coins when they were used as money. Although silver and gold have always had intrinsic value, in the sense that they can be used for jewelry and dental fittings, they would have been worth much less if they had not been used as money. The reason that they were valued so highly was that people were willing to accept them readily in exchanges.

Although it may seem a little like magic, confidence in its general acceptability is the stuff money is made of. The message printed on a dollar bill—"This note is legal tender for all debts public and private"—gives a dollar some commercial value. But the value of money ultimately depends on an unwritten social agreement that it is valuable. And there are good reasons for demanding money.

## The Demand for Money

**Transactions demand for money:** the desire to hold money balances in order to carry out anticipated purchases of goods and services.

**Precautionary demand for money:** the desire to hold money balances in order to finance unexpected or emergency purchases of goods and services.

**Speculative demand for money:** the desire to hold money balances in anticipation of a decrease in the price of other assets and in anticipation of future profits.

Because of the benefits of using and holding on to money, there is a demand for money, just as there is a demand for other goods. Holding money also involves an opportunity cost: the forgone benefits or return on some other asset not acquired—for example, the furniture one could have purchased or the profits one could have earned by investing in a business. Despite the costs, there are three good reasons for holding on to or demanding money. One is the need for money as a medium of exchange; this is called the transactions demand for money. The **transactions demand for money** is the desire to hold money balances in order to carry out anticipated purchases of goods and services. A second is the need for security; this is called the precautionary demand for money. The **precautionary demand for money** is the desire to hold money balances in order to finance unexpected or emergency purchases of goods and services. A third reason for demanding money is the desire to be able to take advantage of future opportunities; this is called the speculative demand for money. The **speculative demand for money** is the desire to hold money in anticipation of a decrease in the price of other assets and in anticipation of future profits.

The demand for money is influenced by personal income, interest rates, the general price level, and expectations about future prices, as well as other economic variables to be considered later. Specifically:

A rise in people's incomes will generally increase the transactions demand for money. Higher incomes mean more purchases, hence a greater need for money balances to finance those purchases.

A rise in interest rates will raise the opportunity cost of holding on to money, discouraging people from maintaining large money balances for any purpose. People will try to economize on their use of money.

An increase in the price level will increase the demand for money to finance transactions, which now require more dollars.

If people expect prices to rise, they will buy now to avoid higher prices in the future, reducing the money balances they individually seek to hold. If people expect prices to fall, they will hold on to money so as to take advantage of lower prices later.

## The Money Stock

Aside from dollar bills and coins, several other financial assets serve as mediums of exchange and stores of purchasing power. Demand deposits, or money in checking accounts, are highly liquid. So are savings accounts and certificates of deposit, which are like government savings bonds but are issued by banks.

How do economists measure the amount of money that exists in the economy at any point in time? The answer depends on how one defines the money stock. A broad definition is easily given. The **money stock** is the sum of all identified forms of money held by the public (as opposed to the banks) at a given point in time. Actually measuring the money stock is a more complicated problem. How many dollars are there? Which dollars should be counted? These questions are still subject to much debate. Different groups of economists measure the money stock in different ways, and how one calculates the total amount of money in the economy changes with changes in the method of measurement.

**Money stock:** the sum of all identified forms of money held by the public (as opposed to the banks) at a given point in time.

Two measures of the money stock are used widely in economics journals and the financial sections of newspapers and magazines. The better known is M1, which includes cash and checking accounts. **M1** is the total of the public's (as opposed to the banks') holdings of currency (paper bills and coins), demand deposits at commercial banks (bank accounts against which withdrawals can be made on demand, or by check), traveler's checks, and other bank accounts against which checks can be written, such as NOW (negotiable order of withdrawal) and ATS (automatic transfer services) accounts. NOW accounts differ from regular demand deposits in that they earn interest. ATS accounts permit the automatic transfer of funds from savings accounts to checking accounts; this allows depositors to earn interest on the idle money in their checking accounts. If M1 is used as a measure of money, in December 1984 the money stock was $554.5 billion (see Table 7.1). Of that total, $158 billion (28 percent) was held in currency and $391.3 billion (71 percent) in demand deposits and other checkable deposits.

**M1:** the total of the public's (as opposed to the banks') holdings of currency (paper bills and coins), demand deposits at commercial banks, traveler's checks, and other bank accounts against which checks can be written, such as NOW (negotiable order of withdrawal) and ATS (automatic transfer services) accounts.

M2 includes savings as well as cash and checking accounts. **M2** is M1 plus savings accounts and small (less than $100,000) time deposits (bank accounts that generally are not subject to transfer by check, and sometimes not to withdrawal on demand) and certificates of deposit, plus money market accounts and other highly liquid assets. If M2 is used as a measure of money, in December 1984 the money stock was $2,376.3 billion—more than four times the size of M1 (see Table 7.1).

**M2:** M1 plus savings accounts and small (less than $100,000) time deposits and certificates of deposit, plus money market accounts and other highly liquid assets.

M1 and M2 reflect the two basic uses for money. M1 emphasizes the medium-of-exchange role. It consists of only those types of money that are used directly in trade—coin, paper bills, and demand deposits. M2 measures money as a store of purchasing power. When paper bills, coins, and demand deposits are not being actively used in exchange, they are being held as a store of purchasing power. Adding savings accounts, small certificates of deposit, and money market funds to M1 yields a measure of the nation's total store of purchasing power.

# Perspectives in Economics: A Short History of Money

*Dennis Placone*

At various times in history, different forms of money have been used in trade. The very first monies were full-bodied commodity money. A **full-bodied commodity money** is a medium of exchange or store of value that has some intrinsic value as a consumer good or factor of production. In other words, it has some economic use apart from its monetary role. In parts of the ancient Roman Empire, rock salt was used as a form of money. Barley and silver served as monies three hundred years before the birth of Christ; seashells and tobacco, in colonial times in North America. Gold, cattle, woodpecker scalps, corn, and cigarettes have all been used as a medium of exchange.

All these goods were common to the communities or societies that used them. Therefore their market values were generally well known. People would accept such goods in trade, even if they did not have an immediate use for them, because they could always be sold at a known price. And if for some reason a commodity money lost part of its value as a money, it could always be used as a good instead. Barley could be ground into meal; cattle could be butchered; woodpecker scalps could be fashioned into ornaments; cigarettes could be smoked. Gold and silver monies, in particular, gradually became common around the world, because they were more useful, portable, divisible, durable, and recognizable in value than other commodity monies.

Full-bodied commodity monies were generally not created by government. Governments have sometimes attempted to influence or control the value of commodity monies, however. In 1791 the U.S. government sought to establish a bimetallic money standard by buying and selling gold and silver at official fixed prices. The task was not as simple as it had imagined, however. The price of gold was set at 15 times the price of silver, even though the market price of gold was 15.5 times the price of silver. As a result people bought gold from the federal treasury and sold it at a profit on the world market. Because silver was officially undervalued and gold officially overvalued, gold was driven out of circulation in the United States and sent abroad, where it was more highly valued.

Such an outcome was to be expected. People will always attempt to use money that is overvalued, because they expect that its relative market value may fall. They will tend to horde undervalued money, expecting that its value will rise. The U.S. government tried to halt the outflow of gold in 1834 by readjusting the official price to be 16 times the price of silver. But at the new official price, silver was undervalued and gold overvalued. Soon silver was driven out of circulation and replaced by gold.

As economic systems became more complex, new, more convenient forms of money emerged. The transactions costs of using gold and silver were high, because substantial resources had to be invested to mine and protect them. To cut those costs, banks developed representative commodity monies. **Representative commodity monies** are certificates or notes that can be converted into given quantities of a specific commodity, like gold or silver. Banks found that people would accept such notes in the belief that they could be redeemed for the gold banks held in their vaults. At first banks backed the notes fully, holding a dollar's worth of gold for every dollar note outstanding. But banks soon found they could issue notes for more than the value of the gold in their vaults. People would continue to circulate the notes in trade, confident they could be redeemed when desired.

So long as people felt secure in using notes as money, the representative commodity monetary system worked. But problems eventually emerged. From 1834 to 1860, over sixteen hundred state-chartered banks, most of them largely unregulated, issued notes. Many banks issued so many notes that they could not always redeem them at full face value. Runs on banks, in which panicked noteholders attempted to cash in their notes for gold, became common. Some banks collapsed when they could not redeem all the notes presented to them. Counterfeiting sometimes provoked a run on a bank. Because each of the sixteen hundred banks issued notes of its own design, the average trader could not always tell a counterfeit or worthless note from a genuine one. Counterfeit bills increased the information cost of using notes and reduced their general acceptance.

Because of these difficulties, governments began to issue paper money. In the United States, the federal treasury issued gold and silver certificates that could be redeemed for metal coin, and "greenbacks"—unbacked paper currency issued to finance the Civil War. The general acceptance of these monies was encouraged by the treasury's willingness to accept them in payment of taxes and by the requirement that creditors accept them in payment of debt. (If creditors refused to accept greenbacks and gold and silver certificates as payment, debtors were legally absolved of their obligations.)

When the Federal Reserve System was established in 1913, private bank notes became illegal and were replaced by Federal Reserve Notes, the paper money we use today. At first Fed notes were backed by a government pledge to redeem the notes in gold and silver. The number of notes in circulation was determined partly by the amount of gold held by the government. These notes were considered so sound by foreigners that they tended to be in short supply in the United States. To increase the money stock and raise prices, President Franklin Roosevelt took the United States off the gold standard in 1933. Roosevelt declared that dollars would no longer be redeemed in gold at the Treasury or the Federal Reserve. Indeed, he outlawed private hoarding of gold and required people who held it to sell it to the government for $22.50 an ounce. (Later the price of gold was set officially at $35 an ounce.) In 1968 Congress revoked the Fed's obligation to redeem silver certificates in silver.

The U.S. monetary system is now based entirely on inconvertible paper currency, or fiat money. **Fiat money** is a medium of exchange or store of value that cannot be redeemed for anything other than a replica of itself. A fiat dollar can be exchanged only for another dollar. The general acceptability of fiat money does not depend on either its intrinsic market value (as was the case with corn), or its redemption value (as was the case with silver certificates). It depends entirely on people's confidence in its continued usefulness in trade.

**Table 7.1.** Two Measures of the Money Stock, December 1984 (in billions of dollars)

| | M1 | M2 |
|---|---|---|
| Currency (paper bills and coins) | $158.0 | $ 158.0 |
| Travelers checks | 5.2 | 5.2 |
| Demand deposits | 248.3 | 248.3 |
| Other checkable deposits | 143.0 | 143.0 |
| Overnight repurchase agreements net plus overnight Eurodollars | | 57.6 |
| Money market mutual fund balances | | 168.1 |
| Money market deposit accounts | | 410.0 |
| Savings accounts | | 294.3 |
| Small denomination time deposits | | 897.1 |
| Totals | $554.5 | $2,376.3 |

**Source:** *Economic Report of the President* (Washington, D.C.: U.S. Government Printing Office, 1985), p. 303.

Measurements of the money stock are extremely interesting to economists studying how the size of the money stock affects prices, national production, and unemployment. (In following chapters we will develop that subject in detail.) The particular measure an economist uses in statistical studies of these questions depends in part on his or her perception of money. Those who view money as something that is held, as opposed to something that is traded, will use M2 in their studies. Those who view money primarily as a medium of trade will use M1.

## The Banking System

Demand deposits are an important part of M1 and time deposits an important part of M2. Both kinds of accounts are held at banks, which are an integral part of the monetary system. Broadly speaking, the U.S. banking system may be divided into depository institutions (local commercial banks and savings and loan associations) and the Federal Reserve System, a national institution.

### Depository Institutions

Depository institutions are privately owned businesses. They hold deposits and checking and savings accounts for individuals and firms. They also make loans in return for interest payments on the amount of the loan.

Before 1981 banks could be categorized according to the types of deposits they received. Only commercial banks were permitted to accept demand deposits, funds that could be withdrawn "on demand," or without notice, by way of checks. Government regulation prohibited the payment of interest on demand deposits. Commercial banks also held some savings accounts, or time deposits, on which they paid a modest interest rate. Savings institutions (savings and loan associations, credit unions, and savings banks) concentrated on time deposits, on which they were allowed to pay a slightly higher interest rate than commercial banks.

These distinctions were obliterated by the Depository Institutions Deregulation and Monetary Control Act of 1980. Savings institutions can now carry what amount to checking accounts. All institutions can now pay interest on accounts with checking privileges. The act was intended to increase competition among banks by giving them greater flexibility.

Before 1981 banks came under the regulatory control of either a state banking commission or the Federal Reserve System, which is in effect the central bank of the United States. In 1980 only the largest banks, about 35 percent of the nation's thirteen thousand banks, belonged to the Federal Reserve System. Those member banks held about 80 percent of all demand deposits. As of 1981, however, all depository institutions—commercial banks, savings banks, savings and loan associations, and credit unions—became subject to partial control by the Federal Reserve System. To understand how banks operate, then, and how the money stock is controlled, we must examine the structure and powers of the Federal Reserve System.

## The Federal Reserve System

The Federal Reserve System, created by an act of Congress in 1913, is made up of twelve Federal Reserve District Banks scattered throughout the nation. Figure 7.1 shows the geographical areas covered by the district banks. The Far West, for example, is served by the Federal Reserve Bank of San Francisco (district 12), which covers Alaska, Hawaii, Washington, Oregon, California, Idaho, Nevada, Utah, and most of Arizona. Each district bank has one or more branch offices.

The Federal Reserve System is headed by a seven-member Board of Governors. Each governor is nominated by the president of the United States and confirmed by the Senate for a term of fourteen years. The Chairman of the Board of Governors, like the chairperson of any collective organization, has limited powers, restricted to persuasion and administration. Nevertheless he is one of the most influential people in the nation when it comes to determining economic policy.

At the district level, each Reserve Bank has a president and is supervised by a board of directors made up of representatives from the district. Each district bank board submits nominations for president of its district bank to the Fed's Board of Governors. The Board of Governors then appoints the twelve district bank presidents.

The primary function of the Federal Reserve System is to establish and conduct the nation's monetary policy. As discussed in Chapter 4, monetary policy is the manipulation of the rate of growth of the nation's money stock to promote a high and stable level of employment and production. More specifically, monetary policy is the management of the growth rate

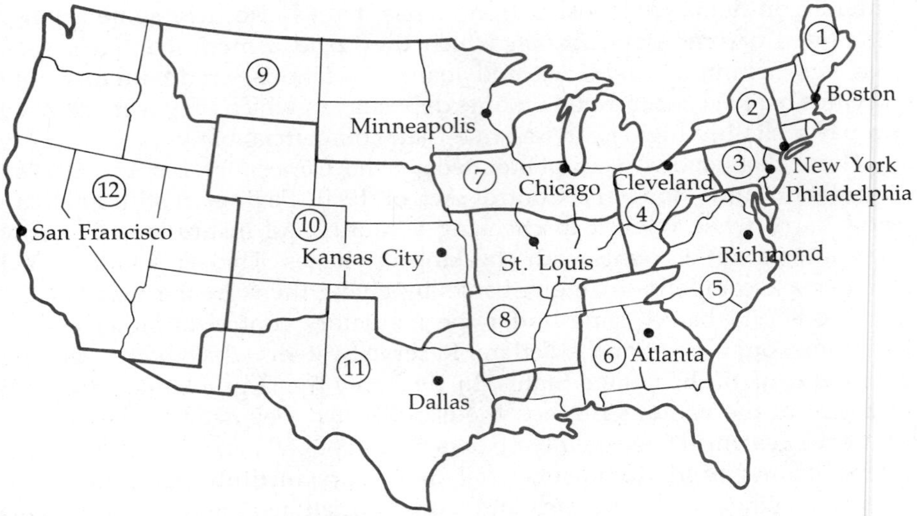


**Figure 7.1.** Federal Reserve District Banks.
The Federal Reserve System has twelve District Banks throughout the nation. Each Reserve Bank supervises the banks in its district. District Reserve Banks also hold reserve deposits for member banks, provide them with currency, and lend them money when necessary. The headquarters of the Federal Reserve System is in Washington, D.C.

of M1 or M2. Major monetary policy decisions are made by the Board of Governors and a group called the Federal Open Market Committee. The committee meets on the third Tuesday of every month to review the Fed's monetary policy. Members study the latest figures on GNP, unemployment, and consumer and wholesale prices before determining whether to increase or decrease the money stock, by how much, and by what action. Most decisions are implemented by ordering the purchase or sale of government bonds on the open bond market, actions that result in a change in the money stock.

**Reserves:** the cash a bank has in its vault plus its deposits at the Federal Reserve Bank.

**Reserve deposits:** the accounts that banks hold in Federal Reserve Banks. (A bank's reserve deposit balance plus its vault cash equals its total reserves.)

The Federal Reserve System also serves as the central bank of the United States, a banker's bank that offers banks many of the same services that banks provide to their customers. When banks get deposits from their customers, they are entitled to claim an equal amount of reserves at the Fed. **Reserves** are the cash a bank has in its vault plus its deposits at the Federal Reserve Bank. As explained in detail on pages 157–158, reserves rise and fall with a bank's deposits. When banks gain customer deposits, their reserves rise, and vice versa. Reserves also change with loans to a bank's customers. They fall when the bank makes a loan, and they rise when the loan is repaid. The Federal Reserve System manages the reserve deposits for banks in its jurisdiction. **Reserve deposits** are the accounts that banks hold in Federal Reserve Banks. (A bank's reserve deposit balance plus its vault cash equals its total reserves.)

Reserve Banks also make loans to all depository institutions and provide currency when needed. For instance, if a bank needs more currency to meet daily withdrawals, the manager can call the district Reserve Bank or one of its branch offices and order more. The bank pays for the currency with a reduction in its reserves. (The switch of funds from reserves to currency does not by itself reduce total bank reserves, since both currency and reserve deposits count as reserves. Bank reserves are reduced, however, when more cash is taken out of the bank than is deposited.) Like some large commercial banks, the Federal Reserve Banks also provide check-clearing services for banks. They collect, sort, and distribute checks to their banks of origin.

## Checks and the Transfer of Money

When you write a check to your sister you know that eventually your bank balance will fall and hers will rise. But how does your money move from one bank to another? Actually nothing tangible ever moves. The figures on the banks' books are simply adjusted to account for your check.

To see how the process works, we must look at some simplified bank records called T accounts (so called because they look like a large T). Each side of the T represents one half of an accounting statement, or balance sheet, listing the bank's assets and liabilities (see Figure 7.2). The assets half includes all properties the bank owns. The liability half includes all claims that nonowners have against the bank. Assets are recorded on the left-hand side of the T, liabilities on the right-hand side. As the name balance sheet implies, the two sides of the T must balance. According to standard bookkeeping technique, an equal asset exists for every liability.[1]

Suppose you write a check for $10 to your university bookstore. Figure 7.2 shows the bookkeeping entries that will result. When the bookstore deposits your check, its demand deposits go up. Since the bookstore's checking account represents a legal claim that the bookstore has against its bank, First and Merchants National Bank, we classify the increase in the bookstore's deposits as a liability of First and Merchants. Thus we enter $10 in the name of the bookstore on the right-hand side of First and Merchants' balance sheet. This is entry *a*.

How does First and Merchants collect the money it has just received from your university's bookstore? The simplest is to send your check to the Federal Reserve. At the Fed, First and Merchants' reserve deposit rises (entry *b*), and the reserve deposit of your bank, Northwestern National, falls (entry *c*). But while First and Merchants' reserve deposit is a liability to the Fed, it is an asset to First and Merchants. Thus the check you wrote to the bookstore also results in a $10 increase in the assets column of First and Merchants' own bookkeeping records (entry *d*).

---

1. Actually, the balance sheet also includes an additional set of entries, called capital accounts, which represent the claims of the owners against the assets.

**First and Merchants National Bank**

| *Assets* | *Liabilities* |
|---|---|
| Reserve deposits:<br>+ $10<br>(entry *d*) | University bookstore's demand deposit<br>+ $10<br>(entry *a*) |

**Federal Reserve Bank**

| *Assets* | *Liabilities* |
|---|---|
| | First and Merchants reserve deposit<br>+ $10<br>(entry *b*)<br>Northwestern National reserve deposit<br>− $10<br>(entry *c*) |

**Northwestern National Bank**

| *Assets* | *Liabilities* |
|---|---|
| Reserve deposits:<br>− $10<br>(entry *f*) | Your demand deposit<br>− $10<br>(entry *e*) |

**Figure 7.2.** Money Transfers in T Accounts.
If you write a check on your Northwestern National Bank account to your university bookstore, your demand deposit at Northwestern (bottom) will fall by the amount of the check. At the same time the bookstore's demand deposit at First and Merchants (top) will rise by the same amount. Northwestern's reserve deposit at the Federal Reserve will fall, while First and Merchants' reserve deposit will increase.

Once the appropriate entries are made on the Fed's accounting records, your check is returned to your bank. Only when the check reaches your bank, perhaps three or four days after you wrote it, is your checking account balance reduced (entry *e* on Northwestern's balance sheet). Because your bank's reserve deposit with the Fed is down by $10 (entry *c*), Northwestern National must also deduct $10 from its own assets (entry *f*).

Several points should be made about these transactions.

1. The check causes your bank balance to fall and the bookstore's bank balance to rise (entries *e* and *a*).
2. The check causes an adjustment in the Fed's reserve deposits. Your bank's reserve deposit goes down; the other bank's reserve deposit goes up (entries *c* and *b*).

3. The Fed's reserve deposits are not the same as the deposits you and your bookstore maintain at your local banks. They are bookkeeping entries based on the demand deposits of member banks. Thus reserve deposits are not money. They are not used directly in trade, as demand deposits are.
4. Reserve deposits are assets to the member banks that maintain them (that point will become clearer in the next section). Thus any check you write causes your bank's assets at the Fed to fall, and the assets of another bank to rise (entries *f* and *d*). (This statement assumes that the person who writes the check and the person who receives it maintain accounts in different banks. If the two parties have accounts with the same bank, one person's deposit will go up and the other's down, but the bank's assets at the Fed will remain the same.)
5. Most important, when anyone writes a check, the nation's money stock does not change. Money is simply moved from one account to another.

## The Creation of Money

When gold was used as a medium of exchange, the creation of money was much like the production of jewelry. Gold ore was mined from the ground and smelted, and the pure metal was molded into coins. How much money was created depended primarily on the amount of gold in the ground and the cost of getting it out. Today, in industrial nations like the United States, money is created principally through the commercial banking system. Banks create money; they create it every time they make a loan.

How is it done? Simply lending out someone else's money would amount to transferring money already in existence from one person to another. When banks create money it is by writing checks to, or increasing the deposits of, borrowers. Suppose you have negotiated a $5,000 car loan with Northwestern National Bank. You sign the necessary papers and the bank gives you a check to deliver to the car dealer. When the dealer deposits the check, money is created.

It is money's general acceptability in trade that enables your bank to create money out of thin air, as it were. So long as the car dealer is willing to accept the bank's check, and other people are willing to accept the checks the dealer writes, something has been created that has general acceptability: money.

### The Reserve Requirement

Banks are not allowed to create unlimited amounts of money. Legally, the amount of money a bank can create depends on the level of its customer deposits. The more customer deposits it has, the more money it can lend and the more money it can create.

**Reserve requirement:** the portion of a bank's reserves that cannot be used to create money.

**Excess reserves:** the amount of a bank's reserves equal to the total reserves minus the required reserves.

The money-creating capability of banks is further restricted by the Federal Reserve. When a bank receives a customer's deposit, its reserve deposit with the Federal Reserve Bank increases. When you ask for a loan, your bank writes its check against this reserve account, and its reserve deposit decreases. The bank cannot write checks indefinitely against its reserve deposit, however. It must maintain a minimum deposit, called the reserve requirement. The **reserve requirement** is that portion of a bank's reserves which cannot be used to create money.

The reserve requirement is expressed as a percentage of the bank's total demand deposits. For example, if the reserve requirement is 15 percent, the bank must maintain a reserve deposit equal to at least 15 percent of its demand deposits. That is, through loans the bank can create money equal to 85 percent of its demand deposits. Thus the amount of money a bank can create depends on its excess reserves. **Excess reserves** are the amount over what the bank is required to hold, or:

$$\text{excess reserves} = \text{total reserves} - \text{required reserves.}$$

A bank's excess reserves depend on the reserve requirement, as shown in the table below. A decline in the reserve requirement increases a bank's excess reserves and money-creating capability. When the reserve requirement goes up, excess reserves and money-creating capabilities go down.

| Reserve Requirement (percentage) | Loans Can Be Equal to: (percentage of demand deposits) |
|---|---|
| 10 | 90 |
| 15 | 85 |
| 17 | 83 |
| 20 | 80 |

A bank with a total demand deposit of $10 million and a reserve requirement of 10 percent can make loans of up to $9 million (90 percent of $10 million). If the reserve requirement is 17 percent, the bank can make loans of only $8.3 million (83 percent of $10 million).

Many students have the impression that the reserve requirement is a means of ensuring that banks have some money on hand to meet the public's withdrawals. Actually, however, the reserve requirement is not intended to serve that purpose or to maintain the financial soundness of the banking system. The purpose of the reserve requirement is simply to restrict the amount of money that banks can create. If banks want security against customer withdrawals, they must maintain reserves above and beyond their required reserves, which are bookkeeping entries only. Banks do not really lend out other people's money when they make loans. Though reserve deposits are calculated on the basis of a bank's demand deposits, they are not the same thing. If they were, banks would not be able to create money. Loans would merely transfer money from depositor to borrower.

## The Multiple Effects of Loans

So far we have considered only the immediate effects of creating money by loan. But the process extends beyond the addition of a specific amount of money to the economy in the form of a loan check. Assume Bank A has total customer deposits of $10 million and a reserve deposit of an equal amount. Its accounts and those of the Federal Reserve are shown in Step I of Figure 7.3. Assume also that the reserve requirement is 20 percent. Bank A can therefore lend against 80 percent of its $10 million in reserves, or as much as $8 million. Bank A decides to lend all $8 million to a local firm that needs new equipment. The firm buys the equipment, handing over Bank A's check to the supplier, who deposits it at Bank B.

**Figure 7.3.** The Creation of Money Through the Banking System.
In Step I, assuming a reserve requirement of 20 percent, Bank A has excess reserves equal to $8 million. In Step II, a loan of $8 million from Bank A ends up as a deposit in Bank B. Bank A's loan also shifts reserves from Bank A to Bank B at the Federal Reserve Bank. In Step III, Bank B can now make a loan for as much as $6.4 million (again, assuming a 20 percent reserve requirement). Bank B's loan ends up as a deposit in Bank C and shifts $6.4 million in reserves from Bank B to Bank C at the Fed. Bank C now has excess reserves equal to $5.1 million that it can loan. This money expansion process can continue as long as excess reserves exist. The maximum addition to the money stock from Bank A's initial $8 million loan would be $40 million.

**Step I**

**Bank A**

| *Assets* | *Liabilities* |
|---|---|
| Reserve deposits:<br>$10 million | Total deposits:<br>$10 million |

**Federal Reserve Bank**

| *Assets* | *Liabilities* |
|---|---|
| | Reserve deposit of Bank A:<br>$10 million |

**Step II**

**Bank A**

| *Assets* | *Liabilities* |
|---|---|
| Reserve deposits:<br>$2 million<br>(entry *e*)<br>Loans:<br>$8 million<br>(entry *d*) | Total deposits:<br>$10 million |

**Bank B**

| *Assets* | *Liabilities* |
|---|---|
| Reserve deposits:<br>$8 million<br>(entry *f*) | Total deposits:<br>+ $8 million<br>(entry *a*) |

**Federal Reserve Bank**

| *Assets* | *Liabilities* |
|---|---|
| | Reserve deposit of Bank A:<br>$2 million (entry *c*)<br>Reserve deposit of Bank B:<br>+ $8 million (entry *b*) |

**Figure 7.3.** *Continued*

**Step III**

**Bank A**

| *Assets* | *Liabilities* |
|---|---|
| Reserve deposits: $2 million<br>Loans: $8 million | Total demand deposits: $10 million |

**Bank B**

| *Assets* | *Liabilities* |
|---|---|
| Reserve deposits: $1.6 million (entry *h*)<br>Loans: $8.4 million (entry *j*) | Total demand deposits: − $8 million |

**Bank C**

| *Assets* | *Liabilities* |
|---|---|
| Reserve deposits: $8.4 million (entry *l*) | Total demand deposits: $8.4 million (entry *e*) |

**Federal Reserve Bank**

| *Assets* | *Liabilities* |
|---|---|
| | Reserve deposit of Bank A: $2 million<br>Reserve deposit of Bank B: $1.6 million (entry *i*)<br>Reserve deposit of Bank C: $8.4 million (entry *k*) |

Bank A's check increases Bank B's total customer deposits, a change shown on Bank B's balance sheet in Step II of Figure 7.3. Bank B's reserve deposit increases by $8 million, a change recorded in the Fed's liability column (entry *b*). At the same time, Bank A's reserve deposit falls from $10 million (Step I) to $2 million (Step II, entry *c*).

Bank A's assets are still worth $10 million, but they are rearranged because of the loan. Total loan assets increase by $8 million (entry *d*), and the reserve deposit decreases to $2 million (entry *e*). Bank B records in its own assets column the $8 million increase in its reserve deposit (entry *f*).

Total demand deposits rise from $10 million in Step I to $18 million in Step II ($10 million of demand deposits in Bank A plus $8 million in Bank B). In other words, the total money stock has increased. This is the reason we say that banks create money when they extend loans.

The money-creating process does not stop with the increases in Bank B's balance sheet. With its newly acquired reserves of $8 million, Bank B can also create money through a loan. It can lend against 80 percent of its additional reserves, or up to $6.4 million. Bank B's loan ends up as a deposit in Bank C, as shown in Step III (entry *g*). Bank B's reserve deposit decreases by $6.4 million to $1.6 million, both in its own records and in the Federal Reserve's (entries *h* and *i*). Bank B's loan account rises by $6.4 million (entry *j*). Finally, Bank C's reserve deposit increases by $6.4 million, both in its own records and in the Federal Reserve's (entries *k* and *l*). As a result of Bank B's loan, total demand deposits in the banking system rise to $24.4 million ($10 million in Bank A plus $8 million in Bank B plus $6.4 million in Bank C). Again the money stock has increased because of a bank loan.

Bank C can now extend loans based on its newly acquired demand and reserve deposits. Like Banks A and B, Bank C can lend against 80 percent of its reserve. As Bank C and successive banks extend new loans up to the legal maximum, the money stock continues to expand. It will not rise indefinitely, however. Each new loan is smaller than the one before it; each adds less to the money stock. Given the reserve requirement of 20 percent and initial excess reserves of $8 million, we can determine the maximum increase in the money stock through a simple formula:

$$= \text{Bank A's excess reserves} \times \frac{1}{\text{reserve requirement}}$$

$$= \$8 \text{ million} \times \frac{1}{0.20} = \$40 \text{ million}$$

Theoretically, once all banks have extended their loans to the legal maximum, the money stock cannot expand further without a change in total reserves or the reserve requirement. In Chapter 8 we will see how the Federal Reserve can change the total reserves and reserve requirement to increase or decrease the money stock.

## Fluctuations in the Money Stock

The foregoing description of the creation of money was based on several assumptions made to simplify the analysis. Money creation does not actually proceed as smoothly as this theoretical model suggests. Day-to-day changes in business conditions cause temporary fluctuations in the money stock. For instance, banks are continually receiving payments on loans. Because they earn their income from such arrangements, they will attempt to relend the payments they receive as quickly as possible. (Banks often loan their excess reserves to other banks for periods as short as a day or less.) But a bank's loan payments do not always match its loan requests; at times they exceed requests. At such times, a bank will have excess reserves. Because it has not made as many loans as possible, it will not have created as much money as it can create. If all banks have problems of this kind, the total money stock will not be as great as it could be.

Moreover, not all bank loans end up as demand deposits in other banks. Part of the money created by banks may end up as currency held in the pockets of the public. Although currency is money, it is not the kind of money that permits banks to claim reserve deposits—not, therefore, the kind of money on which additional loans can be made. To the extent that bank loans end up as currency, the ability of banks to expand loans and increase the money stock is reduced.

For instance, suppose the firm that received the $8 million check from Bank A deposited only $7.5 million in Bank B, taking $500,000 in currency. Bank B would then have been able to lend only $6 million (80 percent of $7.5 million) instead of $6.4 million. Bank C would have received this smaller deposit and would have been able to lend less to Bank D. The total increase in the money supply would have been only $37.5 million instead of $40 million.

Finally, the public's willingness to hold money in the form of both currency and demand deposits will influence the overall level of the money stock. If the public reduces its demand deposits and increases its currency holdings, banks will have lower reserves and will not be able to make as many loans. Unless there are compensating changes (to be discussed in the next chapter), the money stock will fall. Similarly, if the public reduces its currency holdings by depositing currency in its demand accounts, bank reserves will rise. Banks will increase their loans, thereby increasing the money stock.

## Summary and Extensions

Money is a medium of exchange that facilitates trade. In the form of currency and financial assets that can be stored or used to buy goods and services, money is productive. It reduces the time people must spend searching out mutually beneficial trades and increases the time they can spend producing goods and services. Currency, demand deposits, and savings deposits also provide liquidity, or ease of conversion into other assets.

Holding money involves costs as well as benefits. When people hold money, they forgo the goods and services that money could buy. People will not hold money unless the benefits of doing so are at least equal to the benefits of the goods and services it could buy.

Paper money and checks have value simply because they are used as money. People are willing to accept and hold them because they are confident that others will do so. For this reason, modern money is relatively easy to produce. The amount of money that can be created is not limited, for example, by the amount of gold beneath the earth's crust. It is figuratively created with the stroke of a pen, by governments, commercial banks, and the Federal Reserve System.

Government may be tempted to use its money-creating authority to produce money too fast. In recent history, many governments have succumbed to the impulse to inflate the money stock, and the result has been a continuing increase in price levels—that is, inflation—sometimes of runaway proportions. One of the most pressing problems of monetary economies is the question of how to control the money stock wisely. It is no simple problem, as we will see in the next two chapters.

## Major Conclusions

1. Money is a medium of exchange and a store of purchasing power.
2. Money does not have value because of a backing in gold, but because of people's confidence in its general acceptability.
3. People hold money balances to finance transactions (the transactions

demand for money); to cover unexpected expenditures (the precautionary demand); and to take advantage of anticipated increases in interest rates (the speculative demand).
4. The two most widely used measures of the money stock in the United States are M1 and M2. M1 includes currency and demand deposits. M2 includes M1 plus savings account deposits at commercial banks and small certificates of deposit.
5. The Federal Reserve System is composed of twelve district banks and is headed by a Board of Governors, which is responsible primarily for the conduct of the nation's monetary policy.
6. When one person writes a check to another, the demand deposit of the person who receives the check increases, while the deposit of the person writing the check decreases. The bank that pays the check loses reserve deposits, and the bank that receives the check gains reserve deposits. The total stock of money remains the same, however.
7. When banks make loans, they create money.
8. A bank's ability to create money is restricted by its excess reserves and the reserve requirement.
9. The maximum amount of money that can be created equals the excess reserves in the system times the reciprocal of the reserve requirement (that is, one divided by the reserve requirement).
10. The money stock tends to fluctuate because of unevenness in the granting and repayment of bank loans and changes in the amount of currency held by the public.

## Questions to Ponder

1. Suppose you head the government in a nation involved in an unpopular war. You can pay for the war by increasing taxes or by printing more money. Which option would you take? What would be the consequences of your action?
2. Dollar bills are elaborately engraved to prevent counterfeiting. Why? If dollar bills could be easily duplicated, what would happen to the money stock? To the nation's production and price levels? To the value of the dollar?
3. Do S&H Green Stamps qualify as money? Why?
4. Suppose you receive a $15 check from a friend who has an account at another bank. You deposit the check in your account. Using T accounts, sketch the entries that will be made on the books of your bank, your friend's bank, and the Federal Reserve Bank. What happens to the money stock because of the transaction? What happens to the ability of the two banks to make loans?
5. Suppose that your bank has total demand deposits of $20 million; that the reserve requirement is 10 percent; and that the bank has already made loans worth $5 million. How much more money can your bank lend to those who want to borrow?
6. If the reserve requirement is 100 percent, will banks be able to make loans? Will they be willing to handle the public's demand deposits?

## Central Question

*How does the Federal Reserve control the money stock?*

## Key Terms

Discount rate

Open market operations

Equation of exchange

Velocity of money

Chapter 8

# The Federal Reserve and the Money Stock

*Do changes in the quantity of money matter? . . . There is massive historical evidence that they do. Every economic recession but one in the U.S. in the past century has been preceded by a decline in the rate of growth of the quantity of money. And the sharper the decline, the more serious the subsequent recession—though this tendency is far from uniform.*

*Milton Friedman*

As the last chapter discussed, the amount of money banks can create depends on their reserves and the reserve requirement. This chapter describes how the Federal Reserve uses its powers to change the total reserves and the reserve requirement to control the money stock.

The Federal Reserve cannot control the money stock with precision. Its controls resemble the farmer's controls over crop size. The farmer who uses specific quantities of seed and fertilizer has a rough idea of how large his harvest will be. But because natural forces like the weather can change suddenly, the farmer can never be quite sure of the size of the harvest. Similarly, because of the many forces constantly interacting in the national economy, the governors of the Federal Reserve cannot always be sure exactly what will happen to the money stock when they employ one of the Fed's monetary controls. They know the approximate range within which change may occur, and the general direction the change should take, but no more.

## Control of the Money Stock

The Federal Reserve exercises control over the money stock in three ways: (1) through the reserve requirement; (2) through loans to commercial banks; and (3) through the purchase or sale of government securities, mainly three-month bills and notes issued by the U.S. Treasury.

### The Reserve Requirement

The reserve requirement is the portion of a bank's total reserves that cannot be used to create money through loans. It is expressed as a percentage of the bank's demand deposits (from which reserves are generated). That is, the bank's reserves, which include both its deposits at the Fed and the currency in its vault, can drop no lower than the specific percentage of its demand deposits.

Actually, the reserve requirement is not a single figure, but a set of figures that apply to different levels of demand deposits. Table 8.1 shows the reserve requirements on demand deposits as of March 1985. Banks were required to hold 7 percent of their first $2 million in demand deposits in required reserves; 9.5 percent of the next $8 million; and so on. Thus any bank with $350 million in demand deposits was required to hold minimum reserves of $43.35 million.[1] The average reserve requirement for such banks was 12.4 percent of demand deposits ($43.35 ÷ $350).

1. This figure is calculated by multiplying the first $2 million in demand deposits times 7%, the next $8 million by 9.5%, the next $90 million by 11.75%, and the next $250 million by 12.75%, and then adding the products.

**Table 8.1.** Reserve Requirement of Depository Institutions, March 1985[a]

| Demand Deposits | Reserve Requirement (%)[b] |
|---|---|
| $0–$2 million | 7.00 |
| $2–$10 million | 9.50 |
| $10–$100 million | 11.75 |
| $100–$400 million | 12.75 |
| Over $400 million | 16.25 |

[a] Depository institutions include commercial banks, mutual savings banks, savings and loan associations, credit unions, and agencies and branches of foreign banks.
[b] The reserve requirements became effective December 30, 1976.
**Source:** *Federal Reserve Bulletin* (March 1985), p. A7.

The general effect of a change in the reserve requirement is fairly simple. Suppose banks have loaned all the money they can, given the reserve requirement. If the requirement is reduced, they will be able to make more loans. As they do, the money stock will rise. The additional loans will end up as negotiable bank deposits or currency (see Chapter 7), which will supplement the existing money supply.

If the reserve requirement is increased, banks will have to increase their reserves. They will therefore make fewer loans. If banks cannot relend the money they gain when people repay their loans, the money stock must fall. Eventually the ratio of reserves to demand deposits will rise to the new required level.

Though we know that a decrease in the reserve requirement tends to increase the money stock, and vice versa, it is difficult to calculate when or how much the money stock will change. If the Fed lowers the reserve requirement, banks may not expand their loans immediately. Unfavorable business conditions may lead them to hold excess reserves. For instance, suppose banks expect interest rates to rise in the very near future. Instead of increasing their loans immediately, at relatively low interest rates, many banks may wait. Conversely, if the Fed increases the reserve requirement, some banks may not have to contract their loans immediately if they already have on hand all the reserves they need.

At different times, confronted with different market forces, the banking system will respond differently to a change in the reserve requirement. Sophisticated statistical procedures (called econometric model building) can increase the accuracy of the Fed's predictions. But even those methods are not always reliable. If a change in reserve requirements fails to produce the desired effect, the Fed may have to take corrective measures. Because a very small change in the reserve requirement can result in large changes in the money stock, and because banks have difficulty responding to changes in the reserve requirement, the Fed makes such changes infrequently—rarely more than once a year.

| Northwestern National Bank | | Federal Reserve Bank of San Francisco | |
|---|---|---|---|
| *Assets* | *Liabilities* | *Assets* | *Liabilities* |
| Reserve deposits: + $1 million (entry *c*) | Loan from Federal Reserve + $1 million (entry *a*) | Loans to member bank + $1 million (entry *b*) | Reserve deposit of Northwestern + $1 million (entry *d*) |

**Figure 8.1.** Federal Reserve Loan to a Member Bank.
A Federal Reserve loan to Northwestern National Bank increases Northwestern's reserve deposit. Northwestern can use its new reserves to make loans to its customers, which will ultimately increase the money stock.

## Loans to Member Banks

The Federal Reserve can increase or stabilize the money stock through loans to member banks. Just as individuals and business firms borrow from commercial banks, a commercial bank can borrow from the Federal Reserve Bank that serves its region. In return for its IOU, the bank receives an increase in its reserve deposit. This type of transaction is illustrated in Figure 8.1. Suppose Northwestern National Bank wants to borrow $1 million in reserves from the Federal Reserve Bank of San Francisco. Northwestern commits itself to paying the loan back and receives a $1 million increase in its reserves. The loan is listed as a liability on Northwestern's books (entry *a*) and, because interest is collected on it, as an asset on the Federal Reserve Bank's books (entry *b*). The $1 million reserve deposit that Northwestern acquires is an asset to it (entry *c*) and a liability to the Federal Reserve (entry *d*).

Northwestern can use its reserves either to make interest-bearing loans to the public or to ensure that it meets the reserve requirement. If it makes loans, they will increase the money stock. If it uses the new reserves to meet its reserve requirement, it will not have to reduce its outstanding loans, which would contract the money stock. For example, suppose Northwestern's demand deposits are $10 million and its reserves $1 million. If the reserve requirement is 20 percent, Northwestern has $1 million less than it needs to meet the requirement. It could get the extra reserves by reducing its outstanding loans, but that procedure would reduce the money stock. If it borrows $1 million in reserves from the Fed, Northwestern will not have to reduce its loans, and the money stock will not be reduced.

Banks borrow from the Fed for very short periods of time, usually a matter of days. When they pay back their loans, they reduce their reserves, and thus their ability to create money. Usually some banks are borrowing from the Fed while others are repaying their loans, so the total effect of such loans is to increase the money-creating potential of banks. Until late 1984, loans from the Fed hovered around $1 billion. For reasons that were not immediately clear, Fed loans shot up to $8 billion in early 1985. Even then, they amounted to less than 4 percent of total reserves.

Where does the Fed get the reserves that it loans to commercial banks? It creates them. The Fed simply accepts the bank's IOU and increases its reserve deposits, which are only bookkeeping entries.

The Fed can control the number and amount of the loans it grants in two ways. It can refuse to grant a loan (borrowing from the Fed is considered a privilege, not a right). It can also control the level of its lending by changing the interest rate it charges—the so-called discount rate. The **discount rate** is the interest rate the Federal Reserve charges on loans to member banks. A decrease in the discount rate will encourage banks to borrow, because it makes loans less costly. An increase in the discount rate will make loans more costly, discouraging borrowing.

**Discount rate:** the interest rate the Federal Reserve charges on loans to member banks.

In practice, changing the discount rate is not an important tool for controlling the money stock, for the number of loans the Fed makes to member banks is not an especially influential factor. But economists and financial analysts for major banks and brokerage firms often view changes in the discount rate as a signal that the Fed plans to take other actions that will significantly change bank reserves—open market operations, for example. In late 1984, two reductions in the discount rate were taken as signals that the Fed intended to increase the growth rate of the money stock.

## Open Market Operations

By far the most important of the Fed's tools is its ability to sell government securities through its open market operations. **Open market operations** are the purchase and sale by the Federal Reserve of government securities, which can be bills, notes, or bonds. When the Fed buys government securities, it increases bank reserves and the money stock. When it sells government securities, bank reserves and the money stock decline.

**Open market operations:** the purchase and sale by the Federal Reserve of U.S. government securities, which can be bills, notes, or bonds.

Suppose the Fed buys a government bill from a private firm. The manager of the Fed's open market account, who works at the Federal Reserve Bank of New York, first asks dealers in the government securities market for the selling price on the bills they hold. Assume the Fed agrees to pay $1 million for the bill. It is delivered to the Federal Reserve, which issues a check for $1 million to the securities firm. The check ends up as a demand deposit in the firm's bank, increasing the money stock. The bank receiving the deposit can claim an increase in its reserves at the Fed.

Figure 8.2 shows the resulting entries on the books of Northwestern National Bank, which receives the deposit, and of the Federal Reserve. The Federal Reserve's bill holdings, an asset, increase (entry *a*), while the reserve deposit of Northwestern National, an offsetting liability, also increases (entry *b*). Similarly, Northwestern National records an increase in its demand deposits (entry *c*) and in its reserve deposit (entry *d*). Northwestern can now increase its loans up to the limit set by the reserve requirement. In short, it can start the process of money expansion described in Chapter 7 (see pages 161–163).

| Northwestern National Bank | | Federal Reserve Bank | |
|---|---|---|---|
| *Assets* | *Liabilities* | *Assets* | *Liabilities* |
| Reserve deposits: + $1 million (entry *d*) | Demand deposits: + $1 million (entry *c*) | Holdings of U.S. government securities + $1 million (entry *a*) | Reserve deposit of Northwestern + $1 million (entry *b*) |

**Figure 8.2.** Purchase of a Government Bill by the Federal Reserve.
The Fed's purchase of a government bill from a private firm increases the firm's deposit at Northwestern National Bank. It also increases Northwestern's reserve deposit at the Federal Reserve. By acquiring a government security, that is, the Fed increases Northwestern's ability to make loans and expand the money stock.

Where does the money to buy the bill come from? The Fed creates it. So long as people are willing to accept checks written by the Federal Reserve in exchange for their government securities, and so long as banks are willing to accept those checks as demand deposits, that which the Federal Reserve creates is money.

The Federal Reserve can just as easily reduce the money stock, by selling some of the government securities it holds. (In late 1984, the Fed held $162 billion worth of government securities.) When it sells a bill, the Fed receives a check drawn on someone's demand deposit, and the reserves of that person's bank fall. The Fed does not increase its accounts with the money represented by that check, however. It figuratively destroys the money by entering a zero on its books.

This transaction is shown in Figure 8.3. Assume that payment for the bill is made by a check written on an account with Northwestern National. Northwestern's demand deposits fall by the amount of the purchase price, $1 million (entry *a*). At the same time its reserve deposit falls by $1 million (entry *b*). The Federal Reserve loses an asset in the form of the government security (entry *c*) and dispenses with an equal liability in the form of a decrease in Northwestern's reserve deposit (entry *d*). One million dollars has disappeared from the money stock. But that is not all. Assuming that Northwestern has loaned up to its legal maximum before the sale of the bill, it must now reduce its loans in order to build its reserve deposit back up to the legal requirement. Thus the money stock decreases further.

## Summary of Monetary Controls

The members of the Open Market Committee of the Fed have several ways of exerting control over the money stock. If they want to increase the money stock, they may:

| Northwestern National Bank | | Federal Reserve Bank | |
|---|---|---|---|
| *Assets* | *Liabilities* | *Assets* | *Liabilities* |
| Reserve deposits: − $1 million (entry *b*) | Demand deposits: − $1 million (entry *a*) | Holdings of U.S. government securities − $1 million (entry *c*) | Reserve deposit of Northwestern − $1 million (entry *d*) |

**Figure 8.3.** Sale of a Government Bill by the Federal Reserve.
The sale of a government bill by the Federal Reserve decreases the buyer's deposit at Northwestern National Bank. It also decreases Northwestern's reserve deposit at the Fed. Thus the sale of a security by the Fed reduces Northwestern's ability to make loans and create money.

1. Reduce the reserve requirement.
2. Increase the loans made to member banks.
3. Buy government securities on the open market.

If they want to decrease the money stock, they may:

4. Increase the reserve requirement.
5. Reduce the loans made to member banks.
6. Sell government securities held by the Fed.

If the committee takes any of the first three actions and the growth of the money stock accelerates, the Fed is said to be following an expansionary or loose monetary policy. If it takes any of the last three actions and the money stock decreases or slows its rate of growth, the Fed is said to be following a contractionary or tight monetary policy.

The Fed's controls over the money stock are powerful, but it is difficult to apply them precisely within narrow limits. Various forces may work against or in concert with monetary controls. For instance, banks may choose not to lend against all their excess reserves. Even if they do, the money expansion process takes time to work through the banking system. Furthermore, while the Fed is trying to increase reserves, the public may be increasing its currency holdings and reducing its demand deposits, thus reducing reserves and the potential to create money. Finally, the U.S. Treasury has demand deposits both at the Fed and in commercial banks around the nation. If it decides to move some of its deposits from commercial banks to the Federal Reserve, it will reduce reserves.

In short, the Fed's attempts to increase the money stock may simply offset opposing forces that tend to reduce the money stock. Indeed, the Fed often buys government securities (or reduces the reserve requirement, or increases loans to member banks) simply to keep the money stock from falling, rather than to increase it. Similar difficulties may frustrate attempts to contract the money supply.

## A Monetary Explanation of Inflation and Deflation

The ultimate purpose of monetary policy is not simply to change the money stock, but to influence the nation's production, employment, and price levels. In recent years the Federal Reserve has been particularly concerned with the effect of its monetary policy on the rate of inflation.

### Size of the Money Stock and the Value of Money

The value of anything is measured by what it can get in trade. Thus the value of money is what money will buy. If a dollar will buy a quarter-pound hamburger at the local McDonald's restaurant, the exchange value of the dollar is one quarter-pound hamburger. (Contrary to the opinion frequently quoted by the press, the value of the dollar is not about 32 cents. Very few people would trade a dollar for 32 cents.)

In general, the value of the dollar depends on the supply of dollars relative to the supply of goods and services people have to sell. If the supply of dollars people are willing to spend rises faster than the quantity of goods offered on the market, prices will rise. (Competition for the limited number of goods will drive prices up.) As prices rise, the dollar will buy fewer goods, and its value declines. That is why an increase in the money stock is normally associated with a decrease in the value of the dollar. People typically spend more when they have more money, driving prices up and deflating the dollar.

This relationship between the size of the money stock and the value of the dollar has been observed throughout history. When Alexander the Great conquered the Persian Empire and took its capital, Persepolis, he found an immense hoard of gold that the Persian emperors had been accumulating for generations. He spent the gold immediately, partly on his army and partly on himself. As a result, prices all over the Greek world rose sharply. When the supply of money suddenly increased in relation to the supply of goods and services, so many people wanted to spend their newly acquired gold pieces that the prices of goods and services rose, driving the value of the gold down.

There have been other instances of inflation in metallic currencies. Several centuries ago the Spanish discovery of gold and silver mines in the Americas increased the European supply of those metals, depressing their value. The California Gold Rush had much the same effect throughout the world. The most recent example of a gold-backed inflation occurred between 1890 and 1910, when the development of the cyanide flotation process of extracting gold from ore increased the supply of gold and decreased its value.

Modern monies are substantially different from the metallic currencies of the past, but the relationship between the money stock and the price level is the same. The German government financed the First World War largely by borrowing. After the war, instead of raising taxes to pay off its debt, the government printed new money in an effort to inflate it away. The sudden dramatic rise in the money stock caused prices to soar. By

1923, prices were a trillion times higher than their prewar levels. The value of German money diminished so rapidly that people ceased to accept it in trade or even to hold on to it. Germany became a moneyless economy, and economic activity virtually collapsed.

In recent years, governments in Italy, Great Britain, and several South American nations have also printed more money than their economies could absorb. At one point during the 1960s, the annual rate of inflation in Brazil was over 150 percent.

In the Untied States the story has been less dramatic. During the 1950s, both the money stock and the price level increased at an average annual rate of slightly less than 2 percent. In the first half of the 1960s, the average rate of growth of the money stock rose to 3 to 4 percent, and inflation followed at approximately the same rate. In the late 1960s and early 1970s, the average annual growth rate of money increased again to 6 percent, but inflation rose only to 5 percent, partly because of government price controls. In the mid-1970s, price controls were effectively discarded, the annual growth rate of money rose to 7 percent, and inflation accelerated to 9 percent.

Both the money stock and prices hit alarming double-digit rates late in the 1970s. In the early 1980s the Fed sharply reduced money growth to about 5 percent. This dramatic drop in the growth rate of money—indeed, the sudden reversal of policy from a rising to a decreasing rate of growth—was accompanied by two recessions. Real GNP dropped and unemployment increased sharply. When the Fed expanded money growth to nearly 13 percent between 1982 and 1983, however, price increases of the same magnitude did not follow. In fact, from 1982 to 1984, prices increased less than 4 percent, in part because production expanded along with prices. In mid-1983, the Fed again began to tighten up on money growth.

Although inflation has been the general rule throughout history, deflation—a general decrease in prices—has also occurred, usually after wars. Just as nations may be tempted to increase the money stock as a means of financing war-related expenditures, they often try to reduce war-inflated prices afterward by reducing the money stock. The result is deflation. England underwent a long period of mild deflation after the Napoleonic wars; so did the United States after the Civil War. Prices also dropped significantly in the United States in 1920–1921, following the First World War. In each case deflation was caused by a reduction in the money stock.

## The Equation of Exchange

The relationship between the money stock and the price level is expressed by the formula $MV = PQ$, called the equation of exchange. The **equation of exchange** ($MV = PQ$) is a statement of mathematical equality between the product of the money stock ($M$) and the velocity of money ($V$) and the product of the price level ($P$) and the national output level ($Q$). That is, the money stock ($M$) multiplied by the **velocity of money** ($V$), or the average number of times each dollar is used during a given period, equals the prices of goods and services ($P$) multiplied by the quantity of goods

**Equation of exchange ($MV = PQ$):** a statement of mathematical equality between the product of the money stock ($M$) and the velocity of money ($V$) and the product of the price level ($P$) and the national output level ($Q$).

**Velocity of money:** the average number of times a dollar is used during a given period.

and services produced ($Q$). (Prices are normally measured in terms of some recognized index of the price level, like the Consumer Price Index.

On one level, the equation of exchange means simply that the dollar value of people's expenditures ($MV$) must equal the dollar value of what they buy ($PQ$). But the equation also relates changes in the money stock to changes in the price level. If $V$ is held constant, an increase in the money stock, $M$, on the left-hand side of the equation must result in an increase in either $P$ or $Q$ on the right-hand side of the equation. If the economy is at full employment—producing all the goods and services ($Q$) it can—then an increase in $M$ must be largely if not fully translated into an increase in the price level, $P$.

### *Effects of a Change in the Money Stock*

The equation of exchange enables us to draw other conclusions about the relationship between production, the money stock, and the price level. Suppose that the nation's production level, $Q$, is continuously expanding as a result of increases in productivity. If the money stock and velocity remain constant, the price level, $P$, must fall. Otherwise $PQ$ could not remain equal to $MV$. To keep the price level from falling when production is rising, either $M$ or $V$ (or both) must rise. In other words, during times of rising production, increases in the money stock can lead to price stability. Inflation will result only if the money stock, velocity, or both grow faster than the level of production. If production falls while the money stock rises (and velocity remains constant), too many dollars will be chasing too few goods, and prices will rise.

What will happen if the money stock decreases? If $V$ is held constant, a drop in $M$ on the left-hand side of the equation must be offset by a drop in either prices or production on the right-hand side. Generally prices will fall when the money stock falls, because fewer dollars will be competing for the nation's goods and services. The decrease in demand will cause producers to compete with each other through lower prices. Unless the costs of production fall along with prices, unemployment will result. If businesses must pay constant wages while receiving lower prices for their products, they cannot employ as many workers as before. Even if wages decline during times of deflation, they usually do not adjust rapidly enough to prevent unemployment from rising. The extent of the unemployment problem depends on how much and how fast the money stock is reduced and how rapidly wages and prices adjust downward.

### *Effects of a Change in Velocity*

The equation of exchange also tells us that if $M$ is held constant, a decrease in velocity will lead to a decrease in $P$ or $Q$, with the same general result: unemployment. Conversely, an increase in velocity ($V$) can cause prices to rise. That is, assuming that $M$ remains constant, an increase in $V$ on the left-hand side of the equation must lead to an increase in $P$ (the price level), in $Q$ (output), or in both on the right-hand side of the equation.

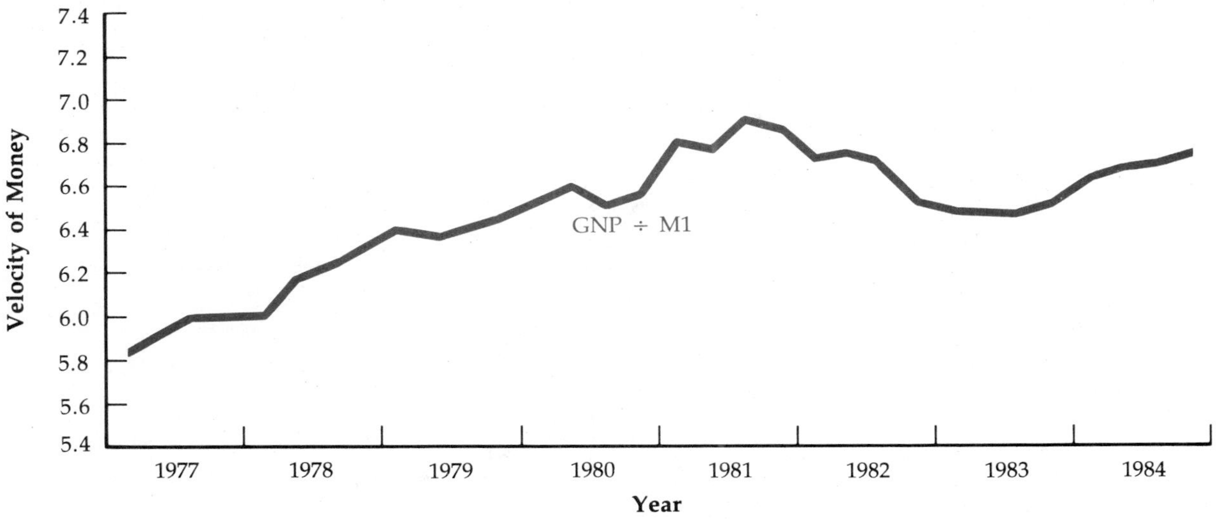


**Figure 8.4.** The Velocity of Money.
The velocity of money, defined as GNP divided by M1, rose gradually from 1976 to 1984. On a quarterly basis, however, it fluctuated considerably.
**Source:** Board of Governors of the Federal Reserve System, *Federal Reserve Chart Book* (February 1985), p. 8.

Increases in velocity, however, are not likely to cause long periods of continuous price increases. Velocity increases because people are using their money more rapidly, holding on to lower and lower money balances. But institutional constraints on velocity, such as regular pay periods, determine the minimum amount of money people must hold. Thus there are limits to how far and how fast velocity can increase—and to how much inflation it can cause.

Still, short-run changes in the velocity of money are possible. The rule is that the velocity of money varies inversely with the amount of money people want to hold. The more money people want to hold, the lower the rate of turnover. As we noted in the previous chapter, people want to hold money for three reasons: to cover expected and unexpected transactions, and in anticipation of higher interest rates. If economic conditions change—for example, if interest rates rise, changing the amount of money demanded—the velocity of money will change. Shifts in the velocity of money are readily seen in Figure 8.4, which shows the quarterly rate from 1976 to 1984.[2]

2. Figure 8.4 shows one measure of velocity, GNP divided by M1. Another measure, GNP divided by M2, showed no upward trend from 1976 to 1984. Both measures varied from quarter to quarter. (See the current issue of the *Federal Reserve Chart Book*.)

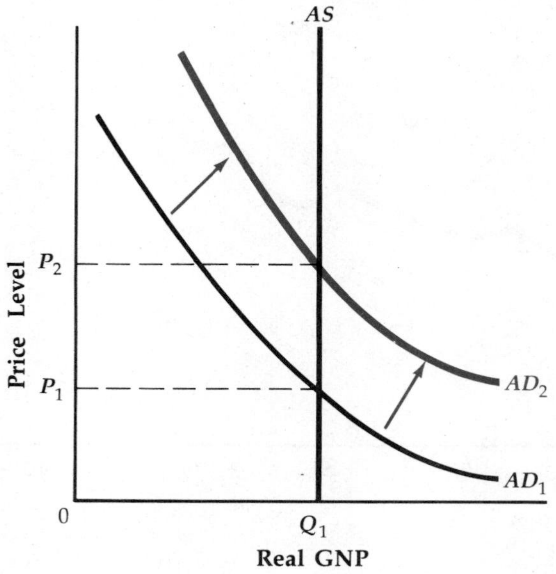


**Figure 8.5.** Effects of an Increase in the Money Stock on Aggregate Demand, Full Employment Assumed.
If the economy is at full employment—the aggregate supply curve is vertical—an increase in the money stock will shift the aggregate demand curve from $AD_1$ to $AD_2$. The price level will rise from $P_1$ to $P_2$, but output will remain the same: $Q_1$.

## Inflation in Terms of Aggregate Demand and Supply

The effects of an increase in the money stock can also be analyzed in terms of aggregate demand and supply. If the economy is at full employment, additional output cannot be produced to compensate for a rise in $M$ or $V$. In effect, the aggregate supply curve is vertical, as shown in Figure 8.5. Aggregate demand, however, will take on its normal downward sloping shape. With a given money stock, the price level will be $P_1$ and the output level $Q_1$ in Figure 8.5. If the money stock expands, people will have more money than they want to hold. As they try to use up their money balances, they will push aggregate demand up from $AD_1$ to $AD_2$. Because output cannot rise past $Q$, the price level will be pushed up to $P_2$. Though the output level stays at $Q_1$, the monetary measure of GNP rises with the increase in prices (GNP goes from $P_1 \times Q_1$ to $P_2 \times Q_1$).

If the economy is not at full employment, output can expand with the price level, and the aggregate supply curve will slope upward as in Figure

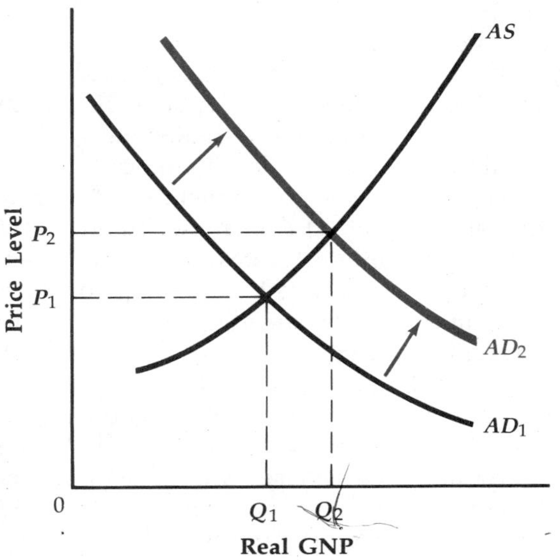


**Figure 8.6.** Effect of an Increase in the Money Stock on Aggregate Demand, Some Unemployment Assumed.
If the economy is not at full employment—the aggregate supply curve is positively sloped—an increase in the money stock will raise output. The aggregate demand curve will shift from $AD_1$ to $AD_2$, as it would under full employment. The resulting rise in prices from $P_1$ to $P_2$ encourages producers to raise output, from $Q_1$ to $Q_2$.

8.6. The increase in the money stock that is reflected in the shift in the aggregate demand curve from $AD_1$ to $AD_2$ will still push the price level up, from $P_1$ to $P_2$, reducing the velocity of money. But more important, output will expand in response to the change in the price level, from $Q_1$ to $Q_2$. In this case, the increase in the money stock increases both production and the price level.

## The Politics of Monetary Policy

To the extent that increases in the money stock cause inflation, the Federal Reserve can be blamed for higher prices. It has sometimes increased the money stock more than was warranted by the nation's production level. But monetary policy is not created in a vacuum. The Fed operates in a system in which government fiscal policy often runs counter to monetary policy. It is subject to political pressure from government. And it must deal with competing economic objectives, such as the reduction of both inflation and unemployment.

## Federal Government Deficits

One of the most troublesome influences on the Fed in recent decades has been the tendency of the government to overspend. Suppose that while the Federal Reserve is attempting to control inflation, the federal government is running up a budget deficit. To make up the difference between what it spends and what it collects in taxes, the government must borrow money by selling bonds in the bond market. This increases the demand for borrowed funds and perhaps the interest rates that businesses, individuals, and government at all levels have to pay. (The extent to which interest rates are raised by government deficit spending, if at all, is for many economists and policy makers an unsettled issue.)

In such situations, members of the House Banking Committee and the administration often accuse the Federal Reserve of adopting an unreasonably tight monetary policy. They will support their claim by citing rising interest rates on loans for everything from houses and cars to school construction and road improvements. Under political pressure, the Fed may then attempt to counteract heavy federal government borrowing by entering the market as a buyer of bonds, in effect increasing the money stock (see pages 171–172). The Fed's purpose is to keep interest rates down. But as we saw earlier, purchases of bonds by the Fed can raise prices. If inflation occurs, is the Fed responsible? In a sense it is. But Congress and the administration must also be held accountable for adopting inflationary spending policies.

## Political Pressures on the Federal Reserve

Theoretically, the Federal Reserve is an independent agency. It is not required to seek the advice or consent of the administration or of Congress, but only to inform Congress of its immediate plans. Congress retains the power to change the Federal Reserve's charter, however, and thereby to curtail its independence—and members of Congress frequently threaten such an action. If it wishes to remain independent, then, the Fed cannot completely ignore administrative and congressional wishes. In the last decade the Federal Reserve has sometimes resisted political pressure from both parties with unusual vigor. (Its resistance was no doubt fortified by the unusually high rates of inflation of the 1970s.) At other times, however, it has expanded the money stock as if its primary purpose were to assure the president's reelection. The result has been an erratic monetary policy, with accompanying fluctuations in the inflation rate.

## Cost-Push Inflation

Another problem for the Fed is the tendency of unions to seek wage settlements that cannot be supported by current market conditions. Such wage increases mean that employers cannot afford to hire as many workers as before. The result will be a rise in unemployment. Again, the Fed may be pressured by the administration and Congress to do something to alleviate the problem. Increasing the rate of growth of the money stock will enable businesses to hire more workers at the new wage rates. Such a policy will also contribute to inflation. Once again, the Open Market Committee of the Federal Reserve is only partially to blame, for it did not negotiate the inflationary wage settlements.

In fact, inflation has no one clearly defined cause. Rather the inflationary process is a set of interconnected causes, some related directly to technical control of the money stock and others related to political and market pressures. Asked what can be done about inflation, Henry Wallich, governor of the Federal Reserve, responded

> The familiar debate about the sources of violence provides an analogy. Do guns kill people? Do people kill people? Does society kill people? Some assert that money, and nothing but money, causes inflation—the "guns kill people" proposition. Some assert that the entire gamut of government policies, from deficit spending to protectionism to minimum wage to farm supports to environmental safety regulations, causes inflation—the "people kill people" proposition. Some argue, finally, that it is social pressures, competition for national product, a revolution of aspirations, which are at the root—the "society kills people" proposition. The first view holds primarily responsible for the inflation the central bank, the second the government, and the third the people that elect and instruct the government.[3]

## Summary and Extensions

The specific actions the Federal Reserve can take to expand or contract the money stock, and their impact on the price level, are technical matters. Its decisions, however, are very much influenced by the political setting in which it operates. The Fed is often pressured into taking actions contrary to its long-run policy objectives.

Occasionally the Fed's actions have been misguided. For instance, its attempts to keep interest rates low by buying government securities have increased the growth rate of the money stock, fueling inflation. As we will see in the chapters that follow, an increase in the inflation rate can also increase interest rates. Those who lend their money will require a higher interest rate to compensate for the depreciation of the dollar. Thus attempts to keep interest rates low can be self-defeating.

## Major Conclusions

1. The Federal Reserve has three fundamental tools for controlling the money stock: (a) the reserve requirement, (b) loans to member banks, and (c) open market operations.
2. The Federal Reserve can increase the money stock by (a) reducing the

---

3. Henry C. Wallich, "Honest Money," *Macroeconomics 1979: Readings on Contemporary Issues* (Ithaca, N.Y.: Cornell University Press, 1979), p. 43.

reserve requirement, (b) increasing loans to member banks (which can be accomplished by lowering the discount rate), and (c) purchasing government securities.

3. The Federal Reserve can reduce the money stock by (a) increasing the reserve requirement, (b) decreasing loans to member banks (which can be accomplished by increasing the discount rate), and (c) selling government securities.
4. The Fed's open market operations are the most important and frequently used control over the money stock.
5. The equation of exchange, $MV = PQ$, states the relationship between the money stock and the price level. A change in either the money stock ($M$) or velocity ($V$) on the left-hand side of the equation will be reflected in an equal change in prices ($P$) or output ($Q$) or both on the right-hand side.
6. The extent to which prices or production levels are changed by an increase in the money stock depends on how close the economy is to full employment. Under conditions of effective full or nearly full employment (that is, when the aggregate supply curve is vertical), any action by the Fed that increases the money stock is likely to increase prices, with little or no effect on output. When unemployment exists, however (that is, when the aggregate supply curve slopes upward to the right), any action by the Fed that increases the money stock is likely to affect both price and production levels.
7. At times, the Fed uses its monetary controls to offset changes in velocity, which would otherwise affect prices and national output.
8. The velocity of money tends to vary significantly over the short run.
9. The Fed may increase the growth rate of the money stock in response to pressure from Congress or the White House to reduce interest rates and unemployment. In the long run, however, such increases in the growth rate of the money stock will probably lead to higher interest and inflation rates.

## Questions to Ponder

1. Suppose people decide to withdraw more money than usual from their demand deposits and convert it into currency. How would this shift affect banks' ability to make loans? What effect would it have on the money stock?
2. What can the Fed do to increase the money stock? What can it do to offset an increase in currency holdings? On the basis of your answers, does it follow that when the Fed buys bonds on the open market, it is always attempting to increase the money stock?
3. What is the relationship between people's willingness to hold money in currency and demand deposits and the velocity of money (the average number of times each dollar is used)? What is the relationship between the rate of interest and people's willingness to hold money? On the basis of your answers, what is the relationship between the interest rate and the velocity of money?
4. Suppose that we reestablish gold and silver coins as the medium of exchange in the United States. Under such a monetary system, would the nation still experience periods of inflation and deflation? Suppose that dimes are made of silver, and that the amount of silver in the dime varies from coin to coin. Which dimes would tend to be used in trade?
5. The Federal Reserve conducts monetary policy in part through the purchase and sale of government bills. If the Federal Reserve bought and sold private bills instead of government bills, would the effect be any different?
6. Suppose all the nation's power groups—large unions, corporations, and governmental units—pushed prices up and held them there, dramatically increasing the price of almost everything. Assume also that the money stock was held constant. What would be the effect on the economy? Explain your answer in terms of the equation of exchange.
7. If a nation's central bank increases the money stock too often and too much, causing high rates of inflation, what can be done to counteract the problem? Why might the central bank take such actions?

## Central Question

*Who gains and who loses from inflation?*

## Key Term

**Variable-rate mortgage**

# Chapter 9

# The Costs and Benefits of Inflation

*In a full-employment situation money creation is strictly equivalent to taxation: Normal methods of taxation can be supplanted by the government's money creation, which . . . will cause inflation and a tax on people's average cash balances.*

*Roger Leroy Miller and Raburn M. Williams*

The costs of inflation are widely recognized, and often exaggerated. When people think about inflation, they tend to consider only the reduction in the purchasing power of their dollar. They often fail to recognize that their wages rise along with prices during inflationary times. Many readers, then, may be puzzled by the reference to the benefits of inflation in the title of this chapter. But people both gain and lose from inflation. Indeed, if it benefited no one and hurt everyone, including government, the political opposition to inflation would probably be overwhelming.

Because government and some segments of the population benefit from rising prices, inflation is difficult to stop once started. Even if the rate of inflation is reduced, as it was between 1980 and 1984, government may find it difficult to hold down, as explained later in this chapter. But before discussing the benefits of inflation—including the incentives government has to inflate prices—we will review its more familiar costs.

## The Costs of Inflation

The damage done by inflation depends primarily on two factors: (1) whether it is anticipated or unanticipated, and (2) what the rate of inflation is. We will begin by considering the effects of unanticipated inflation, a condition experienced in the United States in the mid-1960s and mid-1970s.

As noted in Chapter 8, inflation ran between 1 and 4 percent per year in the United States throughout the 1950s and early 1960s. Americans became accustomed to only moderate price increases. When prices started to rise at rates of 4 to 6 percent during the late 1960s, most people were caught off guard. Disgruntled grocery shoppers demonstrated against escalating prices. Richard Nixon railed against the "exorbitant" 5 percent rate of inflation in his campaign for the presidency in 1968. In August 1971, as public concern about inflation mounted, President Nixon froze the wages and prices of practically all goods and services.

At the time of the wage-price freeze the rate of inflation was 3.5 percent—relatively modest compared with the double-digit rates of 1974 and 1979 to 1980. But the unanticipated inflation of the late 1960s imposed costs that people were not prepared for. For that reason its consequences were perhaps more serious than the results of the later round of price increases. One of the most noticeable consequences, from the average citizen's point of view, was the decline in the relative value of cash savings.

### Losses to Cash Holders

Unanticipated inflation hurts people with dollars in their pockets or in demand and savings accounts. The value of the dollars they are holding goes down, for the dollar buys less at today's prices than it did yesterday. The losses to cash holders are so clear that if people anticipate a high rate of inflation, they will convert their dollars into goods and services at present prices, before their purchasing power goes down. One might argue, then, that people who hold on to their dollars are wagering that the benefits of holding money will exceed the costs. Whether they should be expected to make such bets is an emotional issue. But from an economic perspective, the movement of financial resources into goods and services as the result of anticipated inflation reduces investment and ultimately lowers national production.

## Losses to Institutional Creditors

Institutional creditors, like banks and insurance companies, also lose from unanticipated inflation. Assume that during noninflationary times a bank lends $30,000 to someone who agrees to repay the principal at the end of the year, with 6 percent interest. The bank expects $31,800 [$30,000 + (0.06 × $30,000)] on the termination date. But if prices rise unexpectedly by 10 percent, the *real* value of the dollars the bank receives (that is, what they will buy) will be less than the original value of the loan: $28,620 rather than $31,800. The creditor would have done better to invest the $30,000 in land or some other real good, whose price would have risen along with the prices of other goods and services. In that case, the asset purchased for $30,000 would now be worth $33,000 [$30,000 × (0.10 × $30,000)]. The *real* value, or purchasing power, of the $33,000 piece of property would be no greater than the original purchasing power of the $30,000—the bank would not have gained anything. But it would not have lost anything either.

If inflation is anticipated, banks and other creditors can demand a higher rate of interest on the money they lend, to compensate for the expected lost purchasing power of the dollars they receive in payment. That is why interest rates tend to rise with the inflation rate. High interest rates are generally a consequence rather than a cause of inflation.

## Losses to Bond Buyers

Like banks that make loans, people who buy government and corporate bonds are creditors. When they buy bonds, they lend money to the bond issuer. In return they expect to be paid interest at regular intervals. They also expect to receive the principal (that is, the face value of the bond) on the date of maturity. Since both the interest payments and the principal are normally stated in terms of dollars, an unanticipated increase in the inflation rate can mean an unexpected drop in the purchasing power of the interest and principal.

Like banks, individuals can protect themselves against anticipated inflation by seeking an interest rate that compensates them for the expected loss of purchasing power. Unless they receive such a rate, they will tend to withhold their funds from the bond market, pushing interest rates up.

## Losses to Businesses and Workers

Inflation means that prices in general are on the rise, not necessarily that all prices rise by the same amount. Some prices may not rise at all, and some may even fall.

Some prices tend to change rather rapidly and smoothly, reflecting changes in market forces, like the quantity and velocity of money. The prices of agricultural commodities like wheat and beef tend to mirror changes in their auction markets with reasonable rapidity. But the prices of many other goods take time to adjust upward. Price increases may be delayed when there are long time lags between the placement of an order and the delivery of the product, or when contracts specify the price at the time of delivery. Commercial airplanes, heavy electrical equipment, and many buildings are constructed and sold under these conditions. For the producers of these products, unanticipated inflation can mean cost increases and narrower-than-expected profit margins, or even losses, as well as payment in devalued dollars.

If the prices of products rise at different rates, then wages are likely to follow at different rates, for workers' wages depend in part on the prices charged for their products. In addition, some workers' wages are restrained by contracts that extend over a period of one or more years. In short, some workers' pay may keep pace with inflation; other workers' wages may lag behind price increases. The latter group will suffer a loss.

Not all reductions in the purchasing power of wages can be attributed to inflation, however. In any dynamic economy, there will always be groups of workers whose real wages decline because of the market forces affecting their industries. A decrease in the demand for a particular good, or an increase in the supply of workers in a particular industry, can cause such a decline in wages. Because more people are seeking college teaching positions, for instance, the real salaries of college professors have declined in recent years. The fairly high rate of inflation in the past decade only quickened the downward adjustment. In short, inflation can mean temporary losses in purchasing power for some groups, but not all.

## Losses to Taxpayers

Because of the way income tax systems are structured, almost every income earner is hurt by inflation. Most tax systems are arranged so that they take a higher percentage of a person's money income as it rises. Thus if Ms. Jones's money income rises with inflation, the government will take a greater percentage of it in taxes—even if its real purchasing power merely remains constant. The purchasing power of Ms. Jones's after-tax income declines with inflation.

Suppose, for instance, that the marginal tax rate rises from 10 percent on the first $10,000 of taxable income to 20 percent on the next $20,000, and so on up to 50 percent on incomes over $75,000 (see Table 9.1). If Sue Jones earns $30,000 of taxable income, her tax bill for the year is $5,000 (10 percent of $10,000 plus 20 percent of $20,000). Her after-tax income is $25,000.

**Table 9.1.** Hypothetical Income Tax Schedule

| Income | Marginal Tax Rate (percent) |
|---|---|
| $0 to $10,000 | 10% |
| $10,001 to $30,000 | 20 |
| $30,001 to $50,000 | 30 |
| $50,001 to $75,000 | 40 |
| $75,001 and up | 50 |

Over the following year prices rise by 10 percent, and Sue Jones receives a 10 percent increase in taxable income. While her dollar income rises to $33,000, her real income before taxes remains the same (since $33,000 will buy the same goods and services that $30,000 could buy a year earlier). But the extra $3,000 that permits her to keep pace with inflation puts Sue in a higher tax bracket. It is taxed at the higher marginal rate of 30 percent, increasing her tax bill to $5,900 (10 percent of $10,000 plus 20 percent of $20,000 plus 30 percent of $3,000). After taxes Sue has $27,100 ($33,000 − $5,900) to spend—$2,100 more than she had the previous year. But her purchasing power is only $24,390 ($27,100 × 0.90) after adjustment for the 10 percent inflation rate. In short, Sue loses $610 in purchasing power through what is called bracket creep. The government gains her lost purchasing power.

In 1981 the Reagan administration pushed through Congress an act requiring the Internal Revenue Service to adjust, or index, income tax rates for inflation. Tax indexing became effective in 1985. But in 1984, as the projected federal budget deficit reached $200 billion, some members of Congress began calling for the termination of indexing. It is not yet clear whether indexing will remain law, and what its long-term effects will be. Because indexing reduces the gains government can expect from inflation, it may reduce the government's incentive to inflate the money stock.

## Losses to Pensioners

Retired people who depend on fixed monthly payments from their company pension plans are hurt by rising prices. Congress addressed the problem by providing for cost-of-living adjustments in Social Security checks.

## General Losses from Inflation

During inflationary times, losses in the purchasing power of the dollar can encourage people to hold less money and more real assets, such as land, houses, gold, and collectibles (such as jewelry, artwork, and stamps).

## Perspectives in Economics: Inflation and Inflated Demand for Housing

*Dwight R. Lee*

When the American economy went into a recession in the early 1980s, the housing industry experienced a full-fledged depression. In 1982, new housing starts were less than half the level of three years earlier. Construction and real estate firms went under in record numbers that year, and the future of the housing industry seemed questionable at best.

Most analysts attributed the slump to high interest rates. But the high and rising inflation rates of the previous two decades also played a role. During the 1970s, inflation combined with high interest rates to make investment in housing extremely profitable. Besides increasing the value of real estate, inflation increases the tax-deductible interest that is paid on mortgages. Thus it subsidizes the purchase of a house.

Suppose you are in the 40 percent tax bracket. Every dollar you pay in mortgage interest is deducted from your taxable income. In effect, you get a 40 percent subsidy on every dollar. If there were no inflation, the interest rate on your new mortgage would be about 4 percent. But your after-tax interest rate would be only 2.4 percent (60 percent of 4 percent).

Now assume the inflation rate is 10 percent. The interest rate on your mortgage is now 14 percent (4 percent plus the 10 percent inflation rate), and the after-tax interest rate is 8.4 percent—much higher. But inflation is decreasing the value of the money you owe by 10 percent a year. In real terms, you are not paying interest of 8.4 percent, but negative 1.6 percent. This negative interest rate is in effect a subsidy on the purchase of a new home—a subsidy that increases with inflation.

This tax subsidy had a perverse effect on the type of new housing that was built during the 1970s. By any realistic standard, the size of newly constructed houses should have decreased. The average household size declined from 3.14 people in 1970 to 2.76 in 1980. The price of energy skyrocketed, dramatically increasing the cost of home heating and cooling. And median family income, after adjustment for inflation and federal

To the extent that reduced money holdings mean reduced business investment, inflation can lead to lower levels of production and lower incomes. Lower production levels mean fewer goods and services, hence ultimately even higher prices. These general losses will be spread throughout the economy.

Anticipated inflation can also lead to an overheating of the economy, or unrealistically high production levels. If business people expect higher rates of inflation in the future, they will build up their inventories now, to avoid paying higher prices later. At some point, having accumulated more inventory than necessary, business will cut back on orders for goods. Then production will fall, leading to unemployment and lost income for workers.

In periods of anticipated modest inflation, creditors can adjust their interest rates to compensate for the expected decrease in the value of the taxes, was $436 less in 1980 than in 1970. Nonetheless, during the 1970s the size of the average new house expanded from 1,510 to 1,760 square feet—an increase of nearly 17 percent. Rather than maintaining and expanding the nation's productive capital, Americans have been putting their savings into larger houses for smaller families.

Another factor that contributed to the inflation of housing demand during the 1970s was the increase in federal and state income tax rates. Higher tax rates increase the value of tax benefits, reducing the after-tax cost of housing still further. If your tax rate is 40 percent, the net after-tax cost of a dollar paid in interest is sixty cents. If your tax rate rises to 50 percent, the after-tax cost of your interest dollar falls to fifty cents.

In the early 1980s, critics of the Reagan administration pointed to the depressed housing industry as evidence that government policies, designed to reduce both tax rates and inflation, were not working. Of course the housing industry was suffering partly from the high unemployment of the early 1980s. But in any case, lower inflation and lower tax rates should be expected to deflate the demand for housing. Overall investment may be stimulated by falling inflation and tax rates, but some of these funds should be redistributed away from new housing and into other industries.

In sum, the housing industry benefits from inflation, especially when it is unanticipated. It is hurt by a reversal of the inflationary spiral—especially when a government policy reversal is unanticipated. If the federal government follows an anti-inflationary policy for the remainder of the 1980s, we should expect that smaller houses will be built. "Overbuilt" houses should be divided up or sold to larger families than are living in them at present.

At the same time, lower tax rates have a mixed influence on the housing industry. On the one hand, they increase the disposable income of home buyers, thus adding to the demand for housing. On the other hand, they reduce the tax benefits of a mortgage.

dollar. Similarly, workers can increase their wage demands. But during periods of very high inflation, sometimes called hyperinflation, the value of currency deteriorates so fast that people become reluctant to accept and hold dollars. To avoid significant economic losses, they tend to spend the dollars they receive as fast as they can. Hyperinflation can lead to a moneyless economy, a return to the barter system in which resources are devoted as much to searching out mutually beneficial trades as to production. In such circumstances production levels can fall significantly, as they did in Germany after the First World War.

In the early 1980s, economic growth slowed in Israel, Brazil, and some other Latin American countries, in part because of inflation rates that reached several hundred percent at year. Such economic downturns are felt not just in the nations where they occur, but in creditor nations like the United States, whose banks finance investments throughout the world.

## The Benefits of Inflation

When one person loses from an unanticipated increase in prices, someone else usually gains. (The obvious exception is when inflation contributes to a downturn in total production, in which case almost everyone can lose.) Like the costs of inflation, benefits emerge largely because some people do not anticipate the rise in prices or cannot adjust readily to it. In such a situation, people who do foresee rising prices and move to counteract them will gain at the expense of others. They can buy early, at relatively low prices, and sell later at much higher prices. The possibility of reaping such gains is one factor that tends to draw resources away from production in inflationary times. People use their resources for speculation in the hope that they may be among the gainers from inflation.

### Gains to Debtors

Probably the largest single group of people who gain from unanticipated inflation are debtors who owe money at the time inflation begins. The largest subgroup (not including the government) in this category is homeowners who are paying mortgages with fixed interest charges. They are a significant part of the population, since most single-family dwellings are financed this way. Homeowners benefit because the real value of their debts shrinks. Thus the person with a mortgage during an inflationary period is paying off the loan in dollars that are worth less than the dollars that were borrowed.

Consider a person who purchased a house for $30,000 in 1960, putting $1,000 down and taking out a mortgage for the remaining $29,000 at 6 percent interest. Today the dollar will purchase less than a third of what it could buy in 1960. Therefore the $29,000 mortgage is worth much less today to the bank that holds it than it was in 1960. But because the price of housing has risen slightly faster than other prices, the real or relative value of the house to the buyer has increased. Today the house could probably be sold for over $120,000. Thus while the dollar asset held by the mortgage company has shrunk, the debtor's real asset has appreciated.

The homeowner who has gained on his mortgage may not have gained overall from inflation, however. The homeowner may have some dollar assets, perhaps a government bond that pays 3 percent interest. The decline in the bond's real value because of inflation will partially if not entirely offset the decline in the value of the mortgage.

**Variable-rate mortgage:** a mortgage whose interest rate is adjusted periodically to agree with some market interest rate—for example, the rate on a specific type of government or corporate bond.

In periods of unstable prices, as we have seen, creditors charge higher interest rates to compensate for expected inflation. Because the rate of inflation tends to be variable and unpredictable, banks have moved away from fixed-rate mortgages to loans with variable rates. A **variable-rate mortgage** is one whose interest rate is adjusted periodically to agree with some market interest rate—for example, the rate on a specific type of government or corporate bond. If the designated market interest rate rises, the mortgage interest rate rises also, and vice versa. Market interest rates make good benchmarks for mortgage rates because they tend to move up and down with the inflation rate, as lenders adjust their asking price to the expected rate of inflation.

The variable-rate mortgage does not eliminate the risks associated with inflation. It merely shifts them from the creditor to the debtor, whose mortgaged assets appreciate with inflation. Though debtors can still obtain fixed-rate mortgages, creditors are likely to charge a higher interest rate that incorporates a risk premium. This "risk cost" is another example of how inflation reduces the efficiency of the economy by increasing the cost of doing business.

## Gains to Businesses and Workers

Not all prices adjust upward in times of inflation. Because of institutional barriers to the adjustment of wages and prices, such as lengthy production procedures and long-term labor contracts, some wages and prices rise less rapidly than others. Just as the people whose wages and prices adjust sluggishly are hurt by inflation, those whose wages and prices adjust quickly receive temporary benefits from unanticipated inflation. In particular, statistics show that business profits tend to rise in the early phases of a new and higher inflationary cycle, because product prices tend to rise faster than wages. In such a situation business owners gain at the expense of workers, who may not anticipate the increase in prices soon enough to incorporate it into their wage demands. In a minority of cases, workers are protected by special clauses in their contracts, called COLAs (cost-of-living adjustment clauses).

## Gains to Politicians and Government Employees

Not surprisingly, those who are responsible for increasing the money stock and contributing to inflation tend to benefit from it. This observation holds true whether money is made of gold or paper, though the benefits tend to be smaller with metallic currencies. The discovery of gold in California in the nineteenth century benefited the gold miners who produced and sold it. The miners' benefits were limited to the difference between the cost of mining the gold and the price it commanded when sold, however. To the extent that mining increased the demand for equipment like shovels and pans, some product suppliers also benefited from the increase of the gold supply. The cost of the inflation was shared among everyone who was holding gold at the time, for the new discovery reduced the value of the existing gold.

Because paper money is much less difficult and expensive to produce than metallic currencies, the profits to the producers can be much greater. Modern governments often take advantage of inflation, particularly in wartime. Government can produce paper money in two ways. First, it can increase the money stock directly, either by printing new bills or by raising its bank balance at the central bank (in the United States, the Federal Reserve). The government then uses this newly created money to buy the new roads or military bases it needs. So long as people are willing to accept new dollar bills or checks drawn on the Federal Reserve account, the money stock will increase, and government will benefit from the increase. Politicians who promote government programs, workers who staff them, and people who benefit directly from them will all gain from the inflation. The losers will be those who hold dollar assets and those who must pay higher prices for goods and services because fewer resources are available for nongovernment uses.

The United States government does not increase the money stock in this direct manner, but often takes a more circuitous approach. The federal government runs a budgetary deficit, borrowing the difference between its tax receipts and its expenditures. First the U.S. Treasury sells bonds on the open market, which tends to decrease the price and increase interest rates. The Fed may then come under political pressure to keep interest rates from rising. In response, the Fed orders the Open Market Committee to buy bonds on the open market, which tends to increase the bonds' prices and decrease interest rates. Though the Fed is not bound by law to accommodate the Treasury's wishes, its directors sometimes feel a good deal of political pressure to keep interest rates from rising. If the pressure is great enough, the Fed will cooperate in inflating the money stock.

When the Fed accommodates the Treasury and buys federally issued bonds, the effect on prices is virtually the same as the effect of printing more dollars. The government gains at the expense of everyone holding financial assets valued in dollars, and at the expense of taxpayers, who must pay a higher percentage of their real income to the government as taxes.

Historically the Fed has made only sparing use of its powers to "monetize" the federal debt. Still, since the Second World War the government has benefited significantly as inflation eroded the value of the federal debt. Table 9.2 shows that the federal debt in current dollars (column 1) rose from about \$271 billion in 1946 to \$544 billion 1975 and \$1.6 trillion in 1984. Because of inflation, however, the real value of the debt declined for most of the period. In constant 1967 dollars, the debt fell from \$463 billion in 1946 to \$338 billion in 1975, before rising again in the late 1970s. The federal government gained from inflation at the expense of holders of government securities.

From 1981 to 1984, inflation fell from double-digit levels to less than 4 percent. Yet market interest rates remained high by historical standards. In 1984, for example, home mortgage interest rates exceeded 15 percent in many parts of the nation. It is often argued that the expectation of continued high federal deficits (more than \$200 billion annually) kept interest rates high. According to this theory, lenders feared the government would increase its credit demands, pushing up interest rates, and then repudiate the growing debt by monetizing it, as in the past. Creditors attempted to protect themselves from a new round of inflation by asking higher interest rates on their money.

Thus, by creating money, the government can redistribute resources from private to public use. Directly or indirectly, inflating the dollar increases the government's purchasing power. Because taxes also redistribute purchasing power from the public to the government, inflation can

**Table 9.2.** The Federal Debt in Current and Constant (1967) Dollars, 1945–1984

| Year | Current Dollar Debt | Constant Dollar Debt[a] |
|---|---|---|
| 1946 | 271.0 | 463.3 |
| 1950 | 256.9 | 356.3 |
| 1955 | 274.4 | 342.1 |
| 1960 | 290.9 | 328.0 |
| 1965 | 323.2 | 342.0 |
| 1970 | 382.6 | 329.0 |
| 1975 | 544.1 | 337.5 |
| 1976 | 631.9 | 370.6 |
| 1977 | 709.1 | 390.7 |
| 1978 | 780.4 | 399.4 |
| 1979 | 833.8 | 383.5 |
| 1980 | 914.6 | 370.6 |
| 1981 | 1,003.9 | 368.5 |
| 1982 | 1,147.0 | 396.8 |
| 1983 | 1,381.9 | 463.1 |
| 1984 | 1,576.7 | 506.8 |

[a] Computed with consumer price index.
**Source:** *Economic Report of the President* (Washington, D.C.: U.S. Government Printing Office, 1985), p. 318.

be considered taxation in disguise. Tax collected in this way is obscured by the complex mechanisms of money creation. However, inflation distributes the cost of government programs more haphazardly than normal taxation. And inflation is a kind of taxation without representation because it is never approved by Congress. For politicians who want to vote for public programs but not the taxes to pay for them, inflation may be the ideal tax system.

## Should Inflation Be Stopped?

Many people are hurt by inflation, particularly long-term creditors who live on fixed incomes. Some benefit, particularly debtors and the government. Once inflation has been under way for a time, it becomes hard to stop without harming those who have made rational adjustments to the condition. If it appears that inflation will continue, home buyers will be willing to take on mortgages at a high rate of interest, on the assumption that the loans can be repaid with depreciated dollars. If the inflation rate is reduced, they will have to make high mortgage payments with dollars that do not depreciate as rapidly as expected. Mortgages can be refinanced, or paid off with funds from a new mortgage written at a lower rate. When long-term rates began to fall in 1984, many homeowners refinanced their mortgages. But refinancing often involves a penalty.

The predicament of farmers is more pressing. Many took out loans to buy land and machinery in the late 1970s and early 1980s. They anticipated that rising inflation rates would push up land and crop prices. They expected to cover their debt payments with devalued dollars. When the inflation rate dropped dramatically in the early 1980s, many farmers found themselves saddled with debts that had to be paid off with dollars that were more valuable than expected. The farmers' problems were compounded by falling land and crop prices, caused partly by the reduced profitability of farming and partly by the drop in demand for land as a hedge against inflation. Many farm bankruptcies were due at least in part to the unexpected reversal of the inflationary spiral.

The normative question raised by inflation is whether people should be expected to cope with such changes in the rate of price increase—changes that no individual can control. Monetary stability can be thought of as a public good, a benefit to the general population that the government can produce if the electorate demands it.

## Summary and Extensions

Inflation causes problems mainly when the rate of price increase changes unexpectedly, and when the inflation rate is so high people will not accept dollars in trade. If inflation is anticipated, people can make adjustments in their financial and real assets and in the wages they demand for their labor. Creditors can require higher interest rates for the funds they lend. Laborers can incorporate expected price increases into their labor contracts. Even institutional barriers to price and wage adjustment—fixed salary schedules and contract periods, for example—can be changed to allow for regular adjustment for inflation. Inflation need not redistribute income from creditor to debtor, from employee to employer. As long as the rate of price increase is steady enough that people can expect a similar rate in the future, the costs of inflation will not be prohibitive.

## Major Conclusions

1. Those who stand to lose from inflation include (a) holders of demand and savings deposits, (b) creditors, (c) bond buyers, (d) businesses and workers tied to long-term price and wage agreements, and (e) taxpayers.
2. Those who stand to gain from inflation include (a) debtors, (b) businesses and workers who are free to adjust their prices and wages faster than others, and (c) government.
3. It is primarily unexpected inflation that has redistributional effects.
4. Government creation of money can be interpreted as a hidden tax on the public. An increase in the rate of money creation can lead to an unanticipated increase in the rate of inflation, as well as to increased tax collections.

## Questions to Ponder

1. How has inflation affected your real income, or your parents', during the last few years? List your gains and losses, and indicate the net effect.
2. Who gains and who loses from deflation?
3. Why do the effects of anticipated inflation differ from those of unanticipated inflation?
4. If everyone anticipated the rate of inflation perfectly, and could adjust his prices and wages freely to the new rate, would inflation do any harm?
5. The federal government currently increases the money stock through the sale of government bonds to the Fed. Would the effect on the economy be different if the government printed new dollar bills and dumped them out of airplanes?
6. Can inflation be stopped? Explain.

## Part IV

# National Income and Fiscal Policy

## Central Question

*What macroeconomic forces determine the national income and employment levels?*

## Key Terms

**Real wage rate**
**Full employment**
**Say's law**
**Saving**
**Leakage**
**Injection**
**Investment**
**Planned investment**
**Unplanned investment**
**Equilibrium income level**

# Chapter 10

# Unemployment and the Equilibrium Income Level: An Introduction

*Revolutions occur infrequently in the United States. Or else, when these uprisings happen, there are few observers sufficiently alert to recognize them. Relative unobtrusiveness is only one reason that the "new" economics is so remarkable; with harldy a shot fired, it was named an "economic" revolution in its own time.*

*E. Ray Canterbery*

In this and the following three chapters we will cover macroeconomic theory, past and present. In particular, we will focus on the causes and cures of cyclical changes in national income and employment. To put the so-called Keynesian revolution into historical perspective, this chapter begins with a brief consideration of several earlier theories of unemployment. Then we will develop the basics of what has become known as the Keynesian macroeconomic model—not as John Maynard Keynes himself developed them, but as his followers have. Chapter 11 will extend and qualify that basic model. And Chapter 12 will show how the Keynesian model has been applied in government fiscal policy.

Unfortunately, economic theory—especially macroeconomic theory—does not always provide undisputed policy solutions to the macroeconomic problems of inflation, unemployment, and stagflation. Many of the policy recommendations drawn from Keynesian macroeconomic models are controversial. Alternative theories, discussed in the following section, offer conflicting policies. The debate will not be settled for many years, if ever; we certainly cannot offer conclusions here. Instead we will outline the framework economists use to think about unemployment and inflation, and in that way isolate the points of contention.

## Before Keynes

John Maynard Keynes did not single-handedly bring about the Keynesian revolution. A number of economists who were studying unemployment during the Great Depression made many of the same recommendations as Keynes—including the suggestion that in times of heavy unemployment, the government should run a budgetary deficit to stimulate the economy and create jobs. Their theories may not have been as precisely developed as Keynes's, but their conclusions were identical. For instance, Jacob Viner wrote, "When business activity is declining, or is stagnant and at a low level, reduced taxation, and budget deficits are, from the point of view of the national economy as a whole, sound policy rather than unsound."[1] And Frank Knight wrote, "As far as I know, economists are completely agreed that the government should spend as much and tax as little as possible at a time like this—using the expenditure to do the most good in itself and also to point toward relieving the depression."[2]

To these and other economists, *The General Theory* was nothing new, and they may have been surprised when the book became the manifesto for the new economics. For an idea to become widely accepted, however, it must be effectively presented and promoted. Keynes's contribution probably lies more in the presentation of his theory—in a relatively simple, straightforward manner that attracted both professional and public attention—than in its originality.

---

1. As quoted in J. Ronnie Davis, *The New Economics and the Old Economists* (Ames: Iowa State University Press, 1971), p. 40.
2. Ibid., p. 16.

To appreciate the impact of the Keynesian revolution on people's thinking, we will look briefly at some theories that were in vogue before Keynes. The most influential was the classical explanation for unemployment.

## The Classical Model of the Labor Market

Classical economists assumed that the number of workers employers will hire is inversely related to the wage rate, specifically the real or price-adjusted wage rate. The **real wage rate** is the nominal or money wage rate (the number of dollars a person earns per hour or day) adjusted for inflation or deflation. The real wage rate measures a worker's actual purchasing power. Because the general price level determines how much a given money wage will buy, the real wage rate can be expressed as the ratio *W*/*P*, where *W* is the money wage and *P* is an index (like the consumer price index) representing the general price level:

**Real wage rate:** the nominal or money wage rate (the number of dollars a person earns per hour or day) adjusted for inflation or deflation. The real wage rate measures a worker's actual purchasing power.

$$\text{real wage} = \frac{\text{money wage}}{\text{price index}} = \frac{W}{P}$$

Mathematically, the real wage rises with an increase in the money wage and falls with an increase in the price level.

If the real wage rate rises, then, the number of available jobs falls, and vice versa. Classical economists also assumed a direct relationship between the real wage rate and the number of laborers willing to work. That is, if the real wage rate rises, more workers will give up their leisure time and spend more time at work. Hence an increase in the real wage rate will cause the quantity of labor supplied to rise, and vice versa. The labor supply curve, like other supply curves, slopes upward.

The supply and demand curves for the classical model of the labor market are shown in Figure 10.1. As in other competitive markets, the equilibrium point falls at the intersection of the two curves. At the real wage rate $(W/P)_2$, everyone who is willing to work ($Q_3$) can find a job. In this limited sense, the competitive market process tends toward full employment. In classical theory, **full employment** occurs when the quantity of labor demanded equals the quantity of labor supplied at a market-determined real wage rate.

**Full employment:** the employment level that occurs when the quantity of labor demanded equals the quantity of labor supplied at a market-determined real wage rate.

According to classical theory, if some workers are unemployed, it is because the going real wage is artificially high. In that case the market is not in equilibrium: the real wage is above the intersection of supply and demand. In Figure 10.1, any real wage rate above $(W/P)_2$ will produce unemployment. The number of workers supplied will be greater than the quantity demanded. Union wage rates, minimum wage laws, and other market restrictions can cause such an effect.

Even in a competitive market unhampered by a government- or union-fixed wage rate, unemployment can arise temporarily as a result of changes in supply and demand. Unemployment will persist until the real wage rate adjusts to a new equilibrium point. For instance, suppose the demand for labor in Figure 10.1 falls from $D_1$ to $D_2$ as the result of a change in

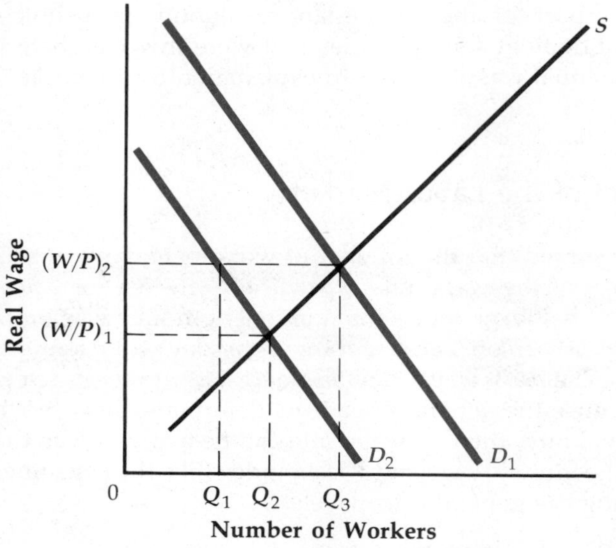


**Figure 10.1.** The Labor Market: The Classical Model.
With supply and demand for labor represented by curves $S$ and $D_1$, full employment will be achieved at a real wage rate of $(W/P)_2$. If the demand for labor in this market falls to $D_2$, the number of workers willing to work ($Q_3$) will at first exceed the number demanded ($Q_1$). Until the real wage rate adjusts downward to $(W/P)_1$, some unemployment will persist.

consumer buying habits. The product made by the workers in this market is now less desirable than some other product made by other workers. This jarring change in demand will throw the market out of equilibrium. The quantity of labor that employers demand at the initial real wage rate, $(W/P)_2$, will fall to $Q_1$. But the number of people willing to work at that rate will remain $Q_3$. Thus $Q_3 - Q_1$ people will be out of work. In a perfectly competitive labor market, the real wage rate (along with the money wage) may fall very quickly, eliminating this gap between the number of jobs available and the number of people seeking them. In the real world, however, markets never work that smoothly. Adjustment requires time—months or even years—and during that period, some people will be unemployed.

An increase in the supply of labor—that is, the number of people willing to work at any given wage—can have a similar effect on unemployment, again temporarily. The supply curve shifts outward, lowering the point of intersection with the demand curve. If the real wage adjusts downward in a competitive manner, the gap between the old real wage rate and the new equilibrium wage will be closed. But as before, there will be unemployment during the transition.

If unemployment persists beyond a transitional period, classical economists would argue that it is because obstructions in the labor market are

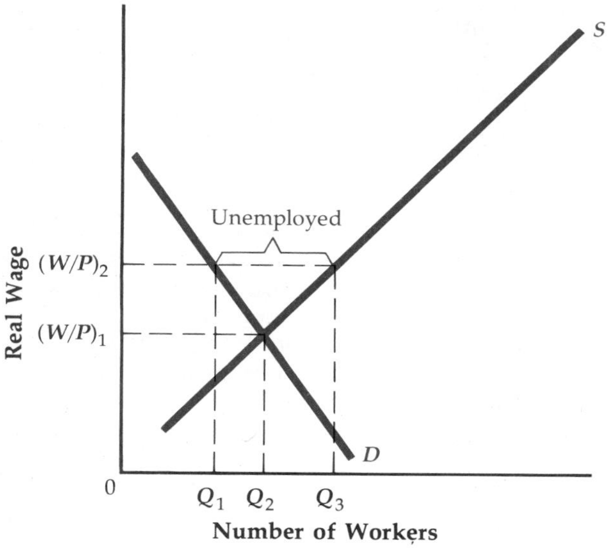


**Figure 10.2.** Obstruction in the Labor Market.
In a free competitive market, the real wage rate will settle at $(W/P)_1$. If the money wage is established at the artificially high level of $(W/P)_2$, however, it will push the real wage rate above equilibrium, causing unemployment equal to the difference between $Q_1$ and $Q_3$.

preventing the real wage rate from falling. Suppose the equilibrium real wage rate is $(W/P)_1$ (see Figure 10.2). If the money wage is raised by union contract to an artificially high rate while the price level remains unchanged [real wage $(W/P)_2$], unemployment equal to the difference between $Q_3$ and $Q_1$ will persist. As we saw in Chapter 8, the government can solve this unemployment problem by creating an increase in the money stock—and with it an increase in the general price level. With an increase in the price level [the denominator in $(W/P)_2$], the real wage rate will fall—assuming, of course, that the money wage rate remains constant. And if the real wage rate falls, the gap between the quantity of labor demanded ($Q_1$) and the quantity of labor supplied ($Q_3$) will evaporate. If unions are able to negotiate perpetual wage increases, however, a government intent on pushing the real wage rate down to the equilibrium point will have to inflate the price level continually. If money wages and prices rise together, the real wage will never reach equilibrium, and unemployment will never disappear.

Classical economists reasoned that an economy would never be completely free from unemployment. Continuing adjustments in the labor market, as well as restrictions that prevent the real wage from adjusting—minimum wage laws and union contracts—would keep unemployment from falling to zero.

## *Economists in History: John Maynard Keynes (1883–1946)*

Probably no single individual has had a more profound influence on modern economic thought than John Maynard Keynes (1883–1946). An erudite British economist who accumulated a sizable fortune by speculating in foreign currencies, he wrote principally on monetary and international economics. His reputation rests primarily on a book published in 1936, *The General Theory of Employment, Interest, and Money*. In this work Keynes attacked the conventional, or "classical," explanation for unemployment, which focused on the supply and demand for labor. Classical economists tended to explain most unemployment in terms of obstacles that prevent wage rates from falling, and therefore from matching the number of people wanting to work with the number of jobs available in specific labor markets. Such obstacles to lower wages include union resistance to wage reductions, minimum wage laws, and unemployment compensation.

Unlike the classical theories, Keynes's theory of unemployment transcended specific labor markets and dealt instead with the economy as a whole. Rather than focusing on obstacles to a drop in the wage rate, he examined the effects of national income, saving, and investment levels on unemployment. Thus while the narrower classical theories were and still are considered to be only partial models, Keynes truly devised a theory of the macroeconomy. His economic model combined the analysis of many different markets under the umbrella of a single general theory of unemployment.

Keynes wrote *The General Theory* during the depth of the Great Depression, a period of very low production, high unemployment, and falling wages and prices. He felt that the classical theories could not explain the persistence of high unemployment despite falling wages. In an effort to explain the events of his day, Keynes hit on the notion that unemployment results in part from the inability or unwillingness of consumers and businesses to buy enough goods and services to keep everyone employed. Because he integrated this model of insufficient aggregate demand with theories of the supply and demand for money and the determination of interest rates, Keynes's work was referred to as a "general theory." Recent events have shown that it is far from universal in its application, however.

Keynes was especially concerned with the welfare of the unemployed during the period when,

## Early Theories of the Business Cycle

Modern economic history has seen a continuing series of business cycles, or alternating periods of recession and recovery. Before Keynes, economists explained these swings in national income and employment as the result of unfavorable growing conditions, excessive production of goods and services, or overexpansion and eventual contraction or collapse of the banking system.

### *Agricultural Theories*

Economic life has always proceeded irregularly. There have always been good years and bad years, as measured, for example, by the gross national according to classical theory, the labor pricing system is readjusting. Falling wages and prices may eventually restore full employment, "but in the long run," Keynes reportedly observed, "we are all dead." Thus he sought solutions for short-term problems—extremely low production and high unemployment—like those of the Depression. During periods of heavy unemployment in the private sector, he argued, the government should stimulate economic activity by spending more or lowering taxes. In other words, the government should deliberately run a budgetary deficit.

Before Keynes, the prevailing philosophy was that government should balance its budget—that is, spend no more than it collects in taxes. Keynes's proposal—raise government spending or lower taxes—appeared to condone fiscal irresponsibility. Thus his recommendation was branded radical, and his analysis referred to as the "new economics" of unemployment. From the vantage point of the 1980s, however, Keynes's theory of the cause and cure of unemployment appears merely conventional. Over the past four decades, his theory has been interpreted, reinterpreted, refined, and extended. A plethora of doctoral dissertations and journal articles have asked not only "What did Keynes really say?" but "What do the interpreters of Keynes say that Keynes said?" By the 1960s, the Keynesian prescription for dealing with unemployment had become accepted doctrine among most economists and politicians. Only now, after the 1970s, a decade of high unemployment and inflation accompanied by large budgetary deficits, has the general faith in the Keynesian model been shaken.

Keynes tried to deal with the high unemployment and falling prices of the 1930s. But today's high unemployment and rising prices are a combination that Keynesian analysis was not designed to handle. Economists are now searching for an approach better fitted to the conditions of the 1970s and 1980s. Some believe the answer lies in a variation of the Keynesian model. Others have virtually abandoned Keynesianism for the newer monetarist, supply-side, or rational expectations models of the macroeconomy. In some respects, many have returned full circle to a more sophisticated version of classical theory. Keynesian theory is still important, however, for it helps to explain much of what has happened in the economy over the last fifty years, and the government policies that have been adopted as a consequence.

product. When a large proportion of the population was engaged in farming, economic ups and downs were caused by changes in the weather. Poor rainfall or an early frost altered farm production, and hence the level and distribution of income. These changes in turn would affect the demand for various goods and various types of labor. For instance, bad growing conditions hurt merchants who made their living by trading with farmers. And the new supply and demand conditions caused transitional unemployment while wage rates adjusted. During poor weather people moved out of the farm labor market, and unemployment increased among suppliers of agricultural equipment and household goods.

Because agriculture still dominated people's lives in the eighteenth and early nineteenth centuries, social scientists of that time looked to natural causes for an explanation of economic instability. One hundred years ago, for instance, the sunspot theory was a favorite explanation for changes in economic activity. Observers had noticed that sunspots were frequently followed by poor growing seasons. Today, of course, agriculture is much less important to national production, and causes other than sunspots must be sought for cyclical unemployment.

### *The Theory of General Glut*

As commerce and industry developed, people realized that economic fluctuations are not necessarily connected to agriculture. Merchants observed that in some periods business was bad in all lines of merchandise, and they could not dispose of their goods at the usual prices in the usual volume. They reasoned that the problem was overproduction. Too much of all goods had been produced, leading to a general glut of merchandise. Resulting cutbacks in production caused unemployment.

This theory now seems unsophisticated, for the modern economy produces several times more than the level the early theorists considered excessive. In fact, the theory of general glut was attacked almost immediately by Jean Baptiste Say, a French economist of the late eighteenth and early nineteenth centuries. Say argued that in a barter economy, the production of one good for sale represented the demand for another, because its production was a means of gaining purchasing power. That is, we produce more than we want to consume so that we may trade with others to acquire what we want but do not produce. This proposition led to the formulation of Say's law. According to **Say's law**, supply creates its own demand—that is, the production of a supply of products creates an equal demand for goods and services.

**Say's law:** the macroeconomic principle that supply creates its own demand—that is, that the production of a supply of products creates an equal demand for goods and services.

In other words, an increase in the quantity of a good produced must mean that people are demanding more of other goods. Their motive for producing more is to be able to trade for more of something else. At times the wrong goods may be produced for sale, or the wrong quantities of goods. The result will be changes in the relative prices of goods and in the supply and demand for various types of labor, as well as transitional adjustments in employment. That does not mean, however, that a general glut exists, or that demand for all goods and services is insufficient.

## Monetary Theories of the Business Cycle

In a barter economy, Say's law is the correct answer to the theory of general glut. Say hinted, however, that his line of reasoning ran into difficulties when money was introduced into an economic system. If producers hold on to the money they receive from the sale of goods, rather than spending it immediately, the total supply of goods will be greater than the total demand. If a person sells the product of his labor for $100, for instance, but does not spend the money, $100 worth of other goods will be left on the market. Thus for the period of time people hold money, overproduction and a reduction in economic activity will result.

Most early monetary theorists blamed fluctuations in economic activity on the structure of the banking system, specifically contractions of the money supply that occurred during times of financial panic. In the eighteenth and nineteenth centuries, the money stock consisted of gold, silver coins, and paper money printed by banks, called bank notes. If a customer took a bank note to a bank and demanded payment, he would receive gold coins. Because banks made money by extending loans through the issuance of bank notes, there was always a risk of overextension—the banks might create too much money. From time to time, a bank would find itself unable to meet depositors' demands for gold and it would go "bankrupt." Bankruptcy might be the result of bad management or extraordinary circumstances, like poor weather, that made it impossible for people to repay loans. Because banks held deposits in other banks, one bank's financial problems could spread throughout the banking system.

The process of contaction proceeded as follows. A bank under pressure to pay off its customers would withdraw its deposits from other banks. Seeing the run on that bank, customers of other banks would lose confidence in the security of their deposits, and they too would attempt to withdraw their deposits. Banks did not (and still do not) hold sufficient reserves to meet their depositors' demands in times of widespread panic. As a result all banks within a city or perhaps even a nation would collapse at virtually the same time, causing a dramatic decrease in the money stock and in the prices of goods and services. (Remember that $MV = PQ$. With $V$ held constant by institutional constraints, a decrease in $M$ on the left-hand side of the equation must lead to a decrease in $P$ and/or $Q$ on the right-hand side—See Chapter 8. The classical economist argued that a decrease in $M$ would have immediate impact on $P$.)

During widespread bank failure, businesses found that the real value of their financial obligations had risen. The price of their assets fell along with their incomes, yet their debts remained the same in dollar terms. Unable to cope with such financial pressures, many businesses also collapsed, further disrupting the flow of economic activity. At the same time, the dramatic decrease in prices increased real wages. (If the numerator of the real wage, $W$, remains constant while the denominator, $P$, falls, the real wage, $W/P$, increases.) The result was a decrease in the quantity of labor demanded and an increase in unemployment. Though in a competitive labor market, nominal and real wages will eventually move toward equilibrium, during a period of bank failure and contraction of the money stock, unemployment tends to persist. This periodic pattern—a collapse of the banking system followed by a rise in unemployment—prompted the classical economist Irving Fisher to suggest that depressions and booms were merely a consequence of "the dance of the dollar." Attempts were made to correct the instability of the early banking system. In the United States, the Federal Reserve System was created to ensure that banks could count on obtaining additional money when they needed it. In times of financial panic, banks can get all the currency necessary to satisfy depositors' demands from the Fed. By squelching bank runs and preventing the collapse of the banking system, the Fed prevents periods of deflation and their accompanying problems of recession and unemployment.

## The Keynesian Perspective: The Essentials

The philosopher Thomas Kuhn has hypothesized that scientific knowledge is advanced in two distinct ways. New discoveries may be made gradually, in a relatively methodical and orderly procedure. Occasionally, however, there is a sudden radical change in the basic paradigm, or world view, held by scientists. Newton caused such a paradigm change in physics. Later Einstein and the quantum physicists brought about others.[3]

Keynes brought about such a paradigm change in economists' view of recessions and unemployment. Instead of taking the classical labor supply and labor demand curves as his frame of reference, Keynes focused on the interrelationship between the overall real national income level (and therefore employment, since the two are closely related) and the aggregate, or total, demand for goods and services. These two macroeconomic factors interact to form the basis of the circular flow of income.

### The Circular Flow of Income

To see the connection between national income level and aggregate demand in the simplest terms possible, imagine an economy without government. (This assumption is highly unrealistic, but it allows us to develop the basic principles of Keynesianism. We will bring government into the analysis later.) This private economy is divided into two broad categories, households and firms, as in Figure 10.3. In this simplified macroeconomic model, households perform two roles. They supply resources such as labor and capital to firms, and they consume the goods and services produced by the firms. Similarly, firms perform two roles. They receive labor and capital from households and sell their products to them.

The two arrows shown in Figure 10.3 would be sufficient to describe a barter economy. Resources go from households to firms, which in turn supply goods to households in exchange for resources. In a monetary economy, however, the system is more complicated. Resources are supplied to firms in exchange for money or income in the form of wages, dividends, and interest. Households then use that money to buy goods and services from the firm. The flow of money is added to the flow of goods, services, and resources in Figure 10.4.

The money received by households (on the left-hand side of the outer flow) mirrors household earnings. It reflects the contribution of household members to the production of goods and services. If firms produce \$100 worth of goods and services, households must earn an aggregate or national income of \$100, simply because the full value of anything produced must ultimately be attributed to someone. On a conceptual level, income and the value of what is produced are equal (though in practice workers generally take home less than the full value of their earnings). In future discussions, the terms national output and national income will be used interchangeably.

3. Thomas S. Kuhn, *The Structure of Scientific Revolutions*, 2d ed. (Chicago: University of Chicago Press, 1970).

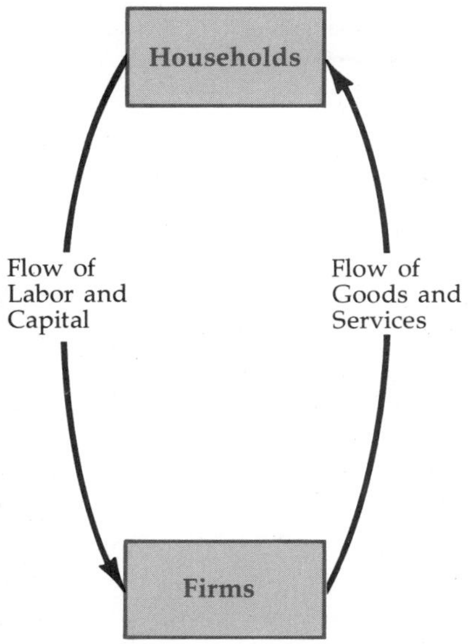


**Figure 10.3.** The Circular Flow of Income in a Barter Economy.
The macroeconomy can be divided into two sectors, households and firms. In a barter economy, resources like labor and capital flow from the households to the firms. Goods and services flow back from the firms to the households.

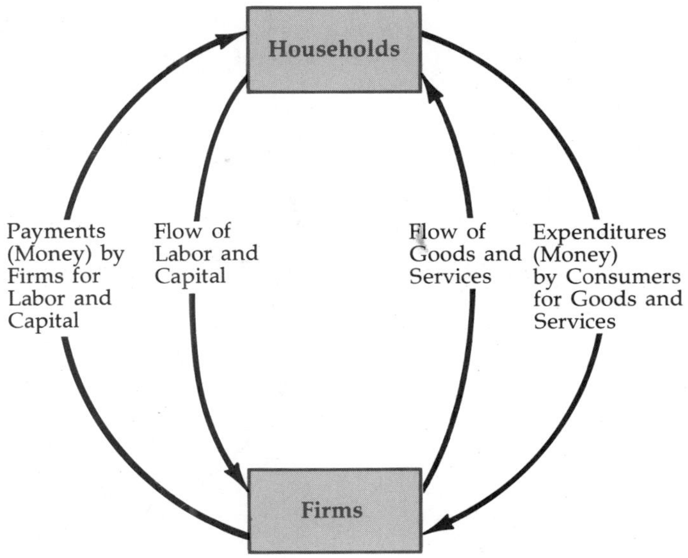


**Figure 10.4.** The Circular Flow of Income in a Money Economy.
In a money economy, firms make money payments to households for the resources they provide. Households then spend the money payments on goods and services produced by the firms.

The circular flow model shows that the ability of firms to sell their products depends on the willingness of households to buy what is produced. And obviously the tendency of households to buy is influenced by the income they earn. Because they determine household income, firms' production plans influence how much households will buy, and thus how much firms will sell. If firms do not produce, households will not have the purchasing power to buy goods and services. Similarly, households' employment opportunities and income depend in part on their aggregate buying decisions. If households in the aggregate refuse to buy goods and services, there will be no basis for employment or paychecks.

Since income and output are by definition equal in value, if households spend all their income on firms' output, all the output will be purchased. But what if firms fail to pay households all they have earned, or households fail to spend what they earn on the goods firms produce? Either households will not receive enough income to buy what has been produced, or firms will not be able to sell all they have produced. In either case, if firms keep producing at full-employment level—that is, at the point where everyone who wants a job can have one—and households continue to spend less than they earn, not all goods will be taken off the market. Unwanted

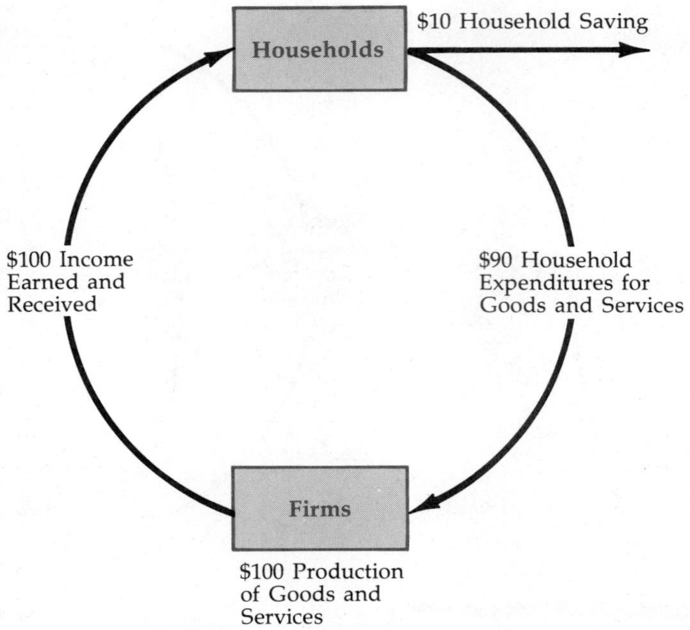


**Figure 10.5.** Leakage from the Circular Flow.
If households save $10 of each $100 they earn, they will buy only $90 of the $100 worth of goods and services produced. If firms then continue to produce at the level of $100, unwanted inventory will pile up. At some point firms will have to curtail production, and unemployment will rise.

inventory (unsold goods) will pile up. To stop the accumulation of unwanted inventory, firms will cut back on production, reducing household income (since fewer man-hours are needed to produce the lower output). To the extent that consumption depends on total income, consumers will reduce their expenditures. The result will be unemployment.

## Saving: A Leakage from the Circular Flow

**Saving:** that portion of income not spent. Represents forgone expenditures on real goods and services.

**Leakage** (outflow): a withdrawal or outflow of income from the circular flow.

The process of income contraction we have been discussing is illustrated in Figure 10.5. Suppose firms pay households $100, but households choose to spend only $90 of their earnings and to save $10. **Saving** is that portion of income not spent; it represents forgone expenditures on real goods and services. Because saving does not go back to firms in the form of purchases, it represents a leakage from the circular flow of income. A **leakage** is a withdrawal or outflow of income from the circular flow. Saving, taxes, and imports are all leakages from the circular flow. As a result of the $10 saving leakage, firms will sell only $90 worth of what they have produced, and will be left with $10 worth of unwanted inventory. If they continue to produce $100 worth of goods and households continue to save $10, inventory will mount by $10 each time $100 worth of goods is produced.

Firms must eventually try to bring their production level into line with their sales. At that point they will reduce both employment and household income—depressing consumer expenditures as well as household saving. To take up this new slack, firms may have to reduce production still further. For example, if producers reduce production to $90 (because households have been spending only $90 out of $100), people may in turn reduce their saving from $10 to $7. But they will still be spending only $83 ($90 of income minus $7 of saving). Goods will continue to go unsold, and production will have to be reduced further.

At this point you may ask why prices do not fall in response to the surplus of goods and services. In practice they may very well fall. But in its most basic form, the Keynesian model of the macroeconomy assumes constant prices—a controversial assumption, as you can imagine. We will sidestep the difficulty for the moment by stating the rationale for the assumption of constant prices. First, the Keynesian model is intended to describe the short run, a period during which prices are more or less inflexible and adjustments in economic activity are expressed at least as much in output as in price. Income, in other words, is assumed to adjust faster than prices.

Second, as prices fall, wages and other payments to households must fall as well. Although a given number of dollars will now buy more, there are fewer dollars in income to buy with. Thus lower prices may not stimulate greater sales. Eventually, prices and wages may decline enough to induce consumers to buy more, if only because their savings are worth more after deflation. As prices fall, the purchasing power of bank account deposits rises, creating a "wealth effect." That is, because people feel wealthier at lower price levels, they tend to spend more. But again, the Keynesian model is designed for the short run. During the time it takes for wages and prices to fall, production and employment can also decline. As Keynes is supposed to have said, "In the long run we are all dead." Though economic problems may eventually work themselves out, that prospect provides small comfort to people who are unemployed during the weeks and months, or even years, of the adjustment process.

## Investment: An Injection into the Circular Flow

**Injection** (inflow): an inflow of income into the circular flow.

The damaging effects of leakages from the circular flow can be partially offset by corresponding injections. An **injection** is an inflow of income into the circular flow. Investment, government expenditures, and exports are all injections. By investment we do not mean the purchase of stocks and bonds by individuals, but the purchase of investment goods by businesses. **Investment** is the purchase of capital goods—plant, equipment, and inventory—that can be used in the production of other goods and services.

**Investment:** the purchase of capital goods—plant, equipment, and inventory—that can be used in the production of other goods and services.

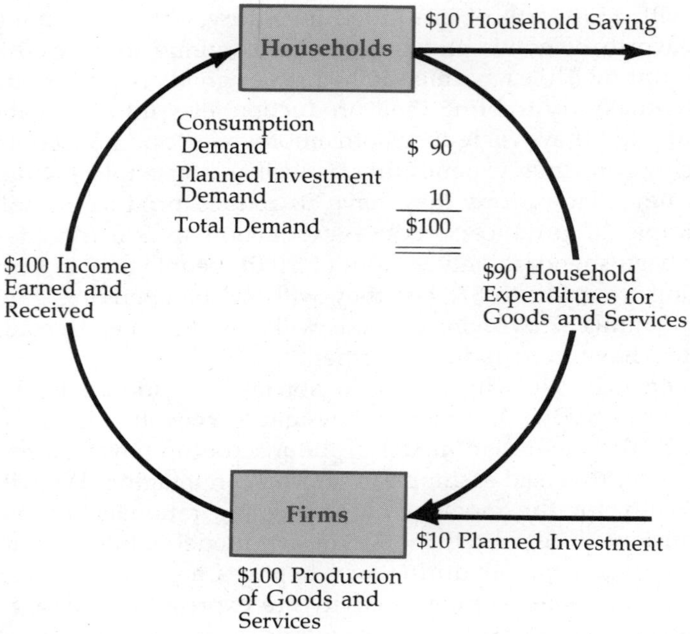


**Figure 10.6.** Injection into the Circular Flow.
When the saving outflow exactly equals the planned investment inflow, the macroeconomy is in equilibrium. The total demand for goods and services exactly equals the quantity of goods and services produced, and firms have no reason to expand or contract production.

**Planned investment:** anticipated, scheduled purchases of plant, equipment, and inventory.

**Unplanned investment:** unanticipated, unscheduled purchases of plant, equipment, and inventory.

Investment may be planned (and therefore desired) or unplanned (undesired). **Planned investment** includes anticipated, scheduled purchases of plant, equipment, and inventory. **Unplanned investment** includes unanticipated, unscheduled purchases of plant, equipment, and inventory. Unplanned investment is purchase by default. It represents goods that were produced to be sold, but ended up as inventory because no one bought them.

Figure 10.6 shows a planned investment expenditure of $10. If this inflow into the circular flow equals the saving outflow, all the goods the economy has produced will be purchased. Households will buy $90 and save $10. Firms will buy the remaining $10 worth of goods in the form of capital goods (plant and equipment) and perhaps some additions to inventory. Total planned expenditures by consumers and investors (*TPE*) will exactly equal the national income-output level (*Y*) at $100. The economy, in other words, will be in equilibrium. Firms will have no reason to produce more or less than they are already producing, for households and firms together will demand no more or less. Equilibrium is achieved when total planned spending equals national income or output. And that is precisely the case in Figure 10.6. Planned investment equals saving at $10, and national income and output do not change.

If an economic system is at full employment, it will tend to remain so as long as planned investment and saving remain constant. If discrepancies between saving and planned investment arise, however, aggregate income and employment will be affected. For instance, if saving rises to $15 while planned investment falls to $5, households and firms will spend a total of only $90 ($85 in consumption and $5 in planned investment). As a result $10 worth of goods will go unsold, ending up as unplanned investment. Firms will then seek to reduce their unplanned inventory by cutting back on production. The result will be a rise in unemployment.

## Maintaining the Equilibrium Income Level

Keynes saw two problems in achieving and maintaining a full-employment national income level. The first had to do with getting wages and prices to adjust enough so that everyone who wanted to work would be employed. The second had to do with ensuring that demand would be sufficient to take off the market all the goods and services produced by the fully employed labor force. In terms of the circular flow model, saving must equal planned investment at the full-employment income level. Keynes questioned the classical theory that interest rates would adjust to bring saving in line with investment.

### Equalizing Saving and Investment: The Classical Theory of Interest Rates

Is there a way to equalize saving and planned investment? Classical economists thought that a change in the market interest rate would bring saving into line with planned investment. That is, people will decide how much to save according to the interest rate. If the interest rate rises, they will save more, and vice versa. With higher interest rates, people will give up more goods and services today in anticipation of even greater quantities in the future.

Planned investment, on the other hand, decreases as the rate of interest increases—and vice versa. Obviously, firms will want each project to earn a rate of return at least as high as the cost of borrowing to finance it. At a 10 percent interest rate, for instance, firms will not wish to invest in any project that yields a return of less than 10 percent. Thus if interest rates are low, firms can afford to undertake a variety of projects, some of which may earn only a modest return. But at high interest rates, they can justify investing only in lucrative projects.

Figure 10.7 shows the relationship of investment and saving to interest rates. The investment curve slopes down, reflecting the inverse relationship between planned investment and interest rates. The saving curve slopes up, indicating the direct relationship between saving and interest rates. People save more (and invest less) as the interest rate rises.

Just how is the interest rate adjusted to bring saving and investment into line? Classical economists argued that in a competitive market, the interest rate will move automatically toward the intersection of the saving and investment curves—$R_2$ in Figure 10.7. If the interest rate is below that level—say $R_1$—the demand for funds to invest ($I_3$) will be greater than the amount of money made available for investment through saving ($S_1$). The interest rate will rise, causing investors to cut back on their planned investment and households to save more. At $R_2$, saving ($S_2$) will equal planned investment ($I_2$). Likewise, if the interest rate is above $R_2$, firms will want to borrow less ($I_1$) than people will want to save ($S_3$), and the interest rate will fall. Again, at $R_2$, the levels of saving and investment are equal. In terms of the circular flow of income, the economy will be in equilibrium. Then, classical theory indicates, unless obstacles in the labor market prevent adjustments in the wage rate and the prices of other resources, the economy will move toward full employment.

## Keynesian Objections to the Classical Theory of Interest Rates

Keynes believed that interest rates cannot be expected to adjust quickly to close a gap between saving and investment. He emphasized that labor will resist wage reductions, which can keep the wage rate above equilibrium, creating temporary but major unemployment problems. Moreover, he argued, the interest rate depends on other forces besides the demand for investment and the supply of savings. People need to hold part of their incomes as cash or bank balances, both to carry out day-to-day transactions and to have some reserve for unexpected purchases or emergencies.

Some people also hold on to money in hopes that its value will rise in the future. This speculative motive for holding money requires additional explanation. If people expect interest rates to go up, they will want to maintain larger-than-usual money balances. For if they lend their money out now, they will be stuck with a low rate of interest in the future. But if they are correct in their expectations, they will be able to lend it at a higher rate later. While speculators wait for a better interest rate, they are neither spending their funds nor lending them to investors. Their speculation keeps the rate above the intersection of the investment and saving curves in Figure 10.7 and causes a leakage from the circular flow that is not offset by a corresponding injection.

Figure 10.8 shows the impact of this discrepancy on the national income level. Planned investment is only \$5, while \$15 is being saved. Consumers will buy \$85 worth of goods and services (\$100 in income minus \$15 in saving) and investors will buy \$5. Total planned spending will therefore be \$90, \$10 short of the value of the goods and services produced (\$100). Because the planned investment inflow does not fully offset the saving outflow, producers will eventually cut back on production, to stop the accumulation of excess inventory. Production, income, and employment

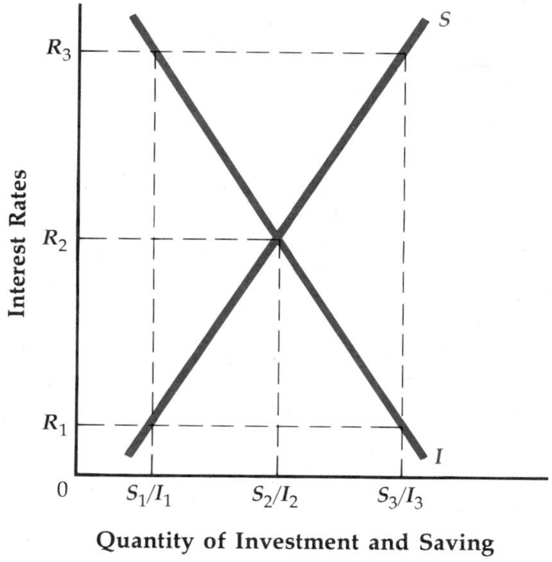


**Figure 10.7.** The Relationship of Saving and Investment to Interest Rates: The Classical Theory.
Classical economists assumed that interest rates would adjust to maintain equality between saving ($S$) and investment ($I$). If saving falls short of the demand for investment, as at interest rate $R_1$, the rate will move up to $R_2$ to bring saving and investment into equilibrium. If saving exceeds investment demand, as at $R_3$, the rate will adjust down to $R_2$.

will spiral downward. With reduced production, fewer workers will be needed and household income will fall, reducing consumption and causing further cutbacks in production and employment.

This downward spiral, fortunately, will not continue indefinitely. Assuming (to simplify the analysis) that planned investment remains constant as saving and income fall, at some point saving and planned investment will become equal. This point is called the equilibrium income level. The **equilibrium income level** is the level at which producers have no reason to change their output level. It is reached when leakages equal injections. The process by which saving falls to meet planned investment is shown in Figure 10.9. As income decreases, the saving curve shifts to the left, reaching equality with planned investment at the higher interest rate of $R_2$. A new equilibrium income level is established—but at a lower national income and a higher unemployment rate.

**Equilibrium income level:** the income level at which producers have no reason to change their output level. Reached when leakages equal injections.

We can now state the central difference between the classical and the Keynesian models. In the classical model, the theoretical focus is on how interest rates adjust to eliminate discrepancies between saving and investment. In the Keynesian model, the theoretical focus is mainly (but not exclusively) on how income adjusts to alleviate those discrepancies.

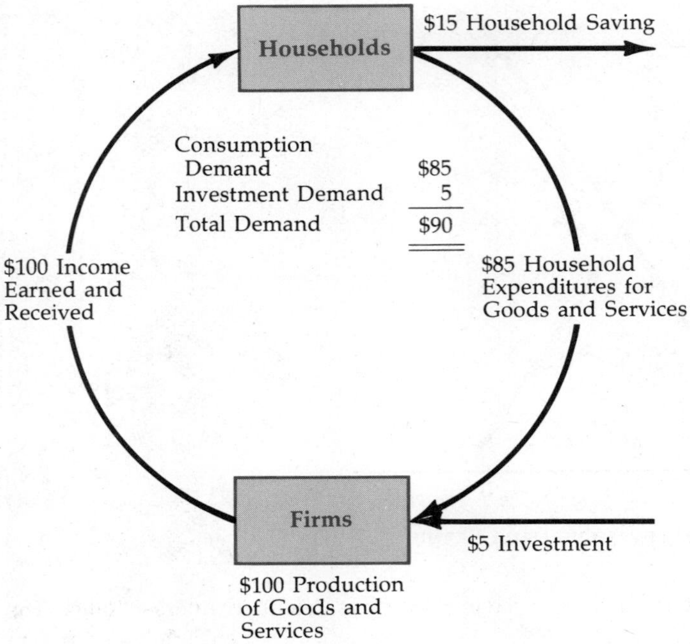


**Figure 10.8.** Disequilibrium in National Income.
When household saving ($15) is greater than investment expenditures ($5), aggregate demand ($90) falls short of the level of production ($100). Unwanted inventory will build up and eventually production will be cut back, reducing national income and raising the unemployment level.

Whereas the classical economists argued that the saving curve would not shift, because interest rates would adjust downward rapidly, Keynes insisted that speculation would slow down interest rate adjustments. Equilibrium would be reached only after production levels—and income—had fallen.

In the Keynesian model, the interest rate usually does adjust downward over the long run, as people alter their expectations about future interest rates. If workers believe that increasing unemployment and a falling national production level will cause interest rates to fall, for instance, they will lend their money at present interest rates rather than holding on to it. In doing so, they will reduce interest rates (because they will be increasing the supply of funds for hire). The lower interest rates will stimulate investment, production, and the demand for goods and services, increasing the need for labor. In the long run, a decline in wages and prices may cause a drop in the real wage rate and an increase in wealth held in dollars. It may bring additional increases in planned consumer and investment expenditures and additional reductions in unemployment. In the meantime, however, unemployment can be a significant social

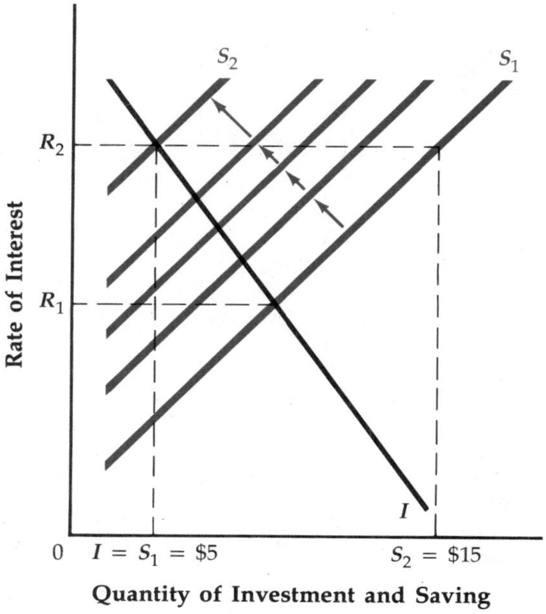


**Figure 10.9.** The Relationship of Saving and Investment to Interest Rates: The Keynesian Theory.
According to Keynesian theory, the speculative demand for money may prevent interest rates from falling to bring saving into line with investment. If saving exceeds investment at interest rate $R_1$, aggregate demand will fall short of national production. Firms will cut back on production, causing further drops in income and saving (see Figure 10.8). As saving falls, the saving curve will shift inward from $S_1$ to $S_2$. Equilibrium will be restored at the higher interest rate $R_2$.

problem. The Keynesian prescription for government spending during a recession was directed at these short-run cyclical unemployment problems. Keynes was fully aware that his policy recommendations would not begin to solve long-run unemployment problems, which can last for decades.

## Adding Government to the Circular Flow

So far we have seen that if households receive from firms an amount of income equal to their earnings, and spend all they receive on goods and services produced by firms, the income flow will remain constant and the macroeconomy will be at equilibrium. Saving, however, constitutes a leakage from the circular flow. And unless planned saving is offset by planned investment, the national income level will fall. If investment exceeds saving, the income level will rise—provided, of course, that unemployed resources can be used in production.

What can government do to modulate swings in economic activity that result from discrepancies between saving and investment? Like saving, government taxes are a diversion of consumer purchasing power away

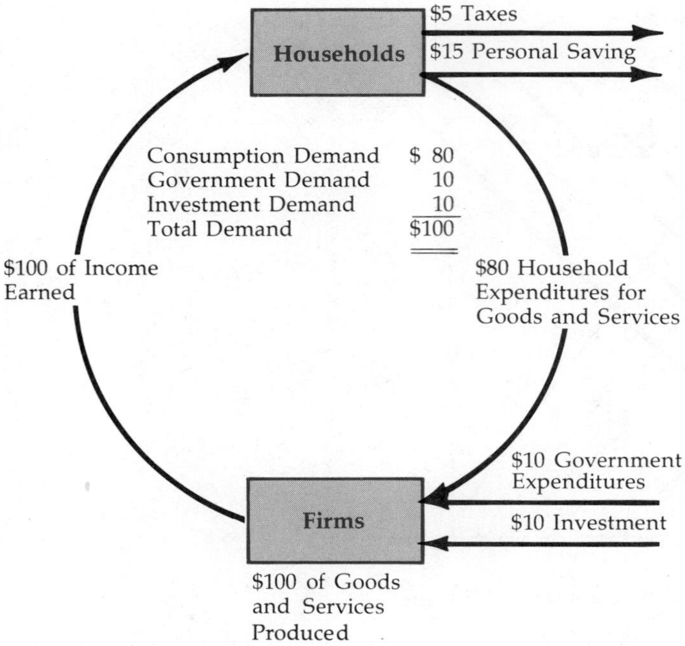


**Figure 10.10.** The Circular Flow of Income, Government Included.
If government is introduced into the circular flow model, equilibrium in national income occurs when total outflows—planned saving plus taxes—exactly equal total inflows—planned investment plus government expenditures. Here taxes at $5 plus saving at $15 equal government expenditures at $10 plus investment at $10.

from the circular flow.[4] Taxes may eventually reenter the circular flow in the form of planned government expenditures. But at the moment government extracts them from the flow, taxes have essentially the same effect as personal saving. For this reason, taxes are shown as an outflow in Figure 10.10. At the same time, government expenditures on goods and services (such as defense systems, buildings, and roads) are paid to firms, and constitute an inflow to the economy. Because they resemble business purchases of capital equipment (investment), planned government expenditures are also represented by an arrow pointing toward the circular flow.

Once government has been introduced into the analysis, we can see that equality in planned saving and investment is not enough to ensure that national income will be at equilibrium. National income equilibrium

4. Corporate income taxes, property taxes, and sales and excise taxes also divert funds from businesses and stockholders to the government. To keep the analysis as simple as possible, we shall ignore these forms of taxation. Their exclusion will not affect the general argument or the conclusions drawn.

occurs when total outflows (planned saving plus taxes) equal total inflows (planned investment plus government expenditures), as in Figure 10.10. Assume again that the economy produces \$100 worth of goods and services. Households earn that amount in income, but they pay \$5 in taxes and save \$15. Planned government expenditures and planned business investment are each \$10. The planned consumption demand of households is therefore \$80 [\$100 − (\$5 + \$15)]; business and government demand is \$20 (\$10 + \$10). Total planned expenditure equals national income at \$100. Since all the goods firms have produced are sold to investors, consumers, or the government, firms have no reason either to raise or to lower production.

Total planned expenditures (*TPE*) is now composed of three types of expenditure: planned consumption (*C*), planned investment (*I*), and planned government spending (*G*).

$$TPE = C + I + G$$

Similarly, people can do three things with the income they earn (*Y*); they can spend it (*C*), save it (*S*), or pay taxes with it (*T*).

$$Y = C + S + T$$

Since in equilibrium, total planned expenditure must equal national income ($TPE = Y$), the components of total planned expenditure must equal national income.

$$Y = C + I + G$$

In Figure 10.10, this condition is met. One hundred dollars of income is earned. Consumers in the aggregate spend \$80 on goods and services; firms spend \$10 on investment goods; and government spends \$10.

$$TPE = \$80 + \$10 + \$10 = \$100 = Y$$

If total planned expenditures equal national income, the components of total planned expenditure must equal the components of national income.

$$C + I + G = C + S + T$$

This equation reduces to $I + G = S + T$, because the *C*s on either side of the equal sign cancel out. In terms of the circular flow model, $I + G = S + T$ simply means that in equilibrium, planned inflows must equal planned outflows. That is the case in our example.

$$\$10 + \$10 = \$15 + \$5$$

## The Function of Deficits

In the last example, planned saving is greater than planned investment. In our earlier model, when planned saving exceeded planned investment, the income level fell and unemployment rose. In this case, however, government expenditures offset the difference between saving and investment. Government planned expenditures exceed taxes by the same amount that saving exceeds investment, $5. The government runs a budgetary deficit in this example, borrowing $5 from savers to make up the difference between taxes and expenditures. In doing so, it keeps the national income level from falling.

According to Keynesian theory, budget deficits should not always be feared or avoided. The stable equilibrium income level achieved with a deficit exceeds the income level to which the economy might fall without a deficit. In our example, if taxes and government expenditures both equaled $10 (that is, if the budget were balanced), consumption demand would be only $75: $100 in income minus $10 in taxes and $15 in saving. Total demand would be $95: $75 in consumption plus $10 in government expenditures and $10 in investment. Five dollars worth of goods and services would not be sold, and firms would have to cut back on production. The national income level would decline in a spiraling process of lower consumption and lower income.

If some resources remain unemployed, government can raise the national income level by increasing outflows over inflows. It can reduce taxes or it can increase expenditures on roads, schools, and hospitals. Or it can reduce taxes and increase expenditures at the same time. Regardless, the Keynesian prescription for unemployment is to run a budgetary deficit—or if the government is enjoying a budgetary surplus, to run a smaller surplus. The overriding goal is to bolster total planned expenditures, which may or may not mean deficit spending.

Suppose, for instance, that the government increases expenditures from $10 to $15, as in Figure 10.11. Consumption demand is still $80, but with the increase in government spending, total planned expenditures rise to $105. Consumers, investors, and government are now demanding more than firms are producing, giving firms an incentive to raise their production levels. Increased production means a higher income level and increased consumption, which in turn induces firms to produce even more goods and services and generate more income. In this way, the national income level moves up.

As the economy moves upward toward the new, higher equilibrium income level, however, planned saving will rise in response. Taxes will also rise if income tax rates are tied to household income levels. For instance, if national income increases from $100 to $110, saving may rise from $15 to $16, and taxes may rise from $5 to $5.25. When the sum of planned saving and taxes equals the new, higher level of planned investment and government expenditure ($25), a new equilibrium income level will be achieved.

Reducing taxes can produce virtually the same increase in national income as increasing government expenditures. The main difference in this case is that people may put a portion of their tax reduction into saving. A $5 reduction in taxes may mean a $1 increase in saving, and as a result total outflows will fall by only $4 instead of $5. Therefore an increase in government expenditures will tend to have a slightly greater effect on the national income level than would an equal decrease in taxes.

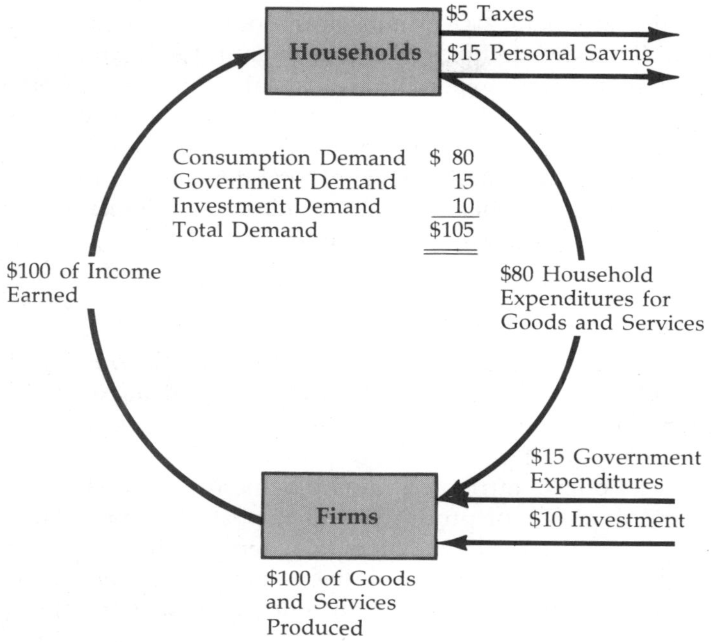


**Figure 10.11.** Rising National Income.
When the total inflows exceed total outflows, total planned expenditures will exceed national income. If some resources, capital, and workers are still unemployed, the national income level will rise.

## Summary and Extensions

The Keynesian revolution must be seen in historical context. The classical approach to reducing unemployment is to speed up the flow of information to workers who are transitionally unemployed and reduce restrictions on wage and labor movements, such as minimum wage laws, union shops, and race and sex discrimination. But Keynes and his followers accepted such restrictions as a political reality, assuming little could be done about them in the short run. Instead they suggested another means of correcting unemployment—an increase in total demand for goods and services.

According to the Keynesian model of the circular flow of income, periods of low production and high unemployment result from a discrepancy between saving and planned investment. With everything else held equal, the national income level will fall and unemployment will rise when planned investment expenditures are less than the level of saving. (If planned investment expenditures exceed the level of saving, the national income level will rise and unemployment will fall.)

To restore national income and production to their former levels, government must somehow increase total demand, offsetting the gap between saving and investment. Government can boost total demand by increasing its expenditures while holding taxes constant. Or it can reduce taxes while holding government expenditures constant. A rise in government expenditures increases total demand directly. Reducing taxes achieves the same effect indirectly. If people take home more pay, they can be expected to spend more, increasing the level of total demand. In the next chapter we will explore these policies in more detail, as we examine a more complicated version of the Keynesian model.

## Major Conclusions

1. John Maynard Keynes is remembered primarily for his *General Theory of Employment, Interest, and Money* (1936), a book that dealt with the high unemployment and low production levels that characterized much of the world economy during the Great Depression.
2. Before Keynes, economists attributed unemployment to normal shifts in the supply and demand for products, and to obstacles in the labor market that prevented wage rate adjustments. Unemployment was also thought to result from changes in the money stock, which affect the real wage rate paid to labor and therefore the quantity of labor supplied and demanded.
3. Keynes argued that unemployment could result from the failure of consumers and businesses to demand all the goods produced by the economy. If businesses and consumers do not plan to buy all that is produced, firms will accumulate excess inventory and will have to cut back on production, increasing the unemployment level.
4. In classical theory, the interest rate adjusts to equalize saving and investment. In the Keynesian model, the national income level adjusts to bring saving and investment into line.
5. In the Keynesian model of the circular flow of income, the conditions for macroeconomic equilibrium can be stated in two ways. First, the macroeconomy will be in equilibrium when total demand for goods and services exactly equals total output. Second, leaving government out of the analysis, the macroeconomy will be in equilibrium when the saving of households and firms exactly equals firms' planned investment expenditures (the purchase of plant and equipment). The equilibrium income level is not necessarily the full-employment level.
6. According to Keynesian theory, as long as some unemployment exists, government can expand national income and employment by increasing total spending. It can do so either by increasing its own expenditures on goods and services or by lowering taxes, thus increasing household and business expenditures.
7. According to the Keynesian model, government budgetary deficits are not necessarily bad. As long as some unemployment exists and saving

exceeds investment, government can raise the national income level by increasing its expenditures. Whether it must run a deficit to do so is not important.

## Questions to Ponder

1. According to the classical model of the labor market (see Figures 10.1 and 10.2), how will a rapid rise in the price level affect employment? What will happen to the money wage rate? To the real wage rate?
2. Suppose investment increases. What will happen to the equilibrium level of income, according to classical theory? According to Keynesian theory?
3. The graph below shows saving and investment as a function of the interest rate. Suppose the interest rate is held above equilibrium at $R_2$. If the equilibrium income level falls, as Keynesian theory suggests it should, what will happen to saving? Why?

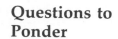

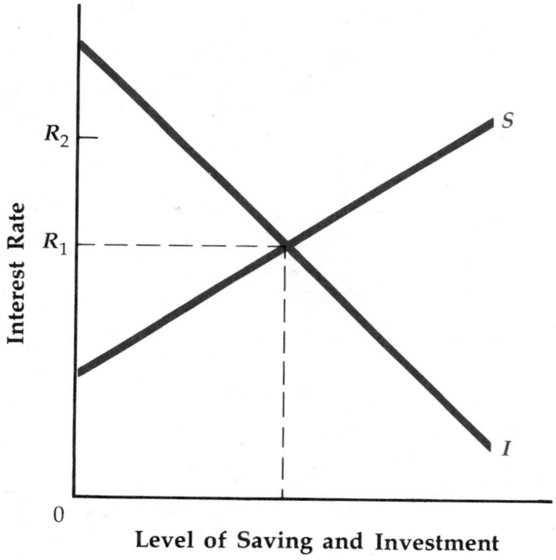


4. Given the information in the graph for question 3, assume that the interest rate declines slowly when saving exceeds investment. Will the equilibrium income level fall by as much as if the interest rate were held rigidly at $R_2$? Explain your answer using both a graph and a circular flow diagram like the one in Figure 10.6.
5. Suppose that saving and investment are equal and the government runs a budgetary deficit. What will happen to the national income level in the Keynesian model?

## Central Question

*How are the equilibrium national income and employment levels determined?*

## Key Terms

Investment function

Marginal propensity to save

Saving function

Dissaving

Consumption function

Marginal propensity to consume

Total expenditure function

Multiplier

Paradox of thrift

Chapter 11

# Unemployment and the Equilibrium Income Level: A More Complicated Model

*It is too early to say, but it does not now appear an extravagant statement, that Keynes may in the end rival Adam Smith in his influence on the economic thinking and governmental policy of his time and age. Both lived at profound turning points in the evolution of the economic order. Both were products of their times. Yet both were also powerful agents in giving direction to the unfolding process of institutional change.*

*Alvin Hansen*

The circular flow model developed in the preceding chapter provided a broad picture of the Keynesian macroeconomy. But the equilibrium national income level and its relationship to savings and consumer expenditures were only lightly sketched. And while the model demonstrated the direction in which national income will move when planned saving and investment are unequal, it did not indicate the extent of the change.

This chapter attempts to add precision to the Keynesian analysis of how the national income and employment levels are determined. First we will develop more fully the concepts of planned saving and investment and their role in determining the equilibrium national income level. Then we will examine national income from the perspective of total spending, using the concept of planned consumption. To keep the analysis simple, government will be excluded from the model. In the next chapter, however, we will reintroduce government in connection with the question of possible remedies for high unemployment and low production levels.

## The Planned Investment and Saving Approach to Income Equilibrium

Chapter 10 presented three essential conclusions of Keynesian analysis. First, if the level of planned saving exceeds the level of planned investment during any given period, total spending on goods and services by households and firms will fall short of the national production level. Unable to sell all they have produced, firms will accumulate excess inventory and will eventually have to cut back on production. When production is curtailed, the national income level will fall. Because less is produced, total earnings (also called national income) must also be less.

Second, if planned investment expenditure exceeds planned saving, total spending for goods and services will exceed the quantity of goods and services produced. Production will fall short of sales, and inventory will dwindle to undesirably low levels. If some workers and other resources are unemployed, firms will hire them and expand production. The national income level will rise.

Third, when planned saving equals planned investment, the producing sector of the economy has no reason to expand or contract production. As long as planned saving and investment remain equal, the circular flow of income will remain constant and the macroeconomy will be at equilibrium.

We can now refine the Keynesian analysis, by adding detail to these fundamental conclusions.

### The Investment Function

The planned investment expenditures of businesses on plant, equipment, and inventory are influenced by many variables, including the market interest rate; the national income level; expectations regarding the profitability of future production; government tax policies; the discovery of new ways of producing goods; and the development of new goods themselves.

As we saw in Chapter 10, planned investment expenditures are likely to be inversely related to market interest rates. That is, investment will rise as interest rates fall and decline as interest rates rise. There are at least two possible explanations for this inverse relationship. First, when interest rates are low, firms are better able to justify borrowing to expand their plant and equipment. A larger number of investment projects will meet their profitability criteria when the cost of borrowed funds is relatively low. Second, a rise in interest rates may persuade some firms to postpone investment until rates decline again.

The level of planned business investment tends to increase or decrease along with the level of national income and with the utilization of the nation's productive capacity. During prosperous periods, when national income is on the rise, businesses are more profitable and thus have more funds on hand to invest. Many businesses will expand their facilities to meet the rising demand for their products. Furthermore, entrepreneurs tend to project present business conditions into the future. Their confidence in future investments rises in prosperous times and falls during depressed periods. Planned investment can therefore be expected to rise and fall with current economic conditions, for it represents plant and equipment that can be used only in the future.

The introduction of new technology can significantly affect the general level of planned investment. The development of the automobile, for instance, stimulated considerable investment in roads, service stations, tourist facilities, and assembly lines. In the future, solar and wind technologies may have a similar effect on the level and distribution of planned investment expenditure. Government tax policies also influence the profitability of current investment. An increase in business taxes will generally reduce planned investment, for firms will have less after-tax income to devote to new plant and equipment.

National income is probably one of the most important factors affecting investment. Its relationship to investment is called the investment function. The **investment function** is the assumed relationship between national income and total planned expenditures on plant, equipment, and inventory. For the moment, however, we will assume that planned investment does not vary, not even with income. Later in our discussion we will discard this simplifying assumption and consider the effect of a change in interest rates or tax policy on investment and national income. For now, given our assumption, the investment function can be represented by a horizontal line, as in Figure 11.1(a), where planned investment is constant at $I_1$, or $400 billion.

**Investment function:** the assumed relationship between national income and total planned expenditures on plant, equipment, and inventory.

## The Saving Function

The level of saving is influenced by many variables. They include current interest rates on bonds and savings accounts; personal income; income tax rates; job security; and current demand for goods and services (since saving is defined as the unspent portion of disposable income). High interest rates increase the relative price of current consumption, for a

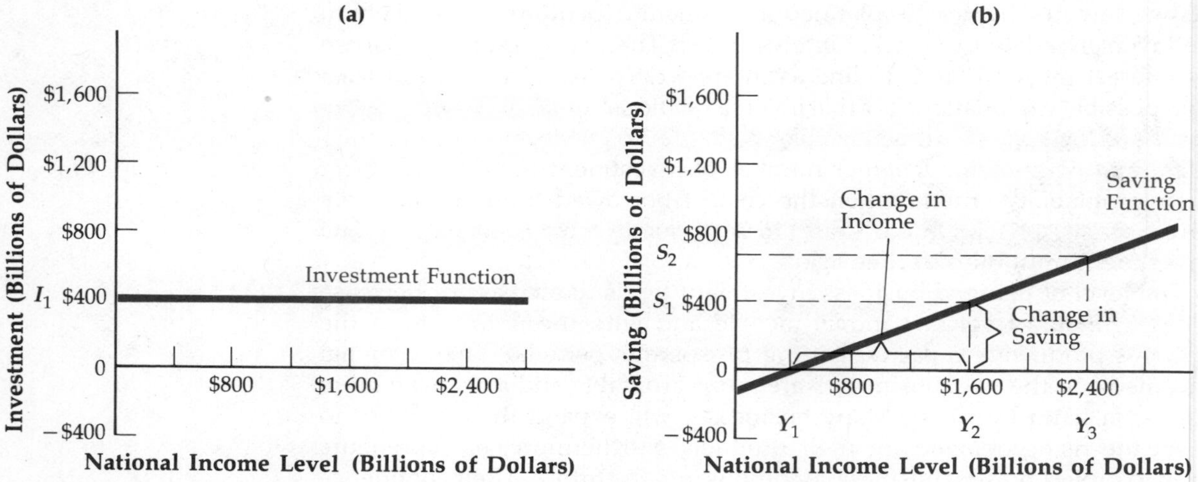


**Figure 11.1.** Planned Investment and Saving.
If it is assumed that planned investment is unaffected by the national income level, the investment function can be drawn as a horizontal line, as in part (a). Investment remains constant at $I_1$ at all income levels. If it is assumed that planned saving is directly related to national income, the saving function must be drawn as an upward-sloping curve, as in part (b). At an income level of $Y_1$, total saving is assumed to be zero. At income levels of $Y_2$ and $Y_3$, saving is $S_1$ and $S_2$, respectively.

failure to save means forgoing relatively more future income. During times of rising interest rates, then, people tend to reduce their consumption, save more of their incomes, and postpone some spending.

When personal income rises, people are encouraged to buy more security (among other goods and services). People purchase security by adding to their savings, thus increasing their financial reserves for less advantageous times. Because personal and corporate income taxes significantly affect workers' take-home pay and firms' after-tax profits, tax rates have an indirect influence on personal saving and corporate dividends and investment. Planned saving generally moves in the opposite direction from taxes. As taxes rise, saving falls, and vice versa.

Expectations about future inflation rates and income levels also influence current planned saving. If people expect prices to rise sharply in the future, they will tend to buy more and save less now, to avoid relatively high future prices. If they expect their future income to drop significantly, they are likely to save more now, to build up the cash reserves they will need.

To keep the discussion simple, we will assume that except for income, all variables that influence the level of saving are given. Like Keynes, we will assume that planned saving varies directly with the national income level. In the aggregate, people will save a portion of any increase in their income. This tendency, known as the marginal propensity to save, can be stated as a ratio. The **marginal propensity to save** (*MPS*) is the percentage of any change in total income that consumers are inclined to save.

**Marginal propensity to save:** the percentage of any change in total income that consumers are inclined to save.

$$MPS = \frac{\text{change in saving}}{\text{change in national income}}$$

To illustrate, if the marginal propensity to save is 10 percent ($MPS = 1/10$), people as a group will be inclined to change their level of planned saving by 10 percent of any increase or decrease in their income. If their incomes rise by $100, they will be inclined to save $10 more than before (10 percent of $100). Likewise a $100 decrease in total income will reduce planned saving by $10. The higher the marginal propensity to save, the greater the change in planned saving that results from any given change in national income.

The upward-sloping curve in Figure 11.1(b) represents this assumed direct relationship between saving and income, called the saving function. The **saving function** is the assumed direct relationship between national income and the amount of income saved (not spent on goods and services). As it is drawn, the saving function incorporates the assumption that there is some income level at which people save nothing—in Figure 11.1(b), level $Y_1$. The U.S. economy operated on the zero-saving income level for several years during the 1930s, when Americans as a group saved nothing. At income levels higher than $Y_1$, the planned saving level is positive—that is, people are adding to their financial assets. For instance, at an income level of $Y_2$, people plan to save a total of $400 billion ($S_1$). At an income level of $Y_3$, they plan to save $666 billion ($S_2$). When their income is less than $Y_1$, people engage in planned dissaving, also called negative saving. **Dissaving** is any net withdrawal from accumulated past savings, or any net increase in borrowing. That is, at levels below $Y_1$, people as a group are withdrawing funds from their savings accounts or borrowing to meet their financial obligations. Regardless of the particular income and planned saving levels, the upward-sloping curve reflects the fundamental assumption that income and saving are directly related.[1]

**Saving function:** the assumed direct relationship between national income and the amount of income saved (not spent on goods and services).

**Dissaving:** any net withdrawal from accumulated past savings, or any net increase in borrowing.

## The Equilibrium National Income Level

Figure 11.2(a) shows both the saving and investment functions. Given the information summarized, we can determine that the economy will move toward an equilibrium national income level of $Y_2$, or $1,600 billion.

1. Geometrically, the slope of a curve like the planned saving function is equal to the opposite side of the triangle $Y_1Y_2E$ divided by the adjacent side, or the change in $S$ divided by the change in $Y$, which is also the marginal propensity to save:

$$\text{slope of saving function} = \frac{\text{change in saving}}{\text{change in national income}} = MPS$$

As the curve is drawn, the change in saving is substantially less than the change in income; the marginal propensity to save is much less than 1. In other words, people are assumed to save only a minor fraction of any change in income—an assumption supported by real-world experience.

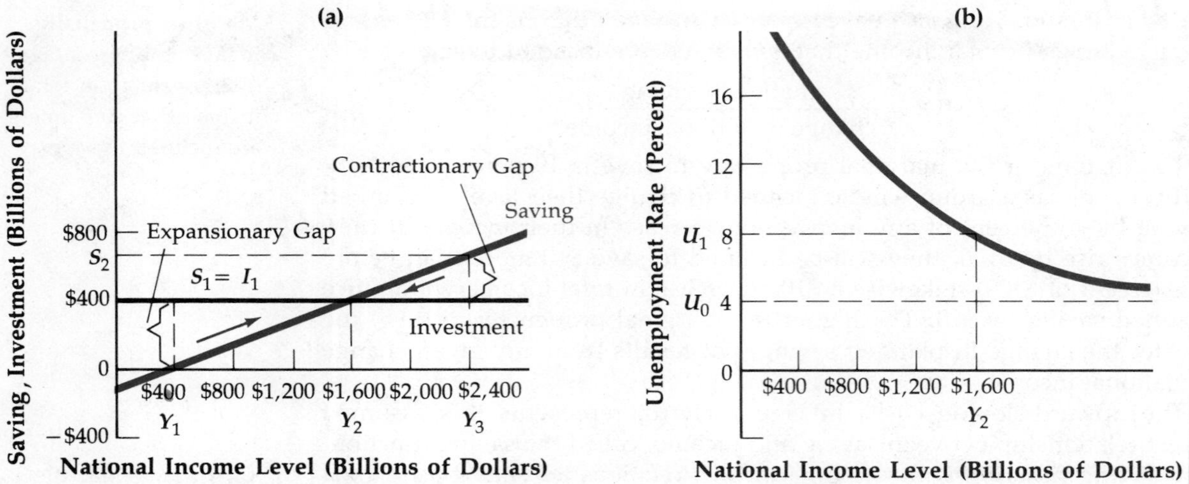


**Figure 11.2.** Determining the National Income Level: The Planned Investment and Saving Approach.
The equilibrium national income level is $Y_2$, or $1,600 billion, the point where saving equals investment. At national income levels above $Y_2$, saving will exceed investment and the national income level will fall. At national income levels lower than $Y_2$, investment will exceed saving and the national income level will rise.
The equilibrium income level may or may not be the full-employment income level. In part (b), the equilibrium income level corresponds to an unemployment rate of 8 percent.

Suppose the economy is generating an income of $Y_3$, or $2,400 billion. Planned investment will be at its assumed constant level of $I_1$, or $400 billion, but planned saving will be at the higher level of $S_2$. Rather than purchasing all $Y_3$ goods, that is, people will be saving part of their income, causing a gap between planned saving and investment. At an income level of $Y_3$, firms will produce more than they will sell. They will pile up unplanned additions to inventory, and at some point will have to cut back on production, thus reducing total income.

This reduction in total income will reduce planned saving. As Figure 11.2(a) shows, the movement back from $Y_3$ will eventually close the gap between planned saving and investment. At $Y_2$ the two will be equal. Once at $Y_2$, firms may try to expand production. If they do, planned saving will increase and unplanned investment (inventory) will again pile up, causing firms to move back toward $Y_2$ again.

If, on the other hand, the economy is operating below $Y_2$—say at $Y_1$—firms in the aggregate will have an incentive to expand production. At $Y_1$, planned saving is zero, but planned investment is at the higher level of $I_1$. Consumers are intentionally spending all they earn, but still firms want to buy additional capital goods. The total spending of households and investors is greater than the level of production. To satisfy the excess demand for goods and services, firms must produce more. In the process they will increase household income; and assuming a positive marginal propensity to save, the level of saving will rise with the increase in income. Eventually planned saving will reach the level of planned investment (assumed to remain constant). This will happen at the national income level of $Y_2$, or $1,600 billion.

This example illustrates a basic point of Keynesian economics. There is some income level toward which the economy will gravitate, and at which it will tend to remain unless economic conditions change. This income level may or may not be the full-employment income level.

As more goods and services are produced, more resources, including workers, are needed for production. As national income rises, therefore, the unemployment rate falls. In Figure 11.2(b), the equilibrium national income level $Y_2$ corresponds to an unemployment rate of $U_1$ (8 percent). That rate is higher than the lowest possible unemployment rate, $U_0$, or 4 percent here.[2]

Here Keynesians depart from the classical notion that the economy will continue to move toward the minimum unemployment level. According to classical theory, if unemployment rises above that minimum rate, a reduction in wage rates will cause the national income level to rise and unemployment to fall. Keynesians, on the other hand, stress that the economy may fail to achieve full employment in the short run because households are saving too much and consuming too little—or because firms are not investing enough.

## The Total Spending Approach to Income Equilibrium

Another way to arrive at the equilibrium-level national income is through the equation of national output with national income. In the preceding section we noted that when the equilibrium income level is achieved, planned saving (an outflow from the circular flow of income) is equal to planned investment (an inflow to the circular flow).

$$\text{planned saving} = \text{planned investment}$$

And Chapter 10 showed that when saving equals investment, total planned expenditures by households and firms exactly equal national output. That is, the equilibrium national income level is achieved when firms sell in the aggregate exactly what they have produced.

$$\text{total planned expenditures} = \text{national output}$$

With all firms selling exactly what they produce, business has no reason either to expand or to contract production.

These two different conditions for equilibrium are mathematically consistent. We know that national income ($Y$) is a mirror image of national

2. At any moment, some workers will be changing jobs. Therefore most economists do not believe that unemployment will ever fall below 4 percent. Many do not believe that an unemployment rate below 6 percent can be sustained.

output. National income is simply a reflection of what is produced in the economy, for without production there is no income. Furthermore, in our simple model, from which government has been excluded, households can do only two things with their income. They can use it for planned consumption ($C$) or for planned saving ($S$). Therefore income must equal consumption plus saving:

$$Y = C + S$$

If planned saving is equal to planned investment ($S = I$), we can rewrite this equation to read:

$$Y = C + I$$

Since national income and output measure the same thing, and since in our model consumption and saving make up total planned spending, the equations above mean that when planned saving and investment are equal, total national output equals total planned expenditure ($TPE$):

$$Y = C + I = C + S = TPE$$

In an economy at equilibrium, then, what is produced by firms is bought either by consumers (as consumer goods) or by businesses (as investment goods).

Thus the equilibrium national income level can be discussed in terms of the forces that determine total planned expenditures. That is the approach Keynes himself emphasized. His theory was built on two relatively simple propositions. First, he argued that the national income level ($Y$) depends on the level of total planned expenditures ($TPE$). That is, the amount of goods and services produced in the economy, and therefore the amount of income earned, depends on the amount of goods and services households and firms in the aggregate want to buy. Second, as we have just demonstrated, the equilibrium income level is the point at which total planned expenditures equal national income.

We now need to consider the forces that determine the levels of planned consumption ($C$) and planned investment ($I$).

## The Consumption and Investment Functions

Like planned saving, households' planned consumption expenditures, or total demands, are influenced by a number of variables. Among them are the interest rates people receive on their savings; personal wealth; the expected rate of inflation; income taxes; and the national income level. Interest rates are likely to be inversely related to planned consumption expenditures. As interest rates rise, people will be inclined to save more and borrow less in order to buy things like furniture and cars. Expected inflation has the opposite effect. If people expect the inflation rate to increase, they are likely to buy more now, to avoid paying higher prices in the future. If income tax rates rise, on the other hand, people will reduce their planned consumption expenditures, for they will have less after-tax income to spend. Finally, an increase in the national income level is likely to increase planned consumption expenditures, simply because more income will enable people to satisfy more of their wants.

Among these variables, special attention must be paid to national income, whose relationship to consumption demand is called the consumption function. The **consumption function** is the assumed direct relationship between the national income level and the planned consumption expenditures of households. Keynesians make three intuitively plausible assumptions about the consumption function. First, as income rises, planned consumption expenditures will rise by a lesser amount. That is, people will not spend all of their extra income; they will save part of it. This inclination of consumers to spend only part of an increase in their income is called the marginal propensity to consume. The **marginal propensity to consume** (*MPC*) is the percentage of any change in income that consumers are inclined to spend. Like the marginal propensity to save, the marginal propensity to consume can be expressed as a ratio.

**Consumption function:** the assumed direct relationship between the national income level and the planned consumption expenditures of households.

**Marginal propensity to consume:** the percentage of any change in income that consumers are inclined to spend.

$$MPC = \frac{\text{change in consumption}}{\text{change in national income}}$$

If the marginal propensity to consume is 90 percent, for instance ($MPC = 9/10$), consumers will be inclined to spend 90 percent of any change in their income. If national income rises (or falls) by \$100, planned consumption expenditures will rise (or fall) by \$90. (The actual figure for *MPC* in the United States is about 92 to 94 percent.)

The marginal propensity to consume and the marginal propensity to save are complementary concepts. Indeed, in our simplified model, whatever portion of an increase in income consumers do not spend, they must save, for $Y = C + S$. If the marginal propensity to save is 0.10, therefore, the marginal propensity to consume must be 0.90. Together, $MPC + MPS = 1$.

Second, Keynesians assume that there is some national income level—a very low one—at which consumers will plan to spend all the income they earn. At that level, consumers may simply be unable to save; they may have to spend everything they earn for subsistence.

Third, at even lower national income levels, consumers will plan to spend more than they earn. If people's income levels are seriously depressed for a short period, they will withdraw funds from their savings accounts to meet their current obligations. If collectively people plan to spend more than they are earning, in effect they are planning to buy more goods than are currently being produced. (Income and output must always be equal.) For a while firms will be able to meet the excess demand by reducing their inventories. But consumption expenditures cannot exceed income indefinitely; firms will eventually run out of inventory.

Figure 11.3(a) shows the upward-sloping consumption function curve, which summarizes graphically the relationship between the national income level and household consumption expenditures. At a national income level of \$400 billion ($Y_1$), the consumption level is also \$400 billion ($C_1$). This is the income level at which people spend all they earn. At a

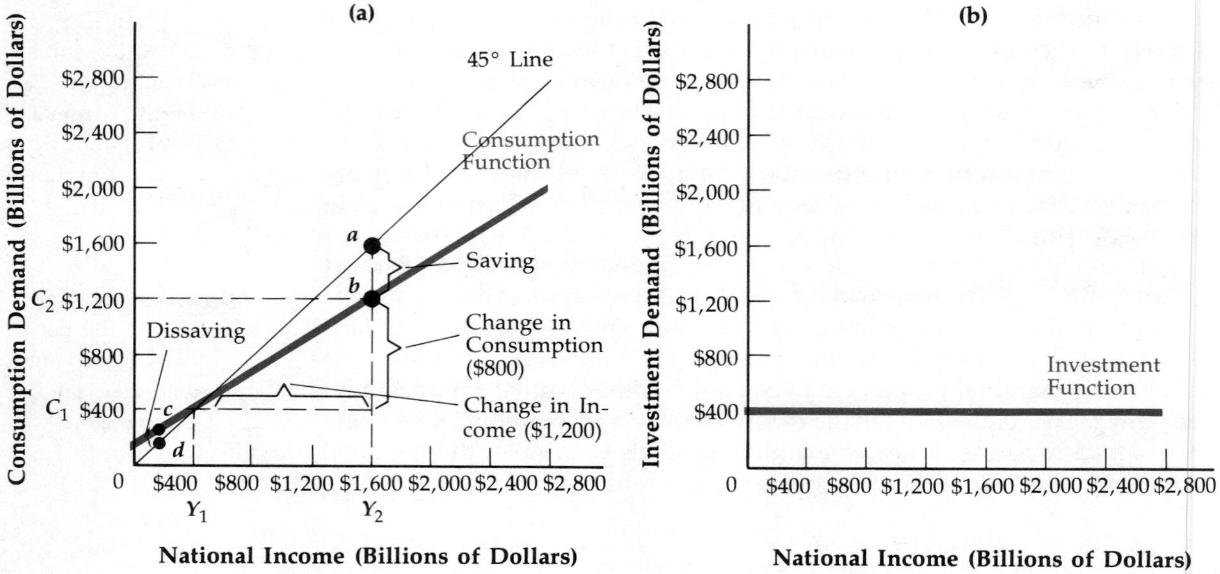


**Figure 11.3.** Planned Consumption and Investment.
Assuming that household consumption expenditures are directly related to national income, the consumption function may be drawn as an upward-sloping curve. At national income level $Y_1$, consumers are spending all they earn and saving nothing. At higher income levels consumption rises, but not as much as national income does. Consumers, in other words, are saving part of their income. For example, at a national income level of $1,600 billion, the consumption level is $1,200 billion; saving is $400 billion, or the distance between points *a* and *b*. Dissaving occurs at income levels below $Y_1$. Investment—part (b)—is assumed to be constant at $400 billion.

higher income level, $1,600 billion ($Y_2$), the consumption level is also higher, $1,200 billion. But the increase in consumption expenditures ($800 billion) is less than the increase in national income that caused it ($1,200 billion). As we saw above, the marginal propensity to consume is less than 1—in this case, ⅔.

$$MPC = \frac{\text{change in consumption}}{\text{change in national income}} = \frac{\$800}{\$1,200} = \frac{2}{3}$$

At all national income levels over $400 billion ($Y_1$), consumers in the aggregate will save some part of their income. The 45-degree line that extends out of the origin shows what the consumption function curve would look like if consumers spent all they earned. At a national income level of $1,600 billion, for instance, $1,600 billion would be spent. If consumers are spending only $1,200 billion at an income level of $1,600 billion, they must be saving the rest, namely $400 billion. This planned level of saving is represented in the figure by the vertical distance between points *a* and *b*. At higher national income levels, the vertical gap between the consumption function and the 45-degree line is larger, and the level of planned saving is greater. The growth of saving is consistent with our definition of the saving function, which specifies that the level of consumer saving is directly related to national income.

At national income levels below $Y_1$, the consumption function curve lies above the 45-degree line. Consumption exceeds the national income level. Consumers are spending more than they are earning, drawing down their savings accounts to meet current expenses. The amount of their dissaving is equal to the vertical distance between the 45-degree line and the consumption function. For example, at a national income level of $200 billion, the planned level of dissaving is $66 billion, or the vertical distance between points *c* and *d* in the graph. And if consumers are spending more than they earn at these low income levels, they must be buying more than is currently being produced. Businesses must also be drawing down their inventories to meet consumer demand.

In our simplified model of the macroeconomy, planned investment and consumption are the only components of total spending ($TPE = C + I$). We have already discussed investment demand (see pages 228–229); nothing more need be added here. For the moment, we continue to assume that planned investment does not vary with national income. We can therefore represent the investment function as a horizontal line, as in Figure 11.3(b).

## The Equilibrium National Income Level

We have demonstrated that equilibrium in national income and employment is established where total planned expenditures equal national income (or output). In our model, total planned spending is composed of two variables, planned consumption and planned investment expenditures. To describe total planned spending graphically, therefore, we must add the investment function from Figure 11.3(b) to the consumption function of Figure 11.3(a). The resulting combined curve, shown in Figure 11.4(a), represents the total expenditure function. The **total expenditure function** is the relationship of total planned expenditures to national income. This is normally assumed to be a direct relationship.

**Total expenditure function:** the relationship of total planned expenditures to national income, normally assumed to be a direct relationship.

In Figure 11.4(a), the line labeled $C + I$ is the total expenditure function. It is the graphical summation of the consumption function curve, $C$, which lies slightly below it, and the horizontal investment function curve. Investment demand is represented by the vertical difference between the consumption function curve, $C$, and the total expenditure function curve, $C + I$. The vertical space between the two curves, $400 billion, is equal to the value of the investment demand curve in Figure 11.3(b).

Given the total expenditures curve in Figure 11.4, we can deduce that the equilibrium national income level is $1,600 billion—the point where the $C + I$ curve crosses the 45-degree line. At that income level ($Y_2$), consumers will buy $1,200 billion worth of goods and services (that is,

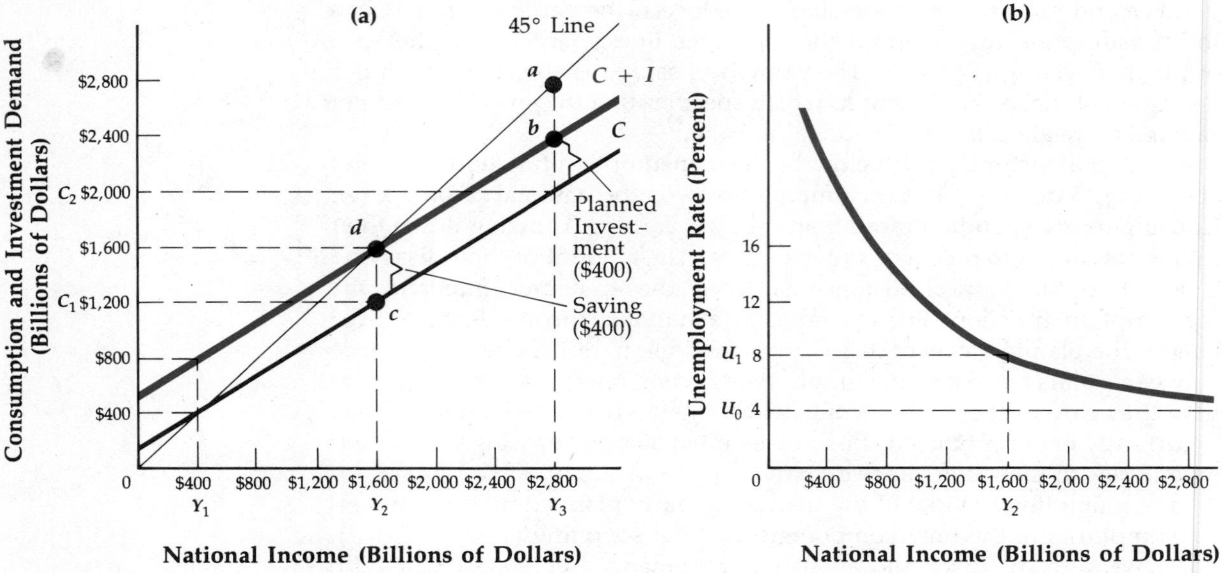


**Figure 11.4.** Determining the National Income Level: The Total Spending Approach.
The equilibrium national income level is $Y_2$, or $1,600 billion, the point where consumption plus investment equals national income. At income levels above $Y_2$, not all that is produced will be bought. At income levels below $Y_2$, consumers and businesses will want to buy more goods and services than are produced.

In part (b), the equilibrium income level corresponds to the unemployment rate $U_1$ (8 percent).

their consumption demand will be $C_1$) and firms will buy $400 billion worth of plant, equipment, and inventory. Total expenditures will equal national income at $1,600 billion.

$$TPE = \$1{,}600 \text{ billion} = Y$$

Consumers and firms will be buying all that is produced.

If the economy is producing either more or less, it will move toward a level of $1,600 billion. For instance, suppose the national income level is $2,800 billion ($Y_3$). Consumers in the aggregate plan to buy $2,000 billion worth of goods and services ($C_2$). Businesses plan to buy $400 billion worth. Total planned spending by consumers and firms will therefore equal only $2,400 billion, or $400 billion less than is being produced. So long as firms continue to produce $2,800 billion worth of output and to sell only $2,400 billion worth, unwanted inventory (unplanned investment) will accumulate. The vertical distance between points *a* and *b* represents this $400 billion of unwanted inventory.

Instead of continually adding to their inventories, firms will at some point reduce their production levels. When they do, the national income level will fall, and planned consumer expenditures will fall with it, though not by as much as national income. If national income initially exceeds total planned spending and falls faster than consumption demand, at some point it must become equal to total demand for goods and services ($C + I$). This equality is achieved, as stated above, at a national income level of $1,600 billion ($Y_2$).

If the national income level is below $Y_2$, it will rise until it reaches that level. Suppose firms in the aggregate are generating only $400 billion worth of goods and services. At that income level, $Y_1$ in Figure 11.4(a), consumers are inclined to spend $400 billion and businesses are inclined to spend another $400 billion. Obviously total planned spending will exceed the quantity of goods and services produced.

$$TPE = C + I = \$400 \text{ billion} + \$400 \text{ billion} = \$800 \text{ billion}$$

To satisfy this high level of demand, firms must draw down their inventories and/or expand production. At some point they are likely to exhaust their inventories and will have to expand production. When they do, more national income will be generated, increasing planned consumption. If demand at first exceeds production, but production (national income) rises faster than planned consumer expenditures, at some point producers will be able to meet total demand. Again, the national income level at which they will be able to do this is $Y_2$, or $1,600 billion.

Note that $Y_2$ is the equilibrium income level arrived at by the saving-investment approach described in Figure 11.2. At $Y_2$, planned saving is equal to planned investment. That fact can be seen in Figure 11.4 as well. At $Y_2$, the vertical distance between the $C$ and $C + I$ curves is the planned investment level ($400 billion). And the vertical distance between point $c$ on the $C$ curve and point $d$ on the 45-degree line is the planned saving level ($400 billion). If both investment and saving are $400 billion, then planned saving is equal to planned investment. Figures 11.2(a) and 11.4(a) are both representations of the same Keynesian model, then, each emphasizing a different aspect of the model.

As Figure 11.4(b) shows, the equilibrium national income level ($Y_2$) is consistent with an unemployment rate of 8 percent ($U_1$). That is higher than the assumed minimum unemployment rate of 4 percent, which can be achieved at a higher production level. But before more is produced, firms and consumers must be inclined to buy more. Thus Keynesian analysis concludes that national income and employment depend on the level of total planned expenditures. In the classical model, unemployment results principally from shifts in the supply and demand for labor and from labor market obstructions to wage adjustments. In the Keynesian model, unemployment is caused by insufficient demand.

The information shown in Figure 11.4 can also be expressed in tabular form. Column 1 of Table 11.1 lists some possible national income levels, from $0 to $2,800 billion. Column 2 shows consumption, reflecting the three Keynesian assumptions described on page 225. At an income level of $0, planned consumption is $133 billion—more than income. At an income level of $400 billion, consumption equals income. Above $400 billion in income, consumption falls short of income. Thus, below $400 billion, consumers are dissaving; above it they are saving (column 3).

**Table 11.1.** National Income Equilibrium (in billions of dollars)

| National Income (1) | Consumption (2) | Saving (+) or Dissaving (−) (3) | Investment Expenditures (4) | Total Planned Expenditures (5) |
|---|---|---|---|---|
| $ 0 | $ 133 | −$133 | $400 | $ 533 |
| 200 | 266 | − 66 | 400 | 666 |
| 400 | 400 | 0 | 400 | 800 |
| 600 | 533 | + 67 | 400 | 933 |
| 800 | 667 | + 133 | 400 | 1,067 |
| 1,000 | 800 | + 200 | 400 | 1,200 |
| 1,200 | 933 | + 267 | 400 | 1,333 |
| 1,400 | 1,067 | + 333 | 400 | 1,467 |
| 1,600 | 1,200 | + 400 | 400 | 1,600 |
| 1,800 | 1,333 | + 467 | 400 | 1,733 |
| 2,000 | 1,467 | + 533 | 400 | 1,867 |
| 2,200 | 1,600 | + 600 | 400 | 2,000 |
| 2,400 | 1,733 | + 667 | 400 | 2,133 |
| 2,600 | 1,867 | + 733 | 400 | 2,267 |
| 2,800 | 2,000 | + 800 | 400 | 2,400 |

Under our simplifying assumption, planned investment is held constant at $400 billion for all income levels (column 4). Total planned expenditures is shown in column 5. By comparing it with column 1, we see that equilibrium with national income is achieved at an output of $1,600 billion. At income levels above $1,600 billion, total planned expenditures fall short of total output. Below $1,600 billion, expenditures exceed output.

# Changes in Total Planned Expenditures

If the levels of planned investment and consumption determine the equilibrium national income level, then changes in the levels of planned investment and consumption will produce a different equilibrium income level. This section discusses the rather complicated effects that changes in planned investment and consumption can have on the equilibrium national income level.

## Changes in Planned Investment

A change in any of the forces that influence investment decisions—interest rates, the national income level, expectations regarding the profitability of future production, and so forth—can change the planned level of investment and thus the national income level. Consider the assumed inverse relationship between the market interest rate and the planned level of investment, shown by the downward-sloping curve $ID_1$ in Figure 11.5. If the interest rate is initially $R_3$, planned investment will be $I_1$. And if this level of planned investment is constant, it can be represented by the planned investment curve $I_1$ in Figure 11.6(b). That level of investment corresponds to an equilibrium national income level of $Y_2$ (part (a) of Figure 11.6) and an unemployment rate of $U_2$ (part (c) of Figure 11.6).

If the interest rate falls to $R_2$ in Figure 11.5, the level of planned investment will rise to $I_2$ in Figure 11.6(b). And total planned expenditures will rise to $C + I_2$ in Figure 11.6(a). At the initial income level of $Y_2$, total planned expenditures $(C + I_2)$ will exceed output. In simple terms, firms will face a greater demand for goods and services than they can satisfy with current production schedules. Given this excess demand, firms will expand production, employing more workers and causing the unemployment rate to fall. Household incomes will rise, and people will save more. Eventually the economy will move toward the new equilibrium income level $Y_3$, where planned saving and investment are once again equal (Figure 11.6(b)). The new lower unemployment rate of $U_1$ is still above the minimum employment rate, however (Figure 11.6(c)).

If investment depends on the interest rate, and income and unemployment on investment, it follows that each interest rate in Figure 11.5 is related to a specific income and unemployment level in Figure 11.6. The minimum level of unemployment ($U_0$, the full-employment rate) will not be achieved until the equilibrium income reaches a much higher level than $Y_3$. Thus investment must rise higher than $I_2$, and the interest rate must fall lower than $R_2$, to achieve the full employment rate $U_0$.

An upward shift in the investment demand curve in Figure 11.5 can have an effect similar to a reduction in the interest rate. Such a shift might be caused by an increase in the expected profitability of an investment, perhaps because of an increase in the productivity of capital goods or a reduction in property taxes. If investment demand shifts from curve $ID_1$ to curve $ID_2$, for instance, and the interest rate remains constant at $R_3$, the level of planned investment will rise from $I_1$ to $I_2$. The equilibrium income level will rise from $Y_2$ to $Y_3$ in Figure 11.6(a), and unemployment will drop from $U_2$ to $U_1$ (Figure 11.6(c)).

A reduction in the level of planned investment expenditures, say from $I_2$ to $I_1$, will have exactly the opposite effect. The equilibrium income level will fall and the unemployment rate will rise. The level of planned investment can be reduced through either an increase in the interest rate or a downward shift in the investment demand curve in Figure 11.5.

As the economy moves toward a new equilibrium income level, a peculiar phenomenon occurs. In Figure 11.6, planned investment expenditures increase by the difference between $I_2$ and $I_1$, but the national income level increases a great deal more—by the difference between $Y_3$ and $Y_2$. In fact, the increase in national income is *three times* the increase in planned investment. The explanation of this phenomenon involves one of the most significant contributions of Keynesian analysis, the concept of the multiplier.

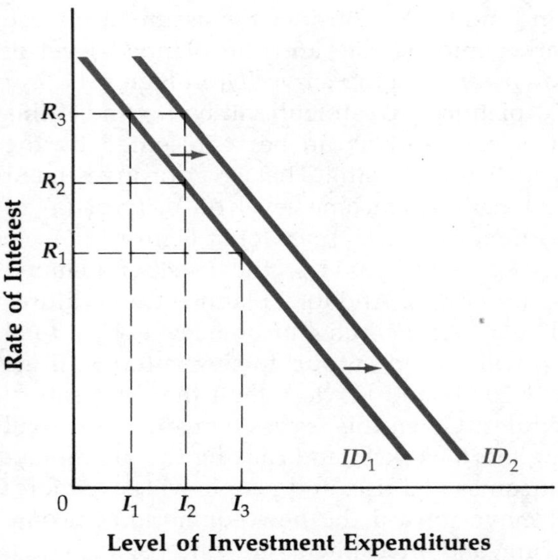


**Figure 11.5.** The Effect of Interest Rates on Planned Investment. Planned investment is inversely related to the rate of interest firms have to pay on borrowed money. If the interest rate falls from $R_3$ to $R_2$, the level of planned investment will rise from $I_1$ to $I_2$. An outward shift in the investment demand curve has the same effect. If the interest rate remains constant at $R_3$ but the investment demand curve shifts from $ID_1$ to $ID_2$, the level of investment will rise from $I_1$ to $I_2$.

## The Multiplier

**Multiplier:** the ratio of a change in national income to the change in total planned expenditures that stimulated it:

$$m = \frac{\text{change in } Y}{\text{change in } TPE}$$

Simply stated, the **multiplier** is the ratio of a change in national income to the change in total planned expenditures that stimulated it.

$$m = \frac{\text{change in } Y}{\text{change in } TPE}$$

In the example just given, the change in total planned expenditures is simply the change in planned investment. The concept of the multiplier is applicable to *any* change in total planned expenditures, however—to consumer and government spending as well as to planned investment. A multiplier of 3 means that the national income level will rise (or fall) by three times the increase (or decrease) in total planned spending—whether the change in *TPE* is due to a change in investment, in consumer demand for goods and services, or in government demand for goods and services. Rearranged slightly, the equation reads:

$$\text{change in } Y = m \times \text{change in } TPE$$

The formula for the multiplier is derived as follows. We know that at the initial equilibrium income level of $Y_2$, planned saving and investment are equal. We also know that planned saving and investment must again

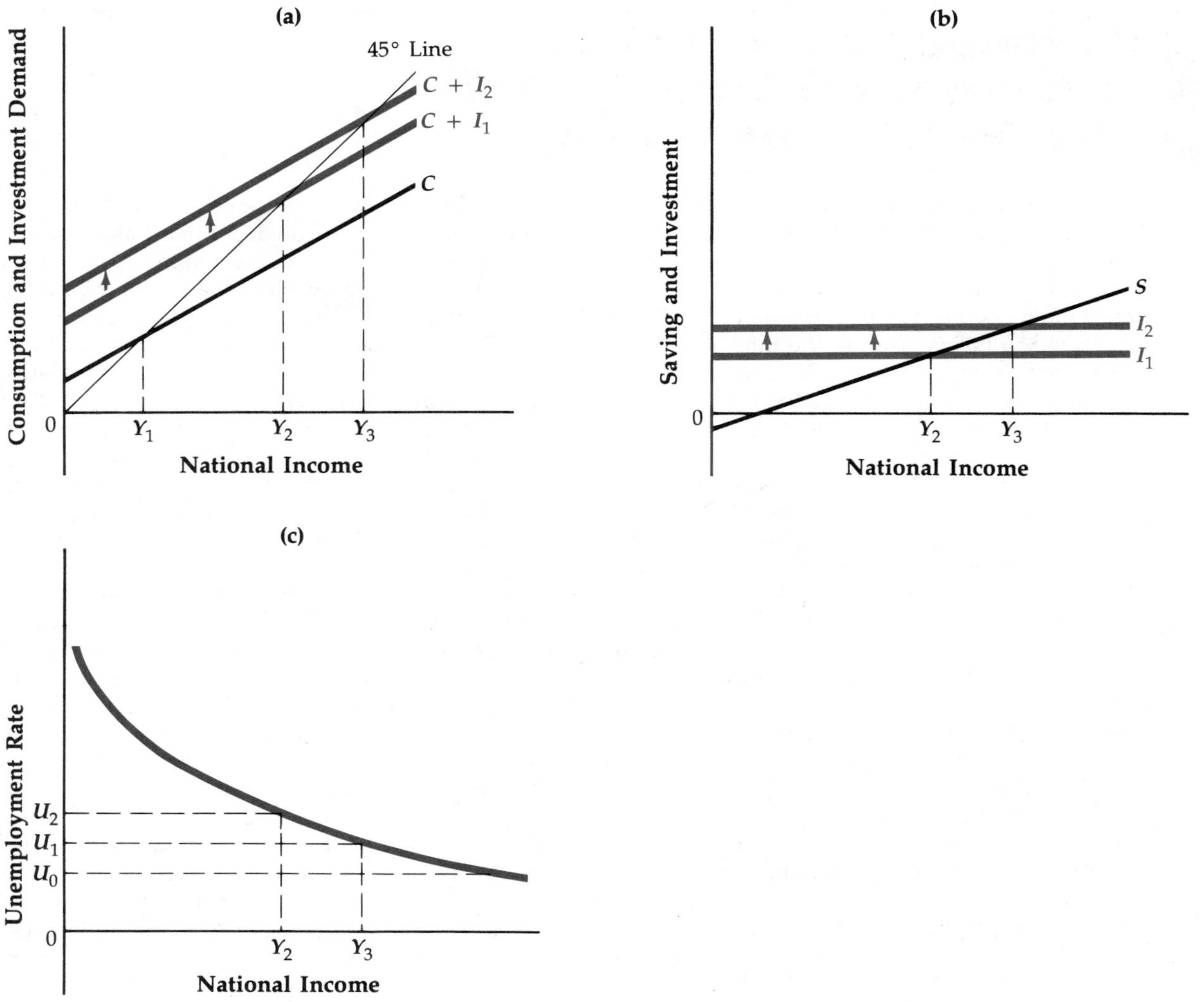


**Figure 11.6.** The Effect of a Change in Planned Investment.
If planned investment spending rises from a level of $I_1$ to $I_2$ in part (b), total expenditures will rise from $C + I_1$ to $C + I_2$ in part (a). As a result the equilibrium national income level rises from $Y_2$ to $Y_3$, and the unemployment rate falls from $U_2$ to $U_1$ in part (c).

be equal at the new equilibrium income level of $Y_3$. Therefore any increase in planned investment that causes firms to produce more must eventually be matched by an equal increase in planned saving. If planned investment goes up by \$10 billion, for instance, causing a movement away from the equilibrium income level, a new equilibrium level will not be reached until planned saving has also risen by \$10 billion.

If we know the marginal propensity to save, we can figure the increase in national income from the increase in saving. Suppose the marginal

## Perspectives in Economics: A Keynesian Explanation of the Great Depression

In 1929, along with much of the rest of the world, the United States began to slide into the worst depression in its history. In that year the gross national product totaled $103 billion. By 1933, at the bottom of the Great Depression, GNP had fallen to $56 billion. During the intervening four years, practically all prices fell sharply. After adjustment for price reductions, the nation's measured output level fell by 31 percent. At the same time unemployment rose to 25 percent of the civilian labor force. Many more people who were underemployed as part-time workers were not counted in the unemployment statistics. The level of private business investment plummeted from $16 billion in 1929 to a little over $1 billion in 1933. The nation was wearing out its plant and equipment faster than it was replacing them. And the stock market crashed. At the peak of the boom in 1929, the total dollar value of stocks listed on the New York Stock Exchange was $90 billion. At the bottom of the market collapse three years later, it was $15 billion—83 percent less.

What caused it all? Keynesian economists point to the decrease in demand, particularly consumption and investment demand, that began in the late 1920s. In the first half of the decade, the demand for plant and equipment had been bolstered by several factors. The First World War had left much of Europe's industrial and agricultural plant and equipment in ruin. European nations looked to the United States for many of the capital goods and consumer products they could not supply themselves. Moreover there was a backlog of domestic demand for new and improved housing and consumer goods of all kinds, because during the war the United States had given priority to the production of war-related goods. Many industries had to expand and retool to meet this shift in domestic demand.

Third, during the 1920s the use of the automobile expanded considerably, and new products such as the radio, the electric stove, and the refrigerator became part of the American way of life. The demand for these new products created a demand for increased capital in the expanding industries that produced them. Finally, people were caught up in a wave of optimism. Some people believed the stock market would continue to rise indefinitely—and planned their expenditures accordingly. And businesses, ignoring a deterioration in underlying economic conditions, continued to base investment decisions on an assumption of sustained growth in demand and profit.

By the middle of the decade, however, most European industries had rebuilt and were able to satisfy their region's demand for many consumer products and capital goods. At the same time the productive capacity of many American industries had caught up with the backlog in consumer demand. In some industries, capacity had obviously been overextended. Table 11.2 shows the pattern in the housing industry. The construction

propensity to save is one-third (that is, people will save one-third of any change in their incomes). We can predict that income will rise by three times the change in saving. If planned saving must rise by $10 billion in order to equal planned investment, then national income must rise by $30 billion. At this point the *MPS* (1/3) times $30 billion equals $10 billion, the increase in saving that is necessary to reestablish equilibrium in national income.

**Table 11.2.** Urban Residential Construction in the United States, 1920–1929

| Year | Dwelling Units | Year | Dwelling Units |
|---|---|---|---|
| 1920 | 247,000 | 1925 | 937,000 |
| 1921 | 449,000 | 1926 | 849,000 |
| 1922 | 716,000 | 1927 | 810,000 |
| 1923 | 871,000 | 1928 | 753,000 |
| 1924 | 893,000 | 1929 | 509,000 |

**Source:** U.S. Bureau of the Census, *Historical Statistics of the United States* (Washington, D.C.: U.S. Government Printing Office, 1975), p. 393.

of new housing fell from its 1925 peak of 937,000 units to 509,000 units in 1929—a drop of 46 percent. Until 1928 this decline in residential construction was more than offset by the rise in nonresidential construction. But in 1929 total construction declined significantly, and purchases of automobiles and electrical appliances fell too.

All these downward trends in demand caused a significant drop in investment demand during the late 1920s. If productive capacity had caught up with consumer demand, there was no need for further investment, either in production or in new plant and equipment. According to Keynesian theory, such a reduction in planned investment will lead to a reduction in production, and thus to lower incomes and further reductions in consumer demand. Through the multiplier process, the economy headed downward into the Great Depression.

Thus the stock market collapse did not cause the Great Depression. The drastic fall in stock prices merely reflected investors' sudden recognition that the economic boom of the twenties was over. But the Great Crash, as it was called, worsened the problem. It dramatically shattered business confidence, causing a further decline in business investment. It also substantially reduced many people's personal wealth. To rebuild their lost security, Americans had to try to save more in times that were already hard. Even those with income resisted buying consumer goods out of fear that the Depression would eventually touch them. Consumers' reductions in planned expenditures also contributed to the downward spiral. Many banks collapsed, causing a sharp reduction in the money supply and the demand for goods based on credit. Finally, because of the growing riskiness of loaning money, interest rates rose to historically high levels, further suppressing investment. Given all these calamities, one might wonder why the Depression, which imposed considerable hardship on many Americans, was not even more severe.

Thus the size of the multiplier is related to the marginal propensity to save. Stated precisely, the multiplier is the reciprocal of the marginal propensity to save, or

$$m = \frac{1}{MPS}$$

Given a specific change in expenditures, the change in national income can be computed by multiplying the reciprocal of the marginal propensity to save[3] times the change in total planned expenditures, or

$$\text{change in } Y = \frac{1}{MPS} \times \text{change in } TPE$$

A concrete example may help explain why a change in planned investment (or consumer demand, or government demand) has a multiplying effect on national income. If businesses buy more plant and equipment— $I_2$ instead of $I_1$ in Figure 11.6—during a given period, their purchases result in higher output and greater income for the suppliers of those investment goods (construction workers and the owners of firms making heavy equipment). Suppliers will spend part of their increased incomes on personal consumption, including such goods as automobiles and refrigerators. The producers of automobiles and refrigerators will then have more income to spend on other items, such as groceries and clothes. In this way, an increase in expenditures for capital goods will affect incomes throughout the economy. But there is a limit to how much an increase in planned investment will raise the national income. As the income level rises, people tend to save more. Eventually the planned saving level will equal the new higher level of planned investment, at which point equilibrium will be attained.

Both the size of the multiplier and the potential change in the national income level are critically related to the value of the marginal propensity to save (or, geometrically, to the slope of the outflow curve). Compare the following sample values for the *MPS* with their associated multipliers.

$$MPS = 0.4 \qquad m = \frac{1}{0.4} = 2.5$$

$$MPS = 0.5 \qquad m = \frac{1}{0.5} = 2$$

$$MPS = 0.6 \qquad m = \frac{1}{0.6} = 1.66$$

Although these hypothetical values are much higher than the real-world *MPS*, they illustrate the inverse relationship between the *MPS* and the multiplier. As the marginal propensity to save rises, the value of the multiplier falls. Since the multiplier determines how much national income will rise with an increase in planned investment (change in $Y = m \times$ change in *TPE*), we can see the impact of *MPS*. The higher the *MPS*, the smaller the change in income with any change in investment—and vice versa. Thus if a nation's marginal propensity to save is very small—say

3. Since the marginal propensity to save and the marginal propensity to consume must add to 1, the multiplier can also be stated as

$$m = \frac{1}{(1 - MPC)}$$

(See the chapter Appendix for a more complete discussion of the multiplier.)

0.05—only a slight change in planned expenditures is required to cause a sharp change in the nation's income level. Finally, the multiplier operates on both increases and decreases in planned spending. A decrease has a negative multiplier effect. The national income level will fall by some multiple of any decline in planned investment. Unemployment will rise.

## Changes in Planned Consumption and Saving

To many people, saving is a virtue. On an aggregate level, however, and within the confines of the Keynesian model of the macroeconomy, saving can have a detrimental short-run effect on income and employment. Suppose the economy is at equilibrium at a national income level of $Y_2$ and an unemployment rate of $U_1$ in Figure 11.7. Total expenditures are $C_1 + I$—part (a)—and saving is $S_1$—part (b). Now suppose people become more thrifty. Anticipating a recession, they decide to set aside more income. The saving curve shifts upward to $S_2$, reflecting this greater saving at each and every level of income. The level of planned saving now exceeds planned investment ($I_1$ in part (b)).

This shift in the saving curve is counterbalanced by a downward shift in the consumption curve in part (a). At the initial income level of $Y_2$, national production now exceeds total expenditure. Firms will not be able to sell all they produce. As their inventories pile up, they will reduce production, laying off workers in the process. Thus as national income falls, unemployment will rise (part (c)).

As income falls, however, saving will fall with it. At the lower national income level of $Y_1$, planned saving will again equal planned investment, and total planned expenditure will again equal national income. But in the process of lowering the nation's income level, the movement toward greater thrift has raised unemployment to $U_2$ (part (c)). Furthermore, at the new equilibrium income level, people can save no more than they could before, at the initial income level of $Y_2$. This perverse result is known as the paradox of thrift. According to the **paradox of thrift,** if people attempt to save more, they will end up earning less in the aggregate, and saving no more (and possibly less) than before. For this reason, Keynesian economists argue that efforts to save can be counterproductive, at least in the short run.

**Paradox of thrift:** the theory that if people attempt to save more, they will end up earning less in the aggregate, and saving no more (and possibly less) than before.

The national income level falls because people consume less when they try to save more. In fact, an increase in planned saving has the same negative multiplying effect on the income level as an equivalent drop in planned investment. In Figure 11.7, planned saving rises by the vertical distance between the two saving curves, $S_1$ and $S_2$. But the national income level falls by a much greater amount—three times as much, to be precise. As before, the marginal propensity to save (the slope of the saving curve) is 0.33, and the multiplier is 3.

Any *decrease* or any *increase* in planned consumption will have a multiplying effect on the economy. The important point is that the multiplier effect moves in the direction of the change in *total* planned expenditures.

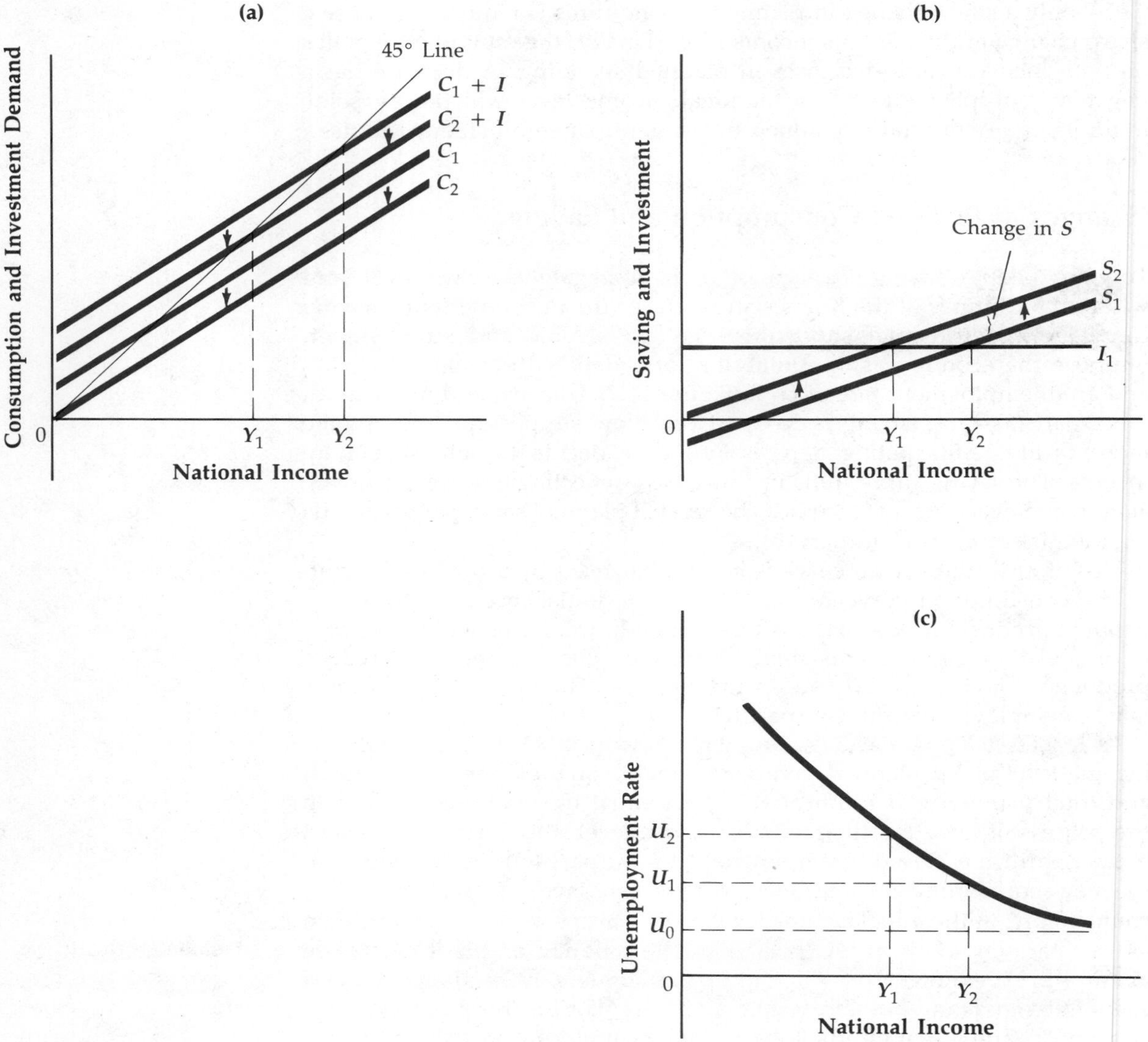


**Figure 11.7.** The Effect of a Change in Planned Saving.
An increase in the level of planned saving will cause the saving curve in part (b) to shift upward, from $S_1$ to $S_2$. This increase in planned saving causes downward shifts in the consumption curve—from $C_1$ to $C_2$ in part (a)—and in the total expenditure curve (from $C_1 + I$ to $C_2 + I$). The result is a decrease in the national income level, from $Y_2$ to $Y_1$, and an increase in the unemployment rate, from $U_1$ to $U_2$, in part (c).

## Summary and Extensions

Many policymakers use the Keynesian macroeconomic model developed in this chapter to explain the business cycle, or the intermittent swings between rising and falling levels of national income and employment. A decrease in planned investment or an increase in planned saving initiates a decrease in the national income level, which is magnified by the multiplier effect. A drop in planned investment, for instance, will lead to cumulative reductions in income and consumption and to further drops in production and income. An increase in planned investment and a decrease in planned saving will have a multiplicative effect in the opposite direction. The smaller the marginal propensity to save, the greater the value and effect of the multiplier.

Keynesian theory contradicts classical prescriptions for dealing with unemployment. To alleviate unemployment, classical economists recommended the elimination of labor market restrictions, such as minimum wage laws and union barriers to wage reductions. But the Keynesian model suggests that unemployment may be decreased by a reduction in the level of saving, and therefore increasing consumption. Through tax and expenditure policies, Keynesians believe that government can actively guide the economy toward the full-employment income level—a topic we will pursue in the next chapter.

## Major Conclusions

1. Using the planned investment and saving approach, one can show that equilibrium in national income and employment is established where the level of planned saving equals the level of planned investment.
2. Using the total planned spending approach, one can show that equilibrium in national income and employment is established where total planned expenditures for goods and services equals national income. (At this equilibrium income level, planned saving will equal planned investment.)
3. Planned investment is influenced by many factors, including the rate of interest firms pay on borrowed money. A decrease in the interest rate will cause an increase in the level of planned investment, and therefore in national income and employment; and vice versa. In the Keynesian model of the macroeconomy, each interest rate is associated with a specific national income level.
4. National income will increase or decrease by some multiple of any change in total planned expenditures. An increase in investment demand, for example, will cause an increase in the national income level greater than the increase in the investment demand.
5. In the Keynesian macroeconomic model, the multiplier is equal to the reciprocal of the marginal propensity to save.
6. According to the Keynesian macroeconomic model, the Great Depression was caused by decreases in planned consumption and investment.

## Questions to Ponder

1. Suppose the nation's marginal propensity to save is 0.2; the level of consumption expenditures increases by $15 at each and every income level; and investment expenditures increase by $10. What will be the amount and direction of the resulting change in national income? What will happen to the unemployment rate?
2. Given the following values for the marginal propensity to save and for changes in investment, compute the multipliers and the resulting changes in national income:

| *MPS* | Multiplier | Change in *I* | Change in *Y* |
|---|---|---|---|
| 1/10 | ________ | +$10 | ________ |
| 1/15 | ________ | −$20 | ________ |
| 3/10 | ________ | +$5 | ________ |

3. Suppose that saving rises by $10 at the same time that investment rises by $10. What will happen to the national income level?
4. The following graph reproduces the saving curve from the other figures in this chapter. The investment function, however, has been drawn as an upward-sloping curve instead of a horizontal line. The implied assumption is that investment is directly related to the national income level. That is, as national income increases, so does investment, and vice versa.

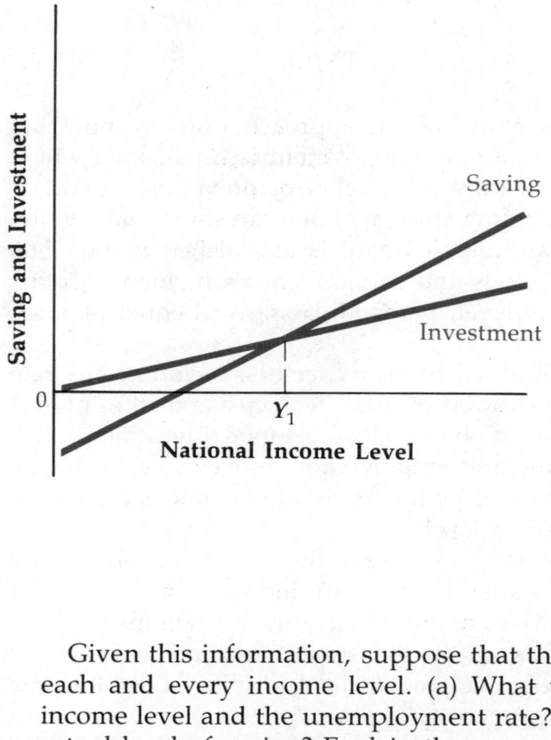


Given this information, suppose that the level of saving increases at each and every income level. (a) What will happen to the national income level and the unemployment rate? (b) What will happen to the actual level of saving? Explain the sequence of events on which your answers are based.

# Appendix: Derivation of the Multiplier

We noted on page 245 that the multiplier is related to the size of the marginal propensities to save and to consume. If investment expenditures rise by $10 billion, to use the example cited there, then planned saving must rise by an equal amount to reestablish equilibrium in national income. And if the marginal propensity to save is one-third, then the national income level must rise to $30 billion before planned saving again equals investment. The multiplier in this example is therefore 3 ($30 billion ÷ $10 billion = 3).

The formal derivation of the multiplier is as follows. To begin, we know that the change in national income will equal the multiplier times the change in total planned expenditures:

$$\text{change in } Y = m \times \text{change in } TPE$$

Furthermore, in the example on page 241, the change in total planned expenditures equals the change in investment. We can therefore substitute change in investment for change in total planned expenditures:

$$\text{change in } Y = m \times \text{change in } I$$

We also know that in an economy in equilibrium, planned saving must equal investment:

$$S = I$$

Before equilibrium in national income can be reestablished, then, any change in planned investment must be matched by an equal change in planned saving:

$$\text{change in } S = \text{change in } I$$

Again, we can substitute one variable for another—change in $S$ for change in $I$—in the multiplier equation:

$$\text{change in } Y = m \times \text{change in } S$$

The equation change in $Y = m \times$ change in $S$ can be rearranged as follows:

$$\frac{1}{m} = \frac{\text{change in } S}{\text{change in } Y}$$

Notice that the right-hand side of this equation is the formula for the marginal propensity to save. Thus:

$$\frac{1}{m} = MPS \quad \text{or} \quad m = \frac{1}{MPS}$$

Or stated verbally, the multiplier is the reciprocal of the marginal propensity to save.

If we know what the marginal propensity to save is, we can find the value of the multiplier. If the marginal propensity to save is one-third, as in our example, the multiplier must be 3:

$$m = \frac{1}{MPS} = \frac{1}{\frac{1}{3}} = 3$$

Since the marginal propensity to save is equal to 1 minus the marginal propensity to consume, the multiplier can also be stated as:

$$m = \frac{1}{1 - MPC}$$

Thus the value of the multiplier can also be computed from the marginal propensity to consume:

$$m = \frac{1}{(1 - MPC)} = \frac{1}{(1 - \frac{2}{3})} = \frac{1}{\frac{1}{3}} = 3$$

## Central Question

*What policy actions should the government take to influence national production, employment, and prices?*

## Key Terms

**Automatic stabilizer**

Chapter 12

# Keynesian Fiscal Policy

*"Fiscal responsibility" is not synonymous with "fiscal restraint." Rather, it calls for an intelligent fitting of tax and spending positions to the needs of the economy.*
*Walter Heller*

The preceding chapter showed how, in the Keynesian model of the macroeconomy, changes in the demand for goods and services can affect national income and employment through the multiplier process. According to that model, the economy's equilibrium income level may not necessarily be its full-employment level. If changes in demand move the economy away from full employment, furthermore, the forces of supply and demand will not necessarily move the economy back toward full employment in the short run.

In this chapter we will consider how, theoretically at least, government fiscal policy can be used to counteract the negative effects of a change in demand. In Chapter 4, fiscal policy was defined as a government's use of tax and expenditure actions to achieve economic goals, such as full employment of the labor force or stable prices. Specifically, we will see how government can move the economy out of a recession by expanding aggregate demand (through a larger budgetary deficit or a smaller budgetary surplus). Conversely, it can reduce inflationary pressures by suppressing aggregate demand (through a larger budgetary surplus or a smaller budgetary deficit). Because such goals have shaped much of our government's economic policy over the past two decades, we will also be able to see the results of Keynesian theory in some real-world situations.

In macroeconomic theory, economic stability and full employment are considered public goods that can only be attained through collective government action. In the midst of a recession, for instance, the national income level can be increased only if firms as a group increase their planned expenditures on plant and equipment, or consumers as a group reduce their planned saving level. But individual households and firms have little incentive to contribute to the production of a public good like economic stability or full employment. A single household or firm is too small by itself to make a significant contribution to such an end, or to realize any substantial benefits from it. Firms and households do not operate in the common interest, but in their own private interest. All tend to become free riders. Thus government action is required for the production of economic stability as it is for the production of national defense.

## Government as Economic Policymaker

To see how government attempts to produce economic stability, we will use graphs (like those in Chapter 11) that relate the various inflows and outflows to the national income level. In our model economy, tax payments and saving are directly influenced by the national income level. As income rises, people save more. Beyond some minimum level, people are required to pay taxes, and to pay more taxes the higher their income. This relationship between taxes, saving, and income is described in Figure 12.1(a). At income level $Y_1$, planned saving and taxes together are assumed to be zero. As income increases, however, planned saving and taxes rise. Any taxes that are collected inevitably reduce the saving outflow. The two outflows, in other words, are not independent. Still, this combined outflow curve has a steeper slope than the outflow curve in the last chapter, which included only saving.

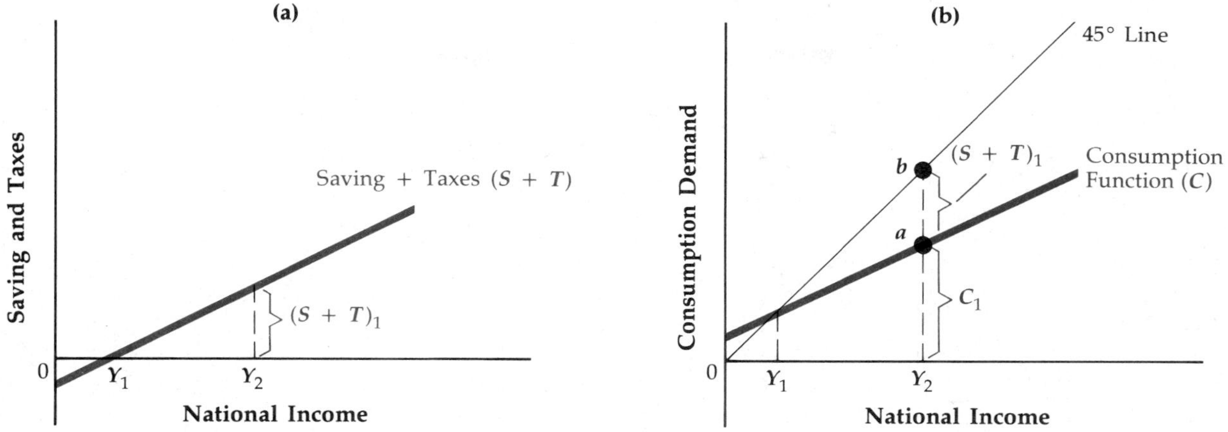


**Figure 12.1.** The Relationship of Planned Saving, Taxes, and Consumption to National Income.
Planned saving and taxes, shown by the upward-sloping curve in part (a), both increase with national income. The slope of this combined outflow curve is steeper than the slope of the outflow curve shown in the last chapter, which included only saving. After taxes, the consumption curve—part (b)—still slopes upward, but less than the consumption curve in the last chapter, for taxes reduce consumption. The vertical distance between the consumption function and the 45-degree line is equal to the combined total of planned saving and taxes shown in part (a).

The effect of taxation on consumption is illustrated in part (b) of Figure 12.1. There the consumption curve has a slightly lower slope than the one in Chapter 11, because taxes reduce consumer expenditures. People simply have less disposable income to spend after taxes. At a national income level of $Y_2$, total planned consumer expenditures are $C_1$, less than they would have been without the tax outflow. Planned saving and taxes are shown here by the vertical distance between the consumption curve and the 45-degree line (*ab*).

Government spending may well be influenced by the national income level. To keep the analysis simple, however, we will assume that neither planned government expenditures nor planned investment expenditures change with a change in national income. The planned government and investment expenditure curves are therefore horizontal, as in Figure 12.2(a) and (b). Combining these two curves yields a higher horizontal curve, like the one in part (c) of Figure 12.2.

Figure 12.3(a) combines the saving and taxes (outflow) curve from Figure 12.1 with the government spending and investment (inflow) curve from Figure 12.2. Figure 12.3(b) combines the consumption curve from Figure 12.1 and the government spending and investment curve from Figure 12.2 into a single total planned expenditure curve, $C + I + G$. With these two graphs we can see the equilibrium national income level.

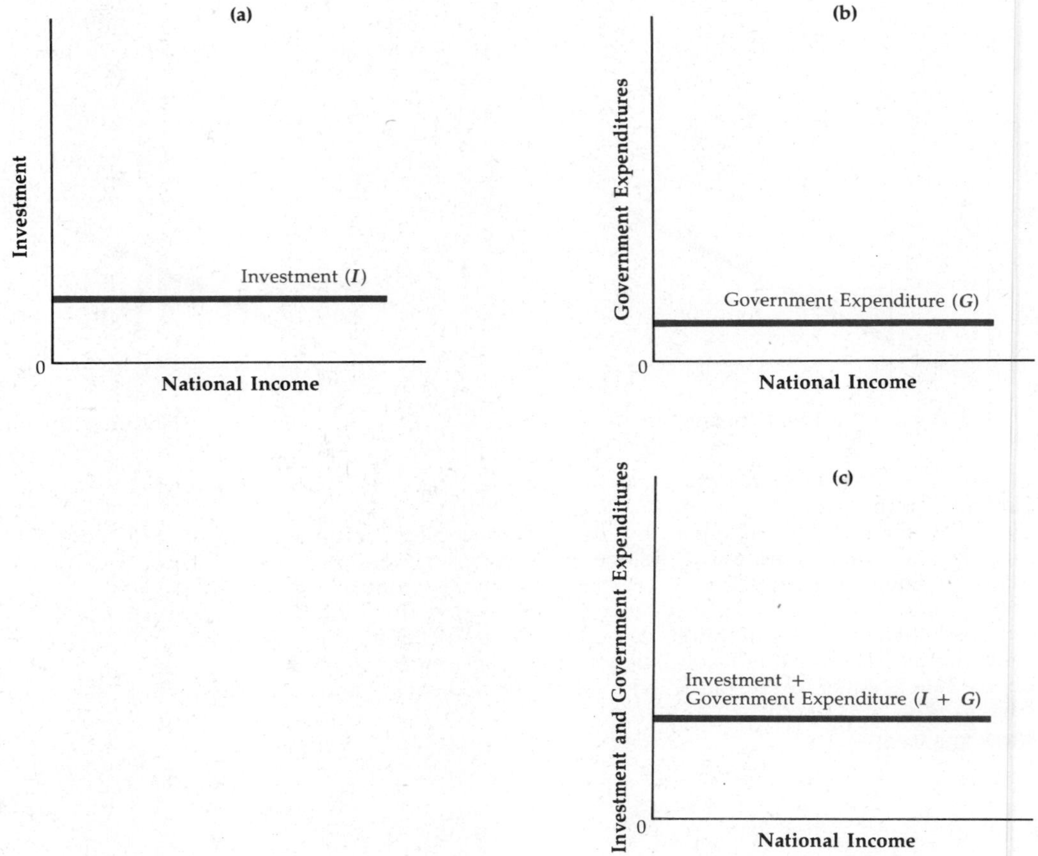


**Figure 12.2.** The Relationship of Investment and Government Spending to National Income.
Planned investment and government spending are assumed to be unaffected by the national income level. Therefore they are drawn as horizontal lines in parts (a) and (b). Planned investment and government spending combined can be represented by the horizontal curve shown in part (c).

From our discussion in the last chapter, we know that the equilibrium national income level will be reached where outflows equal inflows, or where total planned expenditures equal national income. These conditions are met at an income level of $Y_2$ in Figure 12.3(a) and (b). At any other income level, firms will want to cut back or expand production. For instance, at an income level of $Y_3$, outflows (saving plus taxes) are greater than inflows (planned investment plus government expenditures). This "contractionary gap" between outflows and inflows is indicated by the vertical distance between points *a* and *b* in Figure 12.3(a) and (b). Because firms will not sell all they have produced under such conditions, they will

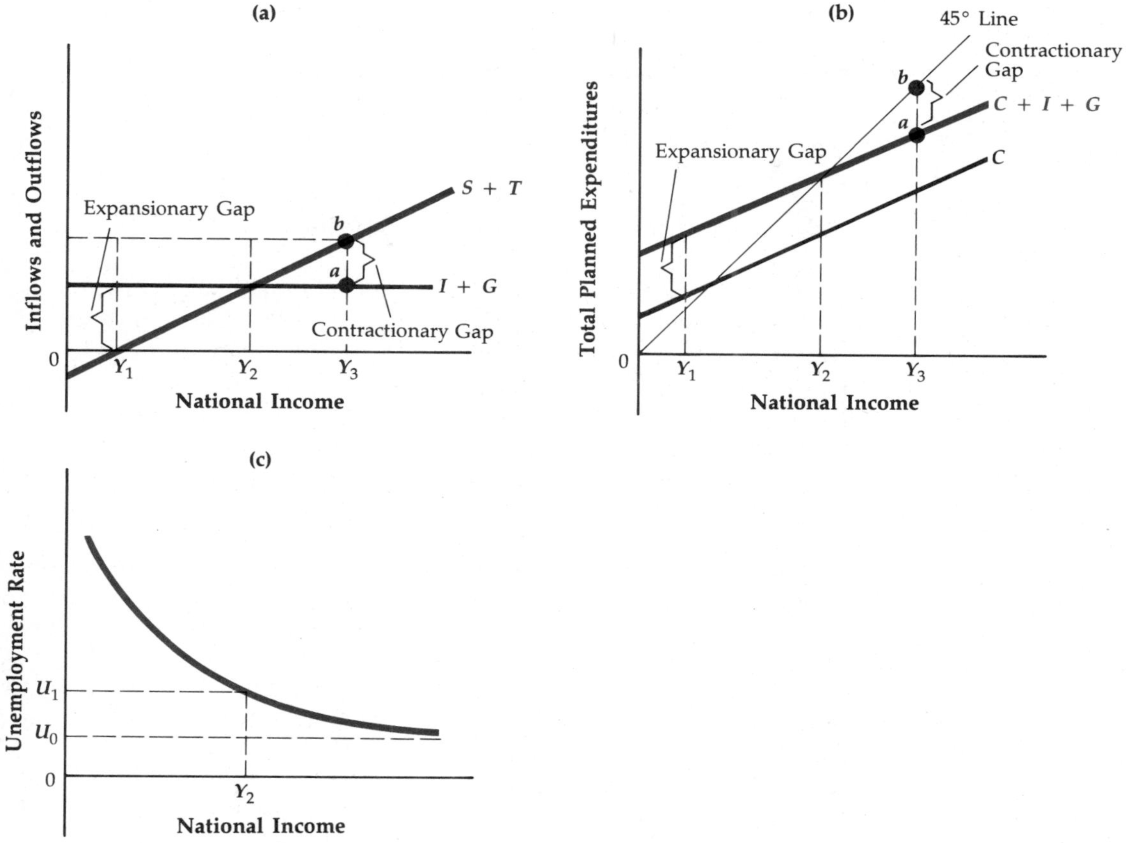


**Figure 12.3.** The Equilibrium National Income Level.
The equilibrium national income level is $Y_2$. At higher income levels, the planned saving and tax outflows exceed the planned investment and government spending inflows—part (a)—and national output exceeds total planned expenditures—part (b). The "contractionary gap" between what is produced and what is demanded by business, consumers, and government will move the economy back down toward $Y_2$. At income levels below $Y_2$, the investment and government spending inflows will exceed the planned saving and tax outflows—part (a)—and total planned expenditures will exceed national output—part (b). An "expansionary gap" between what is produced and what business, consumers, and government want will move the national income back up toward $Y_2$.

reduce production. As a result, the equilibrium national income level will contract toward $Y_2$, along with saving and taxes.

At income levels lower than $Y_2$, planned investment and government expenditure will be greater than planned saving and taxes, producing an "expansionary gap" between the inflow and outflow curves. Firms will be producing less than consumers want, and the excess demand will encourage them to increase production. As they do they will increase the national income level, as well as the outflows of saving and taxes. Eventually outflows will match inflows— at the equilibrium income level $Y_2$. At that level also, total planned expenditures will equal national income—Figure 12.3(b). Still, unemployment will be above the minimum rate of $U_0$, as indicated in Figure 12.3(c).

## Changes in Planned Government Expenditures

We can now examine how government changes the national income level. Suppose the government's budget is balanced (taxes equal expenditures). If it then increases expenditures while holding taxes constant, the national income level will rise. Figure 12.4 illustrates the impact of such an increase in planned government expenditure, achieved in this case by running a budgetary deficit. With the increase in expenditures, the total planned expenditures curve $C + I + G_1$ shifts upward to $C + I + G_2$, in part (a). This shift is mirrored in part (b) by an upward shift of the inflow curve, from $I + G$ to $I + G_2$. An expansionary gap now exists between total planned inflows and total planned outflows. At income level $Y_2$, businesses are not producing enough to satisfy total demand. As they increase production, the national income level rises along with the saving and tax outflows. The economy reaches a new equilibrium income level at $Y_3$, where outflows again equal inflows and total expenditure equals national income. Significantly, unemployment has dropped in the process, from $U_2$ to $U_1$.

Notice that the change in national income ($Y_3 - Y_2$) is greater than the change in government expenditure that initiated it ($C + I + G_2 - C + I + G_1$, or $G_2 - G_1$). Here we see the influence of the multiplier effect (see pages 242–247). When the government spends more, production goes up and people's incomes increase. Consumers then spend more, causing another rise in production, incomes, and consumption. The upward spiral ends when saving and taxes increase enough to equal the increase in government expenditures.

In short, income will increase by some multiple (greater than 1) of the increase in government spending.[1] We know from Chapter 11 that the change in national income equals the multiplier times the change in total planned expenditures.

$$\text{change in } Y = m \times \text{change in } TPE$$

---

1. With the tax outflow added to the saving outflow, the multiplier is not quite as large as it was in the examples in Chapter 11. Like saving, taxes drain off consumers' purchasing power, limiting the effect of any change in government or investment spending. As we pointed out previously, the multiplier equals the reciprocal of the marginal propensity to save. In that analysis, the marginal propensity to save was the same as the slope of the outflow curve, since saving was the only outflow. With taxes added, the slope of the outflow curve is higher; hence the multiplier is lower. How much lower depends on how much the tax drain affects the saving outflow.

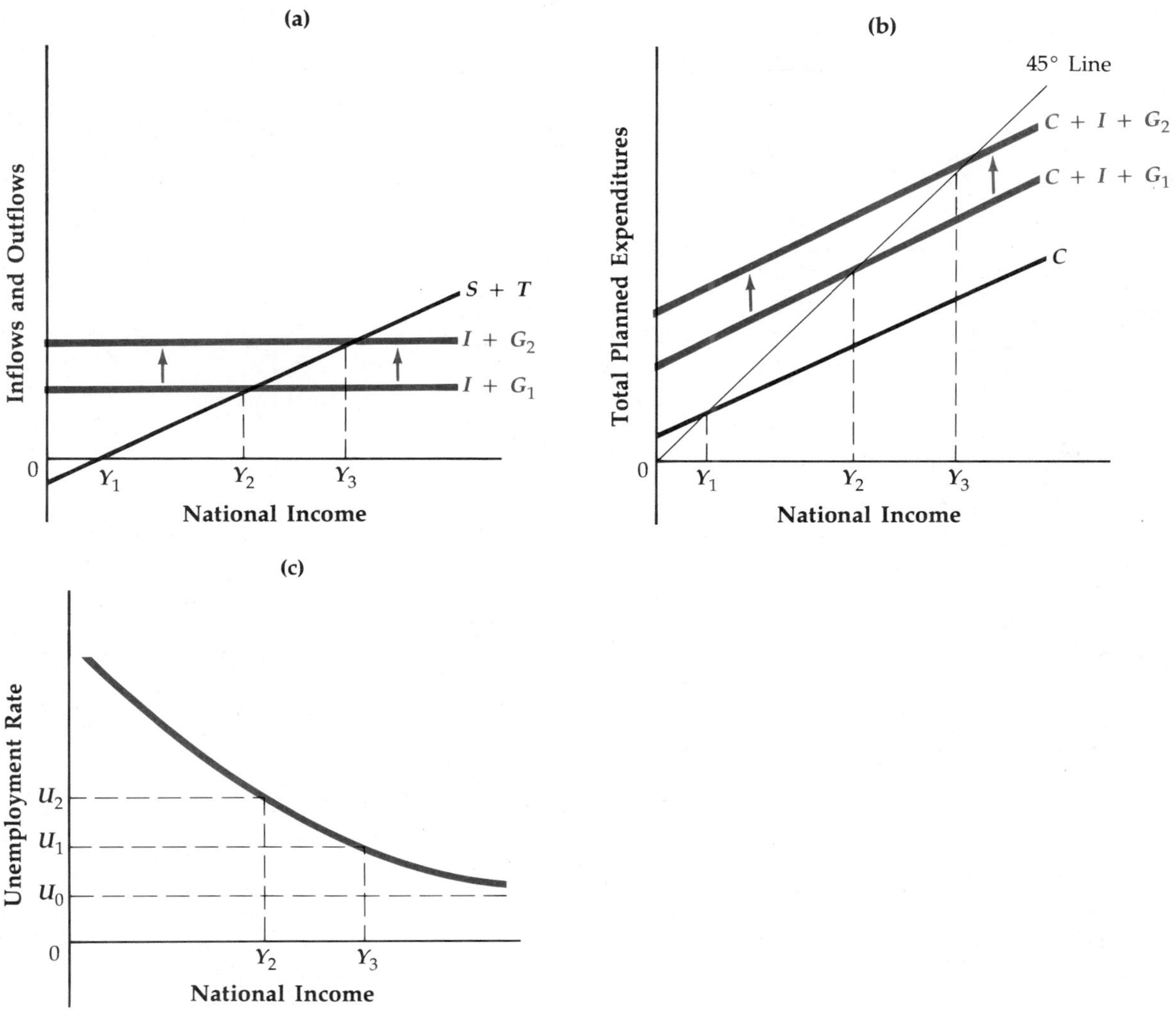


**Figure 12.4.** Increasing Government Spending to Reduce Unemployment.
An increase in government spending will shift the total planned expenditure curve up from $C + I + G_1$ to $C + I + G_2$—part (a)—and the inflow curve up from $I + G_1$ *to* $I + G_2$—part (b). The national income level will move from $Y_2$ to $Y_3$, where total expenditures will again equal national output—part (a)—and inflows will again equal outflows—part (b). Unemployment will drop from $U_2$ to $U_1$.

Since the change in total spending equals the change in government spending, we can restate our equation to read:

$$\text{change in } Y = m \times \text{change in } G$$

Conversely, if the government decreases expenditures while holding taxes constant, the national income level will fall. If the government spends

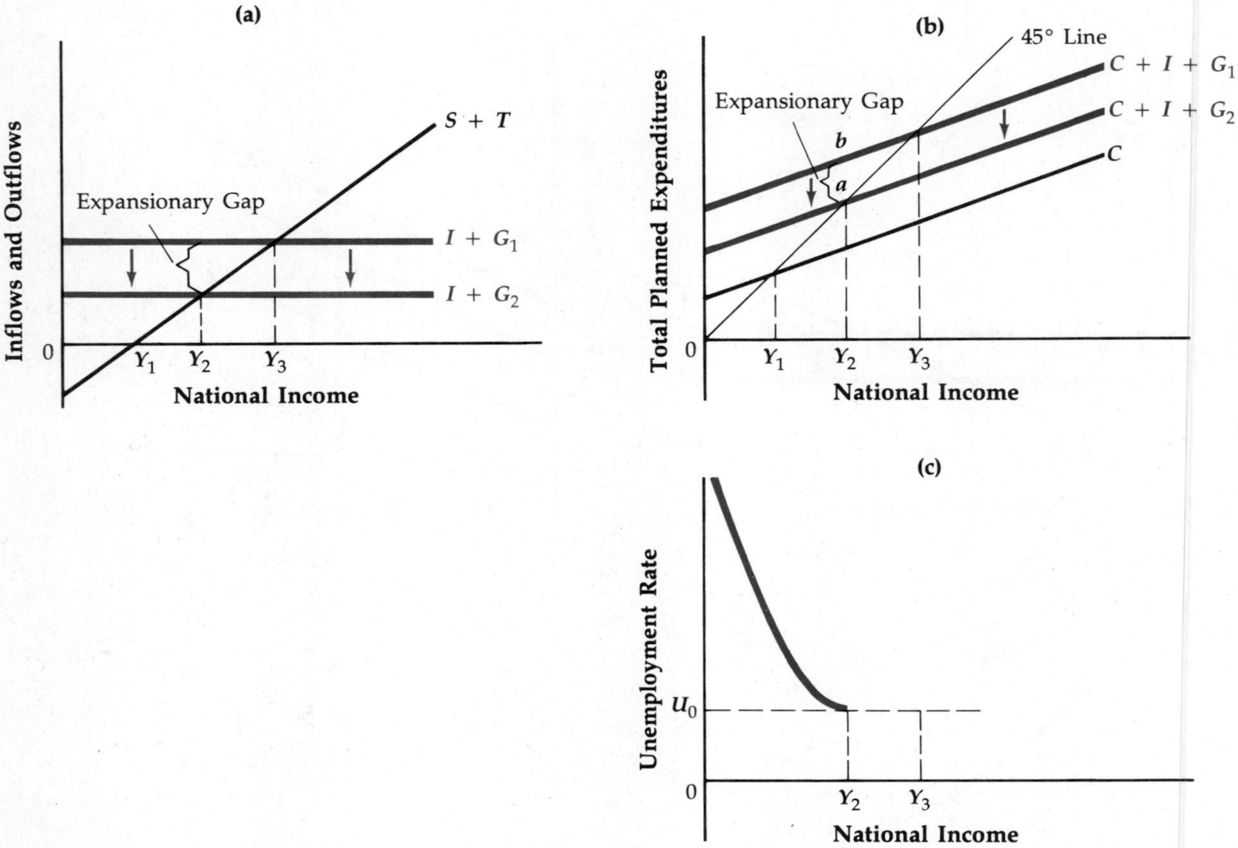


**Figure 12.5.** Decreasing Government Spending to Control Inflation.
If consumers, investors, and government together demand more goods than the economy can produce at full employment ($Y_2$), the gap between demand and output—points $b$ and $a$ in part (b)—will create inflationary pressure on prices. By reducing government expenditures, policymakers can reduce total planned expenditures to $C + I + G_2$, moving the economy away from the inflationary equilibrium income level of $Y_3$ to the noninflationary income level $Y_2$.

less, firms will produce less, workers will receive less income, consumers will consume less, and so forth. The national income level will decline by some multiple of the decrease in government expenditures, and unemployment will rise. In this case the government's fiscal policy causes or contributes to a recession.

Of course no government is likely to cause a recession intentionally. But government policymakers may very well reduce spending in an attempt to control the rate of inflation. In Figure 12.5, for instance, planned government expenditures and investment add up to $I + G_1$. The equilibrium income level is $Y_3$, where the outflow and inflow curves intersect (part (a)). But part (c) shows that the economy reaches the minimum unemployment rate, $U_0$, at a much lower national income level, $Y_2$.

In this case the nation simply does not have a labor force sufficient to produce at an output level of $Y_3$. Yet consumers are demanding that the economy produce at that level (part (b)). A gap exists between what consumers, investors, and government demand—point *b* in part (b)—and what the economy can produce (point *a*). This excess demand should produce inflation, since consumers will bid up the prices of goods that are in short supply. To eliminate the inflationary pressures, government policymakers may decide to reduce government expenditures, thereby reducing total planned expenditures to $C + I + G_2$. The equilibrium national income level will then be $Y_2$, the full-employment level for this economy.

Not all economists accept Keynesian doctrine on the effect of government spending. Some maintain that if the government has to create a deficit or increase its deficit in order to increase spending, the multiplier effect will be significantly weakened. When government borrows, it becomes a competitor in the money market, driving up interest rates and crowding private borrowers out of the market. (For a fuller explanation of crowding out, see pages 318–320.) If the government borrows funds that would otherwise be used elsewhere, these critics charge, any increase in government spending may be partially or totally offset by a decrease in private business ventures, or in state and local government spending.

If the government stimulates demand by spending more than it collects in taxes, it must either increase the money stock or borrow the difference between spending and taxes. The usual method is to borrow the money by selling bonds. Keynes argued that during a severe recession, the government would be borrowing funds that would otherwise remain idle. In a particularly serious recession, he felt, people tend to hold on to their money, fearing that loans to businesses are unsafe or anticipating that interest rates will rise. In that case government borrowing would not lead to a drop in private investment. Any increase in government spending would be fully reflected in the multiplier process.

But not all recessions are severe enough to scare lenders out of investing in private enterprise. What if private investment were to fall at the same time, and by the same amount, as government expenditures increase? Total planned expenditures would not change, and there would be no multiplier effect—no increase in the national income level. Even if private investment fell by less than the increase in government spending—say by \$7 billion when government expenditures rose by \$10 billion—the net change in total planned expenditures would be much reduced (in this example, to \$3 billion). The multiplier effect would still occur, but it would be much smaller than predicted by our earlier analysis.

Especially since the late 1960s, this question has been the subject of considerable controversy. Keynesians cite statistical studies that support the strength of the muliplier effect. Economists of the monetarist, supply-side, and rational expectations schools disagree, as we will see in later chapters. A synthesis on the impact of fiscal policy has begun to emerge,

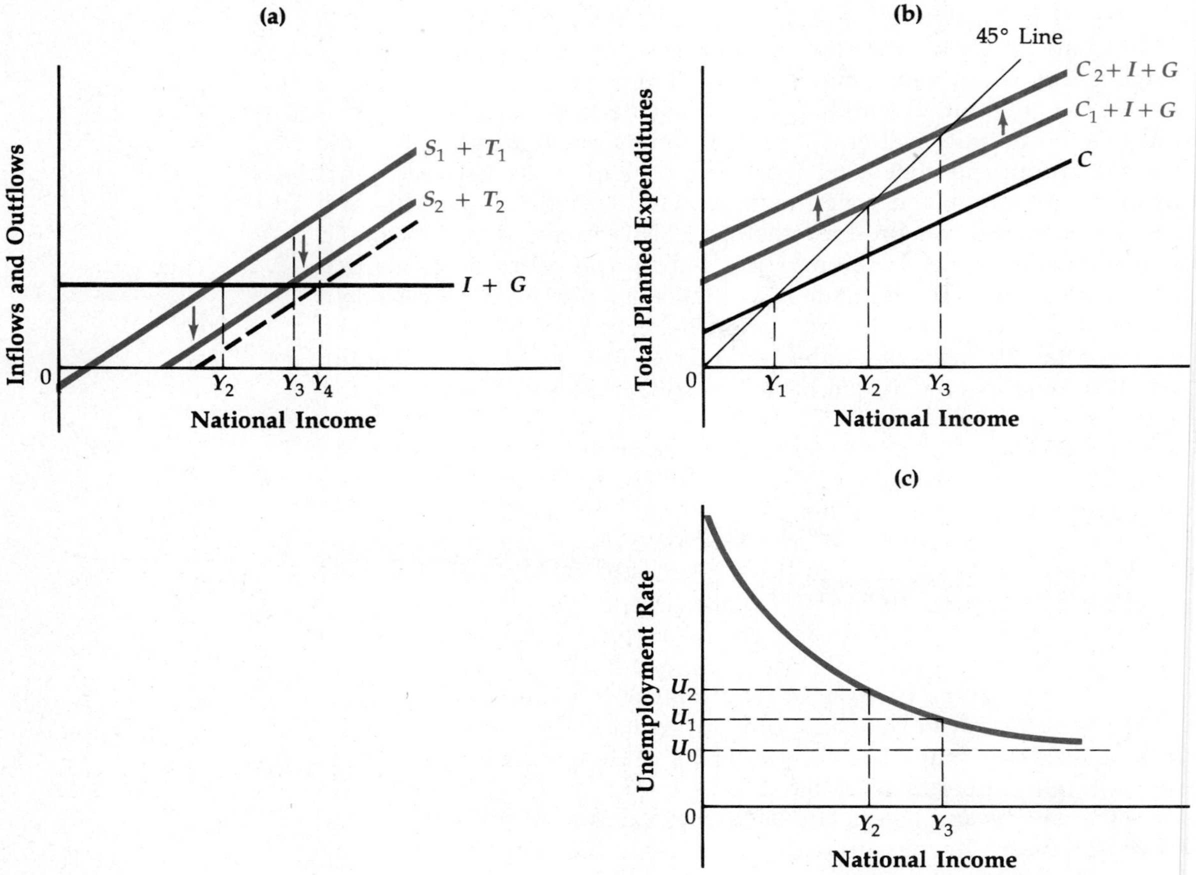


**Figure 12.6.** Decreasing Taxes to Reduce Unemployment.
A reduction in taxes shifts the combined outflow curve $S + T$ downward—part (a)—though not by the full amount of the tax cut, as shown by the dotted line. Some of the cut is saved, increasing the saving outflow at the same time the tax outflow decreases. Total expenditures shift up, as shown in part (b). The equilibrium national income level rises from $Y_2$ to $Y_3$, and the unemployment rate falls from $U_2$ to $U_1$ (part (c)).

however. The economists who adhere to it acknowledge a modest short-run multiplier effect. But they contend that after six months or possibly a year, fiscal action is largely ineffective in influencing aggregate demand and national income.

## Changes in Planned Taxes

A change in tax rates can have similar effects on the equilibrium national income level. If people's saving habits were not affected by the taxes they pay, a reduction in taxes might cause a sizable downward shift in the outflow curve ($S_1 + T_1$), to the dotted line in Figure 12.6(a). The equilibrium national income level would then climb all the way to $Y_4$. In fact, however, people tend to save some part of a tax reduction, particularly if it is a large one. The drop in the tax outflow is partially offset by the resulting increase in the saving outflow. The combined outflow curve shifts only part way, to $S_2 + T_2$. What is not saved is spent, for a reduction in taxes represents an increase in disposable income. Thus the total expenditures curve shifts up to $C_2 + I + G$, as shown in part (b). The national income level rises only to $Y_3$, and the unemployment level falls from $U_2$ to $U_1$.

How much of a tax cut taxpayers will spend can be estimated by multiplying the change in taxes by the marginal propensity to consume.

$$\text{change in } C = MPC \times -\text{change in } T$$

The minus sign is added in the right-hand side of the formula because consumption is expected to change in the opposite direction from taxes. If the marginal propensity to consume is nine-tenths and taxes are reduced by \$30 billion, for example, consumption will rise by nine-tenths of \$30 billion, or \$27 billion. The remaining portion of the tax cut, \$3 billion, will therefore be saved.

A planned tax increase will reduce people's disposable incomes, lowering both saving and consumption. Lower consumption will mean lower production, and eventually still lower incomes. Like a reduction in planned government expenditures, then, a tax increase is often (but not always) intended to reduce the inflationary pressures that arise when total planned expenditures exceed the economy's ability to produce. Lowering the demand for all goods and services dampens competition for scarce resources and slows price increases.

A comparison of this method of altering national income with the change-in-expenditure method discussed earlier leads us to two important conclusions. First, either a reduction in planned taxes or an increase in planned government expenditures will raise the national income level. A decrease in government expenditures or an increase in taxes will lower the national income level, exerting downward pressure on inflation.

Second, a change in planned government expenditures will have a greater effect on the national income level than an equal change in taxes. For instance, suppose the government increases its expenditures by \$10 billion. If the multiplier is 3, the change in the national income level will be \$30 billion (the multiplier times the change in total planned expenditures). If the government reduces taxes by \$10 billion, on the other hand, not all of the reduction will be spent by consumers. If \$3.33 billion ($MPS \times$ \$10 billion) of the cut goes into saving, consumption expenditures will rise by only \$6.67 billion. Because the multiplier process is keyed to the increase in planned consumer expenditures, not to the tax reduction, the change in income will be only \$20 billion (the multiplier times the change in total planned expenditures). Thus if government policymakers want to increase the national income level by reducing taxes, they will have to reduce them by an amount greater than the increase in expenditures needed to achieve the same effect.

## The Balanced-Budget Multiplier

Assume the government's budget is balanced. Now suppose it increases both its expenditures and the taxes it collects by the same amount, thus keeping its budget balanced. Will such an action affect the national income and employment levels? On the surface, it may seem that the two increases will simply offset each other. The rise in expenditures would increase national income by the same amount as a tax increase would reduce it. But Keynesians argue that a simultaneous increase in government expenditures and taxes should have a small positive effect on national income.

To see why, assume that the marginal propensity to consume is ⅔. An increase of $10 billion in taxes will produce a $6.67 billion reduction in consumer expenditures.

$$\text{change in } C = MPC \times -\text{change in } T$$
$$= \tfrac{2}{3} \times -\$10 \text{ billion}$$
$$= -\$6.67 \text{ billion}$$

If the multiplier is 3, this increase in consumption demand will lead to a decrease in national income of $20 billion.

$$\text{change in } Y = m \times \text{change in } TPE$$

Or, in this case, since the change in total spending is equal to the change in consumption,

$$\text{change in } Y = m \times \text{change in } C$$
$$= 3 \times -\$6.67 \text{ billion}$$
$$= -\$20 \text{ billion}$$

But the increase of $10 billion in government spending will increase national income by $30 billion, for the same reason.

$$\text{change in } Y = m \times \text{change in } TPE$$
$$= m \times \text{change in } G$$
$$(\text{since change in } TPE = \text{change in } G)$$
$$= 3 \times \$10 \text{ billion}$$
$$= \$30 \text{ billion}$$

The net change in national income, then, will be $10 billion ($30 billion − $20 billion). This $10 billion rise in national income equals the increase in government expenditures and taxes that caused it. Thus when government expenditures and taxes are increased by the same amount, the combined multiplier, called the balanced-budget multiplier, is 1.

## The Kennedy Tax Cut: A Real-World Case

When President John F. Kennedy took office in 1961, the economy was in a mild recession. He and his economic advisers concluded that the best way to fulfill his campaign promise to "get the economy moving again" was to reduce personal and business taxes, by approximately $12 billion.

Given that an equal increase in expenditures would have had a greater impact, why did Kennedy choose to reduce taxes? Political considerations probably played an important role in the decision. In either case the government would have to run a larger budgetary deficit, and no previous president had ever proposed to run a deficit or increase one simply to stimulate the economy. Indeed deficits had always been equated with fiscal irresponsibility. They were thought to impose a burden on future generations and to court national bankruptcy. In 1961, increasing government expenditures to stimulate the economy was too radical a move politically. Although the tax cut too was controversial, it was more acceptable to the public because it put extra money into the pockets of tax-payers.

There was a technical as well as a political reason for choosing a tax cut, however. Kennedy's economic advisers argued that tax rates were so high they would prevent the achievement of full employment. If the economy started to recover and national income to rise, tax revenues would become so high that people would lack the income necessary to raise consumption. The economy would stop moving upward at some point before reaching full employment. In short, the tax system would impose what the advisers called "fiscal drag" on the recovery. If a tax cut reduced this drain on personal purchasing power, Kennedy's economists argued, the extra money people had to spend would help to speed and extend the recovery.

Keynesian economists argue that the Reagan-backed tax package of 1981, which cut tax rates over the period 1981–1984, stimulated the economy in much the same way as Kennedy's tax cut. There is some debate over whether this most recent tax cut actually had the expected positive effect on national income, however. If the rise in Social Security tax rates and the impact of bracket creep are taken into account, the overall tax rate may not have been cut very much, if at all. Some economists have offered supply-side explanations for the recovery that began in late 1982—an issue that we will take up in Chapter 15. And others attribute the recovery to the rapid rate of increase in the money stock that began late in 1982, not the tax cut. We will consider this monetary explanation for the recovery in Chapter 14.

## Fiscal Policy in the Context of the Business Cycle

We have seen how Keynesians use changes in government spending and taxes to counteract the negative effects of recession and inflation. Eventually, through the multiplier process, a small change in government spending or taxation will be translated into a much larger change in national income. This sort of corrective fiscal policy cannot be expected to eliminate all ups and downs in economic activity, however. Economic recovery takes time; and timing is one of the most crucial aspects of fiscal policymaking.

## Difficulties in the Timing of Fiscal Actions

If policy changes could be put into effect as soon as they were needed, and if they worked almost immediately, fiscal action might be a relatively simple proposition. But almost inevitably the hoped-for increase in national income and employment, or decrease in prices, is slow in coming. Time is lost at several points along the way, starting with the lag in recognizing a problem.

### *Recognition Lag*

Before fiscal action can be taken, government must recognize that a recession or a period of inflation is under way. This process may take several months, given the way some economic data are collected. In the beginning of a recession, signals are likely to be mixed. Some measures, like the number of housing starts per month, may indicate a decline in economic activity. Yet an upward trend may persist in others, like the number of new orders for heavy industrial equipment. Thus government policymakers may not begin to address an economic problem for some time—and then they may not be able to agree immediately on the appropriate fiscal actions.

### *Reaction Lag*

After policymakers have concluded that the economy has changed direction, they will have to convince Congress that a change in taxes or expenditures is needed. Members of Congress may bargain for special benefits for their home districts. Thus policy action is further delayed by politicking. The Kennedy tax cut took sixteen months to go through Congress. The Reagan tax package took almost a year.

### *Impact Lag*

If Congress approves an action, several more months will pass before its impact is felt. A tax cut will take effect as soon as people's take-home pay increases. An increase in government expenditures tends to work more slowly—new projects must be bid on, and contracts negotiated. All in all, the economy can be well on its way to the bottom or top of a cycle before the effects of a fiscal action become evident.

Unfortunately, if an action comes too late, it is likely to make the problem worse. If a fiscal stimulus is passed late in the recovery phase of a recession, it can add to the inflationary pressures that accompany the approach to the peak of a business cycle. Only in a world in which information is readily available and unambiguous can appropriate action be taken at the appropriate time. And because fiscal policies must be formulated in the political arena, appropriate timing is even more unlikely. If Congress uses Keynesian prescriptions to increase political support at home, a political business cycle—one that moves in accord with elections—may develop.

## Use of Automatic Stabilizers

There is an alternative to the use of deliberate policy actions by government, one that does not involve the risk of poor timing. Some taxes and government expenditures vary automatically with changes in the national income level, and generally in the desired direction. These fiscal instruments are called automatic stabilizers. An **automatic stabilizer** is a tax or expenditure that increases total planned spending in times of recession and lowers it in times of economic expansion, without special action on the part of the administration and Congress. Among the more important automatic stabilizers are income taxes and unemployment and welfare benefits.

**Automatic stabilizer:** a tax or expenditure that increases total planned spending in times of recession and lowers it in times of economic expansion, without special action on the part of the administration and Congress.

### *Personal Income Taxes*

Through the tax rate structure, personal income taxes are tied directly to the national income level. As their personal incomes rise, people are required to pay an increasing percentage of their taxable incomes to the government. When national income begins to fall, therefore, the government's tax collections decline as well. This drop in tax revenues partly offsets the drop in consumer purchasing power.

### *Corporate Income Taxes*

Like individuals, corporations must pay a percentage of their profits in taxes to the government. And like personal income taxes, corporate income taxes vary with corporate income, or profits. This stabilizer has a particularly powerful effect on total spending, for corporate profits move dramatically in response to a change in national income. They fall considerably during recessions and rise steeply during economic expansions.

### *Unemployment Compensation and Welfare Benefits*

When the national income level falls, the unemployment level rises. There is then an increase in unemployment compensation, as well as many welfare benefits—food stamps, rent subsidies, and aid to dependent children—increasing the level of government spending. Conversely, a rise in national income reduces unemployment, curtailing these social programs and lowering government spending.

# The Pros and Cons of Deficit Spending

Before Keynes it was generally agreed that government should try to restrict its expenditures to the level of its tax receipts—in other words, balance its budget. Deficit spending during peacetime was equated with fiscal irresponsibility. An underlying assumption was that the federal government was like an individual household. It could not continually incur budgetary deficits without risking bankruptcy. Moreover, because individual debts must be paid back at some point, deficit spending was seen as a burden on future generations.

## Perspectives in Economics: The Political Effects of Keynesian Economics

When Keynes wrote his *General Theory,* British economic policy was formulated by a small group of intellectuals. Keynes developed his arguments for government spending with such a system in mind. He assumed that given good policy recommendations, good men will do good things. He probably did not foresee that his ideas would be taken up by politicians in Washington, who keep one eye on the economy and the other on the opinion polls.

Those who follow the politics of economics have observed that politicians tend to vote for spending programs and against the taxes to pay for those programs.[1] Government expenditures benefit many. To the extent that they benefit a politician's constituency, they increase his or her political support. Taxes, on the other hand, impose costs on political constituencies. They tend to reduce a politician's support. If politicians accept the idea that government budgets must be balanced, some economists argue, they will vote for government expenditures only if the political support they generate exceeds the support lost by raising taxes to pay for the programs. But if politicians do not believe in the

Keynesian theory undermined the popularity of the balanced budget. Keynesians argued that during periods of slack demand and high unemployment, deficit spending creates no present or future costs. On the contrary, because of the implied increase in total spending, deficits allow more people to work, more income to be generated, and more products to be produced. These resources, both people and equipment, would otherwise remain idle. And since the real cost of any government action must be measured against what is forgone, it follows that the real cost of running a deficit during a recession is virtually zero.

Furthermore, to the extent that deficit spending is used to build roads, schools, and national parks, or to encourage private investment through government subsidies, future generations actually benefit from it. They have more capital assets to use in the production of new goods and services. And though they will have to meet the interest payments on the debt, they also have higher incomes with which to meet them. Besides, to the extent the interest is paid to U.S. citizens, such payments do not represent a loss of resources to the nation as a whole. Because we effectively owe the debt to ourselves, we pay the interest to ourselves—or so the argument goes.

During times of full employment, a government deficit does impose a cost on the private sector, because there are no idle resources to be taken up. Resources must be diverted from private to government use. At such times, the cost of a deficit can be measured by what must be given up in the private sector. Most Keynesians agree that deficit spending is generally balanced budget, they will court political support by voting consistently for government expenditures and against taxes. Given widespread acceptance of deficit spending, even politicians who are opposed to deficits may feel forced to accept them in order to survive politically.

In times of inflation, when the government should reduce total planned expenditures and run a budgetary surplus, the political appeal of a deficit becomes even more obvious. Politicians have an understandable aversion to budget surpluses, since they can be created only by raising taxes but not spending—or reducing spending but not taxes. For politicians, surpluses can spell a net loss in political support. Even during periods of excessive demand and inflation, politicians are more likely to vote for a lower surplus, or even a deficit, than for a higher surplus. Keynesian policy may be effective, but it cannot always be productively employed in the political arena.

1. James M. Buchanan and Richard E. Wagner, *Democracy in Deficit: The Destructive Legacy of Lord Keynes* (New York: Academic Press, 1977).

appropriate only during periods of relatively high unemployment.

Keynesians also question the analogy between government and household finances. They point out that even an individual household's debt can grow over time, as the family becomes better able to pay interest and to repay the principal. While a household is paying off some debts, it can incur new ones. People who are paying off a car loan, for instance, can still buy furniture on credit. As people's incomes grow over time, their ability to handle more debt increases.

This is just what has happened in the United States since the Second World War. In 1950 consumer debt (not including home mortgages) totaled \$25 billion; by the end of 1984 it had risen to \$575 billion. Even allowing for inflation, the increase in private debt had been substantial. Yet personal income has grown with it. Personal income increased from \$227 billion to \$3,013 billion between 1950 and 1984.[2] If members of households can increase their indebtedness over time, why not the government?

Furthermore, the idea that all debts will eventually come due cannot really be applied to government. Because people's lives are limited, members of an individual household must pay off all their debts—if necessary, through their estates, after death. But for all practical purposes the government can expect perpetual life. Granted, government bonds do

2. *Statistical Abstract of the United States* (Washington, D.C.: U.S. Government Printing Office, 1985), p. 501.

carry maturity dates, on which bondholders must be repaid the stated amounts. But government can refinance its debt by issuing new bonds and using the funds collected from them to pay off the old debt. Taken collectively, the debt of consumers is never paid off. So why should the government's debt be paid off?

The major constraint on the government's ability to expand its debt is citizens' willingness to buy bonds. The borrowing limit depends on both the stability of the government and people's propensity to save. If a government is in danger of being overthrown, people will of course be reluctant to lend it money. But so long as the government is stable and can pay the going market interest rate out of its tax collections, government bonds will be just as attractive as private bonds, if not more so. U.S. government bonds are generally considered to be safer investments than most corporate bonds, as evidenced by the higher interest rates borne by the latter. Finally, Keynesians would argue, if through deficit spending the government can raise the national income level, and therefore the nation's tax revenues, why worry about increasing the national debt?

We will return to this issue in following chapters, for economists from other schools of thought take issue with the Keynesians' benign view of government deficits.

## Monetary Policy from the Keynesian Perspective

Though modern Keynesians advocate the use of both fiscal and monetary policy to relieve unemployment, Keynesian economics has historically been associated with the management of aggregate demand through fiscal policy. Keynes and his followers doubted that monetary policy could pull the economy out of a particularly severe recession like the Great Depression.

### The Federal Reserve During the Depression

During the Great Depression banks were hit hard on both sides of their balance sheet. While borrowers became less capable of paying back their loans, depositors became skeptical of the solvency of banks and withdrew their deposits. Hundreds of banks failed, and many others came close to bankruptcy.

The banks' predicament was made more difficult by the Federal Reserve. The Fed was established to ensure that banks could borrow the reserves they needed whenever their customers made heavy withdrawals. Yet during the 1930s the Fed severely discouraged banks from borrowing at the discount window. Many banks failed simply because they could not obtain the necessary reserves from the Fed. Bank officers soon became extremely cautious about lending money, and worked to build up their reserve deposits with the Fed and other banks. When the Fed later attempted to increase the money stock, banks held on to part of the newly created reserves for their own protection.

To Keynesians, this buildup of excess reserves demonstrated that during a severe depression, people have a highly elastic demand for money. Even very small decreases in interest rates will cause banks to hold on to whatever reserves they can, and individuals to hold on to whatever money the Federal Reserve creates. The money simply will not be spent. And without an increase in spending, the economy will remain depressed.

Thus Keynes and his followers concluded that monetary policy could not alleviate a severe depression. The only way to stimulate the economy in such circumstances, they argued, was to increase spending or reduce taxes.

## The Liquidity Trap

Keynesians deemphasize monetary policy not just because of its history during the Depression, but because of its role in Keynesian theory. Keynesians reject the classical theory that interest rates adjust to bring the demand for investment goods into line with the supply of savings (see pages 215–219). Instead they stress the demand for money versus the stock of money.

According to Keynesian theory, the demand for money is rooted primarily in the transactions demand and the speculative demand. (In Keynesian terms the transactions demand for money includes both the transactions and precautionary demands, as defined on page 150.) The transactions demand is determined primarily by the national income level. Money is needed to carry on trade, and the greater the national income level, the greater the need for trade. The direct relationship between the national income level and the transactions demand for money is illustrated in Figure 12.7(a).

The speculative demand for money is determined principally by expectations regarding future interest rates. If people think current interest rates are low, they will hold on to their money, waiting for rates to rise. If interest rates are falling, more and more people will begin to expect rates to rise in the future, and will hold on to their money for the present. The quantity of money demanded for speculative purposes will rise. This inverse relationship between interest rates and the speculative demand for money is illustrated in Figure 12.7(b).

Given an income level like $Y_1$ in Figure 12.7(a), the total demand for money will look something like the curve in Figure 12.7(c). Keynes argued that during severe depressions, the interest rate may fall so low that everyone will believe it is going to rise, and everyone will hold on to all the cash they can get. An economy in such circumstances has fallen into a "liquidity trap." The usual monetary policy remedy—expansion of the money stock—can offer no relief.

Suppose, for instance, that the demand for money looks like the downward-sloping curve in Figure 12.8(a), and that the money stock is fixed at $MS_1$. The equilibrium interest rate will be $R_1$, where the demand for money and money stock curves intersect. Notice that with this curve, an increase in the money stock, say from $MS_1$ to $MS_2$, will not lower the

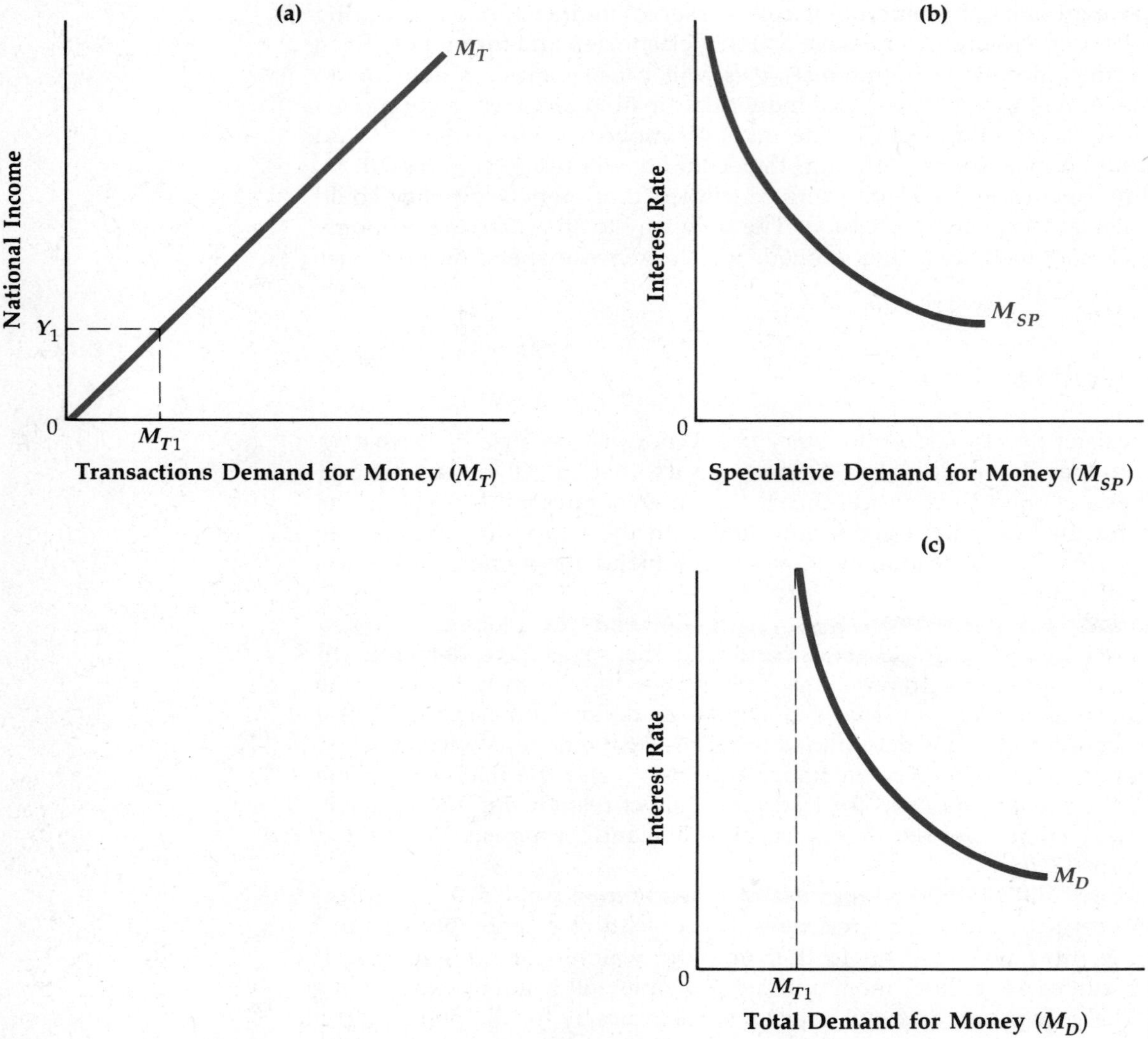


**Figure 12.7.** The Demand for Money: The Keynesian View.
In the Keynesian model, the demand for money is composed of two major components: the transactions demand and the speculative demand. The amount of money demanded for making transactions—part (a)—is directly related to the national income level. The quantity of money demanded for speculation is inversely related to the interest rate (part (b)). The total demand for money—part (c)—is the summation of the transactions demand for money at a given income level—say $Y_1$—and the speculative demand for money.

interest rate any further, as it normally would be expected to do. If the interest rate remains at $R_1$, the investment level will stay at $I_1$ in Figure 12.8(b). With no increase in investment, the national income level must remain depressed.

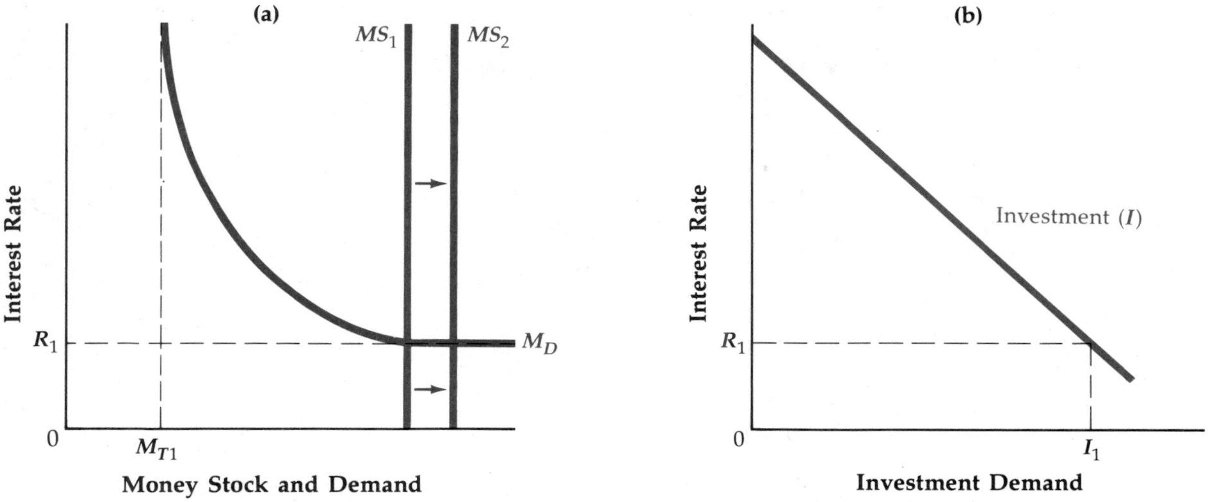


**Figure 12.8.** The Liquidity Trap.
If the money demand curve flattens out at a low interest rate, as in panel (a), and the money stock curve intersects it in its horizontal range, the macroeconomy is said to be in a liquidity trap. An increase in the money stock from $MS_1$ to $MS_2$ will not result in a lower interest rate, and therefore will not increase the level of investment—panel (b).

## The Effect of Changes in the Money Stock

Thus Keynesians explained the apparent ineffectiveness of monetary policy during the Great Depression. They concluded that in severe economic conditions, fiscal policy actions are the only means of stimulating the economy. But many Keynesians now recognize that monetary policy can be a useful means of fighting recession. In fact, the demand for money never flattens out completely, as it does in Figure 12.8(a). Rather, it slopes downward all the way, as in Figure 12.9(a). Hence an increase in the money stock, say from $MS_1$ to $MS_2$, will lead to a lower interest rate and an increase in investment spending, as in Figure 12.9(b). Through the multiplier process, this increase in investment will be translated into a much larger increase in national income, as in Figure 12.9(c).

Though economists now agree on the general effect of an increase in the money stock, debate continues over the magnitude of the effect. The size of the change in national income depends on several factors.

How far the interest rate will fall as the money stock rises depends on how people's demand for money responds to a change in the interest rate.

How much investment spending will increase as the interest rate declines depends on how investment demand responds to a change in the interest rate.

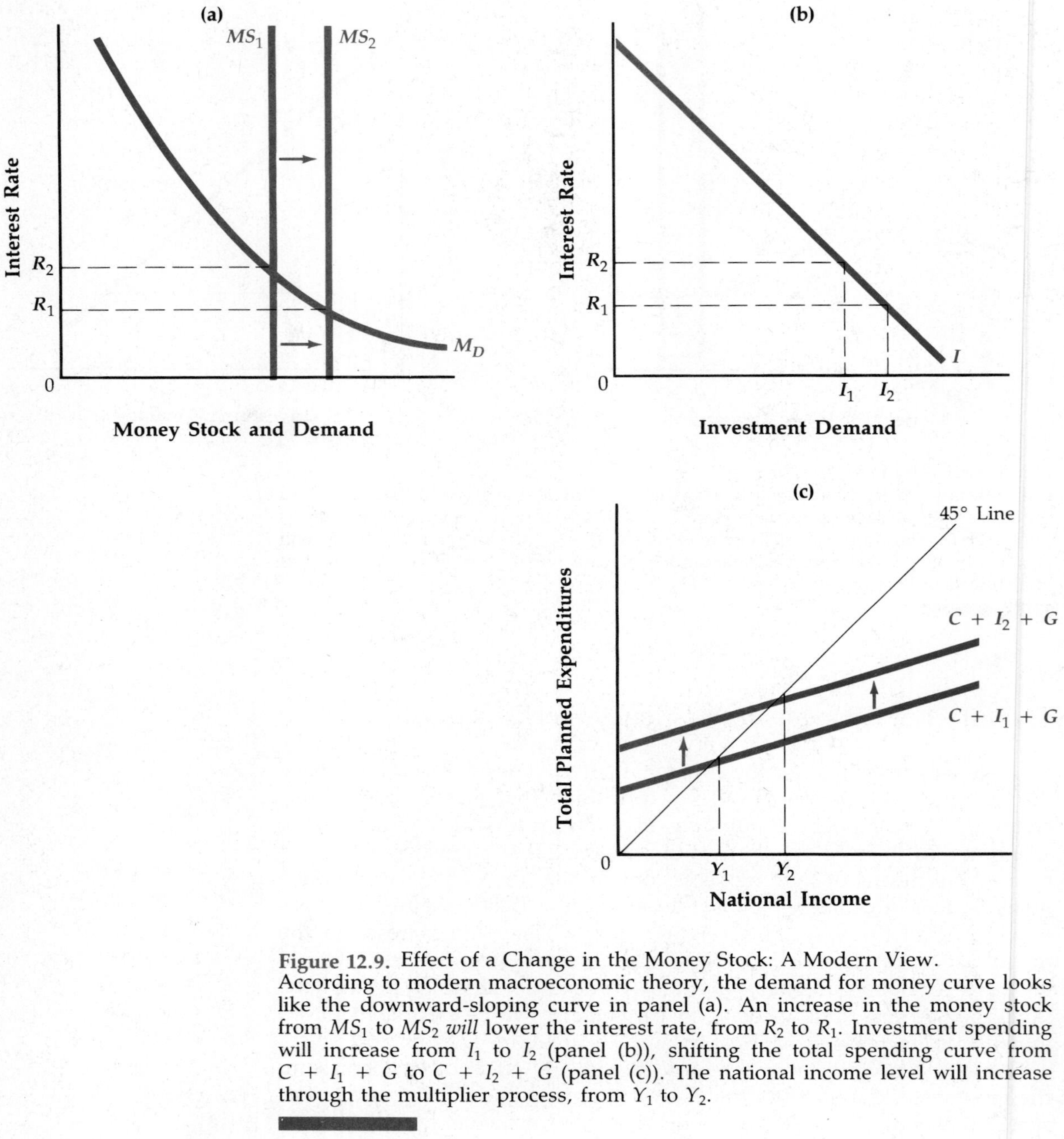


**Figure 12.9.** Effect of a Change in the Money Stock: A Modern View. According to modern macroeconomic theory, the demand for money curve looks like the downward-sloping curve in panel (a). An increase in the money stock from $MS_1$ to $MS_2$ *will* lower the interest rate, from $R_2$ to $R_1$. Investment spending will increase from $I_1$ to $I_2$ (panel (b)), shifting the total spending curve from $C + I_1 + G$ to $C + I_2 + G$ (panel (c)). The national income level will increase through the multiplier process, from $Y_1$ to $Y_2$.

How much the national income level will change as a result of a change in investment spending depends on the size of the multiplier. And the size of the multiplier depends on the marginal propensity to consume and on income tax rates.

## Summary and Extensions

The Keynesian prescription for extremely high unemployment is to increase total planned expenditures, either by increasing government spending or by decreasing taxes. Both methods will increase national income. Either way, though, the government must be willing to create or increase a budgetary deficit or to reduce a budgetary surplus. In times of excessive demand and inflation, the Keynesian prescription is to increase taxes or reduce government expenditures, thus lowering the equilibrium national income level. Such action may require the government to run a budgetary surplus or a smaller deficit.

These same basic effects can be obtained by increasing or decreasing the money stock. An increase in the money stock will tend to lower interest rates, encouraging investment. A decrease in the money stock will do the opposite. Modern-day Keynesians feel that both monetary and fiscal actions can be used effectively, either separately or together, to relieve unemployment and inflation. As we will see in later chapters, however, there is considerable debate about the appropriateness of Keynesian policies. Part of that debate concerns the extent to which fiscal and monetary policy actions affect prices, which we have held constant in the foregoing analysis. That simplifying assumption will be dropped in the next chapter.

## Major Conclusions

1. Government can increase total planned expenditures, and thereby the national income level, by (a) increasing government spending while holding taxes constant; (b) reducing taxes while holding government spending constant; or (c) increasing government spending and decreasing taxes at the same time.
2. Government can reduce total planned expenditures, and thereby inflation, by (a) reducing government spending while holding taxes constant; (b) increasing taxes while holding government spending constant; or (c) reducing government spending while increasing taxes.
3. According to Keynesian theory, increases and decreases in government spending and/or taxes have a multiplier effect on the national income level. Thus the government should adjust its expenditures or its taxes by only a fraction of the desired change in national income.
4. An increase in government spending will have a greater effect on the national income level than a tax reduction of equal size. To increase the national income level through a tax cut, the government must reduce taxes by more than it would have to increase government spending to achieve the same effect.
5. When government borrows money to cover a deficit caused by an increase in its spending, the market interest rate may rise and businesses may reduce their investment spending. This reduction in planned business investment can partially (if not totally) offset the effect of higher government spending on the national income level.
6. Government budgetary deficits should not be incurred needlessly. But they may be acceptable if they emerge from a purposeful fiscal policy designed to stimulate the economy and raise the national income level.
7. Delays in the implementation of fiscal policy should be expected because of recognition lag (delay in recognizing the need for a change

in fiscal policy), action lag (delay in getting Congress to take the necessary action), and impact lag (delay in realizing the effects of the policy change).

8. Automatic stabilizers are fiscal changes triggered automatically by changes in the national income level, without special action on the part of the administration or Congress.
9. The national debt does not have to be paid off; it can be refinanced. When a portion of the national debt comes due, the government can issue new bonds to acquire the funds needed to pay it off.
10. Deficit spending benefits politicians seeking reelection, for their constituents receive more government goods and services without having to pay for them directly through higher taxes. Politicians can thus be expected to support larger deficits than may be necessary to achieve full employment and stable prices.
11. Monetary policy can also influence the national income level. An increase in the money stock will reduce the interest rate, increasing planned investment and total planned expenditures. Like fiscal actions, the increase in total planned expenditures will be translated, by the multiplier process, into an increase in the national income level.

## Questions to Ponder

1. Will an increase in government expenditures of $10 billion have the same effect on the national income level as a $10 billion decrease in taxes? Explain.
2. Will a decrease in the money stock reduce or increase the national income level? Explain your reasoning.
3. If a $10 billion increase in government expenditures causes a $10 billion decrease in investment expenditures, what will happen to the national income level?
4. In recent years, government has allowed a tax credit for investing in new plant and equipment. That is, businesses have been permitted to reduce their tax payments by a percentage of the value of new plant and equipment purchased during the year. Using the Keynesian model of income and employment, explain the possible effects of such an investment tax credit.
5. Does Keynesian theory promote unnecessarily high budgetary deficits? Explain your answer.

## Central Question

*How do aggregate supply and demand interact to determine the national income and price levels?*

## Key Terms

Money illusion
Econometrics
Econometric model
Linear regression

# Chapter 13

# Aggregate Supply and Demand

*Can the United States have high-unemployment prosperity without inflation? For some time, the American people have been asked to tune in tomorrow and find out; but the last episode of the serial has not yet been produced. In no period during the past forty years has the American economy been free of excessive unemployment* and *inflationary tendencies simultaneously. Nor has any other industrial nation found the happier combination; hitting the dual target of high utilization and essential price stability remains the most serious unsolved problem of stabilization policy throughout the Western World.*

*Arthur Okun*

So far we have focused almost exclusively on how changes in total spending affect the national income and employment levels. Little has been said about what happens to the price level when government fiscal or monetary policies change. We have ignored the price level for two reasons. First, Keynesian theory initially assumed that prices do not change very much or very rapidly with changes in total spending. A central point of Keynesian macroeconomics is that changes in total planned spending will be reflected in output and employment—a point that can be illustrated most clearly by holding prices constant. Second, the assumption of constant prices has helped us keep the analysis relatively simple.

This chapter will extend Keynesian macroeconomic theory in two ways. First, we will introduce prices. To explain how price changes can absorb some of the impact of a change in planned expenditures, we will return to the aggregate demand and supply model introduced in Chapter 6. Second, we will show how changes in the conditions of production can affect national income, employment, and prices.

## Aggregate Demand

In Chapter 6 aggregate demand was defined as the presumed negative relationship between the price level and the total quantity of goods and services consumers, businesses, and government want to buy during a given period of time. Aggregate demand is not the same as the market demand for a given product or service. Market demand is the relationship between the price of a given product and the quantity consumers are willing and able to buy. Aggregate demand is the relationship between the general price level (an index of the prices of all products and services) and the total quantity of all goods and services demanded.

Aggregate demand also differs from the total planned expenditure function we discussed in Chapters 10 to 12. That function is the relationship between the national income level and total planned expenditures. Aggregate demand is the relationship between the price level and the total amount of goods and services, or national output, that people want. Aggregate demand permits us to monitor the influence of the price level on total planned expenditures.

Usually aggregate demand is drawn as a downward-sloping curve, like the one shown in Figure 13.1. Its downward slope reflects the negative relationship between prices in general and total product demanded. As the price level goes down, from $P_2$ to $P_1$, total real national income and product demanded rises, from $Y_1$ to $Y_2$. All market demand curves slope downward, but that is not why the aggregate demand curve does so. Its shape is a result of the effects of a change in the price level on interest rates and on people's real wealth.

### The Effect of a Change in Price Level on Interest Rates

Recall our discussion of interest rates in Chapter 12 (see pages 272–276). In Keynesian theory, the interaction of the demand for money and the

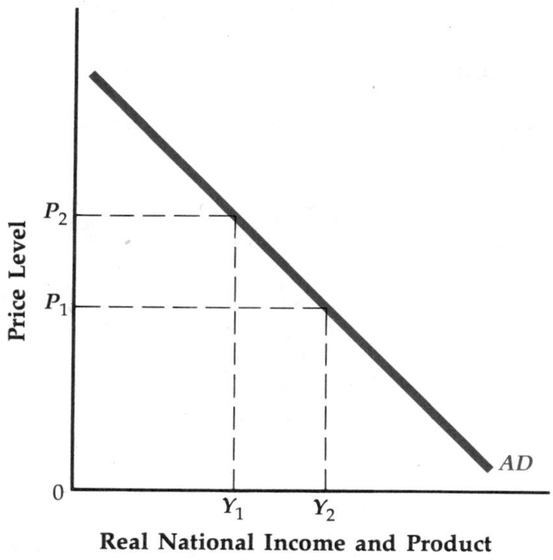


**Figure 13.1.** Aggregate Demand.
Aggregate demand ($AD$) is the assumed inverse relationship between the price level and the total output demanded during a given period of time. If the price level falls from $P_2$ to $P_1$, for example, the total quantity of goods and services demanded by consumers, investors, and government rises from $Y_1$ to $Y_2$.

stock of money determines the interest rate. If the demand for money and the money stock are represented as $MD$ and $MS_1$ in Figure 13.2(a), the interest rate will be $R_2$. Planned investment demand will be $I_1$ (part (b)), and the national income level will be $Y_1$ (part (c)).

A decline in the price level amounts to an increase in the purchasing power of the money stock. Because the amount of money in existence will now cover more transactions, the real money stock has expanded. A reduction in the price level therefore has the same effect as an increase in the money stock, say from $MS_1$ to $MS_2$ in Figure 13.2(a). The interest rate will drop from $R_2$ to $R_1$, increasing planned investment spending from $I_1$ to $I_2$. The increase in planned investment will then be translated, through the multiplier process, into a much greater increase in the national income level, from $Y_1$ to $Y_2$.

We have just deduced an important principle: a reduction in the price level causes an increase in the national income level. Conversely, an increase in the price level will reduce the real money stock, increasing the interest rate and decreasing planned investment and national income. Thus we can say that price level $P_1$ in Figure 13.1 is associated with a national income level of $Y_2$, and price level $P_2$ with a lower national income level, $Y_1$. That is, the price and national income levels are inversely (negatively) related.

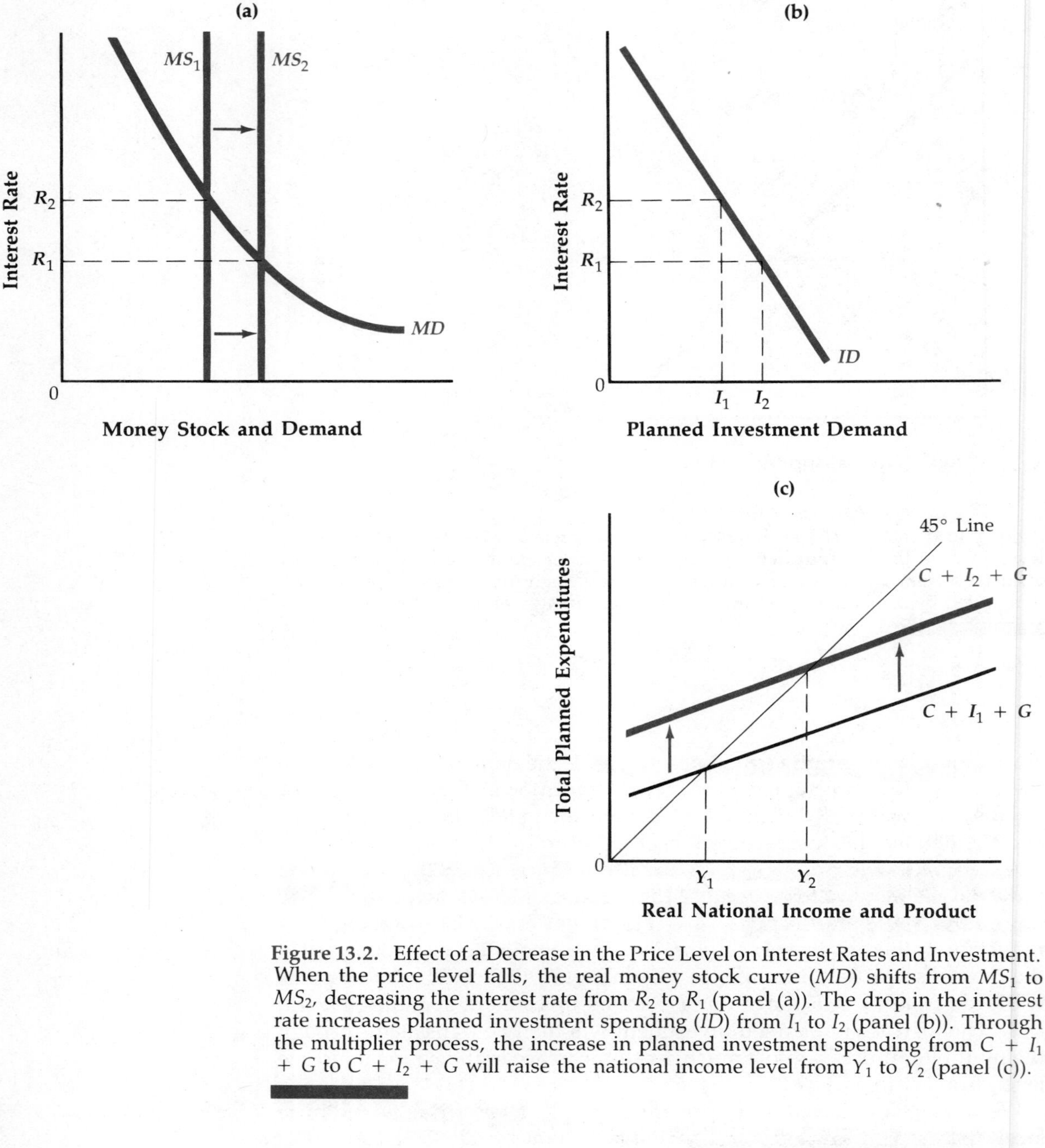


**Figure 13.2.** Effect of a Decrease in the Price Level on Interest Rates and Investment. When the price level falls, the real money stock curve ($MD$) shifts from $MS_1$ to $MS_2$, decreasing the interest rate from $R_2$ to $R_1$ (panel (a)). The drop in the interest rate increases planned investment spending ($ID$) from $I_1$ to $I_2$ (panel (b)). Through the multiplier process, the increase in planned investment spending from $C + I_1 + G$ to $C + I_2 + G$ will raise the national income level from $Y_1$ to $Y_2$ (panel (c)).

## The Effect of a Change in Price Level on Real Wealth

A reduction in the price level can also make people who hold assets valued in dollars—bonds and bank accounts, for example—feel wealthier. With

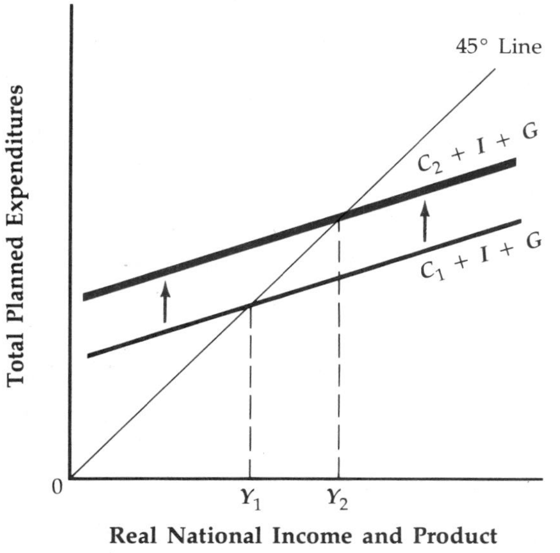


**Figure 13.3.** Effect of a Decrease in the Price Level on Consumption.
When the price level falls, wealth valued in dollars rises, reducing the need for saving and increasing total planned expenditures from $C_1 + I + G$ to $C_2 + I + G$. The result is an increase in the national production and income level, from $Y_1$ to $Y_2$.

lower prices, people's dollar assets will purchase more goods and services. As their real wealth increases, people may feel less need to save and more freedom to spend their money. A reduction in the price level tends to have a "wealth effect" on planned spending, as shown in Figure 13.3. The total planned spending curve shifts up from $C_1 + I + G$ to $C_2 + I + G$, and national income rises from $Y_1$ to $Y_2$. Here again we can deduce the aggregate demand curve is downward sloping. As the price level goes down, from $P_2$ to $P_1$ (Figure 13.1), the national income level goes up, from $Y_1$ to $Y_2$. Conversely, an increase in the price level will make people feel less wealthy, encouraging them to save more. The resulting drop in consumption will shift the total planned spending curve down, reducing the national income level.

## The Size of the Effect of a Change in Price Level

While economists generally agree that the price and national income levels are inversely related, the strength of the relationship remains in dispute. Just how much of an increase in national income can be expected from a decrease in the price level? In practice the size of any change in national income is hard to predict. A reduction in the price level may have a

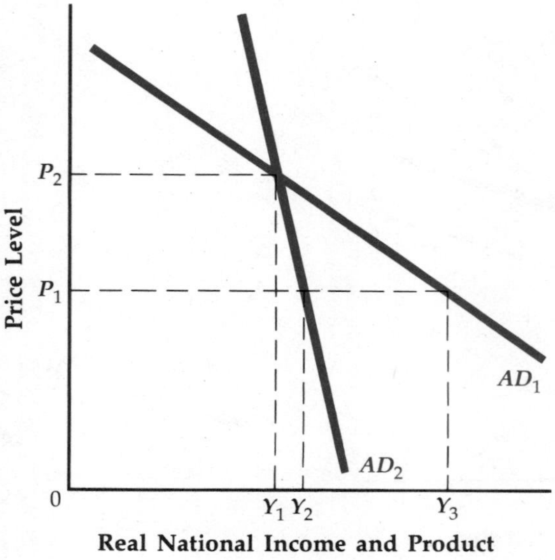


**Figure 13.4.** Size of the Effect of a Decrease in the Price Level.
A decrease in the price level from $P_2$ to $P_1$ may cause a large or a small increase in the total quantity of goods and services demanded and produced. If the aggregate demand curve looks like $AD_1$, the total quantity of goods and services demanded may rise from $Y_1$ to $Y_3$. But if the curve looks like $AD_2$, the quantity of goods and services demanded may rise only to $Y_2$. How much the quantity demanded will increase with any change in the price level depends on several factors, including how the interest rate responds to a change in the real money stock and how investment spending responds to a change in the interest rate.

substantial impact on national income, as in Figure 13.4. If aggregate demand is $AD_1$, a reduction in the price level from $P_2$ to $P_1$ will increase national income from $Y_1$ to $Y_3$. But much depends on the slope of the aggregate demand curve. If it is a much steeper slope—for instance, like $AD_2$ in Figure 13.4—the same reduction in price level will cause a much smaller increase in national income, from $Y_1$ to $Y_2$.

How much a given change in price level will change real national income depends on several factors, including:

how interest rates respond to a change in the real money stock

how investment expenditures respond to a change in interest rates

how consumption expenditures respond to a change in people's real wealth

how much the transactions demand for money changes with a change in the national income level.

The more interest rates respond to an increase in real wealth; the more investors respond to a drop in interest rates; and the more consumers

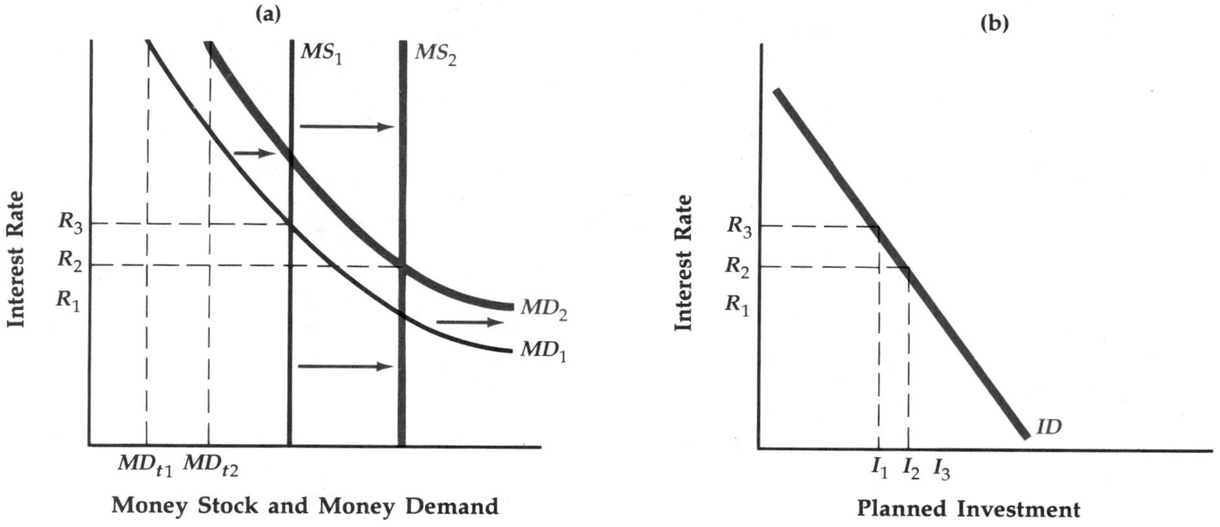


**Figure 13.5.** Effect of an Increase in the Transactions Demand for Money. An increase in the real money stock from $MS_1$ to $MS_2$ (panel (a)) can decrease the interest rate from $R_3$ toward $R_1$ and increase planned investment from $I_1$ toward $I_3$. The resulting increase in national income, however, will increase the transactions demand for money, shifting the total demand for money curve outward from $MD_1$ to $MD_2$. The shift in the demand for money curve (*ID*) will moderate the fall in the interest rate, stopping it at $R_2$. As a result, the rise in investment spending will stop short at $I_2$ (panel (b)), tempering the expansion in national income.

respond to a change in their real wealth, the greater will be the increase in the real national income level. If interest rates do not fall very far when the price level falls, and consumers do not increase their expenditures very much when their real wealth increases, the aggregate demand curve in Figure 13.4 may look more like $AD_2$ than $AD_1$. Although lower prices increase the real wealth of consumers, they decrease the real wealth of creditors, limiting the wealth effect of a drop in the price level. And a fall in interest rates may be partially offset by an increase in the transactions demand for money—the need to hold more money to finance the greater quantity of goods and services produced and consumed.

Suppose, for example, that the price level falls and the real money stock expands from $MS_1$ to $MS_2$, as in Figure 13.5 (part (a)). The interest rate, $R_3$, will begin to fall toward $R_1$. The reduction in the interest rate will spur investment spending (part (b)), increasing national income and with it the transactions demand for money. The money demand curve will shift outward from $MD_1$ to $MD_2$, reflecting this increase in the transactions demand (from $MD_{t1}$ to $MD_{t2}$). As a result, the interest rate falls only to $R_2$, not $R_3$, and planned investment spending rises only to $I_2$ instead of $I_3$. And of course the rise in the national income level is limited as well.

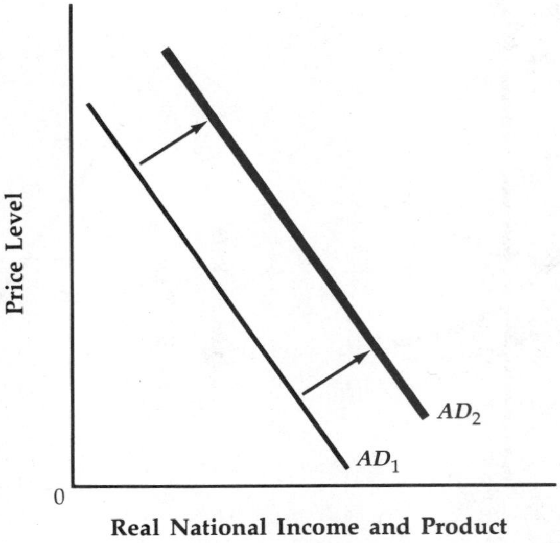


**Figure 13.6.** Change in Aggregate Demand.
An increase in aggregate demand, represented by an outward shift in the aggregate demand curve, can be caused by an expansionary fiscal or monetary policy. A contractionary fiscal or monetary policy will shift the aggregate demand curve inward.

While few economists dispute that the slope of the aggregate demand curve is negative, its exact slope is controversial. For the responsiveness of interest rates, investment, and consumption demand to a fall in the price level all influence the steepness of the curve. Most economists agree that the aggregate demand curve is flatter in the long run than in the short run. With more time, people are better able to respond to changes in the price level.

## Changes in Aggregate Demand

The position of the aggregate demand curve in Figure 13.1 reflects a critical unstated assumption. We held constant all the economic factors that can affect the demand for goods and services—consumer and investment spending, fiscal and monetary policies. But if planned consumer and investment spending increase, they can shift the aggregate demand curve, say from $AD_1$ to $AD_2$ in Figure 13.6. An expansionary fiscal or monetary policy can have the same effect. Conversely, decreases in consumer and investment spending and contractionary fiscal and monetary policies will shift the aggregate demand curve inward.

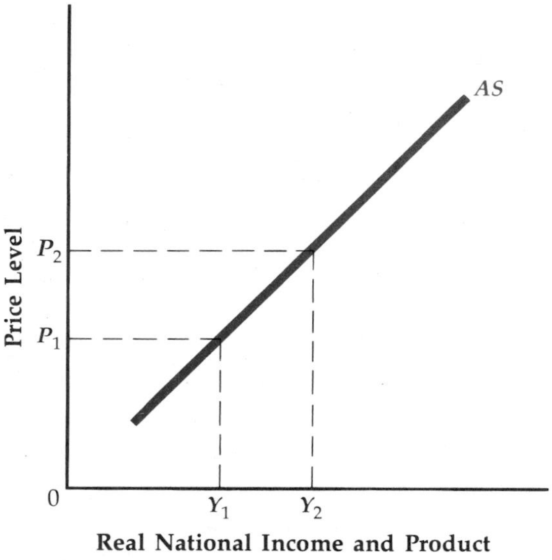


**Figure 13.7.** Short-Run Aggregate Supply.
Short-run aggregate supply is the assumed positive relationship between the price level and total production over a given period of time. If the price level rises from $P_1$ to $P_2$, total output rises from $Y_1$ to $Y_2$.

Economists disagree about the effectiveness of fiscal policy actions in shifting the aggregate demand curve. As we saw in Chapter 12, greater government spending may crowd out private investment and consumption, so that the net effect is a small shift in aggregate demand or none at all. Likewise the Federal Reserve's attempts to increase the money stock may be largely absorbed by increases in the public's money balances. Thus interest rates may not fall very much and investment spending may not rise very much in response to a calculated increase in the money stock.

## Aggregate Supply

In Chapter 6 aggregate supply was defined as the presumed positive relationship between the general price level and the total quantity of goods and services that will be produced in the economy during a given period of time. Aggregate supply was shown graphically as an upward-sloping curve, like the one in Figure 13.7. If the price level rises from $P_1$ to $P_2$, the nation's output of goods and services rises from $Y_1$ to $Y_2$—and vice versa. To be more precise, we should say that the aggregate supply curve slopes upward in the short run. We will take up what happens in the long run later.

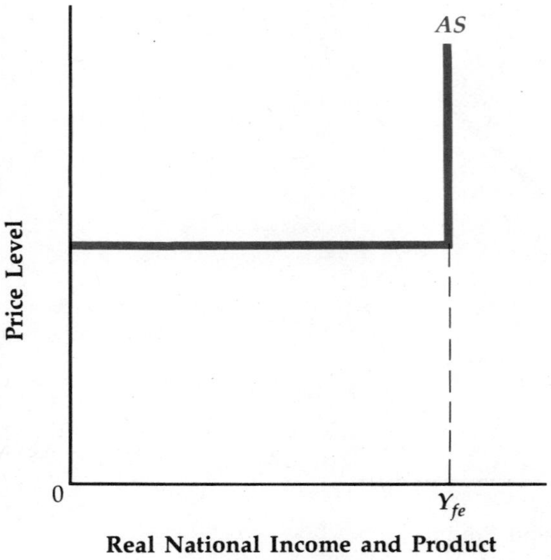


Figure 13.8. Early Keynesian Aggregate Supply Curve.
Early Keynesian theory assumed a constant price level up to the full-employment output level, $Y_{fe}$. As long as some workers remained unemployed, additional output could be achieved without raising prices. After full employment, any further increase in aggregate demand could be realized only at a higher price level.

## Short-Run Aggregate Supply

Early Keynesians did not pay much attention to changes in the price level because they did not believe price increases were a major threat during times of severe recession. They thought the aggregate supply curve resembled the curve in Figure 13.8. Up to a full-employment national output level of $Y_{fe}$, no price increase was needed to induce greater production. At full employment, however, greater demand for output would be reflected in higher prices, as competitors bid up the price of the economy's limited labor resources.

Economists no longer think of the aggregate supply curve in this way. Modern aggregate supply theory assumes that output will increase only if people have some real or imagined incentive—like a price increase—to expand production. The short-run aggregate supply curve in Figure 13.7 illustrates this assumption.

**Money illusion:** the mistaken belief that an increase in market price, stated in dollars, represents an increase in real price.

In the short run, a phenomenon called money illusion provides the incentive needed to expand production. **Money illusion** is the mistaken belief that an increase in market price, stated in dollars, represents an increase in real price. When people find they can sell their labor or their products for a higher price, they initially believe they have received a real increase in payment. Not recognizing that their wage increases are offset by an increase in the prices of the products they buy, workers may work harder and longer hours to take advantage of the apparent increase in real wages. Business owners may expand production. This burst of activity can raise national output, producing an upward-sloping aggregate supply curve like the one in Figure 13.7.

Some of these price increases may indeed be real. Many wage rates, for instance, are set by union contract and cannot be raised with the price level. In the short run, an employer may be able to raise the price of its finished product without having to pay more for labor. The employer will hire more workers, and production will go up. But such an arrangement will not be possible for all employers.

How much output will expand in response to an increase in the price level (how steep or flat the aggregate supply curve is) will depend on several factors:

the availability of unemployed resources

the ease with which unemployed resources can be put into use when prices rise

the extent of the money illusion

the extent to which labor contracts fix wages in current dollar terms

A short-run aggregate supply curve that reflects all these variables can have a slope that changes over the business cycle, as in Figure 13.9. During a recession or depression, the curve can be almost flat. Even a small increase in the price level will cause a significant expansion in national production. In normal times, when the economy is operating near full capacity, the slope is likely to be much steeper. A greater rise in prices will be needed to cover the high cost of drawing into the production process the last few unemployed (and possibly ill-suited) resources. Beyond full employment the aggregate supply curve will become practically vertical. When resources are, for all practical purposes, fully employed, little additional output can be produced, even if prices do rise.

When the recovery phase of the business cycle begins, expansion in output is likely to be relatively rapid and price increases modest. Such was the case with the recovery that began during the first term of the Reagan administration. In 1984 real GNP expanded at a rate of 6.8 percent, while the price level rose only 4 percent. Economists did not expect those favorable conditions to persist as the economy moved out of the recession.

## Long-Run Aggregate Supply

The money illusion on which the short-run aggregate supply curve is founded will not persist indefinitely. With the passage of time, people come to realize that increases in their dollar wages are not necessarily real increases. They will cease to work extra hours to take advantage of those

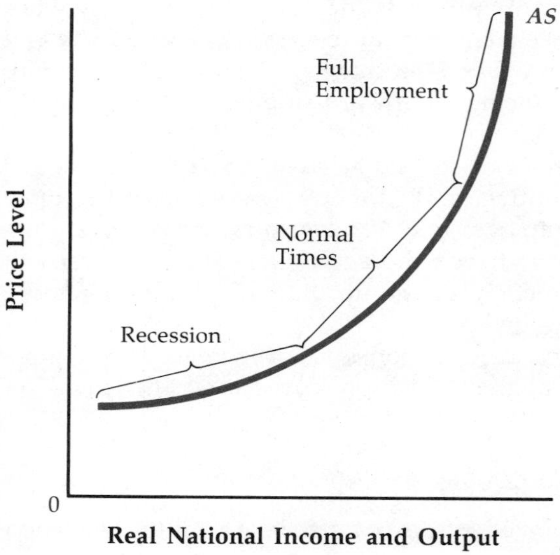


**Figure 13.9.** Short-Run Aggregate Supply in the Context of the Business Cycle. Producers' ability to respond to changing prices depends in part on the availability of unemployed resources. During a recession, when there is substantial unemployment of workers, plant, and equipment, a relatively small increase in the price level may bring a substantial rise in national output. During normal times, when the economy is operating near full employment, a much larger increase in the price level may be necessary to increase national production. When the economy is at or close to full employment, national production may respond very little to an increase in prices.

dollar increases. And as soon as they can, workers will adjust their labor contracts to reflect higher prices. In the process, the short-run aggregate supply curve—and the level of production—will shift backward.

It is not clear just how far back aggregate supply will shift. Many economists argue that the long-run aggregate supply curve is vertical—that an increase in the price level will not affect the long-run national output level. In Figure 13.10, suppose the price level rises from $P_1$ to $P_2$ because of an increase in aggregate demand following an expansion in the money stock. Production may expand for a while along the short-run aggregate supply curve $AS_{sr1}$, from $Y_1$ to $Y_2$. But people will eventually adjust to the change in the price level. At that point the aggregate supply curve will fall back toward $AS_{sr4}$ and the original national output level of $Y_1$. The new price level will be $P_3$, however. So the long-term effect is the same as if the economy had moved straight up the vertical curve $AS_{lr}$. Prices have increased, but national output has not.

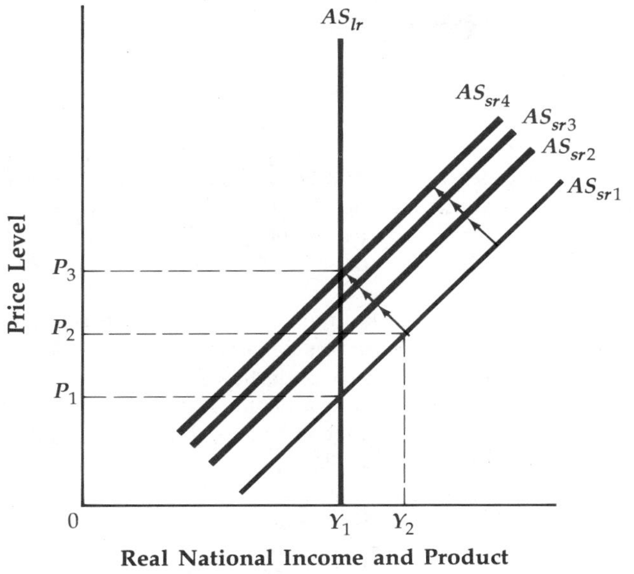


**Figure 13.10.** Long-Run Aggregate Supply Curve.
An increase in the price level from $P_1$ to $P_2$ may temporarily raise national output from $Y_1$ to $Y_2$. But in the long run, after people realize that their real wages have not risen, the supply of labor and other resources may contract, shifting the short-run aggregate supply curve upward from $AS_{ar1}$ to $AS_{sr4}$. The end result may be a price level of $P_3$ and no long-run expansion in national production. In other words, the long-run aggregate supply curve ($AS_{lr}$) is vertical.

## Changes in Aggregate Supply

The aggregate supply curve responds not only to price changes, but to anything that affects the availability of resources or people's incentive to work harder and produce more goods and services. For example, sudden cutbacks in oil production can cause energy shortages, crippling the production of a vast array of goods and services. Such "supply shocks" can shift the short-run aggregate supply curve backward, as in Figure 13.12, reducing national production from $Y_3$ to $Y_1$ and increasing the price level from $P_1$ to $P_3$.

The cutback in energy will not necessarily bring such a dramatic shift in the *long-run* aggregate supply curve, however. The higher price level, and the higher price of energy in particular, will encourage the discovery of alternative energy sources. The long-run aggregate supply curve may shift back only to $AS_{lr2}$, where the increase in price level (to $P_2$) and the decrease in national income (to $Y_2$) will be more moderate. We should not expect the national income level to return all the way to $Y_3$, however. New energy sources will probably be more costly to use, if only because resources will have been consumed just to make them available.

# Perspectives in Economics: Econometrics

*N. Keith Womer*

The real economic world is highly complex. Every day millions of agents make billions of economic decisions. Goods are bought and sold, wages are paid, and investments are made in countless numbers. This daily market is so complicated that economists cannot study it directly. Instead, they must attempt to understand specific aspects of the market by developing and testing economic theories.

Economic theories are based on observations of the real world formalized into precisely stated assumptions. They are not conclusions, but tentative hypotheses whose predictive power must be tested scientifically.

**Econometrics** is the science of the statistical testing of economic theory and predictions. The *metric* in *econometrics* signifies measurement—the measurement of economic relationships. Using economic theory, relevant economic data, and statistical methods, econometricians construct and test econometric models. An **econometric model** is a statistical equation or set of equations that describes economic data.

The data econometricians use are sometimes collected directly, but are more often derived from data that have been collected for other purposes. From these data economic relationships must be carefully estimated through statistical analysis. Then the hypotheses about those relationships can be tested.

This approach can be used to reject or tentatively accept hypotheses. Rejected hypotheses form the basis for revisions of economic theory. Tentatively accepted hypotheses have not been proved. At best, they have been shown to be consistent with observed data. Much of the econometrician's work involves uneasy compromises among economic hypotheses, available data, and the requirements of statistical technique.

Consider the problem of estimating and testing the consumption function, for instance. Keynes stated, "The fundamental psychological law . . . is that men are disposed, as a rule and on the average, to increase their consumption as their income increases, but not by as much as the increase in income." The testable hypothesis derived from Keynes's theory is that the marginal propensity to consume (*MPC*) is positive but less than one.

Statistical technique requires that the relation between two variables be specified precisely. The relation between consumption and income is hypothesized to be linear. That is, if observations of consumption and income were plotted on a graph, the points would fall approximately on a straight line. If the consumption function is linear, the technique of linear regression can be used to estimate it. **Linear regression** is a statistical technique used to find the equation describing the straight line that comes closest to the plotted points of a curve.

Random samples of accurate data on individual consumption and income are difficult to obtain. Econometricians usually use yearly data on aggregate consumption and income together with population statistics to estimate per capita income and consumption. Then they often divide their data by a price index, to adjust for the effects of inflation. An aggregate consumption function derived from such constructed data is illustrated in Figure 13.11. Each point shows the level of consumption associated with a particular income level; the line shows the consumption function derived from the data. Mathematically, that line or function may be expressed as $C = 68.7 + 0.89\,Y$. $C$ equals the consumption function. The estimated intercept (constant term) of the consumption function is \$68.70, and 0.89 is the estimated marginal propensity to consume.

This estimate seems to support Keynes's theory. Our computed marginal propensity to consume, 0.89, is positive and less than one, just as he argued. Such a computation may have been generated by chance, however. To be confident that our computed *MPC* is a close approximation of the true *MPC*, we must run additional statistical tests.[1] If those tests yield the expected results, we can conclude with a high degree of confidence

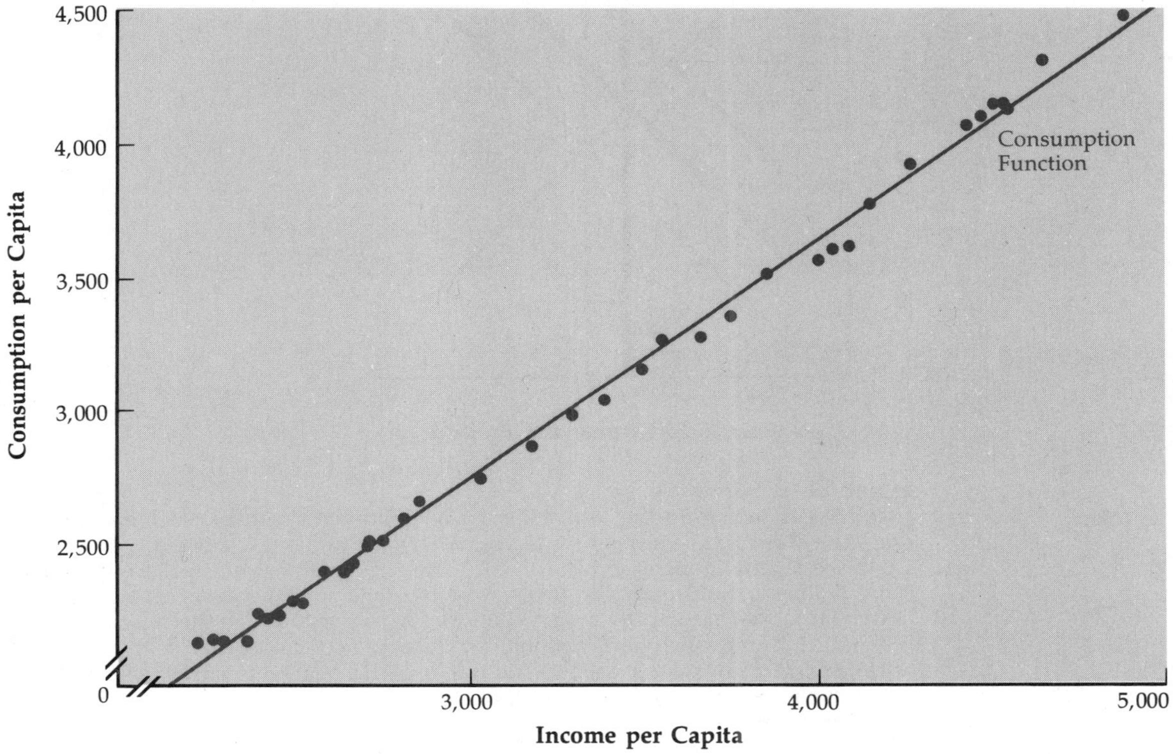


that the true *MPC* is not very different from our computed *MPC*. Though we have not *proved* Keynes's hypothesis, it has survived a challenge. If repeated tests yield the same findings, we will become even more confident that Keynes was correct.

1. To test the estimated marginal propensity to consume, an econometrician would first compare the errors around the consumption function (in the figure, the vertical distance between the data points and the straight line) with randomly selected data. If the errors appear to be random, then the econometrician will measure the precision of the estimate by computing a statistic called the standard deviation.

**Figure 13.11.** Estimated Consumption Function. The relation between consumption and income is linear. If data on consumption and income are plotted on a graph, the points will fall approximately on a straight line. Mathematically, the relation shown here may be expressed as $C = 68.7 + 0.89\,Y$.

**Source:** *Economic Report of the President* (Washington, D.C.: U.S. Government Printing Office, 1985), pp. 248 and 254.

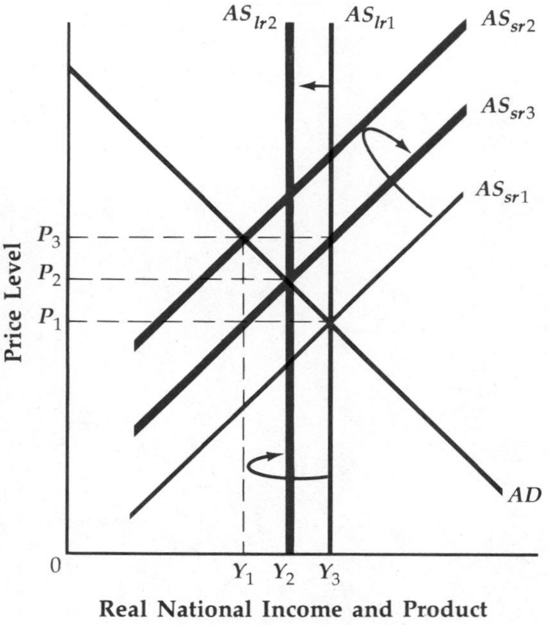


**Figure 13.12.** Supply Shock.
A sudden reduction in the availability of an important resource, such as oil, can cause the short-run aggregate supply curve to shift to the left, from $AS_{sr1}$ to $AS_{sr2}$. The price level will increase from $P_1$ to $P_3$, and the national output level will fall from $Y_3$ to $Y_1$. Substitute resources may be developed because of the shock, however, so that the short-run aggregate supply curve shifts to the right again to $AS_{sr3}$. In the long run, then, national production may climb back to $Y_2$ and the price level may drop back to $P_2$. Thus the long-run aggregate supply curve does not shift as far to the left as the short-run curve.

## The Equilibrium National Income and Price Levels

By putting the aggregate supply and aggregate demand curves in the same graph, as in Figure 13.13, we can see that in the short run the economy will gravitate toward the national income and price levels of $Y_2$ and $P_1$, respectively. At price levels above $P_1$—for example, $P_2$—the total quantity of goods and services producers want to offer ($Y_3$) will exceed the total quantity of goods and services consumers, businesses, and governments want to buy ($Y_1$). The price level will fall back toward $P_1$ as firms compete to get rid of their unwanted inventory. The price decline will stimulate spending by increasing the real money stock. Interest rates will fall, the level of planned investment will increase, and planned consumption expenditures will rise. Total planned expenditures will climb from $Y_1$ to $Y_2$. At the same time, recognizing that the rewards of their labor have shrunk, people will cut back on production. National output and income will drop from $Y_3$ to $Y_2$.

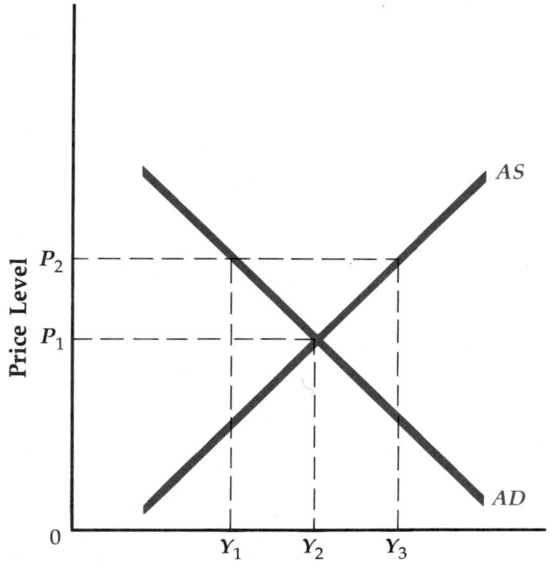


**Figure 13.13.** Short-Run Equilibrium in Real National Income and Prices. Given these aggregate supply and aggregate demand curves, the macroeconomy will move toward a price level of $P_1$ and a national production level of $Y_2$. At a price level above $P_1$—for example, $P_2$—the total quantity of goods and services produced will exceed the total quantity of goods and services demanded. The price level will fall. As it falls, more goods and services will be demanded, while fewer will be produced.

Similarly, at price levels below $P_1$, the total planned expenditures of consumers, businesses, and government will exceed the total quantity of goods and services produced. The prices of goods and services will be bid up, reducing the real money stock and hence people's real wealth. Interest rates will rise, reducing planned investment expenditures. Consumption expenditures will fall as people attempt to rebuild their real wealth by saving. And because of fixed wages and money illusion, production will rise as producers and workers try to exploit the price increase.

## The Real Effect of Expansionary Fiscal and Monetary Policies

What does the combined aggregate supply and demand model suggest about the likely effect of Keynesian fiscal and monetary policies to increase total planned expenditures? If government reduces taxes, increases its expenditures, or expands the money stock—all steps that should cause total planned spending to rise—the aggregate demand curve will shift

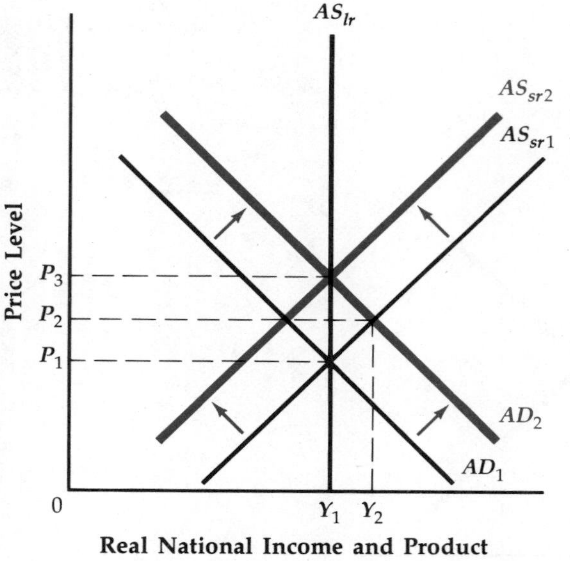


**Figure 13.14.** The Effect of an Expansionary Fiscal or Monetary Policy on Real National Income and Prices.
Expansionary fiscal and monetary policy can shift the aggregate demand curve upward, from $AD_1$ to $AD_2$. In the short run the shift in aggregate demand will cause an expansion in national production, from $Y_1$ to $Y_2$, and an increase in the price level, from $P_1$ to $P_2$. But in the long run the aggregate supply curve will shift up from $AS_{sr1}$ to $AS_{sr2}$. Long-run equilibrium will be achieved at an even higher price level, $P_3$, and national production will return to its original level, $Y_1$.

outward. The result of the shift is shown in Figure 13.14. The national income level expands from $Y_1$ to $Y_2$. And the price level increases from $P_1$ to $P_2$.

In the long run, however, the aggregate supply curve will shift inward to $AS_{sr2}$ as people adjust their work efforts to the price increase. If the long-run aggregate supply curve is vertical, the end result will be a return to the original equilibrium national income level of $Y_1$, but at a higher price level: $P_3$ instead of $P_1$. In fact, over a period of months or years, expansionary fiscal and monetary policies can produce a business cycle of their own. First a recovery period of expansion in production and employment is stimulated by monetary or fiscal policy. Then the resulting drop in short-run aggregate supply causes a new contraction in production and employment.[1]

1. In addition, over the long run the aggregate demand curve can shift back toward $AD_1$, reflecting the reduced investment demand caused by the increase in government spending. The effect of such a reduction in investment spending will be a price level lower than $P_3$.

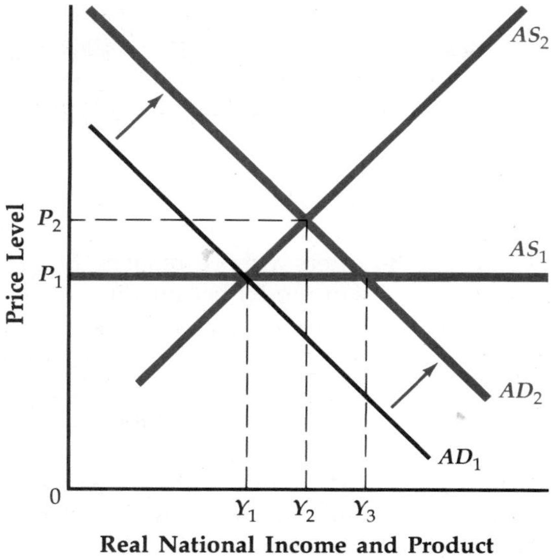


**Figure 13.15** The Multiplier Effect on Real National Income and Prices.
With no change in price level—that is, with a horizontal aggregate supply curve like $AS_1$—an increase in aggregate demand from $AD_1$ to $AD_2$ will cause national production to rise from $Y_1$ to $Y_3$. But if prices rise with aggregate demand—that is, if the aggregate supply curve slopes upward, as $AS_2$ does—the same increase in aggregate demand will raise national production only to $Y_2$. The increase in the price level absorbs part of the impact of the expansion of aggregate demand and reduces the size of the multiplier.

## The Real Size of the Multiplier

The Keynesian economic models used in Chapters 11 to 13 assumed that prices would remain constant. Under that assumption, we can expect a change in total planned expenditures to be fully reflected, through the multiplier process, in a change in national income and production. In that case, however, the aggregate supply curve would have to be horizontal, like curve $AS_1$ in Figure 13.15. Given such a supply curve, an increase in aggregate demand from $AD_1$ to $AD_2$ would cause national income and production to rise from $Y_1$ to $Y_3$. But if prices must adjust upward to create an incentive for increased production and income, as modern theorists believe, then the aggregate supply curve will look like $AS_2$. In that case the shift in aggregate demand from $AD_1$ to $AD_2$ will yield a smaller increase in national income and production, from $Y_1$ to $Y_2$.

If prices rise, then, the multiplier effect will be weaker, for the increase in the price level will absorb part of the stimulus to demand. The higher price level will reduce the real money stock, causing interest rates to rise and planned investment spending to fall. And by reducing consumers' real wealth, it will reduce consumption demand. In short, if prices adjust to changes in demand, expansionary fiscal and monetary policies will not be as effective in relieving production and employment problems as early Keynesian theory would suggest. (Conversely, decreases in total planned expenditures will not depress the economy as much as early Keynesian theory would imply.)

## Summary and Extensions

The aggregate demand and supply model offers a more realistic picture of the economy than the traditional Keynesian model because it includes the effect of price changes on the supply of goods as well as on the quantity demanded. Changes in the price level can lower the value of the multiplier, though the effect may not be dramatic. If the aggregate demand curve has a steep slope, the effect of price changes on total planned spending may be modest.

Changes in aggregate supply may also have a limited effect. The short-run aggregate supply curve slopes upward only to the extent that people mistake a nominal increase in the price of their labor or products for a real one. Money illusion can wear off fast, for workers and producers soon learn that an increase in the overall price level will raise the prices of things they buy as well as the prices of things they sell. They will adjust their contracts accordingly. The long-run aggregate supply curve, then, is likely to be steeper than the short-run aggregate supply curve. It may be practically vertical, so that output ultimately changes very little with changes in total planned spending.

## Major Conclusions

1. The aggregate demand curve slopes downward because of the way prices affect interest rates and consumption. When the price level falls, the real money stock rises and the interest rate falls, increasing investment demand. Consumers' real wealth also increases, fueling consumer demand.
2. The slope of the aggregate demand curve depends on the extent to which a drop in the price level reduces the interest rate and increases planned investment spending, planned consumption, and the transactions demand for money.
3. Expansionary fiscal and monetary policies will shift the aggregate demand curve outward. Contractionary fiscal and monetary policies will shift the curve inward.
4. The short-run aggregate supply curve slopes upward partly because of money illusion and partly because resource owners cannot raise prices immediately when the general price level increases.

5. The long-run aggregate supply curve is steeper than the short-run aggregate supply curve. It may actually be vertical. Over time, people learn that a rise in the dollar price of resources does not necessarily represent a real increase in price. They adjust resource prices upward to match the increase in the price level.
6. Changes in tax rates can affect aggregate supply as well as aggregate demand, for they affect people's incentives to work, save, and invest. If both curves shift, the price level may go up or down, depending on the relative size of the shifts.
7. The equilibrium national income level is established by the intersection of the aggregate supply and demand curves. The price level adjusts upward or downward to bring supply and demand into balance.
8. A shift in the aggregate demand curve has a greater effect on national income in the short run than in the long run. Expansionary fiscal and monetary policies therefore have a greater impact in the short run than in the long run.
9. Changes in the price level will moderate the multiplier effect of a shift in total planned spending.

## Questions to Ponder

1. Explain the difference between the market demand curve and the aggregate demand curve.
2. Explain the difference between the total planned spending function and the aggregate demand curve.
3. In each of the following cases, explain what will happen to the price and national income levels:
   a. Aggregate demand increases.
   b. Aggregate supply decreases.
   c. The expected profitability of investment rises.
   d. The money stock expands.
   e. Tax rates rise.
4. Why will an increase in aggregate demand have a greater effect on national income in the short run than in the long run?
5. Suppose a major new energy source is discovered. What will happen to the national income and price levels in the long run?
6. Explain how the size of the multiplier is affected by an adjustment in the price level.
7. How does the responsiveness of planned investment to a change in the interest rate affect the slope of the aggregate demand curve?
8. What can government do to shift the long-run aggregate supply curve outward?

## Part V

# Alternative Views of the Macroeconomy

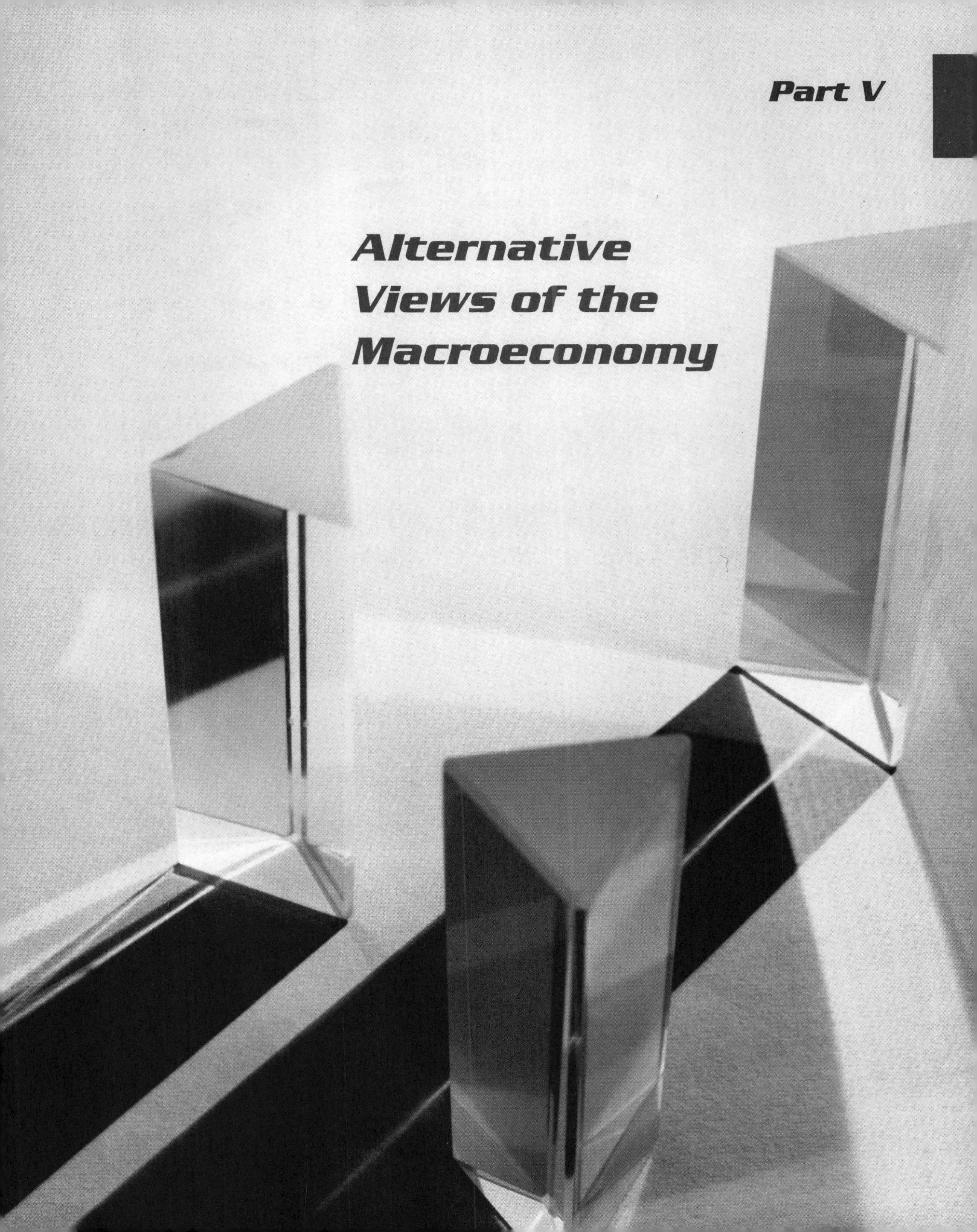

## Central Question

*From the perspective of the monetarists, what are the causes of unemployment and inflation, and how can they be remedied?*

# Chapter 14

# The Monetarist View of Unemployment and Inflation

*My position regarding the cause of inflation and high market interest rates is that they both stem from the same source—an excessive trend rate of expansion of the nation's money stock. Monetary policy, therefore, can contribute to solving both of these problems over a period of a few years by fostering a noninflationary rate of growth of the money supply.*
Darryl Francis

We have stressed that Keynesian theory is controversial. Many of the objections to Keynesian theory come from economists of the monetarist school. This chapter will examine the monetarist interpretation of the macroeconomy, which is based largely on changes in the money stock.

Some caution is advisable in classifying economic thought as monetarist or Keynesian (or supply-side or rational expectations). Economists from different schools agree with each other on some points, which we will note when pertinent. And economists from the same school of thought often disagree. Keynesians have disputed the fine points of macroeconomic theory and policy among themselves, though they generally agree that macroeconomic problems can best be analyzed by focusing on total planned expenditures. Similarly monetarists do not always agree on particulars, though most agree that changes in the money stock explain many of our macroeconomic problems. This chapter outlines the broad theoretical framework that incorporates most monetarist thought.

## The Rise of Monetarism

Keynes developed his *General Theory* during the Great Depression, when the industrialized nations of the West faced rapidly falling prices and high unemployment. Government spending then seemed a good tonic for an ailing economy, and Keynes's theories were widely adopted by legislators and government administrators. Over the past three decades, however, the United States has faced some problems for which Keynesian prescriptions are less suitable. We have had to contend with high and rising rates of inflation, accompanied by high rates of unemployment and growing federal expenditures. Events have apparently disproved the theory, accepted by many Keynesians, that unemployment and inflation are inversely related, and many economists, frustrated by the disparity between theory and reality, have begun to search for a better model of the macroeconomy.

To date, the most significant alternative to the Keynesian macroeconomic model is the monetarist model. The monetarists hold that the root cause of most cyclical swings in unemployment and inflation is abrupt changes in the rate of growth of the money stock. Without attention to the size of the money stock, they argue, fiscal policy will have only limited influence, if any, on the short-term problems of unemployment and inflation. Steady control of the monetary throttle will solve most problems of inflation, high interest rates, and cyclical unemployment.

## The Monetarist View of Unemployment

In developing their theory of the macroeconomy, the monetarists (like Keynesians and others) have borrowed heavily from microeconomic theory. They begin with the basic classical propositions about the market. Long-term unemployment is seen as a consequence of obstacles in the labor market, which prevent real wage rates from falling enough to bring the number of workers demanded in line with the number of people willing

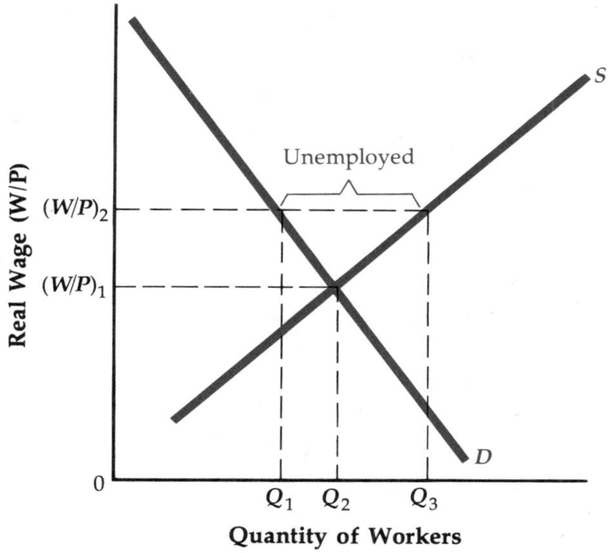


**Figure 14.1.** The Influence of the Price Level on Unemployment.
Assuming that the demand for labor slopes downward, the supply of labor slopes upward, and the real wage rate is fixed at $(W/P)_2$, $Q_3 - Q_1$ workers will be unemployed. As long as the money wage rate and the price level remain constant, unemployment will not fall.

to work. Minimum wage laws, union contracts, and restrictions on labor mobility (such as lack of information) all impede the achievement of an equilibrium wage level and full employment. Full employment may be promoted by wage concessions. Recently unions have been experimenting with this approach in declining industries like steel manufacture.

Consider Figure 14.1. There, as in classical theory, the demand for labor is inversely related to the real wage rate (the money wage rate divided by the price index), while the supply of labor is directly related to the real wage rate. If the real wage rate is prevented from falling below $(W/P)_2$, $Q_3$ workers will want to work, but only $Q_1$ workers will be hired. The difference between $Q_3$ and $Q_1$ is the number of people unemployed. According to monetarist theory, if the money wage rate and the price level remain constant or increase at the same rate, the real wage will not change and $Q_3 - Q_1$ unemployment will persist. If the price level rises while the money wage rate stays the same, the real wage rate will fall, reducing or eliminating unemployment.

## The Phillips Curve

The relationship between unemployment and changes in the price level can be seen more clearly in Figure 14.2, which reproduces the Phillips curve from Chapter 6. The unemployment rate, shown on the horizontal

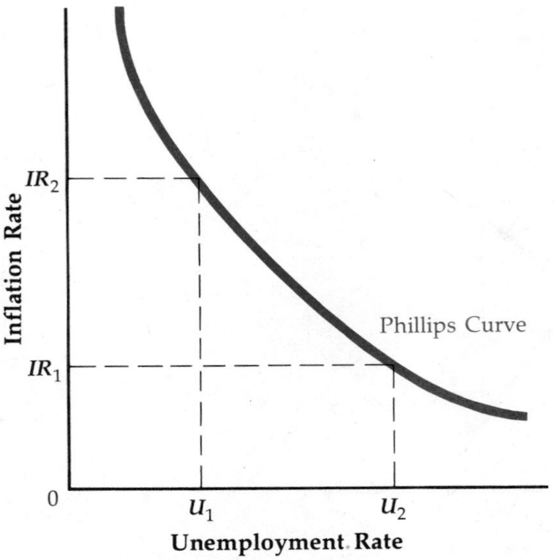


**Figure 14.2.** The Phillips Curve.
Keynesian economists have argued that the unemployment and inflation rates are inversely related. Thus an unemployment rate lower than $U_2$ can be achieved only at the cost of an inflation rate higher than $IR_1$. An unemployment rate of $U_1$, for example, could be obtained only at an inflation rate of $IR_2$.

axis, is obtained by dividing the number of unemployed workers by the total number of workers. Changes in the price level are indicated by the inflation rate, shown on the vertical axis. The graph shows that an inflation rate of $IR_1$ is consistent with an unemployment rate of $U_2$. To achieve a lower unemployment rate, $U_1$, the inflation rate must rise to $IR_2$. Early Keynesians argued that fiscal policy should be directed toward achieving some desired combination of unemployment and inflation rates as shown on the Phillips curve.

Monetarists have contended that the tradeoff between inflation and unemployment generally lasts only for the short run, however. When the inflation rate first accelerates, employers realize that prices are rising faster than wages. As the real wage falls, employers move down their labor demand curve, hiring more workers, and unemployment declines. But eventually workers become aware of the higher price level and see that their real wage rate has fallen. Unions will then bargain for higher wage increases. In competitive labor markets, where the demand for labor will rise because of the rising prices of final products, wages will be bid up. In the end, the economy will return to its original real wage and unemployment rates—but at a higher rate of inflation.

Figure 14.3 shows the sequence of events graphically. In the short run, higher inflation moves the economy up the Phillips curve to the lower unemployment rate of $U_1$. But as workers' expectations concerning prices

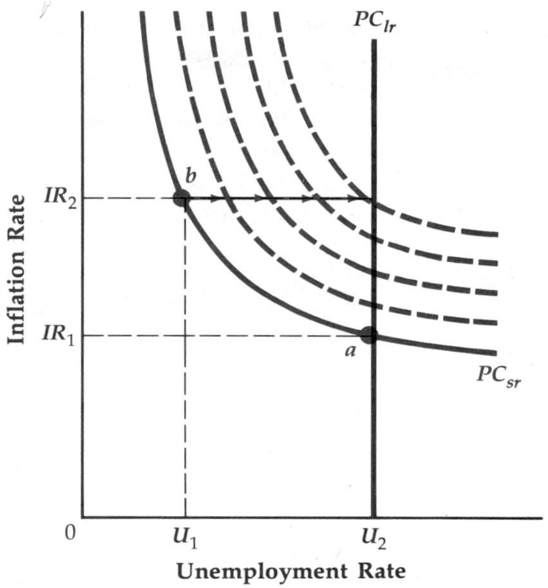


**Figure 14.3.** Short-Run and Long-Run Phillips Curves.
The rate of unemployment can be temporarily reduced by an unexpected increase in the price level. The economy will move up its short-run Phillips curve ($PC_{sr}$), from point *a* to point *b*. In the long run, however, money wages will catch up with the higher prices, and the short-run Phillips curve will shift outward. Unemployment will climb back to $U_2$, but at a higher rate of inflation. In the long run, the Phillips curve is vertical ($PC_{lr}$).

change, the Phillips curve will shift out to the right. While the inflation rate remains at $IR_2$, the unemployment rate will gradually rise back to $U_2$. In the long run, then, the Phillips curve is vertical. There is no tradeoff between unemployment and inflation. (This point is now accepted by many Keynesians.) If the unemployment rate is to remain below $U_2$, prices will have to be increased at progressively higher rates, forcing workers to play catch-up in their wage demands. Even then, though, workers may begin to anticipate the price spiral, and demand bigger and bigger wage increases as a matter of course.

A reduction in the rate of inflation will have the opposite effect. An unexpected slowing of the rise in prices will cause the real wage to rise. The gap between the number of workers wanting jobs and the number hired will widen (Figure 14.1). The economy will move down its short-term Phillips curve (Figure 14.3), from point *b* to point *a*, and unemployment will rise to $U_2$. In the long run, however, the increase in the number of unemployed will intensify competition for jobs, slowing the rate of increase in money wages. The real wage will fall back toward its original level, and employers will demand more workers. The short-term Phillips curve will shift inward, and the unemployment rate will move back toward $U_1$—but at a *lower* rate of inflation.

The crux of the monetarist position on unemployment is that there is no long-term tradeoff between unemployment and inflation. A higher rate of inflation may reduce unemployment temporarily. But in the long run the economy will return to its natural rate of unemployment. The natural rate of unemployment is the percentage of the labor force that is unemployed in the long run because of structural problems in the economy and frictional restrictions on employment. The way to reduce the natural rate of unemployment is to eliminate obstacles to wage adjustments and speed up the movement of the unemployed to expanding labor markets. It is *not*, as the Keynesians would claim, to increase total spending or expand the money stock.

### The Historical Evidence

The past few decades have supplied considerable evidence in support of the monetarists' claim that the tradeoff between unemployment and inflation is only temporary. Figure 14.4 shows U.S. inflation and unemployment rates from 1953 to 1984. Instead of a neatly downward-sloping Phillips curve, the pattern looks more like a contrail left by a stunt plane. The unemployment rate moved up and down, averaging 5.6 percent per year. The inflation rate, until late in the period, moved higher and higher.

Monetarists argue that the relatively high unemployment rates of the last few decades resulted from obstacles to the adjustment of wages and to the movement of labor from one industry to another. They attribute short-term decreases in the unemployment rate to unexpected increases in the rate of inflation. And they believe the gradual increase in the unemployment rate seen in recent decades results from the growth in benefits to the unemployed and in government regulations that increase frictional and structural unemployment.

## The Monetarist View of Inflation

The monetarists maintain that temporary changes in the level of inflation and unemployment (and resulting changes in national income) are linked directly to the rate of growth of the money stock. Their position can be summarized mathematically by referring to the equation of exchange developed in Chapter 8.

$$MV = PQ = Y$$

where $M$ = the money supply, $V$ = the velocity (or turnover rate) of money, $P$ = an index of the price level, $Q$ = quantity of goods and services, and $Y$ = the national income level. This link between the growth rate of the money stock and the inflation rate is rooted in the individual's demand for and supply of money.

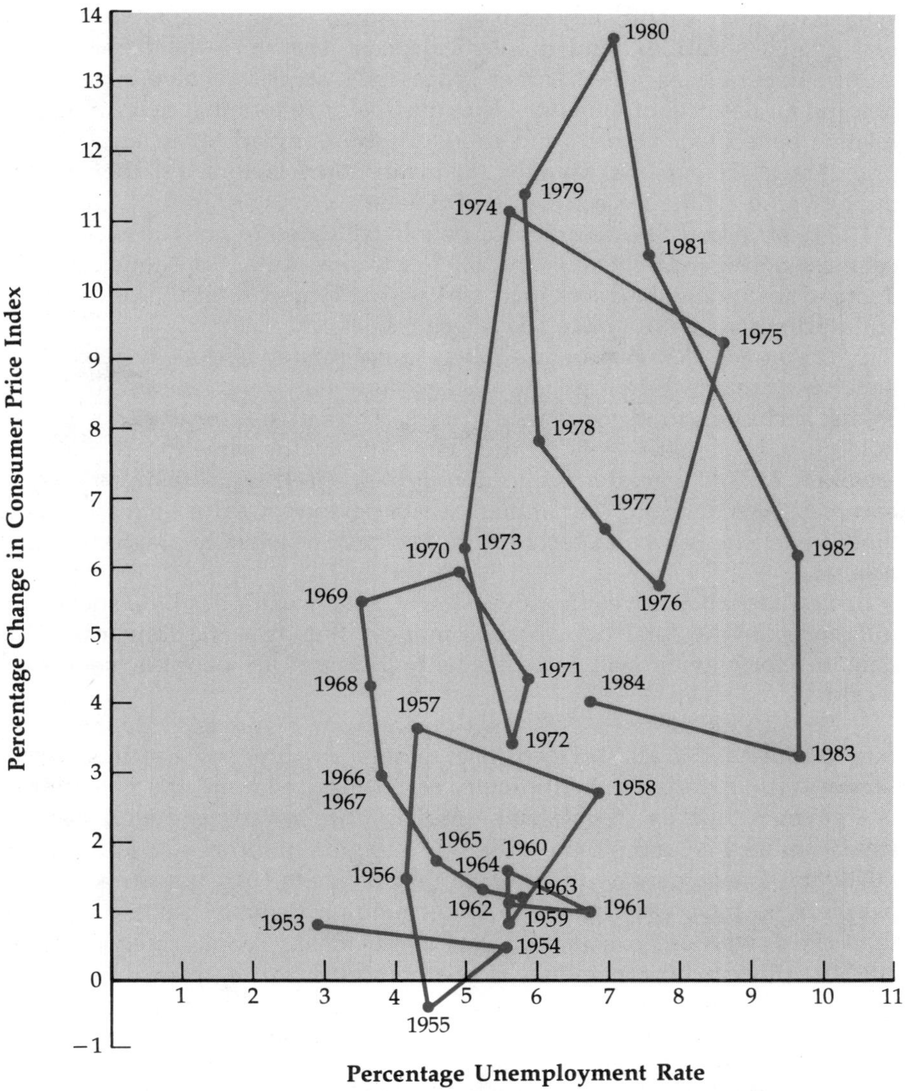


**Figure 14.4.** Inflation and Unemployment in the United States, 1953–1984. Between 1953 and 1984, the unemployment rate fluctuated between 3 and 9.5 percent, while inflation varied annually between practically zero and 14 percent. If a downward-sloping Phillips curve exists, it lasts only a few years. It appears to have shifted up and down over time.

## The Demand for Money

To monetarists and many other economists, money is just one among many assets, such as goods and securities, that people hold for the services they provide. Television sets give people viewing pleasure. Securities yield income. Money enables people to carry out their day-to-day transactions.

Whatever their wealth, people will seek some optimum combination of real goods, securities, and money balances. Therefore the demand for money depends, as noted earlier (page 150), on the relative benefits of holding money and other assets. The five major factors that determine the relative benefits of money, and therefore the demand for it, are: (1) the price level, (2) personal wealth, (3) institutional factors, (4) the rate of interest, and (5) the expected rate of inflation.

1. *The price level.* If prices go up, people will need to hold larger money balances to carry out the same number of transactions. Consequently, the demand for money balances increases with an increase in the price level, and declines when the price level declines.

2. *Personal wealth.* A person's demand for money is directly related to his or her wealth. When people hold money, they forgo the use of other assets, including food, clothes, and cars. Thus it is easier for the rich to hold on to money than it is for the poor. And by the same token, the rich are likely to hold a greater proportion of their assets in the form of money balances than the poor do. Similarly, as a person's wealth increases over time, he or she can be expected to hold a proportionately greater money balance.

Because a nation's wealth grows slowly, total wealth has little short-run influence on the total demand for money. But over the long run, the demand for money will increase with increases in people's collective wealth.

3. *Institutional factors.* A person's demand for money also depends on how frequently he or she is paid and must in turn pay for goods and services. It depends on the difficulty of getting credit and the penalty for late payment of bills. People who are paid once a week will tend to hold smaller money balances than those who are paid monthly and must cover thirty days' expenses with their money balances. On the other hand, people who have easy access to credit require a smaller money balance than those who are considered to be credit risks. People categorized as creditworthy can borrow money to see themselves through any unforeseen financial emergencies. Because salary and bill payment patterns do not change very much or very rapidly, institutional factors have a steadying influence on the demand for money.

4. *The rate of interest.* Money that is held in checking accounts frequently does not earn interest. The forgone interest is the opportunity cost of holding money balances in the form of cash and demand deposits. As the interest rate rises, so does the opportunity cost of holding money. Thus people can be expected to vary their demand for money with changes in the interest rate. When the rate goes up, they will substitute bonds for money balances—theoretically, at least. Empirical studies suggest that interest rates have only a very slight effect on the demand for money.

5. *The expected rate of inflation.* If the rate of inflation increases and people expect it to continue to increase, the cost of holding money balances will go up. Because people will expect to pay more for goods and services in the future, they will prefer to use their wealth to buy goods and services at current prices. Their demand for money will decline.

## The Effect of Changes in the Stock of Money

If the Federal Reserve increases the money stock, what will happen to prices as a result? People as a group will have more money than they need in relation to the price level, their wealth, institutional payment patterns, interest rates, and the expected rate of inflation. They will use their excess money to buy bonds or goods and services. An increased demand for bonds will cause a drop in the market interest rate, thereby increasing planned investment. And an increased demand for goods and services should cause an increase in the price level, as businesses and consumers bid against each other for the limited supply. This increase in the price level will lead in turn to greater employment and a higher national income level. Eventually, however, competition for labor will push wages up, which will return real wage rates to their normal levels and readjust the unemployment rate to its natural level—but at a higher price level.

In the real world the price level is generally on the rise, because the money stock is constantly growing. It must grow, if only because the labor force and production grow constantly. Only if the Federal Reserve increases the *rate* of growth of the money stock will the rate of inflation increase. The monetarists argue that if the rate of inflation rises continually, it will eventually exceed the rate of growth of the money stock. A 6 percent growth rate in the money stock might produce an inflation rate of 7 or 8 percent, for example.

The explanation of this phenomenon is reasonably straightforward. As the rate of inflation increases, the value of money held in currency or bank accounts falls at progressively faster rates. The cost of holding on to money rises. Consequently, people will hold fewer dollars in their bank accounts. Instead, they will buy more goods whose value has the potential to increase over time, such as real estate. As people increase their purchases, dollars will turn over faster (at a higher velocity). The price level will rise not only because more dollars are being used, but because the dollars in existence are being used more frequently. In terms of the equation of exchange ($MV = PQ$), both $M$ and $V$ will rise, forcing an equal rise in either $P$ or $Q$ or in the two together.

If the money stock *contracts* and people suddenly have fewer dollars to hold, depositors may find they have fewer dollars in their money balances than they want. To build up their money balances, some will convert (sell) a portion of their financial assets, such as bonds. Others will refrain from buying cars, furniture, and other consumer goods. With fewer dollars chasing after goods and services, manufacturers will have to lower their prices to sell their products. In this way a decrease in the money stock leads to a lower price level.

When the rate of growth in the money stock declines, fewer dollars will come onto the market. Upward pressure on prices will be diminished, and the rate of inflation will fall. Once the rise of prices has slowed, people's expectations about future inflation will adjust downward. The cost of holding money will drop, and people will again be able to justify keeping a larger portion of their assets in money balances. The velocity of money will fall, causing an equal fall in the *PQ* side of the equation of exchange.

In the monetarists' model, then, the short-run velocity of money is directly related to the rate of inflation. As the rate of inflation rises, so does the velocity of money, and vice versa. This stable relationship comes about because the rate of inflation determines how much money it is rational to hold.

## From Monetary Growth to Unemployment

We are now ready to consider the sequence of events that follows an increase in the money stock, from the monetarists' perspective. The Federal Reserve begins the process, perhaps by buying government securities on the open market. Though more money has been put into circulation, people's need for money is relatively stable. Rather than holding the extra money that comes their way, they will use it to buy more real goods and securities, including bonds. The increased demand for bonds will lower interest rates, raising planned investment.

Together with increased consumer spending, the increase in investment will mean greater aggregate demand for goods and services—and higher prices. In terms of Figure 14.5, the aggregate demand curve shifts up from $AD_1$ to $AD_2$, and the price level begins to rise from its initial equilibrium level, $P_1$, toward $P_2$. As we saw in Figure 14.1, higher prices will temporarily reduce the real wages paid to labor. This short-run sequence of events thus reduces short-run unemployment and increases national production. The national income level moves up, from $Y_1$ to $Y_2$ in Figure 14.5.

In the long run, however, workers will demand higher wages in compensation for their higher cost of living. The real wage rate will return to its previous level, reducing employers' demand for labor and increasing unemployment. These adjustments in labor supply will be reflected by an inward shift in the short-run aggregate supply curve, from $AS_{sr1}$ to $AS_{sr2}$. The price level will rise even further, to $P_3$, and the national income level will fall back to $Y_1$. Together these changes will reestablish equilibrium at the original output, but at a higher price level. The long-run aggregate supply curve, like the long-run Phillips curve, is vertical.

The sequence of events that follows a decrease in the money stock is exactly the opposite. Starting at the initial equilibrium point of $P_3$ and $Y_1$, the aggregate demand curve will shift down from $AD_2$ to $AD_1$. As price and output levels begin to fall, unemployment will temporarily increase. (When the real wage rises, employers demand fewer workers.) In the long run, however, higher unemployment will produce greater competition for jobs, lower money wages, and a drop in the real wage rate. Unemployment will return to its natural rate, and the aggregate supply curve will shift out, from $AS_2$ to $AS_1$. When national production returns to its initial level, $Y_1$, the price level will be lower.

This analysis can also be described in terms of change in the growth rate of the money stock. Assume an established rate of growth in the

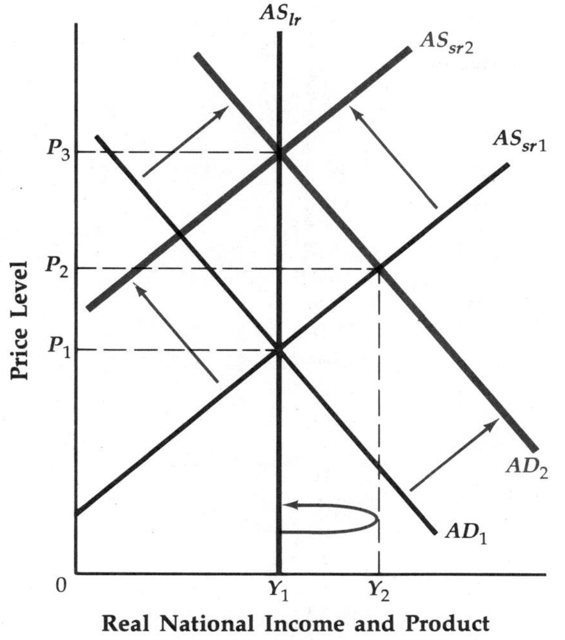


**Figure 14.5.** The Impact of an Increase in the Money Stock on Aggregate Supply and Demand.
An increase in the money stock will shift the aggregate demand curve up from $AD_1$ to $AD_2$, temporarily increasing the national income and price levels. When money wages adjust to the higher living cost, however, the aggregate supply curve will shift down from $AS_{sr1}$ to $AS_{sr2}$. In the long run the national income level will return to $Y_1$, but at a higher price level, $P_3$. The opposite sequence of events will occur if the money stock declines.

money stock, which has produced an established rate of inflation to which workers have adjusted their wage demands. An increase in the growth rate of money will increase both demand and prices. Prices will rise faster than wages, the real wage will decrease, and employment and production will go up—temporarily, until workers can raise the rate of their wage increases. The process ends with a higher inflation rate, but a growth rate in national production that depends, in the long run, on the growth in technology and the availability of resources.

A decrease in the rate of growth in the money stock can cause money wages to rise faster than prices, at least temporarily. Unemployment will rise at first, but after long-run adjustments in the growth rate of money wages, it will return to its original level. For this reason the monetarists argue that the inflation rate can be lowered by reducing the rate of growth of the money stock—if people can endure a temporary increase in unemployment, lasting perhaps four years or more. Once the economy has reached its new equilibrium level, a steady rate of growth in the money stock of around 4 percent will moderate (but not eliminate) the

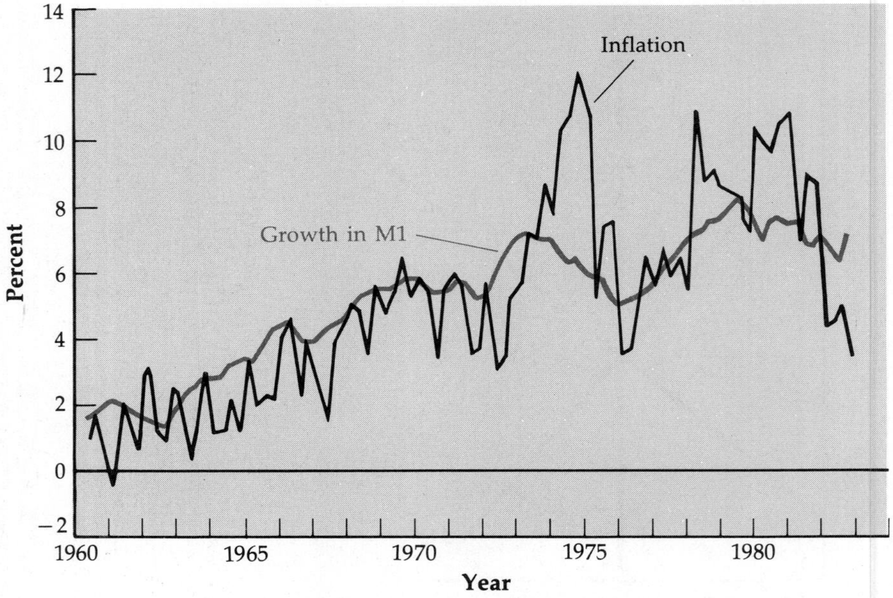


**Figure 14.6.** Inflation and the Rate of Growth of the Money Stock, 1960–1982. The M1 growth line represents a twelve-quarter moving average of M1 growth. The inflation line represents a quarter-to-quarter rate of change in the GNP deflator. The vertical line between the third and fourth quarters of 1979 indicates a change in the Federal Reserve operating procedures. In the short run the rate of inflation has diverged from the rate of growth in the money stock. But over the long term, swings in the rate of inflation have tended to follow swings in the rate of growth in the money stock.
**Source:** Federal Reserve Bank of St. Louis *Review*, 65, May 1983, p. 11.

ups and downs of the business cycle. Steady growth of the money stock should also steady the inflation and unemployment rates. In the monetarists' view, the unpredictable fluctuations in the growth rate of the money stock are the primary cause of fluctuations in the unemployment rate.

## The Historical Evidence

To support their theory, the monetarists cite statistical studies of the relationship between growth in the money stock and the rate of inflation. One such study concluded that every major economic downturn in U.S. history resulted from a contraction of the money stock. Likewise, every period of rapid price increases has been accompanied by an equally rapid increase in the size of the money stock.[1]

---

1. Milton Friedman and Anna J. Schwartz, *A Monetary History of the United States, 1867–1960* (Princeton, N.J.: Princeton University Press, 1963).

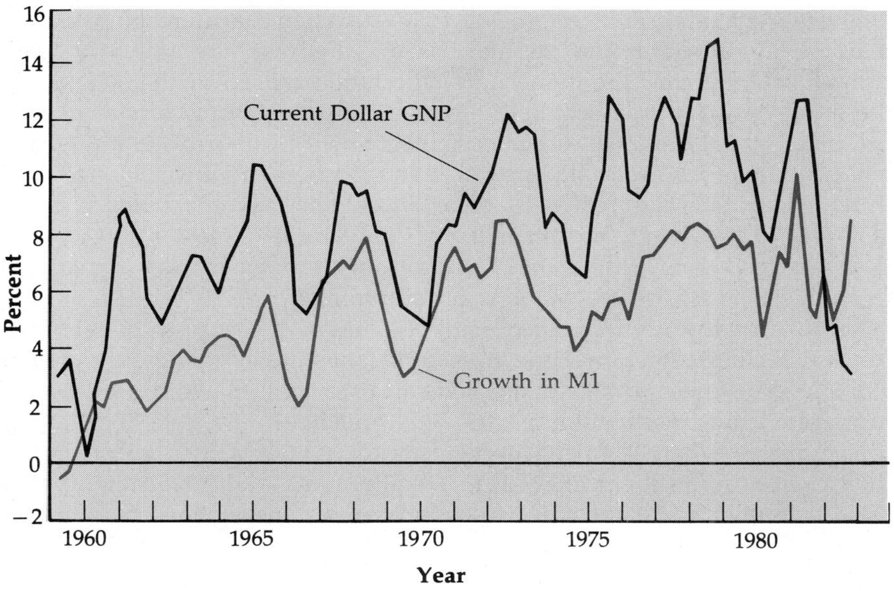


**Figure 14.7.** Growth Rates of the Gross National Product and the Money Stock, 1960–1982.
Each line represents a four-quarter growth rate. The vertical line between the third and fourth quarters of 1979 indicates a change in Federal Reserve operating procedures. Over the long run, the growth paths of the money stock and current dollar GNP have tended to move together. Short-run discrepancies have occurred, however.
**Source:** Federal Reserve Bank of St. Louis *Review*, 65, May 1983, p. 10.

Figures 14.6 and 14.7 plot the recent rate of growth of the money stock (M1) against the inflation rate and the rate of growth in current dollar gross national product. While the growth path of the money stock does not exactly match the patterns for inflation and GNP, swings in the growth of the money stock appear to be reflected in shifts in the inflation and GNP growth rates. Deviations among the three patterns can be attributed to time lags between growth in the money stock and its effects; to supply shocks such as OPEC's oil embargo of 1973 (see Figure 14.6); and to largely random changes in the velocity of money (see Figure 8.4 in Chapter 8).

## The Monetarist View of High Interest Rates

According to early Keynesian theory, an increase in the rate of growth of the money stock will reduce interest rates. As the money stock grows, more funds become available for loans, lessening competition among borrowers. Monetarists agree, but argue that the decrease in rates will be temporary. In the long run, greater growth in the money stock will bring higher interest rates. (Many Keynesians also now accept this point.)

The monetarists' argument goes as follows. When the interest rate drops, many lenders will refuse to make loans, because the rate does not compensate them for the higher rate of inflation caused by the increase in the money stock. For example, if a lender can receive only 5 percent, but the inflation rate exceeds 6 percent, the money the borrower pays back will have less real purchasing power than the money that was loaned. But if the lender invests in real assets (like land) whose nominal value is rising at a rate of 7 percent, he can make a small profit. Unless interest rates rise, lenders will withhold their funds from the loan market and invest them in assets whose real value will not diminish.

Because of the higher rate of inflation, then, the supply of lendable funds will fall. At the same time households, businesses, and governments will speed up their purchases of goods and services, to avoid future price increases. Consumers will buy cars and appliances now, to avoid paying higher prices when the new models come out. Businesses will increase their current investment in plant and equipment. And governments will build schools and roads now to avoid higher construction costs in the future. To accomplish these goals, individuals, businesses, and governments will want to borrow more money.

This demand will increase at a time when lendable funds are in short supply because lenders are unwilling to make loans at the prevailing low interest rates. As a result market interest rates will increase. Together, faster growth in the money stock and a higher inflation rate should push rates up higher than they were initially. But the higher rates do not necessarily discourage investment—a point generally accepted in all schools of macroeconomic thought. Firms may pay higher interest rates for the money they borrow, but part of their interest payment is returned to them in price increases on the goods they sell. During a period of double-digit inflation, for example, a business may have to pay interest of 15 percent or more on the money it borrows to buy its raw materials. It can justify paying such a high rate because it knows that the price of the final goods it produces will rise over time, enabling it to meet the interest payments.

In short, the nominal, or market, rate of interest includes both the real rate of interest, which reflects the rate of return on capital goods, and the rate of inflation.

$$\text{market interest rate} = \text{real interest rate} + \text{expected inflation rate}$$

The way to reduce market interest rates, monetarists and others contend, is to reduce the rate of inflation. That means to control the growth of the money stock. As always, control of the money stock is a predominant issue in the monetarists' interpretation of macroeconomic problems.

## The Monetarist View of Deficits

Monetarists have long argued that government fiscal policy is important because it determines the extent to which the nation's resources will be used for public rather than private purposes. That is, government expenditures impinge on the nation's limited resources, crowding individuals and firms out of the market. Monetarists attach little importance to the multiplier effect of government spending. In fact, many monetarists contend that an increase in government spending will have little if any effect on the nation's short-run income. For greater government spending necessarily means less spending by private firms and individuals. Increased government spending, in other words, does not translate into a significant and enduring increase in aggregate demand (unless it is accompanied by an increase in the money stock). Nor does it matter how the additional government expenditures are financed. If taxes are raised, consumption and business investment will fall, more or less offsetting the increase in government spending. If a deficit is incurred and the money stock is held constant, consumption and investment will still be reduced, because the government will absorb funds that would have been borrowed by consumers and businesses.

The monetarists' position on deficits can be expressed in terms of the equation of exchange, $MV = PQ = Y$. If deficit spending raises the national income level ($Y$), as the Keynesians suggest, it follows that $MV$ must rise with it. If the money stock ($M$) is held constant, then velocity ($V$) must rise. Keynesians maintain that velocity does rise, because the government borrows and then puts into active use money that would otherwise have remained idle. But the monetarists contend that velocity remains more or less stable. Velocity, they say, is determined primarily by the expected rate of inflation, by institutional payment customs, and by personal wealth. Payment customs and personal wealth do not vary much in the short run, and velocity changes depend on changes in the rate of inflation—which in turn, according to the monetarists, depend on changes in the growth rate of the money stock. Therefore government deficits do not materially affect the national income level—or so the argument goes.

Monetarists recognize that the velocity of money depends to some extent on people's willingness to hold money balances. And their willingness to hold money balances is in turn inversely related to market interest rates. People can see that deficit spending puts upward pressure on interest rates, because more demand is chasing after the same amount of money. The higher interest rates go, the less money people will hold and the faster money will circulate. Theoretically, then, government deficits can induce people to hold less money, thereby increasing its velocity and boosting the national income level. But statistical studies apparently don't support this theory; they seem to show that interest rates have only a slight effect on the velocity of money.

How then do the monetarists explain the effects of the 1964 and 1981 tax cuts? In both cases the federal government ran a budget deficit and the national income level went up. Monetarists contend that increases in the rate of growth of the money stock, not deficit spending, sparked those increases in national income. Many (but not all) monetarists point out that after 1964, federal deficits led to greater borrowing by the Treasury, greater overall demand for lendable funds, and upward pressure on interest rates. In an attempt to keep interest rates down, the Federal Reserve expanded the money stock faster than in previous years. In other words, the government's fiscal policy had a significant short-run effect on unemployment, national income, and inflation only because it caused the Federal Reserve to increase the rate of growth in the money stock.

Similarly the recovery that began in late 1982 stemmed from a reversal of monetary policy. Beginning in 1979, the Fed had dramatically reduced the rate of growth in the money stock in order to fight double-digit inflation. Then, in late 1982, the Fed switched to a policy of rapid money growth. Because the economy was then in a serious recession, the change was not reflected in a higher rate of inflation.

## The Importance of a Stable Rate of Monetary Growth

Because they believe money is crucial to the health of the macroeconomy, monetarists contend that government macroeconomic policy should be directed toward establishing a stable, predictable rate of growth of the money stock—say 4 percent a year. That is, the Federal Reserve should establish a policy of increasing the money stock at a given, more or less fixed rate. With the money stock growing at a fixed rate, a steady, largely predictable rate of inflation should result. For as we saw in Chapter 9, it is unanticipated inflation that redistributes the nation's income from creditors to debtors. Inflation would not be nearly as difficult a social problem if it were predictable.

Steady growth of the money stock and a predictable inflation rate would also reduce the risk of holding wealth in dollar assets. Lower risk would mean lower interest rates. And steady growth would eliminate many of the cyclical swings in economic activity that have resulted, according to the monetarists, from past shifts in monetary policy. The critical need, monetarists argue, is to establish a known and stable rate of increase in the money stock; its exact level is much less important. An annual growth rate of about 4 percent would allow for a modest annual rise in the production of goods and services (2 to 3 percent) because of increases in productivity and in the size of the labor force, as well as a relatively stable price level (inflation would be 1 to 2 percent or less). But other rates might serve just as well.

The money stock should increase rather than remain stable or contract. If the money stock remained fixed, prices would have to fall with an increase in output, since a growing quantity of goods and services would have to be purchased with a given quantity of money. Deflation—a drop in the money stock—can cause just as much redistribution of income as inflation. And it may give rise to special problems as well—especially since people have had little experience with deflation in recent history.

In addition, the monetarists argue that the time lags between recognizing macroeconomic problems and implementing monetary policies are often too long to make the policies effective. Moreover, monetarists frequently contend, monetary policymakers do not know enough about how changes in the growth rate of the money stock influence the economy to successfully "fine tune," or manipulate, macroeconomic activity. Monetary policy actions (for example, purchases of government securities) often have highly variable and largely unpredictable time lags, ranging from a few months up to two years. Therefore, Fed policy action taken today may affect prices and output six months from now, but they may not take effect for two years. Monetary actions may start to influence prices and output at a time when the actions will be counterproductive. Monetarists maintain that the Fed should try to control what it can best control (but still imperfectly)—the rate of growth of the money stock.

Critics of monetarist theory make several counterarguments. First, it is difficult to decide which measure of the money stock—M1 or M2 (or M3, not considered here)—should be controlled. Current measures of money are largely arbitrary, and new forms of money not included in the official money stock can be created. Suppose the Fed established a policy of increasing M1 at a rate of 4 percent. If people begin using money market accounts (not included in M1) as a store of purchasing power, the result could be an increase in the velocity of M1 and a higher-than-expected inflation rate.

Second, critics argue that the velocity of most money measures changes in response to a variety of economic factors. If those changes are not offset by changes in the growth rate of the money stock, the inflation rate could be affected.

Third, critics maintain that the growth of the money stock depends only in part on the growth of bank reserves and the reserve requirement, both variables that are directly controlled by the Fed (see Chapter 8). Many other variables—from interest rates to the public's demand for currency—can also affect the size of the money stock. As a consequence, the Fed may not be able to control the money stock precisely, or even within a certain range. As noted before, in 1979 the Fed made a serious effort to control money growth (or so it was thought). But over the next four years the money stock grew at monthly rates that ranged from more than 15 percent to less than −1 percent.

Critics of monetarism argue that if the Fed really wants to stabilize prices, it should worry about what is happening to prices, not to the money stock. That is, the rate of growth of the money stock should be adjusted from time to time to stabilize the rate of inflation. Monetarists counter that the Fed doesn't know enough about the link between money growth and inflation to stabilize prices in that way. Indeed, for most of this century the Fed has had the authority to control prices by controlling the money stock. Yet its record, especially in recent decades, is a blemished one.

Monetarists charge that the Fed has done a poor job of managing the growth rate in the money stock. They point out that between 1979 and 1982, the Fed slammed on the monetary brakes too hard. It permitted wide fluctuations in the rate of growth in the money stock, increasing the risk cost of holding money. Those wide swings, and the corresponding swings in real GNP, are evident in Figure 14.8.

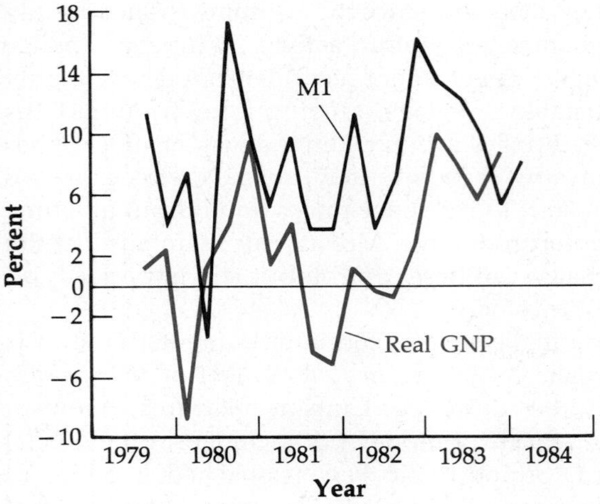


**Figure 14.8.** Change in the U.S. Money Stock and Real GNP, 1979–1983. During the early 1980s, the Fed permitted wide swings in the quarter-to-quarter rate of change in the money stock (black line). Changes in the money stock were accompanied by equally large swings in the quarter-to-quarter rate of change in real GNP (color line).
**Source:** Oppenheimer Capital Corporation, *Manhattan Report*, 4, No. 3 (1984), 4.

In comparison, monetarists point to the success of monetarist policy prescriptions in Japan, which began to stabilize its money stock in 1974. The results of its policy change are shown in Figure 14.9. Before 1974, wide swings in the money stock were accompanied by almost equally wide swings in current dollar and real GNP. After 1974, swings in both the money stock and GNP were moderated. Real and current dollar GNP began to merge, indicating a reduction in the inflation rate.

## Summary and Extensions

Money is not the only determinant of unemployment, inflation, and the national income level in the monetarist model. Technological growth, union power, personal wealth, and other factors also have long-term effects. Money is an extremely important variable, however. The rate of growth of the money stock is the prime determinant of the rate of inflation. Changes in the rate of money growth will cause cyclical swings in both unemployment and inflation. In the short run, then, monetary policy matters a great deal and fiscal policy relatively little, except insofar as government expenditures draw resources away from the private sector. (Inefficient use of resources dampens economic growth.)

Whereas the Keynesian model of the macroeconomy provides a strong argument for government intervention and control of the economy, the

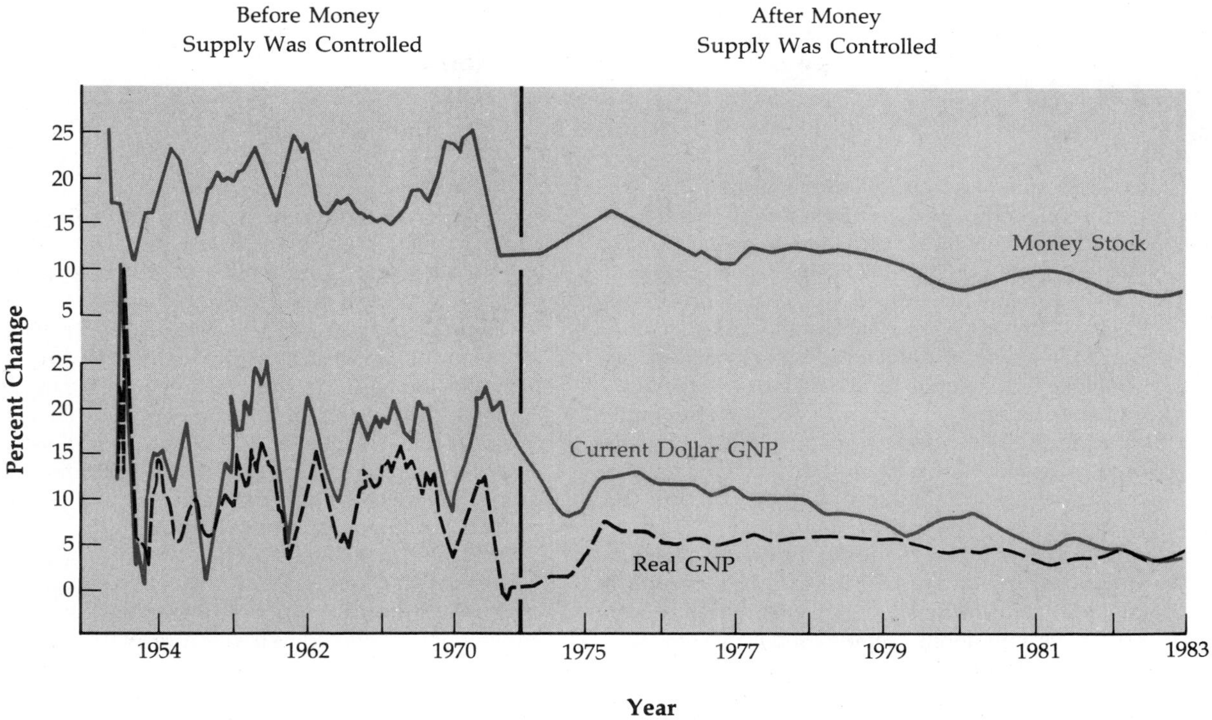


**Figure 14.9.** Changes in the Japanese Money Stock and Real and Current Dollar GNP, 1954–1983.
Before 1974, when the money supply was not controlled, Japan experienced wide swings in the rate of change in the money stock. After 1974, the rate of change in both the money stock and GNP slowed and smoothed out. Current dollar and real GNP converged in the early 1980s, indicating a moderating of the inflation rate.
**Source:** G. T. Management (Asia) Ltd., *Manhattan Report*, 4, No. 3 (1984), 6.

monetarist model provides a strong argument against government involvement—except for control of the money stock. Keynesians argue that government manipulation of the budget and the money stock can foster economic stability and full employment. Monetarists, on the other hand, contend that, by itself, government manipulation of the budget will not lead to a lasting effect on the overall employment level. Furthermore, any increase in the rate of growth of the money stock will only temporarily reduce unemployment and increase inflation. In the long run, the unemployment rate will return to its natural level, which is determined by obstacles in the labor market. Thus the only lasting solution to unemployment, according to the monetarists, is to eliminate as many of those obstacles as possible.

## Perspectives in Economics: Hitting the Money Growth Rate Targets

Monetarists argue that inflation can be contained by careful control of the growth rate of the money stock. The practical problem is which measure of money, M1 or M2, should be controlled. (Critics say monetarists sidestep this question too easily.) Changes in the velocity of money, and in the willingness of banks to make loans and of people to hold various forms of money—currency, demand deposits, and savings accounts—complicate the problem. Because people can shift their money from one form to another, attempts to limit the growth of one measure may simply provoke an explosion in the growth of another.

In the early 1970s, the Federal Reserve began to announce target ranges for the growth rates of M1 and M2.[1] Not until 1979, however, did the Fed become serious about keeping money growth rates within their announced target ranges. How well has the Fed met its goals? Figure 14.10 shows the growth of M1 and M2 from 1982 to 1984 (color lines). The black lines represent the upper and lower limits of the target ranges for the two measures, expressed in percentages. For example, beginning in November 1982, the Fed's target range for the growth rate of M1 was 4 to 8 percent. As you can see, the Fed missed its target by a wide margin. In early 1983 the Fed revised its target range to 5 to 9 percent and missed its target again, at least for the next four months. In late 1983 the Fed refigured its goals on the basis of a larger money stock and lowered its target range to 4 to 8 percent. This time it managed to keep the money stock within announced limits.

The Fed was much more successful in controlling for the growth of M2. Only for two months during 1983 and 1984 did M2 stray from its target range. Perhaps the Fed was more serious about meeting its goals for M2 than for M1. Some monetarists, however, have questioned the Fed's dedication to controlling the size of the money stock. No one at the Fed was fired because M1 exceeded its target growth rates in 1982 and 1983.

Monetarist critics of the Fed believe that the Japanese government's success in meeting its money growth rate targets shows that control of the money stock is possible. Japanese money growth has been much more stable than U.S. money growth. The rate of growth has fallen gradually, and along with it, the inflation rate. The United States could achieve the same success, critics claim, if the Fed took monetarist policy prescriptions seriously.

1. The Federal Reserve is required to report to Congress twice a year, in February and July, to announce new target ranges for money growth and to explain the previous year's performance.

## Major Conclusions

1. From the monetarist point of view, the primary cause of short-run swings in both the unemployment and inflation rates is abrupt changes in the rate of growth of the money stock.
2. Increases in the rate of growth of the money stock will produce unanticipated increases in the rate of inflation, a temporary reduction in the real wages paid to workers, and a temporary decrease in unemployment. In the long run, however, people will begin to anticipate a rise in inflation, and will work their expectations into their wage demands. Once money wages start to rise, unemployment will rise back to the level dictated by obstacles in the labor market, such as minimum wage laws.

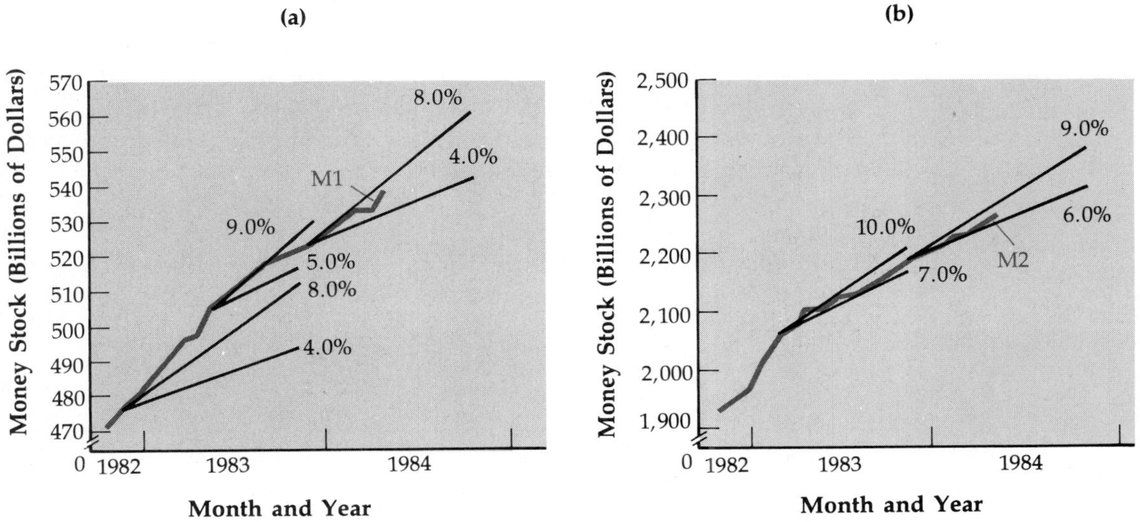


**Figure 14.10.** Growth of the Money Stock and Federal Reserve Target Ranges, 1982–1984.
From late 1982 to late 1983, the growth of M1 (part (a)) exceeded the Fed's announced target ranges (black lines). Growth of M2 (part (b)) was much better contained.
**Source:** Federal Reserve Bank of Cleveland, *Economic Trends* (July 1984), pp. 16 and 17. Figures seasonally adjusted.

3. Decreases in the rate of growth of the money stock will produce an unanticipated reduction in the rate of inflation, a temporary increase in the real wages paid to workers, and a temporary increase in unemployment. In the long run, however, money wage rates will not rise as fast, real wage rates will fall, and unemployment will drop back to the level dictated by obstacles in the labor market.
4. There is no long-run tradeoff between unemployment and inflation, as suggested by the Phillips curve.
5. An increase in the anticipated rate of inflation will cause a simultaneous increase in the demand for, and a decrease in the supply of, lendable funds. The result will be a rise in the market interest rate. Conversely

a reduction in the anticipated rate of inflation will produce lower interest rates. In the monetarist model of the macroeconomy, high rates of inflation eventually raise the interest rate instead of lowering it, as in the Keynesian model.

6. In the monetarist model, government spending crowds out private (consumer and investment) spending. Indeed, the monetarists argue, a decrease in planned investment spending will virtually offset any increase in government spending intended to stimulate the economy. Deficit spending therefore has little or no effect on the national income and employment levels.
7. The monetarist prescription for a healthy economy is a stable, predictable rate of growth in the money stock.

## Questions to Ponder

1. In the monetarist model of the macroeconomy, why will an increase in the rate of growth of the money stock not permanently reduce unemployment?

2. What actions would a monetarist president take to increase his or her chances of reelection in one year? In four years? If a president could be reelected more than once, would the options change?
3. "Given the equation of exchange, $MV = PQ = Y$, deficit spending alone can increase the national income. Deficit spending will increase the price level, which will lead in turn to an increase in $V$." According to the monetarist model, what is wrong with this statement?
4. Suppose the money stock begins to grow faster. What will happen to market interest rates in the short run? What will happen to them in the long run?
5. Suppose the Federal Reserve decreases the rate of growth in the money stock. What will happen to market interest rates in the short run? In the long run?
6. In the monetarist model, how does the Federal Reserve contribute to business cycles?
7. What policies would a monetarist recommend to solve the nation's long-run unemployment problem?

## Central Question

*What are the basic tenets of supply-side economics?*

# Chapter 15

# Supply-Side Economics

*The source of the gifts of capitalism is the supply side of the economy. In the capitalist economies of the West, this simple recognition is the core of all successful economic policy. It is a principle sometimes as obscure to conservatives, with their often excessive preoccupation with the statistics of money and deficit spending, as it is to liberals, with their obsession for aggregate demand and consumer spending. Wisdom on the subject can sometimes be found in strange places. Even Karl Marx knew enough not to stress, as the crux and keystone of capitalism, control over the means of* **consumption.** *Or even of the supply of money.*

*George Gilder*

Keynesian economics was spawned during the Great Depression, when a substantial portion of the labor force was unemployed and prices were actually falling. It achieved academic and public prominence during the 1960s, when the inflation rate, at least for the first part of the decade, was a modest 2 to 3 percent, and the nagging social concern was unemployment. Keynesianism suggested that unemployment and inflation could be alleviated, if not eliminated, by government management of total spending. Unemployment could be reduced by an increase in total spending. Inflation could be reduced by a decrease in total spending (see Chapter 13).

If the goals of reduced inflation and reduced unemployment conflict, many Keynesians would say that policymakers should seek some socially acceptable short-run compromise. That is, they should aim for some combination of inflation and unemployment rates lying on the economy's Phillips curve. In the long run unemployment can be alleviated by education, on-the-job training, and poverty relief programs. And as improved labor skills and mobility increase production, the inflation rate will gradually go down. Monetarists would recommend controlling inflation by a gradual downward adjustment in the growth of the money stock.

Such was the general wisdom until the 1970s, when stagflation suddenly cast Keynesian theory into doubt. As one administration after another was foiled in its attempt to reduce inflation and unemployment simultaneously, many economists came to suspect that Keynesian theory was not the answer to all economic ills. The search began for new ways of analyzing and solving macroeconomic problems.

This chapter examines briefly one of the alternative schools of thought that arose from the crisis of the 1970s. Supply-side theorists see high tax rates as a major source of stagflation. Their overriding theme is that reductions in marginal tax rates will give people greater incentives to work, save, and invest. Their extra effort will raise productivity and national income, reducing unemployment and inflation. In short, supply-side economists offer microeconomic, or market, solutions to macroeconomic problems.

## Tax Rates and Supply-Side Incentives

Much Keynesian economics implicitly assumes a positive relationship between tax rates and tax collections. Lower tax rates will produce lower tax revenues, allowing total spending to rise—thus stimulating production and employment by increasing demand. Supply-side economists, on the other hand, emphasize the effect of tax rates on the supply of goods and services produced. Tax rates affect people's willingness to earn a living and to report their income to the Internal Revenue Service. Thus many macroeconomic problems should be solved by reducing government impediments to production and increasing people's incentives to work, save, and invest in productive activities.

Three major propositions underlie supply-side theory. As you may surmise—and as supply-side economists freely admit—these propositions are based on the work of much earlier economists, including Adam Smith.

## Basic Propositions of Supply-Side Theory

The first and most basic proposition of supply-side economics is that beyond some point, high marginal tax rates on personal income can reduce people's willingness to work. We have already defined the marginal tax rate as the percentage of any additional income that must be paid to the government. Marginal tax rate normally indicates the tax rate applied to the last increment of taxable income. The U.S. federal tax system is progressive, meaning that the marginal tax rate on additional income rises as earned income rises.[1] A taxpayer with a modest income may have a 25 percent marginal tax rate bracket; if he earns one more dollar, he must pay an additional twenty-five cents in taxes. A taxpayer with a very high income can face a marginal tax rate of 50 percent. Because of taxes, people's take-home pay is less than their earned income. Taxpayers must consider how much their additional earned income will be taxed in deciding whether to work more or harder.

Supply-side theorists propose that lower marginal tax rates on personal income should encourage people to enter the labor force and work longer hours. And lower marginal tax rates on business income should increase business demand for labor by increasing the after-tax return on labor. A reduction in marginal tax rates thus should increase both the supply of labor and the demand for it. Employment will expand in response to conventional microeconomic forces—that is, to a reduction in the after-tax price of labor. (The use of any other resource would also be expected to increase if its price declined.)

The second basic proposition of supply-side economics is that high marginal tax rates discourage people from investing in education and improving their work-related skills. They can also encourage businesses to invest abroad, where tax rates are lower, rather than in domestic operations. Again, high tax rates reduce the after-tax return on investments, lowering the nation's capital stock, both human and nonhuman. Growth in productivity will slow, depressing future national income levels. A reduction in marginal tax rates, therefore, should produce a more forward-looking, dynamic economy, in which more is invested in education, job training, and plant and equipment. The result will be a higher future national income level achieved through greater productivity.

The third basic proposition is that high marginal tax rates encourage people to work in the underground economy, where their incomes cannot be traced by the Internal Revenue Service. Barter and trade for cash, the clandestine sale of illegal goods and services such as drugs and prostitution, and the nonreporting of legitimate income all flourish under such conditions. High marginal tax rates also encourage people to spend considerable sums of money in search of tax loopholes. To the extent that efforts to

1. In 1985, the maximum marginal tax rate was 50 percent, and the Reagan administration was actively considering lowering it to 35 percent. At the same time, it was considering eliminating various deductions that high income earners use to lower their taxable incomes.

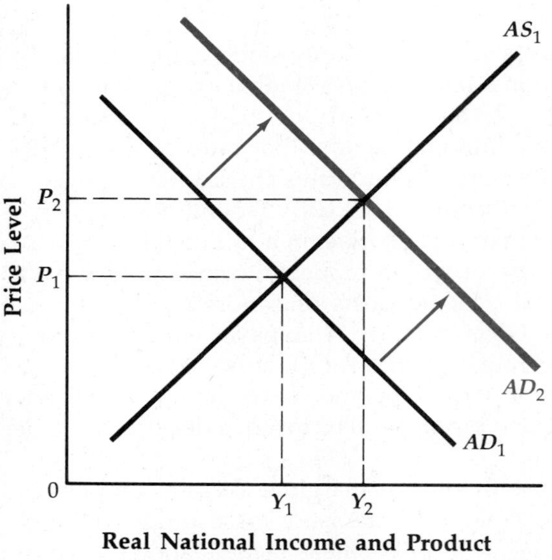


**Figure 15.1.** The Effect of a Cut in Tax Rates: The Keynesian Model. According to Keynesian theory, a cut in tax rates will increase aggregate demand from $AD_1$ to $AD_2$. As a result, the price level will rise from $P_1$ to $P_2$, and the national income level will climb from $Y_1$ to $Y_2$.

avoid taxes use up otherwise productive resources, they reduce the efficiency of the economy. So a reduction in tax rates should increase not only the amount of income people report, but the nation's total income.

## The Effects of a Reduction in Tax Rates

Because high marginal tax rates retard growth in the nation's productive capacity, supply-side economists contend they heighten the inflationary effect of an increase in the money stock. If $MV = PQ$ and $Q$ is retarded, a rise in $M$ must be matched mostly by a rise in $P$. If tax rates are reduced, then, and the supply of goods grows more rapidly in relation to the money stock, inflationary pressures should subside. As employment opportunities rise with the increase in production incentives, fewer people will find it desirable to work in the underground economy. Most people will be better off—earning more and able to keep a large share of their earnings.

Furthermore, a reduction in marginal tax rates need not reduce tax collections. Tax revenues are a function of two key variables, national income and tax rates. Stated mathematically, tax revenues equal the tax rate times the national income ($TR = rY$). If a given percentage decrease in tax rates is accompanied by a larger percentage increase in national income, the government's tax collections will rise. Suppose, for example,

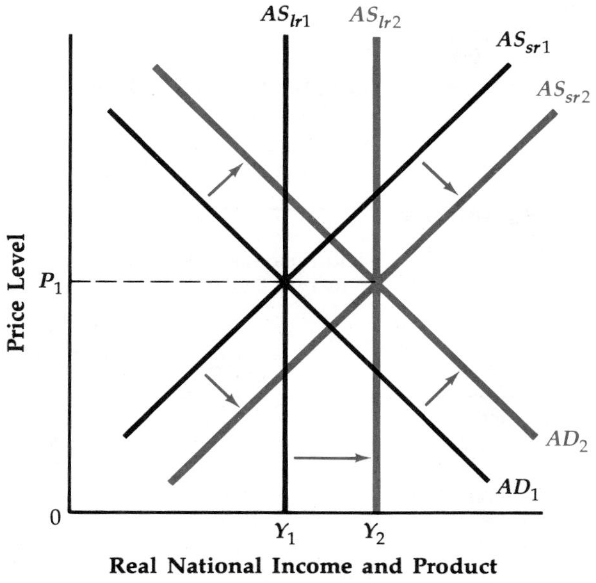


Figure 15.2. The Effect of a Cut in Tax Rates: The Supply-Side Model. According to supply-side theory, a cut in tax rates shifts both the aggregate demand curve and the short-run aggregate supply curve outward. At the new equilibrium point (the intersection of $AD_2$ and $AS_{sr2}$), national income will be higher ($Y_2$ instead of $Y_1$), but the price level will be the same. If the tax cut is perceived as permanent, the long-run aggregate supply curve will also shift, from $AS_{lr1}$ to $AS_{lr2}$. In that case the increase in national income will be permanent.

that the national income is $3.5 trillion, and the average tax rate is 40 percent. Suppose further that if tax rates are reduced from 40 to 36 percent, the national income will rise from $3.5 trillion to $4.2 trillion. Total tax revenues rise from $1.4 trillion (40 percent of $3.5 trillion) to $1.51 trillion (36 percent of $4.2 trillion). Under these circumstances, government spending can actually be expanded—or so the argument goes.

The effect of supply-side proposals can also be described in terms of aggregate demand and supply. As we have seen in previous chapters, a reduction in tax rates will raise aggregate demand, shifting the aggregate demand curve outward, from $AD_1$ to $AD_2$, in Figure 15.1. The price level will rise from $P_1$ to $P_2$, and the national production level will climb from $Y_1$ to $Y_2$. In the long run, however, national production will probably return to $Y_1$, because the long-run aggregate supply curve is vertical.

Supply-side economists add that the aggregate supply curve will also be affected by the tax rate reduction. In the short run, because people have a greater incentive to work, save, and invest, the aggregate supply curve will shift outward, from $AS_{sr1}$ to $AS_{sr2}$, in Figure 15.2. This increase in aggregate supply will tend to dampen, if not totally offset, the price effect of the increase in aggregate demand. A tax rate reduction, in other words, will not be as inflationary as Keynesian theory might suggest.

## Perspectives in Economics: The Impact of Tax Rates Across Countries

*Alan Reynolds*

Tax revenues are often expressed as a percentage of GNP, but governments cannot pay their bills with percentages. To finance real increases in spending, governments need real increases in tax revenues.

The table [Table 15.1] shows what happened to the growth of real revenues, from 1975 to 1982, among countries where taxes were a relatively high or low percentage of gross domestic product (GDP). The tax percentage is a static snapshot; the growth of real revenue over several years is a dynamic motion picture.

Without exception, countries with persistently high tax rates have sustained an actual loss of real tax revenues over the entire seven-year period. Those that attempted to counter this loss with even steeper tax rates, such as Belgium, had even larger revenue losses.

Countries in which taxes extracted the smallest share of GDP—Japan and Spain—have experienced by far the most rapid increase in real tax revenues. The reason, of course, is that real GDP (or GNP) is the tax base for real revenues, and production invariably grows most rapidly in low-tax countries, as Keith Marsden of the World Bank recently observed . . . last December 18 [1984].

**Table 15.1.** Rates and Revenues (1975–82; Percentage Change in 1972 Dollars)

| | Average Tax Rate (% of GDP) | Change in Real Tax Revenues[a] |
|---|---|---|
| Sweden | 49.2% | −12.4% |
| Netherlands | 44.6 | − 6.8 |
| Belgium | 44.6 | −15.7 |
| Denmark | 43.4 | −10.6 |
| France | 40.7 | 6.2 |
| Austria | 40.5 | 7.0 |
| Germany | 37.0 | 7.6 |
| United Kingdom | 35.7 | 29.1 |
| Canada | 32.8 | 6.7 |
| Switzerland | 30.9 | 5.4 |
| United States | 30.0 | 20.1 |
| Portugal | 27.9 | 12.1 |
| Japan | 24.3 | 54.1 |
| Spain | 22.7 | 59.8 |

[a] Adjusted by deflator for U.S. government purchases. Includes state and local government taxes.

The United Kingdom alone appears to have obtained sizable real revenue gains despite fairly high tax rates. But the seven-year average hides what really happened. British taxes dropped to 33.3% from 35.3% of GDP from 1976 to 1979, and real revenues increased 39%. The average tax rate then rose to 39.6% by 1982, with real revenues falling 20% from 1980 to 1982. Industrial production in the U.K. is now barely higher than it was in 1982 and unemployment is near 13%, so high tax rates undoubtedly continue to depress real revenue.

Revenues as a share of GNP or GDP measure an average tax rate, or "tax ratio," at any moment in time. But an increase in that tax rate implies an increase in the marginal tax rate on added output and income. When that happens, economic growth stagnates or contracts. Inflation may nonetheless continue to raise nominal tax revenues, but it inflates government spending, too. Meanwhile, the tax suffocation of real output raises real government spending to alleviate the added poverty. With real spending up and real revenues flat or down, budget deficits become large and chronic. Deficits of 10% to 13% of GDP have become routine in places like Belgium and Sweden, and will remain that way until they cut marginal tax rates.

Japan also runs perpetual deficits, with a government debt nearly as large as that of Belgium and Sweden. Yet Japan is able to finance that debt at long-term interest rates that are half those of the overtaxed nations, including France (whose debt is only half as large as Japan's). Monetary stability in Japan is part of the explanation though

Belgium, too, is quite intolerant of inflation or deflation. Perhaps a better explanation of Japan's high credit rating is that its seemingly large deficits and debt are actually small relative to the rapid growth of real tax revenues. Just as a growing company can easily handle a growing debt, so can a growing national economy. Overtaxed nations, particularly the troubled developing countries, are an inherently bad credit risk, because the ultimate source of real revenues—added GNP—is limited by punitive tax rates.

Those who are proposing a tax increase for the U.S. do not seem to realize that the U.S. is already having an enormous tax increase. Since tax rates were reduced to 18.6% from 20.2% of GNP in 1983, federal tax collections rose almost 7% in real terms last year and are expected to rise an additional 6% to 7% this year. That is an increase in real revenues of almost Japanese proportions.

Such significant revenue effects from economic growth are typically delayed a year. In the first year of recovery, many companies have accumulated losses that initially reduce their taxes, and individual taxes, too, are often paid on the unexpected increases in the previous year's earnings.

A 6% to 7% increase in the U.S. government's real earnings can scarcely be the subject of great public sympathy. Most households and companies expect to get by with a much smaller increase in their own revenues. Attempts to improve the government's budget at the expense of the budgets of the private sector invariably fail, as the European welfare states are learning the hard way.

From 1963 to 1965, federal taxes in the U.S. dropped to 17.7% from 18.5% of gross national product, and real tax revenues soared (with the usual lag) by 19% in the following two years. That was better than we are doing in 1984–85, but the Kennedy tax cuts were more dramatic, and nobody in those days thought 7.2% unemployment constituted an argument for brutal monetary policy. From 1978 to 1981, by contrast, federal taxes rose to 20.8% from 19.1% of GNP, and real tax revenues fell 12% in the following two years. It may be objected that the rising tax rates of 1979–81 just happened to be followed by stagnation and recession. But that was also true of the rising tax rates in 1974, 1969, 1958–59, 1953–54 and 1937–38. What we are missing is a single example of high or rising tax rates that were not followed by stagnation or recession, here or abroad.

When taxes rise as a percentage of GNP, it may simply mean that GNP slowed down even more than tax revenues. Indeed, this is what should be expected when taxes claim a rising share of added output. Robert Barro's revolutionary new text, "Macroeconomics," concludes that "an increase in the marginal tax rate . . . leads in the short run to less work, output and investment. Further, in the long run, there are reductions in the stock of capital, as well as in the levels of output and consumption."

With lower real GNP, we should expect much lower real tax revenues. Barro estimates that "a decline by 1% in real GNP causes real federal revenues to decrease by 1.8%." For any government to attempt to acquire a larger percentage of a smaller real GNP, it must move toward the top of the table, losing real revenue in the process. A 40% share of nothing is nothing.

In the back of every U.S. budget, federal spending is shown in real, inflation adjusted terms. But taxes are only shown in nominal terms, as a percentage of nominal GNP.

Those who demand a "tax increase" must make up their minds. If they want a big increase in real tax revenues, we already have that. If instead they want taxes to be a larger percentage of any remaining GNP, then that must be recognized as a well-tested plan to shrink real revenues, increase real transfer payments, and double the budget deficits.

Reprinted with permission from Alan Reynolds, "Less Will Get You More," *Wall Street Journal,* January 23, 1985, p. 32.

If the tax rate reduction is perceived as permanent, it can also shift the long-run aggregate supply curve outward, from $AS_{lr1}$ to $AS_{lr2}$, in Figure 15.2. Again, the shift occurs because people have greater incentives to work and add to the nation's capital stock. The outward shift in the long-run aggregate supply curve means that some or all of the income effect of the tax rate cut can be permanent. It also means that the money stock can be expanded more than Keynesian theory might suggest. Whether the price level rises or falls, and by how much, depends on the relative impact of the cut on aggregate supply versus aggregate demand, and on the extent to which the money stock is increased when tax rates are lowered.

Does this scenario sound too good to be true? As you can imagine, many economists have serious reservations about some of the supply-side predictions. Nevertheless, the Reagan administration based its economic recovery strategy partly on such thinking. In 1981 it pushed through Congress a three-year, 25 percent cut in personal income tax rates.

## A Critique of Supply-Side Theory

One of the more serious criticisms of supply-side theory has to do with the proposition that lower tax rates encourage people to work harder.

### The Labor-Leisure Tradeoff

Critics of supply-side economics charge that high marginal tax rates do not necessarily reduce the number of hours people work. In fact, they can actually increase the amount of time spent at work. Thus a tax cut could reduce production.

Figure 15.3 shows the critics' view of the labor-leisure tradeoff. Assume the typical citizen-taxpayer has sixty hours to use for work or play each week. Time spent on work yields money income, as shown on the vertical axis. At an hourly wage rate of $10, a worker can earn a maximum of $600 per week. To earn money income, the worker must give up the direct benefits of leisure time, shown on the horizontal axis. In other words, the worker has a production possibilities curve that extends from a point somewhere on the horizontal axis to another point somewhere on the vertical axis.

The tax rate structure will affect the slope of the production possibilities curve. Without any income taxes, the worker's curve may look like $Y_4T_1$. Assume that the worker chooses point *a* on that curve. In doing so, she gives up thirty hours of leisure for $300 a week in income. She could move further up the curve and earn more money income. But presumably she values her leisure time more than the additional goods she could purchase with the additional money. In short, combination *a* maximizes the worker's utility.

Now suppose the government imposes a 30 percent tax on personal income. The worker will take home only $7 out of the $10 she earns for each hour of work. The relative cost of leisure, then, has gone down. Each

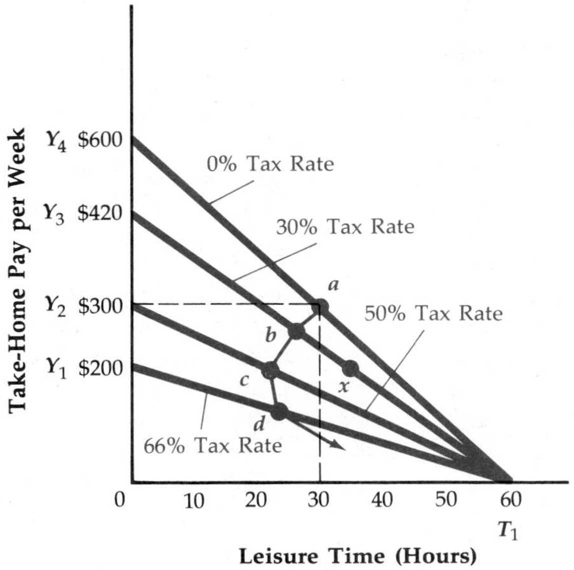


**Figure 15.3.** The Labor-Leisure Tradeoff.
At a tax rate of zero, a worker can consume along transformation curve $Y_4T_1$. A worker making $10 an hour might choose to consume at point *a*, earning $300 a week and taking thirty hours of leisure time. As the tax rate increases, however, the worker's transformation curve pivots downward. On curve $Y_3T_1$, the worker might choose point *x*, which offers less disposable income but more leisure time. Or she could move to point *b*, which minimizes the loss in income, but at the cost of less leisure time. The higher the tax rate, the lower the transformation curve, and the more leisure time the worker will have to give up to maintain her income.

hour now spent talking with friends means only $7 worth of goods forgone. At the same time the relative price of goods purchased with money has gone up. More leisure time must now be forgone for each good that is purchased. Thus a 30 percent tax rate pivots the production possibilities curve, from $Y_4T_1$ to $Y_3T_1$. The worker's maximum take-home pay is now $420 ($7 × 60 hours).

Supply-side economic theory suggests that when a 30 percent income tax is imposed, a worker will move from point *a* to a point like *x* on the new curve, choosing more leisure time and less work. But others argue that the worker may just as well move to point *b*, taking less leisure time and working more. Such a choice seems reasonable, at least for low tax rates. The person who has less take-home pay can be expected to buy less of most goods and services—including recreation. In short, lower tax rates do not necessarily mean greater national income. People may decide to work harder and longer to make up for the purchasing power lost because of a tax increase.

At very high tax rates a tax cut would probably increase the number of hours worked. Suppose the income tax rate is raised gradually, pivoting the transformation curve downward, from $Y_4T_1$ to $Y_1T_1$. At some point (in

Figure 15.3, when the tax rate is higher than 50 percent) the worker's tendency to work longer hours to make up for lost income is bound to halt. Consider the extreme case. If the income tax rate is 100 percent, the worker's consumption transformation curve will be perfectly flat, overlapping the horizontal axis. The rational individual can then be expected to work zero hours. (Would you work if all your income were taxed away?) At such an extreme rate, a tax cut could only encourage a worker to work more.

No government levies a 100 percent income tax, however. At lower rates, the effect of a tax cut is harder to predict. The outcome depends on both the actual level of the tax rate and the individual's personal preferences. A reduction in a very high tax rate may cause a worker to trade leisure for income, moving from point *d* to point *c*. Supply-side theory is based on this kind of response. But actual tax rates may be lower. If the taxpayer's choice lies in the *c* to *b* range, she may decide to take more leisure and work less.

From a strictly theoretical perspective, we cannot know whether a tax cut will cause people to work more. The question is an empirical one. A great deal of empirical evidence suggests that the labor supply curve slopes upward, and that workers respond positively to increased compensation. We might also agree that people will be better off if they are free to dispose of their own income—regardless of how many hours they work. But the actual effects of implementing supply-side policies cannot be predicted in the abstract.

Unfortunately, supply-side theorists' arguments about the impact of tax cuts on saving and investment are also inconclusive. Lower tax rates can encourage greater saving and investment, but they can also discourage it. Critics of supply-side economics point out that after the Reagan tax cut of 1981, the saving rate in the United States actually fell. Furthermore, even if a tax cut has a positive effect on saving and investment, it may not be very large.

Regardless of the actual outcome, many policymakers may continue to favor supply-side policy, reasoning that lower tax rates minimize government's distorting effects on the market process.

## The Laffer Curve

Critics also take issue with the idea that tax cuts inevitably increase tax revenues. Tax revenues may go up or down, depending on the responsiveness of workers, savers, and investors to the tax cut.

At the bottom of this controversy is the so-called Laffer curve, named after the supply-side economist Arthur Laffer. The Laffer curve relates total tax revenues to tax rates, as in Figure 15.4. At low tax levels, an increase in tax rates produces an increase in tax revenues. For example, an increase in the tax rate from $r_1$ to $r_2$ would expand tax revenues from $TR_1$ to $TR_2$. Beyond some point, however, an increase in tax rates can be expected to reduce tax revenues. For example, an increase in the tax rate from $r_3$ to $r_4$ would reduce tax revenues from $TR_3$ to $TR_2$.

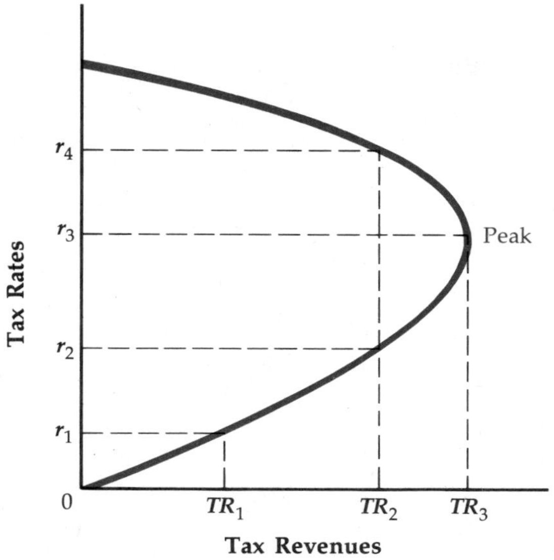


**Figure 15.4.** The Laffer Curve.
At low tax rates, represented by the lower half of the Laffer curve, an increase in tax rates, say from $r_2$ to $r_3$, can produce an increase in tax revenues (from $TR_2$ to $TR_3$). Beyond the peak of the Laffer curve, however, an increase in tax rates will lower tax revenues. For instance, an increase in the rate from $r_3$ to $r_4$ will decrease revenues from $TR_3$ to $TR_2$.

Why does the Laffer curve have the shape it does? At low tax rates, so the argument goes, people have little incentive to avoid taxes. Trading off income for leisure or saving and investment for consumption is not profitable. Finding ways to escape taxes or to move productive activity underground is not worth the trouble. At high tax rates it is costly not to avoid taxes, however. The result is that beyond some peak point, as shown in Figure 15.4, the reported tax base falls off enough that total tax collections go down.

The general shape of the Laffer curve can also be deduced from demand analysis. Because income buys goods, people have a demand for it. How much income they demand depends partly on its price, which is called the tax price in supply-side economics. The more taxes take out of earned income, the less income people will earn—a proposition that yields the downward-sloping income demand curve in Figure 15.5. At a tax rate of zero, citizens will earn a national income equal to $Y_2$. If the government raises its tax rate to $r_1$, tax revenues will rise from zero to $r_1Y_1$. This movement from zero to $r_1$ tax rate in Figure 15.5 is equivalent to a movement up the bottom half of the Laffer curve in Figure 15.4.

If the tax rate is raised indefinitely, at some point tax revenues will fall. If the tax price is raised all the way to $r_2$, people will earn nothing, and again the government will collect no taxes. In short, so long as the amount

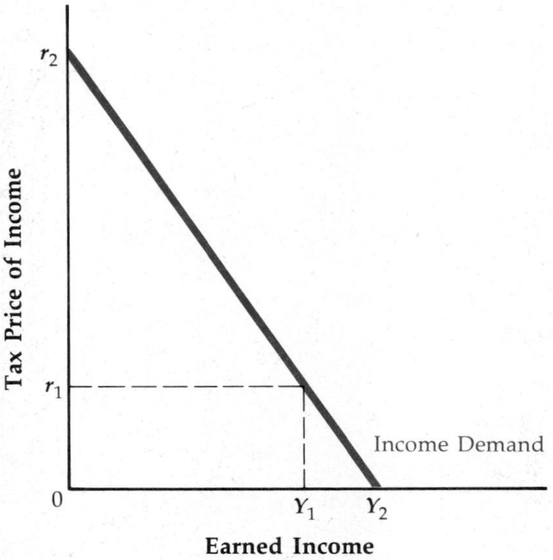


**Figure 15.5.** Effect of the Tax Price on the Demand for Income.
At a tax price, or rate, of zero, the amount of earned income demanded by workers is $Y_2$. The revenues collected by government are also zero. A tax rate of $r_1$ will lower earned income to $Y_1$, but increase government revenues from zero to $r_1Y_1$. Beyond some tax price, however, an increase in the tax rate with mean lower tax revenues. At a tax price of $r_2$, workers will demand no earned income, and government revenues will again be zero.

of income people demand varies inversely with the tax rate, the Laffer curve must have a backward-bending portion.

Whether a particular tax cut will reduce tax revenues depends on three factors: where the present tax rate places the nation on the Laffer curve; how much people respond to a change in the tax rate; and the size of the tax rate cut. If tax rates are above $r_3$ in Figure 15.4, for example, a tax rate cut will expand tax revenues. At tax rates below $r_3$, the effect of a cut will be just the opposite. A drop in tax rates all the way from $r_4$ to $r_1$ will also lead, on balance, to a reduction in tax collections.

Most economists accept the general shape of the Laffer curve. But many dispute the supply-side claim that marginal tax rates in the United States are so high, at least for high-income groups, that the nation is on the upper portion of the Laffer curve. There, of course, a tax rate cut would increase tax revenues. Without more empirical evidence, many economists will regard this claim with skepticism. Why indeed would politicians ever have raised taxes to such a level? By reducing personal income so much that total government spending (and benefits to their constituencies) declined, they would surely have jeopardized their chances of reelection. The critics contend that no one gains from being on the upper half of the Laffer curve.

## The Threat of Inflation

Finally, critics question the supply-side argument that, on balance, the nation is better off because of a tax rate cut. Cuts in marginal tax rates can increase deficit spending, which can eventually increase inflation.

Economists' response to this issue depends on whether they adhere to Keynesian or monetarist theory on matters of demand management. Keynesians tend to argue that in times of inflation, deficit spending will increase aggregate demand, thus adding to inflationary pressures. A cut in marginal tax rates may mean an immediate drop in tax collections and thus an increase in disposable income for consumers. Eventually it may stimulate an expansion of aggregate supply as well, but not until people have had a chance to respond to reduced tax rates by working, saving, and investing more. If spending increases rapidly but output increases slowly, the result will be a higher rate of inflation. (In terms of the equation of exchange, $MV = PQ$, deficit spending increases the velocity of money, $V$, necessitating an increase in $P$ or $Q$ on the other side of the equation. $P$ will increase more rapidly than $Q$.)

Supply-side economists, on the other hand, tend to argue that the increase in the supply of goods and services stimulated by a tax cut will counteract any inflationary pressures from a deficit. Indeed they recommend that the Fed adopt an expansionary monetary policy when tax rates are reduced, to avoid deflation. Supply-side theorists criticized the Fed for adhering to monetarist theory from 1981 to 1984, the period of the Reagan tax cut. Growth of the money stock, they maintain, does not invariably lead to inflation. So long as monetary growth accommodates rapid growth in production, inflation should not be a problem. In 1984, they point out, the rate of inflation did not keep pace with the growth of the money stock, because output expanded unusually fast—at an annual rate of over 7 percent for much of that year.

Supply-side theorists generally agree with monetarists that government expenditures will crowd out private expenditures. Government expenditures, in their view, are the ultimate tax on the economy. But they are not particularly distressed by the prospect of deficit spending crowding out private investment through higher interest rates. Lower tax rates should mean more resources available for investment. First, people will save more, supply-side theorists believe. Their greater saving (or nonconsumption) will free resources for use by investors, shifting purchases from consumption to investment. Second, the greater national income generated in response to reduced tax rates will also mean more resources available for investment. And reduced tax rates should draw back home those investment resources previously employed outside the country.

Supply-side theorists argue too that deficits created by tax rate cuts are likely to be short-lived (just how short-lived is a matter of dispute). With the increased national income generated by lower tax rates, government revenues will rise, wiping out or reducing the deficit. Over a period of years, then, government should run fewer deficits, borrow less, and crowd out less private investment than if tax rates were never reduced. (Keynesians made similar arguments in support of the 1964 Kennedy tax cut, but

# Perspectives in Economics: Soaking the Rich Through Tax Cuts

*Richard Vedder and Lowell Gallaway*

Almost a year ago [1984], the release of Internal Revenue Service data on 1982 income tax returns showed that higher-income Americans paid more in income taxes in 1982 than in 1981, whereas lower- and middle-income Americans paid less. The preliminary IRS data for 1983 tax returns are in, and repeat the pattern of the 1982 returns. Upper-income earners *are* paying a greater share of the tax burden after the Reagan tax-rate cuts.

A year ago, this interpretation was still open to question by critics and skeptics, while supply-siders proclaimed that since the top income-tax rate fell from 70% to 50% in 1982, the 1982 IRS data showed the tax cut was working just as they said it would. The incentives for higher-income Americans to engage in tax avoidance and even tax evasion were reduced and they responded accordingly. The fact that the number of returns from citizens with an adjusted gross income (AGI) of more than $1 million grew by nearly 60% amid the greatest recession in years was ample evidence that the tax cuts were working.

All of this, of course, was mildly embarrassing to Democratic presidential hopefuls who were spending most of last year trashing the Reagan administration for its tax policies that supposedly benefitted the rich and hurt the poor. However, a horde of commentators rose to their defense and attacked the supply-side view. They argued that the 1982 data were not typical. John Berry of the Washington Post suggested that the stock-market boom explained the rising affluence (and tax payments) of the rich, somehow assuming that the tax-rate reductions had no bearing on that boom. Joseph Minarik of the Urban Institute argued that because of inflationary "bracket creep," the payments from the rich typically rose and the 1982 results merely reflected a long-term trend.

Still others used different arguments. Donald Kiefer, a researcher for the Congressional Research Service, claimed that the wealthy, anticipating the tax-rate reductions, engaged in income-shifting tactics in late 1981 that swelled 1982 taxable income. Finally, some people maintained that because of rising nominal income, the definition of "rich" and "poor" was changing, meaning that a simple analysis of the data by constant-income classes led to distorted findings.

While supply-siders believe the bulk of these criticisms to be misdirected or exaggerated, the fact remains that conclusions were being drawn on the basis of a single year's observations. As Mr. Vedder said in a Joint Economic Committee study published last November ". . . the final word will be the 1983 data."

Well, the preliminary 1983 IRS data are in and they further support the contention that as after-tax rates of return rise the supply of labor and capital also increases. As the first table [Table 15.2] indicates, affluent Americans (say, those with an AGI of more than $100,000) paid substantially more than in 1981. Poor and middle-income Americans (those making under $50,000 AGI) paid less in 1983 than in 1982, and far less than in 1981. While tax payments rose 28% from 1981 to 1983 for the affluent group, they decreased nearly 12% for the low- and middle-income groups.

The increase in payments from the super rich was particularly dramatic—those with an AGI of $1 million or more paid 108% more in 1983 than in 1981, and the number of "tax millionaires" more than doubled in the greatest explosion of millionaires in U.S. history.

These results are not surprising. In the afore-

**Table 15.2.** Tax Payments By Income Groups, 1981 to 1983

| Income Class[c] | Taxes Paid[a] | | | % of Total Taxes Paid[b] | | |
|---|---|---|---|---|---|---|
| | 1981 | 1982 | 1983 | 1981 | 1982 | 1983 |
| $0–$15,000 | $26,571 | $23,949 | $21,037 | 9.1% | 8.4% | 7.4% |
| $15,000–$30,000 | 80,475 | 74,196 | 67,000 | 27.6 | 26.0 | 23.6 |
| $30,000–$50,000 | 88,322 | 86,363 | 84,736 | 30.3 | 30.2 | 29.8 |
| $50,000–$100,000 | 52,156 | 51,732 | 55,179 | 17.9 | 18.1 | 19.4 |
| Over $100,000 | 43,633 | 49,387 | 55,781 | 15.0 | 17.3 | 19.6 |
| Over $1,000,000 | 4,901 | 6,955 | 10,231 | 1.7 | 2.4 | 3.6 |

[a] In millions of dollars; refers to total tax liability.
[b] These percentages do not add to 100 because of rounding.
[c] Adjusted gross income.

mentioned JEC study, an analysis of 29 years of tax data from 1954 to 1982 revealed that upper-income Americans have become highly sensitive to variations in marginal tax rates on both ordinary and capital-gains type income. The study revealed that some Americans were in the backward-bending portion of the Laffer Curve—where reductions in tax rates so stimulate growth in the tax base that total tax receipts from the group rise. Profs. James Gwartney of Florida State University, Richard Stroup of Montana State University and James Long of Auburn University have reached virtually identical conclusions using quite a different methodology and different data sources.

The rise in tax payments reflected mainly a boom in what might be termed "entrepreneurial" income—income from small businesses, partnerships, farms, etc., or from working. The second table [Table 15.3] indicates that passive or *rentier* income, in the form of dividends, interest, royalties and the like, grew far less rapidly. It would appear that a big surge in entrepreneurial activity has occurred in response to the increase in the part of income that individuals keep after taxation.

The one argument of the critics that has not been addressed is the notion that rising nominal income normally pushes more Americans into higher tax brackets, increasing the pool of persons with incomes in excess of a given amount. One way to deal with this argument is to look at the relative income of Americans, that is, to examine, say the top 10% of income recipients, regardless of what their income may be. Analysis using this procedure indicates that the shift in tax payments toward the rich is somewhat less dramatic than shown in the first table, but it is occurring nonetheless. The share of total income taxes paid by the top 1% of income recipients grew from 17.44%

*Continued*

# Perspectives in Economics: Soaking the Rich Through Tax Cuts

*Continued*

to 20.64% between 1981 and 1983, with the share of middle-income groups showing a noticeable decline.

A single index of progressivity is the "tax Gini coefficient." A value of 1 indicates perfect progressivity—one rich person pays all the taxes—while a value of 0 describes a situation in which everybody pays the same absolute tax, regardless of income. The tax Gini rose from .6488 to .6560 between 1981 and 1983, a move in the direction of greater progressivity. In other words, the 1981 tax cut seems to have been successful in promoting a key part of the liberal agenda of the past half-century, namely, "redistributive justice."

All of this, of course, speaks to the great tax debate beginning now in Washington. The Treasury, Kemp-Kasten and Bradley-Gephardt proposals all continue in the spirit of the 1981 legislation, further reducing marginal tax rates, raising the rate of return on investment in both human and physical capital, and stimulating growth, fairness and administrative simplicity in the tax system. The evidence from the period 1981 to 1983 indicates that these initiatives also hold the promise of making a welcome addition to the U.S.'s long-term economic vitality.

Reprinted with permission from Richard Vedder and Lowell Gallaway, "Soaking the Rich through Tax Cuts," *Wall Street Journal*, March 21, 1985, p. 30.

**Table 15.3.** Changing Income of the Very Rich, 1981 and 1983[a]

| | AGI Reported (in millions of dollars) | | % of Total AGI | |
|---|---|---|---|---|
| Income Source | 1981 | 1983 | 1981 | 1983 |
| Rentier income[b] | $ 4,509 | $ 7,147 | 40.5 | 28.2 |
| Entrepreneurial income[c] | | | | |
| Business[d] | 329 | 4,012 | 3.0 | 15.8 |
| Financial[e] | 4,105 | 8,718 | 36.9 | 43.4 |
| Human capital[f] | 2,186 | 5,452 | 19.6 | 21.5 |
| Total entrepreneurial income | 6,620 | 18,182 | 59.5 | 71.8 |
| Total income | 11,129 | 25,329 | | |

[a] Very rich includes returns with an AGI of over $1,000,000.
[b] Dividends, interest, rent, royalty income, and estate and trust income.
[c] All income other than rentier income.
[d] Small business corporations, farms, partnerships, and business and professional income.
[e] Primarily capital gains.
[f] Wages and salaries.

they believed that the increase in national income would result from an increase in aggregate demand.)

To ensure that government does not crowd out private investment, supply-side economists often recommend eliminating "fat," "waste," and "counterproductive programs" from the federal budget. (Exactly what constitutes fat and waste varies, as you can imagine, from one economist or policymaker to another.) Budgetary deficits can also be avoided by authorizing tax rate cuts to take effect in the future, thus encouraging businesses to invest now to take advantage of lower tax rates on future income. Future productivity, production, and national income will rise, and when tax rates are actually lowered, government revenues will be no lower than they otherwise would have been.

In general, supply-side economists have opposed efforts to eliminate government deficits by increasing tax rates. Smaller deficits may mean reduced demand for lendable funds. But if tax revenues increase, the result will be a reduced supply of lendable funds. People will earn less and have less to save after taxes. Some supply-side theorists contend that a tax rate increase can only compound the deficit problem.

## Economic Need Versus Political Reality

According to many of its supporters, supply-side policy is not a quick fix, but a long-term economic plan based principally on improving incentives for investment by lowering tax rates. Its advocates do not believe that government can fine-tune the economy. Instead, they assert, time is needed to turn incentives into real plant and equipment and improved human skills. To make the needed investment, businesses and individuals must be convinced that tax rates will not only be cut, but will be held down for some time to come.

Therein lies the Achilles' heel of Reaganomics, which was grounded in a three-year tax cut package. After the tax cut, taxpayers had little reason to believe the immediate future would be any different from the immediate past. Like the so-called tax cuts of the 1970s, the Reagan cuts seemed less likely to be permanent reductions than midcourse corrections in the generally upward movement of tax rates. Since long-term growth depends on expectations about future tax rates, many people remained cautious about investing, fearing that their earnings would go up in the smoke of higher taxes.

But the needs of political leaders, who must keep their eyes on the near term and the next election, may be inconsistent with the needs of investors, who look to the long term and the after-tax return on their investments. Politicians seeking the funds to provide benefits to their constituents may take advantage of people's short-run inability to respond to tax increases. Much of taxpayers' current income may depend on past investments in physical and human capital, which are not readily changed in the short run. People will not destroy their plant and equipment or cast off their work-related skills just because tax rates rise. Thus politicians may decide to maximize short-run revenues, positioning the nation at the peak of the

## Perspectives in Economics: Flat Tax Proposals

*Thomas M. Humbert*

According to a January 1985 New York Times/CBS poll, the American public believes that the U.S. tax system is grossly unfair. An estimated half of all Americans believe they pay more than their fair share in taxes. Two out of three feel that income tax rates should be lowered and most deductions eliminated.

The current attack on the income tax system comes from throughout the political spectrum. Agreement appears widespread that loopholes in the current system, including numerous credits, deductions, exclusions, and exemptions, allow some Americans to escape paying what they should, while others face extremely high tax rates. The system may be considered unfair on two counts. First, loopholes, deductions, and credits violate the principle of horizontal equity—that taxpayers of similar income and circumstances should pay the same taxes. At the same time, they violate the principle of vertical equity—that persons of different circumstances should be taxed according to their differing ability to pay.

Supply-side economists believe that the current system is also inefficient and counterproductive. Because of all the special provisions in the tax code, marginal tax rates are much higher than they otherwise would have to be. These high marginal rates reduce the after-tax return on economic activity. They discourage work, saving, and investment and encourage taxpayers, especially those with high incomes, to seek out tax shelters and loopholes or participate in the underground economy. Business deductions, credits, and loopholes may also divert investment from heavily taxed to lightly taxed activities, distorting the flow of resources to their most productive uses. The end result is not only a less productive economy, but lower tax revenues than could be had under a more equitable tax system.

Most reformers seek a tax system that does not alter individual economic behavior. All activities would be taxed equally, so that the relative prices of leisure and labor or of savings and consumption would not change appreciably. In effect, the system would be neutral. A neutral tax system is a system that does not alter the relative prices of goods and services or of work and leisure.

Not everyone agrees on what constitutes a neutral income tax system, but many see it as a flat tax system. A flat income tax system is one in which the marginal income tax rate is constant, or the same for all income levels. It is a proportional tax system. A pure flat tax would eliminate all deductions, exemptions, and loopholes, and tax all income at the same low tax rate. Reformers estimate that a flat tax of 12 percent on all income would produce the same amount of revenue as the current system (1985), in which marginal tax rates range from 14 to 50 percent. Many supply-side theorists believe that such a tax would produce less distortion in the allocation of the nation's resources. It would also make the tax system substantially less complex and more equitable, and stimulate economic growth.

In January 1985, President Ronald Reagan responded to public criticism of the tax system by

short-run Laffer curve. In the long run, of course, taxpayers will respond to higher tax rates by reducing their investments. Such a response would mean a long-run contraction in the nation's capital stock, income, and tax revenues.

If politicians do lower tax rates, however, the short-term result can be disastrous for them. Tax revenues will drop, at least in the short term, because people will not be able to expand their investments immediately announcing his support for a "modified flat" income tax system. The modified system he proposed significantly lowered marginal income tax rates, but did not equalize tax rates. It was a progressive tax system. By early 1985, two modified flat tax plans had been introduced in Congress, and one had been recommended by the Department of the Treasury. All three plans increased both the standard deduction and exemptions for dependents, to eliminate taxation of the poor. All three retained deductions that were politically popular or promoted activities considered socially desirable, like home ownership and charitable giving. And all three plans retained the graduated tax schedule characteristic of the old tax code.

The Bradley-Gephardt plan, introduced by Senator Bill Bradley (D.-N.J.) and Congressman Richard Gephardt (D.-Mo.), broadened the tax base by eliminating many loopholes and credits. But it retained deductions for charitable giving, a limited amount of home mortgage interest, state and local income and property taxes, payments to IRA and Keogh accounts (retirement plans), and business expenses. And it proposed three marginal tax brackets: 14, 26, and 30 percent.

The Kemp-Kasten plan, introduced by Representative Jack Kemp (R.-N.Y.) and Senator Robert Kasten (R.-Wisc.), eliminated most loopholes, except deductions for home ownership, charitable giving, savings and investment, and private health insurance. Unlike the Bradley-Gephardt plan, it levied a single 24 percent tax rate on all taxpayers. But it gave lower-income families a break by doubling the size of their personal exemptions, increasing their standard deduction, and excluding 20 percent of their wages and salaries from taxation. (This exclusion would gradually be phased out.)

Why did no one propose a pure flat tax, especially when supply-side economists believed that it would stimulate economic growth? First, legislators feared that the adoption of a pure flat tax would cause a massive redistribution of the tax burden, greatly favoring the wealthy at the expense of the poor and middle classes. Second, any attempt to eliminate deductions for mortgage payments or interest on tax-exempt municipal bonds would most assuredly have been politically unpopular. It would have inflicted considerable hardship on home buyers, who had incurred heavy mortgage payments on the assumption the interest would be tax-deductible. And it would have penalized buyers of municipal bonds, who had accepted lower-than-normal rates in return for the bonds' tax-exempt status.

Thus the various modified flat tax plans proposed so far represent compromises among the conflicting goals of efficiency, simplicity, and equity. Proponents of tax reform in Congress recognize that the ideal of the flat tax is both politically difficult and economically controversial. Many strongly believe that a modified flat tax would be a substantial improvement over the current system, as well as a stimulant to the nation's economic growth.

in response to the tax cut. If government expenditures are not reduced, the result can be a larger budget deficit. Politicians may then be accused of fiscal imprudence. When the federal budget deficit reached $200 billion in the mid-1980s, after passage of the Reagan tax package, supporters of the tax cut were frequently chided for their irresponsibility. Critics reminded supply-side theorists that some of them had predicted that the tax cut would bring a smaller deficit, not a larger one. Moreover, politicians who vote for tax cuts can be accused of neglecting current social needs, since lower tax revenues restrict the government's ability to provide social services. Thus the political benefits of a tax rate cut may be available only to future political leaders.

Because of the conflict between the needs of the economy and the realities of the political system, some supply-side theorists have suggested the establishment of constitutional checks on the government's spending and taxing powers.

## Summary and Extensions

The debate between supply-side theorists and other economists hinges largely on empirical questions. How much more will people work, save, and invest in response to a specific tax rate cut for a specific number of years? Will government tax revenues go up or down in response to a tax rate cut? Will a tax rate cut raise or lower inflation in the short run and the long run? Economists have only recently begun to address these questions from the perspective of supply-side theory. Unfortunately the answers are not yet clear.

As evidence of the validity of their theory, supply-side economists point to the effect of the 1964 Kennedy tax cut package and to the rise in national income after 1982 and the Reagan tax cuts. But as we have seen, Keynesian theory attributes the rise in national income that followed those cuts to growth in aggregate demand. And monetarist theory attributes it to growth in the money stock. Because the forces of aggregate supply and demand interact, no one can be certain whether an increase in economic activity is a response to the pull of aggregate demand, as Keynesians and monetarists would contend, or to the push of aggregate supply.

Supply-side economists also point with pride to the very positive effects of state and local tax cuts in California and Puerto Rico during the 1970s. Both economies grew faster after property and income tax rates were reduced. But though many economists agree that a tax rate cut is likely to have some positive effect on growth, they differ as to how much of the growth in these economies was actually due to the tax cut. Other factors, such as changes in energy costs and in the comparative advantage of producing in those areas, may have been responsible for much of the economic growth in California and Puerto Rico.

## Major Conclusions

1. One of the most important tenets of supply-side theory is that lowering tax rates gives people an incentive to work, save, and invest more than they would otherwise. Therefore a reduction in tax rates stimulates the economy through increased production rather than increased demand.

2. Another important tenet of supply-side theory is that a cut in tax rates can alleviate unemployment by increasing people's incentives to work and employers' incentives to create jobs. A tax rate cut can also lower the inflation rate by encouraging investment, thus stimulating the economy through greater productivity and expanded production.
3. Because tax collections depend on the national income level as well as on tax rates, a reduction in tax rates can (but will not necessarily) increase tax collections. Therefore a reduction in tax rates need not force cutbacks in government programs; it might actually allow an expansion. Similarly, an increasse in tax rates will not necessarily expand government revenues; it might reduce them instead.
4. In supply-side theory, a tax rate cut will shift the short-run aggregate supply curve outward, moderating the price effect of the outward shift in the aggregate demand curve. It will also shift the long-run aggregate supply curve outward.
5. The actual consequences of supply-side policy depend on three variables: (a) the responsiveness of workers, savers, and investors to a change in the tax rates; (b) the effect of a change in the tax rates on the total tax revenues collected; and (c) the relative impact of a change in the tax rates on aggregate supply and aggregate demand, and therefore on the rate of inflation.

## Questions to Ponder

1. Keynesians contend that a reduction in tax rates will stimulate production by increasing consumption demand. Supply-side economists say that it will stimulate production by increasing the supply of labor. Is there any real difference between the two theories?
2. Why does the Laffer curve not slope continually upward toward the right, instead of eventually bending backward?
3. What happens if tax rates are lowered when an economy is on the upper half of the Laffer curve? When it is on the bottom half?
4. Suppose the nation is in a period of inflation, and you have been asked to formulate a remedy using the Keynesian model of the macroeconomy. Suppose further that the rich are taxed at very high rates, which place them on the upper portion of the Laffer curve, while the poor are taxed at very low rates, which place them on the bottom half of the Laffer curve. What would your solution be? Would your recommendations be politically acceptable?
5. List all the empirical issues involved in the Keynesian–supply-side controversy. What are the difficulties in resolving them?
6. List the current administration's tax and spending policies, and label them as monetarist, Keynesian, or supply-side.

## Central Question

*What are the basic propositions and conclusions of rational expectations theory?*

Chapter 16

# Rational Expectations

*You may fool all the people some of the time; you can even fool some of the people all the time; but you can't fool all of the people all the time.*
*Abraham Lincoln*

Keynesian theory suggests that unemployment can be alleviated by increasing government spending and/or expanding the money stock. Increased spending works directly on unemployment by increasing aggregate demand. Expansion of the money stock works indirectly by lowering interest rates, thus increasing investment demand.

Both government spending and the money stock virtually exploded during the late 1960s and early 1970s—but did not reduce unemployment as Keynesian theory would have predicted. Instead, unemployment and inflation both rose during the 1970s (see Chapter 14). That experience frustrated many economists, who believed that the validity of any science, physical or social, resided in the correctness of its predictions.

The last chapter described supply-side economists' attempts to reformulate and redirect macroeconomic theory and policy. This chapter examines rational expectations theory, another alternative to the traditional Keynesian model. To improve the predictive power of macroeconomic theory, this school emphasizes the role that expectations play in people's reactions to fiscal and monetary policy.

A cornerstone of the rational expectations theory is the assumption that people will behave rationally—an idea that underlies microeconomic theory as well. That is, people are assumed to be capable of ranking their options from most preferred to least preferred, and of acting on the basis of those priorities. They will develop expectations about the consequences of government fiscal and monetary policies, and will act on those expectations in the future. Rational expectations theorists contend that Keynesian predictions have been incorrect in the past because they did not recognize that government policies cause changes in people's expectations and behavior.

A central (and somewhat extreme) conclusion of many rational expectations models is that fiscal and monetary policy will have no effect on national income and employment, in either the short or the long run. That is, government cannot systematically control the ups and downs of the business cycle by altering its budget or the size of the money stock. People will inevitably learn to anticipate the consequences of such policies and will act to nullify them.

Before we can appreciate this theoretical innovation, we must first understand the role of expectations in traditional Keynesian thought.

## Expectations in Keynesian Theory

The Keynesian model does not ignore expectations. They play a part in determining the investment, consumption, and money demand functions.

### Investment

Expectations about the future profitability of business are critically important in determining the position and slope of the planned investment curve. In Keynesian theory, investment expenditures are inversely related

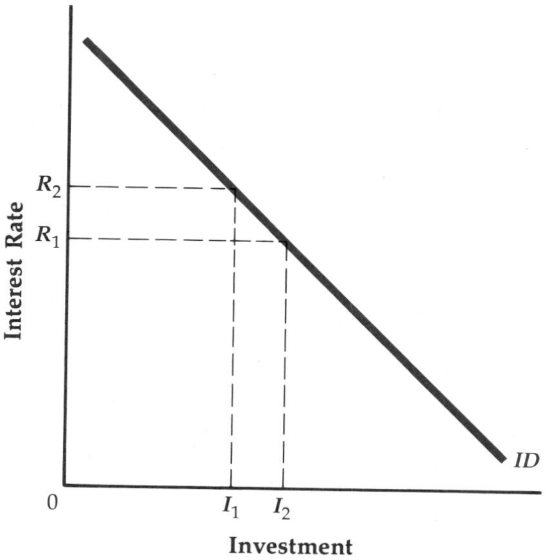


**Figure 16.1.** Investment Demand Curve.
The level of investment spending varies inversely with the interest rate. When the interest rate falls from $R_2$ to $R_1$, investment spending rises from $I_1$ to $I_2$.

to the interest rate. When the interest rate falls—for example, from $R_2$ to $R_1$ in Figure 16.1—investment spending increases, from $I_1$ to $I_2$. But the actual position of the investment demand curve, *ID*, depends on business people's assessment of the future profitability of their investment projects. The anticipated rate of return on an investment project determines whether a firm will borrow funds at prevailing interest rates.

An assumption implicit in Keynesian theory is that the investment demand curve does not change much in response to fiscal policy. Therefore when government demand rises, aggregate demand rises with it (see Figure 16.2). Keynesians do not normally consider the possibility that if government increases its deficit, business expectations may change, shifting the investment demand curve down, in the opposite direction from government demand. Investment may drop, but because of a rise in the interest rate, not a shift in investment demand. On balance, Keynesians believe, the increase in government spending will outweigh any decrease in investment, shifting the aggregate demand curve up. The national income and price levels will rise, from $Y_1$ and $P_1$ to $Y_2$ and $P_2$ in Figure 16.2.

## Consumption

Expectations also play a role in determining consumption patterns. People's consumption decisions are based not only on current income, but on expected future income. The Keynesian analysis implicitly assumes that

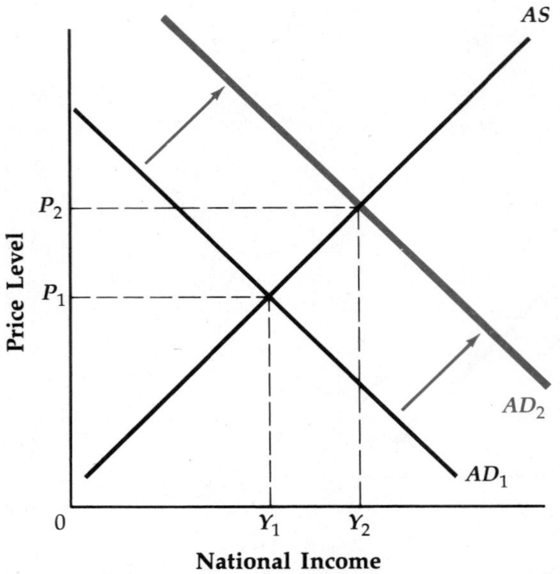


**Figure 16.2.** Fiscal Policy in the Keynesian Model.
In Keynesian theory, an increase in government spending is not fully offset by a reduction in investment and consumption spending. As a result, an increase in government spending can cause the aggregate demand curve to shift out, from $AD_1$ to $AD_2$. The national income level rises from $Y_1$ to $Y_2$, and the price level climbs from $P_1$ to $P_2$.

consumers' expectations, and therefore their consumption and saving patterns, remain more or less stable even if government fiscal and monetary policy change. In other words, when the government takes expansionary fiscal or monetary actions, the consumption function will not shift downward or upward, negating or reinforcing the effect of government policy. According to Keynesian theory, government expenditures affect consumption mainly through actual rather than anticipated changes in real income, prices, and interest rates.

## Demand for Money

Finally, expectations play a role in the construction of the Keynesian demand for money curve. When interest rates fall, more and more people begin to expect them to rise again. They hold on to their money instead of lending it. The quantity of money demanded is therefore inversely related to the interest rate. The lower the rate, the higher the quantity of money demanded. And the demand for money can be represented by a downward sloping curve, as in Figure 16.3.

The actual market interest rate is established by the stock of, and demand for, money balances. (See Chapter 12 for a review of how interest rates

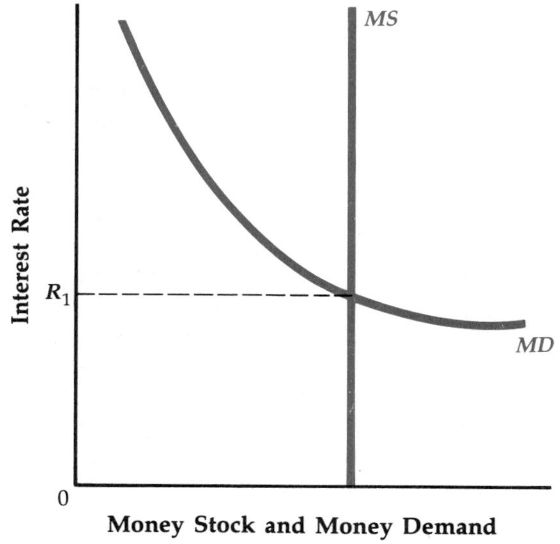


Figure 16.3. The Stock of and Demand for Money.
The money stock, *MS*, is controlled by the Federal Reserve and is more or less fixed, or vertical. The quantity of money demanded, *MD*, is inversely related to the interst rate—the higher the cost of money, the lower the demand. The market interest rate, $R_1$, is established by the intersection of the two curves.

are determined.) That is, the amount of money created by the Federal Reserve (which determines the stock or supply of money) interacts with people's expectations about future interest rates (which influence their demand for money) to determine the interest rate. In Figure 16.3, the equilibrium interest rate is $R_1$, the rate at which the money stock and demand curves intersect.

A change in expectations can change the demand for money and therefore the interest rate—which in turn can influence investment. Thus a change in expectations can be translated into a change in aggregate demand, national production, and employment. Keynesians have generally assumed, however, that the demand for money is relatively stable, at least in the short run. Hence they do not worry that government fiscal and monetary policy will be frustrated by changes in expectations that affect the demand for money.

## Rational Expectations

Rational expectations theorists argue that Keynesian thinking does not account fully for changes in people's expectations about the consequences of fiscal and monetary policy. They contend that in pursuit of their own self-interest, people will gather a rationally determined amount of information on the past consequences of government policy. Then they will act accordingly. For instance, if expansionary fiscal policy has led to higher interest rates in the past (because of the government's increased demand for borrowed funds), people will come to expect higher interest rates as a result of increased government spending, and will take steps to protect themselves. Those who have bonds will attempt to sell them, driving bond prices down and interest rates up in the process. Thus the expectation of higher interest rates leads almost immediately to higher interest rates. (A contractionary fiscal policy can have the opposite effect. People will anticipate lower interest rates, and in the process of reacting to their expectations, they will drive interest rates down.) In Keynesian terms, the demand for money curve shifts up with an increase in government spending.

Suppose, for example, that the government increases its expenditures from $G_1$ to $G_2$ in Figure 16.4(a). Because experience has taught them that greater government spending is accompanied by greater budget deficits, people begin to expect interest rates to rise. This change in expectations will cause the demand for money curve to shift upward, as in Figure 16.4(b). People are now selling their bonds at high prices, so they can hold on to greater cash balances until bond prices drop and interest rates rise. So while the increase in government expenditures increases aggregate demand, the resulting upward shift in the demand for money curve boosts the interest rate from $R_1$ to $R_2$ (Figure 16.4(b) and (c)).

As the interest rate rises, the level of investment falls from $I_2$ to $I_1$ (see Figure 16.4(c)), counteracting the rise in government spending. In this instance the decrease in business investment, $I_2 - I_1$, just balances the expansion in government spending, $G_2 - G_1$. Aggregate demand remains constant (Figure 16.4(d)), and national income and employment are unaffected by the government's action.

Similarly, people may observe that prices rise faster when the Federal Reserve increases the rate of growth of the money stock. According to rational expectations theory, if there is such an acceleration in monetary growth, they will come to expect a higher rate of inflation. Business people will buy plant and equipment now, in anticipation of higher prices later. Wage earners will push for higher wages to protect their future purchasing power. Thus the very anticipation of price increases sets in motion forces that lead to higher prices. Any lag between the adoption of an expansionary monetary policy and the resulting increase in inflation is reduced (if not eliminated altogether) by the impact of people's expectations.

Various quite different models are used by theorists working in this relatively new area. In an effort to keep their models simple, many rational expectations theorists employ unrealistic assumptions about how expectations are formed. For example, some theorists base their models on these three extreme assumptions:

No cost is involved in gathering information about the nature and structure of the economy and the consequences of fiscal and monetary policies.

Prices and wages are perfectly flexible, both upward and downward.

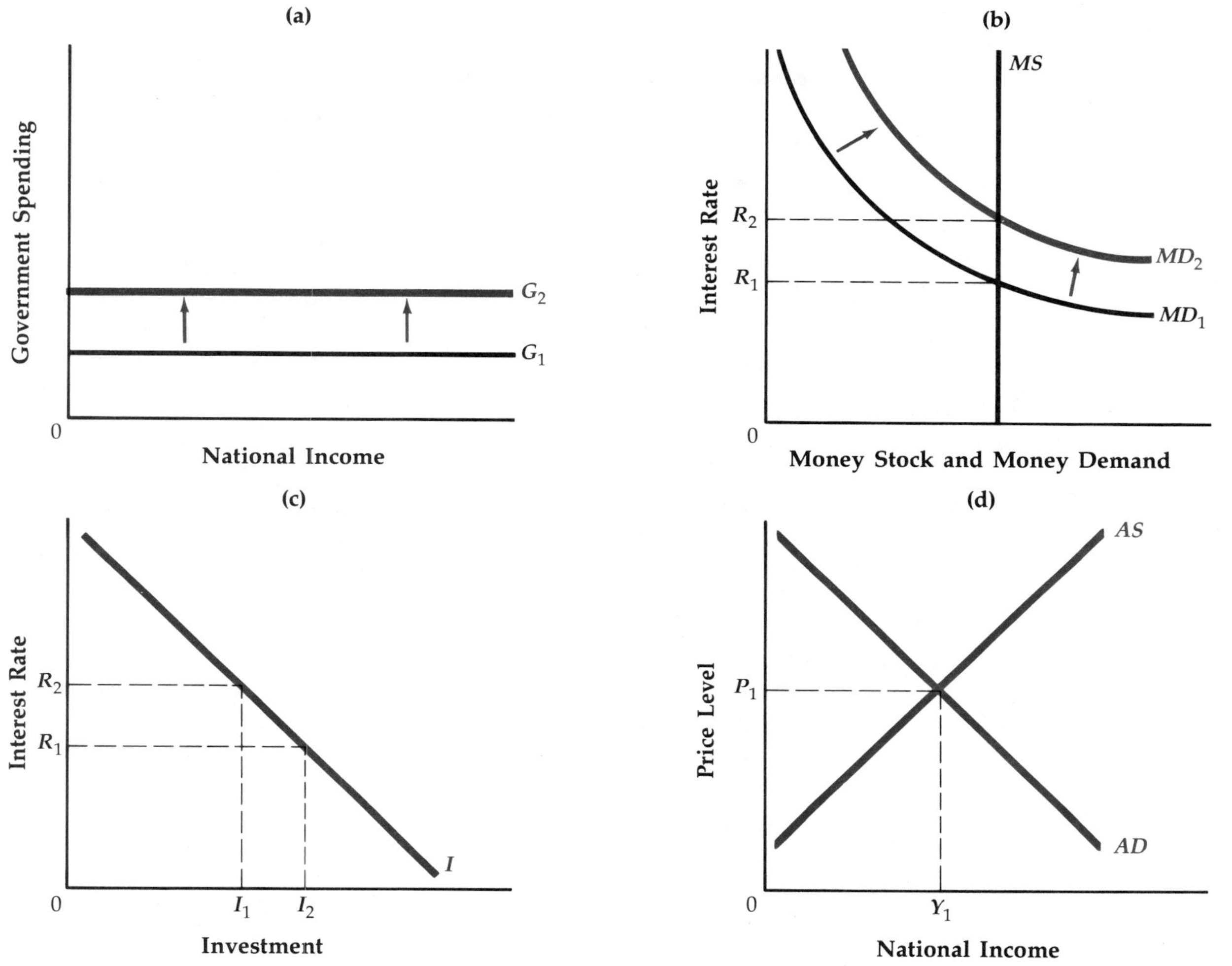


**Figure 16.4.** The Impact of Expectations on the Demand for Money.
Suppose that government increases its expenditures from $G_1$ to $G_2$ (part (a)) and runs a larger deficit or a smaller surplus than people expect. According to rational expectations theory, the demand for money curve will shift up from $MD_1$ to $MD_2$, raising the market interest rate from $R_1$ to $R_2$ (part (b)). But the higher interest rate will cause investment spending to fall from $I_2$ to $I_1$ (part (c)). The drop in investment offsets the impact of increased government spending, so that aggregate demand and supply do not change (part (d)). The nation's equilibrium price and income levels remain the same ($P_1$ and $Y_1$).

Transactions based on expectations of government policy changes and their consequences are costless.

Such assumptions make it relatively easy to conclude that people will fully and accurately anticipate the consequences of government policy, eliminating any time lag between the government action and its consequences.

Of course, in the real world, markets and people do not work with the perfection implied in these assumptions. Recognizing that discrepancy, rational expectations theorists may conclude that on average, people will fairly quickly formulate reasonably correct expectations about the consequences of government policy. Although some time may elapse between the government's action and its consequences, the lag will be much shorter than is usually assumed.

Clearly people learn from experience. The Keynesian assumption that expectations are not changed by government policies may have been a useful working hypothesis during periods like the early 1960s, when people had had relatively little experience with such policies. But when expansionary policy is pursued year after year, people will eventually begin to anticipate its consequences. When that happens, economic predictions based on constant expectations will begin to miss their mark. Before we can predict what will happen in response to fiscal and monetary policy actions, rational expectation theorists contend, we must understand one principle. People develop certain expectations based on past experience. When the rules of the game are changed, people's experience and expectations will change. When government changes its fiscal and monetary policies, it changes the rules of the game. People's expectations will change accordingly. Their behavior will be different, and so will the consequences of government policies. Indeed, once people come to understand what government is doing (or thinking of doing) to the economy, government will lose its ability to do anything to change the nation's real output and employment levels.

## Rational Expectations Theory from Other Perspectives

We have seen that rationally determined expectations can nullify the intended effect of government policy. To understand the principles of individual behavior that lie behind the phenomenon, we must return to monetarist theory.

In Chapter 14 we observed that the quantity of labor demanded and supplied is related to the real wage, $W/P$ (see Figure 16.5). Assuming that the market clears at the intersection of the labor supply and demand curves, the equilibrium real wage rate will be $(W/P)_2$ and the equilibrium employment level will be $Q_1$. As we saw in Chapter 14 (pages 313–317), more rapid growth in the money stock will accelerate inflation. If prices rise faster than money wages, the real wage rate will fall, and employers will want to hire more workers. That is what happens in Figure 16.5. The real wage rate falls from $(W/P)_2$ to $(W/P)_1$, and employers increase employment from $Q_1$ to $Q_2$. As long as workers believe (incorrectly) that the increases in their money wages are increases in their real wages—that the real wage has gone *up,* to $(W/P)_3$—the quantity of labor supplied will expand from $Q_1$ to $Q_2$.

The resulting increase in employment will reduce the unemployment rate and increase real output. But once workers realize that their real wage

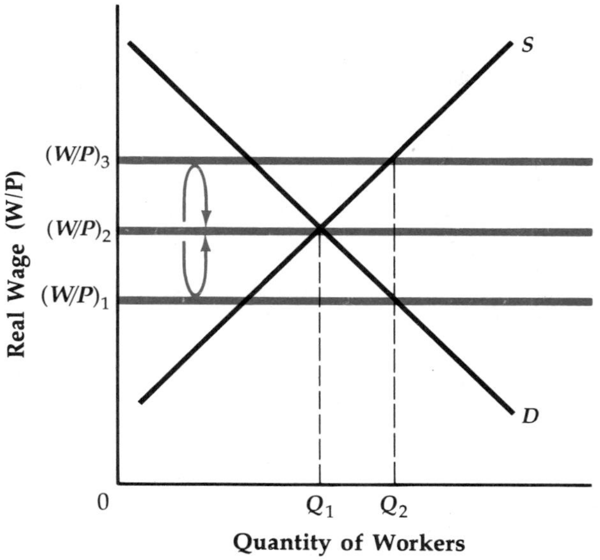


Figure 16.5. The Effect of Expansionary Monetary Policy on the Labor Market. Suppose an expansion in the money stock increases the price level. If employers interpret the increase as a reduction in the real wage, from $(W/P)_2$ to $(W/P)_1$, they will expand the quantity of labor they demand, from $Q_1$ to $Q_2$. As long as workers interpret the resulting rise in their money wage as an increase in real wages, from $(W/P)_2$ to $(W/P)_3$, the quantity of labor supplied will also rise, from $Q_1$ to $Q_2$. The national output and income levels will rise. But in rational expectations theory, workers and employers are not fooled by inflation. Almost immediately wages will adjust to account for price increases, so that the real wage remains at $(W/P)_2$. Thus the quantity of labor employed will remain $Q_1$, and national output and income will not expand.

has actually declined to $(W/P)_1$, they will demand higher money wages. The real wage will climb back up to $(W/P)_2$, negating the effects of the government-induced monetary expansion. Thus expansionary monetary policy can succeed only in the short run.

This process produces a long-run Phillips curve that is vertical rather than downward sloping (see Figure 16.6). When the inflation rate rises from $IR_1$ to $IR_2$, workers may at first be fooled into taking jobs at the lower real wage. Unemployment will drop from $U_2$ to $U_1$. But when workers realize that the real wage has fallen, they will begin to turn down jobs offered at that rate. The unemployment rate will return to its previous level, $U_2$. Once workers have learned to anticipate the effects of monetary expansion, the Phillips curve will be vertical even in the short run.

Thus monetarists draw essentially the same conclusion as rational expectations theorists. The main difference between the two schools of thought lies in the speed of the adjustment process. According to rational expectations theory, people will learn to react very quickly, if not immediately, anticipating higher prices and interest rates as a result of expansionary fiscal and monetary policy. Instead of moving back along the

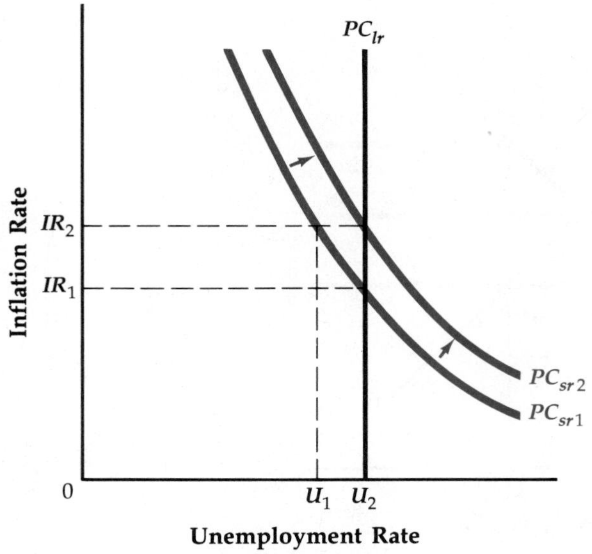


**Figure 16.6.** The Effect of Expansionary Monetary Policy on Unemployment. In Keynesian and monetarist theory, an increase in the inflation rate can move the economy up along the short-run Phillips curve $PC_{sr1}$, reducing the unemployment rate from $U_2$ to $U_1$. But in rational expectations theory, wages adjust immediately or almost immediately to the increase, shifting the Phillips curve from $PC_{sr1}$ to $PC_{sr2}$. The economy moves straight up along its vertical long-run Phillips curve, $PC_{lr}$, and the unemployment rate remains at $U_2$.

short-run Phillips curve $PC_{sr1}$ in Figure 16.6, the economy will move straight up the vertical long-run Phillips curve almost immediately. In other words, the short-run Phillips curve is also vertical, or practically so. And instead of the gradual rise in interest rates and fall in investment spending predicted by the monetarists, rational expectations theorists forecast that the change in expectations underlying the money and investment demands will bring an almost immediate, if not instantaneous, rise in interest rates and fall in investment.

Rational expectations theory can also be seen in terms of aggregate supply and demand. So long as workers are deceived by an increase in the price level from $P_1$ to $P_2$ in Figure 16.7, employment will increase, shifting the aggregate demand curve from $AD_1$ to $AD_2$. National income will rise from $Y_1$ to $Y_2$. But as soon as workers wake up and demand higher wages, the aggregate supply curve will shift to the left, from $AS_1$ to $AS_2$. National income will return to $Y_1$ as producers cut back on production because of higher wages. Again, the monetarist and rational expectations views differ primarily as to the amount of time required for the adjustment. Monetarists tend to argue that people can be fooled for a short period of time. Rational expectations theorists argue that the downward adjustment of aggregate supply is immediate, or almost immediate.

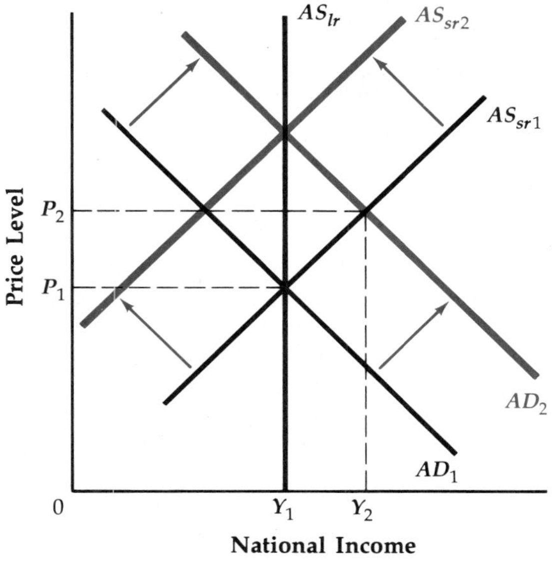


**Figure 16.7.** The Effect of Expansionary Monetary Policy on Aggregate Supply and Demand.
The increased consumption and investment spending caused by an expansionary monetary policy will shift aggregate demand from $AD_1$ to $AD_2$. The price level will rise from $P_1$ to $P_2$; and so long as workers are fooled into believing their real wages have risen, the national output level will rise from $Y_1$ to $Y_2$. Rational expectations theorists contend, however, that monetary policy will be ineffective once people have learned that an expansionary monetary policy leads to a higher price level. Workers will demand higher wages, shifting the aggregate supply curve in from $AS_{sr1}$ to $AS_{sr2}$ almost immediately. The result will be virtually no change in the national income level. In rational expectations theory, the short-run aggregate supply curve is almost vertical, like the long-run aggregate supply curve ($AS_{lr}$) in monetarist theory.

According to rational expectations theorists, the short-run aggregate supply curve is virtually vertical, just like the monetarists' long-run aggregate supply curve.

Thus the expansionary fiscal and monetary policy of the late 1960s and 1970s failed to reduce unemployment, because people anticipated and reacted to it, nullifying its effects. After only a few years of Keynesian fiscal policy, the government had played its hand too long. Some theorists argue that the same phenomenon explains the high real interest rates of the early and mid-1980s. People had learned to associate high federal deficits with high inflation and interest rates. Watching the deficit increase under President Reagan, they moved to protect themselves against another resurgence of inflation, in part by demanding high interest rates for their money. Like Lincoln, rational expectations theorists stress that you can't fool all of the people all the time.

# Perspectives in Economics: Is the Federal Deficit a Burden?

*Robert J. Barro*

Everyone's talking about "large" recent budget deficits. In fact, the consensus is that the federal government's first priority should be to reduce the deficit. But be suspicious of this type of consensus: The last time I remember one this strong was in 1971 when every sensible person was supposed to believe that wage-price controls were a good idea. The current popular view on deficits falls into the same category—it is incorrect and is also likely to be discarded within a couple of years.

The appropriate first question is, how do today's deficits relate to history? Recent deficits—currently about 4%–5% of gross national product, or about $170 billion for fiscal 1984—are in line with what we would expect from experience, given the state of the economy. And they're in line with what we ought to be running. Under current conditions, I would be concerned if the deficit were either much larger or much smaller than it is.

Past U.S. deficits have had three main elements. The first is temporary federal expenditures, which arise primarily in wartime. In these cases a large budget deficit lessens the need to raise tax rates on a temporary basis. Since high tax rates blunt the incentives that help the economy deal with a war or other emergency, these kinds of deficits are a good idea. Wartime finance has, in fact, been the principal long-run source of the stock of public debt in the U.S. and other industrialized countries. But this factor has not been a consideration in recent years.

The second element is the business cycle. The federal deficit rises during recessions in order to avoid either large increases in tax rates or major cuts in government expenditures at these times. This process is well known and underlies the construction of a full-employment deficit (which attempts to filter out the part of the deficit or surplus that derives from the business cycle). This element was the most important source of the budget deficits during the recessions of 1975–76 and 1980–83. Despite the strong recovery since early 1983, the continuing effect of the last recession still matters for the current deficit. I estimate that the remaining shortage of output below the full-employment level accounted for about $60 billion out of the total deficit of $170 billion for fiscal 1984.

The third item is net federal interest payments, which totaled $111 billion for fiscal 1984. This element, which was of minor significance until the rise of inflation in the late 1960s, has become the key force behind current budget deficits. The question is, how much of interest payments should be financed by a deficit rather than by higher taxes?

One part that is reasonable to finance by a deficit is that corresponding to expected inflation. If the government pays for this part with new debt, then—on this count—it just plans for a constant real debt over time. Using an estimate for expected inflation of 6% for 1984 (somewhat above the actual rate), the resulting contribution to the deficit was 6% times a stock of debt of about $1.2 trillion, or $70 billion–$75 billion.

A second element of interest payments appropriate to finance by a deficit is that corresponding to temporarily high real interest rates. These payments are analogous to other types of temporarily high government expenditures—such as wartime spending—that call for a deficit rather than an increase in taxes. In this way the government avoids unnecessary fluctuations in tax rates over time. I estimate that this component accounted for about 2½% (excess of current real interest rates above normal) times $1.2 trillion of debt, or roughly $30 billion of the fiscal 1984 deficit.

Overall, it was reasonable to finance about $100 billion–$105 billion of interest payments by a deficit. Adding in the $60 billion contribution from the residual effects of the recession leads to a total of $160 billion–$165 billion, or almost all of the actual figure of $170 billion.

The historical view of deficits and the accounting for the present situation also tell us what to expect for the future. Basically, deficits will fall greatly in fiscal years 1985 and 1986 only if there is rapid economic growth or if there are substantial declines in interest rates. Typical forecasts of these variables lead to projections of budget deficits for both years of about $170 billion, the same as in 1984. The potential for economic growth to reduce deficits below this figure is limited to about $60 billion, which is the contribution of prior recessions to the 1984 deficit. Thus, the main element that could reduce the deficit further is lower interest rates, whether because of reduced inflationary expectations or decreased real interest rates.

My forecast of a budget deficit of $170 billion for fiscal 1986 contrasts with the Congressional Budget Office's estimate last summer of $200 billion–$210 billion (the figure has been revised upward, but new accounting procedures and growth projections make the old number more appropriate for this comparative analysis). Basically, the CBO projection is for given spending and tax programs, whereas my forecast factors in the likely congressional responses. In other words, I see some combination of cuts in spending or increases in taxes that will total $30 billion–$40 billion for 1986.

It should be clear that there is a major interplay between recessions, interest rates and inflation on the one hand, and federal budget deficits on the other hand. But the channel that has been documented is from the economic variables to the deficit, and not the reverse. For example, recessions cause deficits (as is well known), but there is no evidence that shifts in the deficit have important effects on economic activity. Notably, the large deficits for 1983–84 did not prevent a strong investment-led economic recovery.

Similarly, an increase in interest rates (when it reflects either higher expected inflation or a temporary increase in real rates) can lead to a larger deficit. But, despite the efforts of many researchers to detect it, there is no evidence that shifts in deficits lead to higher interest rates, especially to the higher real rates that would deter investment.

The strongly held popular view is that large budget deficits—and the consequent rise in the real stock of public debt—tend to raise real interest rates and thereby crowd out private investment. Basically, this crowding-out view of deficits is a myth, which is reinforced mainly by repetition. It isn't supported by economic theory or empirical investigation.

In light of what has caused our recent deficits, and what they themselves are unlikely to cause, the national mania these days is rather hard to justify.

Robert J. Barro, "A Deficit Nearly on Target," *Wall Street Journal*, January 30, 1985, editorial page.

## Problems with Rational Expectations Theory

Although it is supported by the monetarist and aggregate demand and supply models, rational expectations theory and its implications are disputed by many economists. Several criticisms must be noted. The first two concern the extreme nature of the assumptions underlying rational expectations theory.

### The Cost of Acquiring Information

Critics point out that rational expectations theory expects too much of people. Economists spend years studying and modeling the macroeconomy and still cannot accurately predict the timing and impact of government policy, they observe. How then can ordinary people be expected to make such predictions, virtually without cost or delay? Though this criticism may reflect the wounded professional dignity of economists, it is also consistent with common sense. In an imperfect world, adjustment to government policy may not be as costless, accurate, and rational as rational expectations theorists assume.

Because of the cost of obtaining information on economic conditions, people do not become perfectly informed. As a result they sometimes over- or underestimate the consequences of government policy actions. Thus an expansion in the money stock could have a perverse effect: an increase in labor's wage demands, a reduction in employment, and a contraction in national income. Or the opposite could occur. That is, fiscal policy could have some temporary positive effect on employment and national income. Because of miscalculations and the time lags required to correct them, government fiscal and monetary policy can have at least some short-run effects on employment and national income. Policy need not be completely impotent, say critics of rational expectations theory.

### Rational Ignorance

Rational expectations theory assumes that it is in people's self-interest to become aware of government policy. If government takes fiscal and monetary actions to influence citizens' welfare, people should have the necessary incentive to understand what government is doing. But critics stress that the macroeconomy is terribly complex, and that individuals have little incentive to keep abreast of government actions. One person can do little to influence the outcome of government policy. To varying degrees, people may be rationally ignorant about government policy—especially economic policy, a comparatively technical subject.

Rational expectations theorists counter that it is not necessary to assume that everyone keeps abreast of government policy. Just a few people may adjust their expectations in response to government actions. Their response will produce a change in pricing signals, which will lead others to adjust their behavior. But the criticism is still relevant. If prices must be adjusted and then readjusted, for a short period at least, people are effectively fooled. Government fiscal and monetary actions can therefore have some short-run effect.

## Changes in the Composition of National Output

Many rational expectations theorists conclude that fiscal and monetary policy has neither short-run nor long-run effects. But critics protest that if government actions change the composition of demand and the relative prices of goods and services, they necessarily affect the composition of the nation's output. For instance, expansionary fiscal policy can produce more government goods and services and fewer private goods and services, including private investment. Expansionary monetary policy can lower interest rates (at least in the short run), thus increasing investment. Such changes in the composition of output necessarily have a long-run effect on the national output level. For example, a reduction in private investment because of greater government spending can mean a reduction in the nation's future capital stock, productivity, and income level.

Many rational expectations theorists accept this criticism. Their point is that, contrary to Keynesian analysis, government cannot systematically influence the employment and production levels by managing aggregate demand.

## Contract and Wage Rigidities

Many rational expectations models assume that prices and wages are perfectly flexible. But there are many institutional rigidities in the real-world pricing system. Many producers, for instance, are bound by labor contracts that strictly prohibit wage and price adjustments for certain periods of time. As a result, wages cannot always be raised in response to a higher inflation rate. At least temporarily, real wages can fall while employment and national production expand.

To this criticism, rational expectations theorists may reply that experience will teach labor leaders to develop contracts that permit wage adjustments for inflation, including clauses for automatic cost-of-living increases.

# Summary and Extensions

Rational expectations theory is relatively new; only in the last several years has it received much attention. Because the theory is new, economists are still working to develop it and to test its usefulness in improving macroeconomic prediction. Many questions remain unsettled. For instance:

Why would a government devise a macroeconomic policy if it would not (and people knew it would not) have any effect on the economy?

Do government policymakers overestimate their own power?

How is economic information transmitted in the macroeconomy?

## *Perspectives in Economics: Expectations and the Effects of Federal Deficits*

*William F. Shughart II*

Almost two centuries ago the British economist David Ricardo (1772–1823) suggested that government expenditures will have the same effect on an economy whether the funds are raised through taxes or through deficit spending (borrowing). Ricardo's theorem is still debated among economists. It is especially controversial today, both because of the emergence of rational expectations theory and because the federal deficit is projected to run from $200 to $250 billion a year for the rest of the decade.

How do expectations influence the economy's response to a budget deficit? Deficit spending implies that the government will eventually have to raise taxes to pay off its creditors. Ricardo proposed that individuals will react to the expectation of higher future taxes just as they would to an increase in current taxes. Others have argued that individuals do not respond to deficits as they do to taxes. Instead, they see deficit spending as a way of shifting part of their tax liability to future generations. Whether or not one should be concerned about deficits depends, obviously, on which of these two views one subscribes to.

Suppose the government decides to increase spending this year by $1, but will return to its former level of spending next year, and each year thereafter. This year's extra spending could be financed by imposing a $1 tax surcharge this year. Taxpayers would then have $1 less to spend as they wished, but the government's budget would remain balanced.

Alternatively the government could pay for this year's extra spending by running a budget deficit. That is, the government would borrow $1 by issuing a bond on which the principal plus interest is due some time in the future. To keep the example simple, assume the loan would be repaid in one year. Although current taxes would not go up, next year's taxes would have to rise enough to cover the $1 of principal plus the interest on the bond, *r*. And the public would be aware of the impending increase.

Taxpayers could meet their increased future liability by buying a $1 bond that pays the same interest rate as the government's, *r*. By sellng the bond next year, they would have just enough money—1 + r—to pay their taxes. As in the first case, they would be one dollar poorer this year. Therefore the extra dollar's worth of public spending would have the same effect whether it is financed by raising taxes or by running a deficit.

Needless to say, these questions cannot be fully answered here. Refinements in theory can be expected with time, and tentative answers will be devised. For now, many see rational expectations as a rather sterile and unrealistic theory. It has made one important contribution to our understanding of government policy, however. That is the observation that the effectiveness of fiscal and monetary policy depend partly on the extent to which people correctly anticipate the impact of government policy and react accordingly. Insofar as government fiscal and monetary policy is effective, people have been fooled. The real value of rational expectations theory may lie in improved predictions and better understanding of the limits of government policy.

Of course, the government does not normally promise to repay the funds it borrows in one year. Government securities usually mature in four, ten, or even twenty years. In fact, the government can borrow money indefinitely, simply by issuing a new bond to pay off an old one when it comes due (a practice known as "rolling over" debt). In this way the government can delay repaying the principal, but it will still have to raise taxes enough to meet the interest payments on its debt.

Suppose, for instance, that a $1 increase in spending is financed by a bond that the government does not intend to retire when it matures. In that case, taxes in each future year must be higher by the amount of the interest, *r*. But again, taxpayers can meet their future tax liability by buying $1 worth of bonds this year. The *r* dollars in interest income they receive in each subsequent year will pay for their extra taxes. Ricardo's theorem still holds. The effect is the same whether the government raises taxes or borrows money to cover its extra spending.

But taxpayers do not live forever. Can they be expected to act as if they will? Some economists think that a concern for the welfare of their children would lead taxpayers to plan beyond their own lifetimes. They would make up for any tax burden the government imposed on their children by giving them larger inheritances. Otherwise part of their tax burden would be shifted to future generations.

Recent evidence suggests that the assumption that taxpayers would plan beyond their lifetimes may be wrong. An analysis of eighty-three federal budgets from 1900 through 1982 shows that holding other things constant (such as the size of government, interest payments on existing debt, and economic growth), increases in the average lifespan are associated with declines in deficit spending. In other words, individuals may prefer deficits to taxes if they do not expect to be living when the government's bonds mature. If so, deficit spending may well be the equivalent of a tax on future generations. As such, it will reduce the amount of capital future generations will inherit, benefiting the living at the expense of those yet to be born.

Adapted from W. F. Shughart II and R. D. Tollison, "A Contingent Liability Theory of Deficit Finance," manuscript, January 1985.

## Major Conclusions

1. In Keynesian economics, expectations underlie the investment, consumption, and money demand curves. But Keynesians tend to assume that changes in people's expectations do not entirely offset the impact of fiscal and monetary policy on aggregate demand.
2. Rational expectations theory assumes that people will acquire information on the consequences of government fiscal and monetary policy, and will act on that information. The aquisition of information will change people's expectations for the future, altering the effectiveness of government policies.
3. In its strictest and most extreme form, rational expectations theory assumes that prices and wages are completely flexible; that the acqui-

sition of information on government policy is costless; and that adjustments based on changed expectations of the results of government policy are also costless. Given these assumptions, rational expectations theorists conclude that government fiscal and monetary policy will be completely ineffective, both in the short run and in the long run.

4. Both monetarists and rational expectations theorists conclude that fiscal and monetary policy will have no long-run effect on the national income level. Monetarists believe, however, that fiscal and monetary policy may have a short-run effect on the national income level. Rational expectations theorists argue that even the short-run effect is practically nil.
5. Criticism of rational expectations theory focuses on the assumptions that underlie it. Critics contend that information is costly to acquire and that citizens have an incentive to remain ignorant of government policy. Some delay between the initiation of government fiscal or monetary policy and its impact on prices and interest rates must therefore be expected. Critics charge too that fiscal and monetary policies alter the composition of the nation's output—between public and private goods, between investment and consumption goods—and thus affect production and national income in the long run. Finally, critics point out that

prices are not perfectly flexible. Labor contracts often fix wages, creating a time lag within which government policy can have some effect.

## Questions to Ponder

1. This chapter focused on the effects of expansionary fiscal and monetary policies. What should be the effects of contractionary fiscal and monetary policies (a) when they are not expected and (b) when they are expected?
2. Suppose the marginal cost of acquiring information increases as more information is obtained. How would the increasing cost of information affect the theory of rational expectations?
3. Suppose money wages cannot be adjusted downward and the real wage is consequently held above equilibrium. With the aid of a graph, explain how an expansionary fiscal policy would affect employment (a) if its consequences were expected and (b) if its consequences were not fully expected.
4. We have discussed four commonly cited objections to rational expectations theory. Can you think of any others?
5. How do expectations figure in Keynesian theory?
6. How do monetarism and rational expectations theory differ?

# Part VI

# The International Economy

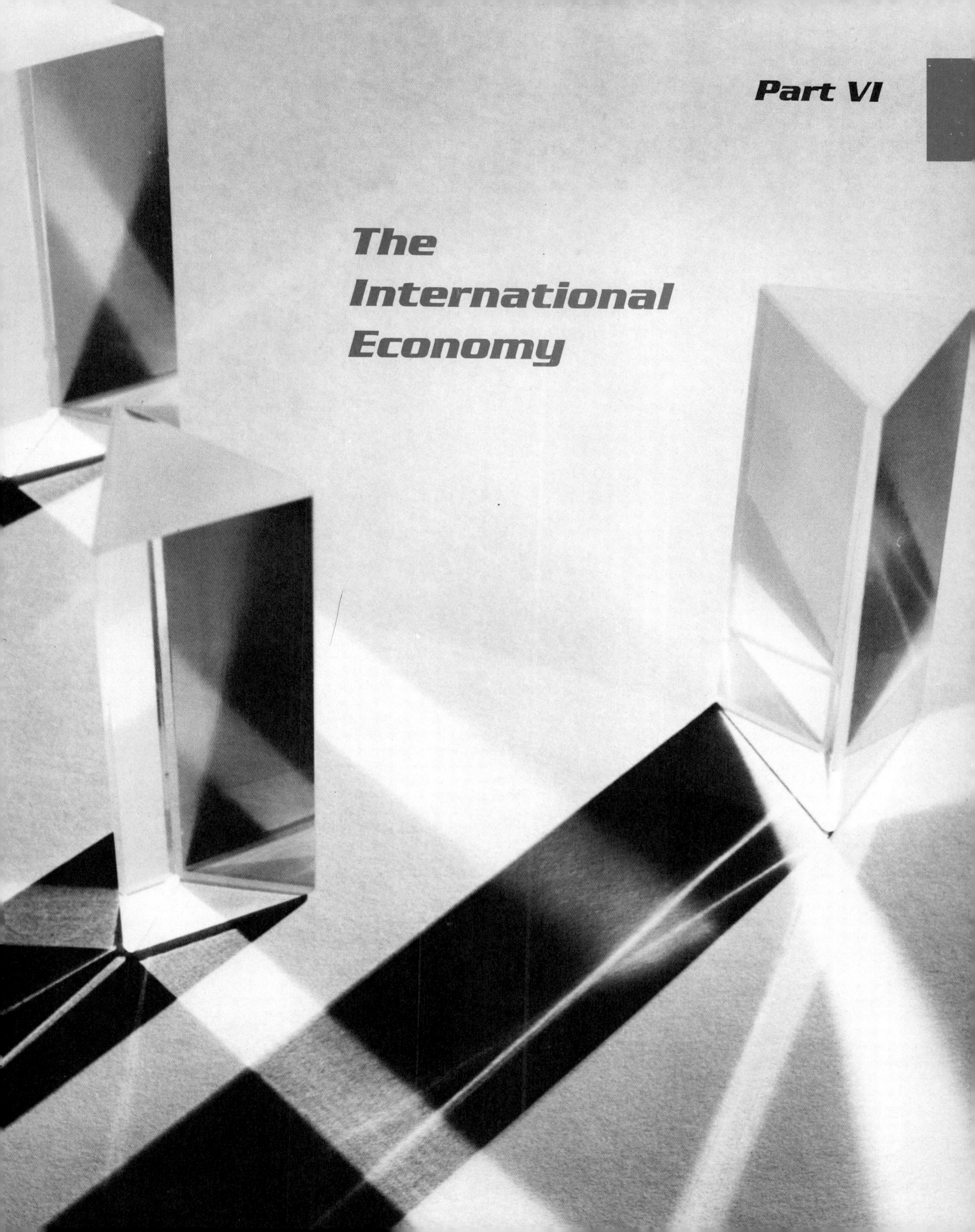

## Central Question

*How and to what extent do nations benefit from international trade?*

## Key Terms

International balance of payments
Merchandise trade balance
Current account
Current account deficit
Current account surplus
Capital account
Capital account surplus
Capital account deficit
Absolute advantage
Merchandise trade surplus
Merchandise trade deficit
Tariff
Quota

Chapter 17

# International Trade

*It can be of no consequence to America, whether the commodities she obtains in return for her own, cost Europeans much, or little labor; all she is interested in, is that they shall cost her less labor by purchasing than by manufacturing them herself.*
David Ricardo

Nations never really trade; people do. This simple point is important, for it allows us to approach international trade as an extension of models already developed, rather than a completely new topic. Earlier discussions focused on the local or national marketplace. In this and the following chapter, our marketplace will be the world.

Of course, there are differences between international and domestic trade—enough to make international economics an important subdiscipline of the profession. Some differences are obvious, like the many different national currencies involved in international exchange. Others go largely unrecognized. An intangible but significant factor is the difference in people's attitudes toward domestic and international trade. As Abraham Lincoln is supposed to have said, "Domestic trade is among us; international trade is between us and them." Yet people all over the world trade with each other for the same reason: they stand to gain from the transaction.

Understanding that trade is between people, not nations, is important for another reason. If we focus solely on gains from trade to nations, we may overlook the distributional effects of international commerce—the gains and losses to individuals. As we will see, while international trade increases a nation's total income, it reduces some individuals' incomes and increases others'. To evaluate objections to free trade among nations in proper perspective, we must recognize these hidden gains and losses.

Objections to free trade can be explained easily in terms of market theory. A major principle of economic theory is that each individual competitor has a vested interest in reducing competition. Competition forces product prices down and spurs product development, restricting business income. Thus it is natural for domestic firms to seek protection from their foreign competitors. But protection only increases the prices consumers must pay. Carried to an extreme, protection based on the narrow interests of particular sectors of the economy can reduce everyone's income. On this basis rests the case for free international trade.

After examining the advantages of international trade from a purely national perspective, we will look at the distributional, or individual, effects. The chapter closes with a discussion of the pros and cons of protectionism.

**International balance of payments:** a summary statement of all international transactions between one nation—for example, the United States—and the rest of the world.

**Merchandise trade balance:** the difference between the dollar value of goods—raw materials, agricultural and manufactured products, and capital and consumer products—imported and exported.

## Collective Gains from Trade

The benefits of international commerce to the United States are revealed in the international balance of payments statistics. The **international balance of payments** is a summary statement of all international transactions between one nation—for example, the United States—and the rest of the world. International transactions include exports and imports of goods, services, gifts, interest and dividend payments, and travel expenditures, as well as the flows of financial capital (purchases of stocks and bonds and real capital assets) across national boundaries. The bulk of the United States' international transactions are exports and imports, which are summarized in the merchandise trade balance. The **merchandise trade balance** is the difference between the dollar value of goods (raw materials,

**Table 17.1.** International Transactions, 1983 (in billions of dollars)

| | |
|---|---|
| Merchandise trade | |
| Exports | $200.3 |
| Imports | −261.3 |
| Investment income | |
| Receipts | 77.0 |
| Payments | −53.5 |
| Net military transactions | .5 |
| Net travel | −4.6 |
| Other services | 8.7 |
| *Balance on goods and services* | −$32.9 |
| Remittances, pensions, and gifts | −8.7 |
| *Balance on current account* | −$41.6 |
| International capital flows | |
| U.S. investments abroad (capital outflows) | −$49.5 |
| Foreign investments in the United States | 81.7 |
| *Balance on capital account* | $32.3 |
| Statistical discrepancy | 9.3 |
| *Balance of current account, capital account, and statistical discrepancy* | $ 0.0 |

**Source:** *Economic Report of the President* (Washington, D.C.: U.S. Government Printing Office, 1985), pp. 344, 345.

agricultural and manufactured products, and capital and consumer products) imported and exported. In 1983 the United States exported goods and services valued at $200.3 billion, or approximately 6 percent of its GNP (see Table 17.1). It imported $261.3 billion worth of goods and services, or almost 8 percent of its total production. Imports exceeded exports by $61 billion.

The difference between exports and imports was offset by other international transactions. In 1983 Americans received approximately $77 billion in interest and dividends from investments in foreign nations. Foreigners, on the other hand, received only about $53.5 billion in interest and dividends from investments in American businesses and securities. American tourists spent $4.6 billion more abroad than foreign tourists spent here. But "other services" sold to foreigners exceeded "other services" to Americans by $8.7 billion. When remittances, pensions, and gifts were added, the United States had a current account deficit equal to $41.6 billion.

The **current account** is the record of all the nation's international transactions other than capital flows and statistical discrepancies, including its merchandise trade, its investment income, its military transactions, its travel expenditures, its other services, and its remittances, pensions, and gifts. A **current account deficit** is the dollar amount by which a nation's

**Current account:** the record of all the nation's international transactions other than capital flows and statistical discrepancies, including its merchandise trade, its investment income, its military transactions, its travel expenditures, its other services, and its remittances, pensions, and gifts.

**Current account deficit:** the dollar amount by which a nation's imports of goods and services, interest and dividend payments to foreigners, gifts to foreigners, travel expenditures abroad, and other remittances to foreign nations exceed its exports of goods and services, interest and dividend receipts from foreign nations, gifts from abroad, foreign travel expenditures in this nation, and other remittances from abroad.

**Current account surplus:** the dollar amount by which a nation's exports of goods and services, interest and dividend receipts from foreigners, gifts from foreigners, foreign travel expenditures in this nation, and other receipts from abroad exceed the nation's imports of goods and services, interest and dividend payments to foreigners, gifts to foreigners, travel expenditures abroad, and other remittances to foreign nations.

**Capital account:** the record of U.S. investments abroad and foreign investments in the United States.

**Capital account surplus:** the dollar amount by which foreign investments in the United States—that is, capital inflows—exceed U.S. investments abroad—that is, capital outflows.

**Capital account deficit:** the dollar amount by which U.S. investments abroad—that is, capital outflows—exceed foreign investments in the United States—that is, capital inflows.

imports of goods and services, interest and dividend payments to foreigners, gifts to foreigners, travel expenditures abroad, and other remittances to foreign nations exceed its exports of goods and services, interest and dividend receipts from foreign nations, gifts from abroad, foreign travel expenditures in this nation, and other remittances from abroad. In contrast to the 1980s, during the 1960s and 1970s, the United States frequently ran a current account surplus. A **current account surplus** is the dollar amount by which a nation's exports of goods and services, interest and dividend receipts from foreigners, gifts from foreigners, foreign travel expenditures in this nation, and other receipts from abroad exceed the nation's imports of goods and services, interest and dividend payments to foreigners, gifts to foreigners, travel expenditures abroad, and other remittances to foreign nations.

Part of the income received from the sale of American goods abroad went into purchases of foreign stocks and bonds and overseas investment by U.S. firms. Such investments are not included in current account statistics, because they are not imports. Instead, they are included in the nation's capital account. The **capital account** is the record of U.S. investments abroad and foreign investments in the United States. In 1983 Americans invested $49.5 billion abroad, while foreigners invested $81.7 billion here. Thus the nation ran a capital account surplus of $32.3 billion. A **capital account surplus** is the dollar amount by which foreign investments in the United States—that is, capital inflows—exceed U.S. investments abroad—that is, capital outflows. In contrast to the 1980s, during the 1960s and 1970s, the United States frequently ran a capital account deficit. A **capital account deficit** is the dollar amount by which U.S. investments abroad—that is, capital outflows—exceed foreign investments in the United States—that is, capital inflows.

Many of the imports Americans bought were finished products like automobiles and television sets, their Japanese or German origins clearly identified. Other imports were raw materials, like crude oil and tin, or parts used in the production of other goods, like transistors and auto parts. Some of the imported raw materials were used to make products that were ultimately exported to other countries. More will be said about export-import balances in the following chapter. The point here is that all these international transactions were undertaken for mutual gain. Americans who bought foreign goods did so because they offered a better price-quality package than their U.S. counterparts. Americans who invested in foreign countries did so because they expected to earn a higher rate of return than would be possible on U.S. properties.

The gains from international trade are clearest when there is no domestic substitute for an imported good. For example, the United States does not have any known reserves of chromium, manganese, or tin. For those basic resources, which are widely used in manufacturing, American firms must rely on foreign suppliers. The gains from trade are also clear for goods that are very costly or difficult to produce in the United States. For example, cocoa and coffee can be raised in the United States, but only in a greenhouse. Obviously it is less costly to import coffee in exchange for some other good, like wheat, for which the U.S. climate is better suited.

Foreign competition also offers benefits to the American consumer. By challenging the market power of domestic firms, foreign producers who market their goods in the United States reduce product prices and expand domestic consumption. Foreign competition also increases the variety of goods available. Without competition from the twenty or more foreign automobile producers who sell in the American market, the three or four U.S. automakers would each get a much larger percentage of the market. They would be less hesitant to raise their prices if consumers had fewer alternative sources of supply. Collusion among major manufacturers would also be much more likely without the presence of foreign competitors.

International trade also promotes specialization, whose benefits are fairly clear. By concentrating on producing a small number of goods and selling to the world market, a nation can reap the benefits of greater efficiency and economies of scale. Resource savings that are not obvious at first may be gained. Indeed, after considering the following example, some readers may doubt that international trade can be mutually beneficial.

Consider a world in which only two nations, the United States and Japan, produce only two goods, textiles and beef. Assume that the United States produces both textiles and beef more efficiently than Japan. That is, with the same resources, the United States can produce more beef and more textiles than Japan can. It has an absolute advantage in the production of both goods. An **absolute advantage** in production is the capacity to produce more units of output than a competitor can for any given level of resource use.

**Absolute advantage:** the capacity to produce more units of output than a competitor can for any given level of resource use.

Table 17.2 shows such a situation. With the same labor, capital, and other resources, the United States can produce thirty units of textiles; Japan can produce twenty-five. If the same resources are applied to beef production, the United States still outproduces Japan, by ninety units to twenty-five. Under such conditions, one might think that trade with Japan could not possibly benefit the United States. But the relevant question is not how efficient the United States is in absolute terms, but whether the people of the United States can make a better deal by trading with Japan than they can make by trading among themselves.

**Table 17.2.** Comparative Cost Advantages, Beef and Textiles, United States and Japan

| | Maximum Units of Textiles (Zero Beef Units) | Maximum Units of Beef (Zero Textile Units) | Domestic Cost Ratios in Each Nation | Mutually Beneficial Trade Ratio, Both Nations |
|---|---|---|---|---|
| United States | 30 | 90 | 1 textile costs 3 beef | 1 textile trades for 2 beef |
| Japan | 25 | 25 | 1 textile costs 1 beef | |

## Perspectives in Economics: The Balance on Current Account

*Edward L. Hudgins*

International economic transactions can be measured in several ways. The merchandise trade balance includes the dollar value of imports and exports. The balance on current account, a more complete measure, includes investment income receipts and payments and other minor transactions as well.

During the twenty-five years following World War II, the United States ran yearly surpluses in its merchandise trade. A **merchandise trade surplus** is the dollar amount by which exports of goods exceed imports of goods. Between 1946 and 1970, exports averaged $4 billion more than imports. Total exports increased from $11.8 billion to $42.5 billion, while imports went from $5 billion to $40 billion.

Except for two years since then, however, the United States has run a steadily increasing merchandise trade deficit. A **merchandise trade deficit** is the dollar amount by which imports of goods exceed exports of goods. Between 1977 and 1982, the deficit averaged $30 billion. In 1983 it climbed to $61 billion, and in 1984 doubled again to reach $123 billion.

During the same period, the balance on current account was more favorable. Ever since World War II, interest income from U.S. investments abroad has exceeded interest payments on foreign investments in the United States. In fact, the surplus interest income has usually been greater than the trade deficit. But from 1977 to 1979, the United States ran deficits on current account of $7.96 to $15.4 billion. That was nothing, however, compared with the staggering deficits of 1983 and 1984 (see Figure 17.1).

The major cause of these deficits in the balance on current account was an increase in imports. After a general decline during the 1970s, the U.S. dollar regained much of its historical strength abroad, allowing Americans to purchase more imports. The surplus of investment income receipts also decreased in these years, in part because of increased investment in the United States by both Americans, who began to invest less abroad, and by foreigners, who began to invest more in the United States.

Some economists see the deficit on current account as a problem. As long as the investment

To determine which is the better deal we must compare the costs of production. If each nation produces and trades the products in which it has a comparative cost advantage, trade can raise both their incomes. Remember that a comparative advantage is the capacity to produce a product at a lower cost than a competitor, in terms of the goods that must be given up. The United States may have an absolute advantage in the production of both beef and textiles, but it may have a comparative advantage only in the production of beef. In other words, the United States must forgo fewer units of textiles to obtain a unit of beef than Japan. Having a comparative advantage in beef necessarily means the United States cannot have a comparative advantage in textiles—a point that will become clear shortly.

In a sense, the United States trades with itself every time it produces either beef or textiles. If it produces beef, it incurs an opportunity cost: it gives up some of the textiles it could have produced. If it produces textiles, it gives up some beef. In Table 17.2, every time the United States produces

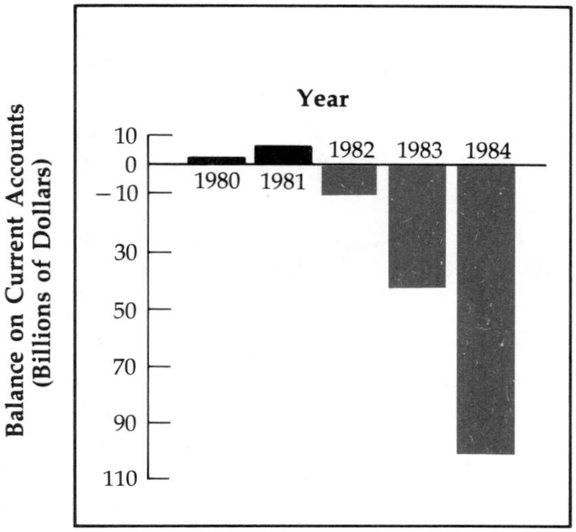


**Figure 17.1.** U.S. Balance on Current Account, 1980–1984.
In 1980 and 1981 the United States recorded a small surplus on current account. By 1984, however, the nation was running a record deficit of $101.6 billion on current account—more than twice its deficit in 1983.
**Source:** U.S. Department of Commerce, *Survey of Current Business* (July 1985).

income surplus matches the trade deficit, they maintain, excess imports can be covered. But if the United States does not earn the equivalent of its excess imports in net investment income, it is in effect buying on credit. In the long run the United States will become a debtor nation, unable to import goods or to attract investment capital because of its high debt payments.

But other economists feel a deficit on current account reflects a passing situation, not an economic problem that demands government action. Excess imports, they argue, may be considered as paid for by the increased buying power of the dollar. That is, the strong dollar has benefited Americans by lowering the prices of imported goods. If too many dollars flow out of the United States, furthermore, the dollar will decrease in value. Over the long run, exports will increase and imports will decrease. Finally, excess dollars that flow out of the United States in payment for imports may well return in the form of foreign investment. Such an inflow of capital would help, not harm, American industry.

one unit of textiles, it gives up three units of beef. (It can produce either thirty units of textiles or ninety of beef—a ratio of one to three.) Thus the United States can benefit by trading beef for textiles if it can give up fewer than three units of beef for each unit of textiles it gets from Japan.

Japan, on the other hand, gives up an advantage of one unit of beef for each unit of textiles it produces. If Japan can get more than one unit of beef for each unit of textiles it trades, it too can gain by trading. In short, if the trade ratio is greater than one unit of beef for one unit of textiles but less than three units of beef for one unit of textiles, trade will benefit both countries. The United States will gain because it has to give up fewer units of beef—two, perhaps, instead of three—than if it tried to produce the textiles itself. It can produce three units of beef, trade two of them for a textile unit, and have one extra beef unit left over. Or it can trade all three units of beef for one and one-half units of textiles. Japan can produce one unit of textiles and trade it for two units of beef, gaining one textile unit in the process.

**Table 17.3.** Mutual Gains from Trade in Beef and Textiles, United States and Japan

| | United States | Japan | Total, U.S. and Japan |
|---|---|---|---|
| Production and consumption levels before international trade | 15 textiles<br>45 beef | 3 textiles<br>22 beef | 18 textiles<br>67 beef |
| Production levels in anticipation of international trade (complete specialization assumed) | 0 textiles<br>90 beef | 25 textiles<br>0 beef | 25 textiles<br>90 beef |
| At an exchange ratio of 2 beef for 1 textile, United States and Japan agree to trade 40 beef for 20 textiles. | | | |
| Consumption levels after international trade | 20 textiles<br>50 beef | 5 textiles<br>40 beef | 25 textiles<br>90 beef |
| Increased consumption (before-trade consumption levels subtracted) | 5 textiles<br>5 beef | 2 textiles<br>18 beef | 7 textiles<br>23 beef |

Both nations can gain from such a trade because each is specializing in the production of a good for which it has a comparative cost advantage. Even though the United States has an absolute cost advantage in both products, Japan has a comparative advantage in textiles. One unit of textiles costs Japan one unit of beef; the same unit of textiles costs the United States three units of beef. Similarly, the United States has a comparative cost advantage in the production of beef. One unit of beef costs the United States only one-third unit of textiles; it costs Japan a whole unit. If each specializes in the commodities for which it has a comparative cost advantage, the two nations can save resources for use in further production.

Table 17.3 shows the gains in production each nation can realize under such an arrangement. Before trade, the United States produces 15 units of textiles and 45 of beef; Japan produces 3 units of textiles and 22 of beef. Total production is therefore 18 units of textiles and 67 units of beef. With trade, the United States produces 90 units of beef and Japan produces 25 units of textiles. At an international trade ratio of 1 unit of textiles to 2 units of beef, suppose the two nations agree to trade 40 units of beef for 20 units of textiles. The United States gets more beef—50 units as opposed to 45—and more textiles—20 units as opposed to 15. Japan also gets more of both commodities. Through specialization, total world production has risen from 18 to 25 units of textiles and from 67 to 90 units of beef. Both nations can now consume more of both commodities. In a very important sense, the world's aggregate real income has increased.

The same gain in aggregate welfare is shown graphically in Figure 17.2. On the left-hand side of the figure, the U.S. production possibilities curve extends from 30 units of textiles on the horizontal axis to 90 units of beef

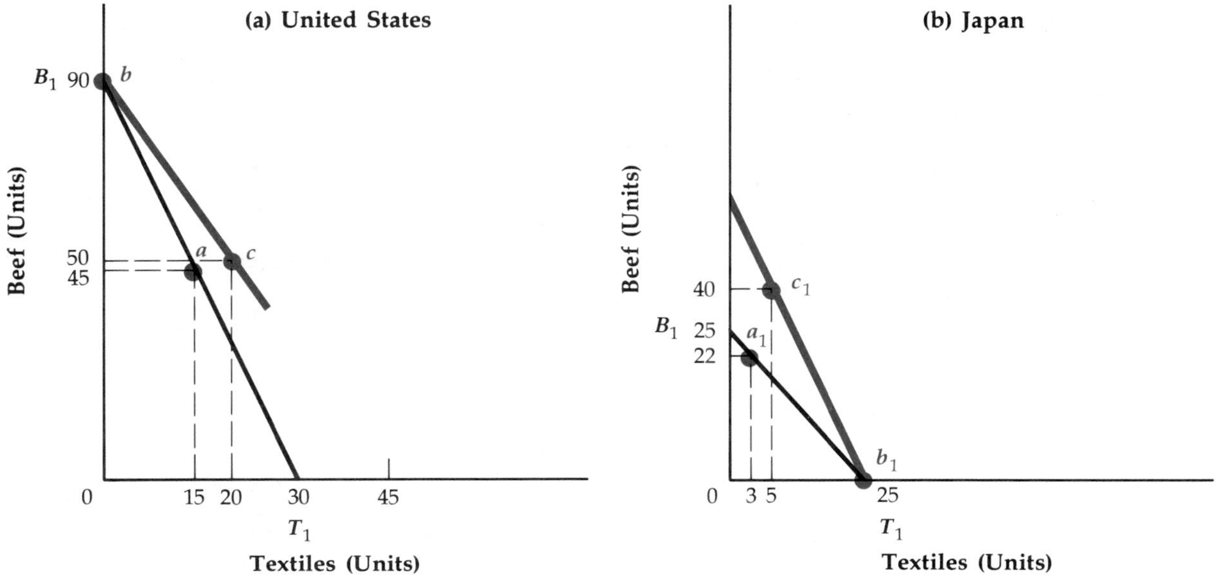


**Figure 17.2.** Production Gains from International Trade.
The United States can produce any combination of beef and textiles along its production possibilities curve $B_1T_1$ (left-hand panel). Without trade, it will choose to produce at point *a*, 45 units of beef and 15 units of textiles. If given the opportunity to trade two units of beef for one unit of textiles, however, the United States will specialize completely in beef (point *b*) and trade beef for textiles along the color line. Through trade, the United States moves from *a* to *c*, exporting 40 units of beef (90 units produced minus 50 consumed) and importing 20 units of textiles. In the process the nation increases its consumption of both beef and textiles, from 45 units of beef and 15 units of textiles to 50 units of beef and 20 units of textiles. (The color line does not intersect the horizontal axis because the United States cannot get more than 25 units of textiles from Japan.)

At the same time trade permits Japan (right-hand panel) to shift its consumption from the black production possibilities curve to the color curve. By producing at $b_1$ and exporting 20 units of textiles in exchange for 40 units of beef, Japan too can expand its consumption, from $a_1$ to $c_1$.

on the vertical axis. Japan's production capability is shown on the right. Without trade, the United States chooses to produce at point *a*, 15 textile units and 45 beef units. But at an exchange ratio of 2 beef units for 1 textile unit, the United States can move up and to the left on its production possibilities curve. At the extreme, it will produce at point *b*, 90 units of beef and no textiles. It can then trade along the color outer line, exchanging 40 beef units for 20 textile units (point *c*). Through trade, the United States realizes a gain in aggregate welfare represented by the distance between points *a* and *c*. In other words, international trade permits the United States to consume at a point beyond its own limited production possibilities curve (the black line in the graph). In the same way, Japan realizes a gain in welfare equal to the difference between its consumption before trade, $a_1$, and its consumption after trade, $b_1$.

## The Distributional Effects of Trade

As we have seen, even a nation that has an absolute advantage in every production process can benefit from trade. In reality, no such nation exists, but that just underscores the point that even in the unlikeliest conditions we can make the case for free trade. If voluntary trade takes place, furthermore, we must assume that both parties gain. Why else would they agree to the arrangement?

Yet international trade remains a controversial subject, for while nations gain from trade, individuals within those nations may not. Individual gains tend to go to the firms that produce goods and services for export.

### Gains to Exporters

Exporters of domestic goods gain from international trade because the market for their goods expands, increasing demand for their products. The increase in their revenue can be seen in Figure 17.3. When the demand curve shifts from $D_1$ to $D_2$, producers' revenues rise from $P_1Q_2$ (point *a*) to $P_2Q_3$ (point *b*). The increase in revenues is equal to the shaded L-shaped area $P_2bQ_3Q_2aP_1$. Producers benefit because they receive greater profits, equal to the shaded area above the supply curve, $P_2baP_1$. Workers and suppliers of raw materials benefit because their services are in greater demand, and therefore more costly. The cost of producing additional units for export is equal to the shaded area below the supply curve, $Q_2abQ_3$.

This graphic suggests why farmers supported the sales of wheat to the Soviet Union that began in the early 1970s. They complained loudly when the U.S. government suspended sales temporarily for political reasons. But many consumers and members of Congress objected to the wheat sales, on the ground that they would increase the domestic price of wheat and therefore of bread. In a narrow sense, consumers of exported products have an interest in restricting their exportation. Yet in the broad context of international trade, restrictions can work against the private interests of individuals, including even consumers of bread. Trade is ultimately a two-way street. To import goods and services that can be produced more cheaply abroad than at home, a nation must export something else. No nation will continually export part of what it produces without getting something in return. To the extent that exports are restricted to suit the special interests of some group, imports of other commodities also are restricted. Restrictions on the exportation of wheat may hold down the price of bread, but they can also increase the price of imported goods, like radios and television sets.

### Losses to Firms Competing with Imports

While consumers gain from increased imports, domestic producers may lose from increased competition. Foreign producers can gain a foothold in the domestic market in three ways: (1) by providing a better product than

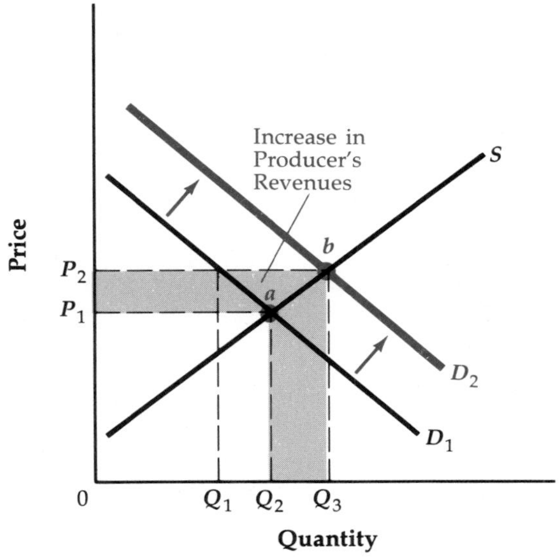


**Figure 17.3.** Gains from the Export Trade.
The opening up of foreign markets to U.S. producers increases the demand for their products, from $D_1$ to $D_2$. As a result, domestic producers can raise their price from $P_1$ to $P_2$ and sell a larger quantity, $Q_3$ instead of $Q_2$. Revenues increase by the shaded area $P_2bQ_3Q_2aP_1$.

domestic firms; (2) by selling essentially the same product as domestic firms, but at a lower price; and (3) by providing a product previously unavailable in the domestic market. Most people welcome the importation of a previously unavailable product. But producers who face competition from foreign suppliers have an incentive to object to importation. If imports are allowed, the domestic supply of a good increases. Domestic competitors will sell less, and they may have to sell at a lower price. In short, the employment opportunities and real income of domestic producers decline as a result of foreign competition.

Figure 17.4 shows the effects of importing foreign textiles. Without imports, demand is $D$ and supply is $S_1$. In a competitive market, producers will sell $Q_2$ units at a price of $P_2$. Total receipts will be $P_2 \times Q_2$. But the importation of foreign textiles increases the supply to $S_2$, dropping the price from $P_2$ to $P_1$. Because prices are lower, consumers increase their consumption from $Q_2$ to $Q_3$ and get more for their money.

But domestic firms, their employees, and their suppliers lose. Because the price is lower, domestic producers must move down their supply curve ($S_1$) to the lower quantity $Q_1$. Their revenues fall from $P_2Q_2$ to $P_1Q_1$. In other words, the revenues in the shaded L-shaped area $P_2aQ_2Q_1bP_1$ are lost. Of this total loss in revenues, owners of domestic firms lose the area above the supply curve, $P_2abP_1$. Workers and suppliers of raw materials lose the area below the supply curve, $Q_2abQ_1$. This is the cost domestic

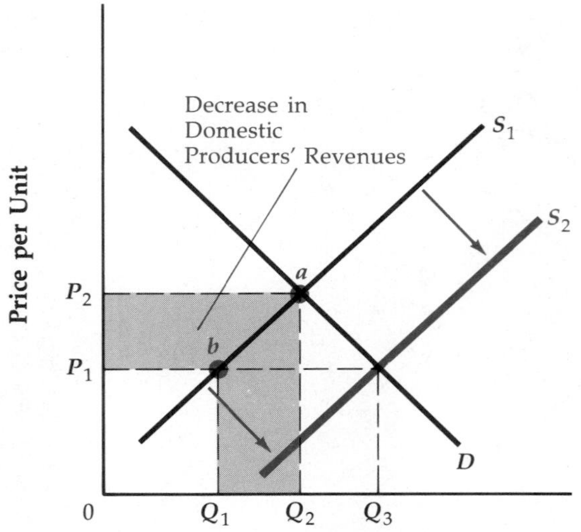


**Figure 17.4.** Losses from Competition with Imported Products.
The opening up of the market to foreign trade increases the supply of textiles from $S_1$ to $S_2$. As a result, the price of textiles falls from $P_2$ to $P_1$, and domestic producers sell a lower quantity, $Q_1$ instead of $Q_2$. Consumers benefit from the lower price and the higher quantity of textiles they are able to buy. But domestic producers, workers, and suppliers lose. Producers' revenues drop by an amount equal to the shaded area $P_2abP_1$. Workers' and suppliers' payments drop by an amount equal to the shaded area $Q_2abQ_1$.

firms would incur in increasing production from $Q_1$ to $Q_2$, the payments that would be made to domestic workers and suppliers in the absence of foreign competition. If workers and other resources are employed in textiles because it is their best possible employment, the introduction of foreign products can be seen as a restriction on some workers' employment opportunities.

## The Effects of Tariffs and Quotas

Because foreign competition hurts some individuals, domestic producers, workers, and suppliers have an incentive to seek government restrictions on imports. Two forms of protection are commonly used, tariffs and quotas. A **tariff** is a special tax on imported goods. A **quota** is a limit on the amount of a good that can be imported.

**Tariff:** a special tax on imported goods.

**Quota:** a limit on the amount of a good that can be imported.

If tariffs are imposed on foreign goods, the supply of textiles will decrease—say from $S_2$ toward $S_1$ in Figure 17.4—and the price of imports will rise. Domestic producers will raise their prices too, and domestic production will go up. If the tariff is high and all foreign textiles are excluded, the supply will shift all the way back to $S_1$. A small tariff will have a more modest effect, shifting the supply curve only partway back toward $S_1$. The price of textiles will rise, and domestic producers will expand their production, but imports will continue to come into the country.

A quota has the same general effect as a tariff. It reduces the market supply, raises the market price, and encourages domestic production. There are three main differences between quotas and tariffs, however. First, quotas firmly restrict the amount of a product that can be imported, regardless of market conditions. A quota may specify how much oil may be imported each day or how much sugar each year. Tariffs, on the other hand, permit any level of importation for which consumers are willing to pay. Thus if demand for the product increases, imports may rise.

The first Reagan administration imposed quotas on steel, copper, textiles, and autos from Japan. In 1984 the so-called voluntary restraint program forced Japan to restrict auto sales in the United States to 1.84 million cars. Because Japanese supply was not allowed to keep pace with the rapidly expanding U.S. demand, the price of Japanese cars rose, more expensive models were imported, and consumers faced longer waiting lists for Japanese cars. In addition, the prices of American cars rose. These consequences led to the termination of the voluntary restraint program in 1985.

The second major difference from tariffs is that quotas are typically specified for each important foreign producer. Otherwise, all foreign producers would rush to sell their goods before the quota was reached. When quotas are rationed in this way, more detailed government enforcement is required. Tariffs place no such restriction on individual producers.

Finally, quotas enable foreign firms to raise their prices and extract more income from consumers. One economist estimated that the Reagan administration's voluntary restraint program permitted Japanese auto producers to raise their prices high enough to take an additional $2 billion out of the American market.[1] Tariffs, on the other hand, force foreign firms to lower their prices to offset the increase from the tariff. They also generate income for the federal government.

Because of the private benefits to be gained from tariffs and quotas, we should expect an industry to seek them so long as their market benefits exceed their political cost. Politicians are likely to expect votes and campaign contributions in return for tariff legislation, and producers will usually make the necessary contributions, because the elimination of foreign competition promises increased revenues. The difference between the increase in profits due to import restrictions and the amount spent on political activity can be seen as a kind of profit in itself.

Consumers, on the other hand, have reason to oppose tariffs or quotas on imported products. Such legislation inevitably causes prices to rise. Consumers typically do not offer very much resistance, however, because the effects of tariffs and quotas are hard to perceive. Unlike a sales tax, the cost of a tariff is not rung up separately at the cash register. And many consumers do not reason through the complex effects of a tariff on

1. Robert Crandell, "Import Quotas and the Automobile Industry: The Costs of Protectionism," *Brookings Review* (Summer 1984), pp. 8–16.

consumer prices. In fact, many, if not most, consumers accept the proposition that what is good for the textile, automobile, steel, or copper industry is good for the nation and themselves. "Buy American" slogans and advertisements emphasizing the need to preserve American jobs are generally effective in swaying public opinion.

As a group, consumers have less incentive to oppose tariffs than industry has to support them. The benefits of a tariff accrue principally to a relatively small group of firms, whose lobby may already be well entrenched in Washington. These firms have a strong incentive to be fully informed on the issue and to make campaign contributions. But the harmful effects of a tariff are diffused over an extremely large group of consumers. The financial burden borne by any one consumer may be very slight, particularly if the tariff in question is small, as most tariffs are. As a result, the individual consumer has little incentive to become informed on tariff legislation or to make political contributions. Though consumers as a whole may share an interest in opposing tariffs, collective action must still be undertaken by individuals. And individuals will not incur the cost of organizing unless they expect to receive compensating private benefit.

At some level of increased cost, of course, consumers will find the necessary incentive to oppose tariff legislation. For this reason Congress rarely passes tariffs high enough to make importation totally unprofitable. But even low tariffs reduce the nation's real income while redistributing it toward protected sectors. The size of the pie is reduced, but the protected few get a bigger slice.

## The Case for Free Trade

We have seen how international trade can increase the total incomes of the nations engaged in it. By extension, we can conclude that anything that restricts the scope of trade between nations generally reduces their real incomes. To the extent that trade is a two-way street—that exports trade for imports, at least in the long run—a reduction in imports brings a reduction in exports. From our imports the Japanese get the dollars they need to buy American exports. If we reduce our imports, they will have fewer funds with which to buy from us. For this reason, U.S. farmers, who sell approximately one-third of their crops in foreign markets, actively opposed the protectionist movement led by textile, steel, and copper firms in the first half of the 1980s.

Yet what is true for one sector of the economy is not necessarily true for all. If all sectors are protected by tariffs, it is possible (but not inevitable) that all experience a drop in real income. Figure 17.5 illustrates the case of an economy with two industries, automobiles and textiles. Both industries must compete with imports. If neither seeks protection, both will operate in cell I, at a combined real income of $50 ($20 for the textile industry and $30 for the automobile industry). If the textile industry seeks protection but the auto industry does not, they will move to cell II, where tariffs raise the textile industry's income from $20 to $23. The automotive

| | Textile Industry Without Tariff Protection | Textile Industry With Tariff Protection |
|---|---|---|
| **Automobile Industry Without Tariff Protection** | Cell I<br>Real Income, Textile: $20<br>Real Income, Auto: $30 | Cell II<br>Real Income, Textile: $23<br>Real Income, Auto: $25 |
| **Automobile Industry With Tariff Protection** | Cell III<br>Real Income, Textile: $15<br>Real Income, Auto: $34 | Cell IV<br>Real Income, Textile: $17<br>Real Income, Auto: $26 |

**Figure 17.5.** Effects of Tariff Protection on Individual Industries: Case 1.
If neither the textile nor the automobile industry obtains tariff protection, the economy will earn its highest possible collective income (cell I). But each industry has an incentive to obtain tariff protection for itself. If the textile industry alone seeks protection (cell II), its income will rise while the auto industry's income falls. If the auto industry alone seeks protection, its income will rise while textile income falls. If both obtain protection, the economy will end up in cell IV, its worst possible position. Income in both sectors will fall.

sector's income falls to $25, so that the two industries' combined real income falls to $48. Consumers get fewer textiles at a higher price.

Similarly, if the auto industry seeks protection while the textile industry does not, the economy will move from cell I to cell III. Again, total real income falls from $50 to $49, but this time the auto industry is better off. Its income rises from $30 to $34, while the textile industry's income falls to $15. Obviously, if one industry seeks protection, the other has an incentive to follow suit. If the textile industry counters with a tariff of its own, the economy will move from cell III to cell IV, and the industry's real income will rise from $15 to $17.

Without some constraint on both sectors, then, each has an interest in seeking protection regardless of what the other does. Yet if the economy winds up in cell IV, total real income will be lower than under any other conditions: only $43. Obviously the best course for the economy as a whole is to prohibit tariffs altogether. And in an economy with only two sectors, the cost of reaching an agreement is manageable. In the real world, however, there are many economic sectors, and the costs of reaching a decision are much greater.

In Figure 17.5, both industries end up with lower real incomes in cell IV. But in reality, the effects of multiple tariffs will be different in different sectors of the economy. Although total real income will fall, several sectors may realize individual gains. Consider Figure 17.6. Though total real income falls from cell I ($50) to cell IV ($48), the auto sector's income rises (from $30 to $31). In this case the textile sector bears the brunt of tariff protection, and the auto sector has a compelling interest in obtaining protective tariffs. The sectors of the economy that are most adept at manipulating the political process will be least willing to accept free trade.

Thus the case for free trade is a subtle one. As always, special-interest groups—entrepreneurs, labor organizations, consumer groups—will pursue their individual interests, competing for favors and benefits the same way they compete in the marketplace. Yet if all are to be treated equally by government, we must choose between free trade for all and protection for all. Economists generally choose free trade for all, because of its obvious benefits to the nation as a whole. There are some legitimate exceptions to that rule, such as the required domestic production of public goods, which are discussed below. Yet even trade restrictions necessary for the public good are abused by those who would secure protection for private purposes.

## The Case for Restricted Trade

Proponents of tariffs rarely argue publicly that they will serve private interests, raise prices, and reduce the availability of goods. Instead, they typically advocate tariffs as the most efficient means of accomplishing some national objective. Any private benefits that would accrue to protected industries are generally portrayed as insignificant side effects.

But though most arguments in favor of tariffs camouflage the underlying issues, one is partially valid. It has to do with the maintenance of national security.

### The Need for National Security

Protariff arguments based on national security stress the need for a strong defense industry. If imports are completely unrestricted, certain industries

| | Textile Industry Without Tariff Protection | Textile Industry With Tariff Protection |
|---|---|---|
| **Automobile Industry Without Tariff Protection** | Cell I<br>Real Income, Textile: $20<br>Real Income, Auto: $30 | Cell II<br>Real Income, Textile: $23<br>Real Income, Auto: $25 |
| **Automobile Industry With Tariff Protection** | Cell III<br>Real Income, Textile: $15<br>Real Income, Auto: $34 | Cell IV<br>Real Income, Textile: $17<br>Real Income, Auto: $31 |

**Figure 17.6.** Effects of Tariff Protection on Individual Industries: Case 2.
In this more realistic case, the auto industry gains from tariff protection, even if both sectors are protected (cell IV). The textile industry's income falls from $20 (cell I) to $17 (cell IV). But the auto industry's income rises from $30 (cell I) to $31 (cell IV). Thus the auto industry has no incentive to agree to the elimination of tariffs.

needed in time of war or other national emergency could be undersold and run out of business by foreign competitors. In an emergency, the United States would then be dependent on possibly hostile foreign suppliers for essential defense equipment. (Although the nation could convert to production of war-related goods, the conversion process might be prohibitively lengthy and complex.) Tariffs may create inefficiencies in the allocation of world resources, but that is one of the costs a nation must bear to maintain a strong national defense.

Given the unsteady popularity of U.S. foreign policy and the uncertain support of allies, this argument has some merit. Other nations, like Israel, have found that they cannot count on the support of all their allies in time of war. Because France disagreed with Israeli policy in the Middle East, it held up shipment of spare parts for planes it had sold to Israel earlier. The United States could conceivably find itself in a similar position if it relies on foreign firms for planes, firearms, and oil.

Special-interest groups can easily abuse the national defense argument for tariffs. The textile industry, for example, promotes itself as a ready source of combat uniforms during wartime. Even candle manufacturers have petitioned Congress for increased tariff protection, on the grounds that candles are "a product required in the national defense."[2] In years past, U.S. oil producers, contending that a healthy domestic oil industry is vital to the national defense, have lobbied for protection from foreign oil imports. But although few would dispute the need for a reliable source of oil in wartime, the effects of a tariff are not entirely straightforward. By making foreign oil more expensive, a tariff increases consumption of domestic oil. Since oil is a finite resource, a tariff can ultimately make the United States more dependent on foreign energy sources in time of emergency.

Recent history illustrates the danger of dependence on foreign suppliers. In 1973, the OPEC oil cartel used U.S. dependence on its oil reserves as a bargaining tool in its efforts to reduce U.S. support for Israel. President Gerald Ford responded in 1974 by supporting a tariff on imported oil, to stimulate exploration for new domestic energy reserves. If the United States could become energy independent by the end of the 1980s, Ford argued, it would reduce the threat of political blackmail from the Middle East. And in 1983, for the same reason, the Reagan administration granted tariff protection to specialty steel products, which are used extensively in high-technology defense systems.

## Other Arguments

Most of the other arguments in support of tariffs are weak from a practical as well as a theoretical perspective. It is sometimes argued that because workers are paid less in foreign countries, U.S. industries cannot hope to compete with foreign imports. But trade depends on the relative costs of production, not absolute wage rates in various nations. U.S. wages may be quite high in either absolute or relative terms. But if U.S. workers are more productive than others, the costs of production can be lower in the United States than elsewhere.

The important point is what tariffs do to trade. In an earlier example of trade in textiles and beef, the United States was more efficient than Japan in the production of both products. That is, generally speaking, fewer resources were required to produce those goods in the United States than in Japan. Very possibly, the incomes of textile and beef workers would be higher in the United States than in Japan. But because Japanese firms had

2. "Petition of the Candlemakers—1951," in *Readings in Economics*, ed. Paul Samuelson (New York: McGraw-Hill, 1973), 7th ed., p. 237.

a comparative cost advantage in textiles (measured in terms of the number of units of beef forgone for each textile unit), they were able to undersell textile firms in the United States. If the U.S. imposed tariffs or quotas on imported textiles because Japan had a comparative advantage in that product, it would destroy the basis for trade between the two nations. Reducing imports will tend to reduce exports, at least in the long run.

A second questionable argument for tariffs is based on the faulty idea that the United States loses when money flows overseas in payment for imports. As Abraham Lincoln is reported to have said, "I don't know much about the tariff, but this I do know. When we trade with other countries, we get the goods and they get the money. When we trade with ourselves, we get the goods and the money."

Lincoln was clearly right when he said he did not know much about the tariff. He failed to recognize the real income benefits of international trade, which are reduced by tariffs. He seems to have confused the nation's welfare with its monetary holdings. It is true that if Americans buy goods from abroad, they get the goods and foreigners get the money.[3] But what are foreigners going to do with the money they receive? If they never spend it, Americans will be better off, for they will have gotten some foreign goods in exchange for some paper bills, which are relatively cheap to print. At some point, however, foreign exporters will want to get something concrete in return for their labor and materials. They will use their dollars to buy goods from U.S. manufacturers. Again, trade is a give-and-take process, in which benefits flow to both sides.

A third argument often made is that foreign nations impose tariffs on U.S. goods; unless we respond in kind, foreign producers will have the advantage in both markets. This argument has a significant flaw. By restricting their imports, foreign nations reduce their ability to sell to the United States and other nations. To buy Japanese goods, for instance, Americans need yen. They get yen by selling to Japan. If Japan reduces its imports from the United States, Americans will have fewer yen to buy Japanese goods. So the Japanese are restricting their own exports with their tariffs. They harm themselves as well as Americans. If Americans respond to their actions by imposing tariffs of their own, they will reduce trade even further. The harm is compounded, not negated.

One sound reason for increasing tariffs is to strengthen our bargaining position in international trade conferences. By matching foreign restrictions, the United States may be able to force a multilateral reduction of tariffs. To the extent that all tariffs are reduced by such a strategy, world trade will be stimulated.

According to the fourth argument, tariffs increase workers' employment opportunities. If the government imposes tariffs on imported goods, the demand for American goods will rise. More workers will have jobs and can spend their income on goods and services produced by other Americans.

---

3. Actually, the transaction may not involve the transfer of paper money. It is more likely—as explained in the next chapter—that payment will be made by transferring funds from one bank account to another. The importer's bank balance will drop, and the exporter's bank balance will increase.

## Perspectives in Economics: The Pros and Cons of Textile Protection

Import controls are a highly controversial issue in states like North and South Carolina, where foreign competition seriously threatens the textile industry, which dominates the local employment market. The following are typical arguments for and against protection, as advanced by representatives of the textile industry and the Reagan administration. They illustrate not only the different viewpoints Americans may take on such an issue, but the extent to which opponents often talk at cross-purposes.

### The Case for Import Restrictions

The U.S. government has an obligation to encourage private enterprise to provide jobs for American citizens. We cannot remain a world power, or provide assistance to our allies and to developing countries, if our basic industries are crippled by competition from state-supported foreign industries. Currently the American market is inundated with textiles produced in countries where labor is much cheaper than in the United States. We aren't asking for protection—just the opportunity for fair competition with foreign producers.

Specifically, the government should:

Roll back import quotas to 1983 levels.

Reduce by one-third the import quotas of the Big Six: Taiwan, South Korea, Hong Kong, China, Japan, and Italy.

Limit imports to no more than 20 percent of domestic sales in every category.

Enforce to the letter restrictive trade agreements already on the books.

Work to establish worldwide quotas that would curb overall import growth, allowing imports to grow no faster than domestic markets.

Establish an enforceable import licensing system, with strong penalties for violations of agreements.

Reciprocate promptly when other nations restrict the importation of American products.

It is true that in the short run, more workers are likely to be hired because of tariffs. But in the long run reduced imports will result in reduced exports. The market for U.S. goods will shrink, increasing unemployment in the export industries.

Furthermore, if Americans reduce their demand for foreign goods to increase employment in the United States, their domestic recession will be transmitted to other nations. With fewer sales of foreign goods, fewer workers will be needed in foreign industries. Foreign governments may retaliate by imposing tariffs of their own. Tariffs will temporarily increase their employment levels and can be used as a bargaining tool in trade negotiations as well. The end result will be a reduction in total worldwide production and real income.

Finally, tariff advocates sometimes claim that new industries deserve protection, because they are too small to compete with established foreign firms. If protected by tariffs, these new industries can expand their scale of production, lower their production costs, and eventually compete with foreign producers. But it is very difficult for a government to determine which new industries may eventually be able to compete with foreign rivals. Over the long period of time that an industry needs to mature,

Reduce the budget deficit, which is keeping the value of the dollar artificially high and encouraging imports.

These steps would allow U.S. companies time to modernize and produce better-quality products and consumer service; to develop new uses for products; and to work with the state and federal governments to encourage product research.

## The Case Against Import Restrictions

Protection from imports is obviously beneficial to parts of the textile industry, but by no means all of it. And measures that may be good for the textile industry are not necessarily good for the general economy. The benefits of trade protectionism are received by executives, stockholders, and workers in the textile industry—at the expense of other Americans. For protectionism drives up the prices of both foreign and domestic textiles, depressing consumers' real incomes. And many consumers earn less than those who benefit from protection.

Tariffs and quotas in one industry, like textiles, increase the costs of other industries, like ready-made apparel. Because they inspire retaliation by other countries, they make it more difficult for still other industries—for example, the soybean industry—to export their products. Protectionism also reduces the incentive of producers to increase their productivity and maintain their competitiveness. It retards economic diversification, encouraging a nation to stake its economic future on industries that are not fully competitive. In short, protectionism destroys American jobs just as surely as it saves them.

The U.S. textile industry buys a great deal of machinery from abroad, because foreign-made machinery is a better buy than domestically made machinery. The case against protectionism is simply a case for granting all consumers the same right to buy from abroad.

conditions, including the technology of production, may change significantly. For a so-called infant industry to become truly competitive, furthermore, it must develop a comparative cost advantage, not just economies of scale.

Moreover, the mere likelihood that a firm will eventually be able to compete with its foreign rivals does not in itself warrant protection. Not until firms have become established will consumers receive the benefit of lower prices. In the interim, tariff protection hurts consumers by raising the prices they must pay. Proponents of protection must be able to show that the future benefits to be gained by establishing an industry exceed the current costs of protecting it.

Finally, if a firm can expand, cover all its costs of production, and eventually compete with its foreign rivals, private entrepreneurs are not likely to miss the opportunity to invest in it. Through the stock and bond markets, firms with growth potential will be able to secure the funds they need for expansion. If a firm cannot raise capital from private sources, it may be because the return on the investment is too low in relation to the risk. Why should the government accept risks that the private market will not accept?

## Summary and Extensions

The schedule of tariffs applied to goods coming into the United States is now larger than the Los Angeles telephone directory. Surely all those tariffs were not imposed in pursuit of the national interest, as in the maintenance of a strong defense industry. Most probably reflect the political influence of special-interest groups.

The case against such special-interest tariffs was wittily stated by the nineteenth-century French economist Frederic Bastiat. Pretending to represent the candle manufacturers of his day, he wrote to the French Chamber of Deputies in 1845:

> Gentlemen:
> . . . We are subjected to the intolerable competition of a foreign rival, who enjoys, it would seem, such superior facilities for the production of light, that he is enabled to *inundate* our *national market* at so exceedingly reduced price, that, the moment he makes his appearance, he draws off all customs for us; and thus an important branch of French industry . . . is suddenly reduced to a state of complete stagnation. This rival is no other than the sun.
>
> Our petition is, that it would please your honorable body to pass a law whereby shall be directed the shutting up of all windows, doors, skylights, shutters, curtains, in a word, all openings, holes, chinks, and fissures through which light of the sun . . . penetrates into our dwellings.[4]

Bastiat suggests that passage of his proposed law would be consistent with the Chamber's attempts to check the importation of "coal, iron, cheese, and goods of foreign manufacture, merely because and even in proportion as their price approaches zero."

Clearly, tariffs force consumers to pay more for domestic goods. To that extent they reduce aggregate real income. Unfortunately, because they benefit special-interest groups—and because the political process is easily exploited by special-interest groups—tariffs, like taxes, are probably inevitable.

## Major Conclusions

1. When two nations trade with each other, both parties gain from the transaction.
2. Even if one nation has an absolute advantage in the production of all goods and services, trade between nations can be mutually beneficial.

---

4. Frederic Bastiat, "A Petition," *Economic Sophisms* (Irvington-on-Hudson, N.Y.: Foundation for Economic Education, 1964; originally published 1845), pp. 56–60.

3. Although nations as a whole always gain from international trade, not all individuals do. Firms that produce for export can gain from foreign trade, along with their employees. But free trade can hurt firms that must compete with foreign producers. And consumers who buy products that are exported must pay higher prices than they would in the absence of trade.
4. Tariffs and quotas reduce the supply of goods on the market, raising prices and encouraging domestic production.
5. Producers who face foreign competition can benefit substantially from, and have a private interest in, tariff or quota restrictions on imports. Consumers have little incentive to oppose tariff legislation, for the cost of opposition is generally greater than the benefit to be gained from it (slightly lower prices).
6. Tariffs and quotas on imports reduce international trade, and therefore the aggregate incomes of the nations that engage in international commerce.
7. Tariffs and quotas sometimes serve the national interest, especially where national defense and security are concerned. Most other arguments in favor of tariffs are seriously flawed.

## Questions to Ponder

1. Using supply and demand curves, show how a U.S. tariff on a foreign-made good will affect the price and quantity sold in the country of origin.
2. How will an import quota on sugar affect the price of sugar produced and sold domestically? Sugar produced domestically and sold abroad?
3. If a tariff is imposed on imported autos and the domestic demand for autos rises, what will happen to auto imports? If a quota is imposed on imported autos and the demand for autos increases, what will happen to auto imports?
4. Given the following production capabilities for cheese and bread, which nation will export cheese to the other? What might be a mutually beneficial exchange rate for cheese and bread?

| | Cheese | | Bread |
|---|---|---|---|
| France | 40 units | or | 60 units |
| Italy | 10 units | or | 5 units |

5. "Tariffs on imported textiles increase the employment opportunities and incomes of domestic textile workers. They therefore increase aggregate employment and income." Evaluate this statement.

## Central Question

*How do firms based in nations with different currencies engage in international trade?*

## Key Terms

International exchange rate

Depreciation of the dollar

Appreciation of the dollar

Floating (flexible) exchange rate system

Fixed exchange rate system

Chapter 18

# International Finance

*The goal of every science is a conceptual model which shows how the pieces of its universe are related. Economists seek to become the Copernicuses of the international financial system, but their task is complicated since this system has changed substantially in the last one hundred years and continues to change.*

Robert Aliber

People rarely use barter in trade. Exchanging one toy for two pens or three pots for the rear end of a steer simply is not practical. Because the bartering seller must also be a buyer, buyers and sellers may have to incur very substantial costs to find one another, even in the domestic market. When people are hundreds or thousands of miles apart, and separated by national boundaries and foreign cultures and languages, as they are in international trade, barter would be all the more complicated. We rarely see exporters acting as importers, exchanging specific exports for specific imports.

In the domestic economy, money reduces the cost of making exchanges. The seller of pots needs only to find a buyer willing to pay with bills, coins, or a check. He does not have to accept goods that may be difficult to store, use, and trade. In the international economy too, money facilitates trade, but well over a hundred different national currencies are in use. The French have the franc; the Japanese, the yen; the Americans, the dollar. To deal with this complication, a system of international exchanges emerged in which importers pay for the goods they buy in their own currency, but the exporters they deal with receive payment in their currency. How this system works, and the problems inherent in it, are the subjects of this chapter.

## The Process of International Monetary Exchange

Imagine you own a small gourmet shop that carries special cheeses. You may buy your cheese either domestically—cheddar from New York, Monterey jack from California—or abroad. If you buy from a domestic firm, it is easy to negotiate the deal and make payment. Since the price of cheese is quoted in dollars and the domestic firm expects payment in dollars, you can pay the same way you pay other bills—by writing a personal check. Only one national currency is involved.

Purchasing cheese from a French cheese maker is a little more complicated, for two reasons. First, the price of the cheese will be quoted in francs. Second, you will want to pay in dollars, but the French cheese maker must be paid in francs. Either you must exchange your dollars for francs, or the cheese maker must convert them for you. At some point, currencies must be exchanged at some recognized exchange rate.

### International Exchange Rates

**International exchange rate:** the price of one national currency stated in terms of another national currency.

Before you buy, you will want to compare the prices of French and domestic cheeses. You must convert the franc price of cheese into its dollar equivalent. To do that, you need to know the international exchange rate between dollars and francs. The **international exchange rate** is the price of one national currency (like the franc) stated in terms of another national currency (like the dollar). In other words, the international exchange rate is the dollar price you must pay for each franc you buy. Table 18.1 gives the dollar prices of several foreign currencies as of the end of February,

**Table 18.1.** Selected International Exchange Rates (dollar prices of foreign currencies), February 28, 1985.

| | Dollar Price of Foreign Currency |
|---|---|
| British pound | $1.0825 |
| Canadian dollar | 0.7246 |
| French franc | 0.0982 |
| Japanese yen | 0.0039 |
| Spanish peseta | 0.0055 |
| Swedish krona | 0.1060 |
| West German mark | 0.2996 |

**Source:** *Wall Street Journal,* March 1, 1985, p. 39.

1985. The franc was then worth almost $0.10, and the British pound cost a little more than $1.08.

Once you know the current exchange rate, conversion of currencies is not difficult. Assume that you want to buy F5,000 (read "5,000 francs") worth of cheese, and that the international exchange rate between dollars and francs is $0.10 (that is, $1 sells for F10). F5,000 at $0.10 apiece will cost you $500.

The international exchange rate determines the dollar price of the foreign goods you want to buy. A different exchange rate would have changed the dollar price of cheese. For instance, suppose the exchange rate rose from $0.10 = F1 to $0.20 = F1. In the jargon of international finance, such a change represents a depreciation (sometimes called a devaluation) of the dollar. A **depreciation of the dollar** (or any other national currency) is a reduction in purchasing power in terms of other national currencies. The dollar is now cheaper in terms of francs: it takes fewer francs (F5) to buy a dollar than previously (F10).

**Depreciation of the dollar** (or any other national currency): a reduction in purchasing power in terms of other national currencies.

The same change represents an appreciation of the franc. An **appreciation of the dollar** (or any other national currency) is an increase in purchasing power in terms of other national currencies. Each franc will now buy a larger fraction of a dollar—$0.20 as opposed to $0.10. From the perspective of the gourmet shop, the important point is that at the higher exchange rate, the dollar price of the cheese purchase is $1,000 ($0.20 × 5,000). If the exchange rate fell from $0.10 = F1 to $0.05 = F1, the price of the French cheese would decline to $250.

**Appreciation of the dollar** (or any other national currency): an increase in purchasing power in terms of other national currencies.

As you can see, your willingness to buy French cheese depends very much on the franc price of cheese and the exchange rate. If the franc price of cheese increases or decreases, your dollar price increases or decreases. Changes in the dollar price of francs have a similar effect. If the dollar depreciates (that is, if the price of francs in dollars rises), the dollar price of French cheese rises. Very likely you will be inclined to import less, since at the higher price your customers will buy less. If the dollar appreciates (that is, if the price of francs falls), the dollar price of French

**Table 18.2.** The Effects of Depreciation and Appreciation of the Dollar on U.S. Exports and Imports

| | Depreciation of Dollar | Appreciation of Dollar |
|---|---|---|
| Price of exports | Decrease | Increase |
| Total dollar value of exports | Increase | Decrease |
| Price of imports | Increase | Decrease |
| Total dollar value of imports | Decrease | Increase |

cheese falls. Very likely you will import more, since you can lower your own price and sell more. In general, a depreciation of the dollar discourages imports; an appreciation of the dollar encourages imports. (The results of changes in the international rate of exchange are summarized in Table 18.2.)

During the first half of this decade the U.S. dollar appreciated in relation to most major currencies. The dollar price of the French franc, for instance, began to tumble in the early 1980s, falling from about twenty-four cents in 1980 to just above eleven cents in late 1984 (see Figure 18.1). As the dollar value of the franc fell, French goods and travel in France became less expensive for Americans. U.S. goods and foreign travel in the United States became more expensive for the French.

## The Exchange of National Currencies

Assume you have figured the dollar price of cheese using the exchange rate and find it satisfactory. Since your American customers pay for their groceries in dollars, that is the only currency you have to make the payment. Yet cheese makers in France need francs to pay for their groceries. Therefore the French cheese exporter must ultimately be paid in francs.

How can you make payment in dollars while the French exporter is paid in francs? A bank will exchange your dollars for you. Banks deal in national currencies for the same reason that business people trade in commodities: to make money. An automobile dealer buys cars at a low price with the hope of selling them at a higher price. Banks do the same thing, except that their commodities are national currencies. They buy dollars and pay for them in francs or yen, with the idea of selling them at a profit.

If you pay for your French cheese in dollars, you write a check against your checking account and send it to the French firm.[1] The French cheese maker will accept the check knowing that your dollars can be traded for francs (that is, sold to a French bank) at the current rate of exchange. If

1. Instruments of exchange other than checks are often used in international transactions. The process, however, is the same.

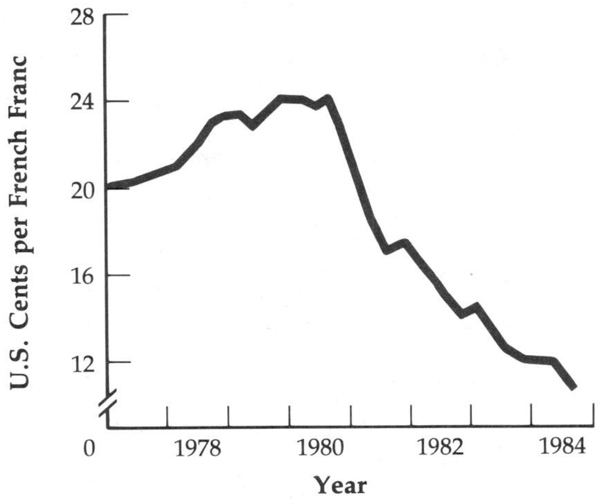


**Figure 18.1.** The Changing Dollar Price of the Franc.
The dollar price of the French franc has fluctuated considerably in recent years. From a high of about 24 cents in 1979, it fell to just above 11 cents in the third quarter of 1984.

the exchange rate is \$0.10 = F1, and you have sent the cheese maker a check for \$500, the exporter will receive F5,000 for your check from the French bank. Remember that banks, even foreign ones, have accounts with other banks, just as individuals do. The French bank will deposit your check with its U.S. banker. Your bank balance will fall, and the French bank's balance at the U.S. institution will rise. Then the French bank will sell (or trade) the dollars it has on account for francs.

In the process of buying and selling dollars, the French bank may make a profit. Suppose, for example, that the French bank buys dollars from the French cheese maker at a rate of \$0.10 = F1 (or \$1 = F10), paying F5,000 for \$500. It can then sell its dollars to a French importer for a higher franc price—say \$0.09 = F1 (or \$1 = F11.11). It will receive F5,555 for its \$500—a net gain of F555.

This hypothetical purchase of French cheese leads to an important observation. Any U.S. import, be it cheese or watches, will increase the dollar holdings of foreign banks. So will American expenditures abroad, whether for tours or for foreign stocks and bonds. Americans must have francs for such transactions; therefore they must offer American dollars in exchange. In most instances, foreign banks end up holding the dollars that Americans have sold.

In the same way, U.S. exports reduce the dollar holdings of foreign banks. Exports are typically paid for out of the dollar accounts of foreign banks. Foreign expenditures on trips to the United States or on the stocks and bonds of U.S. corporations have the same effect. They reduce the dollar holdings of foreign banks and increase the foreign currency holdings of U.S. banks. If American expenditures abroad exceed foreign expenditures here, the dollar holdings of foreign banks will rise—and vice versa.

If American expenditures abroad exceed foreign expenditures here for a long time, foreign banks will eventually accumulate all the dollars they can reasonably expect to use—that is, to sell back to their citizens for the purchase of American goods. Foreign banks then have several options. First, they may sell their dollar holdings to other foreign commercial banks in exchange for francs, marks, or krona. Second, they may sell their dollars to their government—or, more properly, to their government's central bank (for example, the Bank of France).

But the market may already be saturated with dollars. No one, including the central bank, may want to buy dollars at the going price, $0.10 = F1 in our illustration. In that case, foreign banks can induce people to buy dollars by lowering their price. For instance, they can alter the exchange rate from $0.10 = F1 to $0.15 = F1. In so doing they increase the price of francs and decrease (depreciate) the price of dollars.

A change in the exchange rate will have several effects, all tending to reduce the number of dollars coming onto the international money market. As explained earlier, the change will make French goods more expensive for Americans to buy. Thus it will tend to reduce U.S. imports, and accordingly the number of dollars that must be exchanged for foreign currencies. Depreciation will also tend to reduce the price of American goods to foreigners. For instance, at an exchange rate of $0.10 = F1, the franc price of a $1 million American computer is F10 million. At an exchange rate of $0.15 = F1, the franc price of the same computer is F6.66 million—a substantial reduction in price. To buy American goods at the new lower franc price, the French will increase their demand for dollars. Again, the quantity of dollars being offered on the money market will fall, and the growth in foreign dollar holdings will be checked.

## Determination of the Exchange Rate

National currencies have a market value—that is, a price—because individuals, firms, and governments use them to buy foreign goods, services, and securities. There is a market demand for a national currency like the franc. Furthermore, the demand for the franc (or any other currency) slopes downward, like curve *D* in Figure 18.2. To see why, look at the market for francs from the point of view of a U.S. resident. As the dollar price of the franc falls, the price of French goods to Americans also falls. As a result Americans will want to buy more French goods. They will require a larger quantity of francs to complete their transactions.

The supply of francs coming onto the market reflects the French people's demand for American goods, services, and securities. To get American goods, the French need dollars. They must pay for those dollars with francs, and in doing so they supply francs to the international money market. As the dollar price of the franc rises, the price of American goods to the French falls. To buy a larger quantity of American goods at the lower franc price, the French need more dollars; they must offer more francs to get them. Therefore the quantity of francs supplied on the market

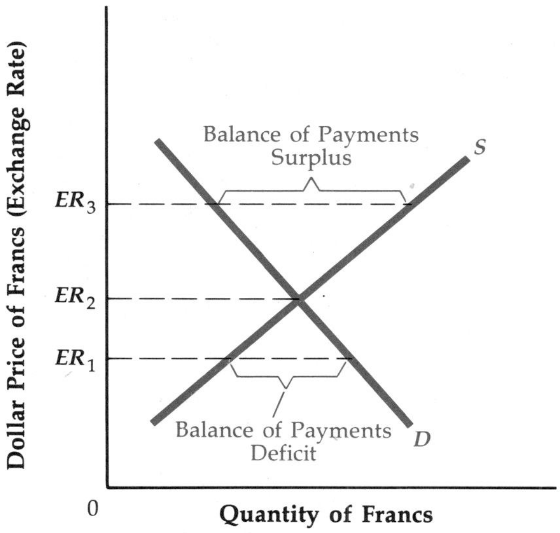


**Figure 18.2.** Supply and Demand for Francs on the International Currency Market. The international exchange rate between the dollar and the franc is determined by the forces of supply and demand. If the exchange rate is below equilibrium at $ER_1$, the quantity of francs demanded, shown by the demand curve, will exceed the quantity supplied, shown by the supply curve. Competitive pressure will push the exchange rate up. If the exchange rate is above equilibrium at $ER_3$, the quantity supplied will exceed the quantity demanded, and competitive pressure will push the exchange rate down. Thus the price of a foreign currency is determined in much the same way as the price of any other commodity.

rises. Thus the supply curve for francs slopes upward to the right, like curve *S* in Figure 18.2.

The buyers and sellers of francs make up what is loosely called the international money market in francs. Banks are very much involved in such markets. They buy francs from the sellers (suppliers) and sell to the buyers (demanders). As in other markets, the interaction of suppliers and demanders determines the market price. That is, given the supply and demand curves in Figure 18.2, in a competitive market the dollar price of the franc will move toward the intersection of the supply and demand curves. The equilibrium price, or exchange rate, will be $ER_2$, the price at which the quantity of francs supplied exactly equals the quantity of francs demanded.

At the market equilibrium point there is no build-up of dollars or francs in the accounts of foreign banks. French and U.S. banks have no reason to modify the exchange rate to encourage or discourage the purchase or sale of either currency. To use a financial expression, the net balance of payments coming into and going out of each nation is zero.

If the exchange rate is below equilibrium level—say $ER_1$—the quantity of francs demanded will exceed the quantity supplied (see Figure 18.2).

An imbalance in the balance of payments will develop. Or in the jargon of international finance, the United States will develop a balance of payments deficit—a shortfall in the quantity of a foreign currency supplied. (This is a conceptual definition. When it comes to defining the balance of payments deficit in a way that can be measured by the Department of Commerce, economists are in considerable disagreement.)

As in other markets, this imbalance will eventually right itself. Because of the excess demand for francs, French banks will accumulate excess dollar balances. French banks will have more dollars than they can sell and fewer francs than they need. Competitive pressure will then push the exchange rate back up to $ER_2$. People who cannot buy francs at $ER_1$ will offer a higher price. As the price of francs rises, French goods will become less attractive to Americans, and the quantity of francs demanded will fall. Conversely American goods will become more attractive to the French, and the quantity of francs supplied will rise.

Similarly, at an exchange rate higher than $ER_2$—say $ER_3$—the quantity of francs supplied will exceed the quantity demanded (see Figure 18.2). A balance of payments surplus—an excess quantity of a foreign currency supplied—will develop. The surplus will not last forever, however. Eventually the exchange rate will fall back toward $ER_2$, causing an increase in the quantity of francs demanded and a decrease in the quantity supplied. In short, in a free foreign currency market, the price of a currency is determined in the same way the prices of other commodities are determined.

## Market Adjustment to Changes in Money Market Conditions

By modifying exchange rates to correct for imbalances in payments, the money market can accommodate vast changes in the economic conditions of nations engaged in trade. A good example is the way the market handles a change in consumption patterns.

Suppose American preferences for French goods increase for some reason. The demand for francs will rise, because Americans will need more francs to buy the additional French goods they desire. If, as in Figure 18.3, the U.S. demand for francs shifts from $D_1$ to $D_2$, the quantity of francs demanded at the old equilibrium exchange rate of $ER_1$ will exceed the quantity supplied. Those who cannot buy more francs at $ER_1$ will offer to pay a higher price. The exchange rate will rise toward the new equilibrium level of $ER_2$. As the dollar depreciates in value, the imbalance in payments is eliminated.

Now suppose Americans' real incomes rise. Assuming that consumption goes up with real income, they will be likely to demand more foreign imports, both directly and in the form of domestic goods that incorporate foreign parts or materials. Either way, an increase in real incomes leads to an increase in the demand for foreign currencies. Again the demand for francs will rise, as in Figure 18.3. The exchange rate will rise with it to bring the quantity supplied into line with the quantity demanded.

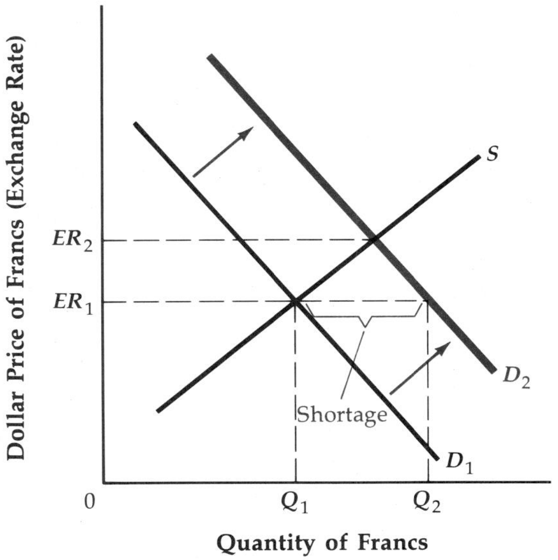


**Figure 18.3.** Effect of an Increase in Demand for Francs.
An increase in the demand for francs will shift the demand curve from $D_1$ to $D_2$. At the initial equilibrium exchange rate, $ER_1$, a shortage will develop. Competition among buyers will push the exchange rate up to the new equilibrium level, $ER_2$.

A change in the rate of inflation can have a similar effect on the exchange rate. If the inflation rates are about the same in two nations that trade with each other, the exchange rate between their currencies will remain stable, *ceteris paribus*. Because the relative prices of goods in the two nations stay the same, people will have no incentive to switch from domestic to imported goods, or vice versa. If one nation's inflation rate exceeds another's, however, the relative prices of foreign and domestic goods change. If prices increase faster in the United States, for example, Americans will want to buy more foreign goods and fewer domestic goods. Foreigners, on the other hand, will have an incentive to buy more goods from their own countries, where prices are not rising as fast as in the United States. In sum, a higher U.S. inflation rate spells a rise in the demand for foreign currencies, a fall in their supply, and a depreciation of the dollar.

Figure 18.4 illustrates the process. As U.S. demand for foreign goods rises, the demand curve for francs shifts outward, from $D_1$ to $D_2$. But as foreign demand for U.S. products falls, the supply curve for francs shifts to the left, from $S_1$ to $S_2$. At the initial equilibrium exchange rate of $ER_1$, a shortage of francs will develop. The exchange rate will rise to $ER_2$, eliminating the shortage and reestablishing balance in the money market. At the higher rate, Americans must pay a higher dollar price for foreign goods. The rise in the exchange rate has evened out the difference in the two nations' inflation rates.

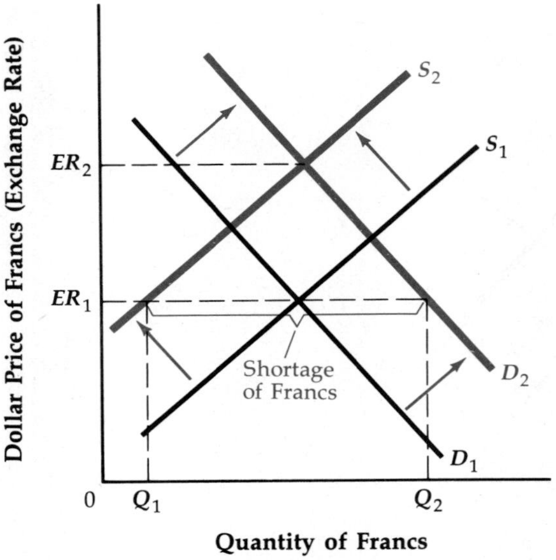


**Figure 18.4.** Effect of an Increase in Inflation on the Supply and Demand for Francs.
If the rate of inflation is higher in the United States than in France, the demand for francs will rise from $D_1$ to $D_2$, while the supply of francs will contract from $S_1$ to $S_2$. The dollar price of francs will rise from $ER_1$ to $ER_2$.

# Control of the Exchange Rate: The Fixed-Rate System

**Floating (flexible) exchange rate system:** an international monetary exchange system in which the prices of currencies are determined by competitive market forces.

**Fixed exchange rate system:** an international monetary exchange system in which the prices of currencies are established and maintained by governments.

So far our analysis of the international money market has assumed a floating, or flexible, system of exchange. A **floating (flexible) exchange rate system** is one in which the prices of currencies are determined by competitive market forces. Until 1971, however, international exchange rates were controlled by governments. Rates were not permitted to move in response to changes in supply and demand. Because rates were fixed for long periods of time by government decree, this system is generally referred to as a fixed exchange rate system. A **fixed exchange rate system** is one in which the prices of currencies are established and maintained by governments. Though the fixed-rate system is no longer in use among major nations, it merits some discussion because of its historical importance.

The fixed exchange rate has one advantage over the floating rate: it is stable. Because even a small change in the exchange rate can cause significant losses to people who have already concluded business deals, a flexible exchange rate can increase the risks involved in international trade. For example, suppose you agree to purchase cheese at an exchange rate of \$0.10 = F1. You promise to pay the exporter \$500, and the French cheese maker expects to receive F5,000. But by the time you send the check, the exchange rate has moved to \$0.11 = F1. The exporter will now receive only F4,545 (\$500 ÷ 0.11). He loses F455.

If the exchange rate moves in the opposite direction, of course, the exporter will gain. In addition, the French cheese maker can hedge against short-term losses by agreeing, at the time he closes the deal, to sell the proceeds at a given exchange rate, perhaps a fraction of a cent less than the current rate of \$.10 = F1. In long-term deals, however, traders inevitably risk losing money because of changes in exchange rates. They incur a risk cost that is translated into higher prices. Under a fixed-rate system, exchange rates move only periodically. The risk cost is reduced, and the prices of foreign goods can be lower.

Like any other form of price control, however, control of foreign exchange rates creates its own problems. If the exchange rate is fixed—at $ER_1$ in Figure 18.3, for example—and the supply and demand curves remain stable, there is no problem. But neither is there any need for government to fix the rate. It will remain at $ER_1$ as long as the supply and demand curves for currency stay put.

Problems can develop when market conditions change but the exchange rate is fixed. If the demand for francs increases from $D_1$ to $D_2$ in Figure 18.3, a shortage of francs will develop on the international money market. Those who want francs at the fixed price will be unable to get all they want. The government may have to ration the available francs and police the market against black marketeering. For if black markets are not controlled, the price of currency will rise—illegally perhaps, but it will rise nonetheless. In the end the exchange rate will not really be controlled.

## Monetary Adjustment Under the Fixed-Rate System

Under the conditions just described, the United States government can keep the exchange rate fixed if it finds some way to fill the gap between the quantity of francs supplied and demanded. Under the fixed exchange system, governments hold currency reserves for just this purpose. Accordingly, the U.S. government sells some of its francs at the officially established price ($ER_1$ in Figure 18.3), eliminating the upward pressure on the exchange rate. To do so, however, the government must have collected reserves at times when the quantity of francs supplied exceeded the quantity demanded. During such periods the government generally buys the excess francs with dollars specially created for the purchase.

If a shortage of francs persists, however—if the imbalance in the balance of payments is fundamental rather than temporary—it can only be corrected by a shift in market conditions. An increase in the demand for U.S. goods, for instance, might correct a persistent imbalance. Until market conditions change, maintaining sufficient currency reserves can become a real problem. A persistent shortage of currencies, often referred to as a liquidity problem, can be remedied temporarily in several ways.

## Perspectives in Economics: The World Debt Crisis

Early in the 1980s, American news magazines began carrying articles on the dramatic rise in debt owed by third-world nations, including Brazil, Mexico, and Argentina. And indeed, when measured in current U.S. dollars, the growth of those three countries' debt was staggering (see Figure 18.5). Between 1972 and 1981 their combined debt grew at an average annual rate of 26 percent. In just nine years, their total debt expanded eight times. No wonder that two of those nations, Argentina and Mexico, were occasionally unable to meet their interest payments.

Soon policymakers began to fear that some countries might default on their debt. The Reagan administration involved itself in the controversy when it became known that several U.S. banks, including the Chase Manhattan Bank of New York, had made sizable loans to the governments of foreign countries. Concerned that default might bankrupt these banks, weakening public confidence in the entire banking system, the U.S. government in 1983 agreed with other members of the International Monetary Fund to an increase in IMF loans. The action gave debt-strapped third-world nations more funds at lower interest rates. (IMF loans are made at below-market rates.)

Critics opposed the administration's efforts to ease the debt burden of foreign countries on several grounds. First, they charged, the IMF loans represented a thinly disguised bailout of U.S. banks that had made bad loans. In effect, U.S. tax dollars had been made available to other nations through the IMF, enabling them to pay the interest they owed U.S. banks.

Second, many banks had charged high interest rates on their foreign loans to compensate for the risk of default. Even if several of their loans went bad, income from their other loans should be sufficient to cover their losses.

Third, the seriousness of the debt crisis had been overblown. A nation's ability to repay its debt may be gauged by the ratio of its debt to its gross national product. Though the debt burdens of Brazil, Mexico, and Argentina rose in comparison with their GNP during much of the 1970s, their debt-GNP ratios began to fall toward the end of the decade (see Figure 18.6). They continued to fall or held steady through 1981.

Fourth, default would not enable a nation to walk away from its debt. It would simply require the debtor nation to find some other way of covering its debt payments besides current tax collections. A nation in default could sell some of its assets, whether land or nationalized industries. Or it could convert its debt to an equity interest in its assets. After all, debtor nations had used much of their borrowings to expand their capital base. From that perspective, the debt crisis was really a crisis in their willingness—not their ability—to make good on their debts.

Fifth, the government's remedy for the presumed debt crisis—subsidized loans from the IMF—could foster a real debt crisis. Low-interest loans might encourage debtor nations to go so far into debt that they could not extract themselves without further aid from the IMF—and indirectly, from U.S. taxpayers.

Proponents of government aid to developing countries, on the other hand, maintained that the third-world debt crisis was real. Many developing countries had had difficulty earning the money to make payments on their debt. Third-world nations tend to rely heavily on agricultural exports, whose prices were depressed in the early 1980s. From that perspective, IMF loans could be seen as a way of helping debtor nations through temporary hard times.

Proponents of aid charged also that U.S. banks and even some governments had urged developing countries to go into debt in the 1970s. Policymakers had apparently reasoned that greater debt meant greater demand for goods and services in developing countries—and thus greater sales of goods and services to them. The OPEC oil price hikes had also increased the indebtedness of third-world nations. To meet the rising oil prices of the mid-1970s, developing countries had to sell more goods and services abroad. At the same time, OPEC

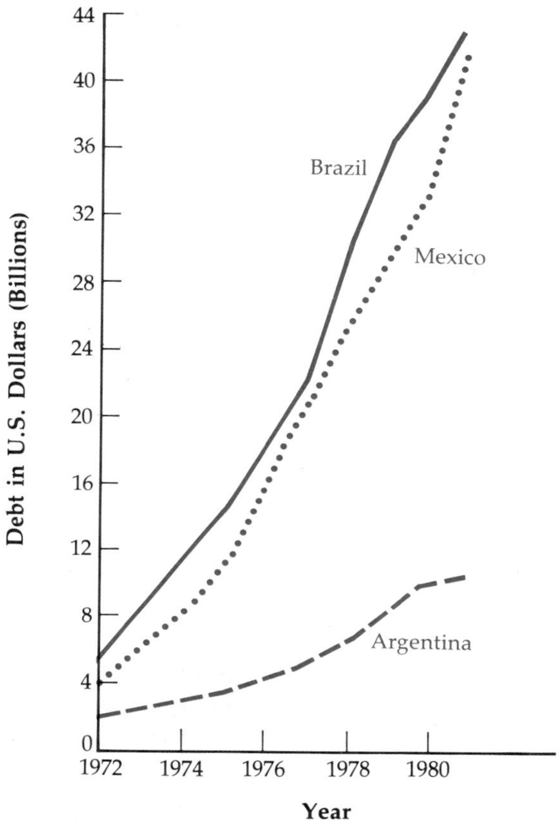

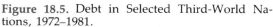

**Figure 18.5.** Debt in Selected Third-World Nations, 1972–1981.
In current U.S. dollars, Brazil's debt rose from approximately $6 billion to $44 billion from 1972 to 1981. In the same period, Mexico's debt jumped from slightly under $4 billion to $42 billion. Argentina's debt grew more modestly, from just over $2 billion to over $10 billion.
**Source:** Jon Osborne, "Paper Crisis," *Reason* (May 1984), p. 31.

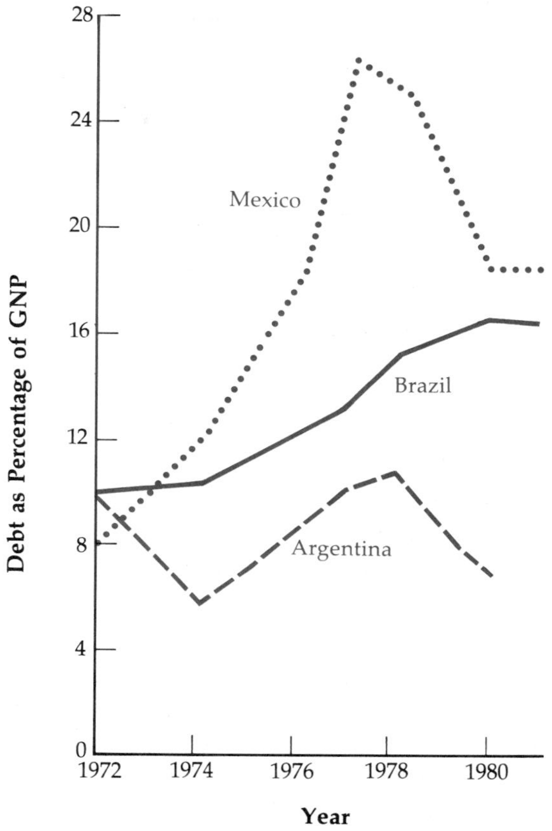


**Figure 18.6.** Debt as a Percentage of GNP in Selected Third-World Nations, 1972–1981.
Mexico's debt-to-GNP ratio jumped dramatically between 1972 and 1977, and then fell sharply after 1978. Brazil's debt-to-GNP ratio grew more gradually until 1980, then turned slightly downward. During the same period Argentina's debt-to-GNP ratio fluctuated.
**Source:** Jon Osborne, "Paper Crisis," *Reason* (May 1984), p. 32.

countries were earning substantially more from their oil exports than they wanted to spend on imports. They had money available for overseas investment, which they channeled to both third-world and developed nations through U.S. banks.

The controversy over what should be done to help developing countries manage their debt arose partly because people interpreted the facts differently. The magnitude of the problem, and the capacity of third-world nations to handle it, remain matters of debate. So does the question of who should be held responsible for the debt—the developing countries that incurred it, or the banks that made the loans to them.

## Gold Reserves

For centuries governments have used gold as an international monetary reserve, defining their national currencies in terms of it. The U.S. government might establish the price of gold at $35 an ounce, for example; the French government, at F350 an ounce. In case of a currency shortage, these gold reserves can be used to fill the gap between quantity supplied and demanded. If a shortage of francs develops on the money market, for instance, the U.S. government can sell some of its gold to France and receive F350 for each ounce. The government can then sell the francs on the money market, filling the gap at the official exchange rate.

In practice, the process may not work exactly that way. Given the shortage of francs, foreign banks may continue to exchange francs for dollars and then sell their dollars to the Bank of France, which will exchange them for gold. The final outcome is the same, however. Gold is traded for francs, and the shortage of francs is eliminated.

Conversely, if there is a shortage of dollars, the French government can keep the price of the dollar from rising above the official level by selling some of its gold to the United States. It then exchanges (sells) its dollars for francs.

## Currency Reserves

From the 1930s until 1971, when exchange rates were allowed to float, most nations kept a combination of gold and currency as monetary reserves. Many kept the U.S. dollar, which has come to be accepted throughout the world as a form of exchange. A Brazilian exporter, for example, might accept dollars from a German importer, because he is confident that they can be converted into Brazilian currency.

Foreign banks too have been willing to hold large amounts of dollars, partly because of the dollar's acceptability in business transactions and partly because banks know foreigners will always demand a large variety of U.S. goods. Before 1971, banks could trade their dollars in for gold at any time. Since gold was more expensive to store, however, they chose to hold dollars. Note that these foreign banks got their dollars from the sale of goods and services to Americans. To the extent that they still hold them for the purpose of carrying out other transactions, people in the United States have struck a tremendous deal. They have traded money—a paper product relatively cheap to produce—for foreign textiles, automobiles, and appliances, which are much more expensive to produce.

## The International Monetary Fund (IMF)

The International Monetary Fund (IMF) was created at the close of the Second World War to expand international reserves further. By depositing part of its gold reserves and a specified amount of its currency in the IMF, a nation receives the right to borrow other foreign currencies at a modest interest rate. It can then use those currencies to fill a gap between outgoing and incoming foreign payments. Borrowing rights are restricted to 125 percent of a nation's deposit with the IMF.

Suppose the United States' deposit is $1 billion. At the established exchange rates, the United States can borrow as much as $1.25 billion worth of francs, pounds, yen, or any other currency. When its need for extra reserves has slackened, the United States can pay back the currencies it has borrowed. The method works well. Over the years member nations have raised their deposits at the IMF, increasing the quantity of foreign currencies they can borrow.

## Currency Swaps

At times nations have increased one another's currency reserves simply by trading their currencies. For instance, the United States might agree to swap some of its dollars for West German marks. Each nation then has more of the other's currency available to cover a balance of payments deficit, should one occur. In addition, during periods of international monetary crisis, when buyers and sellers of a particular currency no longer accept the official exchange rate, nations can lend money to each other. The borrowed funds can be used to fill a balance of payments gap and prevent the exchange rate from rising.

Reserves acquired through currency swaps are meant to be used only to correct temporary imbalances in a nation's international accounts, or to get it through financial difficulties. During periods when incoming payments exceed outgoing payments, nations are expected to rebuild their depleted reserves. In the 1960s, however, the system failed to work as expected. Some nations, particularly the United States and Great Britain, failed to correct their persistent balance of payment deficits. Once they got additional reserves, they used them up. In effect, the United States and Britain were using currency swaps to trade their paper currency for the goods and services of other nations.

To correct a fundamental imbalance of payments, a nation might adopt anti-inflationary policies or impose tariffs on imports. It might also take measures to improve the competitiveness of its industry. (More will be said on this subject later.)

## Special Drawing Rights (SDRs)

Gold has been used for centuries as an international reserve. But it is expensive to mine and store. To use gold as a currency reserve, a nation must not only get it out of the ground, but go to the trouble and expense of storing it. And it must maintain expensive security systems to prevent the gold from being stolen. Though gold has an important role in international finance, its benefits come at considerable expense to all who use it.

Gold reserves have another disadvantage: they increase only as new gold is mined and distributed. Yet growth in world trade can quickly widen the gap between a nation's outgoing and incoming payments. If the exchange rate is to be held constant, the growing gap must be filled with a larger quantity of reserves. Unfortunately, growth in world trade can easily outstrip not only growth in gold reserves, but growth in reserves from other sources.

Fearing that currency imbalances might impede world trade, and recognizing the expense of increasing world gold reserves, members of the IMF developed plans for a new monetary reserve system, called Special Drawing Rights (SDRs) in the 1960s. Unlike other reserves, SDRs are merely bookkeeping entries in the IMF accounts. Once a nation has an SDR account, it can use SDRs to settle imbalances in any currency. It can sell some of its SDRs to France for francs (or to Germany for marks), and use the francs (marks) to fill the balance of payments gap. Because SDRs can be used much as gold is used, they are sometimes called paper gold.

Even though SDRs are only bookkeeping entries, they are a form of international money. The members of the IMF have agreed to accept SDRs in settlement of their accounts, just as they accepted gold in the past. Just as the general acceptability of the U.S. dollar gives the bills in your wallet value in domestic transactions, the general acceptability of SDRs gives them value. Money is what people will generally accept in trade.

## Correcting a Persistent Balance of Payments Deficit

International reserves of gold, foreign currencies, and SDRs are useful in solving temporary balance of payment problems. But if outgoing payments exceed incoming payments for long, a nation's reserves will eventually run out. It will not be able to prop up the value of its currency without resorting to elaborate corrective measures, most of which are either economically inefficient or politically unacceptable.

Tax increases, expenditure decreases, and a reduction in the growth of the money stock may help to reduce inflation temporarily, but at the cost of a drop in total real income. The lower inflation rate will make domestically produced goods more attractive, both at home and abroad. And a lower aggregate real income will mean people will have less to spend, both on domestic goods and on imports. This reduced demand for foreign goods will be translated into a reduced demand for foreign currencies. As a result, the gap between the supply of and demand for any particular foreign currency will narrow, reducing the short-run balance of payments deficit. Many economists believe this was precisely the policy President Dwight Eisenhower followed during his term of office (1953–1961). Politically it is a controversial approach. By lowering total real income and production, this method of correcting a balance of payments deficit can add to the nation's unemployment. Though a reduction in the inflation rate may seem attractive, increased short-term unemployment is a high price to pay for an improved balance of payments.

Tariffs on imported goods and/or restrictions on the flow of funds into foreign investments are another way of correcting a persistent balance of payments deficit. Both approaches tend to reduce the immediate demand for foreign currencies. Though these policies have been used by almost all governments at one time or another, they expose citizens to all the

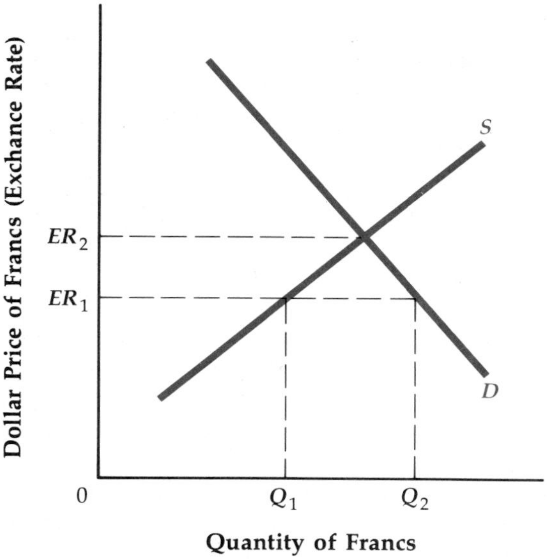


**Figure 18.7.** Balance of Payments Deficit.
Given a supply of francs equal to $S$ and a demand for francs equal to $D$, an exchange rate of $ER_1$ will cause a balance of payments deficit equal to the difference between $Q_2$ and $Q_1$. At $ER_1$, the exchange rate is below equilibrium; more francs are demanded than supplied. Depreciation of the dollar through a rise in the exchange rate, from $ER_1$ to $ER_2$, will eliminate the deficit.

negative effects of restrictions on international trade described in the preceding chapter.

After all else has been tried, a nation may be forced to depreciate its currency. Given a fixed exchange rate of \$0.10 = F1, for instance, the United States could correct a balance of payments deficit by depreciating the dollar (or revising the exchange rate upward) to \$0.20 = F1. The rules of the IMF provide for such a change, which would make U.S. exports more attractive to foreigners and foreign imports less attractive to Americans. Thus it would reduce the quantity of francs demanded and increase the quantity of francs supplied on the international monev market. In Figure 18.7, with the exchange rate at $ER_1$, the balance of payments deficit is the difference between the quantity of francs demanded, $Q_2$, and the quantity supplied, $Q_1$. At $ER_1$, the exchange rate is below equilibrium. Depreciation of the dollar moves the exchange rate up toward the equilibrium rate of $ER_2$, reducing the gap between supply and demand.

## The Demise of the Fixed-Rate System

In August 1971, President Richard Nixon withdrew the United States' commitment to maintain fixed exchange rates between the dollar and other national currencies. In so doing, he allowed the overvalued U.S. dollar to seek a new equilibrium level and to move, or float, with changes in money market conditions. The demise of the fixed exchange rate system—sometimes called the adjustable peg system, since nations could adjust the rates periodically—was inevitable. The United States had run a balance of payments deficit almost every year since 1950. Its gold reserves, valued at $35 an ounce, had dwindled from a high of $23 billion in 1950 to $12 billion in 1971. At the same time, about $80 billion had accumulated in foreign bank accounts. Although many of those dollars were necessary to the transaction of world trade, it was becoming clear that the market was saturated with overvalued dollars.

In the mid-1960s, moreover, people had begun to expect depreciation of the dollar and the British pound. Every year or so there would be a run on the dollar or the pound. Panicky investors would try to exchange their dollars or pounds for some other currency, like German marks. Such crises became progressively more frequent in the late 1960s and early 1970s. By August 1971, they had so destabilized the fixed exchange rate system that it was certain to be abandoned. The only question was the timing of the change to a floating exchange rate system.

Fear of depreciation can disrupt the international money market for two reasons. First, depreciation of a currency reduces the value of foreign holdings of that currency in terms of other world currencies. For example, at an exchange rate of $0.10 = F1, a $100 bank account is worth F1,000. At $0.20 = F1, however, that same $100 is worth only F500. To avoid a loss from an expected depreciation, people will try to sell the currency in question and buy others. In other words, at times of international monetary crisis, the demand for undervalued foreign currencies like francs will increase. The greater demand for francs will widen the gap between the quantity demanded and the quantity supplied, thus increasing the amount of reserves needed to bring the quantity supplied into line with the quantity demanded.

Second, speculators will try to make a profit on any expected depreciation of a currency. If a person holding dollars can buy francs at $0.10 apiece and sell them back at $0.20, he will make a profit of $0.10 on each franc. This speculative activity increases the demand for francs, again widening the gap between the quantity demanded and the quantity supplied. During the 1950s and 1960s, when the British experienced substantial balance of payments deficits, speculation in the pound was active.

## Summary and Extensions

A stable set of international exchange rates is needed for the smooth operation of international trade. Continual and significant variations in exchange rates introduce an unwanted element of risk into international commerce, reducing the volume of trade. But control of exchange rates through a fixed rate system has serious practical defects.

Under a floating exchange rate system, exchange rates vary in response to changes in consumer taste and the technology of production. Such fluctuations are not only useful but necessary. Exchange rates also vary with changes in domestic and foreign inflation rates and national income levels. In short, the international monetary system mirrors the stability or instability of the world's national economies. If the nations of the world are pursuing inappropriate domestic policies, they cannot expect the international monetary system to remain stable.

## Major Conclusions

1. The international exchange rate affects the relative prices of domestic and foreign products.
2. Changes in the exchange rate will change the relative prices of foreign and domestic products, altering import and export levels. Specifically, depreciation of the dollar will lower imports to the United States and increase exports from the United States. Appreciation of the dollar will have the opposite effect.
3. Under a floating exchange rate system, international exchange rates are determined by the interaction of supply and demand.
4. Changes in consumer tastes, in total real income, and in the rate of inflation can alter the exchange rate.
5. Under a fixed exchange rate system, nations use gold and currency reserves, loans from the International Monetary Fund, currency swaps, and special drawing rights to fill gaps between the quantity of a currency supplied and the quantity demanded.
6. A fixed exchange rate system lessens the risk involved in trade, but tends to create balance of payment problems. The United States dropped the fixed exchange rate in 1971.

## Questions to Ponder

1. If a nation appreciates its currency in relation to other national currencies, what will be the effect on other nations' exports and imports? On the willingness of that nation's citizens to invest abroad?
2. Will a tax on imports and a subsidy on exports have the same effect on trade as depreciation of a nation's currency?
3. Suppose the exchange rate between the pound and the dollar is fixed. If both the United States and Great Britain double the price of gold in terms of their own national currencies, what will be the effect on trade between the two nations? Assuming that other nations hold the price of gold in their own currencies constant, how will the change in the dollar and pound prices of gold affect trade between the United States and Britain and the rest of the world?
4. Develop cases for and against the fixed exchange rate system.
5. Do you agree that if a nation runs a persistent balance of payments surplus—that is, if its outgoing international payments fall consistently short of its incoming payments—it is trading goods and services for foreign currencies? Why might a nation be unwilling to incur an extended balance of payments surplus?

## Central Question

*What are the major forms of economic organization, and how do they differ?*

## Key Terms

**Mercantilism**
**Capitalism**
**Communism**
**National economic planning**
**Socialism**

## Chapter 19

# Comparative Economic Systems

*[I]nappropriate, wasteful, and sometimes harmful commodities have been produced and sold as the logical embodiment of the accepted principle which in a capitalist economy governs what is produced—the maximization of profit.*

Barry Commoner

In his *Wealth of Nations* in 1776, Adam Smith explained how the invisible hand of self-interest, tempered by competition, could effectively satisfy society's economic needs. The American economic system rests largely on Smith's theory. Our supermarkets, shopping centers, fast-food chains, and computer companies are bastions of free enterprise. Yet the federal government frequently thrusts a visible hand into the operations of the market, setting standards, propping up prices, interfering with imports, or encouraging employment.

In the Soviet Union, on the other hand, the economy is carefully controlled. Still, financial incentives must be employed to stimulate production, and many goods are sold on the open market. Not long ago, in fact, many economists believed that over time the United States and the Soviet Union, like a married couple, would come to resemble each other more and more.[1] Recent years have given little evidence that the Soviet hierarchy is relaxing its control of the economy, however. And the United States seems to be moving away from government intervention, particularly in transportation, communication, and banking.

At the same time, the economies of Western Europe are showing signs of economic ambivalence. Under Margaret Thatcher's Conservative government in Great Britain, government interference has sometimes taken precedence over the free market. In France, the Socialist regime of Francois Mitterrand has retreated from some traditional socialist objectives. History is similarly ambiguous. In ancient times, trade stretched far across the Mediterranean. Yet the Code of Hammurabi and the construction of the pyramids in Egypt attest to persistent government efforts to manipulate and control economic activity.

This chapter explores some of the various "isms" under which government control and free enterprise blend in the modern world. Despite some important differences, there are many startling similarities in the way various economies operate.

## Mercantilism

The fading of the Middle Ages in Europe brought the gradual consolidation of nation-states, a process that transformed Western society. Particularly in England and France, but later in Germany and Italy, sovereigns wrought dramatic changes. They fostered the development of roads and canals, struck down internal tariffs that hindered trade along rivers, and stabilized systems of coinage. As fragmented and self-sufficient feudal fiefdoms gave way to more centralized political units, commerce blossomed.

While these changes spurred economic development, they were politically motivated. Their ultimate goal was to help sovereigns achieve control. Each new nation aimed to export more goods than it imported, in order

1. Neil H. Jacoby and James E. Howell, *European Economics—East and West: Convergence of Five European Countries and the United States* (Cleveland: World Publishing, 1967).

to enrich its sovereign's treasury. To achieve their desired balance of trade, nations granted monopoly rights to corporations. The formal name for such a policy is mercantilism. **Mercantilism** was a system of economic organization that flourished between 1500 and 1800. It was designed specifically to promote a desired balance of trade through monopoly of production and trading rights.

**Mercantilism:** a system of economic organization that flourished between 1500 and 1800, designed to promote a desired balance of trade through monopoly of production and trading rights.

## The Balance of Trade

Students of American history will recall that the British government discouraged manufacturing in its colonies. It preferred to extract raw materials, ship them to the homeland, enhance their value through the manufacturing process, and return finished goods to the colonies.

When exports outweigh imports, the nation is giving up more goods than it gets in return. You may wonder why sovereigns pursued that goal. As Adam Smith wrote in 1776, "If a foreign country can supply us with a commodity cheaper than we ourselves can make it, better buy it of them with some part of the produce of our own industry, employed in a way in which we have some advantage."[2] But there was method in the royal madness. What the sovereigns coveted was the money income, generally in the form of silver or gold, that made up the difference between their nations' exports and imports. Such funds could be taxed. The ample revenues they provided would equip large armies or support the construction of palatial royal estates.

David Hume first pointed out the fallacy in this reasoning. Adding an increased flow of hard currency to the domestic money supply would simply inflate prices. That in turn would discourage foreigners from buying British products, which would become more expensive in relation to their own. British exports would drop. Simultaneously, foreign items would become relatively more attractive to the British. Their imports would increase. The two trends would eventually combine to eliminate the trade surplus, cutting off the inflow of gold and silver. In the meantime, however, the sovereign would have enhanced his treasury—a victory of narrow personal interests over the general welfare.

## Monopoly Corporations

The establishment of monopoly corporations under mercantilism was designed to assure the surplus of exports that sovereigns desired. For a fee, rulers created special corporations and granted them exclusive control over trade with specific royal colonies. Such chartered companies were particularly appealing to the English monarchs, who found Parliament

2. Adam Smith, *An Inquiry into the Nature and Causes of the Wealth of Nations* (New York: Modern Library, 1937), p. 424.

persistently tightfisted in its support of royalty. In 1601, Queen Elizabeth I chartered the East India Company, granting it for fifteen years the power to "have, use and enjoy the whole entire and only trade and traffic . . . to and from the said East Indies and to and from all the islands, posts, havens, cities, towns and places aforesaid." The charter was repeatedly renewed, until in 1661 it became perpetual. Similar monopoly privileges were granted to settlers of the colonies and to those who would manufacture such items as glass, salt, and soap in England. Royal policy even required that many imports and exports be transported on the nation's own ships. The famous Navigation Acts of 1651 and 1660 served that purpose.

Of all the European rulers, the Dutch relied least on royally chartered monopolies. And it was the Dutch economy, the one with fewest government constraints, that expanded most rapidly in the mercantilist era. At the other extreme, the French government, under Louis XIV's minister of finance, Jean Baptiste Colbert, not only created great monopolies for producing such items as tapestries, but rigorously controlled product quality to enhance the products' export value. All such policies, though supposedly designed to promote the wealth of the nation, clearly enhanced the wealth of the sovereign and of investors in privileged companies more than the welfare of the people.

In the late 1600s, the influence of mercantilist thought began to wane. Following the Glorious Revolution in 1688, the British Parliament abolished the sovereign's right to create monopolies, for emerging commercial interests yearned to trade freely. By the late 1700s, American colonists so despised the confining monopoly power of royal corporations that the framers of the Constitution decided to avoid even mentioning corporations in that document, hoping that none would be created.[3] Not surprisingly, few corporations gained federal charters. Instead, virtually all corporations in the new nation were established by the states. In fact, states vied with one another for the economic development corporations would bring by making corporate charters easier and easier to obtain. Incorporation became so easy that corporations quickly lost all their monopoly privileges. Today's corporate charters certainly do not grant General Motors, IBM, Xerox, and RCA immunity from the forces of competition.

## Modern Mercantilism

Despite the founding fathers' hostility to monopoly rights, vestiges of mercantilism persist in the United States today. A good example is trade barriers that seek to limit foreign competition in the production of everything from steel, copper, cars, and textiles to golf carts, plastic mattress handles, canned pears, and ice cream sandwich wafers. These modern barriers are designed not to provide revenue for the Treasury,

3. A. A. Berle, Jr., *Economic Power and the Free Society* (Santa Barbara, Calif.: Center for the Study of Democratic Institutions, 1957), p. 4.

but to limit the supply and raise the price of protected products. But the general effect is the same: favored producers can sell their products at a higher price. Other vestiges of mercantilism limit entry into certain activities, such as the practice of medicine and law. In some cities, cab drivers must be licensed. The supply of licenses is limited so strictly that in recent years, licenses have sold for $84,000 and more.

Obviously, then, government and business are not natural enemies. They are often in cahoots. When the Carter administration deregulated the protected truck and airline industries, firms fought vigorously to maintain their privileged positions. Even under the conservative Reagan administration, attempts have been made to create new monopoly privileges. A bill submitted to Congress recently would have allowed beer producers to create exclusive monopolies for the distribution of their products. As one congressional representative wrote, "Beer wholesalers apparently are uncomfortable about the uncertainty that accompanies a competitive marketplace."[4] Finally, much like the British Navigation Acts, the Jones Act limits shipping between two American ports to American ships—although foreign vessels often offer lower rates and better service.

Thus, though the days of the exclusive royal charter are long gone, political leaders still serve their constituencies by granting exclusive monopoly privileges and protecting domestic industries. Nationalistic restrictions and favoritism are still with us.

## Capitalism and Its Critics

Mercantilism did not disappear overnight. Nor did Adam Smith's arguments about the power of the invisible hand have overwhelming impact. In the newly formed United States, Secretary of the Treasury Alexander Hamilton argued that tariffs on foreign imports were needed to protect fledgling industries at home. But in England, the Industrial Revolution wrought drastic changes in the economic environment. By the early 1800s, steam engines and innovations in textile manufacture combined to move production out of the home and into the factory. To finance production on such a large scale, producers needed large amounts of capital. A new economic system, called capitalism, quickly emerged. **Capitalism** is an economic system based on private property and free enterprise, in which few or no government barriers to trade or restrictions on entry into business or the professions discourage competition.

**Capitalism:** an economic system based on private property and free enterprise, in which few or no government barriers to trade or restrictions on entry into business or the professions discourage competition.

Capitalism is, of course, the philosophical basis for the free market system that exists today in the United States and many other nations. In its pure form, it has never enjoyed unqualified support anywhere. English writers like William Blake deplored the "dark, satanic mills" that fouled the air over the English countryside. "Supply-and-demand,—Alas!" wrote

4. Charles E. Schumer, "A Beer Bill to Mug Consumers," *Wall Street Journal*, February 22, 1984, p. 32.

# Perspectives in Economics: The Competitive Japanese Economy

*Katsuro Sakoh*

Japan has experienced remarkable economic success since the end of World War II. In 1981 Japan's GNP surpassed that of the Soviet Union, making it the second-largest economy in the world. By 1984 its current dollar GNP had climbed to $1,251 billion, compared with $3,820 billion in the United States—a nation with twice its population. In terms of GNP per capita, Japan ranked tenth in the world.

The driving forces of Japan's phenomenal success have been private entrepreneurs and a well-educated labor force. Unlike European governments, the Japanese government has tried to avoid owning and operating major industries. Instead, it has concentrated on keeping taxes low by holding down expenditures on social welfare, quality of life, and national defense. (Japan's tax-revenue-to-GNP ratio is the lowest of the developed nations.) This relatively low tax burden has allowed the Japanese to achieve a high rate of saving—20 percent, or almost three times that of Americans. In turn, high savings have produced a high rate of capital investment and rapid technological improvements in the private sector.

This free market environment enabled Japan to shift quickly from an agricultural orientation in the 1950s to an industrial orientation in the 1960s and a service orientation in recent years. Today, 57 percent of Japanese workers are employed in service industries—only 12 percentage points less than in the United States. Contrary to popular perception, these changes in economic structure have been carried out mostly by small private companies rather than by government direction. In the private sector as a whole, nearly 70 percent of the labor force works for companies with fewer than 200 employees. Almost all the workers in agriculture; more than three-quarters of the workers in construction, wholesale, retail, and personal service industries; and more than half of the workers in manufacturing are employed by small companies. The majority—perhaps two-thirds—of these workers are not guaranteed permanent employment.

Japan has achieved its economic success despite some formidable obstacles. The nation is small, the size of Montana, with no fossil fuels and few natural resources. To survive and grow, it must import most of its raw materials. During the oil crises of 1973 and 1978, Japan suffered high inflation, severe economic recession and negative growth rates, and large balance of trade deficits. As a result of that recession, the government is carrying a huge budget deficit. In 1983 Japan's debt-to-GNP ratio was 51 percent, compared with 43 percent in the United States.

Though Japan is heavily dependent on foreign trade for its well-being, trade is not the main source of its phenomenal economic growth. Japan's export-to-GNP ratio was only 13 percent in 1984—much lower than the ratio in any major industrial nation except the United States.[1] During the two oil crises of the 1970s, the buying power of Japan's exports deteriorated more than 30 percent. But the nation overcame that handicap by investing heavily in energy-saving measures and more productive technology. Once more, Japan became competitive in the world market. Like its rapid recovery from the devastation of World War II, Japan's strength today is due to its imaginative, hard-working, consumer-oriented private sector.

1. The figures are 48 percent for the Netherlands; 27 percent for West Germany; 25 percent for Canada; 20 percent for the United Kingdom; and 7 percent for the United States.

Thomas Carlyle in 1843.[5] And in 1862 John Ruskin complained, "To this . . . professed and organized pursuit of Money . . . is owing *All* the evil of modern days."[6] Today, the writings of environmentalist Barry Commoner and economist John Kenneth Galbraith, among others, reflect a wariness toward the free market and the quest for profit. But of all the critics of capitalism, none is more notable than the man who made *capitalism* a household word: the German economist Karl Marx.

## Marxian Communism

Marx (1818–1883) did not favor a return to a traditional economy. Indeed, he commended capitalists for rescuing "a considerable part of the population from the idiocy of rural life."[7] But though he accepted the writings of the classical economists Adam Smith and David Ricardo, he viewed capitalist activities as at best a temporary necessity. To Marx, capitalism was merely a brief period of transition between a grim past and the more prosperous future. For Marx had observed a more fully developed capitalism than had Adam Smith, one in which the blessings of the division of labor were obscured by the curse of unemployment. It was unemployment that Marx saw as the fatal weakness of capitalism.

Marx's ideas are often summed up in the phrase "dialectical materialism." The word *dialectic* is derived from the Greek word for the process of developing philosophical ideas. Ancient Greek philosophers originated the technique of posing an idea, or hypothesis, against a contrasting idea, or antithesis. Through discussion thinkers would eventually merge the two ideas to create a new idea, or synthesis. But the process did not end there. The synthesis became the new hypothesis, and a new antithesis spawned a new synthesis.

In the early nineteenth century, the German philosopher Friedrich Hegel applied the concept of dialectics to historical development. He suggested that human evolution could be seen as a continuous process of hypothesis, antithesis, and synthesis. Marx extended the idea by specifying social classes as the opposing forces in the dialectical process. Medieval lords and serfs, pitted against each other, had been replaced by the bourgeois capitalists and the paid laborers ("proletariat") of modern times. Marx noted that each historical era had its own peculiar mode of production—the windmill of earlier times had given way to the steam engine. Thus the dialectical process had a distinctly economic, or material, base.

5. Quoted in Neil H. Jacoby and James E. Howell, *European Economics—East and West: Convergence of Five European Countries and the United States* (Cleveland: World Publishing, 1967), p. 2.
6. Quoted in Bernard Murchland, *Humanism and Capitalism: A Survey of Thought on Morality* (Washington: American Enterprise Institute for Public Policy Research, 1984), p. 7.
7. Karl Marx and Friedrich Engels, *The Communist Manifesto* (New York: Appleton-Century-Crofts, 1955), p. 14.

Like Hegel, Marx saw human history as a broad upward sweep through time. In London, where he took refuge from political persecution at home, Marx developed his theory. He started with the classical labor theory of value. For Adam Smith, that theory had meant emancipation from the mercantilist belief that the value of the world's output was rigidly fixed and could not increase. Trade was not a zero-sum game, Smith saw; what France gained, England would not necessarily lose. But the opening words of *The Wealth of Nations*, "Labour . . . supplies . . . all the necessities and conveniences of life," meant something quite different to Marx. He took the idea one step further and argued that only labor created value. The capitalist was an unnecessary parasite who had freed workers from bondage to the land, but was unnecessary to their future advancement.

The capitalist was, of course, the owner of the means of production: the machinery and tools that workers used. Forces of competition compelled capitalists then and now to acquire more and more capital. To purchase it, Marx charged, capitalists paid workers less than the value of their output—a tendency David Ricardo had already described. Capitalists did not live on the surplus revenues; instead, they used it to purchase more capital.

Meanwhile, instead of benefiting from the improved productivity created by new equipment, workers lost their jobs. As more and more of them were fired, they joined the "reserve army of the unemployed," a ready source of eager labor that depressed wages. Because workers were unable to buy the output of the new factories, capitalists would suffer wrenching business failures. Eventually, Marx believed, the reserve army of the unemployed would become so large and so desperate that it would rise up and overthrow the remaining capitalists in a bloody revolution. Such a violent transition had marked the advent of capitalism in France, and Marx expected history to repeat itself. The coming revolution would usher in the new and final era of communism. **Communism**, as conceived by Marx, was a classless society governed by workers that would emerge from the downfall of capitalism. In practical terms, communism is an economic system in which virtually all the means of production are owned and controlled by the state.

**Communism:** as conceived by Marx, a classless society governed by workers that would emerge from the downfall of capitalism. In practical terms, an economic system in which virtually all the means of production are owned and controlled by the state.

In the period after the revolution, which Marx called the dictatorship of the proletariat, property rights would be abolished and a new society would emerge. Since workers would no longer be the slaves of capitalists, they would spontaneously become more productive. And since the state—like religion—had merely been a device to suppress the workers, it would eventually wither away. Although Marx dwelt only briefly on the nature of the new society, he apparently believed that it would be both productive and satisfying. According to his famous slogan, production and distribution would be based on the principle "from each according to his ability, to each according to his need."

Marx may have been wrong about the threat that capital posed to labor, and naive to believe that a totally classless society was possible. But for many oppressed peoples, his writings have served as a beacon of hope and inspiration. And for many communist leaders, from Lenin to Mao to Castro, his writings have provided the foundation for new revolutionary goals. Still, what is called communism today, especially in the Soviet Union, is very unlike the ideal state Marx envisioned. The economist Joseph Schumpeter once remarked that "There is, between the true meaning of Marx's message and . . . [Soviet] practice and ideology, at least as great a gulf as there was between the religion of humble Galileans and the practice and ideology of the princes of the church or the warlords of the Middle Ages."[8]

## Soviet Communism

In the late nineteenth century, Russia was governed by a repressive monarchy whose abuses encouraged revolutionary activity. There were some spurts of economic development in the 1890s and the early twentieth century, but industry was largely directed and controlled by government, and the economy remained overwhelmingly agricultural. On the eve of the Communist Revolution, then, czarist Russia had not nearly reached the stage of capitalist development that Marx had predicted would precede a workers' revolution.

Nevertheless revolutionary uprisings occurred in early 1917. They were largely a spontaneous reaction to Russia's devastating losses in the First World War. A provisional regime set up under Alexander Kerensky seemed to offer the possibility of a more democratic government. But then a man named Lenin appeared on the scene.

### Leninism

Lenin, whose real name was Vladimir Ilyich Ulyanov, was a native Russian whose father had taught mathematics and physics. As a young man Lenin had been exiled to Siberia because of his efforts to promote more power for the working class. He believed that revolution should be brought about by the concerted effort of a small group of professionals. In 1903, at a meeting in London, his determination on that point had split the Russian revolutionary party in two. Lenin's smaller group had adroitly termed itself the Bolsheviks, which means "majority." The other group became known as the Mensheviks, or the minority.

In 1917 Lenin was in exile again, this time in Switzerland. There he aided the Germans in a devious plan to neutralize their enemy on the eastern front. By helping Lenin return to Russia, Winston Churchill observed, the Germans deployed "the most grisly of all weapons" in a war already distinguished by the use of poison gas and flame throwers. "They transplanted Lenin in a sealed truck like a plague bacillus from Switzerland into Russia."[9]

8. Joseph A. Schumpeter, *Capitalism, Socialism, and Democracy*, 3d ed. (New York: Harper & Row, 1950), p. 3.
9. Quoted in Alan Moorehead, *The Russian Revolution* (New York: Perennial Library, Harper & Row, 1965), p. 171.

In October 1917 Lenin led the Bolsheviks in overthrowing Kerensky's provisional government. As the Germans had hoped, he withdrew Russia from the war, thus eliminating one of their enemies. But several years of struggle were required before Lenin could consolidate his control of the country. During this period of "war communism," industry was nationalized, wages were equalized, and crops were confiscated to feed the army and urban workers. By 1921, when Lenin finally claimed political success, the economy was faltering so badly that he was forced to retreat temporarily from his ideological objectives. His New Economic Policy (NEP) provided more freedom to farmers and small businessmen, in an effort to restore production to previous levels.

This new, more open society did not last, for in January 1924 Lenin died without designating his successor. Joseph Stalin and Leon Trotsky fought for control and by 1928 Stalin was victorious.

## Stalinism

**National economic planning:** the process of deciding collectively on national economic objectives, and of developing policies and programs for accomplishing those objectives.

Stalin's overriding goal was the rapid industrialization of the Russian economy through national economic planning. **National economic planning** is the process of deciding collectively on national economic objectives, and of developing policies and programs for accomplishing those objectives. To achieve his end Stalin set up Gosplan, the Soviet central planning agency. In the first of a series of five-year plans, bureaucrats in Gosplan established mandatory economic goals for various sectors of the economy. The last vestiges of the NEP program were swept away, and the secret police regained the pervasive control they had held first under the czars and then during the period of war communism.

Whereas Lenin had come to believe that greater freedom was the key to enhancing agricultural output, Stalin rejected that view. He abolished private farms and combined them into huge collectives, running some like factories in which workers earned wages. Farmers did not gain the benefit of improvements in productivity. Instead, most of the food was earmarked for workers in urban areas, to support their construction and factory work. In essence, farmers were forced to accept subsistence wages to support the rapid accumulation of capital in industry—an ironic reincarnation of the capitalist system Marx had condemned.

At least initially, Stalin's plans for raising farm productivity through collectivization backfired. The peasants so resented the new system that they retaliated by destroying their crops and slaughtering their livestock. Such discord was inconsistent with Marx's prediction of a placid and productive postrevolutionary society. Conflict was supposed to be the result of class distinctions, and classes had presumably been wiped out. So Stalin resolved the dilemma by blaming the difficulties of forced collectivization on the *kulaks* (prosperous peasant farmers who had done well for themselves under the NEP). Eventually he announced that the kulaks would be "liquidated," and several thousand of them were shot.[10]

10. Calvin Hoover, *Memoirs of Capitalism, Communism, and Nazism* (Durham, N.C.: Duke University Press, 1965), pp. 111–14.

Stalin's repressive policies did not last, but neither did Soviet agriculture flourish. Eventually Soviet planners had to establish incentives to stimulate production. Instead of paying equal wages to all, they rewarded more productive workers. In recent years peasants have been allowed to farm small plots of land near their homes and to sell the produce in local markets. Peasants naturally tend to use these plots to produce agricultural items whose market value is high—milk and eggs, for instance. Still, the productivity of the privately farmed land testifies to the value of incentives. The collectively farmed lands, which produce less valuable foodstuffs like wheat, are not nearly so productive. In recent years, the Soviets have had to import grain regularly from capitalist nations.

The lack of a profit motive also presented problems in Soviet industry. Managers of Soviet plants were expected to meet quotas, not to satisfy the demands of customers. A factory manager who had been told to produce a million pairs of shoes could satisfy his quota most easily by making all of them the same size—and many managers did just that. Knitting factories made caps but not sweaters, because caps were easier to make. Lampshade factories made all their products one color—orange. And in the lighting fixtures industry, where quotas were established in terms of weight, a small number of extremely heavy products was produced.

Such tales may be exaggerated, but they demonstrate the problem of establishing an effective system of incentives. While the Soviet government can take pride in its military and space technology, it has not been able to match Western economies and Japan in the production of consumer goods and services. Competition with the United States spurs Soviet military and space achievements. The lack of competition holds back the Soviet consumer products sector.

Marx's classless society has not yet emerged in the Soviet Union. The ruling class has privileges that workers do not. A reporter who lived in the Soviet Union observed that special stores reserved for the elite "insulate the Soviet aristocracy from chronic shortages, endless waiting in line, rude service, and other daily harassments that plague ordinary citizens. Here the politically anointed can obtain rare Russian delicacies like caviar, smoked salmon, the best canned sturgeon, export brands of vodka or unusual vintages of Georgian and Moldavian wines, choice meat, fresh fruits and vegetables in winter that are rarely available elsewhere."[11]

Soviet industry may have become even more inefficient in recent years. During his brief tenure as premier, Yuri Andropov tried earnestly to improve productivity, but there are few signs that he was successful. Suggestions that the Soviet economy is tottering on the brink of collapse are probably exaggerated, however. Like their czarist predecessors, party members enjoy power and privileges they will not readily forgo. And there are no strong signs of unrest among the Soviet people. In fact, the similarities between czardom and communism in Russia are so great that one is reminded of the old French proverb: the more things change, the more they stay the same.

---

11. Hedrick Smith, *The Russians* (New York: Quadrangle, New York Times Book Co., 1976), p. 26.

## Perspectives in Economics: A Traveler's View of Emerging Capitalism in China

*Laurence S. Moss*

Ten years ago no one imagined China would reach out to embrace capitalist economic methods. During Mao Zedong's Cultural Revolution, bands of teenagers had roamed China's countryside, burning books, destroying historical monuments, and dragging reluctant counterrevolutionaries through the streets. Thousands of citizens were forced to renounce their bourgeois-capitalist ways and close their flourishing commercial institutions.

Today the news media are filled with reports of China's return to capitalism. It is not yet clear how far the dismantling of China's centrally planned economy will proceed. But Premier Deng Xiaoping, China's pragmatic new leader, has obviously set out to accomplish what Mao would never have allowed: the liberalization of trade and the toleration of Western lifestyles.

The change in government policy has been most dramatic in the agricultural sector. In 1958, Mao's Great Leap Forward literally abolished most private landholding, consolidating farm management in huge regional collectives. The merging of small peasant farms and village lands was supposed not only to help in the mechanization of farming and the improvement of productivity, but to foster the spiritual rebirth of the Communist people. Unfortunately, the move did not produce the promised results. The stifling of personal incentives disrupted the whole economy for most of a decade.

Starting in 1980, however, the Chinese government declared a series of agricultural reforms that amounted to wholesale abandonment of collective land management. Most provincial landholdings were abolished, and small village and family farms were restored to their former owners. Farmers are now required to turn over only part of their output to the government. Any surplus is theirs to consume or to trade for cash in the cities. Government officials also encouraged the development of an agricultural futures market by allowing farmers to contract ahead of time for delivery of their crops. The idea was to give farmers an incentive to vary the composition of their output as market conditions warranted.

Trade works best when buyers and sellers can communicate easily with one another. In most Chinese cities the government has now granted sidewalk space to traders, and even blocked off traffic on selected streets. Traders still need licenses, but they are said to be relatively easy to acquire. In hopes of making a profit, a person may set up a trading booth and offer beans, clothing, ginseng roots, or dried beetles to passing shoppers. In one outdoor market in the city of Guangzhou, Western travelers recently saw a vendor offer several packages of Wrigley's chewing gum at premium prices. Another vendor, equipped with a dentist's chair, white apron, and surgical pliers,

## Democratic Socialism

Between the command economy of the Soviet Union and the market system of the United States lies another form of economic organization that, much like mercantilism, involves partial government control of the economy. Under mercantilism, monarchs created monopolies and then left merchants and manufacturers relatively free to operate them, within certain guidelines. Under socialism, the government actually gets into the offered to pull aching teeth for passers-by who found the wait at the state hospital painfully long.

The free market principles operating in the open air markets can also be observed in Chinese factories. Managers are encouraged to negotiate Western-style contracts promising bonuses if a job is completed under budget and penalties if deadlines are not met. In Guangzhou the manager of a jade factory is now allowed to negotiate contracts with business people from Hong Kong without the approval of the Central Communist Party in Beijing (Peking). Only the small bureaucracy of Guangzhou province watches over his dealings. Contracts with foreigners are more likely to be approved if they provide employment for Chinese laborers or help to augment the state-owned Bank of China's foreign exchange holdings. Among other companies J. R. Reynolds (tobacco), Gillette (razor blades), Foxboro (automatic controls), and IBM (computers) have entered into joint ventures in China. To foreign travelers, the most obvious joint ventures are the smart high-rise hotels, some with indoor pools and revolving restaurants, that cater to the thousands of tourists who visit China each day.

In addition to the opportunities now available to entrepreneurs, a private labor market provides extra disposable income to many Chinese citizens. Tourists who read Chinese report seeing hand-painted signs along the roadways offering wages for after-hours labor on construction projects. Taxicab drivers in Beijing say that after they have paid a fixed sum to the government, they are free to work for themselves. Workers use their extra earnings to purchase television sets and refrigerators, or to establish small businesses in the open air market.

Chinese citizens' ability to reorganize production methods or reallocate capital in response to changing market conditions is more limited. The days of total police control of citizens' movements seem to be over. Individuals can now travel freely within each of China's provinces, without signing in and out of police stations. As a result, some middleman activity is possible. Goods can be moved from countryside to city to even out maladjustments in supply and demand. But can individuals start a labor union and strike? Can entrepreneurs issue stocks or engage in other sophisticated venture capital arrangements? In 1985 the government allowed a company in Shanghai to offer stock, but it is not yet clear whether that action was the harbinger of a new China or only a tentative experiment. Only time will tell whether Chinese capitalism will last.

See also Laurence S. Moss, "Capitalism in China" (Babson Park, Mass.: Economics Department, Babson College, 1985).

business of production. **Socialism** (sometimes called democratic socialism) is an economic system in which the government owns major plants in industries such as coal, transportation, steel, and banking, and operates them in the public interest.

**Socialism (or democratic socialism):** an economic system in which the government owns major plants in industries such as coal, transportation, steel, and banking, and operates them in the public interest.

Socialist philosophy tends to reflect Marx's belief that capitalist profits are unearned. Public ownership of industry thus allows unearned profits to be turned over to the public. (Of course, members of the general public can and do hold shares in capitalist corporations. And in return for their profit, capitalists do take risks in funding production.) Another socialist goal has been the elimination of the exploitation of labor.[12] The theory is that if industry is owned publicly, profits can be used to improve working conditions and promote a more equitable distribution of income.

In the United States, the postal service has always been owned by government. Today public elementary and secondary schools and land-grant colleges are all run by state, county, or local governments. (The historian Arnold Toynbee once called the American public schools the most socialistic system of education in the world.) In the 1930s, the federal government entered the electricity business by establishing the Tennessee Valley Authority. More recently it has taken control of ailing railroads to establish Amtrak and Conrail. Still, outright government ownership of plant and equipment is relatively limited.

In Europe, industry has been far more extensively socialized. At the end of the Second World War, Britain's new Labour government nationalized several major industries. In Austria at about the same time, a substantial segment of industry that had been confiscated by the Nazis during the war was placed under government control. More recently, governments in Norway, Sweden, and France have assumed ownership of many industries.

One study of nationalization estimated the percentages of industry owned by the public in several Western European nations as follows:[13]

| | |
|---|---|
| Austria | 65% |
| France | 55 |
| Italy | 45 |
| Norway | 40 |
| Sweden | 30 |
| Great Britain | 25 |
| West Germany | 20 |

## The Effects of Nationalization

Originally, industries were nationalized in order to prevent the exploitation of workers and to distribute unearned profits. Over the years, however, motivations have changed. Government officials began taking over industries simply because they were failing. In Britain, Rolls Royce was nationalized not by a Labour administration with socialist leanings, but by a Conservative government. Similar moves have become common in Norway and Sweden.

In a free-market economy, persistent losses are usually taken as a signal that a firm should reorganize or go out of business. Of course, during recessions and sometimes for other reasons, producers may endure

12. Upton Sinclair described turn-of-the-century labor conditions in wrenching detail in his novel *The Jungle* (1906). See the afterword by Robert B. Downs to the Signet edition (New York: New American Library, 1960).
13. R. Joseph Monsen and Kenneth D. Walters, *Nationalized Companies: A Threat to American Business* (New York: McGraw-Hill, 1983), p. 17.

temporary losses, expecting better times. But continued losses suggest that the firm is producing the wrong product or managing resources inefficiently. Like a thermostat that turns on the furnace when the temperature in a building falls too low, losses reveal a need for change.

Sometimes unprofitable companies can be rescued by astute managers. For instance, Lee Iacocca turned Chrysler from a failing enterprise into a profitable company. His efforts were assisted by government loan guarantees (which critics maintain was a wasteful use of funds). If nothing else, the example shows there are other ways for government to restore a company's profitability besides outright ownership. John Kenneth Galbraith, an economist who favors the nationalization of failing industries, insists that once a company has been nationalized, it should be run according to strict principles of profit and loss. The manager appointed by the state "must have extensive autonomy in decision-making. . . . [Public management] must be held accountable for results by the orthodox standards of cost and return. This is not a capitalist test of efficiency; it is the universal and only test."[14]

What sounds good in theory does not necessarily work in practice, however. Scholars have found that "the government as owner is interested in whether the company contributed to the nation's export drive, whether it managed to avoid laying off employees, and whether it kept domestic prices under control. One rarely hears about the state-owned company's return on investment, its return on capital, or the profitability of its assets."[15] Thus macroeconomic goals—the mercantilist desire to promote exports, the Keynesian urge to achieve high employment, and the monetarist aim to suppress inflation—tend to replace the profit motive in state-run companies.

Political considerations also influence the management of publicly owned firms. When the chairman of British Steel announced plans to reduce employment because of lagging demand in 1975, the secretary of industry objected, and the chairman was replaced. More recently, Conservative Prime Minister Margaret Thatcher refused to fund a new factory for a state-owned microelectronics firm unless it were located in Wales, where unemployment is high. Such political intervention raises costs, which either consumers or taxpayers must ultimately pay for. It also "creates chaos for the managers of nationalized firms."[16] Too often, the short-term interests of politicians conflict radically with the long-run goals of industry.

Nowhere is the conflict between political and economic goals more obvious than in government attempts to deal with inflation. It has been charged that "state companies tend to nearly freeze their prices in the year before national elections and then raise them rapidly in the following year."[17] Even in nonsocialist nations like the United States, politicians

14. John Kenneth Galbraith, quoted in R. Joseph Monsen and Kenneth D. Walters, *Nationalized Companies: A Threat to American Business* (New York: McGraw-Hill, 1983), p. 71.
15. Ibid., p. xi.
16. Ibid., p. 42.
17. Ibid., p. 44.

## Perspectives in Economics: Yugoslavia, a Modified Communist Economy

*Russell Shannon*

Perhaps no nation has a paper currency more appropriate to its economy than Yugoslavia. Instead of a monarch or a president, the face of the 10 dinar note shows a smiling factory worker outfitted with cap, gloves, and shovel. On the back of the note, a sprawling industrial complex belches smoke into the air. For a nation whose industries are publicly owned and guided by workers' committees, the bill seems fitting.

A nation only a bit larger than Wyoming, Yugoslavia has a population density similar to that of industrial states like Ohio and Pennsylvania. Though it is a communist nation, its economy resembles a free market system more than the centrally planned system of the Soviet Union.

In the state-owned factories, self-management by workers is the rule. Workers are elected to a council, which may then select a management committee. The council or committee makes basic decisions about production, pricing, and pay. Profits are divided among workers or reinvested in the operation. Firms tend to be market oriented, because the workers suffer if their products do not satisfy consumers. And workers are paid according to the value of their output. Although parts of this arrangement seem to resemble the free market system, Yugoslavs insist that their approach is true to the Marxist ideal of a dictatorship of the proletariat.

Worker management has produced moderately successful results for the Yugoslavs. From 1952 to 1965, Yugoslavia's per capita growth in GNP was second only to Japan's. In 1980 its output, $73.2 billion worth, almost equaled that of Iran, a nation with half as many more people. Compared with other nations, however, Yugoslavia's per capita GNP, $3,000 in 1980, was small. In the same year, the communist nations of East Germany, Czechoslovakia, and Hungary produced per capita GNPs of $5,000 to $8,000. And the free market nations of Japan, France, and West Germany enjoyed GNPs of $9,000 to $12,500 per capita. Yugoslavia has also been plagued by persistently high inflation—50 percent or more a year—and high unemployment.

Worker-run industries have certain problems. A group of basically untrained, inexperienced managers often cannot run an enterprise efficiently on

sometimes resort to this practice. President Richard Nixon imposed comprehensive wage and price controls just before the presidential campaign of 1972. As a result, the American economy was plagued by shortages. In his memoirs, Nixon admitted that "the . . . decision to impose [controls] was politically necessary and immensely popular in the short run. But in the long run I believe that it was wrong. The piper must always be paid, and there was an unquestionably high price for tampering with the orthodox economic mechanism."[18]

Small wonder that the income statements of nationalized firms are often awash in a sea of red ink. As one book put it, "In the state firm, there is

18. Richard M. Nixon, *Memoirs of Richard Nixon* (New York: Grosset and Dunlap, 1978), p. 521.

a day-to-day basis. In practice, factories must be run by a general director selected by the worker management committee. Directors are supposed to serve limited terms, but frequently retain control for many years. Workers' personal interests may also bias their business decisions. Workers commonly prefer to distribute profits among themselves rather than to reinvest them in the business. As a result, funds for new equipment or for research and development are usually scarce. At the same time, workers may be so anxious to preserve their jobs that they keep an operation going when it is no longer useful to society. And discipline is so lax in worker-run factories that the nation's output is seriously reduced.

Yugoslavia's economic problems probably originate as much in its historical circumstances as in its Marxist ideology, however. Split for centuries between the Austro-Hungarian Empire in the north and the Ottoman Empire in the south, the nation was not united until near the end of World War I. Yugoslavia is a nation of two alphabets, three religions, four languages, five ethnic groups, and six republics. Substantial economic disparities between the northern and southern regions intensify the natural rivalries and conflicts among these groups. For these reasons the central planning approach used in most communist economies simply will not work in Yugoslavia. It was tried in the 1940s under Marshal Tito's government, but failed miserably. The decentralized organization of local workers' groups fits the fragmented nature of Yugoslav society much better.

In 1980 the death of President Tito, one of the few unifying influences in the nation, left Yugoslavia in a precarious situation. As one observer worried, "So extensive is the autarky of the republics that there is now less economic cooperation and exchange among the various Yugoslav republics than among the members of the Common Market."[1] Even under the best of economic systems, the many barriers to Yugoslavia's prosperity, symbolized by the four languages printed on its currency, might still thwart the nation's prospects.

1. Milovan Djilas, "Yugoslav Unity Fragments Without Tito," *Wall Street Journal*, March 13, 1985, p. 35.

a bottom line, but it is political, not financial."[19] The same conclusion also applies to economic planning in a socialist economy.

## The Effects of Economic Planning

Early socialists argued that capitalists took a narrow personal view in their production decisions, preferring individual gain to the general good of society. Government planning, they suggested, would improve economic performance. As the eminent Polish economist Oskar Lange put it, under

19. R. Joseph Monsen and Kenneth D. Walters, *Nationalized Companies: A Threat to American Business* (New York: McGraw-Hill, 1983), p. 128.

socialism, "the Central Planning Board has a much wider knowledge of what is going on in the whole economic system than any private entrepreneur can ever have."[20]

It is probably true that a group of planners can have broader knowledge than a single capitalist. But in a competitive economy of many producers, both actual and potential, the collective knowledge of producers far exceeds that of any planning board. Even with the best of intentions, then, government planning may be more prone to error than the market process.

Consider the case of Japan, which was at roughly the same stage of development as Russia at the turn of the century. Japan's economic growth has now far outstripped the Soviet Union's. Many believe that Japan's central planning agency, the Ministry for International Trade and Industry (MITI), is largely responsible for the nation's success. Yet MITI actively discouraged two Japanese firms, Honda and Toyo Kogyo, from entering the automobile industry. Both have nevertheless achieved great success. As one scholar has noted, in Japanese manufacturing, "cement, paper, glass, bicycles, and motorcycles are huge success stories, even though MITI did little to help or hinder them."[21]

Those who envy Japan's industrial prowess, then, should not credit it to economic planning. The might of MITI is a myth. There is no evidence that state ownership and central control of the economy will produce more efficient results than the free market system. Instead, it might well produce improvements in job security; redistribution of income; and personal gain for politicians.

## Summary and Extensions

In recent years, the governments of Western Europe have been nationalizing ailing industries at an unprecedented rate. The election of a Conservative government in Britain has done little to reverse the trend. In the United States the Reagan administration, supposedly committed to the free market, has restricted imports of steel, textiles, sugar, cars, and motorcycles. And it has slowed the process of deregulation in the trucking industry.

Perhaps Marx was correct, then. Capitalism may be only a temporary phase in the world's economic development. Yet instead of moving toward a new utopian order, the world seems to be reverting back to old mercantilist policies. Whether the party in power is Socialist or Conservative, Republican or Democrat, seems to make little difference. A recent article on French socialist policy was headlined "Mercantilism for the 21st Century."[22]

---

20. Oskar Lange, *On the Economic Theory of Socialism* (New York: McGraw-Hill, 1964), p. 89.
21. Arthur T. Denzau, *Will an "Industrial Policy" Work for the United States?* (St. Louis: Center for the Study of American Business, Washington University, 1983), p. 10.
22. *Business Week,* January 10, 1983, p. 54.

Marx saw the capitalist economy as the servant of producers' self-interest. But the free market economy has proved far more responsive to consumers—and has limited their freedom less—than the planned economy of the communist state.[23] For though capitalism is based on producers' self-interest, in the long run the producers' interest is to satisfy their customers. As Adam Smith wrote, "Consumption is the sole end and purpose of all production."[24] Both mercantilism and socialism shift the focus away from consumers, replacing the invisible hand of self-interest with the visible and often clumsy hand of government.

## Major Conclusions

1. Mercantilism is a system of trade restrictions designed primarily to produce a favorable balance of trade and a horde of gold that can be used to enlarge the powers of government or of private interests. Although the heyday of mercantilist policy was from 1500 to 1800, vestiges of the system exist today as restrictions on foreign imports and on entry into various occupations and industries.
2. Communism, as conceived by Karl Marx, has never existed and will probably never emerge as a viable economic system.
3. Socialism, an economic system that relies heavily on state ownership and control of major sectors of the economy, has flourished in many European countries. Elements of socialism can also be found in the United States.
4. Most industrial economies are a mixture of free market activity and government control.
5. Replacing capitalism with government control is not necessarily in the national interest. Government control is apt to mean lower productivity and greater power for special-interest groups and politicians.

## Questions to Ponder

1. Mercantilists often argued that government control of production was necessary to maintain product quality. Who should determine what degree of quality is proper, the government or the consumer?
2. Are restrictions on imports really in the national interest?
3. Explain Hume's theory that attempts to control a nation's balance of trade would always fail.
4. Although Marx argued that the purchase of new capital equipment eliminates jobs, studies show that new equipment actually creates jobs. Explain how that can happen.
5. How does the history of agricultural production in the Soviet Union illustrate the value of incentives? Does Soviet industry have incentive problems?

---

23. Calvin B. Hoover, *The Economy, Liberty, and the State* (New York: Twentieth Century Fund, 1959), p. 18.
24. *An Inquiry into the Nature and Causes of the Wealth of Nations* (New York: Modern Library, 1937), p. 625.

## Central Question

*What are the major problems facing under-developed countries seeking to increase their national income and wealth?*

## Key Terms

Economic growth

Economic development

# Chapter 20

# Economic Growth and Development

*The bourgeoisie, during its rule of scarce one hundred years, has created more massive and more colossal productive forces than have all preceding generations together. Subjection of Nature's forces to man, machinery, application of chemistry to industry and agriculture, steam navigation, railways, electric telegraph, clearing of whole continents for cultivation, canalization of rivers, whole populations conjured out of the ground—what earlier century had even a presentiment that such productive forces slumbered in the lap of social labor?*

*Karl Marx*

Most of the nations of the world can be classified as rich or poor, have or have-not. Among the have-nots—a category that includes most of the world's countries—are China and India, which together represent more than a third of the world's population. Mass poverty exists in these societies. People often lack basic food, clothing, or shelter, and have little opportunity to obtain the education taken for granted in developed countries. The enormous gap between poor nations and rich increases the potential for world conflict.

This chapter examines the reasons why some countries are far more developed economically—and therefore richer—than others. Less developed countries share certain characteristics, such as low income, high population growth, and technological underdevelopment, that are linked to their economic difficulties. We will also explore some theories of what conditions are required for economic development to occur. And we will look at the obstacles to economic growth, such as inadequate rates of saving. Finally we will consider some of the proposed remedies for economic underdevelopment.

## Prerequisites for Growth and Development

**Economic growth:** the expansion of a nation's capacity to produce the goods and services its people want.

The terms economic growth and economic development are often used interchangeably, but they have slightly different meanings. **Economic growth** is the expansion of a nation's capacity to produce the goods and services its people want. Since the productive capacity of an economy depends fundamentally on the quantity and quality of its resources, as well as on its level of technology, economic growth must involve the expansion and improvement of those factors of production. Especially important are the accumulation of capital through saving and investment; improvements in human skills; and technological advances.

**Economic development:** the enhancement of a nation's capacity to produce through the creation of new kinds of output.

**Economic development** is the enhancement of a nation's capacity to produce through the creation of new kinds of output. It includes but goes beyond the improvements in technology and skills that promote economic expansion.

An economy can have economic growth without economic development, but not vice versa. A nation that relies on oil exports for much of its income can increase its growth rate by pumping more oil. But its economic development may be minimal unless new industries and outputs are created. Development of those new industries requires investment, which must be funded by increases in oil exports. The distinction is similar to the difference between growth and development in human beings. Growth generally means increases in height or weight. Development means changes in learning capacity, physical coordination, or the ability to adapt to new circumstances. The second depends, at least in a person's early years, on the first.

There are a number of prerequisites for economic growth and development. Most of the developed countries have at least several of the following.

1. Sufficient quantity and quality of labor. The existence of a large labor force in itself does not guarantee growth and development—India is an excellent case in point. A labor force must have the education and job skills to deal with new products and methods of production.
2. Sufficient quantity and quality of capital in the form of raw material, machines, and equipment. The supply of capital depends on the level of saving, which is the difference between income and consumption. In countries where people exist at a subsistence level, there is little difference between income and consumption. Thus capital is generally in short supply in the less developed countries.
3. Sufficient quantity and quality of natural resources. This factor is helpful but not crucial. The United States' vast natural resources obviously contributed to its economic development. But Japan, which has few natural resources, has attained a high level of growth and development, because of high savings and the quality of its labor force.
4. A sufficiently high level of technology (the knowledge of how to convert resources into goods and services). Technology is generally more important to the efficiency of production than to the introduction of new goods or the improvement of existing goods. Different combinations of land, labor, and capital simply require different levels and types of technology.
5. Favorable sociocultural factors. It has been said that the Protestant work ethic, which applauds hard work, diligence, and thrift, was partly responsible for the economic development of the United States.[1]

## Characteristics of Less Developed Countries

Three-fourths of the world's population lives in less developed countries, which include most of the nations of Latin America, Africa, and Asia. Some of these countries are in more advanced stages of economic development than others. Though Mexico is far less developed than the United States, the average Mexican citizen enjoys much better living conditions than the average farmer in Bangladesh. Mexico's per capita income is only one-sixth that of the United States, but it is fifteen times greater than that of Bangladesh. Nevertheless, some characteristics are common to the less developed countries. These include low per capita income and a more inequitable distribution of income than that of developed countries.[2]

### Income

Countries are sometimes classified as developed or less developed on the basis of their GNP per capita—a rough measure of the value of goods and

1. Max Weber, *The Protestant Ethic and the Spirit of Capitalism* (New York: Scribner, 1930).
2. See also Harvey Leibenstein, *Economic Backwardness and Economic Growth* (New York: Macmillan, 1957), pp. 40–41.

**Table 20.1.** GNP per Capita for Selected Countries, by Level of Development

| Poorest Countries | | Poor Countries | | Early-Stage Developing Countries | |
|---|---|---|---|---|---|
| Country | Per Capita Income | Country | Per Capita Income | Country | Per Capita Income |
| Bangladesh | $140 | Indonesia | $ 580 | Malaysia | $1,860 |
| Ethiopia | 140 | Egypt | 690 | South Korea | 1,910 |
| Zaire | 190 | Thailand | 790 | Chile | 2,210 |
| India | 260 | Philippines | 820 | Brazil | 2,240 |
| China | 310 | Nigeria | 860 | Mexico | 2,270 |
| Pakistan | 380 | Nicaragua | 920 | Algeria | 2,350 |
| Kenya | 390 | Ivory Coast | 950 | Portugal | 2,420 |
| Sudan | 440 | Guatemala | 1,130 | Argentina | 2,520 |

services produced and available to the average person.[3] Among the poorest countries of the world by this measure are China, India, Bangladesh, and Pakistan. Together they include almost 40 percent of the world's population but produce less than 2 percent of the world's gross national product. The annual GNP per capita for those countries is less than 5 percent of the U.S. level, which was $13,160 in 1982. Bangladesh had a GNP per capita of only $140 in 1982, or about 1 percent of Sweden's. The poverty represented by that abstract figure shows up tangibly in nutritionally inadequate diets, primitive and crowded housing, the absence of medical services, and the general unavailability of schooling.

Table 20.1 shows per capita GNP in countries at various stages of development. The first category, the poorest countries—those with per capita incomes of $500 or less—includes both China and India, the two largest countries in the world. In the second category, Indonesia and Nigeria, with per capita GNPs between $500 and $1,000, are still not much better off than China and India. Sixty percent of the world's population lives in countries that would fall in one of these two categories. In the third category, which includes Mexico and Brazil, countries have higher incomes and at least some industrial base. These countries are in the early stages of economic development. The fourth category includes areas in

3. The United Nations classifies countries as either more developed or less developed. More developed regions comprise all of Europe, the United States, Canada, Australia, Japan, New Zealand, and the Soviet Union. All other regions are classified as less developed. There is not much difference, however, between the per capita income of Portugal, which is considered more developed, and the per capita income of Mexico, which is considered less developed.

| Later-Stage Developing Countries | | Developed Countries | |
|---|---|---|---|
| Country | Per Capita Income | Country | Per Capita Income |
| South Africa | $2,670 | Soviet Union | $ 5,940 |
| Yugoslavia | 2,800 | United Kingdom | 9,660 |
| Venezuela | 4,140 | Japan | 10,080 |
| Greece | 4,290 | Canada | 11,320 |
| Israel | 5,090 | France | 11,680 |
| Hong Kong | 5,340 | West Germany | 12,460 |
| Spain | 5,430 | United States | 13,160 |
| Singapore | 5,910 | Sweden | 14,010 |

Note: The average per capita income of all developed countries is $9,190; the average per capita income of all less developed countries is $750.
**Source:** The World Bank, *World Development Report 1984,* Table 1, pp. 218–19.

an advanced stage of development, like Hong Kong and Spain. And the highest category includes the Soviet Union and the developed market economies of the United States, Japan, and Western Europe.

Some countries with high per capita GNPs defy classification. Kuwait's per capita GNP is $19,870, higher than that of the United States or Sweden. But Kuwait relies on oil exports for its income. Its high per capita income does not reflect advanced economic development. Nor does per capita GNP tell us anything about income distribution. In fact, income is distributed less equally in the less developed countries than in developed countries, as Table 20.2 shows. In Mexico, for example, the top 10 percent of households received about 40 percent of the national income. The bottom 60 percent of households received only about half that amount, 22 percent. In Japan, the top 10 percent of families received about the same amount of income as the bottom 40 percent. Particularly in the poorest of the less developed countries, there is no middle class. An enormous gulf separates rich and poor.

Over time, economic growth and technological development can lead to greater equality in income distribution. But time is not on the side of most less developed countries. In these countries, rapid population growth tends to cancel out increases in national income per capita.

## Economic Growth Versus Population Growth

Economic growth is important to a nation's development for several reasons. It increases the amount of goods and services available to consumers for personal use. It expands the supply of resources available for capital formation. And it gives government the resources it needs to

**Table 20.2.** Income Distribution in Selected Countries, Less Developed and Developed (percentage share of household income, by quintile)

| Country | Year | First Fifth | Second Fifth | Third Fifth | Fourth Fifth | Last Fifth | Top 10 Percent |
|---|---|---|---|---|---|---|---|
| *Less Developed* | | | | | | | |
| India | 1976 | 7.0% | 9.2% | 13.9% | 20.5% | 49.4% | 33.6% |
| Kenya | 1976 | 2.3 | 6.6 | 11.5 | 19.2 | 60.4 | 45.8 |
| Peru | 1972 | 1.9 | 5.1 | 11.0 | 21.0 | 61.0 | 42.9 |
| Malaysia | 1973 | 3.5 | 7.7 | 12.4 | 20.3 | 56.1 | 39.8 |
| Panama | 1970 | 2.0 | 5.2 | 11.0 | 20.0 | 61.8 | 44.2 |
| Brazil | 1972 | 2.0 | 5.0 | 9.4 | 17.0 | 66.6 | 50.6 |
| Mexico | 1977 | 2.9 | 7.0 | 12.0 | 20.4 | 57.7 | 40.6 |
| Argentina | 1970 | 4.4 | 9.7 | 14.1 | 21.5 | 50.3 | 35.2 |
| *Developed* | | | | | | | |
| United Kingdom | 1979 | 7.0 | 11.5 | 17.0 | 24.8 | 39.7 | 23.4 |
| Japan | 1979 | 8.7 | 13.2 | 17.5 | 23.1 | 36.8 | 21.2 |
| Finland | 1977 | 6.8 | 12.8 | 18.7 | 24.9 | 36.8 | 21.2 |
| West Germany | 1978 | 7.9 | 12.5 | 17.0 | 23.1 | 39.5 | 24.0 |
| Sweden | 1979 | 7.2 | 12.8 | 17.4 | 25.4 | 37.2 | 21.2 |
| Norway | 1979 | 6.3 | 12.9 | 18.8 | 24.7 | 37.3 | 22.2 |

**Source:** The World Bank, *World Development Report 1984*, Table 28, pp. 272–73.

discharge its social responsibilities. Table 20.3 shows the average annual growth rates for selected countries, developed and undeveloped, from 1960 to 1982. With few exceptions, growth rates were higher in the developed countries.

In the low-income countries, especially those of Africa, slow growth accentuates and perpetuates poverty. In the poorest country in the world, Chad, income per capita declined significantly from 1960 to 1982. Three other poor countries, Zaire, the Sudan, and Zambia, had static economies. India, with one of the largest populations in the world, grew at a rate of only 1.3 percent annually. To make matters worse, in countries like India, population gains often offset economic growth. Because their resources are consumed at home, poor countries have little to export to earn the income necessary for economic development.

Although the overall rate of population growth has been declining worldwide since the late 1970s, the population is still growing year by year. In 1982 world population increased by 82 million people, bringing the total to 4.7 billion—twice as many as twenty years ago.[4] Current projections suggest the world's population will be about 6.5 billion by the

4. "Population Bulletin of the United Nations," No. 14-182, Department of International Economic and Social Affairs (New York: United Nations), 1983.

**Table 20.3.** Average Annual Growth Rate of GNP Per Capita, Selected Countries, 1960–1982 (percent)

| Less Developed | | | Developed | | |
|---|---|---|---|---|---|
| | Per Capita Income | Growth Rate | | Per Capita Income | Growth Rate |
| Chad | $ 80 | −2.8 | Italy | $ 6,680 | 3.4 |
| Bangladesh | 140 | 0.3 | United Kingdom | 9,660 | 2.0 |
| Ethiopia | 140 | 1.4 | Austria | 9,880 | 3.9 |
| Zaire | 190 | −0.3 | Japan | 10,080 | 6.1 |
| India | 260 | 1.3 | Belgium | 10,760 | 3.6 |
| Haiti | 300 | 0.6 | Finland | 10,870 | 3.6 |
| China | 310 | 5.0 | Netherlands | 10,930 | 2.9 |
| Pakistan | 380 | 2.8 | Australia | 11,140 | 2.4 |
| Sudan | 440 | −0.4 | Canada | 11,320 | 3.1 |
| Indonesia | 580 | 4.2 | France | 11,680 | 3.7 |
| Zambia | 640 | −0.1 | West Germany | 12,460 | 3.1 |
| Nigeria | 860 | 3.3 | Denmark | 12,470 | 2.5 |
| Peru | 1,310 | 1.4 | United States | 13,160 | 2.2 |
| Chile | 2,210 | 0.6 | Sweden | 14,040 | 2.4 |
| Brazil | 2,240 | 4.8 | Norway | 14,280 | 3.4 |
| Mexico | 2,270 | 3.6 | Switzerland | 17,010 | 1.9 |

**Source:** The World Bank, *World Development Report 1984,* Table 1, pp. 218–19.

end of this century. Almost all the increase will come in Latin America, Africa, and Asia, where birth rates are high and mortality rates are declining. These are the countries that can least afford population increases. The population of China and India is projected to increase by 450 million persons by the year 2000. The population of Bangladesh and Pakistan is likely to increase by 150 million.

Table 20.4 shows past population growth rates and projected future rates for selected countries, along with per capita GNP, which reflect a country's capacity to support an increase in population. The countries with very low per capita GNP tend to be those with the highest population growth rates. Income and population growth are inversely related. Sweden, which had a per capita GNP of $14,040 in 1982, has one of the lowest population growth rates in the world. It is projected to have about the same population in the year 2000 as it did in 1982. Bangladesh, which had a per capita GNP of $140 in 1982, is projected to have 64 million more people by the year 2000.

## Social Services

There are two kinds of capital, social overhead capital and physical capital. Social overhead capital includes the structure and equipment required to

**Table 20.4.** Population Growth, Past and Projected, Selected Countries, 1970–2000

| Country | Per Capita GNP, 1982 | Annual Average Population Growth 1970–1982 | Annual Average Population Growth 1980–2000 | Population (millions) 1982 | Population (millions) 2000 |
|---|---|---|---|---|---|
| Bangladesh | $ 140 | 2.6% | 2.9% | 93 | 157 |
| India | 260 | 2.3 | 1.9 | 717 | 994 |
| China | 310 | 1.4 | 1.0 | 1,008 | 1,196 |
| Pakistan | 380 | 3.0 | 2.7 | 87 | 140 |
| Indonesia | 580 | 2.3 | 1.9 | 153 | 212 |
| Egypt | 690 | 2.5 | 2.0 | 44 | 63 |
| Nigeria | 860 | 2.6 | 3.5 | 91 | 169 |
| Malaysia | 1,860 | 2.5 | 2.0 | 15 | 21 |
| Brazil | 2,240 | 2.4 | 2.0 | 127 | 181 |
| Mexico | 2,270 | 3.0 | 2.3 | 73 | 109 |
| Algeria | 2,350 | 3.1 | 3.7 | 20 | 39 |
| Italy | 6,840 | 0.4 | 0.1 | 56 | 58 |
| United Kingdom | 9,660 | 0.1 | 0.1 | 56 | 57 |
| West Germany | 12,460 | 0.1 | −0.1 | 62 | 60 |
| United States | 13,160 | 1.0 | 0.7 | 232 | 259 |
| Sweden | 14,040 | 0.3 | 0.1 | 8 | 8 |

**Source:** The World Bank, *World Development Report 1984,* Table 1, pp. 218–19; Table 19, pp. 254–55.

support and develop human resources—housing, hospitals, and schools. Physical capital consists of directly productive capital: the plant and equipment used in industry and agriculture. Neither kind of capital can be created without a supply of savings. Yet as we have seen, incomes are too low to permit much saving in poor countries. Inevitably, the low rate of saving translates into a low rate of capital formation. The result is that poor countries cannot afford the medical services and educational facilities needed to improve the quality of their labor forces.

Table 20.5 shows the difference among countries in medical and educational services. In Bangladesh, there is one physician to 10,940 persons; in the United States, one to every 520. In Uganda, only 5 percent of high-school-age people are in school, and only 1 percent of college-age people are in college. In Japan, the figures are 92 percent and 30 percent, respectively.

## Agriculture and Technology

One of the most fundamental characteristics of the less developed countries is that a high percentage of the population is employed in agriculture. In most of these countries it would be possible to reduce the number of workers employed in agriculture without changing technology and still

**Table 20.5.** Health and Education in Selected Countries, Developed and Less Developed

| Country | Population per Physician | Percentage of Age Group in Secondary Schools | Percentage of Age Group in Higher Institutions |
|---|---|---|---|
| Bangladesh | 10,940 | 15% | 3% |
| Ethiopia | 58,490 | 12 | 1 |
| Uganda | 26,810 | 5 | 1 |
| India | 3,690 | 30 | 8 |
| China | 1,810 | 44 | 1 |
| Pakistan | 3,480 | 17 | 2 |
| Kenya | 7,890 | 19 | 1 |
| Indonesia | 11,530 | 30 | 3 |
| Nigeria | 12,550 | 16 | 3 |
| Guatemala | 16,710 | 16 | 7 |
| Italy | 340 | 73 | 27 |
| Japan | 780 | 92 | 30 |
| United States | 520 | 97 | 58 |
| Sweden | 490 | 85 | 37 |
| Soviet Union | 270 | 96 | 21 |
| Canada | 550 | 93 | 37 |

**Source:** The World Bank, *World Development Report 1984,* Table 24, pp. 264–65; Table 25, pp. 266–67.

obtain the same output. Farming techniques are primitive, tools and equipment limited. Modern equipment is neither easy to import nor highly demanded. And agricultural output consists mostly of high-calorie cereals and raw materials. Relatively little protein food is produced, since it requires more acres per calorie than cereals do.

Table 20.6 shows the percentage of the labor force employed in agriculture, industry, and services in various countries. In a poor country like Bangladesh, 74 percent of the working-age population is employed in agriculture, compared with 2 percent in the United States. In the highly developed countries, employment in the service industries actually exceeds employment in manufacturing. The United States is such a postindustrial economy: employment in services far exceeds employment in industry and agriculture combined.

Technologically, many less developed countries are divided between two coexisting modes of production. One is modern, capital intensive, export oriented, and often foreign owned and managed. The other is traditional, labor intensive, dedicated to supplying the home market or the family, and domestically owned.[5] The first is technologically advanced

5. Bruce Herrick and Charles P. Kindleberger, *Economic Development*, 4th ed. (New York: McGraw-Hill, 1983), p. 520.

**Table 20.6.** Labor Force Participation Rates in Agriculture, Industry, and Services, Selected Countries

| Country | Per Capita GNP (1982) | Percentage of 1980 Labor Force Employed in | | |
|---|---|---|---|---|
| | | Agriculture | Industry | Services |
| Bangladesh | $ 140 | 74% | 11% | 15% |
| Ethiopia | 140 | 80 | 7 | 13 |
| India | 260 | 71 | 13 | 16 |
| China | 310 | 69 | 19 | 12 |
| Niger | 310 | 91 | 3 | 6 |
| Pakistan | 380 | 57 | 20 | 23 |
| Sudan | 440 | 78 | 10 | 12 |
| Indonesia | 580 | 58 | 12 | 30 |
| Thailand | 790 | 76 | 9 | 15 |
| Syria | 1,680 | 33 | 31 | 36 |
| Brazil | 2,240 | 30 | 24 | 46 |
| Mexico | 2,270 | 36 | 26 | 38 |
| Greece | 4,290 | 37 | 28 | 35 |
| Italy | 6,340 | 11 | 45 | 44 |
| West Germany | 12,460 | 4 | 46 | 50 |
| United States | 13,160 | 2 | 32 | 66 |

**Source:** The World Bank, *World Development Report 1984*, Table 1, pp. 218–19; Table 2, pp. 220–21; and Table 21, pp. 258–59.

and highly productive. The second is technologically dated and underproductive. In small cottage industries, each worker may perform every step in the production process.

This technological dualism can create social divisions, for new products and production methods often require people to change their beliefs and ways of living. Workers accustomed to different modes of production will have different values and different economic goals.

## Theories of Economic Development

Over time economists have developed a considerable body of thought on the conditions necessary for economic development. We will summarize some of the more important theories here.

### Classical Theory

The classical economists of the late eighteenth and early nineteenth centuries—Adam Smith, David Ricardo, Thomas Malthus, and John Stuart Mill—saw technological progress as the key to development. Increasing mechanization permitted the efficient division of labor, improving productivity. Such technological progress depended in turn on the accumulation of capital, which itself depended on the level of profits.

Classical economists worried that profits were linked to population growth. As profits increased, employment and total wages paid would rise with them, encouraging workers to have more children. (It was assumed that an unlimited amount of labor, including child labor, was available at a subsistence wage.) Population growth would tend to absorb profits, creating a drag on economic development. To feed the growing population, farmers would have to put marginal land into use or till the best land more intensively. Diminishing returns would cause prices to rise, pushing up labor costs. Profits would go down, and the accumulation of capital would decline. To stay ahead of the population growth, therefore, technology would have to improve continually.

## Marxist Theory

The German economist Karl Marx contended that economic conditions were the basic forces that shaped society. Marx saw technological change as the prime mover in the development of medieval feudalism into industrial capitalism. But capitalism was merely one stage in the evolution of society toward its final form: the communist state.

Like the classical economists, Marx believed that economic development depended on technological progress, which depended on the accumulation of capital and ultimately on profits. But he saw wages as the key to the whole process. Marx argued that labor was the sole source of value in the productive process. Capitalists would try to pay labor a subsistence wage and claim the surplus value for themselves. Eventually consumption would decline, causing recurrent economic crises. Ultimately economic instability would wreck the capitalist system, preparing the way for the new communist society.

## Rostow's Takeoff Theory

Probably the most prominent of recent theories of economic development is Walt Rostow's takeoff theory.[6] According to Rostow, nations pass through five stages in the process of economic development.

1. *The traditional society.* In this first stage, most resources are concentrated in agriculture. There is no cumulative, self-reinforcing process of material improvement, such as exists in industrial societies. As a result there is little social mobility. All societies before the Renaissance were traditional societies.

2. *Prerequisites for takeoff.* In the second stage, the prerequisites for sustained, systematic social change are created. At least part of the

6. Walt Whitman Rostow, *The Stages of Economic Growth: A Non-Communist Manifesto* (New York: Cambridge University Press, 1971).

population in traditional societies must abandon its fatalistic outlook on life. There must be entrepreneurs willing to take risks in finance and manufacturing. Social respect must come to depend on economic achievement rather than inherited status. Finally, a leading sector—mining, petroleum, or some other industry—must propel the takeoff.

3. *Takeoff.* In this stage, which lasts twenty to thirty years, the pace of social and economic change suddenly accelerates. The process is fueled by an increase in the percentage of the gross national product that is saved and invested, and by the establishment of manufacturing. Social customs, governmental forms and practices, and economic institutions continue to evolve.

4. *The drive to maturity.* This is a period of self-sustaining increases in gross national product, both overall and per capita. During this stage, which lasts about sixty years, industry acquires the most advanced technology available. Manufacturers become capable of producing whatever they wish, subject only to the constraints of the market and the availability of resources.

5. *Mass consumption.* The last stage of economic development is one of mass consumption of durable goods and services. The production of such goods and services enables most of the population to attain a high living standard.

Rostow's theory has been criticized on several counts. It does not fit historical fact very closely. Some countries' economies do not take off suddenly, but develop steadily over a long period of time. The theory is also vague on what causes growth in each stage, and what distinguishes one stage from the next. Nevertheless Rostow's theory offers valuable insight into the changes that must occur before a nation in the traditional stage of development can develop economically.

## Other Theories

Two other theories of economic development deserve brief mention. The *big push theory* offers a potential solution to the vicious circle of low income, low saving, low investment, low productivity, and low income. The idea is that a large infusion of investment, primarily from foreign sources, into different industries will enlarge markets, creating support industries. As industries buy from each other, the economy will grow, income and saving will rise, and the circle will be broken.

The *dependency theory* relates the problems of the less developed countries to their former colonial status. Most less developed countries were once possessions of mercantilist nations like Spain, England, France, the Netherlands, and Portugal. Their natural resources were exploited by the mother countries, and they were prevented from developing technologically. These colonies eventually achieved independence, but they remained economically and psychologically dependent on Europe. Many of the new African countries still rely on foreign military and financial advisers, for example.

## Perspectives in Economics: The Value of Children in Less Developed Countries

*Martin Schnitzer*

If population growth is an obstacle to economic development, why are birth control programs difficult to implement in less developed countries? For one thing, traditional cultural barriers must be overcome. To the male head of the household, a large family may be a symbol of social prestige. And religion may prohibit the use of contraceptives.

But economic factors also play a part. A large family can mean economic security for parents, for each additional child represents an earning asset. The economic motive is especially strong in agricultural areas, where farmers need extra labor to work the land. Parents also depend on children to care for them in their old age. Thus the monetary benefits of having many children may far outweigh the costs.

In the developed countries, it is usually the other way around. As living standards increase, it costs more to provide the goods and services needed to raise children. In addition there is the opportunity cost of raising children—the amount of time parents put into caring for children, compared with other uses they could have made of that time. A woman who leaves the labor force to have children may lose considerable income. No wonder people with high incomes want fewer children than people with low incomes. The alternative uses for their time—making money, enjoying leisure pursuits—are quite attractive.

# Obstacles to Economic Development

Economic development has been proceeding slowly or not at all in many of the less developed countries. Per capita GNP is not only low, but stagnant. In some countries, during some periods, it has actually fallen. The fact is, economic development is an extremely elusive objective. Among the most significant obstacles to its achievement is overpopulation.

## Overpopulation

Perhaps the chief obstacle to economic development in less developed countries is people. Because people provide the most important factor of production, labor, one might conclude that more people would obviously mean more GNP. That assumes access to large amounts of natural resources and capital, however. More people mean not only more labor and output, but more mouths to feed. The more people, the less capital and natural resources per capita. Unfortunately, many less developed countries are experiencing runaway population growth.

**Table 20.7.** Birth and Death Rates and Population Doubling-Time for Selected Countries, Developed and Less Developed, 1982

| **Developed Countries** | Birth Rate (thousands) | Death Rate (thousands) | Doubling-Time (years) |
|---|---|---|---|
| All countries | 16 | 9 | 112 |
| Soviet Union | 20 | 10 | 68 |
| United States | 16 | 9 | 100 |
| Japan | 13 | 6 | 102 |
| West Germany | 10 | 12 | — |
| East Germany | 14 | 14 | — |
| Italy | 11 | 10 | 408 |
| United Kingdom | 13 | 12 | 693 |
| France | 15 | 10 | 151 |
| Canada | 15 | 7 | 85 |
| Sweden | 11 | 11 | 3465 |

### *Population Doubling*

In 1798 the English clergyman Thomas Malthus published *An Essay on the Principle of Population*. Malthus took a pessimistic view. He suggested that the world's population was growing faster than its food supply. On the basis of scattered empirical evidence, including data from the North American colonies, Malthus calculated that populations tended to double every twenty-five years, in geometric progression, whereas the food supply tends to increase arithmetically. For example:

| | | | | | | | | | |
|---|---|---|---|---|---|---|---|---|---|
| Year | 0 | 25 | 50 | 75 | 100 | 125 | 150 | 175 | 200 |
| Population | 1 | 2 | 4 | 8 | 16 | 32 | 64 | 128 | 256 |
| Food | 1 | 2 | 3 | 4 | 5 | 6 | 7 | 8 | 9 |

Malthus based his proposition on two assumptions that have subsequently been disproved: first, that technological change could not increase the food supply faster than the population was increasing; second, that population growth could be limited only by an increase in the death rate. Nevertheless there was some truth in Malthus's predictions. It took over four thousand years of recorded history for China to reach a population of 500 million, but then only a little more than three decades to increase to one billion. And it is true that whatever a nation's size, natural resources, and level of development, a large population and a high birth rate will bring increasing problems in the future.

Table 20.7 shows the birth and death rates and the time required for a doubling of population for selected countries. The United States, with a

| **Less Developed Countries** | Birth Rate (thousands) | Death Rate (thousands) | Doubling-Time (years) |
|---|---|---|---|
| All countries | 32 | 11 | 33 |
| China | 21 | 8 | 54 |
| India | 34 | 14 | 36 |
| Indonesia | 34 | 13 | 33 |
| Brazil | 31 | 8 | 30 |
| Bangladesh | 49 | 18 | 22 |
| Pakistan | 43 | 15 | 25 |
| Nigeria | 49 | 17 | 21 |
| Mexico | 32 | 6 | 26 |
| Philippines | 32 | 7 | 27 |
| Vietnam | 34 | 10 | 30 |

**Source:** Mary M. Kent and Carl Haub, "1984 Population Data Sheet" (Washington, D.C.: Population Reference Bureau, April 1984).

birth rate of 16 per 1,000 and a death rate of 9 per 1,000, will double its population in 100 years.[7] Mexico, with a birth rate of 32 per 1,000 and a death rate of 6 per 1,000, will double its population in just 26 years. West Germany and East Germany, with negative and zero rates of growth respectively, will never double their population unless their growth increases. Worldwide, the population doubling-time for developed countries is 112 years; for less developed countries, it is 33 years. The gap is even wider if we compare Western Europe (442 years), with Africa (24 years). And again we see the link between economic growth and population growth. In 1982, the GNP per capita for Africa was $810; it was $12,000 for Western Europe.

*Urbanization*

Urbanization compounds population problems through congestion. Overcrowding in cities promotes pollution, unemployment, and a greater demand for human services. The increased stress can cause disease—not only communicable diseases like tuberculosis but heart disease, cancer, and other ailments attributable to a breakdown in the body's immunity. The problems of urbanization are particularly acute in less developed countries, which lack the financial resources to provide remedial services.

By the end of this century, at least twenty-two of the world's cities will have populations of more than ten million. Sixty will have more than five

7. Mary M. Kent and Carl Haub, "1984 World Population Data Sheet" (Washington, D.C.: Population Reference Bureau, April 1984.

million.[8] Most of these, like Mexico City, now the second largest city in the world, are located in the less developed countries.

### *Food Shortages*

The larger a nation's population, the greater its demand for food. In most overpopulated countries, the strong demand for food has left little saving and has hampered industrial development. The rural population competes with a rising tide of urban consumers for the limited agricultural output.

Here again we see the vicious circle of poverty in operation. The inability to industrialize reduces the potential of less developed countries to earn money from exports, which could be used to import additional food. Food shortages produce nutritional deficiencies and ultimately ill health. And poor health reduces productivity, output, and income.

## Lack of an Infrastructure

Infrastructure is a broad concept that includes the highways, railways, airports, sewage facilities, housing, and other social amenities provided in developed areas. Once in place, the infrastructure encourages both economic and social development. Because less developed countries generally do not have infrastructures, industrial firms will not normally locate plants there. Products manufactured for mass consumption simply cannot be distributed and used without transportation and communication facilities, skilled labor, and waste disposal plants.

### *Schools*

Educational facilities are a key component of an area's infrastructure. Because education is directly related to the quality of life, it constitutes a form of social capital. A low literacy rate can retard economic development. A high literacy rate can assist it.

Literacy is directly related to a country's stage of economic development. There is a positive correlation between a low standard of living and a high rate of illiteracy. It has been estimated that one-third of the world's people are illiterate,[9] and that most of them live in countries with high birth rates, large populations, and little money to spend on education. This general lack of educational opportunities reinforces the distribution between the haves and the have-nots, perpetuating class differences as well as slowing economic development.

---

8. United Nations, Department of International and Social Affairs, *Population Bulletin of the United Nations*, No. 14, 1983, p. 24.
9. United Nations, Department of International and Social Affairs, *Population Bulletin of the United Nations*, No. 14, 1983, p. 25.

### *Roads*

A system of roads is vital to economic and social development. Without roads, transportation becomes much more expensive. The cost of air transport is prohibitively high for most products, and railroad networks serve only a limited number of major access points.

Poor countries usually do not have the resources to develop and maintain an adequate road system. Their limited capital is simply insufficient to surmount natural barriers to transportation. For example, the lack of highways across the Sierra Madre and Andes mountains has long inhibited the east-west development of Mexico and South America. Transportation is especially hard to develop in countries dominated by mountain ranges, like Bolivia and Peru.

### *Other Facilities*

Dams, bridges, and waste disposal and communication facilities are vitally important assets that less developed countries usually lack. Dams provide the water supply and electric power necessary for economic and social development. Bridges create more efficient transportation by directly linking areas separated by water bodies. Waste disposal facilities control communicable diseases like cholera and typhoid fever, which can be spread by rats and other animals that feed on garbage dumped in city streets. Finally, communication facilities must be reliable enough to allow the transaction of business on a regular basis. In the less developed countries, government-owned telephone and telegraph services are notoriously inefficient.

## Other Obstacles

### *Low Savings Rate*

Savings are an important prerequisite for capital formation, for they free resources for use in the production of plant and equipment. An inability to raise capital is therefore a serious obstacle to economic development. Here again less developed countries are caught in a vicious circle. Small savings mean a small capital stock and a small gross national product. If GNP is small, almost all of it will be consumed in subsistence goods like food, leaving little to be saved. Capital formation will remain low, along with the standard of living and the rate of economic development.[10]

The unequal distribution of income in less developed countries exacerbates the saving problem. The vast majority of workers in these countries do not earn enough income to accumulate any savings. Instead, a minority

10. Ragnar Nurkse, *Problems of Capital Formation in Underdeveloped Countries* (New York: Oxford University Press, 1953).

of households receives most of the income. In Mexico, for example, the top 10 percent of income earners receives about 40 percent of the national income. In Brazil, the top 10 percent receives about 50 percent of the nation's earnings. Members of this privileged group could provide the saving necessary for capital formation, but they usually invest their money in real estate, which offers them a quick, high return on investment, or in foreign assets. Swiss bonds, which cannot be expropriated by a new government, may be extremely attractive to investors living in politically unstable countries.

### *Limited Range of Exports*

The less developed countries tend to export agricultural products, raw fuels, and metals. Many depend on a single product for most of their export income. About 80 percent of Nigeria's total export earnings is from oil, for instance. Needless to say, such dependence on one commodity can make a country extremely vulnerable to the ups and downs of the marketplace.

When oil prices were high in the early 1970s, for example, Nigeria's income increased. It ran a surplus in its balance of payments and used foreign earnings to improve its living standards. Increased public spending improved Nigeria's infrastructure, bettering its opportunities for development. During the early 1980s, however, world demand for oil began to decline. Oil prices fell by about $6 per barrel from a peak of $35 in 1980. As revenues from oil exports declined, Nigeria developed a deficit in its balance of payments. It must now pay off a large foreign debt incurred when oil prices were high, with earnings received when prices are low.

Countries that depend on the export of agricultural products and minerals are usually at a disadvantage in trade with developed countries. The terms of trade—that is, the quantity of exports required to pay for a given amount of imports—tend to favor the developed countries. Brazilian coffee and Mexican oil, for example, are much more subject to shifts in price than American computers or Japanese cars. The demand for agricultural products and minerals tends to be inelastic, so that when prices fall, they are not offset by an increase in demand. When coffee prices decline, then, Brazil will have to give up more income to import the same number of computers or cars. At the same time, America and Japan will give up less income to acquire Brazil's coffee.

### *Sociocultural Factors*

Sociocultural factors can also impede economic development.[11] In countless ways, culture influences individual and group behavior, determining how and when things will be done. Status distinctions based on education,

11. For a discussion of sociocultural factors and their impact on development, see Edmund Leach, *Social Anthropology* (New York: Oxford University Press, 1982); and W. Arthur Lewis, *The Theory of Economic Development* (Homewood, Ill.: Irwin, 1955).

caste, politics, religion, or sex can hold back employment of productive labor. Language differences can make communication and job training difficult. But culture can also contribute to development. If the use of machinery and equipment creates an industrial culture that is alien to the old agrarian ways, the new culture will speed the transition to a developed economy. Cultural conformity keeps groups of people working together, either for or against new ideas and ways of living.

Cultural attitudes and values underlie population problems as well as productivity rates. The norm in most less developed countries is to have large families. Religious prohibitions on birth control contribute to this pattern, but so do the limited social roles of women. Women in these countries occupy a secondary position that allows them little education or opportunity for work outside the home.

Status distinctions and religious values are also important determinants of economic advancement. Business has a lower status than other professions in some less developed societies. And economic development often conflicts with religious tradition. The overthrow of the Shah of Iran in 1979 was led largely by a fundamentalist Moslem clergy in revolt against Western materialism. Finally, traditional tribal conflicts can hamper development.

## Remedies for Economic Underdevelopment

There is no easy way for poor countries to become rich overnight. Many problems must be overcome, notably population growth. The mismatch between population growth and income growth in many less developed countries works against economic development.

Changes in the developed countries' economic and financial policies could relieve some of the difficulties of the less developed countries. Foreign trade can be an instrument of growth. If governments of the developed countries would drop some of their import restrictions, less developed countries would be able to earn more income. Through foreign aid programs, developed countries could also lend funds for investment to developing countries.

### Foreign Aid

Foreign aid is the transfer of income from rich nations to poor nations for the purpose of promoting their economic development. The transfer may be made as outright grants or as loans carrying lower interest rates and longer repayment periods than usual. (In 1982, the average interest rate for public borrowing in Bangladesh was 1.5 percent, and the average length of repayment was thirty-nine years.) Foreign aid may also take a variety of physical forms, from technical assistance to food supplies. Military assistance may be considered a form of foreign aid, although its impact on economic development is debatable.

Since the end of the Second World War, a battery of international financial institutions has sprung up to assist less developed countries in developing their economies. Among these are the International Bank of Reconstruction and Development (IBRD), the International Development Association (IDA), and the International Finance Corporation (IFC). All these organizations attempt to promote economic and social progress through the creation of modern economic and social infrastructures. All three make loans to countries or firms for such purposes as roads, irrigation projects, and electric generating plants. The IFC, for example, makes loans to firms, on the condition that the project benefit the economy of the less developed country and have a reasonable prospect of making a profit. Finally, the World Health Organization (WHO), an agency of the United Nations, assists less developed countries in improving their health services.

Besides these international institutions, the United States and other developed nations have their own programs of assistance for less developed countries. The Overseas Private Investment Corporation (OPIC), an American agency, provides direct loans for development projects at low interest rates. And the Export-Import Bank (Eximbank), though originally created for other purposes, has recently allocated most of its funds for the use of less developed countries. In addition, most Western European countries provide technical or financial assistance to the less developed countries.[12] In the Third World, or politically nonaligned, countries of Africa, Asia, and the Middle East, the Soviet Union is increasingly providing technical and capital assistance. Economic aid to those countries is now a major factor in the contest for power between the United States and the Soviet Union.

Foreign aid is not a miracle cure for economic underdevelopment. Military aid can do little to promote economic development, unless it permits a country to divert defense funds to more productive uses. The benefits of aid may end up in the hands of a few, instead of reaching a broad segment of the population. And if aid is used for consumption instead of investment, it will generate few lasting economic benefits. Moreover, many foreign aid projects take time to develop. Not all produce directly marketable output immediately.

## Other Solutions

In the last three decades many less developed countries have made substantial economic and social progress. In general, this development has come about in one of three ways.

1. Exportation of a major resource, with no real progress toward industrialization. The Arab oil-producing countries have achieved very high per capita incomes through their oil exports, for example.

---

12. Foreign aid as a percentage of gross national product varies considerably by country. In 1983, for example, 0.24 percent of the U.S. GNP went to foreign aid, compared with 1.10 percent for Norway. Japan contributed 0.33 percent of its GNP to foreign aid, West Germany 0.48 percent.

## Perspectives in Economics: Mexico's Economic Development Problems

*Martin Schnitzer*

Mexico is a nation of both extreme wealth and extreme poverty, of vast mineral resources but little arable land. It has one of the fastest-growing steel industries in the world, and is strategically located next door to the world's largest consumer market, the United States. Even though Mexico's advantages could make it one of the world's most prosperous nations, 40 percent of its labor force is unemployed or underemployed. Its population is growing at the alarmingly high rate of 2.5 percent a year. And its financial position is getting worse. From 1982 to 1984, inflation increased to rates of more than 100 percent, and the peso lost more than three-fourths of its value against the dollar. Mexico's foreign debt, around $90 billion, is now among the highest in the world. At the same time export revenues, which are based mostly on oil, are declining.

Mexico's economy is a combination of public and private enterprise. A government-owned monopoly, Pemex, produces all the oil in Mexico. The revenue from oil exports goes to finance a wide variety of development schemes, including a national support system for agriculture and a plan to generate electricity using nuclear reactors. Because in 1982 the government nationalized the banking industry, it now controls access to financial credit. It also influences the geographical location of private firms through its control of the infrastructure, such as ports and roads. In some industries, such as steel, government enterprises compete directly with private firms. Finally, the government controls access to imported goods through exchange controls and import licensing.

Despite government efforts, several factors work against the realization of Mexico's economic potential. The first is overpopulation. Unemployment and underemployment is already high, particularly in the cities. The nation will be hard pressed to find jobs for the 800,000 new workers that will join the labor force each year in the near future. Second, extreme inequality in the distribution of income and wealth limits saving and promotes social unrest. And finally, corruption, another potential cause of unrest, is widespread in Mexico's one-party political system. (Political corruption was a prime factor in Fidel Castro's rise to power in Cuba.)

2. Industrialization and protective tariffs and quotas. The Mexican government, for example, has encouraged manufacturing both directly, through controls on investment and trade, and indirectly, through taxes, subsidies, and other measures influencing resource and product prices. At the same time it has restricted imports to limit the competition faced by new industries.
3. Industrialization and the export of manufactured goods. Japan and South Korea have pursued this approach successfully. Both nations have relied mainly on the incentives of the market system, with some direction and control from the state. A high rate of investment has been a major contributor to economic growth in these nations.

These methods may not be relevant to the poorest countries in the world, which have little of value to export and little potential for industrialization. Investment in India and other poor countries is limited by their inability to absorb capital; by low levels of saving; and by adverse foreign exchange rates. Less developed countries cannot control many of the factors that influence their development prospects—such as the economic well-being of the developed countries, their source of trade and foreign aid.

In the end the key to development may lie in the right combination of government policy and private enterprise initiative. Some East Asian countries have succeeded this way. Government policies have expanded exports by keeping exchange rates competitive, while restricting imports on the basis of price. They have maintained high real interest rates, which have encouraged saving and ensured that investment is directed to the areas of highest return. Yet in these countries resources are allocated by the market, to ensure their most productive use. In China, the government recently introduced a series of measures to restructure the economy and increase the rate of development. Business enterprises are to have greater autonomy; there will be greater reliance on the market to determine output; and government monopolies will be broken up through competition.

## Summary and Extensions

Almost half the world's population lives in countries with a GNP per capita of $500 a year or less. Another 500 million people live in countries with a per capita income of between $500 and $1,500 a year. These countries are in the beginning stages of economic development. Yet many countries with higher per capita incomes, like Mexico and Brazil, are by no means modern industrial economies. Similarly, in the oil-exporting countries, per capita incomes are high, but the level of development is low.

Less developed countries face many challenges in their efforts to advance. The first is to attract enough investment, either through saving or aid, to provide a satisfactory rate of economic growth. They must also build an infrastructure that provides the services necessary for industrial development. Negative sociocultural attitudes must also be overcome. Probably the most important obstacle to conquer is high population growth. If population grows rapidly, most of a nation's investment must be devoted to maintaining per capita income at current levels rather than to increasing it.

## Major Conclusions

1. Although the terms economic growth and economic development are often used interchangeably, they have different meanings. Economic growth involves an expanded capacity to produce goods and services. Economic development involves growth through a reorganization of the resources used and the goods and services produced.
2. Economic growth and development depend on (a) the quantity and quality of a nation's labor force, capital stock, and natural resources;

(b) a nation's level of technology; and (c) socioeconomic factors, such as religion, that influence what goods are produced and how.
3. The per capita GNP of many underdeveloped countries, like India and China, is only a small fraction of the per capita GNP of industrialized countries, like Japan and the United States.
4. In less developed countries, the national income tends to be concentrated more heavily in the hands of high-income earners than in developed countries.
5. Less developed countries typically have lower growth rates than developed countries.
6. The rate of population growth tends to be higher in less developed than in developed countries.
7. In less developed countries a much higher percentage of the labor force is employed in agriculture than in developed countries.
8. There are a number of theories of economic growth and development. (a) Classical theory focuses on the role of capital accumulation in growth and development. (b) Marxist theory focuses on the role of expanding technology and the capitalist incentive to accumulate ever increasing amounts of capital. (c) Rostow's takeoff theory divides growth into five stages, from the early traditional society to the mass consumption society.
9. The major problems facing less developed countries in their efforts to grow and develop include (a) overpopulation and relatively high rates of population growth; (b) an inadequate infrastructure; (c) concentration on the exportation of only a few products or commodities; and (d) a low rate of saving and investment.
10. Remedies for the economic problems of less developed countries include (a) control of population growth; (b) foreign aid; and (c) greater reliance on market incentives in the allocation of scarce resources.

## Questions to Ponder

1. On what basis is a country classified as less developed?
2. What are the typical features of a less developed economy?
3. Distinguish between economic growth and economic development.
4. Describe Rostow's theory of the stages of economic development.
5. What is the typical attitude toward family size in traditional societies? Why?
6. What do you consider the most important obstacle to economic development in the less developed countries? Why?
7. Give some examples of sociocultural factors that block economic development.
8. Why are less developed countries at a disadvantage in their trade with developed countries?
9. When and how are people a liability rather than an asset in achieving economic development?

## Part VII

# The Political Economy

## Central Question

*How is government policy determined, and what are the economic effects of that process?*

## Key Term

**Median voter**

# Chapter 21

# Public Choice: The Economics of Government

*I have no fear, but that the result of our experiment will be, that men may be trusted to govern themselves without a master. Could the contrary be proved, I should conclude, either that there is no God, or that he is a malevolent being.*
Thomas Jefferson

Previous chapters have discussed the effects of various government policies on the market system. We looked at government efforts to control the external costs of pollution. We considered the economic impact of price controls and consumer protection laws on the market for final goods and services. And we examined the effects of government agricultural policy. Throughout the analysis we have focused on assessing the economic efficiency of government policy. We said little about how government policy is determined, or why government prefers one policy to another.

In this chapter, we will shift our focus to the functioning of government itself. Using economic principles, we will examine the process through which government decisions are made and carried out in a two-party democratic system, and consider its consequences. Today, when government production accounts for a substantial portion of the nation's goods and services, no student of economics can afford to ignore these issues.

## The Central Tendency of a Two-Party System

In a two-party democratic system, elected officials typically take middle-of-the road positions. Winning candidates tend to represent the moderate views of the many voters who are neither liberals nor conservatives. For this reason there is generally little difference between Republican and Democratic candidates. Even when the major parties' candidates differ strongly, as Ronald Reagan and Walter Mondale did at the start of their 1984 presidential campaign, they tend to move closer together as the campaign progresses.

Figure 21.1 illustrates politicians' incentives to move toward the center. The bell-shaped curve shows the approximate distribution of voters along the political spectrum. A few voters have views that place them in the wings of the distribution, but most cluster near the center. Assuming that citizens will vote for the candidate who most closely approximates their own political position, a politician who wants to win the election will not choose a position in the wings of the distribution.

Suppose, for instance, that the Republican candidate chooses a position at $R_1$. The Democratic candidate can easily win the election by taking a position slightly to the left, at $D_1$. Though the Republican will take all the votes to the right of $R_1$ and roughly half the votes between $R_1$ and $D_1$, the Democrat will take all the votes to the left. Clearly the Democrat will win an overwhelming majority.

The smart politician, therefore, will choose a position near the middle. Then the opposing candidate must also move to the middle, or accept certain defeat. Suppose, for instance, that the Republican candidate chooses position $R$, but the Democrat remains at $D_1$. The Republican will take all the votes to the left of $R$ and roughly half the votes between $R$ and $D_1$. She will have more than the simple majority needed to beat her Democratic opponent. In short, both candidates will choose political positions in the middle of the distribution.

Politicians can misinterpret the political climate, of course. Even with polls, no one can be certain of the distribution of votes before an election.

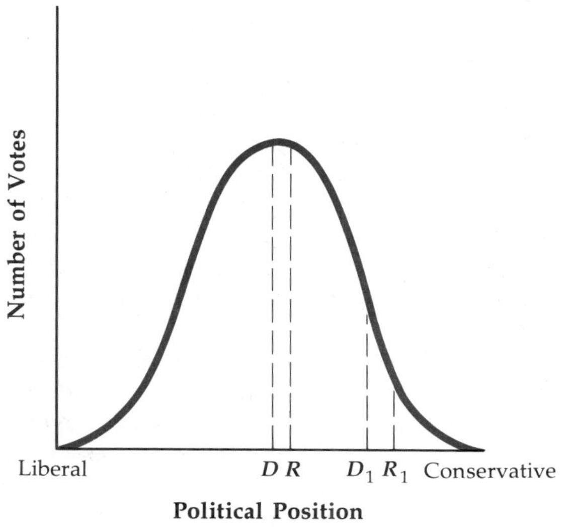


**Figure 21.1.** The Political Spectrum.
A political candidate who takes a position in the wings of a voter distribution, such as $D_1$ or $R_1$, will win fewer votes than a candidate who moves toward the middle of the distribution. In a two-party election, therefore, both candidates will take middle-of-the-road positions, such as *D* and *R*.

Just as producers find the optimum production level through trial and error, politicians may suffer several defeats before finding the true center of public opinion. But inevitably, political competition will drive them toward the middle of the distribution, where the median voter group resides. The **median voter** is the voter in the middle of the political distribution.

**Median voter:** the voter in the middle of the political distribution.

The recent history of presidential elections illustrates how politicians play to the views of the median voter. After an election in which the successful candidate won by a wide margin, the losing party has moved toward the position of the winning party. After Barry Goldwater lost by a wide margin to Lyndon Johnson in 1964, the Republic party made a deliberate effort to pick a more moderate candidate. As a result, the contest between Richard Nixon and Hubert Humphrey in 1968 was practically a dead heat. And after George McGovern was defeated by Richard Nixon in 1972, Democrats realized they too needed a less extreme candidate. Their choices in 1976 and 1984, Jimmy Carter and Walter Mondale, were more moderate.

## The Economics of the Voting Rule

So far we have been assuming that a winning candidate must receive more than 50 percent of the vote. But although most issues that confront civic bodies are determined by simple-majority rule, not all collective decisions are made on that basis, nor should they be. Some decisions are too trivial for group consideration. The cost of a bad decision is so small that it is uneconomical to put the question up for debate. Other decisions are too important to be decided by a simple majority. Richard Nixon was elected president with only 43 percent of the popular vote in 1968 (when a third-party candidate, George Wallace, took almost 14 percent), but Nixon's impeachment would have required more than a majority of the Senate and the state legislatures. In murder cases, juries are required to reach unanimous agreement. In such instances, the cost of a misguided decision is high enough to justify the extra time and trouble required to achieve more than a simple majority.

The voting rule that government follows helps determine the size and scope of government activities. If only a few people need to agree on budgetary proposals, for example, the effect can be to foster big government. Under such an arrangement, small groups can easily pass their proposals, expanding the scope of government activity each time they do so. But under a voting rule that requires unanimous agreement among voters, very few proposals will be agreed to or implemented by government. There are very few issues on which everyone can agree, particularly when many people are involved.

A unanimity rule can be exploited by small groups of voters. If everyone's vote is critically important, as it is with a unanimous voting rule, then everyone is in a strategic bargaining position. Anyone can threaten to veto the proposed legislation unless he is given special treatment. Such tactics increase the cost of decision making.

Government represents people's collective interest. But the type of voting rule used determines the particular interests it represents, and the extent to which it represents them.

## The Inefficiencies of Democracy

As a form of government, democracy has some important advantages. It disperses the power of decision making among a large number of people, reducing the influence of individual whim and personal interest. Thus it provides some protection for individual liberties. Democracy also gives political candidates an incentive to seek out and represent voters' interests. Competition for votes forces candidates to reveal what they are willing to do for various interest groups. Like the market system, however, the democratic system has some drawbacks as well. In particular, democracy is less than efficient as a producer of some goods and services.

The fact that the democratic form of government is inefficient in some respects does not mean that we should replace it with another decision-making process, any more than we should replace the market system, which is also plagued by inefficiencies. Instead, we must measure the costs of one type of production against the other, and choose the more efficient means of production in each particular case. We must weigh the cost of externalities in the private market against the cost of inefficiencies in the public sector. Because neither system is perfect, we must choose carefully between them.

**Table 21.1.** Costs and Benefits of a Public Park for a Five-Person Community

| Individuals (1) | Dollar Value of Benefits to Each Person (2) | Tax Levied on Each Person (3) | Net Benefit (+) or Net Cost (−) [(2) − (3)] (4) | Vote For or Against (5) |
|---|---|---|---|---|
| A | $200 | $100 | +$100 | For |
| B | 150 | 100 | + 50 | For |
| C | 125 | 100 | + 25 | For |
| D | 50 | 100 | − 50 | Against |
| E | 25 | 100 | − 75 | Against |
| Total | $550 | $500 | | |

## Median Voter Preferences

When you buy a good like ice cream in the marketplace, you can decide how much you want. You can adjust the quantity you consume to your individual preferences and your ability to pay. But if you join with your neighbors to purchase some public service, you must accept whatever quantity of service the collective decision-making process yields. How much of a public good government buys depends not only on citizens' preferences, but on the voting rule that is used.

Consider police protection, for instance. Perhaps you would prefer to pay higher taxes in return for a larger police force and a lower crime rate. Your neighbors might prefer a lower tax rate, a smaller police force, and a higher crime rate. But public goods must be purchased collectively, no matter how the government is organized. If preferences differ, you cannot each have your own way. Under a democracy, the preferences of the median voter group will tend to determine the types and quantities of public goods produced. If you are not a member of that group, the compromise that is necessary to a democracy inflicts a cost on you. You probably will not receive the amount of police protection you want.

## The Simple-Majority Voting Rule

Any decision that is made less than unanimously can benefit some people at the expense of others. Because government expenses are shared by all taxpayers, the majority that votes for a project imposes an external cost on the minority that votes against it. Consider a democratic community composed of only five people, each of whom would benefit to some degree from a proposed public park. If the cost of the park, $500, is divided evenly among the five, each will pay a tax of $100. The costs and benefits to each taxpayer are shown in Table 21.1. Because the total benefits of the project ($550) exceed its total costs ($500), the measure will pass by a vote of three to two. But the majority of three imposes net costs of $50 and $75 on taxpayers D and E.

When total benefits exceed total costs, as in this example, decision by majority rule is fairly easy to live with. But sometimes a project passes even though its cost exceeds its benefits. Table 21.2 illustrates such a situation. Again the $500 cost of a proposed park is shared equally by five people. Total benefits are only $430, but again they are unevenly distributed. Taxpayers A, B, and C each receive benefits that outweigh a $100 tax cost. Thus, A, B, and C will pass the project, even though it cannot be justified on economic grounds.

It is conceivable that many different measures, each of whose costs exceeded its benefits, could be passed by separate votes under such a system. If all the measures were considered together, however, the package could be defeated. Consider the costs and benefits of three proposed projects—a park, a road, and a school—shown in Table 21.3. If the park is put to a vote by itself, it will receive majority support from A, B, and C. Similarly, the road will pass with the support of A, C, and E, and the school will pass with the support of C, D, and E. But if all three projects are considered together, they will be defeated. Voters A, B, and D will reject the package (see column 4).

Many if not most measures that come up for a vote in a democratic government benefit society more than they burden it. And voters in the minority camp can use "logrolling" (vote trading) to defeat some projects that might otherwise pass. For instance, voter A can agree to vote against the park if voter D will vote against the school. Our purpose is simply to demonstrate that, in some instances, the democratic process can be less than cost efficient.

## Political Ignorance

In some ways, the lack of an informed citizenry is the severest problem in a democratic system. The typical voter is not well informed about political issues and candidates. In fact, the average individual's welfare is not perceptibly improved by knowledge of public issues.

A simple experiment will illustrate this point. Ask everyone in your class to write down the name of his or her congressional representative. Then ask them for the name of the opposing candidate in the last election. You may be surprised by the results. In one survey, college juniors and seniors, most of whom had taken several courses in economics, political science, and sociology, were asked how their U.S. senators had voted on some major bills. The students scored no better than they would have done by guessing.[1] In the United States as a whole, most voters do not even know which party controls Congress.[2] And public opinion polls

1. Richard B. McKenzie, "Political Ignorance: An Empirical Assessment of Educational Remedies," *Frontiers of Economics* (Blacksburg, Va.: University Publications, 1977).
2. Donald E. Stokes and Warren E. Miller, "Party Government and the Saliency of Congress," *Public Opinion Quarterly*, 26 (Winter 1962), 531–46.

**Table 21.2.** Costs and Benefits of a Public Park for a Five-Person Community, Alternative Schedule

| Individuals (1) | Dollar Value of Benefits to Each Person (2) | Tax Levied on Each Person (3) | Net Benefit (+) or Net Cost (−) [(2) − (3)] (4) | Vote For or Against (5) |
|---|---|---|---|---|
| A | $140 | $100 | +$ 40 | For |
| B | 130 | 100 | + 30 | For |
| C | 110 | 100 | + 10 | For |
| D | 50 | 100 | − 50 | Against |
| E | 0 | 100 | − 100 | Against |
| Total | $430 | $500 | | |

**Table 21.3.** Costs and Benefits of a Park, a Road, and a School for a Five-Person Community

| | Park (1) | | | Road (2) | | | School (3) | | | Total, 3 Projects (4) | | |
|---|---|---|---|---|---|---|---|---|---|---|---|---|
| Individuals | Benefit | Cost | Vote | Benefit | Cost | Vote | Benefit | Cost | Vote | Benefit | Cost | Vote |
| A | $120 | $100 | For | $250 | $ 200 | For | $ 50 | $ 400 | Against | $ 420 | $ 700 | Against |
| B | 120 | 100 | For | 50 | 200 | Against | 50 | 400 | Against | 220 | 700 | Against |
| C | 120 | 100 | For | 250 | 200 | For | 500 | 400 | For | 870 | 700 | For |
| D | 50 | 100 | Against | 50 | 200 | Against | 500 | 400 | For | 600 | 700 | Against |
| E | 50 | 100 | Against | 250 | 200 | For | 500 | 400 | For | 800 | 700 | For |
| Total | $460 | $500 | | $850 | $1,000 | | $1,600 | $2,000 | | $2,910 | $3,500 | |

indicate that most voters greatly underestimate the cost of programs like Social Security.[3]

If voters were better informed on legislative proposals and their implications, government might make better decisions. In that sense, political information is a public good that benefits everyone. But as we have seen before, in large groups people have little incentive to contribute anything toward the production of a public good. Their individual contributions simply have little effect on the outcome.

To remain politically free, people must exercise their right to determine who will represent them. The result is that they often cast their votes on the basis of impressions received from newspaper headlines or television commercials—impressions carefully created by advertisers and press secretaries.

3. Edgar Browning, "Why the Social Insurance Budget is Too Large in a Democracy," *Economic Inquiry,* 13 (September 1974), 373–88.

## Special Interests

The problem of political ignorance is especially acute when the benefits of government programs are spread more or less evenly, so that the benefits to each person are relatively small. But benefits are not always spread evenly; subgroups of voters—farmers, labor unions, or civil servants—often receive more than their proportional share. Members of such groups thus have a special incentive to acquire information on legislative proposals. Farmers can be expected to know more about farm programs than the average voter. Civil servants will keep abreast of proposed pay increases and fringe benefits for government workers. And defense contractors will take a private interest in the military budget.

Congressional representatives, knowing they are being watched by special-interest groups, will tend to cater to their wishes. As a result, government programs will be designed to serve the interests of groups with political clout, not the public as a whole.

## Cyclical Majorities

In their personal lives, most people tend to act consistently on the basis of rational goals. If he prefers good A to good B, and good B to good C, the rational individual will choose A over C repeatedly. But collective decisions made by majority rule are not always consistent. Consider a community of three people, whose preferences for goods A, B, and C are as follows.

| Individual | Order of Preference |
|---|---|
| I | A, B, C |
| II | B, C, A |
| III | C, A, B |

Suppose these three voters are presented with a choice between successive pairs of goods, A, B, and C. If the choice is between good A and good B, which will be preferred collectively? The answer is A, because individuals I and III both prefer it to B. But if A is pitted against C, which will be preferred? The answer is C, because individuals II and III both prefer it to A. Since the group prefers A to B and C to A, one might think it would prefer C to B. But note that if C and B are put up to a vote, B will win. A cyclical, or revolving, majority has developed in this group situation. This phenomenon can lead to continual changes in policy in a government based on collective decision making.

Although there is no stable majority, the individuals involved are not acting irrationally. People with perfectly consistent personal preferences can make inconsistent collective choices when acting as a group. Fortunately, the larger the number of voters and issues at stake, the less likely a cyclical majority is to develop. Still, citizens of a democratic state should recognize that the political process may generate a series of inconsistent or even contradictory policies.

## The Efficiencies of Competition Among Governments

In the private sector, competition among producers keeps prices down and productivity up. A producer who is just one of many knows that any independent attempt to raise prices or lower quality will fail. Customers will switch to other products or buy from other producers, and sales will fall sharply. To avoid being undersold, therefore, the individual producer must minimize its production costs. Only a producer who has no competition—that is, a monopolist—can afford to raise the price of a product without fear of losing customers.

These points apply to the public as well as the private sector. The framers of the Constitution, in fact, bore them in mind when they set up the federal government. Recognizing the benefits of competition, they established a system of competing state governments loosely joined in federation. As James Madison described it in *The Federalist* Papers, "In a single republic, all the power surrendered by the people is submitted to the administration of a single government; and the usurpations are guarded against by a division of the government into distinct and separate departments."[4]

Under the federal system, the power of local governments is checked not just by citizens' ability to vote, but by their ability to move somewhere else. If a city government raises its taxes or lowers the quality of its services, residents can go elsewhere, taking with them part of the city's tax base. Of course, many people are reluctant to move, and so government has a measure of monopoly power. But competition among governments affords at least some protection against the abuses of power.

Local competition in government has its drawbacks. Just as in private industry, large governments realize economies of scale in the production of services. Garbage, road, and sewage service can be provided at lower cost on a larger scale. For this reason, it is frequently argued that local governments, especially in metropolitan areas, should consolidate. Moreover, many of the benefits offered by local governments spill over into surrounding areas. For example, people who live just outside San Francisco may benefit from its services, without helping to pay for them. One large metropolitan government, including both city and suburbs, could spread the tax burden over all those who benefit from city services.

Consolidation can be a mixed blessing, however, if it reduces competition among governments. A large government restricts the number and variety of alternatives open to citizens and increases the cost of moving to another locale by increasing the geographical size of its jurisdiction. Consolidation, in other words, can increase government's monopoly power. As long as politicians and government employees pursue only the public interest, no harm may be done. But in fact, the people who run government have interests of their own. So the potential for acheiving greater efficiency

4. Alexander Hamilton, John Jay, and James Madison, *The Federalist: A Commentary on the Constitution of the United States*, no. 51 (New York: Random House, Modern Library, 1964) pp. 338–39.

## Perspectives in Economics: Differences in Health Care Systems—A Public Choice Perspective

*Cotton M. Lindsay*

In most industrialized nations health care is financed by the government. Health care services are organized in a variety of ways. In Britain and the Soviet Union, physician and hospital services are produced by the government. Government agencies decide which hospitals to expand, how many orthopedic surgeons and urologists to hire at each, and so on. In West Germany and Denmark, the government leaves the allocation of health services to the market. Doctors are free to practice anywhere they choose, and hospitals are allowed to make their own investment decisions. The government simply pays the bills.

The way the governments organize their health sector has a significant effect on the overall allocation of resources. When the government is in the business of producing health care, decisions are made by disinterested civil service employees or by politicians sensitive to public opinion. On the other hand, when the government offers insurance, decisions are made by people who are ill and want medical attention. It is not surprising that the results of the two systems differ markedly.

In Britain, where Parliament must approve the budget for the National Health Service, decisions tend to reflect the needs of the majority of voters—most of whom are healthy and do not want the government to spend a great deal on health care. Voters who appear at the hospital door needing medical care receive only as much care as Parlia-

through consolidation could easily be lost in bureaucratic red tape. Studies of consolidation in government are inconclusive. But it seems clear that consolidation proposals should be examined carefully.

## The Economics of Government Bureaucracy

Bureaucracy is not limited to government. Large corporations like General Motors and AT&T employ more people than the governments of some nations. They are bigger than the major departments of the federal government—though no company, of course, is as large as the federal government as a whole. Yet corporate bureaucracy tends to work more efficiently than government bureaucracy. The reason may be found in the fact that it pursues one simple objective—profit—that can be easily measured in dollars and cents.

Certainly the reason cannot be that stockholders are better informed than voters. Most stockholders are rationally ignorant of their companies' doings, for the cost of becoming informed outweighs the benefits. Even in very large corporations, however, some individuals hold enough stock to make the acquisition of information a rational act. Often such stockholders sit on the company's board of directors, where their interest in ment has paid for. In the United States, where the government is an insurer rather than a producer of health, the sick decide how much to spend on health care. If patients demand more hospital space and the government will pay the bills, hospitals simply expand to provide that space. Indeed, because government pays the bills, people seek even more care than they would be willing to pay for themselves. Even for apparent necessities like medical care, demand curves slope downward.

Because of the difference in interests of the people making the decisions in the two cases, economists would expect government-organized health systems to spend less than insurance-based health systems. And that is precisely what happens. Production costs, and therefore prices, may differ from place to place, and exchange rates may further distort spending data, making comparisons of nominal expenditures misleading. But we can ask what proportion of their gross national product various nations devote to health. Britain's National Health Service cares for citizens' health on a budget amounting to only about 6 percent of the nation's GNP. But West Germany, where health care is insured rather than delivered by the government, about 13 percent of GNP is spent on health. And in the United States, when Congress adopted a special health insurance plan covering the elderly and the poor, health spending increased from 6 to 10 percent of GNP in one decade.

increasing the value of their own shares makes them good representatives of the rest of the stockholders. The crucial point is that this informed stockholder has one relatively simple objective—profit—and can find out relatively easily whether the corporation is meeting it. The voter, on the other hand, has a complicated set of objectives and must do considerable digging to find out whether they are being met.

Because most corporations function in competitive markets, furthermore, the stockholder's drive toward profit is reinforced. General Motors knows that its customers may switch to Toyota if it offers them a better deal. In fact, stockholders can sell their General Motors stock and buy stock in Toyota. Thus corporate executives make decisions on the basis of the consumer's well-being—not because they wish to serve the public good, but because they want to make money.

Government bureaucracies, on the other hand, tend to produce public goods and services for which there is no competition. No built-in efficiencies guard the taxpayer's interests in a government bureaucracy. Both government bureaucrats and corporate executives base their decisions on their own interests, not those of society. But competition ensures that the interests of corporate decision makers coincide with those of consumers. No such safeguards govern the operations of government bureaucracies. Bureaucracies are constrained by political, as opposed to market, forces.

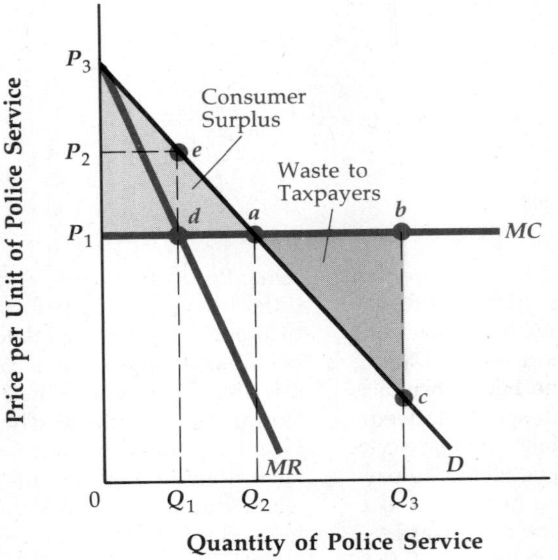


**Figure 21.2.** Bureaucratic Profit Maximization.
Given the demand for police service, *D*, and the marginal cost of providing it, *MC*, the optimum quantity of police service is $Q_2$. But a monopolistic police department interested in maximizing its profits will supply only $Q_1$ service at a price of $P_2$. (A monopolistic bureaucracy interested in maximizing its size would expand police service to $Q_3$.)

From the economist's point of view, one of the advantages of the profit-maximizing goal of competitive business is that it permits one to make predictions. Though some business people pursue other goals—personal income, respect in the business—their behavior can generally be well explained in terms of the single objective, profit. There is no single goal like profit that drives the government bureaucracy. Different bureaucracies pursue different objectives. We do not have time or space to consider all the possible objectives of bureaucracy, but we will touch on three: monopolistic profit maximization; size maximization; and waste maximization.

## Profit Maximization

Assume that police protection can be produced at a constant marginal cost, as shown by the horizontal marginal cost curve in Figure 21.2. The demand for police protection is shown by the downward-sloping demand curve *D*. If individuals could purchase police service competitively at a constant price of $P_1$, the optimum amount of police service would be $Q_2$, the amount at which the marginal cost of the last unit of police service equals its marginal benefit. The total cost would be $P_1 \times Q_2$ (or the area $0P_1aQ_2$), leaving a consumer surplus equal to the triangular area $P_1P_3a$.

Police protection is usually delivered by regional monopolies, however. That is, all police services in an area are supplied by one organization. These regional monopolies have their own goals and their own decision-making process, which do not necessarily match the individual taxpayers'. If police service must be purchased from such a profit-maximizing monopoly, service will be produced to the point where the marginal cost of the last unit produced equals its marginal revenue: $Q_1$. The monopolist will sell that quantity above cost at price $P_2$, making a profit equal to the rectangular area $P_1P_2ed$.

At the monopolized production level, there is still some surplus—the triangular area $P_2P_3e$—left for consumers. But they are worse off than under competitive market conditions. They get less police protection ($Q_1$ instead of $Q_2$) for a higher price ($P_2$ instead of $P_1$).

This analysis presumes that the police are capable of concealing their costs. If taxpayers know that $P_2$ is an unnecessarily high price, the outcome will be the same as under competition. They will force the police to produce $Q_2$ protection for a price of $P_1$.

## Size Maximization

In fact, a government bureaucracy is unlikely to take profit as its overriding objective, if only because bureaucrats do not get to pocket the profit. Instead, government monopolies may try to maximize the size of their operations. For if a bureaucracy expands, those who work for it will have more chance of promotion. Their power, influence, and public standing will improve, along with their offices and equipment.

What level of protection will a police department produce under such conditions? Instead of providing $Q_1$ service and misrepresenting its cost at $P_2$, it will probably provide $Q_3$ service—more than taxpayers desire—at the true price of $P_1$. The bill will be $P_1 \times Q_3$, or the area $0P_1bQ_3$ in Figure 21.2. Note that the net waste to taxpayers, shown by the shaded triangular area *abc*, exactly equals the consumer surplus, $P_1P_3a$. By extending service to $Q_3$, the police have squeezed out the entire consumer surplus and spent it on themselves.

## Waste Maximization

Instead of maximizing the amount of service they offer, bureaucrats may choose to maximize waste. They can increase their salaries, improve their working conditions, or reduce their workloads. All such changes increase the cost of providing a given amount of service.

Figure 21.3 shows how far a bureau can go in increasing the cost of, or budget for, its services. The marginal cost curve $MC_1$ is the minimum cost of providing additional police protection. The optimum quantity of police protection is therefore $Q_2$, the same as in Figure 21.2. But if the police pad their costs, the marginal cost curve will shift up to $MC_2$. The bureau's

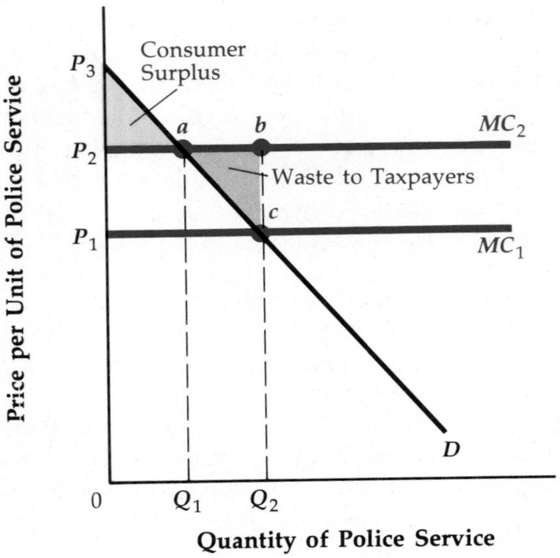


**Figure 21.3.** Bureaucratic Waste Maximization.
Given a demand for police service $D$ and a marginal cost of providing it $MC_1$, the optimum quantity of police service will be $Q_2$. A monopolistic bureaucracy, however, may seek to maximize waste by inflating its costs to $MC_2$. It will supply $Q_2$ units of police protection at a tax price of $P_2$ instead of $P_1$. The shaded area *abc* shows the waste created, which exactly equals the consumer surplus $P_2P_3a$.

budget climbs from $P_1 \times Q_2$ to $P_2 \times Q_2$. Note that beyond $Q_1$, the marginal cost of additional police service is now greater than its marginal benefit, indicated by the demand curve. Again, the police are wasting taxpayers' money, as shown by the shaded triangular area *abc*. By moving their cost curve to $MC_2$, they have managed to extract all the consumer surplus (shown by the triangular area $P_2P_3a$) and to spend it on unnecessary frills.

In real life, most bureaucratic monopolies may pursue both size maximization and waste maximization. For each unit of service they provide, they will try to expand both the size of their operation and the funds spent on it. But they do have to make tradeoffs between the two objectives. Whenever they expand their size, they must forgo a certain amount of expansion in their cost per unit of service. There is, after all, only so much consumer surplus that can be extracted from the system.

Figure 21.4 shows one possible combination of size and budget maximization. In this case the department chooses to expand its service from $Q_1$ to $Q_2$. Having done so, it can expand its cost per unit only to $MC_2$. Again, the shaded triangular area that indicates waste, *abc*, just equals the consumer surplus $P_2P_3a$.

Fortunately government bureaucracies do not usually achieve perfect maximization of size or waste. For one thing, most legislatures have at least some information about the production costs of various services.

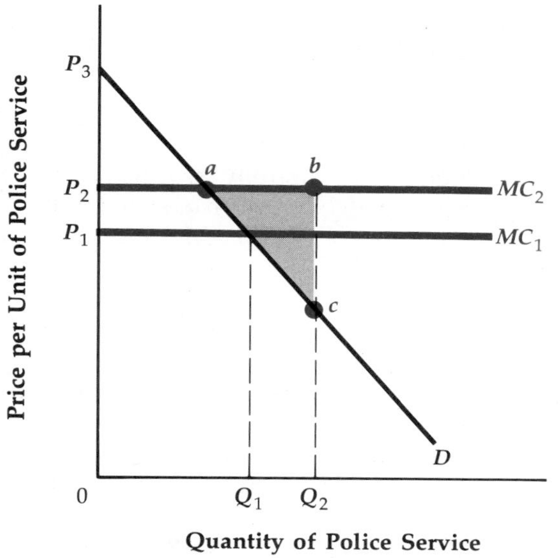


**Figure 21.4.** Size and Waste Maximization Combined.
The monopolistic bureaucracy may choose to increase both its size and the cost of its service. Any increase in one must come at the cost of the other, however, for together the two increases must not exceed the consumer surplus. Here net waste, shown by the shaded triangular area *abc*, is divided between size and cost increases. The area between the two marginal cost curves $MC_1$ and $MC_2$ represents waste maximization. The area below the marginal cost curve $MC_1$ represents size maximization. The whole area *abc* exactly equals the consumer surplus, $P_2P_3a$.

And bureaucrats may not be willing to do the hard work necessary to exploit their position fully. If bureaucracy does not manage to capture the entire consumer surplus, citizens will realize some net benefit from their investment.

## Making Bureaucracy More Competitive

What can be done to make government bureaucracy more efficient? Perhaps the development of managerial expertise at the congressional level would encourage more accurate measurement of the costs and benefits of government programs. But cost-benefit analysis alone will not necessarily help. As long as special-interest groups, including those of government employees, exist, the potential for waste can be substantial.

A better solution to bureaucratic inefficiency may be to increase competition in the public sector. In the private marketplace, buyers do not attempt to discover the production costs of the companies they buy from. They simply compare the various products offered, in terms of price and quality, and choose the best value for their money. A monopoly of any kind, of course, makes that task difficult if not impossible. But the existence of even one competitor for a government bureaucracy's services would allow some comparison of costs. The more different sources of a service, the flatter the demand curve faced by each source, and the more efficient it must be to stay in business.

How exactly can competition be introduced into bureaucracy? First, proposals to consolidate departments should be carefully scrutinized. What appears to be wasteful duplication may actually be a source of competition in the provision of service. In the private sector, we would not expect the consolidation of General Motors, Ford, and Chrysler to improve the efficiency of the auto industry. If anything, we would favor the breakup of the large firms into separate, competing companies. Why then should we merge the sanitation departments of three separate cities?

A second way to increase the competitiveness of government services is to contract for them with private producers. Many government activities that must be publicly financed need not necessarily be publicly produced. In the United States, highways are usually built by private companies but repaired and maintained by government. Competitive provision of maintenance as well as construction might reduce costs. Other services that might be "privatized" are fire protection, garbage collection, and education.

Finally, competition can be increased simply by dividing a bureaucracy into several smaller departments with separate budgets, thus increasing competition. Such a change would reduce the costs citizens must bear to move to an area that offers better or cheaper government services. The loss (or threat of loss) of constituents can put pressure on government to improve its performance.

## Summary and Extensions

This chapter has used cost-benefit analysis to develop an economic model of government. In government as well as private industry, producers in a monopolistic market position will tend to exploit the lack of competition for their service. A government bureau that has no competitors are in an enviable bargaining position vis-à-vis legislators and taxpayers. As the sole producer of a service, it can charge higher prices and deliver poorer service than competitive producers would.

In many cases, then, the performance of government bureaucracies can be improved by the introduction of competition for their services. Where possible, alternative sources of a government-provided good or service should be encouraged. If government bureaus have to compete with other producers by lowering their prices or increasing the quality of their service, they will be forced, like private producers, to reveal not just what they want to do, but the limit of what they will do for the consumer's business.

The democratic system provides checks and balances to control the exploitation of power in government. Voters can vote not to re-elect officeholders who abuse the public trust. They may not do so reliably, however, because of imperfect information. The fact that democracy is not a completely efficient system does not mean that a nondemocratic form of government is preferable.

## Major Conclusions

1. In a two-party democracy, political candidates will tend to represent the interests of the median voter group.
2. The simple-majority voting rule can minimize the cost of reaching collective agreement. But it is not the only possible voting rule, nor does it minimize the cost of all collective agreements. Some issues are too important to be decided by simple majority; others are too trivial to require voters' attention.
3. Democracy is inefficient in several respects. (a) Individual citizens must accept whatever quantity of a public good the government provides, as established by the median voter group. They cannot adjust their consumption to suit their individual preferences. (b) Under the simple-majority voting rule, government programs can be authorized even if their total cost exceeds their total benefit. They may be rejected even if their benefits exceed their costs. (c) Voters have little incentive to become informed about candidates' political positions or the consequences of government policy. (d) Special-interest groups receive a disproportionate share of political influence. (e) Cyclical majorities can create inconsistent or even contradictory policies.
4. Decentralized forms of government, like the federal-state arrangement in the United States, foster efficiency in the public sector by providing citizens with alternatives to their local government.
5. Public bureaucracies can become too large, both because legislators do not know the true cost of government services and because bureaucrats benefit personally from government expansion. Instead of maximizing profits, bureaucratic governments will tend to maximize government size and waste.
6. Government efficiency can be increased by the introduction of competition into the provision of public services. That goal can be accomplished either by increasing the number of departments that provide a service or by requiring government to compete with private firms.

## Questions to Ponder

1. Is it desirable, in your opinion, that government generally adopts policies intended to please the median voter group? Why or why not?
2. It is sometimes said that a rational decision must be based on perfect information. Would it be rational for a voter to acquire perfect information about politics? Would it be possible?
3. What effect does increased competition have on the slope of an individual firm's demand curve? Why? How does a change in the slope of a firm's demand curve affect its efficiency? How do these effects apply to government bureaucracy?
4. "Competition forces producers to reveal what they are willing to do at the limit, not just what they want to do." How does this statement apply to government bureaucracy, and to legislators' ability to control it?
5. Write down all the government-provided services you can think of. Which of them *must* be provided by government bureaucracy? Which could be provided through competitive contract?

# Glossary

## A

**Absolute advantage** the capacity to produce more units of output than a competitor can for any given level of resource use.

**Aggregate demand** the presumed negative relationship between the general price level and the total quantity of goods and services that consumers, business, and government want to buy.

**Aggregate supply** the presumed positive relationship between the general price level and the total quantity of goods and services produced in the economy during a given period.

**Appreciation of the dollar** (or any other national currency) an increase in purchasing power in terms of other national currencies.

**Automatic stabilizer** a tax or expenditure that increases total planned spending in times of recession and lowers it in times of economic expansion, without special action on the part of the administration and Congress. Also known as nondiscretionary fiscal policy.

**Average fixed cost** total fixed costs ($FC$) divided by the number of units produced ($Q$). Or, $AFC = FC \div Q$.

**Average tax rate** the percentage of total income that is paid in taxes. Obtained by dividing total taxes paid by total taxable income.

**Average total cost** the total of all fixed and variable costs divided by the number of units produced ($Q$). Or, $ATC = TC \div Q = AFC + AVC$.

**Average variable cost** total variable costs ($VC$) divided by the number of units produced ($Q$). Or, $AVC = VC \div Q$.

## B

**Bonds** a long-term debt obligation of a corporation, generally traded on the open market.

**Book profit** the profit shown on a company's accounting books.

**Break-even income level** that income level at which a government subsidy is no longer available.

**Budget deficit** the amount by which outlays exceed receipts during a given accounting period.

**Budget line** a curve that shows all the combinations of two goods a consumer can buy with a given amount of income.

**Budgetary (or fiscal) policy** the manipulation of federal expenditures and taxes to promote a high and stable level of employment and production, price level stability, and economic growth. Also known as discretionary fiscal policy.

**Budget surplus** the amount by which receipts exceed outlays during a given accounting period.

**Business cycle** a recurring swing in general economic activity; a smaller pattern of ups and downs within a major long-term trend.

## C

**Capital** (investment goods) any output of a production process that is designed to be used later in other production processes. Plant and equipment—things produced to produce other things—are examples of these manufactured means of production.

**Capital account** the record of U.S. investments abroad and foreign investments in the United States.

**Capital account deficit** the dollar amount by which U.S. investments abroad—that is, capital outflows—exceed foreign investments in the United States—that is, capital inflows.

**Capital account surplus** the dollar amount by which foreign investments in the United States—that is, capital inflows—exceed U.S. investments abroad—that is, capital outflows.

**Capitalism** an economic system based on private property and free enterprise, in which no government barriers to trade or restrictions on entry into business or the professions discourage competition.

**Cartel** an organization of independent producers intent on thwarting competition among themselves through the joint regulation of market shares, production levels, and prices. The principal purpose of such anticompetitive efforts is to raise prices and profits above competitive levels.

**Cash transfer** a money grant provided by government to a select group of citizens.

**Circular flow of income** the integrated flow of resources, goods, and services between or among broad sectors of the economy, like producers, consumers, and government.

**Common access resources** resources owned in common instead of privately by individuals. Thus individuals may not be excluded from their use.

**Common stock** a set of ownership rights in a corporation that entitles the investor to a share of any profits remaining after all other obligations have been met.

**Communism** as conceived by Karl Marx, a classless society governed by workers that would emerge from the downfall of capitalism. In practical terms, an economic system in which virtually all the means of production (not just some, as in socialism) are owned and controlled by the state.

**Comparative advantage** a relatively lower cost of production, or the capacity to produce a product at a lower cost than a competitor, in terms of the goods that must be given up.

**Competition** the process by which market participants, in pursuing their own interests, attempt to outdo, outprice, outproduce, and outmaneuver each other.

**Conglomerate** a firm that results from the merging of several firms from different industries.

**Constant dollar (or real) gross national product** gross national product adjusted for price changes.

**Consumer equilibrium** a state of stability in consumer purchasing patterns in which the individual has maximized his or her utility. Unless conditions—income, tastes, or prices—change, the consumer's buying patterns will tend to remain the same.

**Consumer price index (CPI)** the ratio of the cost of specific consumer items in any one year to the cost of those items in the base year, 1967. Used to gauge price trends in the consumer products sector of the economy.

**Consumption function** the assumed direct relationship between the national income level and the planned consumption expenditures of households.

**Consumption goods** goods that are produced to be used and enjoyed more or less immediately by their purchasers.

**Corporate income taxes** government revenues collected on a corporation's computed profits, as reported on its profit and loss statements.

**Corporation** a legal entity, created by government charter, with the right to conduct business in its own name, much as an individual does. A corporation can buy and sell, sue and be sued in its own name rather than the names of its owners.

**Cost** (opportunity cost) the value of the most highly preferred alternative not taken. Also called real cost. (Compare to money cost.)

**Cost-benefit analysis** the careful calculation of all costs and benefits associated with a given course of action.

**Cost-push inflation** a general rise in prices that occurs when restrictions are placed on the supply of one or more resources, or when the price of one or more resources is increased.

**Cost structure** the way various measures of cost (total cost, variable cost, and so forth) vary with the production level.

**Current account** the record of all the nation's international transactions other than capital flows and statistical discrepancies, including its merchandise trade, its investment income, its military transactions, its travel expenditures, its other services, and its remittances, pensions, and gifts.

**Current account deficit** the dollar amount by which a nation's imports of goods and services, interest and dividend payments to foreigners, gifts to foreigners, travel expenditures abroad, and other remittances to foreign nations exceed its exports of goods and services, interest and dividend receipts from foreign nations, gifts from abroad, foreign travel expenditures in this nation, and other remittances from abroad.

**Current account surplus** the dollar amount by which a nation's exports of goods and services, interest and dividend receipts from foreigners, gifts from foreigners, foreign travel expenditures in this nation, and other receipts from abroad exceed the nation's imports of goods and services, interest and dividend payments to foreigners, gifts to foreigners, travel expenditures abroad, and other remittances to foreign nations.

**Cyclical unemployment** unemployment that is caused by downswings of the business cycle—that is, by a broad-based reduction in the overall level of spending in the economy. Lasts for a period of weeks or months.

## D

**Decrease in demand** a decrease in the quantity demand at each and every price, represented graphically by a leftward, or inward, shift of the demand curve. Also a decrease in the price buyers are willing and able to pay for each and every quantity demand.

**Decrease in supply** a decrease in the quantity producers are willing and able to offer at each and every price, represented graphically by a leftward, or inward, shift of the supply curve. Also an increase in the price producers are willing and able to accept for each and every quantity supplied.

**Demand** the assumed inverse relationship between the price of a good or service and the quantity consumers are willing and able to buy during a given period, all other things held constant.

**Demand for labor** the assumed inverse relationship between the real wage rate and the quantity of labor employed during a given period, everything else held constant. Derived from worker productivity and the market price of the product produced.

**Demand-pull inflation** a general rise in prices that occurs when total planned expenditures increase faster than total production.

**Depreciation of the dollar** (or any other national currency) a reduction in purchasing power in terms of other national currencies.

**Discount rate** the interest rate the Federal Reserve charges on loans to member banks.

**Diseconomies of scale** increases in per-unit cost due to an increase in the rate of production when the use of all resources is expanded; increases in the long-run average cost. Diseconomies of scale occur when an increase in resource inputs is not matched by a proportionate increase in output.

**Disposable income** personal income minus personal income tax payments.

**Dissaving** any net withdrawal from accumulated past savings, or any net increase in borrowing. Same as negative saving.

**Duopoly** an oligopolistic market shared by only two firms.

## E

**Econometric model** a statistical equation or set of equations that describes economic data.

**Econometrics** the science of the statistical testing of economic theories and predictions.

**Economic development** the enhancement of a nation's capacity to produce through the creation of new kinds of output. Includes but goes beyond the improvements in technology and skills which promote economic growth.

**Economic growth** the expansion of a nation's capacity to produce the goods and services its people want. Caused by additions to or improvements in the technology of production.

**Economic losses** the amount by which the accounting expenses, the opportunity cost of capital, and the risk cost of doing business exceed a company's revenue.

**Economic profit** the amount left after all costs, including the opportunity cost of capital and the risk of losing money, have been deducted from company revenues. Normally zero.

**Economic rent** any payment received for the use of a resource or factor of production that exceeds its opportunity cost.

**Economics** the study of how people cope with scarcity—with the pressing problem of how to allocate their limited resources among their competing wants so as to satisfy as many of those wants as possible.

**Economies of scale** decreases in per-unit cost due to an increase in the rate of production when the use of all resources is expanded; decreases in the long-run average cost. Economies of scale occur when an increase in resource inputs brings a proportionally greater increase in output during a given period of time.

**Efficiency** the maximization of output through careful allocation of resources, given the constraints of supply (producers' costs) and demand (consumers' preferences). The achievement of efficiency means that consumers' or producers' welfare will be reduced by an expansion or contraction of output.

**Elastic demand** a relatively sensitive consumer response to price changes. If the price goes up or down, consumers will respond with a strong decrease or increase in the quantity demanded.

**Elasticity coefficient of demand** ($E_d$) the ratio of the percentage change in the quantity demanded to the percentage change in price. $E_d$ = percentage change in quantity ÷ percentage change in price. Measures buyer response to price changes.

**Employer cartel** any organization of employers that seeks to restrict the number of workers hired in order to lower wages and increase profits.

**Entrepreneur** an enterprising person who discovers profitable opportunities and organizes, directs, and manages productive ventures. Entrepreneurs are often considered to be a resource in themselves. Distinguished from labor because they manage other resources.

**Equation of exchange** ($MV = PQ$) a statement of mathematical equality between the product of the money stock ($M$) and the velocity of money ($V$) and the product of the price level ($P$) and the national output level ($Q$).

**Equilibrium income level** the income level at which producers have no reason to change their output level. Reached when leakages equal injections, or when total spending equals total output.

**Equilibrium price** the price toward which a competitive market will move, and at which it will remain once there, everything else held constant. The price at which the market "clears"—that is, at which the quantity demanded by consumers is matched exactly by the quantity offered by producers.

**Equilibrium quantity** the output (or sales) level toward which the market will move, and at which it will remain once there, everything else held constant. Reached when the quantity demanded equals the quantity supplied (at the equilibrium price).

**Excess reserves** the amount of a bank's reserves equal to the total reserves minus the required reserves.

**Excise taxes** taxes levied on specific products or services, for specific purposes. Normally stated as a percentage of the purchase price.

**Exclusive dealership** an agreement between a manufacturer and its dealers that forbids the dealers from handling other manufacturers' products. Declared illegal in the Clayton Act.

**Explicit cost** the money expenditure required to obtain a resource, product, or service.

**External benefits** benefits of production and consumption that are received by people not directly involved in the production, consumption, or exchange of a good. Positive effects on some third party. Also known as spillover benefits.

**External costs** costs of production and consumption that are imposed on people not directly involved in the production, consumption, or exchange of a good. Negative effects on some third party. Also known as spillover costs.

**Externalities** the positive (beneficial) or negative (harmful) effects that market exchanges have on people who do not participate directly in those exchanges. Third-party, or "spillover," effects.

## F

**Fiat money** a medium of exchange or store of value that cannot be redeemed for anything other than a replica of itself. (A fiat dollar can be exchanged only for another dollar. It is money simply because the government states that it is money.)

**Final goods and services** those goods and services that are purchased for consumption rather than for further processing or resale.

**Fiscal policy** the manipulation of federal expenditures and taxes to promote a high and stable level of employment and production, price level stability, and economic growth. Also known as budgetary policy or discretionary fiscal policy.

**Fixed cost** any cost that does not vary with the level of output.

**Fixed exchange rate system** an international monetary exchange system in which the prices of currencies are established and maintained at some fixed level or within some fixed range by governments.

**Floating (flexible) exchange rate system** an international monetary exchange system in which the prices of currencies are determined by competitive market forces.

**Frictional (transitional) unemployment** unemployment that occurs when people move from one job to another requiring similar skills. Generally temporary, lasting only a few days or weeks. Caused by normal shifts in the supply of and demand for products.

**Full-bodied commodity money** a medium of exchange or store of value that has some intrinsic value as a consumer good or factor of production. Money that has some economic use apart from its monetary value.

**Full employment** the employment level that occurs when the quantity of labor demanded equals the quantity of labor supplied at a market-determined real wage rate. Estimated at about 93 to 96 percent of the labor force.

**Full wage rate** the sum of the money wage rate and the monetary equivalent of the nonmonetary benefits of a job.

## G

**General sales tax** a tax on most, but not necessarily all, consumer purchases.

**Gross national product (GNP)** the current market value in dollars of all final goods and services produced in the economy in a given period.

**Guaranteed income level** the income level below which a family's or individual's income will not be allowed to fall. In effect, the government income subsidy at the zero adjusted earned income level.

## H

**Horizontal merger** the joining of two or more firms in the same market—for example, two car companies—into a single firm.

**Human capital** the acquired skills and productive capacity of workers.

## I

**Imperfect price discrimination** the practice of charging a few different prices for different consumption levels or different market segments (based on location, age, income, or some other identifiable characteristic). A fairly common practice.

**Implicit cost** the forgone opportunity to do or acquire something else, or to put one's resources to another use.

**Implicit marginal income tax** the amount by which a government subsidy is reduced when earned income rises.

**Implicit marginal income tax rate** the amount by which a government subsidy is reduced when earned income rises, stated as a percentage of the additional earned income.

**Increase in demand** an increase in the quantity demanded at each and every price, represented graphically by a rightward, or outward, shift in the demand curve. Also an increase in the price buyers are willing and able to pay at each and every quantity demanded.

**Increase in supply** an increase in the quantity producers are willing and able to offer at each and every price, represented graphically by a rightward, or outward, shift in the supply curve. Also an increase in the price producers are willing and able to accept for each and every quantity supplied.

**Indifference curve** a curve that shows the various combinations of two goods that yield the same level of utility.

**Inelastic demand** a relatively insensitive consumer response to price changes. If the price goes up or down, consumers will respond with only a slight decrease or increase in the quantity demanded.

**Inferior good or service** any good or service for which demand falls with an increase in income, or rises with a decrease in income.

**Inflation** a rise in the general level of prices over a period of time.

**Injection** (inflow) an inflow of income into the circular flow. Investment, government expenditures, and exports are injections.

**In-kind transfer** any good or service provided by government to a select group of citizens.

**Interest** a payment for deferred consumption, which in a competitive lendable funds market tends to reflect the productivity of capital. Normally expressed as a percentage or rate, as in interest rate.

**Interest rate** the annual payment for deferred consumption, expressed as a percentage of the dollar amount loaned (which is equal to the deferred consumption).

**Interlocking directorate** the practice of having the same people serve as directors of two or more competing firms.

**Intermediate goods and services** goods and services that are purchased for further processing or resale.

**International balance of payments** a summary statement of all international transactions between one nation—for example, the United States—and the rest of the world. International transactions include exports and imports of goods and services, gifts, interest and dividend payments, and travel expenditures, as well as the flows of financial capital (purchases of stocks and bonds and real capital assets) across national boundaries.

**International exchange rate** the price of one national currency (like the franc) stated in terms of another national currency (like the dollar).

**Investment** the purchase of capital goods—plant, equipment, and inventory—that can be used in the production of other goods and services.

**Investment function** the assumed relationship between national income and total planned expenditures on plant, equipment, and inventory.

**Investment goods** (capital) any output of a production process that is designed to be used later in other production processes. Plant and equipment—things produced to produce other things—are examples of these manufactured means of production.

**Irrational behavior** behavior that is inconsistent or clearly not in the individual's best interests, and that the individual recognizes as such at the time of the behavior.

**Isocost curve** (from the Greek word *iso*, meaning "same") a curve that shows the various combinations of resources that can be employed at a given expenditure (cost) level and given resource prices.

**Isoquant curve** (from the Greek word *iso*, meaning "same") a curve that shows the various technically efficient combinations of resources that can be used to produce a given output level.

## L

**Labor** any way in which human energy, physical or mental, can be usefully expended.

**Labor force** all persons sixteen years of age or older who are willing and able to work and who are counted as either unemployed or employed. Labor force = number unemployed + number employed.

**Labor force participation rate** the number of people employed divided by the number of people in the labor force.

**Land** One of the four major resource categories. Includes the surface area of the world and everything in nature—minerals, chemicals, plants—that is useful in the production process.

**Law of demand** the assumed inverse relationship between product price and quantity demanded, everything else held constant. If the relative price of a good falls, the individual will buy more of the good. If the price rises, the individual will buy less.

**Law of diminishing marginal returns** the law that if successive units of one resource—labor, fertilizer, or any other resource—are applied to a fixed quantity of another resource—land, for instance—then at some point in the production process, the added output gained from each additional unit of the variable resource will begin to diminish.

**Law of diminishing marginal utility** the rule that as more of a good is consumed, its marginal utility or value relative to the marginal value of the good or goods given up diminishes.

**Leading indicator** an index of business activity that tends to move up or down several months before measures of general economic activity, like real GNP, do so.

**Leakage** (outflow) a withdrawal or outflow of income from the circular flow. Saving, taxes, and imports are leakages.

**Linear regression** a statistical technique used to find the equation describing the straight line that comes closest to the plotted points of a curve.

**Liquidity** the ease with which any asset can be converted into another form, especially into money.

**Long run** the period during which all resources (and thus costs of production) can be changed—either increased or decreased. Calendar time varies from firm to firm and industry to industry.

**Long-run equilibrium** the price-quantity combination that will exist after firms have had time to change their production facilities (or some other resource that is fixed in the short run).

**Luxury good or service** any good or service for which demand rises faster than income.

## M

**M1** the total of the public's (as opposed to the banks') holdings of currency (paper bills and coins), demand deposits at commercial banks, traveler's checks, and other bank accounts against which checks can be written, such as NOW (negotiable order of withdrawal) and ATS (automatic transfer services) accounts.

**M2** M1 plus savings accounts and small (less than $100,000) time deposits and certificates of deposit, plus money market accounts and other highly liquid assets.

**Macroeconomic policy** the manipulation of taxes, federal expenditures, and the money supply to promote a high and stable level of employment and production, price level stability, and economic growth.

**Macroeconomics** the study of the national economy as a whole, or of its major components. Macroeconomics deals with "the big picture," not the details, of the nation's economic activity.

**Marginal cost** the additional cost incurred by producing one additional unit of a good, activity, or service.

**Marginal cost of labor** the additional cost to the firm of expanding employment by one additional worker.

**Marginal product** the increase in total output that results when one additional unit of a resource—for example, labor, fertilizer, or land—is added to the production process.

**Marginal propensity to consume** the percentage of any change in income that consumers are inclined to spend.

**Marginal propensity to save** the percentage of any change in total income that consumers are inclined to save.

**Marginal rate of return on investment** the additional income earned from an additional purchase of capital goods.

**Marginal revenue** the additional revenue a firm acquires by selling an additional unit of output.

**Marginal tax rate** the percentage of any additional income that is subject to taxation.

**Marginal utility** the additional satisfaction received from consuming one additional unit of a good or service.

**Market** the process by which buyers and sellers determine what they are willing to buy and sell, on what terms. That is, the process by which buyers and sellers decide the prices and quantities of goods to be bought and sold.

**Market demand** the summation of the quantities demanded by all consumers of a specified good or service at each and every price.

**Market (nominal) interest rate** the total payment that can be expected on a loan, expressed as a percentage of the loan. Also called the money interest rate.

**Market shortage** the amount by which the quantity demanded exceeds the quantity supplied at a given price. Graphically, the shortfall in supply that occurs at any price below the intersection of the supply and demand curves.

**Market surplus** the amount by which the quantity supplied exceeds the quantity demanded at a given price. Graphically, the excess supply that occurs at any price above the intersection of the supply and demand curves.

**Mean family income** the average family income level, or the total income of all families divided by the total number of families.

**Median family income** the midpoint of the family income distribution, above and below which an equal number of families fall.

**Median voter** the voter in the middle of the political distribution.

**Mercantilism** a system of economic organization that flourished between 1500 and 1800, designed to promote a desired balance of trade through monopoly of production and trading rights.

**Merchandise trade balance** the difference between the dollar value of goods—raw materials, agricultural and manufactured products, and capital and consumer products—imported and exported.

**Merchandise trade deficit** the dollar amount by which imports of goods exceed exports of goods.

**Merchandise trade surplus** the dollar amount by which exports of goods exceed imports of goods.

**Microeconomics** the study of the individual markets—for corn, records, books, and so forth—that operate within the broad national economy.

**Monetary policy** the manipulation of the rate of growth of the nation's money supply to promote price level stability and a high and stable level of employment and production.

**Money** any generally accepted medium of exchange or trade that also serves as a store of purchasing power.

**Money cost** a monetary measure of the benefits forgone when a choice is made. (Compare to real cost.)

**Money illusion** the mistaken belief that an increase in the market price, stated in dollars, represents an increase in real price (in the price of the good or service relative to other items).

**Money stock** the sum of all identified forms of money held by the public (as opposed to the banks) at a given point in time.

**Monopolistic competition** a market composed of a number of producers whose products are differentiated and who face highly elastic, but not perfectly elastic, demand curves.

**Monopoly** a sole seller of a good or service. Because a monopoly has no competitors, it can cut back on production (thus limiting the quantity supplied), charge higher prices, and reap greater profits than other firms.

**Monopoly power** the ability of a firm to raise the market price of its good or service by reducing production.

**Monopsony** the sole buyer of any good, service, or resource. (Should not be confused with monopoly, the single seller of a good or service.)

**Monopsony power** the ability of a producer to alter the price of a resource like labor by changing the quantity employed.

**Multiplier** the ratio of a change in national income to the change in total planned expenditures that stimulated it: $m$ = change in $Y$ ÷ change in $TPE$. Magnifies the effect of relatively small changes in total planned expenditures on national income.

## N

**National economic planning** the process of deciding collectively on national economic objectives, and of developing policies and programs for accomplishing those objectives.

**National income** the total payment made to owners of productive resources for the use of those resources during a given period. Equals the total income earned by all resources employed during the same period. Also equals the total cost of producing the goods and services included in the net national product.

**Natural monopoly** an industry in which long-run marginal and average costs decline with increases in production, so that a single firm dominates production.

**Natural rate of unemployment** the minimum percentage of the labor force that is unemployed because of structural problems in the economy and transitional movement among jobs.

**Negative income tax** an income redistribution system under which people below a breakeven income level receive cash grants. The lower the income, the higher the grant.

**Net national product (NNP)** gross national product minus an allowance for replacement of worn-out plant and equipment (called the capital consumption allowance). Because replacement of old equipment has been subtracted, net national product is a better measure of the real growth of production than gross national product.

**Nominal (market) interest rate** the total payment that can be expected on a loan, expressed as a percentage of the loan. Also called the money interest rate.

**Normal good or service** any good or service for which demand rises with an increase in income, and falls with a decrease in income.

**Normative economics** that branch of economic inquiry that deals with value judgments—with what prices, production levels, incomes, and government policies ought to be.

## O

**Oligopoly** a market composed of only a handful of producers—as few as two and as many as twelve or more—whose pricing decisions are interdependent.

**Open market operations** the purchase and sale by the Federal Reserve of U.S. government securities, which can be bills, notes, or bonds.

**Opportunity cost** the value of the most highly preferred alternative not taken. Also called real cost. (Compare to money cost.)

**Opportunity cost of capital** the return that might have been realized on the best alternative investment not undertaken.

## P

**Paradox of thrift** the theory that if people attempt to save more, they will end up earning less in the aggregate, and saving no more (and possibly less) than before.

**Partnership** a business venture owned and managed by two or more persons.

**Peak** the phase of the business cycle that occurs when general economic activity is no longer rising.

**Perfect competition** a market composed of numerous sellers and buyers of an identical product, such that no one individual seller or buyer has the ability to affect the market price by changing the production level. Entry into and exit from a perfectly competitive market is unrestricted.

**Perfectly elastic demand** a demand that has an elasticity coefficient of infinity. Expressed graphically as a curve horizontal to the *X* axis.

**Perfect price discrimination** the practice of selling each unit of a given good or service for the maximum possible price. Under perfect price discrimination, the seller's marginal revenue curve is identical to the seller's demand curve.

**Personal income** that part of national income that is paid to individuals as opposed to businesses.

**Personal income taxes** government revenues collected from individual earnings, after allowance for certain exemptions and deductions.

**Phillips curve** a graphical representation of the presumed inverse relationship between unemployment and inflation.

**Planned investment** anticipated, scheduled purchases of plant, equipment, and inventory.

**Positive economics** that branch of economic inquiry that is concerned with the world as it is rather than as it should be. Deals only with the consequences of changes in economic conditions or policies.

**Poverty income threshold** the income level below which people are classified as being poor. The minimum income believed necessary for basic subsistence.

**Precautionary demand for money** the desire to hold money balances in order to finance unexpected or emergency purchases of goods and services.

**Preferred stock** a set of ownership rights in a corporation that entitles the investor to a fixed share of profits after taxes.

**Present value** the value of future costs or benefits in terms of current dollars.

**Price** whatever a person must give up in exchange for a unit of goods or services purchased, obtained, or consumed. A rate of exchange, typically expressed in dollars per unit.

**Price ceiling** a government-determined price above which a specified good cannot be sold. Usually a legal price that is set by the government below the equilibrium price.

**Price discrimination** the practice of varying the price of a given good or service according to how much is bought and who buys it.

**Price elasticity of demand** the responsiveness of consumers, in terms of the quantity purchased, to a change in price.

**Price floor** a government-determined price below which a specified good cannot be sold. Usually a legal price that is set by the government above the equilibrium price.

**Price searcher** a consumer or producer large enough in relation to the entire market that its purchases and sales will affect the market price. Through its consumption or production decisions, the price searcher helps to determine the market price. From the various price-quantity combinations available, it chooses that one combination that maximizes utility or profit. Also called a price maker.

**Price taker** a consumer or producer so small in relation to the entire market that its purchases and sales cannot affect the market price. The price taker must either accept or reject the market price, deciding how much to buy or sell on the assumption that the market price will not change.

**Private goods** goods that are bought or produced and used by people as individuals or as members of small voluntary groups.

**Private sector** all the economic transactions undertaken voluntarily by individuals, either alone or in association with others. Also known as the nongovernment sector.

**Production possibilities curve** a graphical representation of the various combinations of goods that can be produced when all resources are fully and efficiently employed. Sometimes called a production possibilities frontier or a product transformation curve.

**Progressive tax system** any means of collecting government revenues in which the percentage of income that is paid in taxes rises with income.

**Property rights** legally defined and permissible uses, both private and collective, of resources, goods, and services.

**Property tax** a tax on specified assets, usually real estate, cars and boats, household goods, bank account balances, and stocks and bonds.

**Proportional tax system** any means of collecting government revenues in which all income earners pay the same tax rate (the same percentage of their income in taxes).

**Proprietorship** any business venture owned and run by a single individual.

**Public goods** goods that are bought or produced and used by large groups of people or by governments. Public goods can benefit many people at once.

**Public sector** the activities of federal, state, and local government. Government decisions are normally made collectively, either by voters in a referendum or by Congress, and are financed primarily by forced taxation.

**Pure interest rate** the return one can expect from an investment in the absence of risk and inflation.

**Pure monopoly** a single seller of a product for which there are no close substitutes. Protected from competition by barriers to entry into the market.

## Q

**Quasi-rent** the difference between the price of a resource and its opportunity cost, when the opportunity cost is not zero.

**Quota** a limit on the amount of a good that can be imported.

## R

**Rate of return on investment** the income earned from the purchase of capital, expressed as a percentage of the purchase price.

**Rational behavior** consistent behavior that maximizes an individual's satisfaction.

**Real (constant dollar) gross national product** the gross national product adjusted for price changes.

**Real wage rate** the nominal or money wage rate (the number of dollars a person earns per hour or day) adjusted for inflation or deflation. Measures a worker's actual purchasing power.

**Recession** a downward movement in general economic activity, especially in national production and employment. (A downward movement in real GNP must last for two quarters to be classified by the U.S. Department of Commerce as a recession.)

**Recovery** an upward movement in general economic activity, especially in national production and employment.

**Regressive tax system** any means of collecting government revenues in which the percentage of income that is paid in taxes declines as income rises.

**Representative commodity money** certificates or notes that can be converted into given quantities of a specific commodity, like gold or silver.

**Reserve deposits** the accounts that banks hold in Federal Reserve Banks. (A bank's reserve deposit balance plus its vault cash equals its total reserves.)

**Reserve requirement** that portion of a bank's reserves that cannot be used to create money (that is, to make loans).

**Reserves** the cash a bank has in its vault plus its deposits at the Federal Reserve Bank.

**Resources** things used in the production of goods and services. Also referred to as factors of production or inputs.

**Right-to-work laws** a state statute that allows unionized firms to hire nonunion workers, and to continue to employ them whether or not they join the existing union.

**Risk cost** the loss that can be anticipated because

of the failure of a certain percentage of a firm's ventures.

## S

**Saving** that portion of income not spent. Represents forgone expenditures on real goods and services.

**Saving function** the assumed direct relationship between national income and the amount of income saved (not spent on goods and services).

**Say's law** the macroeconomic principle that supply creates its own demand—that is, that the production of a supply of products creates an equal demand for goods and services.

**Scarcity** the fact that we cannot all have everything we want all the time. Put simply, there isn't enough of everything to go around.

**Short run** the period during which one or more resources (and thus one or more costs of production) cannot be changed—either increased or decreased. Calendar time varies from firm to firm and industry to industry.

**Short-run equilibrium** the price-quantity combination that will exist so long as producers do not have time to change their production facilities (or some other resource that is fixed in the short run).

**Socialism** an economic system in which the government owns major plants in industries such as coal, transportation, steel, and banking, and operates them in the public interest. Sometimes called democratic socialism.

**Specialization of labor** the process of dividing and assigning different production tasks to individuals with differing skills and talents.

**Speculative demand for money** the desire to hold money balances in anticipation of a decrease in the price of other assets and in anticipation of future profits.

**Stagflation** the combination of persistently high rates of unemployment and inflation.

**Structural inflation** a general rise in prices that occurs when producers cannot shift production in response to changes in the structure of the economy. Changes in the demand for a product, in the technology of its production, and in the competition producers face can all cause structural inflation.

**Structural unemployment** unemployment that occurs with major changes in the skills needed by workers. Caused by changes in the structure of industry due to technological innovation or changes in the relative competitiveness of an industry.

**Sunk cost** a cost incurred in the past, which cannot be altered by current decisions.

**Supply** the assumed relationship between the quantity of a good producers are willing and able to offer during a given period and the price, everything else held constant. Generally, because managerial costs tend to rise with expanded production, this relationship is presumed to be positive.

**Supply of labor** the assumed positive relationship between the real wage rate and the number of workers (or worker-hours) offered for employment during a given period, everything else held constant. Depends on the opportunity cost of workers' time.

## T

**Tariff** a special tax on imported goods.

**Technology** the knowledge of how resources can be combined in productive ways.

**Theory** a set of abstractions about the real world.

An economic theory is a simplified explanation of how the economy, or part of the economy, functions or would function under specific conditions. A good theory must predict and explain outcomes.

**Total cost** the sum of fixed costs (*FC*) and variable costs (*VC*) at each output level. Or, $TC = FC + VC$.

**Total expenditure function** the relationship of total planned expenditures to national income, normally assumed to be a direct relationship. (Total expenditures equal consumption spending plus investment spending plus government spending plus exports minus imports.)

**Transactions demand for money** the desire to hold money balances in order to carry out anticipated purchases of goods and services.

**Transitional (frictional) unemployment** unemployment that occurs when people move from one job to another requiring similar skills. Generally temporary, lasting only a few days or weeks. Caused by normal shifts in the supply of and demand for products.

**Trend** a long-run directional change, up or down, in some economic variable—for example, real GNP.

**Trough** the bottom of the business cycle, the point at which general economic activity ceases to fall.

**Tying contract** an agreement between seller and buyer that requires the buyer of one good or service to purchase some other product or service. Declared illegal in the Clayton Act.

## U

**Unemployment rate** the ratio of the number of people estimated to be unemployed to the number of people estimated to be in the labor force, stated as a percentage. Unemployment rate = number unemployed ÷ labor force.

**Union shop** a place of employment where a worker, once employed, must join the recognized union as a condition of continued employment.

**Unitary elastic demand** a consumer response to a price change in which the percentage change in price exactly matches the percentage change in quantity demanded. A change in price therefore does not alter consumer expenditures.

**Unplanned investment** unanticipated, unscheduled purchases of plant, equipment, and inventory.

**Usury laws** a legislated upper limit on the interest rates that lending institutions may charge to borrowers.

**Utility** the satisfaction a person receives from the consumption of a good or service, or from participation in an activity.

## V

**Variable cost** any cost that changes with the level of output.

**Variable rate mortgage** a mortgage whose interest rate is adjusted periodically to agree with some market interest rate—for example, the rate on a specific type of government or corporate bond.

**Velocity of money** the average number of times a dollar is used during a given period.

**Vertical merger** the joining of two or more firms that perform different stages of the production process into a single firm.

**Very long run** the time period during which the technology of production and the availability of resources can change because of invention, innovation, and discovery of new technologies and resources.

# Index

Boldfaced page numbers indicate the first occurrence of key terms; page numbers followed by (tab) indicate information from tables; page numbers followed by (fig) indicate figures; and page numbers followed by n indicate material from notes.